PROFESSIONAL JUDGMENT

A READER IN CLINICAL DECISION MAKING

~

Jack Dowie and Arthur Elstein

CAMBRIDGE
UNIVERSITY PRESS

PUBLISHED BY THE PRESS SYNDICATE OF THE UNIVERSITY OF CAMBRIDGE
The Pitt Building, Trumpington Street, Cambridge, United Kingdom

CAMBRIDGE UNIVERSITY PRESS
The Edinburgh Building, Cambridge CB2 2RU, UK   www.cup.cam.ac.uk
40 West 20th Street, New York, NY 10011–4211, USA   www.cup.org
10 Stamford Road, Oakleigh, Melbourne 3166, Australia
Ruiz de Alarcón 13, 28014 Madrid, Spain

First published 1988
6th printing 1999

Printed in the United Kingdom at the University Press, Cambridge

British Library Cataloguing in Publication data
Professional judgment: a reader in clinical decision making
1. Medicine – Decision Making
I. Dowie, J. A.   II. Elstein, A. S.
610   R723

Library of Congress Cataloguing in Publication data
Professional judgment: a reader in clinical decision making
(edited by) J. A. Dowie and A. S. Elstein.
p. cm.
Reprints of papers originally published in various
periodicals and monographs.
Companion vol. to: Judgment and decision making
edited by Hal R. Arkes, Kenneth R. Hammond. 1986.
ISBN 0 521 34628 2   ISBN 0 521 34696 7 (pbk.)
1. Medicine — Decision making.
I. Dowie, J. A.   II. Elstein, Arthur S. (Arthur Shirle), 1935- .
R723.5.P76 1988 616—dc19 87-20599 CIP

ISBN 0 521 34696 7 paperback

CE

— ~ —

TO HILARY AND ROCHELLE

CONTENTS

CONTRIBUTOR AFFILIATIONS

Henry J. Aaron   The Brookings Institution, Washington, D.C. 20036, USA

Hal R. Arkes   Department of Psychology, Ohio University, Athens, OH 45701, USA

Ruth Beyth-Marom   Everyman's University, Ramat Aviv 61392, ISRAEL

John E. Billi   Department of Internal Medicine, University of Michigan Medical School, Ann Arbor, MI 48109, USA

Georges Bordage   Bureau de Pédagogie Médicale, Faculté de Médecine, University Laval, Quebec, P.Q., G1K 7P4, Canada

Charles L. Bosk   Department of Sociology, University of Pennsylvania, Philadelphia, PA 19104, USA

Norman F. Boyd   Ontario Cancer Institute, Toronto, Ont., M4X 1K9, Canada

Michael H. Boyle   Department of Pediatrics, Faculty of Health Sciences, McMaster University, Hamilton, Ont., L8N 3Z5, Canada

James B. Bushyhead   University of Washington, Seattle, WA 98195, USA

Daniel Candee   Department of Research in Health Education, University of Connecticut Health Center, Farmington, CT 06032, USA

Caryn Christensen   Center for Educational Development, University of Illinois at Chicago, IL 60612, USA

Jay J.J. Christensen-Szalanski   Department of Management Sciences, University of Iowa, Iowa City, IA 52242, USA

A. Ciampi   Montreal Children's Hospital Research Institute, 2300 Tupper Street, Montreal, P.Q., H3H 1P3, Canada

Charles H. Clanton   Stanford University, Stanford, California, USA

Robyn M. Dawes   Department of Social and Decision Sciences, Carnegie-Mellon University, Pittsburgh, PA 15213, USA

F. Tim de Dombal   Clinical Information Science Group, St James Hospital, Leeds, UK

Peter Doubilet   Department of Radiology, Brigham and Women's Hospital, Boston MA 02115, USA

Michael F. Drummond   Health Services Management Centre, University of Birmingham, Birmingham, UK

David M. Eddy   Center for Health Policy, Research and Education, Duke University, Durham, NC 27706, USA

Hillel J. Einhorn   University of Chicago (deceased)

Arthur S. Elstein   Center for Educational Development, University of Illinois at Chicago, IL 60612, USA

Stephen A. Eraker   Department of Medicine, University of Michigan, Ann Arbor, MI 48109, USA

Baruch Fischhoff   Department of Social and Decision Sciences, Carnegie-Mellon University, Pittsburgh, PA 15213, USA

John Fox   Biomedical Computing Unit, Imperial Cancer Research Fund, London, WC2A 3PX, UK

G. Anthony Gorry   Department of Community Medicine, Baylor College of Medicine, Houston, TX 77030, USA

Larry D. Gruppen   Department of Postgraduate Medicine and Health Professions Education, University of Michigan Medical School, Ann Arbor, MI 48109, USA

Robert M. Hamm   Institute of Cognitive Science, University of Colorado, Boulder, CO 80309, USA

Allan R. Harkness   Department of Psychology, University of Minnesota, Minneapolis, MN 55455, USA

Vincent L. Hoellerich   Department of Anesthesiology, Massachusetts General Hospital, Boston, MA 02114, USA

Margaret Holmes   Department of Medicine, Michigan State University, East Lansing, MI 48824, USA

Gerald B. Holzman   Department of Obstetrics and Gynecology, Medical College of Georgia, Augusta, GA 30902, USA

Ruth B. Hoppe   Department of Medicine, Michigan State University, East Lansing, MI 48824, USA

Sargent P. Horwood   Department of Pediatrics, McMaster University Medical Center, Hamilton, Ont., L8N 3Z5, Canada

Jerome P. Kassirer   Department of Medicine, Tufts University School of Medicine/New England Medical Center, Boston, MA 02111, USA

Jay Katz   Yale University School of Law, New Haven, CT 06520, USA

Karen Klein   Urban Woman and Child Health Clinic, Jamaica Plain, MA 02130, USA

Benjamin J. Kuipers   University of Texas, San Antonio, Texas, USA

Hilary Llewellyn-Thomas   Ontario Cancer Institute, Toronto, Ont., M4X 1K9, Canada

Dennis J. Mazur   Veterans Administration Medical Center, Portland, OR 97207, USA

Ali McGuire   Health Economics Research Unit, University of Aberdeen, Aberdeen, AB9 22D, UK

Barbara J. McNeil   Department of Radiology, M.I.T., Cambridge, MA 02139; and Brigham and Women's Hospital, Boston, MA 02115, USA

William A. Metheny   Department of Obstetrics and Gynecology, Medical College of Georgia, Augusta, GA 30912, USA

Kashinath D. Patil   Department of Family Practice, University of Nebraska College of Medicine, Omaha, NE 68105, USA

Stephen G. Pauker   Division of Clinical Decision Making, Tufts University School of Medicine/New England Medical Center, Boston, MA 02111, USA

Peter Politser   Department of Health Policy and Management, Harvard School of Public Health, Boston, MA 02115, USA

Bill Puka   Department of Philosophy, Rensselaer Polytechnic Institute, Troy, NY 12180, USA

Michael M. Ravitch   Office of Medical Education, Northwestern University School of Medicine, Chicago, IL 60611, USA

Marilyn L. Rothert   College of Nursing, Michigan State University, East Lansing, MI 48824, USA

David R. Rovner   Department of Medicine, Michigan State University, East Lansing, MI 48824, USA

Paul D. Saville   Charleston, West Virginia 25304, USA

Donald A. Schön   Department of Urban Studies and Education, M.I.T., Cambridge, MA 02139, USA

William B. Schwartz   Tufts University School of Medicine, Boston, MA 02111, USA

John C. Sinclair   Department of Pediatrics, McMaster University Medical Centre, Hamilton, Ont., L8N 3Z5, Canada

Heather J. Sutherland   Ontario Cancer Institute, Toronto, Ont., M4X 1K9, Canada

Robert Tibshirani   Department of Preventive Medicine and Biostatics, Faculty of Medicine, University of Toronto, Toronto, Ont., M5S IAI, Canada

James E. Till   Ontario Cancer Institute, Toronto, Ont., M4X IK9, Canada

George W. Torrance   Faculty of Business, McMaster University, Hamilton, Ont., L8S 4M4, Canada

Robert S. Wigton   Department of Internal Medicine, University of Nebraska College of Medicine, Omaha, NE 68105, USA

Fredric M. Wolf   Department of Postgraduate Medicine and Health Professions Education, University of Michigan Medical School, Ann Arbor, MI 48109, USA

Robert L. Wortmann   Department of Medicine, The Medical College of Wisconsin, Milwaukee, WI 53225, USA

~

EDITORS' PREFACE

Our aim in assembling this collection has been to provide an inter-disciplinary introduction to judgment and decision making in the clinical professions. By 'clinical professions' we mean those in which (1) professionals, either by themselves or as part of a team, have responsibility for the management of individual cases (commonly called patients or clients, depending upon the profession); (2) that responsibility is based significantly, although not exclusively, on the expressed or implied consent of the individual concerned; and (3) elements of risk and uncertainty are unavoidable, due to the nature of the problems to be dealt with and/or the imperfect character of the knowledge and information available to deal with them. (While aware of views that challenge the conventional interpretation of the professional–client relationship, in the extreme portraying it as yet another device whose latent function is to maintain bourgeois hegemony, we feel that most of the issues addressed in our collection remain of practical import, whatever structural perspective is adopted.)

A clear implication of our main title is that we believe the issues and approaches discussed in this collection have general relevance to all clinical professions. However, to avoid providing only a shallow and inadequate level of empirical detail, we have concentrated exclusively on clinical medicine. We feel, moreover, that it is important to provide anyone seeking insight into judgment and decision-making processes in the real world – or real worlds, as some writers would argue – with some substantial contact with the economic and other contexts in which these activities occur. The collection therefore offers multiple interdisciplinary perspectives on a single area of application. In this way, it contrasts with, but also complements, two companion readers: *Judgment and Decision Making: An Interdisciplinary Reader*, edited by Hal Arkes and Kenneth Hammond (Cambridge University Press, 1987) has a largely psychological and social psychological focus, but surveys a number of application settings; *Judgment under Uncertainty: Heuristics and Biases*, edited by Daniel Kahneman, Paul Slovic, and Amos Tversky (Cambridge University Press, 1982) concentrates on basic psychological decision processes and is the least applied of the three volumes. We have chosen to present a broader range of perspectives on judgment and decision making, and to limit the survey largely to the clinical domain as the arena within which these activities are carried out.

Our guiding philosophy has been to indicate the variety of approaches and treatments now being adopted towards professional judgment and decision making within the domain marked out. The reader will accordingly find a mixture of papers, some more discursive, some more analytical, some reviewing an area of empirical research, some exemplifying the research in detail. A vast number of papers could have been included, equal in quality to those selected, and we are all too aware of the extremely subjective nature of the judgment and decision processes which have produced this set of thirty papers and not another. Very mindful of the critique of human judgment and decision making expressed in several of the papers in our collection, we plead the necessity of arriving at a *satisfactory*, rather than an *optimal*, solution to the problem of choice with too many alternatives.

We are keenly aware that for the general reader, these papers cannot stand alone. Yet our ability to supply the desirable explanatory and background material has been severely constrained by the size of the volume. The papers presented are thus highly selective and introductory; essentially they are ones which, we think, constitute useful points of entry, in one way or another, to the various literatures and sub-literatures of a growing field. Given the diverse nature of the collection, we felt that it would be most useful to readers if we provided one lengthy introductory overview of the papers, giving a sense of the territory traversed in the volume and of some of the underlying issues, rather than discussing each paper as it appears.

Wherever possible, papers have been reproduced in their entirety.

We take this opportunity to acknowledge the support of our respective institutions, the Open University and the University of Illinois at Chicago, during the time we have been engaged in this intercontinental as well as interdisciplinary effort. The efforts of the junior editor were supported in part by grants from the Josiah Macy, Jr, Foundation (B–8520004) and the National Library of Medicine, LM–04583; Laurie J. Belzer and James M. Dod assisted in the early phases of bibliographic search and appraisal. We are very grateful to Chris Nichols for her unstinting help and support in the preparation of this volume.

~

INTRODUCTION

PART I: THE ART AND SCIENCE OF UNCERTAINTY

Clinicians have traditionally held clinical judgment and decision making in high regard and been suspicious of attempts to explore them systematically with a view to making explicit their precise character. This is true even when such efforts are undertaken for the presumably laudable purpose of helping novices to acquire the ability to make good clinical judgments and decisions with minimal distress to themselves, their teachers and – not least – their patients. But it is especially true in relation to those who seem to wish to demystify for the sake of demystification, or hope thereby to facilitate the achievement of some such (apparently) non-clinical goal as economic efficiency or the redistribution of welfare in the community.

The suspicions remain widespread despite, or perhaps because of, the increased attention focussed on clinical judgment and decision making in recent years, from both inside and outside the medical profession. The broad reasons for this growing interest are fairly well appreciated. Internally, the growth of biomedical knowledge on the one hand and technological developments on the other have vastly expanded the range of investigative and therapeutic possibilities confronting the practitioner and those on the way to becoming practitioners: the clinical and educational interests reinforce one another because of the central place of clinical training in the profession. Externally, rising public expectations concerning both the length and quality of life have, along with the general growth of "consumerism", changed the attitudinal basis of professional-client relations. At the same time they have brought major changes in the institutional and legal contexts within which these relations occur. The profession has undoubtedly contributed in some measure to these "external" developments, because the growth of its technical knowledge and technological capability has been used as the basis for claims to increased funding and other resources. Much of the increased interest from outside therefore represents calls for greater accountability for professional judgments and decisions.

The conceptually separable questions of *how* clinicians make judgments and decisions and of *how well* they make them have both become of greater interest to a wide range of parties, the evaluative question being the dominant concern of those who see themselves as bearing the costs, monetary or personal, of inferior judgments and decisions. The wide variation in clinical practices uncovered by virtually all studies of clinical behaviour – whether the comparison is 'between colleagues, communities or countries – has been one empirical focus for those attempting to assess professional performance. The significant percentage of discrepancies between clinical diagnoses and pathological findings which emerges in most autopsy studies is another (Goldman *et al.* 1983 and references cited therein). While both types of study are always questionable on a variety of methodological grounds the idea that clinical judgment and decision making are in "perfect health" and that, at most, "fine tuning" is required, has become increasingly hard to sustain to independent observers. This criticism of everyday clinical judgment is complemented by a growing number of techniques and systems that claim to provide clinicians with the means to improve their judgments and decisions, accompanied by evidence that (under at least some circumstances) these claims are warranted.

It is not difficult to accept that attitudinal and behavioural changes in society at large have brought new uncertainties to the clinicians in their dealings with individual patients. It is more paradoxical, though only until the matter is given second thought, that increased biomedical knowledge and technological capability have increased rather than reduced the complexity and difficulty of the clinician's task. Eddy [1] sees contemporary medical practice as being saturated with uncertainties:

Whether a physician is defining a disease, making a diagnosis, selecting a procedure, observing outcomes, assessing probabilities, assigning preferences, or putting it all together, he is walking on very slippery terrain. It is difficult for nonphysicians, and for many physicians, to appreciate how complex these tasks are, how poorly we understand them, and how easy it is for honest people to come to different conclusions. (p. 45)

After exploring the nature of the uncertainties present in each of the components into which he divides the clinical task, Eddy concludes that the management decision for a single patient requires, in principle, such a complex synthesis of imperfect information that it "would be an extremely hard task for a research team; there is no hope that it could occur with any precision in the head of a busy clinician" (p. 54). For him the appropriate clinical response is not the denial or avoidance of the uncertainties, reactions which far too often characterize practice and produce, among other things, conflicting policies defended with great confidence by different clinicians. The uncertainties should be *explicitly* – indeed "scientifically" – confronted, using the relevant techniques and languages that have been developing alongside the biomedical knowledge that clinicians so admire and use.

Over the past few hundred years languages have been developed for collecting and interpreting evidence (statistics), dealing with uncertainty (probability theory), synthesizing evidence and estimating outcomes (mathematics), and making decisions (economics and decision theory). These languages are not currently learned by most clinical policymakers; they should be. (p. 58)

On the contrary, Schön sees [2] clinical wisdom and expertise residing precisely in the ability to accomplish the tremendously difficult synthesizing task described by Eddy *without* resort to formal analysis. Expert clinicians move efficiently to the appropriate *resolution* of problems, where "resolution" encompasses the "framing" or "setting" of the problem as well as its "solving" once it has been framed. The framing of the client's problem is not amenable to the systematic, formal, analytical modelling Eddy recommends, even if the solving of already framed problems is. Eddy's call for greater openness and the public evaluation and justification of clinical policies (i.e. "what I do for my patients"), using the language of the decision sciences, comes up against Schön's belief that a substantial part of clinical expertise, and probably the most important part, comes in the form of "knowledge-*in*-action". In contrast to "knowledge-*for*-action" (which can be acquired from books or colleagues) this sort of knowledge is only revealed *in action* – in the doing of the task, whether it be tightrope walking or clinical diagnosis. There is no reason to expect the performer to be able to articulate it, or even for outside observers to be able to capture and make it into "knowledge-for-action" by others. Based on the protracted and unique personal experience of the person concerned, it only exists in that individual professional's actions.

It would be tempting and not altogether misleading to characterize Eddy as a pessimist about the quality of professional judgment and decision making and Schön as an optimist. Eddy certainly seems broadly unimpressed with the quality of clinical practice at *all* levels, including that of the highest experts: even the best clinicians are performing below levels of achievements which are feasible. If they were to face up fully to the difficulties of the clinical task and address the uncertainties that characterize all aspects of it much more explicitly and analytically, the overall quality of practice would be raised. For Schön, on the other hand, the best experts are *by definition* performing at the highest possible level (given the resource and other contexts of their practice), so it is only a question of bringing those who are not currently exhibiting "best practice" judgment and decision making up to this level. This can be done by increasing their "knowledge-in-action" and by encouraging and facilitating the other hallmark of the best clinicians, which is their ability to "reflect-in-action". This is not reflection *on* action *after* the action is over, but reflection on action *in* action, that is during the action.

The practitioner allows himself to experience surprise, puzzlement, or confusion in a situation which he finds uncertain or unique. He reflects on the phenomena before him, and on the prior understandings which have been implicit in his behavior. He carries out an experiment which serves to generate both a new understanding of the phenomena and a change in the situation.

When someone reflects-in-action, he becomes a researcher in the practice context. He is not dependent on the categories of established theory and technique, but constructs a new theory of the unique case . . . He does not keep means and ends separate, but defines them interactively as he frames a problematic situation. He does not separate thinking from doing, ratiocinating his way to a decision which he must later convert to action . . . Thus reflection-in-action can proceed, even in situations of uncertainty and uniqueness, because it is not bound by the dichotomies of Technical Rationality. (pp. 75–6)

It is difficult to pin down the precise nature of Schön's "reflection-in-action" (and hence its distinction from reflection *on* action), because its character is said to vary with the length of the "action present", "the zone of time in which action can still make a difference to the situation". This zone may vary from seconds to years depending on the type and duration of action (acute surgery, community geriatric care). It will also vary for one practitioner with different patients and for the same patient through time. Equally in need of clarification is the idea of "a theory of the unique case". But what is very clear is that for Schön the activity is essentially *craftlike* in character. He greatly respects what has traditionally been referred to as the artistic, or intuitive, aspect of clinical practice.

Are the manifold uncertainties of contemporary clinical practice to be seen as the legitimate basis for regarding clinical judgment and decision making as significantly – even "essentially" – artistic in character? Albeit, of course, an *art* that uses, and gains credibility from, the knowledge produced by the medical and other *sciences*. Or are claims to artistry just the way the profession dresses up its refusal to apply the same scientific approach to its own cognitive processes and behaviour that it insists upon in relation to processes and knowledge at the levels of organ and cell? Those, like Eddy, who take the latter view would insist that even if clinical practice *can* be usefully regarded as an art or craft this does not, and should not, prevent the results of that activity being evaluated scientifically or at least systematically. Those, like Schön, who are deeply impressed by the dangers of applying to human activity the positivism of the natural sciences, question the possibility of evaluating craft activities "scientifically". The "variations in practice" detected by investigators are precisely what one would expect if individual clients' problems are being framed appropriately – and differently – even if by some "scientific" criterion the frames are equivalent.

The long-standing debate as to whether clinical practice is essentially artistic or scientific, to which Eddy and Schön may be regarded as recent contributors, is, fortunately, giving way to more productive and research-based discussion about the precise mixture of activities in which clinicians engage. From this it has become clear (Sober 1979) that if clinical judgment is an art it is not because it is a fundamentally non-logical, qualitative activity which is emotionally concerned with the unique individual. Clinical judgment can only be successful to the extent that it is also – implicitly if not explicitly – logical, quantitative, detached and statistical. Hamm [3] introduces a theoretical framework in which the dichotomy between "intuitive art" and "analytical science" gives way to a continuum of modes of practice, in which the nature of clinical inference and decision making varies with the structure and context of the task and the way of thinking adopted by the clinician in response to that structure and context.

Cognitive Continuum Theory, developed by Kenneth Hammond, identifies *intuitive judgment* and *scientific experiments* (of the sort done in physics and chemistry) as the poles of a continuum of modes of inquiry (or practice) which we, as humans, have more or less available to us. We select a mode for practice on the basis of the structural characteristics of the task facing us and the time and other resources available in the context. Broadly speaking the less well structured a task is – or is perceived to be – the more we will be induced to adopt the way of thinking (mode of cognition) in which *intuition* is dominant (i.e. intuitive judgment). The better structured the task is – or is perceived to be – the more we will be induced to draw on the mode in which analysis is dominant (i.e. scientific experiment).

While both task structure and cognitive mode are continuous variables, six characteristic combinations of them – six main modes of practice – are identified in Cognitive Continuum Theory. The intermediate modes are variously labelled, depending on whether the focus is on inference or decision, but may be generally referred to as "peer-aided judgment", "system-aided judgment", "quasi-experiment" (e.g. epidemiological studies) and "controlled trial". As we move through these modes from "intuitive judgment" to "scientific experiment" the possibility of manipulation by the clinician/researcher increases: at the intuitive judgment end one is engaged in developing a "theory of the single case" with little possibility of holding other things equal and observing the effect of changing one variable (e.g. *this* patient's age), precisely what a scientific experiment offers. Increasing in parallel is the openness of his/her activity to examination and replication but also, of course, is the time (and usually other resourcing) necessary to carry out the manipulation. For the *clinician* the most relevant modes are therefore the three more intuitive ones and many of the papers in this collection may be interpreted as contributions to the debate about the "proper" or "best" mode of practice for clinical activity. In most cases they advance the case for moving towards more explicit peer-aided judgments (Mode 5) and to system-aided judgments (Mode 4), where "system" embraces such things as data-based aids, knowledge-based decision support systems and particular types of decision analysis.

It is important to note that Cognitive Continuum Theory is fundamentally descriptive, designed for empirical testing to see whether judges' modes of practice *are* substantially determined by the structure of the particular task they are undertaking – rather than by, for example, some personality-based preference for a particular blend of intuition and analysis irrespective of the task. But while Cognitive Continuum Theory identifies a number of attributes on which to "objectively" index task structure (among others, the number and redundancy of the cues available to the clinician) it is clearly possible that the *perceived* structure of a given situation will vary from person to person. Others would go further and argue that structures are never given (and perceived) but always *generated*, this being the view of those like Schön who hold problem-framing rather than problem-solving to be the heart of clinical judgment. Arguments in the real world about the appropriate mode of practice will then be arguments about *what* sort of task is being undertaken and how much time and how many resources *are* available to tackle it, rather than about the mode of cognition appropriate for an agreed type of task. Alternatively these arguments may be completely *normative* ones (e.g. about the cues and time and resources which *should* be available to clinicians), in which case the *descriptive* validity of the theory is irrelevant.

There is no suggestion in Cognitive Continuum Theory that clinicians' ability to draw correct inferences or arrive at optimal decisions for their patients is *guaranteed* by the adoption of the mode of cognition (and hence practice) appropriate to the task. While practitioners at all levels of expertise are seen as having each of the modes of cognition available in their repertoire, they may be more or less expert within any of them, be it more intuitive or more analytical. This is not so in the alternative model introduced by Hamm, that of Hubert and Stuart Dreyfus. They postulate only two practice modes, retaining a fundamental dichotomy between *intuition* and *analysis*, and, in contrast to the determination-by-task thrust of Cognitive Continuum Theory, argue that it is the clinician's level of expertise that determines whether an intuitive or analytical approach is taken to the various components of the clinical task. Put at its simplest, a novice is one who tackles each of the clinical sub-processes (which they identify as "perception", "action", "orientation" and "decision") analytically and the expert is one who tackles all of them intuitively. Instead of intermediate modes of *practice* we have, in the Dreyfus schema, intermediate levels of *expertise*, through which clinicians graduate by increasing the number of sub-processes which they approach intuitively. (They can only do this having established a sound analytical ability at each first.)

There are clear echoes of Schön in the Dreyfus' assertion that "better thinking is done intuitively, because experts, who think better, think intuitively" (p. 99). Unfortunately, it is difficult to see any way of empirically testing such a proposition and the question of whether a valid *independent and objective* evaluation of expert performance in the clinical professions is possible underlies much of the tension between the artistic-intuitive and rational-analytic views of clinical reasoning. If an evaluative study shows experts performing less well than non-expert humans or some impersonal system such as an equation, is it, by conclusion, methodologically defective? This question reverberates through the papers in the next section.

PART 2: MODELLING THE CLINICIAN AND THE CLINICAL TASK

In this section we are concerned primarily with two major approaches to the description of *how* clinicians make judgments and decisions, although the question of *how good* these judgments and decisions are arises frequently, and so, by implication, does that of the appropriate normative standard for evaluation.

The policy-capturing or *clinical judgment analysis* approach to the modelling of clinician behaviour in a task seeks to capture, in the form of a mathematical equation, the relationship between the inputs (cues or indicants) available to the clinician and his/her outputs (judgments or decisions). It consciously makes no claim to model what goes on inside the clinician's head, which is officially treated as a "black box", though the temptation to make inferences about what is going on in there is not always easy to resist. The *process-tracing approach* has, in its pure form, precisely the reverse aim: to model only what goes on inside the clinician's head. Since, however, such modelling is of little *practical* use in either educational or decision support development if it is unable to predict the clinician's behaviour reasonably well, the pure forms of process tracing have tended to give way (e.g. in computer simulations) to modes which incorporate intelligent reasoning of various sorts, whether or not it is reported by the clinician. Elstein and Bordage [4] provide introductory summaries of the earlier literature in these two traditions.

Statistical approaches

The judgment tradition, adopting the theoretical framework provided by Egon Brunswik's lens model, has been remarkably successful in showing that the intuitive judgments of clinicians can be successfully reproduced by simple (linear, additive) equations. In the absence of gold standard verdicts this sort of analysis is restricted to comparing the cue weights captured from a clinician's behaviour with the weights they *say* they *think* they give the cues, or comparing them with a colleague's captured weights. Significant differences between captured and expressed weights and between colleagues' captured weights (even when they report the same expressed weights) are typically found.

Wigton, Hoellerich and Patil [5] found little variation in the captured group average weights of faculty members, house officers and students in diagnosing simulated cases of pulmonary embolism, but great individual variation within each group. Most surprising to them, they found no convergence towards a consensus weighting as experience increased – surprising because they had deliberately selected a task where definitive laboratory tests were lacking and clinical experience would therefore be the main basis of clinical judgment. The paper canvasses the possible reasons for its findings, assuming that they are not experimental artifacts, but also notes (in relation to that assumption) the significant methodological problems presented by all studies based on case vignettes ("paper patients"), and the possibility that the variations in diagnostic policy had little or no therapeutic significance.

It is the two latter responses – "I don't believe the results would hold in real clinical life" and "So what, it doesn't matter for management" – that have dominated clinicians' reactions to the results coming from policy-capturing studies, particularly those which have brought in gold standard verdicts for each case and thereby introduced evaluations as well as comparisons. The performance of a judge can, in these circumstances, be compared with that of the equation captured from his behaviour. If the equation outperforms the judge (has a higher number of correct diagnoses, roughly speaking) then the judge can "bootstrap" himself – achieve a better performance – by replacing himself with this equation. The equation probably does better because it eliminates the "noise" in his judgments that arises from very "human" variations in mood and attention, while retaining his consistent "signal" (i.e. the judge's policy, in the terminology of this literature).

But if a gold standard verdict exists it is possible to model the relationship between it and the cues directly, leaving out the judge entirely. If the conclusion that judges could usually be bootstrapped was controversial, vastly more so was the oft-repeated finding that a purely statistical modelling of clinical tasks would outperform the judge (and even his captured, "bootstrapping", equation). The demonstrated superiority of statistical over clinical judgment – of Mode 3 over Mode 6 in Cognitive Continuum terms – became the centre of intense methodological debate. The clinical fraternity and their defenders claimed that the competition was being set up in a way that ensured "the computer" would win. Cues were presented in clusters rather than sequentially, and as pre-coded information rather than as part of the texture of the real world. The judgments asked of the clinician had to be supplied in quantitative form; and so on. Whatever the validity of these objections a deeper and somewhat more appealing explanation eventually emerged, ironically from those responsible for many of the original findings.

This deeper explanation is discussed by Dawes [6] in a paper which expands on his claim that

in a wide variety of psychological contexts, systematic decisions based on a few explicable and defensible principles are superior to intuitive decisions – because they work better, because they are not subject to conscious or unconscious biases on the part of the decision maker, because they can be explicated and debated, and because their basis can be understood by those most affected by them. (p. 151)

(The empirical illustration in this case is graduate school admission procedures, but the arguments transfer to many other clinical situations.)

Why do regression equations "work better" than clinical judgments? Dawes suggests that it is because most of the clinical tasks we undertake are ones in which, as far as current knowledge permits us to know, the relationship between the cues we know to have some relevance and the thing we are predicting is "conditionally monotonic": a higher value on each of these cues is associated with a higher value on the variable being predicted, irrespective of the values of the other cues. This is precisely the statistical situation in which regression equations are very good predictors, so that the clinicians were right, though in a very different way from the one they thought, when they felt the competition favoured "the computer". It is the difficult tasks we are left to tackle clinically, rather than in a routine way based on secure causal knowledge, that are the ones in which "the computer", grinding out its regression equations, is more or less bound to win. In other words the clinician is the person left with the tasks that we know relatively little about – relative to their immense complexity – and her attempts to deal with these in a sophisticated way, on the basis of highly developed knowledge and skills, often lead to inferior performance and wasted mental energy. The consolation to the clinician is that it is only she who can establish the relevant set of non-redundant cues for the computer to work on.

What about the procedural and ethical arguments against system-aided (or system-*made*) judgments, which are invariably raised when the output performance case has had to be conceded? Dawes points out that the defence that clinical judgment avoids "dehumanizing judgment by numbers" is one that needs to be examined carefully in the light of the tradeoffs between process and outcome, as well as wider considerations of justice. In this examination is it really the clinician who should be deciding whether a "more human process" is worth the increased number of inferior decisions or unfairnesses it can produce compared with the regression equation?

Clinicians have great difficulty accepting that their expansive and complex technical knowledge does not necessarily guarantee that they can do better, in most clinical cases that come to them, than something as simple as "add up how many cues are in favour of each possible judgment and go with the highest score". Arkes, Dawes and Christensen [7] raise the alarming possibility that resistance to the use of simple decision rules, which cannot be outperformed because existing knowledge does not allow it, increases with expertise and the size of the stake. It seems to be precisely when highly qualified experts are engaged in tasks where the consequences of error are rated extremely serious that we will find most reluctance to use a simple mechanical rule – and end up with a higher than necessary number of errors as a result.

Einhorn [8] looks for a wider framework within which to interpret the persistence of the clinical versus statistical controversy, despite the one-sided results. Arkes *et al.* set up their experimental task in such a way that there was no way of improving on the performance of their simple decision rule, which in fact had a 70 percent success rate. Implicitly many of their respondents, and particularly the more expert, refused to believe that they could not do better than this, an attitude which reflects a wider belief that even if we cannot predict perfectly now, perfect prediction should be our goal. It is unacceptable to "settle for" a given number of errors (in this case 30 percent) when it is *possible* that 100 percent success may be achieved. Insofar as such an attitude motivates search for greater knowledge it may indeed further the movement towards the goal of perfect prediction *in the long run*, but will an increased number of current errors result from pursuing that possibility? For the "statisticians" the empirical evidence is that there is *at least* a short-run cost of this sort to be paid – and a long-run one too if the world is *not* really determinate or determinable. Einhorn suggests that the clinical versus statistical controversy is therefore between people who hold fundamentally different beliefs about the degree of predictability of that part of the world about which they are making judgments and/or have very different valuations of the two sorts of error which one may make: treating a situation which is "truly" random as being systematic and predictable and treating a

situation which is "truly" systematic as random and unpredictable. These errors can be labelled false positive and false negative ones respectively if it is the presence of "system" that is being diagnosed, false positives reflecting an "illusion of control" and false negatives reflecting an "illusion of helplessness". Again the obvious question that needs to be asked is whether it is either the clinicians or statisticians whose world views or error valuations ought to count in this decision.

The final paper in this section, by de Dombal [9], is a brief report on one of the few data-based decision aids that has been widely used and evaluated in routine clinical use. While based on a simple independent Bayesian model, rather than the regression or conjoint measurement techniques encountered in previous papers, it still represents a statistical – "gold standard capturing" – approach. (Wigton *et al.* did compare the weights captured from their clinicians' judgments on simulated cases with weights derived from an analysis of patients who had actually undergone angiography for pulmonary embolism. There were substantial differences, especially on the heart rate cue, but the authors are well aware that differences in the clinical setting may invalidate the use of these "actual" weights as gold standard comparisons for their clinicians.)

In a "naive" Bayesian system, such as the Leeds abdominal pain one, a carefully compiled data base is used to calculate the likelihood ratios for a set of symptoms and signs in relation to a specified condition (or set of conditions) – how much more likely an indicant is to be present (or absent) in people with the condition than in those without it. Assuming independence between the indicants these likelihood ratios are then multiplied – or added if logarithms are taken– to generate the probability of someone presenting with a particular pattern of signs and symptoms having the target condition(s). But since the predictive value of a sign or symptom will be influenced by the prevalence of the condition in the presenting population, as well as by the sensitivity and specificity of the indicant (summarized in the likelihood ratio), the calculation for a particular patient starts out from a prior probability representing that prevalence, modifying this by the likelihood of the evidence observed in that particular person.

If such a system were used as a decision *maker* we would need to think of it as a Mode 3 approach. Collecting and analyzing the distribution of indicants in a population is the essence of the epidemiological approach, which is firmly located in that mode. There is nothing in principle to prevent such a decision making use of the system, but de Dombal, as a practicing clinician, is vigorously opposed to this – and even to the comparative evaluation of probabilities produced by the system and those of clinicians diagnosing the same patients without knowledge of its outputs (or inputs for that matter). Because of the ethical and legal context of clinical action he argues that "clinical judgment must take precedence" and that the only valid comparison is between *aided clinicians* and *unaided clinicians*, that is, between clinicians using the system's output as "just another test result" in arriving at their own judgment, and clinicians who do not have the system available as an aid. In such a comparison and in a variety of hospitals (Adams *et al.* 1986) the introduction of the system appears to have had a significant effect on diagnostic performance and decision making, though the evidence indicates that a substantial part of the effect is coming from the highly structured history-taking and physical examination that data collection for the computer enforces, as well as from the motivating force of the presence of a "competitor". As de Dombal points out, the system is in fact "coercing" clinicians into doing thoroughly what they always claimed as their central function.

Process-tracing approaches

The process-tracing approach (also introduced in the paper by Elstein and Bordage) rests on close analysis of verbal reports obtained from expert clinicians as they solve diagnostic problems or make therapeutic decisions. The adequacy of the theoretical formulation of the problem-solving process constructed on the basis of this analysis can be tested in several ways: by comparison with more general cognitive principles to see if the clinical formulation is consistent with them; by the clinical judgment of experts; and by resort to computer simulation. For this last test, the theory of clinical reasoning is written as a computer program, and if the program runs and solves the problem pretty much as the clinicians did, or makes the same mistakes as they did, it can be said to be a necessary and sufficient representation of the reasoning process.

In most domains that have been examined, including clinical medicine, expertise has been shown to be heavily dependent on a well organized store of *knowledge*. Experts know more than novices and what they know is organized or compiled so as to be retrievable and applicable to new situations. Experts more easily recognize apparently new problems as transformations or variants of old, familiar problems, facilitating speed and efficiency. But differences in *strategy* between experts and novices have been harder to detect. Numerous investigators, including Eddy and Clanton [10], have identified some form of hypothetico-deductive reasoning as a basic strategy of diagnostic troubleshooting and inference. Both experts and novices solve diagnostic problems by generating a set of hypotheses or problem formulations based on very limited data – and perhaps selection of a "pivotal" finding – and using these formulations to guide subsequent data collection. The workup then functions not simply to gather a complete data base, but to test these hypotheses, confirming one or more as possible, discriminating between similar competitors, and reformulating the list along the way, if necessary (Kassirer, Kuipers and Gorry [11]). Efficiency is facilitated by generating early a set of plausible or reasonable hypotheses, so as to avoid fruitless and expensive pursuit of rare diagnoses. While the hypothetico-deductive approach characterizes both experts and novices, experts have a better sense of the structure of the environment, and therefore, what the reasonably likely possibilities are. They are therefore generally quicker, more efficient, and more accurate, it is concluded.

The expert's store of knowledge contains rules for procedures – what to do next or what to do if certain conditions are met – as well as propositional knowledge of normality and disease. Thus, experts know how to do certain things – they have practical clinical skills – and they know how to determine when these actions should be taken – that is, they have rule structure which governs performance. This implicit rule structure is sometimes referred to as "clinical judgment" and experts tend to take this knowledge for granted – it will probably often be in the highly compiled form that Schön calls "knowledge-in-action" – until they are confronted with the question of why novices stumble at this level despite the fact that they can satisfactorily answer questions about disease mechanisms. The difficulty novices experience in practice makes clear that planning and procedural skills are not identical with retrospective identification of causal mechanisms and that procedural knowledge and propositional knowledge are not identical.

Experts have richly developed networks for efficient access to and retrieval from their store of knowledge. Flexibility and adaptability to the task environment are salient expert characteristics; they do not hesitate to change paths – to reframe the problem – if that seems indicated, and they are quick to recognize a new problem as a variant of a familiar type. The rule structure for clinical puzzles appears to be complex and case-specific and this has provided a challenge for those developing decision-support systems or clinical algorithms. Information-processing research has explored several ways of handling this complex task: prototypes, frames and deep structural models that relate apparently idiosyncratic or unusual features of a case to deeper underlying principles.

The aim of research on knowledge-based decision support systems, such as MYCIN and CADUCEUS, is to create a computer program that emulates the expert clinician. The system should give the same advice or reach the same diagnostic or therapeutic decisions as the expert – and it should be able to explain its reasoning to a user much as expert human consultants explain their reasoning (in Mode 5 discussions). It is far more important, from the perspective of the potential clinical user, that the system display commonsense and intuitively clear "clinical judgment" than that it be quantitative, explicit, and consistent with any formal theory of decision making. It is natural, given these aims and constraints, that within this research community experts are viewed as knowledgeable, intelligent and flexible and that their performance and judgment are the criteria by which the computer's performance is assessed. The criterion for validation of the system's advice is the expert's judgment. If the system fails to perform as does the expert being modelled, the rule structure or data base is adjusted until it does. While in principle one could ask if the expert had made a mistake and if the machine had in fact improved upon human reason, the more usual approach in systems design is imitative; the objective is not so much to improve upon expert judgment as to make it available to the average practitioner. Expert systems research, conducted very much in the *spirit* of Schön and the Dreyfuses, displays a great confidence in experts. It doubts that the *average* level of clinical performance meets that standard, mainly because of deficiencies in the knowledge base and knowledge representation of non-experts.

In marked contrast to the statistical approach, the form of reasoning in these expert systems is symbolic and non-quantitative. Fox [12] points out that conditional probabilities or likelihood ratios

represent a *relationship* between the symptoms and diseases, but in an abstract form. They say nothing about what a symptom is, what a disease is, whether "measles" is a symptom or a disease, or whether a symptom is caused by a disease or just statistically associated with it. Each number records the *scale* of a relationship but not its *sense*. In knowledge-based systems we try to represent knowledge in a way that preserves the natural sense as well as the scale of relationships. (p. 232)

Published samples of work on knowledge-based systems suggest that the explanations they provide are much more concerned with tracing back causal mechanisms or the temporal course of a disease than with the analysis of how imperfect information has been combined. *Quantitative* elements – expressions of informed expert judgments – are involved in many knowledge-based systems (e.g. "confirmatory factors" in MYCIN; "evoking strength", "import values" and "frequency values" in CADUCEUS). But these elements are left implicit in the programming and are of concern more to the authors of the programs than to the users. They resemble probabilities for they can range from 0.0 to 1.0, but their logical status is far less clear and the design of the expert system does not require that they obey the conventional laws of probability.

Fox is impressed with the ability of knowledge-based techniques to represent an experienced clinician's knowledge qualitatively, informally and naturally, each of these being treated as a virtue for a decision aid. His paper surveys the basic ingredients of knowledge-based systems: the triptych of knowledge base (in the form of rules, for example), inference engine (in the form of data-driven "forward chaining" or goal-driven "backward chaining"; or a combination of both) and data on the particular patient. It then attempts a realistic assessment of the claims for expert systems in the light of medical experience, which is in fact all developmental and experimental experience, because there is virtually no fully evaluated clinical use of the sort reported for the Leeds data-based system. Fox makes clear that some of the major advantages claimed for such systems (e.g. that they can be developed incrementally because of the separation of the domain-focussed knowledge base from the domain-independent "inference mechanism" or "shell") will have to be reassessed in the light of this experience. Developers will also need to take much more seriously the way in which uncertainties of all sorts are represented in, and propagated through, the program. He is also very concerned that, compared with the more established statistical approaches, expert systems do not embody, or fit naturally into, a *decision-making* technology. None has any facility for incorporating values and costs explicitly into its process. Such things are implicitly introduced by way of their embedding in the expert's procedures. While procedures or rules may be a socially natural way of expressing policies and the values they reflect, they do not provide a way of dealing with conflicts of opinions about what is the "intuitively appropriate" rule. Fox sees the answer to these problems in the development of a *knowledge-based* decision theory. This would store different ways of making decisions in the knowledge base (including a purely statistical approach as one option), along with rules for when to choose a particular procedure. In other words the system would have a way of deciding how to decide. This "meta-decision" facility is a necessary part of a comprehensive decision support system, since no available theory, statistical or other, says how a particular decision task should be structured/framed. As Fox says "Bayes' rule can be used to calculate numbers, but not to calculate its own appropriateness" (p. 241).

That, however, doesn't stop committed Bayesians recommending that all problems should be structured in a way that enables them to apply their *statistical* technique. Nor does it stop Fox remaining convinced that *verbal* rules express our intuitions about what it is desirable to do in any situation better – more "naturally" – than mathematics. For him decision support systems, if they are to be intelligible and accountable should avoid, or use only when absolutely necessary, formal abstract representations of knowledge, of which numbers and equations are key examples. In the next section we move to the other extreme – to examine an approach which involves following just one, formal abstract rule, "maximize expected utility", in all situations.

PART 3: THE DECISION ANALYTIC APPROACH TO
CLINICAL DECISIONS

Decision analysis

Decision analysis (Doubilet and McNeil [13]) is an approach to rational decision making under uncertainty. It is concerned with situations in which alternative actions are available and where some chance of a poor or undesired outcome exists even if the "right" decision has been made, and where, therefore, one would wish to distinguish between employing a rational coherent process to reach a decision and achieving a good outcome. The theory can also incorporate problems of optimal allocation of scarce resources and of deciding whether it is worth obtaining a particular piece of information, given the costs and risks associated with data collection and the presumed quality of the information once it is in hand. Given all these qualities, clinical interest in decision analysis has grown considerably in recent years.

The theoretical foundation of decision analysis is the theory of expected utility, a way of ordering preferences for actions that follows logically and coherently from a few axioms. Because expected utility theory has an axiomatic base, it has had great appeal as the foundation for a rational theory of decision making and choice under uncertainty. Given agreement with the axioms one *should* accept and act on the basis of the conclusions of the analysis; in this sense it is a *prescriptive* approach which has no necessary interest in whether or not it provides a valid *description* of behaviour, or reaches the same conclusions as those actually arrived at by people.

Decision analysis decomposes any decision problem into discrete components and provides a procedure for synthesizing these components into an overall measure of the attractiveness of each possible action – its expected utility – so that the *optimal* strategy can be selected. Data required are of two types – measures of uncertainty and measures of (un)desirability. In the vocabulary of decision theory, uncertainties are expressed as probabilities and desirabilities as utilities. The expected utility of an alternative is determined by weighting (multiplying) the utilities of its outcomes by their probabilities and one should rationally choose the alternative with the highest result, i.e. maximize expected utility.

One of the few places where decision analysis is used in clinical practice in its full quantitative rigor is the New England Medical Center, where consultations are regularly undertaken by the Division of Clinical Decision Making. The results of these consultations appear as Clinical Decision Conferences in the journal *Medical Decision Making*. Our selected paper by Klein and Pauker [14] concerns the treatment of a pregnant woman for deep venous thrombosis. It is presented here as a relatively straightforward example of the decision analytic approach being used in an actual clinical case, but it gains extra interest from the existence of disparate risks to mother and foetus – pulmonary embolism without anticoagulation therapy, foetal complications with it – and the consequent need to consider parents' attitudes towards unfavourable outcomes for both mother and foetus as well as the physician's assessments of alternative drug therapies.

In this analysis extensive sensitivity analysis was undertaken in order to see how variations in the numerical assessments of probability and utility, necessary to determine the optimal strategy, affected the strategy which emerged as optimal. If a small change in an assessment leads to a different option having the highest expected utility then the decision is very sensitive in relation to that assessment. "Threshold" values can be calculated to show the point at which "switch-overs" occur and it is these threshold values that are extensively plotted and analyzed in the final section of the paper. First one variable, and then two and three variables simultaneously, are allowed to vary. The sort of complex conclusions that is made possible by three-way sensitivity analysis is that:

If the burdens of the two types of fetopathy [abnormality and death] are equal, and if the efficacy of heparin equals that of warfarin (75 percent), then the two alternatives would be equivalent. If fetal death is less severe a burden than fetal abnormality . . . then the balance swings towards heparin; if [the opposite] then the balance swings towards warfarin. Finally, all other things being equal, decreases in the efficiency of heparin (with warfarin efficacy held constant) will enlarge the region in which warfarin is to be preferred. (p. 295)

It is one of the paradoxes of decision analysis that its explicit confrontation with the multiple dimensions of decisions, such as the one in the above case, produces criticisms that the conclusions are both too simple and too complex. The accusation that it is too simple is especially likely to be heard when the conclusion conflicts with the "intuitive" judgments of clinicians. Our next study, Elstein, Holzman, Ravitch *et al.* [15], therefore undertook the task of comparing the recommendations of clinicians in relation to estrogen replacement therapy for menopausal women with those of a decision analytic model. The decision analysis took each physician's own subjective probabilities and utilities for each outcome and combined them to arrive at a recommended action. The findings showed that the decision analysis embodying *their own* assessments of the risks and benefits recommended replacement estrogen far more often than the clinicians "themselves" did. Their decisions seemed generally to be guided by the "minimax regret principle": they favoured the action with the smaller maximum loss, in this case outcomes associated with cancer.

Even though they knew that progestin with estrogen would reduce cancer risk to about the level of no treatment, they avoided this regimen. In addition, they seemed to feel more responsible for bad outcomes caused by their *action* (cancers caused by estrogen treatment they had prescribed) than for bad outcomes that "just happened" following inaction (spontaneous fractures due to osteoporosis). Significantly for programmes of continuing medical education, their behaviour could not be attributed to ignorance of the facts. While there were clear individual differences in the accuracy of probability estimates, on average they were remarkably accurate. The estrogen replacement decision hinged on the way information was integrated, not on unawareness of specific risks and benefits.

Handling uncertainty

Work done in the area known as "behavioral decision theory" approaches clinical reasoning from the opposite direction to that of information processing psychology: a formal, explicit, quantitative model of inference and decision making is employed as the standard of comparison. The model is statistical decision theory, or expected utility theory, embodied in the procedures and techniques known as decision analysis. Research derived from this model investigates the extent to which human decision making corresponds to this model, the reasons for observed discrepancies, and the psychological processes employed in carrying out the probability and utility assessments required by decision analysis.

A central conception in behavioral decision theory as well as information processing psychology is that of bounded or limited rationality. This principle expresses the idea that our capacity to carry out rational thought is limited or bounded, in part by the limited size of working memory. As a consequence, problem solvers are required to represent complex problems in simplified problem spaces and to find ways ("heuristics") to cut down mental effort and reduce cognitive strain. Information processing psychology sees experts as adaptive and clever in spite of these limitations on their rationality. Despite the fact that human experts make mistakes, expert systems research, as we have seen, esteems clinical judgment so highly that it finds it worthwhile to design computer programs that will mimic these judgments insofar as it is possible. Behavioural decision theory takes a much more guarded view of unaided human inference. The research in this tradition has identified systematic errors and biases in information processing and judgment among physicians at various levels of experience and has shown that clinical inference often fails to obey the rules of statistical decision theory. Departures from the prescriptive theory can be demonstrated in each of the four major phases of the analytic process: hypothesis (i.e. option) generation, probability assessment and revision, utility assessment and combining the separate assessments to reach a decision.

In the early days of this research the maximization of expected utility was taken as a fairly good approximation of what people actually do – or at least what they try and want to do. More recently, the validity of this hypothesis as even a first approximation of actual decision making has come under increasing criticism. The most troubling problems for decision theorists have arisen in situations where decision makers not only do not obey the expected utility rule but, when their inconsistency is pointed out to them, insist that they do not want to change their decisions. These observations have cast some doubt on the normative status of this major theory of rational decision making and have occasioned much lively debate about the status of the theory and of our understanding of what it means to be rational.

However, as suggested in an earlier section, many of the errors and biases that have been identified from the standpoint of behavioural decision theory also have relevance within the information-processing approach to clinical reasoning, so there is considerable overlap in practice, if not in principle. This is what gives Fischhoff and Beyth-Marom's [16] taxonomy of the possible "ways to stray" from the Bayesian approach to hypothesis testing a wider significance. Using Bayes Theorem in its odds form as their basic reference, they systematically analyze the ways in which omissions and errors in component elements, or their combination, may distort the conclusion reached. This provides not only a framework for classifying (and reinterpreting) existing research results that claim to discern defects in human inference, but also an agenda for future research – if there is no empirical evidence pointing to a conceptually possible bias does this represent "an opportunity to observe suboptimal behaviour that researchers missed or an opportunity to exhibit suboptimal behaviour that subjects 'missed?'" (p. 324)

The following "ways of straying clinically" seem worth particular emphasis, because of their appearance in both the "pessimistic" stream of research in behavioural decision theory and in research in the clinical information processing tradition.

1 Failure to retrieve correct hypothesis from memory. Many diagnostic problems are so complex that the correct solution is not contained within the initial set of formulations. Restructuring and reformulating must occur as problem solving proceeds. However, as a problem solver works with a particular set of hypotheses, psychological commitment takes place and it becomes more difficult to restructure the problem. One might feel, ideally, one ought to work purely inductively, "waiting till all the data are in" and then reasoning from them, but this is never done in practice because this strategy is so inefficient in time and other costs, including the

patient's condition. (This does not prevent its explicit or implied recommendation in many teaching situations.) Some schemata are needed to
provide structure for reasoning and hypotheses provide the needed
framework. Early problem formulation is necessary – but also potentially
biasing.

2 Pursuit of exotic categories at the expense of more probable diseases.
This bias might occur because rare diseases are over-represented in the
literature and in training centres and these circumstances lead novices in
particular to overestimate their likelihood. In addition, very small probabilities tend to be overestimated. It is also difficult for everyday judgment
to keep separate accounts for probability and utility. If the rarer disease is
more serious, there is a good chance that clinicians will respond to the
regret they would feel about missing that diagnosis instead of to a
weighted combination of probability and value. The pleasure that comes
from identifying a rare disease that other clinicians have missed may set
off a search that is motivated by probability-contaminated values.

3 Misinterpretation of data. The most common error in processing
data is to interpret data which should be non-contributory to a particular
hypothesis, and which might even suggest that an alternative be considered, as consistent with hypotheses already under consideration. The
data best remembered tend to be those that fit the hypotheses generated.
Where findings are distorted in recall, it is generally in the direction of
making the facts more consistent with typical clinical pictures. Positive
findings tend to be overemphasized and negative findings discounted and
there is a tendency to seek information that would confirm a hypothesis
rather than the information that would permit testing of two or more
competing hypotheses (Wolf, Gruppen and Billi [17]). Clinicians also tend
to collect more data than are needed, because they are often unaware of
the redundancies in the data and more data tend to increase confidence
without increasing accuracy. In summary, clinicians have difficulty
extracting all the information embedded in a data set, but like to keep
adding to it. In these circumstances, some inefficiency in inference due to
information overload is practically inevitable.

4 Probability revision. From the standpoint of decision theory, the
process of reaching a diagnosis can be conceptualized as probability
revision with imperfect information. The formal rule for probability
revision in the light of such evidence is Bayes' theorem. In the past decade,
many studies have demonstrated a lack of appreciation of the statistical
properties of clinical evidence, neglect of Bayes' theorem in revising
diagnostic probabilities, and mistaken intuitions about the effects of low
prevalence on the interpretation of test results. In particular, these studies
have repeatedly shown confusion between a test's *performance rates*
which (combined in the likelihood ratio) yield its *diagnostic value* and its

predictive values. Unless the problem is so structured so as to call attention to the relevance of Bayes' rule, there is a strong tendency to equate test sensitivity with the predictive value of a positive test and test specificity with the predictive value of a negative one.

Some studies have begun to identify the processes clinicians use when revising probabilities that lead to Bayesian violations. For example, base rates are often neglected in favour of individualizing information, perhaps because case material is more vivid and memorable. Balla, Iansek and Elstein (1985) found that the impact of prior established disease was underestimated and the posterior probability of new disease over-estimated when two conditions were met: the new disease possibility had less ominous prognostic implications, and the probability of observing the findings in the new disease was greater than its probability in the established condition. In this situation, base rate neglect – a "cognitive bias" – and wishful thinking – a "motivated bias" – combine to yield erroneous probability estimates.

We have selected two papers from the empirical literature on prob-ability assessment. Each gives some further support to those who are "pessimists" about clinicians' judgmental ability, but also, in its different way, contributes to the "optimistic" counter school of thought that has become increasingly dissatisfied with the pessimists' portrayal of humans, and even clinical experts, as cognitive cripples.

Overconfidence was one of the findings of Christensen-Szalanski and Bushyhead [18] in their investigation and evaluation of clinician's use of probabilities in the management of possible pneumonia cases in an outpatient clinic. In line with most other studies (apart from those of weather forecasters and horserace odds forecasters) they found their subjects' probabilities poorly *calibrated*: at all levels of probability the proportion of cases confirmed to have pneumonia (by a radiological gold standard) was much less than expected. For example, less than 20 percent of people assigned a pneumonia probability between 80 and 100 percent actually had it. In order to establish whether this "overconfidence" reflected a motivated bias the authors also asked their physicians for their relative vaiuations of the alternative forms of diagnostic correctness and error. Since they did not rate a True Positive as better or worse than a True Negative, nor a False Positive differently from a False Negative, the authors conclude that the bias was a cognitive one. (If one does have differential valuations the normatively correct procedure is, as we have seen in the previous section, to arrive at "uncontaminated" probability assessments, but to select actions on the basis of the utilities of the outcomes as well as their probability. In this sense the "overdiagnosis" of a disease like pneumonia is justifiable, but not the overassessment of its probability.)

The second bias looked for in this study was the tendency to ignore or under use "base rate" information about populations or groups, compared with case-specific information about the particular patient. This question was investigated by comparing the "actual" predictive values for pneumonia of a large number of symptoms – both the predictive value of a symptom when present and its predictive value when absent – with physicians' *implicit* predictive values, measured as the mean probabilities of pneumonia for patients with and without a symptom. Finding a significant positive correlation in both "present" and "absent" cases the authors conclude that their physicians *had* taken base rate information into account, since only by doing so could they arrive at such valid predictive values.

This paper makes a substantive contribution in making clear that any simple claim about widespread multiple biases in clinical assessments of probability is likely to be insupportable (overconfidence was found, but not neglect of base rates). But it is of wider interest methodologically, because of the attempt made to overcome the laboratory basis of most bias studies. Christensen-Szalanski and Bushyhead have addressed the issue of whether a bias (e.g. neglect of base rate) is exhibited when the relevant information must be drawn from *experience* rather than being provided as part of the experimental design. They feel that previous studies

which tested the participant's ability to use base-rate information when presented in quantitative word problems, did not test ability to use base-rate information obtained *from experience* . . . The experience of a 3 percent base rate is more salient and thus may be easier for physicians to incorporate into their judgment processes than reading a sentence that states the base rate is 3 percent. (p. 371)

But even they have to concede that one quite plausible explanation of the failure of their physicians (as a group) to exhibit base rate neglect is methodological: the requirement that they fill in a checklist of signs and symptoms when examining patients may have meant a much greater attention to all information, particularly absent-cue information, than would have been the case in "real life". The paper is, by virtue of its practitioner focus and base rate results, in line with the "optimistic" stream of thought that questions the bias literature on the ground that the latter is, in its methodology, biased in favour of discovering bias. But it demonstrates yet again the difficulty of moving much beyond highly tentative conclusions in judgment and decision-making research and hence the danger of not placing the burden of proof *equally* on optimistic defender of the status quo and pessimistic sceptic.

The bias with perhaps the most fundamental implications for the way clinical activity and teaching are organized is the "hindsight" one. Hindsight bias leads to – indeed is defined as – the assigning of a higher probability to that outcome of an event that is known to have occurred than was (or would have been) actually assigned to it while it remained uncertain. People tend, the suggestion goes, to "remember" having assigned a higher probability to the correct outcome (winning team, correct diagnosis) before the result was known than they actually did at the time. The bias is difficult to investigate for fairly obvious reasons. It is less likely to be exhibited if genuine "prior" probabilities are elicited beforehand – they may be recalled when the hindsight questions are asked – but if they are not elicited then one is clearly investigating the subject's *reconstruction* of his/her state of mind. Arkes, Wortmann, Saville and Harkness [19] rely on group differences to explore the existence of hindsight bias among practicing clinicians and their results give qualified confirmation of the existence of the bias among people with substantial subject knowledge. Earlier studies demonstrated its presence mainly among people with little or no knowledge of the area about which they were making probability assessments. This doesn't matter in principle because it is the difference between foresight and hindsight judgments that is being investigated not – as in our preceding study – how good either of those assessments are.

Five groups of clinicians were presented with a case history of a patient which permitted four possible diagnoses. All were asked for their individual assessment of the probabilities of the four diagnoses, but only one group (the "foresight" one) was left in the dark about the actual outcome. Each of the other four ("hindsight") groups was told that a different one of the four diagnoses was the correct one. A majority of the "hindsight" clinicians gave higher probabilities to the known-to-have-occurred outcome than that given by the "foresight" group. However, when analysis by "correct diagnosis" was undertaken, it became clear that the bias was exhibited only by the groups who had been told that the two least likely diagnoses were correct (least likely according to the foresight group). In other words the hindsight bias was present only for events initially judged to be least plausible.

The authors feel that, despite this qualification, their results confirm that hindsight bias is compelling and they see it as having major implications for clinicians. If one believes one "knew it all along" one not only has little motivation to learn, but also lacks the cognitive basis on which learning can occur: if one believes one's prior odds *were* the same as one's posterior odds *are*, then any evidence one has observed is implicitly assigned a likelihood ratio of 1 to 1 (i.e. treated as uninformative). Making sense out of what is known to have occurred or to be the case is a *very* different cognitive activity from constructing a set of possibilities (a differential diagnosis) and assessing their likelihood. To the extent that referral systems and clinical teaching fail to require genuinely independent, *ex ante*, analyses by staff and students, they permit and encourage hindsight bias – and hence overconfidence – with deleterious consequences for diagnostic accuracy and clinical decision making.

Handling values

The various bounds and biases which may characterize clinical inference will clearly (if they exist) impinge on the way in which practitioner and client arrive at "their" management decision. Any inferential shortcomings among patients will exacerbate the likelihood of an inferior decision, unless they are fortuitously offsetting. Eraker and Politser [20] explore some of the main ways in which they may interfere with the incorporation of the patient's preferences into the clinical decision being made about them. They are particularly concerned that physicians better understand the way patients perceive the risks and benefits of investigation and treatment – that is, the *value* or *utility* side of the clinical decision. In this respect decision analysis may be a useful tool for both physician and patient, if applied with caution and in the light of the assumptions it makes.

In decision analysis, the assessment of utilities is based on the assumption that a pre-existing set of coherent values exists in someone's head and is awaiting measurement. The problem is thus conceptualized mainly as a measurement task. The techniques used for utility elicitation are supposed to do just that – *elicit* preferences, not *form* them. Furthermore, since pre-existing preferences are being elicited, the numbers obtained ought to be equivalent over formally "equivalent" presentations of the problem. The evidence for framing and context effects in utility assessment seriously challenges this idealized notion. For example McNeil and her colleagues (1982) asked medical students and physicians about their preferences for alternative therapies for cancer when the outcomes of these therapies were framed as the probabilities of living or dying within a fixed period of time. These frames are clearly formally equivalent presentations of the problem, since the two probabilities are complementary. Nevertheless, patterns of preference showed a marked sensitivity to the wording of the problem, which is inconsistent with expected utility theory. Apparently innocuous changes in the wording of a question can exert powerful effects on responses to these questions.

Our next selected reading, by Llewellyn-Thomas, Sutherland, Tibshirani *et al.* [21], raises other serious questions about the fit between the psychological processes people ordinarily employ in judging health states and the axioms of utility theory. In the standard gamble method of eliciting utilities, the one with the best-established axiomatic basis, the utility of any specified "intermediate" health state is defined as the expected value of a gamble involving best and worst outcomes with specified probabilities, provided that the decision maker is indifferent between remaining in that intermediate state with certainty and playing that gamble. The probabilities in this reference gamble are adjusted until the indifference point is found, and the expected value of the gamble can then be calculated by multiplying the probabilities of the best and worst outcomes by their values. If the relative values of the "best" and "worst" outcomes are arbitrarily defined as 1.0 and 0.0, the utility of any intermediate outcome is given by the probability of the "best" outcome needed to make the decision maker judge that intermediate state equivalent to the gamble. In theory, at least, the calculated utility of an intermediate state should be consistent even if the best and worst anchors of the gamble are changed. As the gamble outcomes are changed, the decision maker should change the indifference probabilities just enough to hold the utility of the intermediate outcome constant. This consistency would imply that people can and do locate health states on a continuous underlying scale. The Toronto researchers (and others, too) raise serious questions about the validity of this assumption.

Llewellyn-Thomas and her colleagues found that the utility assigned to a particular state varied with the outcomes used in the gambles presented. The utilities of intermediate states were significantly higher when death was not used as the "worst" outcome. The point is not that the patients responded in such a way as to suggest that death was an overriding consideration – in fact, the reverse – but that the alternatives offered in the gamble did strongly influence the utility calculated for each of these states. Evidently, the probability adjustments made were not accurate enough to hold the utilities of these intermediate outcomes relatively constant, in clear violation of expected utility theory. The results were compatible with the "prospect theory" interpretation that subjects framed gambles involving death in terms of losses and gambles not involving death in terms of gains (Kahneman and Tversky, 1979), but the study did not permit firm conclusions about this being the underlying source of the violation.

These investigators also found that the *style* in which the health states were expressed influenced the utility assessment. Vivid first person narrative scenarios consistently produced lower utilities than detached, more impersonal summaries of five health states. This is yet another confirmation of the proposition that different methods of utility elicitation are likely to yield different numbers. In some instances, these differences can change the recommended course of action. It therefore becomes increasingly difficult to speak of *the* utility of a particular outcome for a person, independent of the language used to describe it and the context of judgment. Human judgment appears to be more context dependent than expected utility theory prescribes. Yet the normative theory *per se* offers no guidance as to the proper way to word the options or what outcomes should be used as the reference outcomes for a standard gamble. One recommendation for avoiding the bias that may be inherent in a particular framing or phrasing is to present the options in several different ways, and to explore the meaning and significance of variations in responses. This caution applies not only to clinicians who may use utility elicitation techniques to involve their patients in decision making, but also to all clinicians who are conscientiously thinking about options and choices on behalf of their patients. Given these thorny issues, decision analysis is likely to prove more useful as a conceptual framework for stimulating thought about the structure and ingredients of "the problem" than it is to provide a recipe for its quick and easy solution. Interpreted in this way it is to be clearly disassociated from Technical Rationality of the sort that so concerns Schön and others, becoming a valuable resource for "reflection-in-action" as well as retrospective reflection-on-action and (as more normally) prospective reflection-for-action.

As itself a clinical activity, there is a case for decision analysts reflecting on themselves and their own behaviour, which is often undertaken at Mode 6 level. Fischhoff [22] points out that:

When it comes time to apply [their] tools . . . decision analysts must more or less rely on their own wits. There is no codified body of knowledge telling them when to use formal models and when to rely on intuitive judgments, how to approach decision makers and how to coax from them their true problems, which elicitation methods to use and when to trust their results, which parameters should be subjected to sensitivity analysis and what range of alternative values should be used, how to make certain that the assumptions and conclusions of an analysis are understood and heeded, or when decision analysis is likely to improve the understanding of a decision problem and when it is not likely to be cost effective. Such knowledge as does exist regarding these topics is largely anecdotal. It is acquired by trial and error in the field, perhaps aided by apprenticeship with a veteran practitioner. (p. 409)

In considering the future of decision analysis at the clinical level Fischhoff feels it helpful to look at the history of a somewhat older clinical activity – psychotherapy. In all its myriad forms it has been and is dedicated, like decision analysis, to helping its clients to understand their world better, and function better in it. It, too, typically urges the benefits of confronting explicitly the *uncertainties* and motivational and *value conflicts* that are seen to be at the heart of current difficulties. Three key points emerge from the comparison.

One is the great importance of – but equally great difficulty of – proper evaluation of the activity, including whether it "degrades gracefully" in the hands of less than expert practitioners. (Is a poorly done decision analysis, or psychoanalysis, better or worse than none at all?) A second is the need for mutual adaptation between analysts and clients, rather than the uncompromising insistence by clients that the analysis be "acceptable" by the standard of their status quo (cognitively or organizationally), or by analysts that the full theoretical rigor of the technique is always needed. (The education value of an analysis may be as important as its recommendation of a particular alternative.) And the third is the importance of accepting that in the widest sense neither decision analysis nor psychotherapy can be value-neutral. They are both based on the assumption that their clients can help themselves address their current problem, or decision, better if they have greater insight into themselves and their world. But the decision analytic assumptions that the client's world is sufficiently ordered and that he or she has the necessary beliefs and preferences to enter into the analysis, can be no more than that – assumptions. Those who see reason as having a relatively minor role to play in the determination of human action and the structuring of societies will not be attracted by the assumption or by the technique. While they need not necessarily be agreed with, an awareness of the subtler ideological context of clinical activity should inform the decision analyst's own "reflective practice".

PART 4: THE CONTEXTS OF CLINICAL DECISIONS

Clinical judgments and decisions are not isolated cognitive events. They can be meaningfully conceptualized only in relation to a task and that task will of necessity occur in some context. (The "unreality" of laboratory contexts has been a prominent feature of clinicians' criticisms of research reported in earlier papers in this collection.) Clinicians operate in particular institutional settings and wider social contexts and these influence more or less heavily and more or less directly the actions open to them as well as their ways of deciding which of these actions to undertake (their mode of practice). These influences are, in the extreme, of such dominating force that they are appropriately referred to as ideologies. Some would argue, as we have just noted, that the whole notion of clinical judgment and decision making – focussing as it does on the single case – is ideology-based. And it *is*, compared to a form of practice in which the whole community is charged with responsibility for its health care, and judgments and decisions, such as there are, are collective in character and community-oriented. But even within our chosen clinical paradigm there are clearly wide variations in the structures – political, economic, ethical, legal and sociological – within which practitioners (and their clients) think and behave.

The economic context

Medical care and its provision has been one of the most contentious political issues within the Western democracies and the debates over the appropriate mix of responsibility between private and public sectors, between insurance-based and tax-based funding, and between fee-for service and alternative modes of practitioner remuneration continue to flourish. Indeed their intensity is, if anything, increasing as the possibilities open to practitioners expand in the light of new knowledge and technological capability – and client expectations and (seemingly) dissatisfaction also grow. Clinical freedom and autonomy are at the heart of these debates insofar as they involve the use of resources which might have been used in some alternative way – which is almost all resources, including the clinician's, and client's time.

Economic analysis takes as its starting point the scarcity of resources compared with the uses which could be made of them. It takes for granted, in contradiction of the medical principle, that "everything *cannot* be done" for patients in general (as opposed to – possibly – doing it for some small number of patients). It assumes that the use of some resources to generate benefits in one way involves foregoing the benefits that would have been generated by using them in some other way. The fundamental fact of *scarcity* leads to the logical necessity of *choice* and to the conceptualization of the cost of resources as their cost *in some use*, to be properly measured by the benefits foregone in their most productive alternative use. The economic or *opportunity cost* of a new piece of equipment (e.g. a scanner) is not the amount of money it costs, but the highest amount of benefits that could be generated if this money was not spent on a scanner. If those foregone benefits are lower than the benefits generated by the scanner then the latter represents the optimal use of that amount of money and the resources it represents. It they are higher the resources cannot rationally be allocated to the scanner.

It is not uncommon for clinicians and other caring professionals to dismiss completely the relevance of economic analysis to their work. To the extent that this rejection is based on the assertion that one central professional "resource" – "caring" or in some sense "love" – is *not* scarce, does not have to be allocated, and indeed may increase rather than be drawn down during the process of care, the argument reflects a correct understanding of what economists are saying. But even if "professional love" is an important characteristic which distinguishes professional-client relationships from ordinary exchange-based ones, it does not in any way eliminate the need for choice in respect of the undeniably scarce resources over which the professional has control or influence. While love itself may be infinite, the time available to spend with each of the possible recipients is definitely finite, as are the various investigative and therapeutic resources which the professional may wish to employ in this client's interest.

Should clinicians reject any role in the allocation of scarce resources between patients (including potential patients) as an ethically inappropriate one, incompatible with his/her responsibility to the individual currently under treatment? Most clinicians do seem to have a highly developed *intuitive* sense of what in economic jargon would be called the marginal opportunity cost of what they are doing – and appear to act on the basis of it. At a personal level they are constantly making implicit assessments of whether it is better to spend an extra period of time with patient A or to move on to patients B (and C . . .). The criterion for this decision is clearly a comparison of the benefits to B (and C . . .) with those to A. Rejection of such a "cost-benefit assessment" would seem the essence of poor clinical judgment, yet there is considerable resistance to the principle as soon as it is made *explicit* and held up as a normative ideal, especially for the allocation of resources between groups of people requiring different types of treatment (and often therefore different types of clinician).

Such a stance leaves the decisions elsewhere – to the distribution of income and wealth in society in respect of private medicine and to the decisions of legislators and budget holders in relation to public systems. Schwartz and Aaron [23] have examined one of the most socialized of the western systems of medical care provision – the British National Health Service – with a view to seeing how clinicians behave in a system where the total amount of resources is determined at governmental level and there are clear indications that "everything *possible* is not being done" for each patient, let alone every potential patient. Whether or not the rates at which various procedures are done in the United States are an appropriate reference is debatable, but, along with the existence of long waiting lists in Britain, such rate differentials demonstrate that very different attitudes to the need for treatment and to the timing of response to that need, prevail in the two countries. While noting the existence of the safety valve of a private sector, Schwartz and Aaron emphasize the way both the British people and British clinicians have "adapted to" the everyday consequences of the idealistic philosophy on which the NHS is based: maintenance of the ideal of access to all necessary care at time of need and free at the point of consumption, is accompanied by behavioural adaptation to the economic reality that means the ideal will always remain just that. They see clinician adaptation as having been crucial to the continued functioning of a system which *in their view* systematically denies many patients useful, even lifesaving, care. This adaptation is psychological and implicit and has no formal basis:

Explicit limitation of medical resources puts physicians in a position that many of them find awkward. Neither the training nor the ethics of medicine prepare most physicians to make the required decisions in economic terms. Therefore, wherever possible, British doctors recast a problem of resource scarcity into medical terms. They have developed standards of care that incorporate economic reality into medical judgments. (p. 429)

The question which follows is clearly, why, if this is being done implicitly and intuitively (at Modes 6 and 5), it should not be done more formally. The relevant language and theory – that of economic evaluation – is introduced by Drummond [24] who points to its relevance at both the *planning* level, where the decisions concern the allocation of resources across programmes of medical care provision, and at the *clinical* level, where practitioners are making investigative and therapeutic decisions concerning individuals. The lack of any formal link between these levels is a major problem and one that is not necessarily solved even when economic evaluations are carried out at each level separately. But engaging in such analysis is the prerequisite of a "rational" use of resources within each level.

Economic evaluations take three major forms, depending on the measure of output (benefits) used. The least controversial form is cost-effectiveness analysis, which gains its appeal (and relative lack of controversy) from the fact that it uses some everyday "natural" indicator as its measure of output – "life years gained", "bed days saved". A programme (or clinical option) which produces more life years gained than another involving the same resource cost is more cost-effective. But such analysis cannot help when the first programme involves higher costs as well as higher gains, and neither can it help when more than one sort of output is of concern and the programmes differ in their ability to generate them (e.g. life years gained and improved social functioning). Evaluations in these sorts of situation require us to inject some relative worth assessments and bring all the outputs into a common currency.

If that currency is *money* then we have cost-benefit analysis. In this all the benefits of a programme are summed up in a monetary amount and since this sum can be directly compared with the costs of the programme (or clinical option) we are in a position to say whether or not it is worth undertaking it at all – in an absolute sense. One should not (given that one is satisfied that all the benefits have been correctly identified, measured and commuted into money values) spend resources where the return is less than the cost. Of course the parenthesized qualification is the source of intense controversy and, in conjunction with opposition to the whole idea of "rational optimization" in human affairs, the basis of massive resistance to the idea of full-blown cost-benefit analysis in areas such as health care provision. One cannot (and should not) it is said place a monetary value of human life, or on a life year gained, or even on an increased probability of a life year gained – not to mention any of the other tangible and intangible attributes of health that medical care may help generate.

Confronted by this sort of reaction, but impressed more by the fact that choices and behaviour in the real world have the effect of *actually* placing relative valuations on all these things, economists have produced a compromise measure: a technique somewhere between cost-benefit and cost-effectiveness analysis called cost-utility analysis, with its increasingly familiar acronym, the QALY (Quality Adjusted Life Year). As its name implies this form of evaluation draws on utility theory and elicitation techniques to produce an output measure on which, in principle, all competing uses of health and medical care resources can be compared. But by not placing any *monetary* value on these it makes no assertion about the absolute worth of any of these programmes, merely that programmes (or clinical options) which generate more QALYs should be favoured relative to those which generate fewer.

Having established the logical case for cost-utility analysis Drummond is particularly keen to acknowledge the difficulties in the elicitation of the necessary utilities and establishing the "proper" rate at which the future should be discounted. (A zero discount rate seems attractive, but is incompatible with almost all human behaviour.) There is, moreover, the problem of how one divides up the world. What groups of actions and what groups of patients are to be regarded as homogeneous enough to be lumped together and what groups are to be regarded as worth of separate status? Who and what is put into a category will influence very much the number of QALYs generated per unit of expenditure and hence its claim on resources. Finally, even if one were to have arrived at a fully satisfactory set of QALY outputs for a fully satisfactory categorization of action/patient combinations, should one use the resulting league table in the obvious and straightforward manner? This would involve starting with the most (QALY) productive programme (e.g. hip replacements), spending all the money necessary to cope with that condition, then moving on to the second most productive use (e.g. pacemakers) . . . and so on down the list. Even if it were done less mechanically than this, the clear implication is that those with conditions which medical care can do little about in terms of generating increased quality or quantity of life will receive few resources. Is this *just*? It will not be unjust because the importance of "caring" (as compared with "curing") has not been properly incorporated in the utility measure – there is nothing in the technique which excludes caring – but it may well be unjust by some non-utilitarian criterion.

The methodological difficulties in carrying out economic evaluations are well illustrated in the study by Boyle *et al.* [25] into the provision of intensive neonatal care for very low birth weight infants. They attempted all three forms of evaluation and not unexpectedly found that by any measure of output (using a 5 percent discount rate) the results were more favourable for relatively heavier infants than for relatively lighter ones. For example the cost per QALY gained was seven times higher for newborns weighing 500–999 g than for ones weighing 1000–1499 g. There were however variations *within* each of these subgroups, which demonstrates the importance of the classification issue mentioned earlier. The broad results held up under sensitivity analysis and the authors feel that their results are reasonably free from bias in terms of both population characteristics and cost calculation – and are therefore capable of being generalized to other "similar" settings. But their concern with how well these possible biases have been dealt with in other studies made them unwilling to make comparisons beyond their internal one. And of course the relative cost-utility of intensive care for VLBW infants in the 500–999 g class can only be judged if that for all other programmes in competition for the same resources can be established.

Both Drummond and Boyle *et al.* are conscious of treading a tightrope in making the case for economic evaluation. On the one side they are convinced that we are doing no one a service by telling ourselves that costs of our chosen actions are "only money", when they are actually the benefits (extra quantity and/or quality of life) that other individuals would enjoy if we had chosen to do something else. On the other side they recognize the formidable, and far from irrational, objections that may be raised to any practical implementation of formal techniques, even if their desirability in principle is conceded. One such objection is that formal analyses are subject to possible manipulation in the interests of particular groups (e.g. by the definitions or measurement techniques adopted) just as much as the alternative, current, more informal methods. Here one is moving into personal assessments of the efficiency and equity of the "political markets" that represent the status quo in resource allocation: the macro markets that produce national and regional budgets and the micro markets of particular institutions, professional groupings and departmental teams. Whether the techniques that characterize the work-ings of such markets – of which "shroud waving" is perhaps the most prominent – are socially more effective than formal approaches, which severely constrain the sort of arguments that can be advanced and call for fundamental agreement on measures and explicit relative valuations, is not easy to establish. Introducing the latter may "merely" shift the political debate to a higher level. But, having said that, it should make it more open on fundamental issues, and this is something which may be regarded as valuable in its own right. As with decision analysis the ultimate case for economic evaluation may not be the merits of the technique in problem *solving*, but in a way it facilitates debate about problem *framing*.

The ethical and legal context

Economic analysis fits most easily with one of the two major categories of ethical theory – the consequentialist or utilitarian – and we have so far underplayed the role played, in its rejection by clinicians (and caring professionals in general), by their adherence to principles derived from the other – the absolutist or deontological. Broadly speaking a utilitarian ethic judges the "goodness" of an action by its *consequences*, whereas a deontological ethic judges it by whether or not it is in accordance with relevant rights and duties and in this sense by its *internal character*, irrespective of its consequences. Candee and Puka [26] are careful to emphasize that these broad approaches do not offer any *detailed* guidance for particular clinical decisions – they are philosophies not recipes or algorithms – but they accept the challenge of arguing through the same case from within each perspective.

The particular strength of their attempt lies in their willingness to offer illustrative numerical values in the case of the utilitarian approach and a detailed listing of the relevant rights and duties in the case of the deontological one. Their aim is to make it clear that it is only by giving *particular* responses that one can arrive at an ethical decision within either approach. It is not to defend their own ones, except insofar as they *are* particular ones and can therefore be legitimately criticized only by an offering of an alternative set of responses at the same level. They naturally offer no suggestion as to whether a utilitarian or deontological approach is "better" or any guidance as to how the two sorts of analysis (or their results in a particular case) might be integrated – if one wanted to take both *consequences* and *rights and duties* into account. Most clinicians, and indeed most people, claim to attach importance to both these aspects of an action and Candee and Puka apparently go along with this, while being able to offer only encouragement and the suggestion that a limited exercise may still be useful.

An individual may not actually go through the process of constructing utilitarian tables or listing all claims, rights, and duties in every moral dilemma. A simple list of pros and cons, and a consideration of one or two rights will probably suffice in most cases. But, having seen the process that underlies detailed ethical reasoning, the health professional is in a better position to guide her thought and to know which questions must be answered before she or he can rest comfortably with any moral decision. (p. 488)

One thing that emerges clearly from any detailed consideration of a decision with ethical implications – and almost all decisions have them – is that the designation of which individuals or groups are to be included in the analysis is crucial in determining the answers that may finally be arrived at. In determining the *scope* of the analysis one is assigning "property rights" to individuals or groups, property not in the sense of material goods but of power to control or influence the allocation of resources. At its simplest, to be regarded as an "insider" rather than an "outsider". International boundaries provide a clear example but there are many *intra*national boundaries which are relevant to resource allocation in health care, such as those between professionals and administrators, between professionals and clients and between patients and their relatives. McGuire [27] explores the impact of the pattern of property rights in contemporary western health care systems and suggests that they exacerbate what he sees as the undesirably individualistic bias of medical care.

Medical ethics, and particularly the various ethical codes that have been compiled from the time of Hippocrates, have been dominated by the ethic of duty towards the individual patient currently under the care of the practitioner. The justification for this has been that the practitioner gets his authority in relation to the person he treats (and can only validly get such authority) from their *individual* consent to him/her acting as their *agent*. Unless that patient can trust the doctor to act on his behalf, *and only on his behalf*, this whole-hearted consent, which is of great clinical as well as legal significance, will not be forthcoming. However, in respecting this trust – and the assumption of total self-interest by the patient on which it is based – the practitioner is necessarily forsaking the interest of all other individuals who might be in need of care and is, in that sense, not considering the "social" or "common good".

The strong property rights enjoyed by clinicians in the disposition of health care resources come partly from their agency relationship with patients and the power it gives them to determine what and how many resources are *consumed*. But they also arise from the fact that governments and other regulators and interested parties (e.g. insurance groups) have delegated many of their powers to the profession in the form of self government and licencing. Clinicians therefore have great power to determine what and how much is *produced*. These powers have traditionally been exercised only in relation to the *short-run* allocation of resources, and the "firefighting" nature of much clinical activity, as well as the inherent uncertainty of the clinical task, have been key factors justifying the need for "clinical freedom and autonomy", the outward manifestation of structural power.

Having distinguished two sorts of economic inefficiency – technical inefficiency (using excessive amounts of resources to produce a unit of some output, e.g. a hip replacement) and allocative inefficiency (allocating resources among different forms of output, such as hip replacements and coronary by-pass operations, in a way that does not maximize social benefits) McGuire suggests that the individualistic bias of medical ethics has until recently mainly encouraged *technical* inefficiency. But as overall budget pressures increase, and calls for cost containment come from those who have retained power over long-run resource allocation, they are likely to have growing consequences for *allocative* efficiency. The existing property rights of doctors, symbolized by their clinical freedom, are therefore under threat from this direction (as well as from "consumerist" pressures) and the resolution can, in McGuire's view, come in only one of two ways. One possibility is a de-individualization (or socialization) of medical ethics, so that the common good becomes an ever-present consideration in the individual clinical decision. Given this, doctors could be allowed to retain unreduced power over short-run allocation. The other possibility is the retention of the individualistic ethic at the clinical level, but the loss by clinicians of much of their powers over resource allocation even in the short run. Clinicians are thus faced with either taking the wider consequences of their actions into account themselves, or having their area of discretion reduced so that others can control those consequences.

McGuire, like Drummond and the advocates of many of the formal techniques surveyed earlier, is far from complacent about the ability of *non-clinical* parts of the health care structure to satisfactorily encapsulate the common good in their increasingly short-run interventions. Clinicians are in many ways much better placed to assess the relationship between particular interventions and health states. But it is their strong orientation to addressing this relation in the acute individual case (e.g. heart surgery) rather than in chronic community ones (e.g. geriatric care) that McGuire personally feels is presently disqualifying them from retaining this role.

Clinicians' actions take place not only within a particular institutional structure but within a particular jurisdiction. Legal developments have added to the uncertainty characterizing clinical judgment and decision making. Irrespective of any contractual relationship between professional and client, the practitioner owes a legal "duty of care" to the patient and it is the basis on which he/she can be held to be in breach of that duty which has exercised courts and legislatures on both sides of the Atlantic in recent years. Historically the breach of most concern has been negligence in relation to management actions – in the carrying out of appropriate investigations and treatment (e.g. failing to do a test, amputating the wrong leg). Recently the emphasis has shifted from such malpractice to breaches in the obtaining of the patient's consent and particularly in the adequacy of a doctor's disclosure of information. A central issue has been whether the same standard should be applied to breaches in respect of the obtaining of consent as in the carrying out of management. But how that standard should be defined is also itself at the centre of debate. Broadly speaking there are two choices to be made in determining a standard.

One choice, common to many areas of law, is that between a so-called "objective" test and a so-called "subjective" test. In a subjective test the relevant question is "Was this action reasonable to this particular person at this particular time?" In an objective one it is "Would this (same) action have been reasonable to some generalized person – the person on the Clapham omnibus, the ordinary prudent person, the reasonable person?". An action which might be held to pass the subjective test might not be held to pass the objective one, or vice versa, depending on the divergence between the particular person's judgments in a particular situation and the court's reconstructed conception of what its generalized person's thinking would have been.

The other choice in the professional setting is between adopting a *professional* or *client*-based standard. In an objective test the standard for adequate disclosure could be either what the reasonable practitioner in this medical community would offer or what the reasonable patient in this social community would expect. In a subjective test it could be what either this particular practitioner or this particular patient felt was reasonable in the situation at the centre of dispute. As Mazur [28] reports until recently there has been little support for either of the subjective standards in legislatures or courts, it being felt that a subjective patient standard would place an unfair burden of risk on the practitioner and encourage excessively defensive practice, while a subjective practitioner standard would offer too little protection for patients against idiosyncratic professionals. He does, however, identify recent signs in the United States of a move to acknowledge that the preferences of the individual concerned should be the relevant ones in medical decisions, rather than those of some mythical average, reasonable person. A profession dedicated to acting in the best interests of *individual* patients can hardly object in principle to such a legal development, but the chances of a subjective patient standard achieving widespread acceptance seem small in any system of law based heavily on precedent. Actions producing outcomes of identical probability as far as the practitioner is concerned would or would not be reasonable depending on the patient. The court would have to determine the affected individual's strengths of preference *at the time of decision*, in hindsight, and in knowledge of the harmful outcome having occurred.

In the resolution of the choice between the reasonable practitioner and reasonable patient standards there has been much more movement in recent decades, the reasonable patient standard making substantial inroads, particularly in North American jurisdictions. In the United Kingdom, however, recent cases have confirmed that in consent as well as malpractice cases the practitioner is to be judged by whether or not his/her behaviour was in accordance with that of a body of respectable medical opinion: decisions on what should be *disclosed* have been held to be as much a matter of clinical judgment as those on what should be *done*. The practical significance of a caveat which suggests that the law may not uphold "respectable medical opinion" if it has not been "rightly" arrived at, remains to be tested. And, even in North America, the ubiquitous presence of some form of "therapeutic privilege" – a valid defense against an accusation of inadequate disclosure is the (reasonable) belief that the disclosure would in itself have interfered with the best interests of the patient – represents a major obstacle to the aggrieved client. Those concerned with patients' rights have accordingly been more attracted by the court's affirmation that the practitioner is under an obligation to answer truthfully and accurately any questions put by patients. In other words, while her obligations to *volunteer* information are to be determined by what is held to be reasonable practice in the community, failure to supply requested information is not so limited. The sensible patient will therefore ask questions rather than wait for information, thereby limiting the application of a professional standard to the determination of whether the practitioner's *responses* were reasonable.

The law has always been immensely respectful of the modes of practice we have labelled "intuitive judgment" and "peer-aided judgment". As the amount of "system-aided judgment" increases, new uncertainties confront both the practitioners and the legal system. If a data-based aid, such as the Leeds abdominal pain diagnostic system one, is developed and proves satisfactory in controlled trials the clinician using it is not, of course, relieved of clinical responsibility at law, which is one of the reasons for the repeated injunction that "clinical judgment must take precedence". When such systems are under development – and much the same goes for knowledge-based systems – the main fear is that their use will, in the event of an action being brought in relation to some harm caused, be held to be a breach of clinical duty. But when evidence pointing to the clinical benefits of using such a system accumulates, the legal pendulum begins to swing in the other direction: as it becomes increasingly likely that employing the system as an aid improves clinical performance, then *not using it* becomes the potential breach. Arguments as to whether or not such Mode 4 approaches constitute acceptable practice and currently reflect a "respectable body of professional opinion" therefore have undoubted legal significance at any point in time.

It seems most unlikely that professional communities – or the law – will accept the output of such systems as "*just* another test result or set of test results", given that they manifestly reshape and interact (even "interfere") with the judgment and decision-making processes of the clinician, rather than merely constituting an input into them. Decision analysis poses particularly interesting challenges – and possibilities – to both practitioners and those regulating their behaviour through the law. It is a process explicitly dedicated to assisting the practitioner (in conjunction with the patient) to arrive at the best decision for an individual patient. The question arises: if this is an appropriate technique for aiding clinical decision making then is it not equally appropriate for the retrospective evaluation of clinical decisions, in particular a legal examination of whether or not some action (in relation to either disclosure or management) was "reasonable"? There are indications that the courts informally employ the main conceptual elements of decision analysis in assessing the reasonableness of alternative possible actions and of the likelihood and severity of harms they may result in, as opposed to the likelihood and magnitude of the benefits that may result. What they have, with rare exception, been unwilling to do is to adopt a quantitative approach or to accept that the maximization of expected utility is the appropriate strategy for identifying the best action (or even to accept that an action so identified is necessarily a "reasonable" one). Mazur is hopeful that, in the future evolution of the doctrine of informed consent, both jurists and physicians will take advantage of decision analytic techniques to clarify, and make more precise, principles that are currently the source of confusion and communication problems. We thus have yet another echo of Eddy's original call, with an extension now from the problems of medical foresight to those of judicial hindsight.

The professional context

Clinicians' conceptions of "negligence" – and of "errors" and "mistakes" – are determined largely, not by ethical theories or legal cases, but by the ways of thinking, talking and behaving that they have been socialized into during their training, and have had constantly reinforced in the daily life of the hospital or clinic. Bosk [29], in our extract from his ethnographic study of surgical training, summarizes his conclusions concerning the implicit categorization of "error" which was in operation in the institution he studied – errors as defined by those whose superior status enabled them to define actions as being erroneous and who had the power to impose sanctions of one sort or another in respect of them. He discerns a fundamental distinction between "clinical" errors and "moral" errors and his surprising conclusion is that moral errors are held to be much more serious and sanction-worthy than clinical (technical or judgmental) ones. When a surgeon makes a clinical error he is performing his role conscientiously, it is just that in the case of "technical errors" his skills weren't up to the task and in the case of "judgmental errors" he simply didn't select the "correct" management strategy. A moral or normative error occurs when he fails to discharge his role obligations conscientiously, for example fails to display sufficient commitment to, or diligence in, a task. Bosk does not want to imply that clinical errors are treated as unimportant, simply that they are the occasion for understanding and forgiving, subject to their being remembered and learnt from. (*Repetition* of a clinical error constitutes moral error, because it reflects a failure to be sufficiently dedicated to its removal.) Moral errors on the other hand are the occasion for conspicuous measures of social control, ranging from public humiliation to professional disqualification.

The reason why errors in technical performance, with their apparent possibility of "objective" evaluation, are subordinated to moral errors, with their inherently "subjective" judgments of an individual's character and intentions, is found by Bosk partly in the nature of the professional-client relationship. It *is* as an agency relationship and the last line of defence for the professional (when things go wrong for the client) is that "as your agent, I did everything possible". This, to Bosk, is a moral defence and not a technical one – although the *result* (the outcome) may be unsatisfactory or open to debate, the practitioner argues that his *conduct* (the process) is not. But the origins of the ordering lie also and more fundamentally in the greater uncertainty which characterizes the evaluation of clinical performance:

With errors of technique, it is never completely clear whether the fault lies in the individual or in the field . . . [but] [d]edication, hard work and a proper reverence for role obligations are all readily apparent . . . [P]hysicians do not expect the application of medical knowledge to be perfect. There will always be honest errors. However, physicians do expect perfect compliance with the norms of clinical responsibility. They see this compliance as their best defence and remedy for the honest and inevitable errors they will all occasionally make. Negligence is defined in terms of clinical norms – moral values – and not technical standards. (pp. 527, 532)

From outside a profession the interesting question becomes whether its moral responsibility in facing up to its uncertainties has been sufficiently diligent. Whether, in other words, the limits of clinical error are drawn too loosely and the definition of "honest error" too widely. If, as the law has tended to do, the profession is regarded as the best judge of whether or not there has been moral dereliction in this respect, there is little further to say. One can then only consider the contributions of those who *from within it* have questioned the arguments in support of the status quo. We began with a paper by Eddy which suggested that the appropriate response to increasing clinical uncertainty was not complacent faith in intuitive judgment (however well-based on clinical experience) but the learning of languages and techniques designed for this very purpose. We end with one

by Katz [30] which asks why clinicians are unlikely to respond favourably
to the call for greater acknowledgement of, and formal dealing with,
clinical uncertainty.

For Katz clinicians are "only human" in their reluctance or inability

to maintain a consistent, self-conscious appreciation of the extent to which
uncertainty accompanies them on their daily rounds and to integrate that
uncertainty with whatever certainties inform their conduct ... They will
acknowledge medicine's uncertainty once its presence is forced into conscious
awareness, yet at the same time will continue to conduct their practices as if
uncertainty did not exist. (p. 542)

There are the well-rehearsed theories for such a disregard or denial of
uncertainty – ranging from unconscious oedipal conflicts to functional
adaptation to the existence of doubt (uncertainty can paralyze action,
unrealistic optimism may produce greater happiness than realistic
uncertainty) – but Katz is concerned with the way in which the profession
and its structure itself fosters this attitude. Specialization is one of the key
sources of unwarranted clinical certainty. It may genuinely lead to
increased certainty in particular technical matters, but this warranted
certainty is easily extrapolated beyond its justified scope in the pursuit of
income, or in the prosecution of intra-professional rivalries, or perhaps
(and most often) simply in the desire to do good for patients. Medicine has
become a congeries of competing, *relatively* unwarranted certainties,
rather than exhibiting a more generally diffused uncertainty. And within
institutions and communities, the social pressures to conformity, coupled
with the ability of superiors to sanction failure to "do things as *we* do
them here" as a moral error (role violation), irrespective of whether the
practice is acceptable or prescribed *elsewhere*, sustain the wide variations
in practice identified by Eddy.

Even if practitioners themselves fully and explicitly confronted the
uncertainties of their practice, should they communicate these to their
patient? The law, as we have seen, recognizes a "therapeutic privilege", by
which it is the clinical judgment of the doctor that should determine
whether or not information is disclosed to the patient. Its justification is
the possible detrimental effect of the disclosure of information on the
patient's morale and compliance with needed treatment – need as
professionally determined – and more generally the importance of trust
and confidence in the practitioner's ability to achieve a desired result in
bringing about that result. Katz is, in keeping with his own fundamental
message, uncertain about the empirical significance of the placebo effect.
But that is consistent with his believing that there is a reasonable chance
that the confidence and trust between professional and client that is at its
heart may be better generated by both parties acknowledging they are

voyagers on the high seas of uncertainty, rather than engaging in one-way or mutual deception. If this leads to the oft-predicted defection of their patients to "quacks", professionals should accept it: "In promising more than medicine can deliver, physicians adopt the practices of quacks and are themselves transformed into quacks." (p. 558) If the objection is that conveying uncertainty takes more *time* then we need to ask whether the technology for its conveyance can be improved, as well as whether the effect of more effective communication of uncertainty might not be to save resources currently absorbed by the impulse – even bias – towards action (rather than inaction). But ultimately the question is whether the price is not worth paying, an assessment that is not for the profession to make.

We conclude, then, with someone whose fundamental concern is that patients' supposed intolerance of uncertainties is, in significant part, a result of identifying with doctors' incapacity to live with them. Given the relative status of the two parties it is up to the professionals to open up the dialogue on clinical judgment and decision making which would rule out this possibility. The challenge is to begin this dialogue and, at the same time, provide comfort and hope.

REFERENCES

Adams, I.D., Chan, M., Clifford, P.C. *et al.* (1986) "Computer aided diagnosis of acute abdominal pain: a multicentre study", *British Medical Journal*, 293, 800–3

Balla, J.I., Iansek, R. and Elstein, A. (1985) "Bayesian diagnosis in presence of pre-existing disease", *Lancet*, February 9, 326–9

Goldman, L., Sayson, R., Robbins, S. *et al.* (1983) "The value of the autopsy in three medical eras", *New England Journal of Medicine*, 308, 1000–5

Kahneman, D. and Tversky, A. (1979) "Prospect theory: an analysis of decision under risk", *Econometrica*, 47, 263–91

McNeil, B.J., Pauker, S.G., Sox, H.C. *et al.* (1982) "On the elicitation of preferences for alternative therapies", *New England Journal of Medicine*, 3306, 1259–62

Sober, E. (1979) "The art and science of clinical judgment: an informational approach", in Englehardt, H.T., Spicker, S.F. and Towers, B. (eds.) *Clinical judgment: a critical appraisal*, Reidel, 29–44

PART I

~

THE ART AND SCIENCE OF UNCERTAINTY

I

———— ~ ————

VARIATIONS IN PHYSICIAN PRACTICE:
THE ROLE OF UNCERTAINTY*

David M. Eddy

Why do physicians vary so much in the way they practice medicine? At first view, there should be no problem. There are diseases – neatly named and categorized by textbooks, journal articles, and medical specialty societies. There are various procedures physicians can use to diagnose and treat these diseases. It should be possible to determine the value of any particular procedure by applying it to patients who have a disease and observing the outcome. And the rest should be easy – if the outcome is good, the procedure should be used for patients with that disease; if the outcome is bad, it should not. Some variation in practice patterns can be expected due to differences in the incidence of various diseases, patients' preferences, and the available resources, but these variations should be small and explainable.

The problem of course is that nothing is this simple. Uncertainty, biases, errors, and differences of opinions, motives, and values weaken every link in the chain that connects a patient's actual condition to the selection of a diagnostic test or treatment. This paper describes some of the factors that cause decisions about the use of medical procedures to be so difficult, and that contribute to the alarming variations we observe in actual practice. It examines the components of the decision problem a physician faces, and the psychology of medical reasoning, focusing in particular on the role of uncertainty. Finally, it suggests some actions to reduce uncertainty and encourage consistency of good medical practice.

Uncertainty creeps into medical practice through every pore. Whether a physician is defining a disease, making a diagnosis, selecting a procedure, observing outcomes, assessing probabilities, assigning preferences, or putting it all together, he is walking on very slippery terrain. It is difficult for nonphysicians, and for many physicians, to appreciate how complex these tasks are, how poorly we understand them, and how easy it is for honest people to come to different conclusions.

* First published in *Health Affairs*, 3 (1984), 74–89. Reprinted by permission.

DEFINING A DISEASE

If one looks at patients who are obviously ill, it is fairly easy to identify the physical and chemical disorders that characterize that illness. On the other hand, a large part of medicine is practiced on people who do not have obvious illnesses, but rather have signs, symptoms, or findings that may or may not represent an illness that should be treated. Three closely related problems make it difficult to determine whether or not a patient actually has a disease that needs to be diagnosed or treated.

One problem is that the dividing line between "normal" and "abnormal" is not nearly as sharp as a cursory reading of a textbook would suggest. First, the clues on which we base the diagnosis of many diseases can be very difficult to see, with frequent errors in both directions (missing an existing disease and "finding" a nondisease). Second, even if the diagnosis were correct and a disease were acknowledged to be present, the "disease" might not actually cause the patient any harm. Dysplasia of the cervix is a good example of both problems. It is an abnormal finding in the sense that most women do not have it, and it is associated with the development of cancer of the cervix. On the other hand, it is notoriously difficult to diagnose with certainty because dysplastic cells are only slightly different in appearance than normal cells (see example to follow under "Making a diagnosis"), and in the majority of cases it disappears spontaneously (assuming it was there in the first place). Obesity, hyperplasia of the tonsils, fibrocystic disease of the breast, and dozens of other conditions pose similar dilemmas.

A second problem is that many "diseases", at least at the time they are diagnosed, do not by themselves cause pain, suffering, disability, or threat to life. They are considered diseases only because they increase the probability that something else that is truly bad will happen in the future. This raises two more sources of uncertainty. (1) If a condition presages a bad outcome, one must judge the probabilities. Most conditions of this type do not always cause a "real" disease, and the "real" disease can usually occur without the condition. In situ lobular carcinoma of the breast presages a future invasive breast cancer less than 50 percent of the time, and the great majority of invasive breast cancers occur without a history of in situ lobular carcinoma. (2) Just because a condition can precede a "real" disease and can indicate a higher probability that the disease will develop, does not necessarily mean that it causes the disease, or that treating the condition will prevent it from occurring. Ocular hypertension and glaucoma are good examples; loss of visual field and blindness appear to occur whether or not the ocular pressure is lowered.[1]

The difficulty of defining a disease is compounded by the fact that many of the signs, symptoms, findings, and conditions that might suggest a disease are extremely common. If a breast biopsy were performed on a random sample of senior citizens, fully 90 percent of them could have fibrocystic disease. If obesity is a disease, the average American is diseased. By the time they reach seventy, about two-thirds of women have had their uteruses removed. Because the average blood pressure increases with age, some physicians feel a need to relabel "hypertension" to keep the majority of older people from having this disease.

And the ambiguities grow worse as medical technology expands. More and more diseases are being defined by an abnormal result on some test, leaving uncertainty about its real meaning to a patient and the appropriate treatment. Silent gallstones were silent until the oral cholecystogram was introduced, dysplasia of the cervix did not exist before the Pap smear, and many people's coronary artery disease showed up only on a treadmill test. Finding "diseases" early may be worthwhile, but it is difficult to know what else is being scooped up in the net.

Given these uncertainties about what constitutes a disease, it should not be surprising that there are debates about the definitions of many diseases, and when there is agreement about a definition, it is often blatantly and admittedly arbitrary. A quick review of the literature reveals multiple definitions of glaucoma, diabetes, fibrocystic disease of the breast, coronary artery disease, myocardial infarction, stroke, and dozens of other conditions. Morbid obesity is defined as 100 percent above the ideal weight. But what is "ideal", and why 100 percent? The lesson is that for many conditions a clinician faces, there is no clear definition of disease that provides an unequivocal guide to action, and there is wide room for differences of opinion and variations in practice.

MAKING A DIAGNOSIS

Suppose everyone agreed that a particular collection of signs, symptoms, and test results constituted an unequivocal definition of a disease. Would this eliminate the uncertainty? Unfortunately, even when sharp criteria are created, physicians vary widely in their application of these criteria – in their ability to ask about symptoms, observe signs, interpret test results, and record the answers. The literature on "observer variation" has been growing for a long time. To cite some of the classics:

Cyanosis, or blueing of the face and fingers, is considered a sign of low oxygen content in the blood. One investigator compared the abilities of twenty-two doctors to note cyanosis in twenty patients, the true diagnosis of cyanosis being confirmed by oximeter under controlled conditions. Only 53 percent of the physicians were definite in diagnosing cyanosis in subjects with extremely low oxygen content. And 26 percent of the physicians said cyanosis existed in subjects with normal oxygen content.[2]

Perhaps the error rates are less severe if the physician can study "hard" evidence like X-rays, electrocardiograms, or laboratory procedures:

A set of 1,807 photofluorograms containing thirty "positive" and 1,760 "negative" films (as defined by unanimous agreement of seven experts), were read independently by ten physicians. As many as 32 percent of the positive films were missed, and 2 percent of the negative films (thirty-five films) were incorrectly called positive. When individual readers read the same films on two separate occasions, they disagreed with themselves about 20 percent of the time.[3]

A group of experts compiled 100 electrocardiogram tracings, fifty of which showed myocardial infarctions, twenty-five of which were normal, and twenty-five of which showed some other abnormality (according to the experts). These EKGs were then given to ten other cardiologists to test their diagnostic abilities. The proportion of EKGs judged by the ten cardiologists to show infarcts varied by a factor of two. If you had an infarct and went to physician A, there would be a 28 percent chance the physician would have missed it. If you did not have an infarct and went to physician B, there would be a 26 percent chance that physician would have said you had one.[4]

How much confidence can we have in taking a person's medical history?

Four physicians interviewed 993 coal miners about several common symptoms, including cough, sputum, shortness of breath, and pain. After each physician completed all his interviews, he was asked to record the proportion of miners who reported each symptom (for example, to state the proportion of miners who answered yes to the question, "Do you have a cough?"). The proportion of miners reported to have various symptoms varied from 23 percent to 40 percent for cough, 13 percent to 42 percent for sputum, 10 percent to 18 percent for shortness of breath, and 6 to 17 percent for pain.[5]

Perhaps the hard eye of the microscope can yield definitive answers.

Thirteen pathologists were asked to read 1,001 specimens obtained from biopsies of the cervix, and then to repeat the readings at a later time. On average, each pathologist agreed with himself only 89 percent of the time (intraobserver agreement), and with a panel of "senior" pathologists only 87 percent of the time (interobserver agreement). Looking only at the patients who actually had cervical pathology, the intraobserver agreement was only 68 percent and the interobserver agreement was only 51 percent. The pathologists were best at reading more advanced disease and normal tissue, but were labeled "unsatisfactory" in their ability to read the precancerous and preinvasive stages.[6]

Similar studies have been reported for the presence of clubbing of the fingers, anemia, psychiatric disease, and many other signs, symptoms, and procedures.[7] Even if there were no uncertainty about what constitutes a disease and how to define it, there would still be considerable uncertainty about whether or not a patient has the signs, symptoms, and findings needed to fit the definition.

SELECTING A PROCEDURE

The task of selecting a procedure is no less difficult. There are two main issues.

First, for any patient condition there are dozens of procedures that can be ordered, in any combination, at any time. The list of procedures that might be included in a workup of chest pain or hypertension would take more than a page, spanning the spectrum from simply asking questions, to blood studies, to X-rays. Even for highly specific diagnostic problems, there can be a large choice of procedures. For example, if a woman presents with a breast mass and her physician wants to know its approximate size and architecture, the physician might contemplate an imaging procedure. The choice could include mammography, ultrasonography, thermography, diaphanography, computed tomography, lymphography, Mammoscan, and nuclear magnetic resonance imaging. A physician who chose mammography would still have to decide between xeromammography and film mammography, with several brands being available for the latter. There are about a dozen procedures that apply the principles of thermography. And why should a diagnostic workup be limited to one test? Why not follow a negative mammogram with a computed tomogram (or vice versa)? For the detection of colorectal cancer, a physician can choose any combination of fecal occult blood tests (and there are more than a dozen brands), digital examination, rigid sigmoidoscopy, flexible 30 cm sigmoidoscopy, flexible 60 cm sigmoidoscopy, barium enema (either plain or air contrast), and colonoscopy. These choices are not trivial. Most procedures have different mechanisms of action and a long list of pros and cons. Different brands of fecal occult blood tests have very different sensitivities and specificities, and film mammography and xeromammography differ in their radiation exposure by a factor of about four. These procedures are for relatively well-defined diseases; imagine the problems of selecting procedures to evaluate symptoms like fatigue, headache, or fever that can have about a dozen causes.

Second, adding to the uncertainties of defining and choosing a procedure is the fact that the value of any particular procedure depends on who performs it, on whom it is performed, and the circumstances of performance. The potential for variability in the people who perform procedures can be appreciated by considering one of the simplest procedures, the Pap smear. A gynecologist reviewed the technique used by sixty of his colleagues to take a Pap smear, and found that only fifteen of them performed the test properly. With this amount of slippage in such a simple test, one can only imagine the variation in quality that occurs with a more complicated procedure like coronary artery bypass surgery. With respect to who receives the procedure, the outcome of a test will depend on the probability the patient has the disease in question, on the physical condition of the patient (for example, young breasts absorb X-rays differently than older breasts), and on the patient's psychological condition (some people can tolerate passing a colonoscope all the way to the cecum, while others cannot). Finally, the circumstances under which a procedure is performed can have a dramatic effect on its value. Blood pressures go up for insurance examinations. Ocular pressures fluctuate by several millimeters of mercury every day. An IQ test can be a joy for a person with a good night's sleep, and a tragedy for a person with a head cold. The message is that a "procedure" is not a procedure. Each procedure has many faces, and many factors influence the quality and consequences of its use.

OBSERVING OUTCOMES

In theory, much of the uncertainty just described could be managed if it were possible to conduct enough experiments under enough conditions, and observe the outcomes. Unfortunately, measuring the outcomes of medical procedures is one of the most difficult problems we face. The goal is to predict how the use of a procedure in a particular case will affect that patient's health and welfare. Standing in the way are at least a half dozen major obstacles. The central problem is that there is a natural variation in the way people respond to a medical procedure. Take two people who, to the best of our ability to define such things, are identical in all important respects, submit them to the same operative procedure, and one will die on the operating table while the other will not. Because of this natural variation, we can only talk about the probabilities of various outcomes – the probability that a diagnostic test will be positive if the disease is present (sensitivity), the probability that a test will be negative if the disease is absent (specificity), the probability that a treatment will yield a certain result, and so forth.

One consequence of this natural variation is that to study the outcomes of any procedure it is necessary to conduct the procedure on many different people who are thought to represent the particular patients we want to know about, and then average the results. This in turn raises additional problems. First, many of the diseases are fairly rare, and it is necessary to average over many people to get a sample large enough to yield reliable results. This usually requires using many physicians, drawing patients from many settings, and performing the experiments at different times. Each of these elements introduces additional variation.

Some diseases are so rare that, in order to conduct the ideal clinical trials, it would be necessary to collect tens of thousands, if not hundreds of thousands, of participants. A good example concerns the frequency of the Pap smear. One might wonder why the merits of a three-year versus one-year frequency cannot be settled by a randomized controlled trial. Because of the low frequency of cervical cancer, and the small difference in outcomes expected for the two frequencies, almost one million women would be required for such a study.

An additional problem is that most procedures have multiple outcomes and it is not sufficient to examine just one of them. For example, a coronary artery bypass may change the life expectancy of a sixty-year-old man with triple vessel disease, but it will also change his joy of life for several weeks after the operation, the degree and severity of his chest pain, his ability to work and make love, his relationship with his son, the physical appearance of his chest, and his pocketbook. Pain, disability, anxiety, family relations, and any number of other outcomes are all important consequences of a procedure that deserve consideration. But the list is too long for practical experiments and many of the items on it are invisible or not measurable at all. We either lack suitable units (for example, for anxiety or pain), or the units exist but no experiments are fine enough to detect a change (for example, the increased incidence in breast cancer due to radiation from mammography).

Beyond this, many of the outcomes needed to evaluate a medical procedure take years to observe. There is no way to measure the ten-year survival of a patient following a porto-caval shunt without waiting ten years. To pursue the example of the Pap smear, the long duration of the preinvasive stages of the disease means that if the study with one million women were initiated, it would have to be continued for more than two decades to learn the results.

Finally, even when the best trials are conducted, we still might not get an answer. Consider the value of mammography in women under fifty, and consider just one outcome – the effect on breast cancer mortality. Ignore for the time being the radiation hazard, false-positive test results, inconvenience, financial costs, and other issues. This is one of the best-studied problems in cancer prevention, benefiting from the largest (60,000 women) and longest (more than fifteen years) completed randomized controlled trial, and an even larger uncontrolled study involving 270,000 women screened for five years in twenty-nine centers around the country. Yet we still do not know the value of mammography in women under fifty. The first study showed a slight reduction in mortality, but it was not statistically significant. The larger study suggested that mammography has improved since the first study, and that it is now almost as good in younger women as in older women, but the study was not controlled and we do not know if "almost" is good enough. Even for women over fifty, where the first study showed a statistically significant reduction in breast cancer mortality (of about 40 percent at ten years), there is enough uncertainty about the results that no fewer than four additional trials have been initiated to confirm the results. These trials are still in progress.

Unable to turn to a definitive body of clinical and epidemiological research, a clinician or research scientist who wants to know the value of a procedure is left with a mixture of randomized controlled trials, nonrandomized trials, uncontrolled trials, and clinical observations. The evidence from different sources can easily go in different directions, and it is virtually impossible for any one to sort things out in his or her head. Unfortunately, the individual physician may be most impressed by observations made in his or her individual practice. This source of evidence is notoriously vulnerable to bias and error. What a physician sees and remembers is biased by the types of patients who come in; by the decisions of the patients to accept a treatment and return for follow-up; by a natural desire to see good things; and by a whole series of emotions that charge one's memory. On top of these biases, the observations are vulnerable to large statistical errors because of the small number of patients a physician sees in a personal practice.

The difficulty of measuring outcomes has three important implications: We are uncertain about the precise consequences of using a particular procedure for a particular patient. We cannot, over the short term at least, resolve this uncertainty. And whatever a physician chooses to do cannot be proved right or wrong.

ASSESSING PREFERENCES

Now assume that a physican can know the outcomes of recommending a particular procedure for a particular patient. Is it possible to declare whether those outcomes are good or bad? Unfortunately, no. The basic problem is that any procedure has multiple outcomes, some good and some bad. The expected reduction in chest pain that some people will get from coronary artery bypass surgery is accompanied by a splitting of the chest, a chance of an operative mortality, days in the hospital, pain, anxiety, and financial expense. Because the outcomes are multiple and move in different directions, tradeoffs have to be made. And making tradeoffs involves values.

Just as there is a natural variation in how each of us responds to a medical procedure, there is a variation in how we value different outcomes. The fact that General Motors alone produces more than fifty distinct models of automobiles, not to mention dozens of options for each model, demonstrates how tastes about even a single item can vary. Imagine the variation in how different people value pain, disability, operative mortality, life expectancy, a day in a hospital, and who is going to feed the dogs.

In fact, for the outcomes of medical procedures, variations in the values of different people can be huge. Consider a single outcome of a fairly simple procedure – the scar from a breast biopsy. One of the ingredients to a physician's decision to recommend a biopsy for a woman with a breast mass is the physician's assessment of how the woman values the cosmetic affects of the surgery. How important is it to her not to have a small scar on her breast? While it is difficult to know precisely, one can pose questions such as the following to women.

Pretend that you have just had a breast biopsy. You have already received the results of the biopsy and know that you do not have cancer. There is no more medical information to be obtained from further studies. However, following the biopsy, you have on the upper outer quadrant (at about 3 o'clock) of your left breast a small one-inch scar that is slightly indented from the removal of a piece of tissue about the size of a pecan. I am a wizard and I can snap my fingers and make that scar disappear without a trace. I cannot erase the memory of your hospitalization, any anxiety you had prior to surgery, or any of the other events surrounding your biopsy, but if I snap my fingers, your scar will disappear. How much will you pay me to snap my fingers?

When about twenty women were asked this question in an informal setting, the answers ranged from less than $100 to $10,000. In addition to the wide variation in the answers, it is pertinent that husbands typically gave lower numbers than their wives, and physicians gave the lowest numbers of all.

To the inherent variation in values individual patients place on different outcomes must be added two additional sources of uncertainty and variation in assessing values. First, because decisions about procedures are typically made by physicians on behalf of their patients, the physicians must infer their patients' values, and keep them distinct from their own personal preferences. This raises the second problem, communication. It is difficult enough to assess one's own values about the outcomes of a complicated decision (think about switching jobs); consider having someone else try to learn your thoughts and do it for you. The room for error in communication can be appreciated by returning to the experiment in which four physicians asked 993 coal miners about cough, shortness of breath, pain and sputum. The variation in their reports of responses to a simple question like, "Do you have a cough?" was large; imagine a question like, "How do you feel about operative mortality?"

PUTTING IT ALL TOGETHER

The final decision about how to manage a patient requires synthesizing all the information about a disease, the patient, signs and symptoms, the effectiveness of dozens of tests and treatments, outcomes, and values. All of this must be done without knowing precisely what the patient has, with uncertainty about signs and symptoms, with imperfect knowledge of the sensitivity and specificity of tests, with no training in manipulating probabilities, with incomplete and biased information about outcomes, and with no language for communicating or assessing values. If each piece of this puzzle is difficult, it is even more difficult for anyone to synthesize all the information and be certain of the answer. It would be an extremely hard task for a research team; there is no hope that it could occur with any precision in the head of a busy clinician. Hence the wide variability in the estimates physicians place on the values of procedures.

Two final examples document how difficult it is to combine information from many sources to estimate the value of a particular procedure. The fecal occult blood test can be used to detect blood in the stool of asymptomatic people for the early detection of colorectal cancer. Flexible sigmoidoscopy (60 cm) can detect precancerous adenomas and cancers. At a recent meeting of experts in colorectal cancer detection, all of whom were very familiar with fecal occult blood testing (and most of whom had participated in two previous meetings on cancer detection in the previous four years), the attendees were asked the following question: "What is the overall reduction in colorectal cancer incidence and mortality that could be expected if men and women over the age of fifty were tested with fecal occult blood tests and 60 cm flexible sigmoidoscopy every year?" The answer to this question is obviously central to any estimate of the value of fecal occult blood testing, and it is pertinent that the experts were

Exhibit 1 Effect of screening annual fecal occult blood test and annual flexible scope

Reduction in incidence

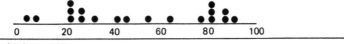

Reduction in mortality

unanimous in their belief that the fecal occult blood test was valuable and should indeed be recommended annually to men and women over fifty. The answers were distributed as shown in Exhibit 1. It is tempting to say that nonexperts, or people who did not share the belief that the fecal occult blood test is valuable, would have shown a wider variation, but the variation expressed by this group could hardly be any wider. As startling as the degree of variation in the estimates, is that the attendees were surprised by the results; they had never communicated this number to each other, and had no idea they had such differences of opinion.

The second example is a classic. A survey of 1,000 eleven-year-old schoolchildren in New York City found that 65 percent had undergone tonsillectomy. The remaining children were sent for examinations to a group of physicians and 45 percent were selected for tonsillectomy. Those rejected were examined by another group of physicians and 46 percent were selected for surgery. When the remaining children were examined again by another group of physicians, a similar percent were recommended for tonsillectomy, leaving only sixty-five students. At that point, the study was halted for lack of physicians.[8]

CONSEQUENCES

The view of anyone who wants a close look at the consequences of different medical procedures is, at best, smoky. Some procedures may present a clear picture, and their value, or lack of it, may be obvious; putting a finger on a bleeding carotid artery is an extreme example. But for many, if not most medical procedures, we can only see shadows and gross movements. We usually know the direction in which various outcome measures can move when a medical activity is undertaken, but we typically do not know the probabilities they will move in those directions, or how far they will move. We certainly do not know how a particular individual will respond. Words like "rare," "common," and "a lot" must be used instead of "One out of 1,000," or "seven on a scale of one to ten."

There is also a strong tendency to oversimplify. One of the easiest ways to fit a large problem in our minds is to lop off huge parts of it. In medical decisions, one option is to focus on length of life and discount inconvenience, pain, disability, short-term risks, and financial costs. A physician can also draw on a number of simplifying heuristics. Anyone uncomfortable dealing with probabilities can use the heuristic, "If there is any chance of (the disease), the (procedure) should be performed." If one cannot estimate the number of people to be saved, one can use the heuristic, "If but one patient is saved, the effort is worthwhile." If one cannot contemplate alternative uses of resources that might deliver a greater benefit to a population, there is the heuristic, "Costs should not be considered in decisions about individual patients." There is a general purpose heuristic, "When in doubt, do it." Or as one investigator wrote, "An error of commission is to be preferred to an error of omission." Unfortunately, a large number of incentives encourage simplifications that lead to overutilization. It is time-consuming, mentally taxing, and often threatening to colleagues for a physician to undertake a deep analysis of a confusing clinical problem. A physician is less likely to be sued for doing too much than too little. Most physicians' incomes go up if they do more, and go down if they do less. Hospitals get to fill more beds and bill for more procedures, laboratories collect more money for services, and companies sell more drugs, devices, and instruments. The more that is done, the more the providers win. The losers are patients, consumers, and taxpayers – anyone who has to undergo a valueless procedure or pay the bill.

In the end, given all the uncertainties, incentives, and heuristics, a physician will have to do what is comfortable. If it is admitted that the uncertainty surrounding the use of a procedure is great, and that there is no way to identify for certain what is best, or to prove that any particular action is right or wrong, the safest and most comfortable position is to do what others are doing. The applicable maxim is "safety in numbers." A physician who follows the practices of his or her colleagues is safe from criticism, free from having to explain his or her actions, and defended by the concurrence of colleagues.

This tendency to follow the pack is the most important single explanation of regional variations in medical practice. If uncertainty caused individual physicians to practice at random, or to follow their personal interpretations and values, without any attempts to match the actions of their neighbors, the variations in practice patterns would average out, and no significant differences would be observed at the regional level. Differences between regions are observed because individual physicians tend to follow what is considered standard and accepted in the community. A community standard evolves from statements published in national journals and textbooks, from the opinions of established physicians, and from new ideas brought to the community by new physicians. The community standards themselves exist because enough is known to enable the leaders of a community to develop opinions which, when followed by their colleagues, become community standards. The differences between community standards exist because not enough is known to establish which opinion is correct. We call the community standards for a particular practice clinical policies, and anyone who makes an unambiguous recommendation about a medical practice is a policymaker.[9]

WHAT HARM IS DONE?

First, it should be clear that some variation in practice is appropriate. The differences in patients' risks, signs and symptoms, responses to treatment, and values are real. Differences in physicians' talents and the available facilities are also real. If physicians were able to tailor their practices to take these individual differences into account, variations would be both inevitable and desirable. The problem is that uncertainty so clouds every aspect of this problem that many of the appropriate variations cannot occur, and many of the variations we see are not motivated by logic or a deep understanding of the issues.

There is no doubt that uncertainty about the consequences of different medical activities can harm both the quality and cost of medical practice. It is also true, however, that most of the simplifications and heuristics point in one direction, toward overutilization. When this happens the price is paid in terms of inconvenience, pain, distress, days in the hospitals, unnecessary risks, and money.

CONCLUSIONS

Many of the problems described in this paper are insurmountable. There is no way to shorten the time needed to observe ten-year survival rates, and there is no way to increase the frequency of rare diseases, reduce the number of outcomes that are important to a patient, or decrease natural variations in response to treatment. Nor do we want to suppress the differences that exist in patients' preferences.

However, while we can not eliminate uncertainty, we can decrease the amount of it and develop strategies to minimize its damage. In fact, the profession and society have not begun to exploit the available techniques for reducing uncertainty and maximizing expected outcomes. The evaluation of medical practices and the development of clinical policies deserve much more attention and a higher priority than they currently get. Wennberg and others have described how data bases and other techniques can improve the available information. The next task is to improve our ability to process the information we get. This calls for several actions, all designed to develop a tradition that insists on the collection and evaluation of information to understand and describe the consequences of medical practices.

First, physicians can do more to admit the existence of uncertainty, both to themselves and to their patients. While this will undoubtedly be unsettling, it is honest, and it opens the way for a more intensive search for ways to reduce the uncertainty.

Second, people who want to promote policies regarding the use of medical procedures can learn the necessary languages. Over the past few hundred years languages have been developed for collecting and interpreting evidence (statistics), dealing with uncertainty (probability theory), synthesizing evidence and estimating outcomes (mathematics), and making decisions (economics and decision theory.) These languages are not currently learned by most clinical policymakers; they should be.

Third, physicians who follow existing policies can examine more carefully the supporting evidence and logic. The mere fact that a policy is established and accepted does not make it correct.

Fourth, to encourage and assist the two previous actions, any policy statement, whether it be made by an individual physician at a hospital conference, or a third-party payer considering reimbursement, should be accompanied by (1) a list of medical and economic outcomes that were considered in making the policy, (2) the policymaker's estimates of what can be expected to happen with respect to each of the listed outcomes if the policy is followed, and (3) the supporting evidence for those estimates. Any policymaker unable to supply that information should not be making policies.

Fifth, editors and reviewers of journals can encourage publication of good papers that synthesize existing information, estimate the outcomes of different policies, and present the rationales for different actions. Such work, while not traditional, is both difficult and important.

Sixth, editors and reviewers can require that any author who recommends a policy supply the information listed in action 4. No good journal today will report the results of an experiment without a description of the design and methods; it is no less important to describe the reasoning behind a policy statement.

Seventh, the government can support far more evaluation research to analyze medical practices. The National Institutes of Health spend more than $5 billion each year to learn more about diseases and develop tests and procedures. The budget of the major federal unit charged with determining how medical procedures should be used, the National Center for Health Care Technology (NCHCT), was $4 million, less than one thousandth as large. Even that was considered too much, and the budget was recently cut to zero. Not only should the NCHCT be revived, it should be expanded by a factor of ten to 100. Research to evaluate medical practices is like the windows in a car; without them there is little way to know where you are going.

Finally, patients can push the process by asking questions. If informed of an operative mortality rate, they can ask, "What percent?" If told about the discomfort of a particular procedure, they can ask how it compared to having a tooth pulled under novocaine, or some other event they can identify with. If a procedure is recommended, a patient can ask why, what might be found, with what probability, what difference will it make, and so forth. Many physicians will be uneasy, and some even angry, when asked questions of this type because they may not know the answers. But there are few things better than asking questions to force research to get the answers.

I believe these actions should be taken. Some of the uncertainty and the resulting variations in practice patterns that exist are unavoidable, but much of the uncertainty can be managed far better than is done now. The problems that exist today are not the fault of any individuals; the fault lies with the profession and society as a whole for not developing the traditions and methods needed to assess medical practices. Today the problem is bad; five years from now, if not improved, it will be a tragedy.

NOTES

1 D.M. Eddy, L.E. Sanders, and J.F. Eddy, "The Value of Screening for Glaucoma with Tonometry," *Survey of Ophthalmology* 28 (1983): 194–205.

2 J.H. Comroe and S. Botelho, "The Unreliability of Cyanosis in the Recognition of Arterial Anoxemia," *The American Journal of the Medical Sciences* 214 (1947): 1–6.

3 J. Yerushalmy, "Reliability of Chest Radiography in the Diagnosis of Pulmonary Lesions," *American Journal of Surgery* 89 (1955): 231–240.

4 L.G. Davies, "Observer Variation in Reports on Electrocardiograms," *British Heart Journal* 20 (1958): 153.

5 A.L. Cochrane, P.J. Chapman, and P.D. Oldham, "Observers' Errors in Taking Medical Histories," *Lancet* 1 (1951): 1007–1009.

6 J. Ringsted, F. Amtrup, C. Asklund, P. Baunsgaard, H.E. Christensen, L. Hansen, C. Jakobsen, N.K. Jensen, J. Moesner, J. Rasmussen, I. Reintoft, J. Rolschau, H. Starklint, N. Thommesen, and J. Vrang, "Reliability of Histo-Pathological Diagnosis of Squamous Epithelial Changes of the Uterine Cervix," *Acta Pathologica Microbiologica et Immunologica Scandinavica*, Section A: Pathology 86 (1978): 273–278.

7 D.A. Pyke, "Finger Clubbing: Validity as a Physical Sign," *Lancet* 2 (1954): 352–354; V.F. Fairbanks, "Is the Peripheral Blood Film Reliable for the Diagnosis of Iron Deficiency Anemia?" *American Journal of Clinical Pathology* 55 (1971): 447–451; P. Ash, "The Reliability of Psychiatric Diagnoses," *Journal of Abnormal and Social Psychology* 44 (1974): 272–276; and A.T. Beck, C.H. Ward, M. Mendelson, J.E. Mock, and J.K. Erbaugh, "Reliability of Psychiatric Diagnoses: 2. A Study of Consistency of Clinical Judgments and Ratings," *American Journal of Psychiatry* 119 (1962): 351–357.

8 American Child Health Association, *Physical Defects: The Pathway to Correction* (1934), 80–96.

9 D.M. Eddy, "Clinical Policies and the Quality of Clinical Practice," *The New England Journal of Medicine* 307 (1982): 343–347.

2

———— ~ ————

FROM TECHNICAL RATIONALITY TO REFLECTION-IN-ACTION*

Donald A. Schön

THE DOMINANT EPISTEMOLOGY OF PRACTICE

According to the model of Technical Rationality – the view of professional knowledge which has most powerfully shaped both our thinking about the professions and the institutional relations of research, education, and practice – professional activity consists in instrumental problem solving made rigorous by the application of scientific theory and technique. Although all occupations are concerned, on this view, with the instrumental adjustment of means to ends, only the professions practice rigorously technical problem solving based on specialized scientific knowledge.

The model of Technical Rationality has exerted as great an influence on scholarly writing about the professions as on critical exposés of the role of the professions in the larger society. In the 1930s, for example, one of the earliest students of the professions asserted that

it is not difficult to account in general for the emergence of the new professions. Large-scale organization has favored specialization. Specialized occupations have arisen around the new scientific knowledge.[1]

In a major book on the professions, published in 1970, Wilbert Moore embraced Alfred North Whitehead's distinction between a profession and an avocation. An avocation is "the antithesis to a profession" because it is "based upon customary activities and modified by the trial and error of individual practice."[2] In contrast, Moore said, a profession

involves the application of general principles to specific problems, and it is a feature of modern societies that such general principles are abundant and growing.[3]

The same author argues further that professions are highly specialized occupations, and that

* Edited extracts from Chap. 2 of *The Reflective Practitioner: How Professionals Think in Action*, by Donald A. Schön. © 1983 by Basic Books, Inc., Publishers. Reprinted by permission of Basic Books, Inc., Publishers.

the two primary bases for specialization within a profession are (1) the substantive field of knowledge that the specialist professes to command and (2) the technique of production or application of knowledge over which the specialist claims mastery.[4]

Finally, a recent critic of professional expertise sees the professional's claim to uniqueness as a ". . . preoccupation with a specialized skill premised on an underlying theory."[5]

The prototypes of professional expertise in this sense are the "learned professions" of medicine and law and, close behind these, business and engineering. These are, in Nathan Glazer's terms, the "major" or "near-major" professions.[6] They are distinct from such "minor" professions as social work, librarianship, education, divinity, and town planning. In the essay from which these terms are drawn, Glazer argues that the schools of the minor professions are hopelessly nonrigorous, dependent on representatives of academic disciplines, such as economics or political science, who are superior in status to the professions themselves. But what is of greatest interest from our point of view, Glazer's distinction between major and minor professions rests on a particularly well-articulated version of the model of Technical Rationality. The major professions are "disciplined by an unambiguous end – health, success in litigation, profit – which settles men's minds,"[7] and they operate in stable institutional contexts. Hence they are grounded in systematic, fundamental knowledge, of which scientific knowledge is the prototype,[8] or else they have "a high component of strictly technological knowledge based on science in the education which they provide."[9] In contrast, the minor professions suffer from shifting, ambiguous ends and from unstable institutional contexts of practice, and are *therefore* unable to develop a base of systematic, scientific professional knowledge. For Glazer, the development of a scientific knowledge base depends on fixed, unambiguous ends because professional practice is an instrumental activity. If applied science consists in cumulative, empirical knowledge about the means best suited to chosen ends, how can a profession ground itself in science when its ends are confused or unstable?

The systematic knowledge base of a profession is thought to have four essential properties. It is specialized, firmly bounded, scientific, and standardized. This last point is particularly important, because it bears on the paradigmatic relationship which holds, according to Technical Rationality, between a profession's knowledge base and its practice. In Wilbert Moore's words,

If every professional problem were in all respects unique, solutions would be at best accidental, and therefore have nothing to do with expert knowledge. What we are suggesting, on the contrary, is that there are sufficient uniformities in problems

and in devices for solving them to qualify the solvers as professionals . . .
professionals apply very general principles, *standardized* knowledge, to concrete
problems . . .[10]

This concept of "application" leads to a view of professional knowledge
as a hierarchy in which "general principles" occupy the highest level and
"concrete problem solving" the lowest. As Edgar Schein has put it,[11] there
are three components to professional knowledge:

1 An *underlying discipline* or *basic science* component upon which the
   practice rests or from which it is developed.
2 An *applied science* or *"engineering"* component from which many of
   the day-to-day diagnostic procedures and problem-solutions are
   derived.
3 A *skills and attitudinal* component that concerns the actual performance of services to the client, using the underlying basic and applied
   knowledge.[12]

The application of basic science yields applied science. Applied science
yields diagnostic and problem-solving techniques which are applied in
turn to the actual delivery of services. The order of application is also an
order of derivation and dependence. Applied science is said to "rest on"
the foundation of basic science. And the more basic and general the
knowledge, the higher the status of its producer.

When the representatives of aspiring professions consider the problem
of rising to full professional status, they often ask whether their knowledge base has the requisite properties and whether it is regularly applied
to the everyday problems of practice. Thus, in an article entitled "The
Librarian: From Occupation to Profession,"[13] the author states that

the central gap is of course the failure to develop a general body of scientific
knowledge bearing precisely on this problem, in the way that the medical
profession with its auxiliary scientific fields has developed an immense body of
knowledge with which to cure human diseases.

The sciences in which he proposes to ground his profession are "communications theory, the sociology or psychology of mass communications, or
the psychology of learning as it applies to reading."[14] Unfortunately,
however, he finds that

most day-to-day professional work utilizes rather concrete rule-of-thumb local
regulations and rules and major catalog systems . . . The problems of selection and
organization are dealt with on a highly empiricist basis, concretely, with little
reference to general scientific principles.[15]

And a social worker, considering the same sort of question, concludes that
"social work is already a profession" because it has a basis in

theory construction via systematic research. To generate valid theory that will
provide a solid base for professional techniques requires the application of the

scientific method to the service-related problems of the profession. Continued employment of the scientific method is nurtured by and in turn reinforces the element of *rationality* . . .[16]

It is by progressing along this route that social work seeks to "rise within the professional hierarchy so that it, too, might enjoy maximum prestige, authority, and monopoly which presently belong to a few top professions."[17]

If the model of Technical Rationality appeared only in such statements of intent, or in programmatic descriptions of professional knowledge, we might have some doubts about its dominance. But the model is also embedded in the institutional context of professional life. It is implicit in the institutionalized relations of research and practice, and in the normative curricula of professional education. Even when practitioners, educators, and researchers question the model of technical rationality, they are party to institutions that perpetuate it.

As one would expect from the hierarchical model of professional knowledge, research is institutionally separate from practice, connected to it by carefully defined relationships of exchange. Researchers are supposed to provide the basic and applied science from which to derive techniques for diagnosing and solving the problems of practice. Practitioners are supposed to furnish researchers with problems for study and with tests of the utility of research results. The researcher's role is distinct from, and usually considered superior to, the role of the practitioner.

In the evolution of every profession there emerges the researcher-theoretician whose role is that of scientific investigation and theoretical systematization. In technological professions, a division of labor thereby evolves between the theory-oriented and the practice-orientated person. Witness the physician who prefers to attach himself to a medical research center rather than to enter private practice . . .[18]

In similar vein, Nathan Glazer speaks of the sociologist, political scientist, or economist who, when he is invited to bring his discipline to the school of a minor profession, manifests a level of status disturbingly superior to that of the resident practitioners. And in schools of engineering, which have been transformed into schools of engineering science, the engineering scientist tends to place his superior status in the service of values different from those of the engineering profession.[19]

The hierarchical separation of research and practice is also reflected in the normative curriculum of the professional school. Here the order of the curriculum parallels the order in which the components of professional knowledge are "applied." The rule is: first, the relevant basic and applied science; then, the skills of application to real-world problems of practice. Edgar Schein's study of professional education led him to describe the dominant curricular pattern as follows:

Most professional school curricula can be analyzed in terms of the form and timing of these three elements [of professional knowledge]. Usually the professional curriculum starts with a common science core followed by the applied science elements. The attitudinal and skill components are usually labelled "practicum" or "clinical work" and may be provided simultaneously with the applied science components or they may occur even later in the professional education, depending upon the availability of clients or the ease of simulating the realities that the professional will have to face.[20]

Schein's use of the term "skill" is of more than passing interest. From the point of view of the model of Technical Rationality institutionalized in the professional curriculum, real knowledge lies in the theories and techniques of basic and applied science. Hence, these disciplines should come first. "Skills" in the use of theory and technique to solve concrete problems should come later on, when the student has learned the relevant science – first, because he cannot learn skills of application until he has learned applicable knowledge; and secondly, because skills are an ambiguous, secondary kind of knowledge. There is something disturbing about calling them "knowledge" at all.

Again, medicine is the prototypical example. Ever since the Flexner Report, which revolutionized medical education in the early decades of this century, medical schools have devoted the first two years of study to the basic sciences – chemistry, physiology, pathology – as "the appropriate foundation for later clinical training."[21] Even the physical arrangement of the curriculum reflects the basic division among the elements of professional knowledge:

The separation of the medical school curriculum into two disjunctive stages, the preclinical and the clinical, reflects the division between theory and practice. The division also appears in the location of training and in medical school facilities. The sciences of biochemistry, physiology, pathology and pharmacology are learned from classrooms and laboratories, that is, in formal academic settings. More practical training, in clinical arts such as internal medicine, obstetrics and pediatrics, takes place in hospital clinics, within actual institutions of delivery.[22]

Technical Rationality is the heritage of Positivism, the powerful philosophical doctrine that grew up in the nineteenth century as an account of the rise of science and technology and as a social movement aimed at applying the achievements of science and technology to the well-being of mankind. Technical Rationality is the Positivist epistemology of practice. It became institutionalized in the modern university, founded in the late nineteenth century when Positivism was at its height, and in the professional schools which secured their place in the university in the early decades of the twentieth century.

Practical knowledge exists, but it does not fit neatly into Positivist categories. We cannot readily treat it as a form of descriptive knowledge of the world, nor can we reduce it to the analytical schemas of logic and mathematics. Positivism solved the puzzle of practical knowledge in [this way]. Practical knowledge was to be construed as knowledge of the relationship of means to ends. Given agreement about ends,[23] the question, "How ought I to act?" could be reduced to a merely instrumental question about the means best suited to achieve one's ends. Disagreement about means could be resolved by reference to facts concerning the possible means, their relevant consequences, and the methods for comparing them with respect to the chosen ends of action. Ultimately, the instrumental question could be resolved by recourse to experiment. And as men built up scientific understandings of cause and effect, causal relationships could be mapped onto instrumental ones. It would be possible to select the means appropriate to one's ends by applying the relevant scientific theory. The question, "How ought I to act?" could become a scientific one, and the best means could be selected by the use of science-based technique.

In the late nineteenth and early twentieth centuries, the professions of engineering and medicine achieved dramatic successes in reliably adjusting means to ends and became models of instrumental practice. The engineer's design and analysis of materials and artifacts, the physician's diagnosis and treatment of disease, became prototypes of the science-based, technical practice which was destined to supplant craft and artistry. For according to the Positivist epistemology of practice, craft and artistry had no lasting place in rigorous practical knowledge.

EMERGING AWARENESS OF THE LIMITS OF TECHNICAL RATIONALITY

Both the general public and the professionals have become increasingly aware of the flaws and limitations of the professions . . . the professions have suffered a crisis of legitimacy rooted both in their perceived failure to live up to their own norms and in their perceived incapacity to help society achieve its objectives and solve its problems. Increasingly we have become aware of the importance to actual practice of phenomena – complexity, uncertainty, instability, uniqueness, and value-conflict – which do not fit the model of Technical Rationality.

From the perspective of Technical Rationality, professional practice is a process of problem *solving*. Problems of choice or decision are solved through the selection, from available means, of the one best suited to established ends. But with this emphasis on problem solving, we ignore problem *setting*, the process by which we define the decision to be made, the ends to be achieved, the means which may be chosen. In real-world practice, problems do not present themselves to the practitioner as givens. They must be constructed from the materials of problematic situations which are puzzling, troubling, and uncertain. In order to convert a problematic situation to a problem, a practitioner must do a certain kind of work. He must make sense of an uncertain situation that initially makes no sense. When professionals consider what road to build, for example, they deal usually with a complex and ill-defined situation in which geographic, topological, financial, economic, and political issues are all mixed up together. Once they have somehow decided what road to build and go on to consider how best to build it, they may have a problem they can solve by the application of available techniques; but when the road they have built leads unexpectedly to the destruction of a neighborhood, they may find themselves again in a situation of uncertainty.

It is this sort of situation that professionals are coming increasingly to see as central to their practice. They are coming to recognize that although problem setting is a necessary condition for technical problem solving, it is not itself a technical problem. When we set the problem, we select what we will treat as the "things" of the situation, we set the boundaries of our attention to it, and we impose upon it a coherence which allows us to say what is wrong and in what directions the situation needs to be changed. Problem setting is a process in which, interactively, we *name* the things to which we will attend and *frame* the context in which we will attend to them.

Even when a problem has been constructed, it may escape the categories of applied science because it presents itself as unique or unstable. In order to solve a problem by the application of existing theory or technique, a practitioner must be able to map those categories onto features of the practice situation. When a nutritionist finds a diet deficient in lysine, for example, dietary supplements known to contain lysine can be recommended. A physician who recognizes a case of measles can map it onto a system of techniques for diagnosis, treatment, and prognosis. But a unique case falls outside the categories of applied theory; an unstable situation slips out from under them. A physician cannot apply standard techniques to a case that is not in the books. And a nutritionist attempting a planned nutritional intervention in a rural Central American community may discover that the intervention fails because the situation has become something other than the one planned for.

Technical Rationality depends on agreement about ends. When ends are fixed and clear, then the decision to act can present itself as an instrumental problem. But when ends are confused and conflicting, there is as yet no "problem" to solve. A conflict of ends cannot be resolved by the use of techniques derived from applied research. It is rather through the non-technical process of framing the problematic situation that we may organize and clarify both the ends to be achieved and the possible means of achieving them.

Similarly, when there are conflicting paradigms of professional practice, such as we find in the pluralism of psychiatry, social work, or town planning, there is no clearly established context for the use of technique. There is contention over multiple ways of framing the practice role, each of which entrains a distinctive approach to problem setting and solving. And when practitioners do resolve conflicting role frames, it is through a kind of inquiry which falls outside the model of Technical Rationality. Again, it is the work of naming and framing that creates the conditions necessary to the exercise of technical expertise.

We can readily understand, therefore, not only why uncertainty, uniqueness, instability, and value conflict are so troublesome to the Positivist epistemology of practice, but also why practitioners bound by this epistemology find themselves caught in a dilemma. Their definition of rigorous professional knowledge excludes phenomena they have learned to see as central to their practice. And artistic ways of coping with these phenomena do not qualify, for them, as rigorous professional knowledge.

This dilemma of "rigor or relevance" arises more acutely in some areas of practice than in others. In the varied topography of professional practice, there is a high, hard ground where practitioners can make effective use of research-based theory and technique, and there is a swampy lowland where situations are confusing "messes" incapable of technical solution. The difficulty is that the problems of the high ground, however great their technical interest, are often relatively unimportant to clients or to the larger society, while in the swamp are the problems of greatest human concern. Shall the practitioner stay on the high, hard ground where he can practice rigorously, as he understands rigor, but where he is constrained to deal with problems of relatively little social importance? Or shall he descend to the swamp where he can engage the most important and challenging problems if he is willing to forsake technical rigor?

In such "major" professions as medicine, engineering, or agronomy there are zones where practitioners can function as technical experts. But there are also zones where the major professions resemble the minor ones. Medical technologies such as kidney dialysis generate demands in excess of the nation's willingness to invest in medical care. Engineering that seems powerful and elegant when judged from a narrowly technical perspective may also carry unacceptable risks to environmental quality or human safety. Large-scale, industrialized agriculture destroys the peasant economies of the developing worlds. How should professionals take account of such issues as these?

There are those who choose the swampy lowlands. They deliberately involve themselves in messy but crucially important problems, and when asked to describe their methods of inquiry, they speak of experience, trial and error, intuition, and muddling through.

Other professionals opt for the high ground. Hungry for technical rigor, devoted to an image of solid professional competence, or fearful of entering a world in which they feel they do not know what they are doing, they choose to confine themselves to a narrowly technical practice.

The field of "formal modelling" offers an interesting context in which to observe the two responses.

During World War II, operations research grew out of the successful use of applied mathematics in submarine search and bomb tracking. After World War II, the development of the digital computer sparked widespread interest in formal, quantitative, computerized models which seemed to offer a new technique for converting "soft" problems into "hard" ones. A new breed of technical practitioner came into being. Systems analysts, management scientists, policy analysts, began to use formal modelling techniques on problems of inventory control, business policy, information retrieval, transportation planning, urban land use, the delivery of medical care, the criminal justice system, and the control of the economy. By the late 1960s, there was scarcely a described problem for which someone had not constructed a computerized model. But in recent years there has been a widening consensus, even among formal modellers, that the early hopes were greatly inflated. Formal models have been usefully employed to solve problems in such relatively undemanding areas as inventory control and logistics. They have generally failed to yield effective results in the more complex, less clearly defined problems of business management, housing policy, or criminal justice.

Formal modellers have responded to this unpleasant discovery in several different ways. Some have continued to ply their trade in the less demanding areas of the field. Some have abandoned their original training in order to address themselves to real-world problems. Others have decided to treat formal models as "probes" or "metaphors" useful only as sources of new perspectives on complex situations. But for the most part, the use of formal models has proceeded as though it had a life of its own. Driven by the evolving questions of theory and technique, formal modelling has become increasingly divergent from the real-world problems of practice. And practitioners who choose to remain on the high ground have continued to use formal models for complex problems, quite oblivious to the troubles incurred whenever a serious attempt is made to implement them.

The dilemma which afflicts the professions hinges not on science per se but on the Positivist view of science. From this perspective, we tend to see science, after the fact, as a body of established propositions derived from research. When we recognize their limited utility in practice, we experience the dilemma of rigor or relevance. But we may also consider science before the fact as a process in which scientists grapple with uncertainties and display arts of inquiry akin to the uncertainties and arts of practice.

Let us then reconsider the question of professional knowledge; let us stand the question on its head. If the model of Technical Rationality is incomplete, in that it fails to account for practical competence in "divergent" situations, so much the worse for the model. Let us search, instead, for an epistemology of practice implicit in the artistic, intuitive process which some practitioners do bring to situations of uncertainty, instability, uniqueness, and value conflict.

REFLECTION-IN-ACTION

When we go about the spontaneous, intuitive performance of the actions of everyday life, we show ourselves to be knowledgeable in a special way. Often we cannot say what it is that we know. When we try to describe it we find ourselves at a loss, or we produce descriptions that are obviously inappropriate. Our knowing is ordinarily tacit, implicit in our patterns of action and in our feel for the stuff with which we are dealing. It seems right to say that our knowing is *in* our action.

Similarly, the workaday life of the professional depends on tacit knowing-in-action. Every competent practitioner can recognize phenomena – families of symptoms associated with a particular disease, peculiarities of a certain kind of building site, irregularities of materials or structures – for which he cannot give a reasonably accurate or complete description. In his day-to-day practice he makes innumerable judgments of quality for which he cannot state adequate criteria, and he displays skills for which he cannot state the rules and procedures. Even when he makes conscious use of research-based theories and techniques, he is dependent on tacit recognitions, judgments, and skillful performances.

On the other hand, both ordinary people and professional practitioners often think about what they are doing, sometimes even while doing it. Stimulated by surprise, they turn thought back on action and on the knowing which is implicit in action. They may ask themselves, for example, "What features do I notice when I recognize this thing? What procedures am I enacting when I perform this skill? How am I framing the problem that I am trying to solve?" Usually reflection on knowing-in-action goes together with reflection on the stuff at hand. There is some puzzling, or troubling, or interesting phenomenon with which the individual is trying to deal. As he tries to make sense of it, he also reflects on the understandings which have been implicit in his action, understanding which he surfaces, criticizes, restructures, and embodies in further action.

It is this entire process of reflection-in-action which is central to the "art" by which practitioners sometimes deal well with situations of uncertainty, instability, uniqueness, and value conflict.

Knowing-in-action   Once we put aside the model of Technical Rationality, which leads us to think of intelligent practice as an *application* of knowledge to instrumental decisions, there is nothing strange about the idea that a kind of knowing is inherent in intelligent action. Common sense admits the category of know-how, and it does not stretch common sense very much to say that the know-how is *in* the action – that a tightrope walker's know-how, for example, lies in, and is revealed by, the way he takes his trip across the wire, or that a big-league pitcher's know-how is in his way of pitching to a batter's weakness, changing his pace, or distributing his energies over the course of a game. There is nothing in common sense to make us say that know-how consists in rules or plans which we entertain in the mind prior to action. Although we sometimes think before acting, it is also true that in much of the spontaneous behaviour of skillful practice we reveal a kind of knowing which does not stem from a prior intellectual operation.

As Gilbert Ryle has put it,

What distinguishes sensible from silly operations is not their parentage but their procedure, and this holds no less for intellectual than for practical performances. "Intelligent" cannot be defined in terms of "intellectual" or "knowing *how*" in terms of "knowing *that*"; "thinking what I am doing" does not connote "both thinking what to do and doing it." When I do something intelligently . . . I am doing one thing and not two. My performance has a special procedure or manner, not special antecedents.[24]

And Andrew Harrison has recently put the same thought in this pithy phrase: when someone acts intelligently, he "acts his mind."[25]

Michael Polanyi, who invented the phrase "tacit knowing," draws examples from the recognition of faces and the use of tools. If we know a person's face, we can recognize it among a thousand, indeed, among a million, though we usually cannot tell how we recognize a face we know. Similarly, we can recognize the moods of the human face without being able to tell, "except quite vaguely,"[26] by what signs we know them. When we learn to use a tool, or a probe or stick for feeling our way, our initial awareness of its impact on our hand is transformed "into a sense of its point touching the objects we are exploring."[27] In Polanyi's phrase, we attend "from" its impact on our hand "to" its effect on the things to which we are applying it. In this process, which is essential to the acquisition of a skill, the feelings of which we are initially aware become internalized in our tacit knowing.

Psycholinguists have noted that we speak in conformity with rules of phonology and syntax which most of us cannot describe.[28] Alfred Schultz and his intellectual descendants have analyzed the tacit, everyday know-how that we bring to social interactions such as the rituals of greeting, ending a meeting, or standing in a crowded elevator.[29] Birdwhistell has made comparable contributions to a description of the tacit knowledge embodied in our use and recognition of movement and gesture.[30] In these domains, too, we behave according to rules and procedures that we cannot usually describe and of which we are often unaware.

In examples like these, knowing has the following properties:

- There are actions, recognitions, and judgments which we know how to carry out spontaneously; we do not have to think about them prior to or during their performance.
- We are often unaware of having learned to do these things; we simply find ourselves doing them.
- In some cases, we were once aware of the understandings which were subsequently internalized in our feelings for the stuff of action. In other cases, we may never have been aware of them. In both cases, however, we are usually unable to describe the knowing which our action reveals.

It is in this sense that I speak of knowing-*in*-action, the characteristic mode of ordinary practical knowledge.

Reflecting-in-action If common sense recognizes knowing-in-action, it also recognizes that we sometimes think about what we are doing. Phrases like "thinking on your feet," "keeping your wits about you," and "learning by doing" suggest not only that we can think about doing but that we can think about doing something while doing it. Some of the most interesting examples of this process occur in the midst of a performance.

Big-league baseball pitchers speak, for example, of the experience of "finding the groove":

- Only a few pitchers can control the whole game with pure physical ability. The rest have to learn to adjust once they're out there. If they can't, they're dead ducks.
- [You get] a special feel for the ball, a kind of command that lets you repeat the exact same thing you did before that proved successful.
- Finding your groove has to do with studying those winning habits and trying to repeat them every time you perform.[31]

I do not wholly understand what it means to "find the groove." It is clear, however, that the pitchers are talking about a particular kind of reflection. What is "learning to adjust once you're out there"? Presumably it involves noticing how you have been pitching to the batters and how well it has been working, and on the basis of these thoughts and observations, changing the way you have been doing it. When you get a "feel for the ball" that lets you "repeat the exact thing you did before that proved successful," you are noticing, at the very least, that you have been doing something right, and your "feeling" allows you to do that something again. When you "study those winning habits," you are thinking about the know-how that has enabled you to win. The pitchers seem to be talking about a kind of reflection on their patterns of action, on the situations in which they are performing, and on the know-how implicit in their performance. They are reflecting *on* action and, in some cases, reflecting *in* action.

When good jazz musicians improvise together, they also manifest a "feel for" their material and they make on-the-spot adjustments to the sounds they hear. Listening to one another and to themselves, they feel where the music is going and adjust their playing accordingly. They can do this, first of all, because their collective effort at musical invention makes use of a schema – a metric, melodic, and harmonic schema familiar to all the participants – which gives a predictable order to the piece. In addition, each of the musicians has at the ready a repertoire of musical figures which he can deliver at appropriate moments. Improvisation consists in varying, combining, and recombining a set of figures within the schema which bounds and gives coherence to the performance. As the musicians feel the directions of the music that is developing out of their interwoven contributions, they make new sense of it and adjust their performance to the new sense they have made. They are reflecting-in-action on the music they are collectively making and on their individual contributions to it, thinking what they are doing and, in the process, evolving their way of doing it. Of course, we need not suppose that they reflect-in-action in the medium of words. More likely, they reflect through a "feel for the music" which is not unlike the pitcher's "feel for the ball."

Much reflection-in-action hinges on the experience of surprise. When intuitive, spontaneous performance yields nothing more than the results expected for it, then we tend not to think about it. But when intuitive performance leads to surprises, pleasing and promising or unwanted, we may respond by reflecting-in-action. Like the baseball pitcher, we may reflect on our "winning habits"; or like the jazz musician, on our sense of the music we have been making; or like the designer, on the misfit we have unintentionally created. In such processes, reflection tends to focus interactively on the outcomes of action, the action itself, and the intuitive knowing implicit in the action.

Reflecting-in-practice   If we are to relate the idea of reflection-in-action to professional practice, we must consider what a practice is and how it is like and unlike the kinds of action we have been discussing.

The word "practice" is ambiguous. When we speak of a lawyer's practice, we mean the kinds of things he does, the kinds of clients he has, the range of cases he is called upon to handle. When we speak of someone practicing the piano, however, we mean the repetitive or experimental activity by which he tries to increase his proficiency on the instrument. In the first sense, "practice" refers to performance in a range of professional situations. In the second, it refers to preparation of performance. But professional practice also includes an element of repetition. A professional practitioner is a specialist who encounters certain types of situations again and again. This is suggested by the way in which professionals use the word "case" – or project, account, commission, or deal, depending on the profession. All such terms denote the units which make up a practice, and they denote types of family-resembling examples. Thus a physician may encounter many different "cases of measles"; a lawyer, many different "cases of libel." As a practitioner experiences many variations of a small number of types of cases, he is able to "practice" his practice. He develops a repertoire of expectations, images, and techniques. He learns what to look for and how to respond to what he finds. As long as his practice is stable, in the sense that it brings him the same types of cases, he becomes less and less subject to surprise. His knowing-in-practice tends to become increasingly tacit, spontaneous, and automatic, thereby conferring upon him and his clients the benefits of specialization.

On the other hand, professional specialization can have negative effects. In the individual, a high degree of specialization can lead to a parochial narrowness of vision. When a profession divides into subspecialties, it can break apart an earlier wholeness of experience and understanding. Thus people sometimes yearn for the general practitioner of earlier days, who is thought to have concerned himself with the "whole patient," and they sometimes accuse contemporary specialists of treating particular illnesses in isolation from the rest of the patient's life experience. Further, as a practice becomes more repetitive and routine, and as knowing-in-practice becomes increasingly tacit and spontaneous, the practitioner may miss important opportunities to think about what he is doing. He may find that he is drawn into patterns of error which he cannot correct. And if he learns, as often happens, to be selectively inattentive to phenomena that do not fit the categories of his knowing-in-action, then he may suffer from boredom or "burn-out" and afflict his clients with the consequences of his narrowness and rigidity. When this happens, the practitioner has "over-learned" what he knows.

A practitioner's reflection can serve as a corrective to over-learning. Through reflection, he can surface and criticize the tacit understandings that have grown up around the repetitive experiences of a specialized practice, and can make new sense of the situations of uncertainty or uniqueness which he may allow himself to experience.

Practitioners do reflect *on* their knowing-in-practice. Sometimes, in the relative tranquility of a postmortem, they think back on a project they have undertaken, a situation they have lived through, and they explore the understandings they have brought to their handling of the case. They may do this in a mood of idle speculation, or in a deliberate effort to prepare themselves for future cases.

But they may also reflect on practice while they are in the midst of it. Here they reflect-in-action, but the meaning of this term needs now to be considered in terms of the complexity of knowing-in-practice.

A practitioner's reflection-in-action may not be very rapid. It is bounded by the "action-present," the zone of time in which action can still make a difference to the situation. The action-present may stretch over minutes, hours, days, or even weeks or months, depending on the pace of activity and the situational boundaries that are characteristic of the practice. Within the give-and-take of courtroom behavior, for example, a lawyer's reflection-in-action may take place in seconds; but when the context is that of an antitrust case that drags on over years, reflection-in-action may proceed in leisurely fashion over the course of several months. An orchestra conductor may think of a single performance as a unit of practice, but in another sense a whole season is his unit. The pace and duration of episodes of reflection-in-action vary with the pace and duration of the situations of practice.

When a practitioner reflects in and on his practice, the possible objects of his reflection are as varied as the kinds of phenomena before him and the systems of knowing-in-practice which he brings to them. He may reflect on the tacit norms and appreciations which underlie a judgment, or on the strategies and theories implicit in a pattern of behavior. He may reflect on the feeling for a situation which has led him to adopt a particular course of action, on the way in which he has framed the problem he is trying to solve, or on the role he has constructed for himself within a larger institutional context.

Reflection-in-action, in these several modes, is central to the art through which practitioners sometimes cope with the troublesome "divergent" situations of practice.

When the phenomenon at hand eludes the ordinary categories of knowledge-in-practice, presenting itself as unique or unstable, the practitioner may surface and criticize his initial understanding of the phenomenon, construct a new description of it, and test the new description by an on-the-spot experiment. Sometimes he arrives at a new theory of the phenomenon by articulating a feeling he has about it.

When he finds himself stuck in a problematic situation which he cannot readily convert to a manageable problem, he may construct a new way of setting the problem – a new frame which, in what I shall call a "frame experiment," he tries to impose on the situation.

When he is confronted with demands that seem incompatible or inconsistent, he may respond by reflecting on the appreciations which he and others have brought to the situation. Conscious of a dilemma, he may attribute it to the way in which he has set his problem, or even to the way in which he has framed his role. He may then find a way of integrating, or choosing among, the values at stake in the situation.

An ophthalmologist says that a great many of his patients bring problems that are not in the book. In 80 or 85 percent of the cases, the patients' complaints and symptoms do not fall into familiar categories of diagnosis and treatment. A good physician searches for new ways of making sense of such cases, and invents experiments by which to test his new hypotheses. In a particularly important family of situations, the patient suffers simultaneously from two or more diseases. While each of these, individually, lends itself to familiar patterns of thought and action, their combination may constitute a unique case that resists ordinary approaches to treatment.

The ophthalmologist recalls one patient who had inflammation of the eye (uveitis) combined with glaucoma. The treatment for glaucoma aggravated the inflammation, and the treatment for uveitis aggravated the glaucoma. When the patient came in, he was already under treatment at a level insufficient for cure but sufficient to irritate the complementary disease.

The ophthalmologist decided to remove all treatment and wait to see what would emerge. The result was that the patient's uveitis, a parasitic infection, remained in much reduced form. On the other hand, the glaucoma disappeared altogether, thus proving to have been an artifact of the treatment. The ophthalmologist then began to "titrate" the patient. Working with very small quantities of drugs, he aimed not at total cure but at a reduction of symptoms which would allow the patient to go back to work. (Seven lives depended on his 5,000 ocular cells!) The prognosis was not good, for uveitis moves in cycles and leaves scars behind which impede vision. But for the time being, the patient was able to work.

In an example such as this, something falls outside the range of ordinary expectations. The physician sees an odd combination of diseases never before described in a medical text. The practitioner allows himself to experience surprise, puzzlement, or confusion in a situation which he finds uncertain or unique. He reflects on the phenomena before him, and on the prior understandings which have been implicit in his behavior. He carries out an experiment which serves to generate both a new understanding of the phenomena and a change in the situation.

When someone reflects-in-action, he becomes a researcher in the practice context. He is not dependent on the categories of established theory and technique, but constructs a new theory of the unique case. His inquiry is not limited to a deliberation about means which depend on a prior agreement about ends. He does not keep means and ends separate, but defines them interactively as he frames a problematic situation. He does not separate thinking from doing, ratiocinating his way to a decision which he must later convert to action. Because his experimenting is a kind of action, implementation is built into his inquiry. Thus reflection-in-action can proceed, even in situations of uncertainty or uniqueness, because it is not bound by the dichotomies of Technical Rationality.

Although reflection-in-action is an extraordinary process, it is not a rare event. Indeed, for some reflective practitioners it is the core of practice. Nevertheless, because professionalism is still mainly identified with technical expertise, reflection-in-action is not generally accepted – even by those who do it – as a legitimate form of professional knowing.

Many practitioners, locked into a view of themselves as technical experts, find nothing in the world of practice to occasion reflection. They have become too skillful at techniques of selective inattention, junk categories, and situational control, techniques which they use to preserve the constancy of their knowledge-in-practice. For them, uncertainty is a threat; its admission is a sign of weakness. Others, more inclined toward and adept at reflection-in-action, nevertheless feel profoundly uneasy because they cannot say what they know how to do, cannot justify its quality or rigor.

For these reasons, the study of reflection-in-action is critically important. The dilemma of rigor or relevance may be dissolved if we can develop an epistemology of practice which places technical problem solving within a broader context of reflective inquiry, shows how reflection-in-action may be rigorous in its own right, and links the art of practice in uncertainty and uniqueness to the scientist's art of research. We may thereby increase the legitimacy of reflection-in-action and encourage its broader, deeper, and more rigorous use.

NOTES

1 A.M. Carr-Saunders, *Professions: Their Organization and Place in Society* (Oxford: The Clarendon Press, 1928). Quoted in Vollmer and Mills, eds., *Professionalization* (Englewood Cliffs, N.J.: Prentice-Hall, 1966), p. 3.
2 Wilbert Moore, *The Professions* (New York: Russel Sage Foundation, 1970), p. 56.
3 Ibid.
4 Ibid., p. 141.

5 Jethro Lieberman, *Tyranny of Expertise* (New York: Walker and Company), p. 55.
6 Nathan Glazer, "Schools of the Minor Professions," *Minerva* (1974): 346.
7 Ibid., p. 363.
8 Ibid., p. 348.
9 Ibid., p. 349.
10 Moore, *The Professions*, p. 56.
11 Edgar Schein, *Professional Education* (New York: McGraw-Hill, 1973), p. 43.
12 Ibid., p. 39.
13 William Goode, "The Librarian: From Occupation to Profession," reprinted in Vollmer and Mills, *Professionalization*, p. 39.
14 Ibid.
15 Ibid.
16 Ernest Greenwood, "Attributes of a Profession," reprinted in Vollmer and Mills, *Professionalization*, p. 11.
17 Ibid., p. 19.
18 Ibid., p. 12.
19 Harvey, Brooks, "Dilemmas of Engineering Education," *IEEE Spectrum* (February 1967): 89.
20 Schein, *Professional Education*, p. 44.
21 Barry Thorne, "Professional Education in Medicine," in *Education for the Professions of Medicine, Law, Theology and Social Welfare* (New York: McGraw-Hill, 1973), p.30.
22 Ibid., p. 31.
23 Of course, the problem of the lack of agreement about ends has engaged the attention of many of the protagonists of the positivist epistemology of practice. Approaches to this problem have ranged from the search for an ultimate end, to which all others could be subordinated; to a "universal solvent" for ends, as in the utility functions of the welfare economists; to the "piecemeal social engineering" proposed by Karl Popper. For a discussion of these, their defects and merits, see Charles Frankel, "The Relation of Theory to Practice: Some Standard Views," in *Social Theory and Social Intervention*, Frankel et al., eds. (Cleveland: Case Western Reserve University Press, 1968).
24 Gilbert Ryle, "On Knowing How and Knowing That," in *The Concept of Mind* (London: Hutcheson, 1949), p.32.
25 Andrew Harrison, *Making and Thinking* (Indianapolis: Hacket, 1978).
26 Michael Polanyi, *The Tacit Dimension* (New York: Doubleday and Co., 1967), p. 4.
27 Ibid. p. 12.
28 The whole of contemporary linguistics and psycholinguistics is relevant here – for example, the work of Chomsky, Halle, and Sinclair.
29 Alfred Schultz, *Collected Papers* (The Hague: Nijhoff, 1962).
30 Ray L. Birdwhistell, *Kinesics and Context* (Philadelphia: University of Pennsylvania Press, 1970).
31 Jonathan Evan Maslow, "Grooving on a Baseball Afternoon," in *Mainliner* (May 1981): 34.

3

~

CLINICAL INTUITION AND CLINICAL ANALYSIS: EXPERTISE AND THE COGNITIVE CONTINUUM*

Robert M. Hamm

1 OVERVIEW

This paper addresses medical students' and clinicians' concerns about how to reason well. It describes the many kinds of thinking people can do successfully, ranging from very intuitive cognition to the very analytical. Two theories of intuitive and analytical cognition, by Kenneth Hammond and by Hubert and Stuart Dreyfus, are discussed. It will be shown that the kind of task that a doctor is working on has an important role in determining the kind of thinking that is likely to be used. That the match between the task characteristics and the kind of thinking influences the accuracy of the thinking. And that the extent of the doctor's experience also influences the kind of thinking used and its likely success.

2 INTRODUCTION

At some point in their medical training, most likely near the time when they first take responsibility for patient care, most doctors develop an intense interest in thinking – How should one *think* to discover the cause of a patient's 3-day fever? Given an uncertain diagnosis, and available treatments that "usually work" but that have painful side effects, how should one *think* when deciding on a treatment plan?

It is natural that clinical decision makers should try to copy the thinking of the experts. This is especially true for medical students: seeking to think correctly about their first patients, they look for guidance to the experienced doctors who teach in medical schools. But these experts offer a number of different models:

1 When presenting case histories in their lectures, professors show reasoning that is elegantly logical in its use of science in the diagnosis of hidden diseases and the selection of correct treatments.

* Especially prepared for this volume, drawing on an 1984 article in *Medical Decision Making*, 4, 427–47.

2 On teaching rounds, the clinical professors lead the medical students and residents in a systematic consideration of all the evidence about the patient, yet they use their own perceptions and judgments, justified by reference to informal rules of thumb, to guide the diagnostic conclusions and treatment decisions.

3 When an expert clinician sees a patient, without explaining things to students, it is not evident that any "reasoning" is being used at all. The clinician seems to know what to do after a few questions.

The thinking processes that expert clinicians reveal in these three contexts are very different. While it may take 20 minutes of teaching rounds for the doctor and students to arrive at a tentative diagnosis, experienced clinicians typically formulate initial hypotheses within 15 seconds of talking with a new patient (Elstein *et al.*, 1978). Computer scientist William Clancey discovered the vast differences in experts' reasoning processes, when he sought to modify MYCIN, an "expert system" program that mimics how specialists diagnose bacteremia and meningitis, so that it could tutor students with the teaching style of one of the specialists. To make an expert system, a computer scientist will ask an expert (or experts) to explain how he or she reasons, and encode the explanations as rules in the computer program. The reasoning that Clancey's expert revealed when modeling tutoring to help produce an expert *tutoring* program was so different from the reasoning that a team of experts revealed when modeling diagnosis for the expert *diagnosing* program that it was necessary to rewrite the knowledge in the program extensively before it could be used for teaching (Clancey, 1983). Clancey's situation is analogous to that of the medical student seeking to model his or her own thinking after an expert clinician's thinking. The medical student will find that the expert's thinking processes in different situations seem to be completely incompatible. Which process (if any) should the student emulate?

Faced with such an impasse, the medical student, or indeed anyone interested in improving clinical judgment and decision making, might wish to consult psychology or cognitive science to see what scientists have to say about expert thinking. Perhaps researchers in these fields have discovered how experts really think, and can tell relatively inexperienced clinicians the best way to reason about diagnoses and decisions, even if the expert clinicians have no perspective on their own cognitive processes. There has in fact been extensive study of expert reasoning on diagnosis, problem solving, and decision making tasks (Chi and Glaser, 1985; Ericsson and Simon, 1984; Greeno and Simon, 1984; Hammond, McClelland, and Mumpower, 1980; Kahneman, Slovic, and Tversky, 1982), including tasks in the domain of medicine (Elstein, Rovner,

Holzman, *et al.*, 1982; Elstein, Shulman, and Sprafka, 1978; Johnson, 1982; Neame *et al.*, 1985; Wigton, Hoellerich, and Patil, 1986).

Most psychologists and cognitive scientists assume that thinkers receive perceptual inputs about their situation (e.g., by looking at and listening to the patient, by reading test results); interpret these inputs according to categories of knowledge that reside in memory, thus producing a representation of the situation (Rouse and Morris, 1986); consider how to use their skills to attain their goals in the represented situation; modify their representations as they get new information or gain new insight; produce, evaluate, and select plans of action; and finally carry out those plans. But there is considerable disagreement about how these various steps *are* done and *should* be done, about what aspects of the process change as one becomes more expert, and about which of these steps are most essential for accurate thinking. For example, it is generally acknowledged that people are capable of applying rules to the inputs to guide their categorizations and actions. It is also acknowledged that they are capable of perceiving and acting without explicitly applying rules. But researchers disagree about whether such rules are essential for accurate performance, or actually impede it. The clinician who has gone to the research literature for insight should keep in mind that thinking needs to be understood in context. The two important contexts to be covered here are the *task* and the thinker's *expertise*.

These contexts will be examined in terms of the important distinction between analytical and intuitive cognition, which can help a doctor understand how to think well in different medical contexts and at different stages in one's learning of medicine. The paper draws on the theoretical and empirical contributions of Kenneth Hammond, a psychologist whose Cognitive Continuum Theory describes analysis and intuition as distinct kinds of thinking, and shows how cognition depends on task characteristics (Hammond, 1980, 1981, 1986b). It also covers the theory of philosopher Hubert Dreyfus and operations researcher Stuart Dreyfus, who have characterized the development of expertise in terms of changes in the use of analytical and intuitive thinking (Dreyfus and Dreyfus, 1986).

In the perspective of these theorists, certain questions become sensible that are not commonly asked in psychological and cognitive science research, questions that are directly pertinent to the predicament of the medical student or clinician seeking guidance about how to think well:

1 What kinds of thinking, analytical or intuitive (or a mixture), should be used in various medical situations?
2 How does the practitioner discover or decide which mode of cognition to use?

3   How can the appropriate kind of thinking be performed as well as possible?

The clinician reading the research literature will need to keep this perspective in mind in order not to be discouraged by the apparent irrelevance of much research to his or her present problems. It is not that research is "too abstract" or "about unrealistically simple tasks." The problem, rather, is that researchers themselves lack perspective on the full range of kinds of thinking that people can do (Hammond, 1986b). Although Cognitive Continuum Theory (Hammond, 1980, 1983, 1986b) can serve as a framework for describing the many tasks that people are capable of performing, and the many kinds of thinking ("modes of cognition") that they can employ on these tasks, most researchers in psychology and cognitive science have chosen to situate their work within more limited horizons. While this narrow focus enables them to make progress in understanding the way people think on the particular tasks the researchers are studying, it also leads them to make exaggerated claims about the generality of their findings (Hammond, 1986a). The medical student or clinician seeking guidance in "how to think" is likely to reject the entire psychological research endeavour upon reading advice based on research on a task that is quite different from the current case.

3   A FRAMEWORK FOR PLACING COGNITION IN CONTEXT

Because the Cognitive Continuum is a framework in which different kinds of thinking and different kinds of task can be placed, it can provide structure for advice about how one can improve one's thinking on various tasks. The elements of this framework are: a range of kinds of cognition, a range of task conditions, and a range of modes of practice (Hammond, 1978, 1980, 1981).

3.1   The cognitive continuum

The venerable distinction between analysis and intuition has stimulated little research because intuition has been defined only as "the absence of analysis". Hammond (1980) sought instead to define the intuitive pole of the cognitive continuum in terms of specific features: Intuitive thought involves rapid, unconscious data processing that combines the available information by "averaging" it, has low consistency, and is moderately accurate. The expert clinician seeing a patient in the office, as described above, is using intuitive cognition. Analysis, the other end of the cognitive continuum, has the opposite features: Analytic thought is slow, conscious, and consistent; it is usually quite accurate (though it occasionally produces large errors); and it is quite likely to combine information using organizing principles that are more complicated than simple "averaging". The professor's lecture exemplifies analytical reasoning about a case. In its claim that intuition involves the combination of cues by the simplest psychological process, averaging, Cognitive Continuum Theory goes against the argument that experts make "configural" use of information in their clinical judgments (see Dawes, 1979; Goldberg, 1970; and Holt, 1970).

Analytical and intuitive thinking are defined as poles of a "continuum" because most thinking is neither purely intuitive nor purely analytical, but rather lies somewhere in between. This "in between" or "quasirational" cognition can have intermediate values on the features (e.g., it could take a moderate amount of time), or it can have a mixture of features (some features that are characteristic of analysis and others that are characteristic of intuition), or finally, it can involve alternation back and forth between analysis and intuition (Hammond, 1981; Hamm, 1985). The reasoning of the clinical professor leading students on teaching rounds exemplifies this quasirational cognition.

As an exercise, the reader may compare doctors' or students' reasoning, in situations he or she has observed, with the features listed above in order to place it on the cognitive continuum.

3.2 The task continuum, and the influence of task on cognition

Knowing that there are different kinds of thinking does not tell one which kind to use. For a clinician to convert the notion of a cognitive continuum, ranging from analysis to intuition, into guidance about how to think, two other ideas central to Hammond's theory are pertinent:

1 The doctor's task induces him or her to select a corresponding mode of cognition. Thus, some cases will induce a physician to think about them analytically, others will elicit intuitive cognition. The pertinent task features are reviewed in the remainder of Section 3.2.

2 The accuracy of cognition depends in part on whether the doctor selects the appropriate mode of cognition. If a physician tries to take an intuitive approach to a case which induces analysis, or vice versa, it will be difficult to reason accurately. The relation between task and accuracy is discussed in Section 3.3.

The first idea gives a basis for understanding why we would see an expert clinician thinking analytically in one situation and intuitively in another. The second idea gives grounds for evaluating whether someone's thinking is appropriate for the task. Section 3.4 covers the use of these ideas in combination to guide one's thinking.

In Cognitive Continuum Theory, tasks are considered to occupy a position on a task continuum, ranging from analysis-inducing to intuition-inducing, indicated by task features that influence the model of cognition that the thinker will adopt. These features include the complexity of the task, the ambiguity of the content of the task, and the form of task presentation. The following are examples of features in each category (Hammond, 1980, 1981, 1986b).

1 Complexity of task structure.
   a Number of cues – the more pertinent cues there are, the more likely the task will induce intuition. Given much information about a case, the doctor will probably use intuition to make the diagnosis.
   b Redundancy of cues. The more the cues can be predicted from each other, the more likely intuitive cognition will be used.
   c Identity of the accurate organizing principle. If a simple linear weighted average organizing principle is known to be most accurate, this is likely to encourage the doctor to use intuition. If, on the other hand, it is known that a complicated procedure for combining the evidence is most likely to produce an accurate answer, then a clinician would be likely to reason analytically.

2 Ambiguity of task content.
   a Availability of the organizing principle. If a complex organizing principle is readily available, the doctor is likely to use it, hence to be analytical.
   b Familiarity of the task content. Unfamiliarity induces an intuitive approach, involving the averaging of available cues, due to the unavailability of more complicated principles for organizing the cue information (Hammond, 1980, pp. 60–63; see Section 6.2, below).
   c The possibility of high accuracy. If the doctor knows that it is possible to be highly accurate on a particular diagnostic or treatment selection task, he or she is likely to use analysis.

3 Form of task presentation.
   a Task decomposition. If the task is presented in a manner that guides the doctor to address a sequence of subtasks, this will induce analytical cognition.
   b Cue definition (manner of presentation of information). If the information is presented pictorially, it induces intuition. If the cues are measured objectively and presented to the doctor in a quantitative form, it induces analysis.
   c The permitted or implied response time. If only a brief time is available, the doctor will adopt intuitive cognition. For example, a doctor with 20 patients scheduled for three hours in the clinic knows that intuition is the mode the institution expects.

Hammond, Hamm, Grassia, and Pearson (1987) varied these task features to determine their effect on expert highway engineers' modes of cognition. The task conditions were varied along two independent dimensions – "deep" and "surface" task features. The "deep" task feature bundles varied the content of the task and the degree of nonlinearity of the optimal organizing principle (among other features). The "surface" task feature bundles varied the mode of presentation of information, the number of cues, and the cue redundancy (among other features). It was found, as Cognitive Continuum Theory predicted, that both deep and surface task features had significant effects on the mode of cognition adopted.

The social and institutional context can also be expected to have a role in determining the mode of cognition a doctor uses (Hamm, Clark, and Bursztajn, 1984). Much medical reasoning, particularly in hospital settings, takes place in discussions involving people with different fields of training, different experience, and responsibility for different aspects of the patient's treatment (Climo, 1984). Such a group of people will readily accept some kinds of thinking from a doctor – that which is familiar, that which seems competent, that which seems to eliminate uncertainty (Bursztajn, Feinbloom, Hamm, and Brodsky, 1981). However the group may not accept highly analytical thinking if they do not understand it. And they may reject intuitive thinking on the part of a junior physician if it cannot be justified with reasoning that is more analytical.

The institution too affects the prevailing mode of cognition used in diagnosis and decision making, through the kind of staff training it provides or pays for, the amount of time it allows for reasoning about each patient, the kind of information that is routinely made available (e.g., tests, records, literature), the accessible tools (e.g., computers, software), and the rewards and punishments that are contingent on patient outcomes or physician practices. The medical student will need to be sensitive to the effects of such social and institutional factors on his or her thinking, as well as on others' thinking – even the thinking of doctors with greater experience.

No one task feature or contextual factor can completely determine a doctor's mode of cognition. For example, even when information is presented pictorially (as with chest X-rays), the doctor may know that high accuracy is possible, and hence reason analytically.

The ability of a task feature to induce a mode of cognition depends also on *what the thinker knows*. If one does not know that there is a generally accepted procedure for analyzing lung capacity, then that "task feature" can not make one think analytically in interpreting lung capacity data. For an illustration of this, consider a study of a formal tutorial conversation between a medical student and a teacher, where it was observed that the teacher thought more analytically. In this unpublished study (done in 1985 by Hamm, Hammond, and Grassia; methodology described by Hamm, 1985), the medical student presented a case to the teacher, and then they discussed it as they would on rounds. All statements were coded in terms of their degree of analysis. The teacher was consistently more analytical than the student throughout the whole conversation. Even though both were thinking about the same case, the greater knowledge of the teacher enabled him to think about it and explain it more analytically.

3.3 The relation of cognition/task correspondence and accuracy

Hammond (1980, 1981) argued that people's reasoning is relatively more effective when the mode of thinking they adopt corresponds to the task features. For example, if all the conditions of a case demand analytical cognition but the doctor tries to handle it intuitively, errors can be expected. On the other hand, if the information presentation, the problem context, and the social environment induce intuition, but the doctor tries to use an analytical approach, poor performance can again be anticipated. Empirical evidence for this relationship was found by Hammond, Hamm, Grassia, and Pearson (1987), who measured the extent to which their engineer subjects' cognition (when judging the capacity, safety, and aesthetic value of highways) corresponded to the task features, and found, in a within subject analysis, that the closer the correspondence, the greater the engineers' accuracy.

Clinicians, starting in their medical student days, are therefore advised to learn to identify and control the kind of thinking they are using, and to attend to those characteristics of their situation that would induce analysis or intuition. They can use this awareness to choose appropriate modes of cognition to use on their professional tasks, thus influencing their accuracy on the tasks.

3.4 The six modes of practice

The ideas presented above will be helpful to the clinician but they do not exploit the full power of Cognitive Continuum Theory to provide a basis for a systematic approach to improving the accuracy of one's thinking. The *induction* idea, that features of the doctor's task induce the mode of cognition he or she will use, is helpful because it explains why we see experts thinking differently in different situations. The notion that *correspondence between cognition and task features partially determines accuracy* is also helpful, for it can guide adjustments that one might make to one's cognition, or to the task, to improve the accuracy of one's reasoning. To understand the next possible step, consider this question: If it were possible to have cognition and task be well-matched at any position along the cognitive continuum, at which position would the most accurate reasoning take place? It is plausible that for every patient, there is an ideal task-cognition combination. That is, the doctor's reasoning might be most accurate if the approach to the patient's problem were formulated as a task at a particular position on the task continuum and the cognition were at the corresponding position on the cognitive continuum. Let us use the term "practice" to refer to both the characteristics of the task and the cognition the doctor uses on that task. To rephrase the question, what is the ideal mode of practice for a particular patient?

To make this conception usable, the doctor must have control not only over his or her cognition but also over the task features. Our discussion so far has assumed the doctor is a reactive thinker, who selects a kind of thinking in response to the given (externally controlled) task features. We also imagined the doctor trying out one mode of cognition in a number of situations that have different task features. But we should recognize that people have the ability to change the features of the tasks that face them (Basseches, 1984; Riegel, 1978, 1979). Indeed, it may be easier to control the task features and let *them* drive the selection of cognitive mode, than to simply "will" a change in cognitive mode. This is analogous to Skinner's (1953) observation that it is easier to change the contingencies of reinforcement and let them drive the behavior, than to directly "will" a change in behavior. Thus it is sensible to speak of shifting the features of a particular task, and the cognition one uses on it, until the most accurate position on the continuum of possible modes of practice is found.

In a study by Hammond, Hamm, Grassia, and Pearson (1987), the accuracy of highway experts judging the capacity, safety, and aesthetic value of highways was measured, using three presentation modes (the bundles of surface task features mentioned above) for each judgment task. In each judgment task, the more analytical modes of practice were more accurate. That is, the presentation mode with the more analytical task features (and the corresponding cognition) produced the more accurate judgments. The advantage of analysis would not necessarily be found with other kinds of task content; the point here is the possibility of performing better on a task after changing the task features and the corresponding cognition *together*.

Hammond (1978) divided the task/cognition continuum into six modes of inquiry. The first, most analytical, mode occurs in the laboratory of the hard sciences (physics, chemistry). The sixth, most intuitive, mode occurs wherever an individual judge is operating with minimal support from colleagues or reference to impersonal aids (e.g., a doctor on a home visit). The more analytical the mode of cognition and the more structured the task, (a) the greater the possibility of variable manipulation by the judge in the judging process; (b) the greater the visibility of the judgment process (i.e. openness to inspection or replication by others); and (c) the greater the time (and usually resources) required by the process (see Figure 1). This framework has been applied to the problems of medical *diagnosis* (Hammond, Hamm, Fisch, and Joyce, 1982) and medical *decision making* (Hamm, Clark, and Bursztajn, 1984). As these applications cover the general problems of correct *knowledge* and correct *action*, respectively, I will speak of "modes of practice" rather than "modes of inquiry", with the former term encompassing the latter.

Correct knowledge: epistemological safeguards   Doctors value accurate diagnoses. Different reasoning strategies are used to assure the quality of their causal reasoning in each of the modes of practice (see Table 1). The safeguard used in Mode 1, the most analytical mode, is highly controlled experimentation. The safeguard in Mode 6 is nothing more than an individual's opinion justified by the authority of his or her experience. Table 1 (modified from Hammond, Hamm, Fisch, and Joyce, 1982) distinguishes among the modes by reference to the epistemological safeguards that can be used in each mode. It lists features whose presence or absence characterizes these safeguards. While the usual conditions for the acquisition of medical knowledge involve epistemological safeguards at Modes 1, 2, and 3, the usual conditions for its application in the clinic involve Modes 6 (uncriticized, private judgments), and 5 (group discuss-

Figure 1   The six modes of enquiry (after Hammond 1978, 1981, 1983)

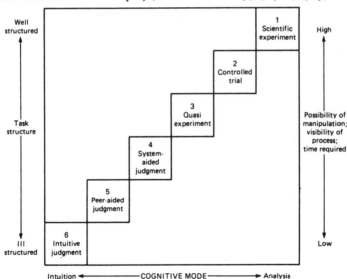

Table 1 *Features characteristic of causal reasoning at each mode on the cognitive continuum*

Feature:	Intuitive			Analytical		
	1 Uncriticized conclusions	2 Discussion	3 Aided subj. inference	4 Epidemiological studies	5 Clinical trials	6 Controlled experiments
Having control of variables extraneous to the causal model	No	No	No	No	No	Yes
Having control of variables intrinsic to the causal model	No	No	No	No	Yes	Yes
Able to measure the causes and effects in the causal model	No	No	No	Yes	Yes	Yes
Having a causal model or judgment with numerical parameters based on subjective judgments, at least	No	No	Yes	Yes	Yes	Yes
Able to justify one's beliefs by pointing to evidence, reasons, rules, or principles	No	Yes	Yes	Yes	Yes	Yes

Table 2 *Features characteristic of decision making at each mode on the cognitive continuum*

	Mode					
	Intuitive				Analytical	
	1	2	3 SEU	4	5	6
Feature:	Uncriticized decisions	Group discussion	with MD's assessments	Epidemiology perspective	Clin. trial perspective	Formal deduction
Decision structure, probabilities of events, and evaluation of outcomes are based on accepted, a priori models	No	No	No	No	No	Yes
Probabilities and evaluations are based on controlled measurement of events and outcomes, at least	No	No	No	No	Yes	Yes
Measurements of event probabilities and outcomes are based on statistical summaries of large amounts of data, at least	No	No	No	Yes	Yes	Yes
Decision model is generated and probabilities and evaluations of outcomes are measured subjectively, at least	No	No	Yes	Yes	Yes	Yes
Actions are justified with reference to reasons, rules, and principles, at least	No	Yes	Yes	Yes	Yes	Yes

ion), and on rare occasions, Mode 4 (for example, using cognitive aids such as Bayes' Theorem with subjectively assessed probabilities; see Weinstein *et al.*, 1980).

Correct action: decision making   Doctors wish to make decisions optimally. The feasible methods for selecting the treatment plans that have the best expected utility for the patient are different for each mode of practice. Table 2 (modified from Hamm, Clark, and Bursztajn, 1984) shows the methods that can be used to select the best decision in each of the six modes of practice, and lists features whose presence or absence distinguishes among these methods. Modes 6 and 5 are most commonly encountered in the clinic (see Climo, 1984; Hamm, Clark, and Bursztajn, 1984). Modes 1 through 4 involve the use of a formal decision analytical framework, including the measurement of the probabilities and utilities. If the probabilities and utilities are subjectively estimated, it would be Mode 4 cognition; if the probabilities can be measured with reference to the relative frequencies of events in a large data base, and the utilities can be measured by systematically surveying a large number of people, it would be typical of Mode 3. Analyses of this sort are frequently published in the journal *Medical Decision Making* (e.g., Matchar and Pauker, 1986).

Inspection of the descriptions of the modes of practice in Tables 1 and 2 should convince the reader that a doctor does not have the option of choosing a mode at will for a given situation. The medical "state of the art", as well as the social and institutional factors which provide the context for the doctor's thinking and acting, can not be so easily changed that every mode of practice can be applied (Bursztajn, Feinbloom, Hamm, and Brodsky, 1981). For example, in my freshman physics laboratory, the assignment was to measure a distance marked on the floor, without laying a yardstick along it. This is a Mode 1 or 2 problem. One classmate's solution was to poll the others and average their guesses. This Mode 4 solution was not acceptable in that context, as his lab partner quickly let him know. And along with that situational unacceptability, in fact *driving* it, was the fact that the answer produced by this method was much less accurate than the more analytic methods' answers. Similarly, for any particular medical problem, the doctor will not have the whole range of modes of cognitive practice as options. But yet there will be options within a narrow range (cf. Adelman, Sticha, and Donnell, 1984). The choice among those options is what we consider next.

Selection of a mode of practice   Consider a medical situation where the doctor has the choice of reasoning at the level of Mode 5 (arriving at a treatment plan through discussing the options with peers, justifying and criticizing each option in turn until a consensus plan is reached) or reasoning at Mode 4 (through applying the decision analytic framework to the options and their potential outcomes, getting subjective estimates of the probabilities that the outcomes would follow each option, plus subjective assessments of the utility of each outcome, and combining these by weighting the outcomes' utilities by the probabilities that they would occur to find the expected value of each option). There is a very obvious tradeoff here, between (a) the more analytic Mode 4 procedure which (1) promises higher accuracy but (2) requires more effort to do and to convince others to accept, and (b) the more intuitive Mode 5 procedure which, while (1) easier, (2) involves knowledge and actions in which one has less confidence (Hammond and Hamm, 1983). This is not an easy choice, and the difficulty does not go away once one has earned one's medical degree.

Doctors' decisions about which mode of practice to use are not as wise as they could be, because the tools that help them reason well at each mode are not well known. Let us consider two types of tools – tools which help bring the normative perspective to bear, and tools which "capture" or make public the doctors' judgment policies so that they can be inspected, compared, or combined.

Normative tools   The general norms for *diagnostic reasoning* are exemplified by Bayes' Theorem and ROC analysis. The general norm for *decision making* is decision theory, applied as outlined in the example two paragraphs above (see Table 2). Formal application of these norms requires cognition at least as analytical as Mode 4. Many doctors may not know that techniques for applying these norms with subjective judgments (Mode 4) are available; some who do may exaggerate the valid criticisms that have been made of these techniques (cf. Bursztajn and Hamm, 1982; Feinstein, 1977); and some who respect the approaches in principle may not know how to *use* them. These factors, rather than a fair evaluation of the advantages and disadvantages of using these normative procedures at Mode 4, may be what causes a doctor to practice at Mode 5 with a particular patient. This is a lost opportunity that could perhaps be recovered through education and advocacy (Lusted, 1984).

But the formal application of Bayes' Theorem or an expected utility formula is not the only way to bring these norms to bear on one's practice. Accurate use of the language of probability, phrased perhaps in the everyday terms of gambling (Bursztajn, Feinbloom, Hamm, and Brodsky, 1981), can keep the normative perspective in mind in discussions at Mode 5 of practice. Using such a conceptual framework accurately is not easy, and requires study of concepts, as well as monitoring of practice for accuracy. Opportunities may be lost if the doctor does not know how to use this informal normative reasoning tool, whether the loss be because the doctor practices at Mode 5 *without* the aid of probabilistic language, or because the doctor shifts to Mode 4 in the belief that the norm can not be respected at Mode 5, when in fact the formal normative tools are infeasible for the particular case.

A similar dilemma is found where medicine interfaces with the law, i.e., in the realm of medical malpractice arguments. Courts have recognized three types of justification – the intuitive "community standards", in which a doctor who does what other doctors do is not negligent (Mode 6); the analytical "Learned Hand rule" which involves evaluating the doctor's practice against an expected value criterion (Mode 3 or 4); and the intermediate "reasonable and prudent person" standard, which involves determining whether the doctor did what a careful thinker would have done in the circumstances – which is presumably to apply flexible, context-sensitive, critical reasoning to the problem (Mode 5), recognizing the issues addressed by the more formal decision analysis without being bound to its methods (Bursztajn, Hamm, Gutheil, and Brodsky, 1984).

Tools of judgment analysis Appropriate methods from cognitive psychology can be used at each mode of cognition to describe the doctor's thinking. Such descriptions can be useful in a number of ways. Let us consider applications of these methods at Modes 6, 5, and 4.

Mode 6 A doctor making uncriticized decisions in social isolation (Mode 6) could be given "cognitive feedback" – could be presented with an objective description of his or her judgment policy, that is, a description of the way the given information is used in producing a decision (Hammond and Boyle, 1971). This description could be compared with the doctor's own conception of how he or she makes those judgments. If there were a standard governing this kind of judgment, the doctor's judgment policy could also be compared with this standard. Either way, the cognitive feedback would give the doctor insight that might lead to changes, so that the doctor's future judgments, although still made intuitively in a Mode 6 context, would be more accurate.

Mode 5 Doctors whose reasoning involves public justification and mutual criticism of courses of action use their own judgments as inputs to the group discussion. Judgment analysis techniques can clarify for group members the source of these inputs. Techniques for describing individuals' judgment policies have been used to call attention to the fact that specialists in rheumatoid arthritis have widely varying policies (Kirwan *et al.*, 1983), which was not otherwise known. These techniques have also been used to show that disagreeing group members in fact have very similar basic judgment policies. Such objective descriptions of doctors' judgment policies could improve the accuracy of the group's thinking and the efficacy of the group's functioning without changing the group's basic mode of practice.

Mode 4 The tools of judgment analysis have also been useful at more analytical modes of practice. Hammond, Sutherland, Anderson, and Marvin (1984) worked with a group of experts who had widely divergent opinions on a particular *case* (the health danger of a nuclear weapons manufacturing facility located just outside of Denver). This group was led to focus on their subjective models of the causal relations among *variables* (instead of on the case), and they were able to agree on a causal model of the health effects of exposure to plutonium dust that applied to the particular case upon which they had previously disagreed. This example involves Mode 4 reasoning, because people discussed their subjective models of the relations among variables, and also Mode 3 reasoning, because when members of the group challenged each other they were asked to use epidemiological evidence to support their beliefs.

4 EVALUATION OF COGNITIVE CONTINUUM THEORY

It has been demonstrated that Cognitive Continuum Theory's formalization of the age-old distinction between intuition and analysis can help the medical student or clinician (a) recognize the kinds of cognition, and the kinds of task that typically elicit them; (b) adjust his or her cognition so that it corresponds to the task, in the hope of increasing its accuracy; (c) change the task characteristics for a given patient to facilitate the form of cognition that is most likely to produce accurate answers for the patient; and finally (d) select appropriate techniques for applying a normative perspective to the case.

The theory provides a general framework, not specific instructions. It does not tell the student exactly how to think intuitively or analytically. Rather than *explaining* cognition and its relation to the task in terms of internal psychological processes and how these are *controlled* by task features, the theory *describes* features of the cognition and how these are *correlated* with task features. The student is oriented towards both the characteristics of the task and the kind of cognition he or she is using on the task, but is left the difficult jobs of assessing the situation, assessing his or her own capabilities, and deciding whether cognition or task must be changed.

Some doctors might hesitate to be guided by Cognitive Continuum Theory because they think it overly simple to explain the various kinds of cognition in terms of just one basic dimension, the analytic/intuitive continuum. In the theory, any number of combinations of task features are said to produce cognition that is at the same point on the cognitive continuum. Thus, if the doctor can look at the patient (intuition inducing) but also knows of an appropriate principle for diagnosing the cause of this type of illness (analysis inducing), cognition at an intermediate point on the continuum would be expected – but cognition at that same point could also be induced if the doctor did not actually see the patient but rather was given numerically measured information about him (analysis inducing) but knew of no appropriate diagnostic principle for this type of illness (intuition inducing). One might think that the reasoning in these two situations would be quite different, but Cognitive Continuum Theory would make no further distinctions between them if they have the same position on the continuum (measured, for example, by the Cognitive Continuum Index developed by Hammond, Hamm, Grassia, and Pearson, 1987).

5 THE DREYFUSES' THEORY OF EXPERTISE

The doctor who finds the cognitive continuum too simple may be more pleased with Dreyfus and Dreyfus' theory of expert cognition (1986). Where Hammond (1980, 1981) would place a doctor's cognition at one particular position on the continuum, Dreyfus and Dreyfus (1986) describe several levels of thinking involved in a task. Different modes of cognition can be used at each level. This idea of a structured task description has not figured prominently in the core of Cognitive Continuum Theory (Hammond, 1980, 1981, 1986b), though Hamm (1985) looked for different modes of cognition on different subtasks of a complicated judgment task.

Dreyfus and Dreyfus describe five stages that one must go through to become, say, an expert physician – novice, advanced beginner, competent, proficient, and expert. Performance at each stage involves these subtasks:

1   At the level of the whole situation, the doctor must be oriented and act.
    a   Orientation. The doctor must understand the facts and the motivating issues in the situation, e.g., he or she must recognize when a patient is an emergency.
    b   Decision. The doctor must formulate goals and plan coordinated actions to reach those goals.
2   At the level of the components of the situation, the doctor must perform a large repertoire of skilled actions.
    a   Perception. The doctor must recognize the relevant aspects of the situation, e.g., recognize signs of various illnesses in every part of the body.

b   Action. The doctor must know what use to make of these
perceptions – what diagnoses to make, what further questions to
ask or tests to order, what actions to take.

Like Hammond, the Dreyfuses consider *analysis* and *intuition* as the
key concepts in understanding people's cognition. Specifically, each of the
above activities can be done intuitively or analytically (see Table 3).
(While Dreyfus and Dreyfus use different phrases to describe the special
characteristics of the analytical and intuitive thinking at each level, I will
speak of only "analysis" and "intuition" here, to emphasize the structure
of the theory.) The developmental stages are distinguished by those
subprocesses of thinking which are handled analytically or intuitively at
each stage. The *novice* must think analytically in order to perform, that is,
must relate the present situation to guiding principles, consciously interpret sense perceptions, and follow rules about what to do if a particular
sign is observed. For example, the medical student first learning to listen to
the lungs does not know what to make of the sounds he or she hears, and is
taught rules relating commonly known sounds to the needed perceptual
categories – e.g., "The fine crepitant rale is best imitated by moistening the
thumb and finger tip, pressing them tightly together and separating them
while they are held near the ear" (Hare, 1902, p. 274), as well as rules
relating *rales* to various lung conditions. The novice leaves the definition
of the "whole situation" to the teacher. The *advanced beginner* has
learned to perceive intuitively, e.g., can instantly distinguish "fine crepitant rales" from "fine bubbling rales", but must still apply rules to know
what diseases these indicate. The *competent* doctor exercises both perception and action components of the skill intuitively, e.g., listens to lungs
and *hears* the patient's condition. However, the competent doctor must
still think analytically about the whole situation. The *proficient* doctor
perceives the whole situation intuitively – the important details stand out,
others recede into the background – but makes decisions analytically
about the strategy for managing the patient. Finally, the *expert* makes
these decisions intuitively as well.

This structured description of the doctor's task, and differentiated
assignment of cognitive mode to the subtasks, give Dreyfus and Dreyfus a
complicated framework from which to advise medical students about
their modes of cognition:

1   Realize that expertise is acquired step by step. One must learn the
components explicitly and learn to act with them analytically. Experience will allow thinking about patients to become intuitive.
2   Avoid trying to think like an expert (intuitively). Without experience
based on an analytic foundation, intuitive performance will be poor.
Not using rules is a privilege of the expert, not a route to becoming
expert more quickly.

Table 3 *Cognitive mode used at each level of the task, at each state of the development of expertise, in the theory of Dreyfus and Dreyfus (1986)*

Level of organization	Lower		Higher	
Subprocess	Perception	Action	Orientation	Decision
	Perceives the elements of the situation	Acts on those elements	Recognizes whole situations	Makes decisions and plans how to attain goals in the situation
Stage				
1 Novice	Analytical	Analytical	Rely on others	Rely on others
2 Advanced beginner	Intuitive	Analytical	Rely on others	Rely on others
3 Competent	Intuitive	Intuitive	Analytical	Analytical
4 Proficient	Intuitive	Intuitive	Intuitive	Analytical
5 Expert	Intuitive	Intuitive	Intuitive	Intuitive

3   Instead, practice intensively using the rules and logic that are available, whether these be the rules for performing a skill or the rules for judging what is important and deciding what to do.

In addition, the field as a whole should not rely too heavily on aids that take the rule-like decisions out of peoples hands, e.g., rule-based expert systems (or to use the Dreyfuses' term, "competent systems"), for this may deny students the opportunity to develop their expertise.

How valid is the Dreyfuses' theory? The authors support it by demonstrating its logic, citing evidence from the literature, and giving examples that connect with the readers' own experience. For example, a study of the acquisition of nursing expertise describes beginning nurses as rule-bound and lacking intuition about what is important (Benner, 1984). On the whole, the description of the move from analysis to intuition with the development of expertise seems correct, although the stage structure of their theory may invite them to make more distinctions than are necessary. Because the authors' disciplines, philosophy and operations research, do not demand that their theory be supported by a program of empirical research, the theory has not been subjected to the kind of test that would build one's confidence in all its details.

6 COMPARISON WITH COGNITIVE CONTINUUM THEORY

The clinician interested in improving his or her reasoning about patients may ask whether it is necessary to understand both theories, since each uses the concepts of intuition and analysis. We now compare the two theories, highlighting especially the important differences that have practical applications. Medical practitioners should be cautious in applying the controversial aspects of either theory until the issues are resolved through research.

Cognitive Continuum Theory emphasizes that the task features determine the doctor's mode of cognition and indirectly his or her accuracy. Such factors, and particularly the effects of social and institutional setting on a doctor's cognition, are largely ignored by the Dreyfuses.

The Dreyfuses, for their part, emphasize the relation of the doctor's thinking to his or her experience. For Hammond, experience figures indirectly in determining a doctor's mode of cognition in a particular case, through factors such as whether an organizing principle is known. But it is not assumed to play the paramount role, as it does in the Dreyfuses' theory.

In contrast with the untested theory of the stages of expertise, Cognitive Continuum Theory, conceived in the field of psychology, was designed to be put to the test. Studies by Goldsberry (1983), Hammond, Hamm, Grassia, and Pearson (1987), Hamm (1985), and Howell (1984) have explored major tenets of the theory, and found support for it, including verification of some nonobvious predictions.

6.1 Similarities between the theories

The most important agreement is the assumption that people have the option of using analytical and intuitive modes of thinking. Though the theories' definitions of intuition (and analysis) are not identical, it is clear that they intend the same basic concepts.

Neither theory views intuition as a mere "automatization" of the processes involved in analysis. Intuition is not just a faster, unconscious performance of the analytic thinking processes, according to Cognitive Continuum Theory. It specifies a number of features on which the *results* of a doctor's intuitive thinking are different from the results of analytical thinking (e.g., in the pattern of errors, the consistency, and the rule relating the answer to the input information). Dreyfus and Dreyfus argue that intuition is different in kind from analysis, because analysis involves symbolic thinking while intuition does not (see Section 6.4 below).

Both theories say that in order to predict the accuracy of a doctor's performance, we must know something about both cognition and its context. For Hammond, the key context is task: performance is relatively most efficacious when the mode of cognition corresponds to the task features, and also when the problem is approached with the appropriate level of cognition and task features. For the Dreyfuses, the relevant context is the doctor's level of expertise – performance is most accurate when the doctor's cognitive mode is appropriate to his or her experience, for each level of the task.

6.2 Similar predictions for different reasons

There are several issues on which the two theories predict the same kind of phenomenon, but for different reasons. For example, both theories value intuition and say it can be better than analysis on the same task, i.e., produce more accurate answers. For the Dreyfuses, this occurs because only intuition can bring into play the doctor's deep understanding of the situation. It is the expert doctor's intuition that enables him or her to deal with unexpected situations, where the usual rules don't apply.

Cognitive Continuum Theory similarly predicts that intuition will be better than analysis in situations that are somewhat novel, but this prediction derives from an understanding of the organizing principles typical of analysis and intuition. Analytic organizing principles use only a few cues, in a precise manner, while intuitive organizing principles use many cues imprecisely, as by giving them approximately equal attention. If the doctor's situation is somehow different from the situation for which the analytic rule was produced, then the doctor may do better using intuitive cognition than by using the precise, but wrong, rule (see Einhorn and Hogarth, 1981). Thus, a particular test may define exactly whether a person has this year's variety of the flu; but at the beginning of next year's flu season the doctor will be better off looking intuitively at a patient seeking a flu-like pattern, than relying on the test, because next year's flu may be a variety to which the test is not sensitive.

Both theories expect the predominant mode of cognition to change from analysis to intuition in the course of the medical education. Hammond and Hamm (1983) attribute this to the change in the medical students' task characteristics, which shift from the analysis-inducing environment of the lecture hall and lab to the intuition-inducing clinic. Dreyfus and Dreyfus would attribute the same change from analysis to intuition to the students' increasing expertise rather than to the task environment.

6.3 Contradictions between the theories

Issues on which the theories disagree about the causes or advantages of the use of particular modes of cognition are the most important aspects of a comparison, for practical and theoretical reasons. Practically, until an issue is resolved, doctors will reasonably hesitate to use the conflicting advice. In the realm of theory, future progress in explaining expert cognition depends on the correctness as well as the richness of a theory's description.

What are the possible forms of quasirational cognition? While Hammond considers analysis and intuition the end points of the Cognitive Continuum, Dreyfus and Dreyfus speak only of the two pure types of cognition. They claim these are very different in principle, carried out by different processes (symbolic versus nonsymbolic). Therefore they would not endorse Hammond's notion of quasirational cognition as the middle range on a continuum, the type of cognition whose intermediate features reflect an intermediate cognitive process. However, the other two forms of quasirationality − mixtures of analysis and intuition, and alternation between analysis and intuition − would be consistent with their theory. Research strategies hinge on this issue (Hammond, 1981).

Are doctors more likely to use analysis or intuition when they are unfamiliar with a task? In Cognitive Continuum Theory, unfamiliarity of task content is a feature that induces intuition because, not having been trained to use any particular analytic principle for organizing their thinking about the situation, doctors will rely on the intuitive method for integrating information − averaging. For the Dreyfuses, the novice is by definition unfamiliar with the task, and can only do it by taking an analytic, step by step approach. The contradiction may be explained, within a Cognitive Continuum Theory framework, by a key difference in the task features. Novices in the teaching contexts the Dreyfuses discuss have these step by step analytical rules available in the minds of their teachers or in their texts − in fact the educational environment is designed to provide them with these analytical organizing principles. However, there are no such aids in the general case Hammond speaks of, and so the clinician with an unfamiliar problem will use the default organizing principle, the averaging characteristic of intuitive cognition.

Does the quality of a doctor's reasoning depend on whether it is done analytically or intuitively? Both theories argue that it does, in particular contexts; but the particulars are quite different. For the Dreyfuses, better thinking is done intuitively, because experts who think better, think intuitively. A major theme of their book is the fallibility of analysis. In Cognitive Continuum Theory, the relation of a doctor's performance to his or her use of intuition is an empirical issue, likely to depend on the task characteristics. Even if experts *prefer* to use intuitive cognition because it takes less time and effort, this does not mean it will be more accurate than analysis. Evidence that experts' intuition can be inaccurate (see Adelson, 1984) includes the discovery of widely divergent intuitive judgment policies used by expert medical specialists (Kirwan *et al.*, 1983) and the finding that clinical psychologists' diagnostic judgments are not as accurate as mathematical models (see Dawes, 1979; Goldberg, 1970).

Should experts' instructions to novices be viewed as repetitions of the lessons that the experts originally heard when they were learning, rather than as indications of how they think? Perhaps this makes sense when one considers the game of chess, one of the Dreyfuses' examples, which has changed little in decades. But for a rapidly changing field such as medicine, teachers' lessons represent their best *current* understanding of good practice. Further, in their practice, the experts use the rules they tell the student. Much of medicine is carried out with a quasirational mode of cognition, say Mode 5 or Mode 4, as when the doctor plays a leadership of coordinating role in a group. The explicit expression of reasoning plays an indispensible role in such a group's decision making, and is not merely a remnant from the doctor's student days that has no function in his or her current thinking.

Do experts usually perform with fully intuitive cognition? The Dreyfuses think so, and judge it good that they do. For Hammond, experts perform at a variety of cognitive modes, depending on task, and this variation is good because research has shown that experts' intuition can be quite inconsistent and inaccurate.

6.4 Complementary aspects of the theories

The Dreyfuses' theory of the different psychological processes that underly analysis and intuition complements the methods Hammond recommends for studying the two modes of cognition. The Dreyfuses believe that the processes involved in analytic cognition are quite distinct from those of intuition, whether these be embodied in human brains or computers. Analytic thinking involves the manipulation of symbolic propositions, the kind postulated to underly *all* problem solving by Newell and Simon (1972). But the processes underlying intuitive thinking are not symbolic, and are currently best modeled by a very different class of computer techniques, parallel distributed systems (e.g., Rumelhart *et al.*, 1986; Smolensky, 1986).

Cognitive Continuum Theory does not describe the kind of information processing that underlies analysis and intuition. But it recommends that different techniques be used for describing the cognitive modes, based on the features of analytical and intuitive cognition (Hammond, 1981; 1983; Hammond, Hamm, Grassia, and Pearson, 1987). It would be appropriate to describe analytical cognition by analyzing verbal protocols and producing computer programs to simulate the cognition discovered there (Ericsson and Simon, 1984), because analysis has rule-like organizing principles and people are capable of reporting these rules. Hammond recommends describing intuitive cognition with statistical models (e.g., Brunswik's Lens Model) that express the answer as a weighted average of the available information, both because such models work well with intuitive cognition (see Hoffman, 1960; Einhorn, Kleinmuntz, and Kleinmuntz, 1979) and because people are not able to report any *rules* of intuition (see Rouse and Morris, 1986).

These approaches are complementary because Hammond's methods map onto the Dreyfuses' processes. The same protocol analysis methods Hammond recommends for describing people's analytic cognition have proven useful for studying the cognition-by-symbol-manipulation process that the Dreyfuses say underlies analysis. The methods Hammond uses for describing people's intuitive cognition (statistical modeling of the relation between the answer and the given information) are based on assumptions (Brunswik, 1956) very similar to the assumptions of the nonsymbolic paradigm of cognition (Smolensky, 1986).

7 CONCLUSION

The medical student or clinician wishing to reason well about patients will gain from recognizing that there are different modes of cognition, analysis and intuition; that each is likely to occur in some contexts but not in others; and that in some situations each is the best thinking the doctor can do for the patient. The two theories reviewed in this paper have different frameworks for explaining the occurrence of the different modes of thinking and recommending their use. Hammond's Cognitive Continuum Theory calls our attention to the task conditions in which the clinician must think. Dreyfus and Dreyfus's theory focusses on the changes in the doctor's own level of expertise.

Together, the two theories provide an explanation for variations in cognition on different tasks and at different stages of a doctor's career. They make suggestions for how to change cognitive mode, task characteristics, or (most difficult) one's own level of expertise, in order to improve accuracy. They also provide a framework for selecting techniques that help one reason normatively under different task conditions.

The theories can not provide step by step instructions on how to discover the appropriate reasoning strategy and use it. Clinicians will need to develop their own abilities to judge task situations and select appropriate modes of cognition.

The existence of important contradictions between the theories will make the clinicians' task all the more difficult. Should they base their actions on the Dreyfuses' assertions that experts are necessarily intuitive, and that intuition is the preferable mode for an expert doctor to use? Or should they follow Cognitive Continuum Theory in assuming that the cognitive mode used by the expert will depend on characteristics of the task, as will the accuracy of intuition? No matter which theory seems more true, one will need to keep a critical eye on the theories, both watching one's own practice for evidence supporting or refuting the theories, and monitoring the research literature for relevant results.

The reader of the research literature should pay attention to the quality of the research. Good research will specify the mode of cognition being investigated, select research methods appropriate to that mode of cognition, and restrict generalizations to the mode of cognition studied. Even better research will look at several modes of cognition, using several methods (cf. Hammond, Hamm, and Grassia, 1986).

The resolution of the issues concerning the definitions of analysis and intuition, the processes underlying them, and the conditions in which each produces accurate reasoning will be one of the interesting challenges facing psychologists and cognitive scientists in the coming years. The medical community will have an important role in demanding, supporting, and carrying out the research that will resolve these questions, and in using its results wisely.

REFERENCES

Adelman, L., Sticha, P.J., and Donnell, M.L. (1984). The role of task properties in determining the relative effectiveness of multiattribute weighting techniques. *Organizational Behavior and Human Performance, 33,* 243–262.

Adelson, B. (1984). When novices surpass experts: The difficulty of a task may increase with expertise. *J. Experimental Psychology: Learning, Memory, and Cognition, 10,* 483–495

Basseches, M. (1984). *Dialectical Thinking and Adult Development.* Norwood, NJ: Ablex Publishing Corp.

Benner, P. (1984). *From Novice to Expert: Excellence and Power in Clinical Nursing Practice.* Reading, MA: Addison-Wesley.

Brunswik, E. (1956). *Perception and the Representative Design of Psychological Experiments.* Berkeley: Univ. of California Press.

Bursztajn, H., Feinbloom, R.I., Hamm, R.M., and Brodsky, A. (1981). *Medical Choices, Medical Chances: How Patients, Families, and Physicians Can Cope with Uncertainty.* New York: Delacorte Press/ Seymour Lawrence.

Bursztajn, H. and Hamm, R.M. (1982). The clinical utility of utility assessment. *Medical Decision Making, 2,* 161–165.

Bursztajn, H., Hamm, R.M., Gutheil, T.G., and Brodsky, A. (1984). The decision-analytic approach to medical malpractice law: Formal proposals and informal syntheses. *Medical Decision Making, 4,* 401–414.

Chi, M.T.M., and Glaser, R. (1985). Problem solving abilities. In R. Sternberg (Ed.), *Human Abilities: An Information Processing Approach* (pp. 227–248). San Francisco: Freeman.

Clancey, William J. The epistemology of a rule-based expert system – A framework for explanation. *Artificial Intelligence,* 1983, 20, 215–251.

Climo, L.H. (1984). Some thorny medical judgments and their outcomes: The view from the public mental hospital. *Medical Decision Making*, 4, 415–424.

Dawes, R.M. (1979). The robust beauty of improper linear models in decision making. *American Psychologist*, 34, 571–582.

Dreyfus, H.L., and Dreyfus, S.E. (1986). *Mind over Machine: The Power of Human Intuition and Expertise in the Era of the Computer*, New York: The Free Press.

Einhorn, H.J., and Hogarth, R.M. (1981). Behavioral decision theory: Processes of judgment and choice. *Annual Review of Psychology*, 32, 53–88.

Einhorn, H.J., Kleinmuntz, D.N., and Kleinmuntz, B. (1979). Linear regression and process-tracing models of judgment. *Psychological Review*, 86, 465–485.

Elstein, A.S., Rovner, D.R., Holzman, G.B., et al. (1982). Psychological approaches to medical decision making. *American Behavioral Scientist*, 25, 557–584.

Elstein, A.S., Shulman, L.S., and Sprafka, A. (1978). *Medical Problem Solving: An Analysis of Clinical Reasoning*. Cambridge, MA: Harvard University Press.

Ericsson, K.A., and Simon, H.A. (1984). *Protocol Analysis: Verbal Reports as Data*. Cambridge, MA: MIT Press.

Feinstein, A.R. (1977). Clinical biostatistics: XXXIX. The haze of Bayes, the aerial palaces of decision analysis, and the computerized Ouija board. *Clin. Pharmacol. Ther.*, 21, 482–496.

Goldberg, L.R. (1970). Man versus model of man: A rationale, plus some evidence, for a method of improving on clinical inferences. *Psychological Bulletin*, 73, 422–432.

Goldsberry, B.S. (1983). In search of the components of task induced judgment decrements (Technical Report No. 83-3). Houston, TX: Rice University, Department of Psychology.

Greeno, J.G., and Simon, H.A. (1984). Problem solving and reasoning. In R.C. Atkinson, R. Hernnstein, G. Lindzey, and R.D. Luce (Eds.), *Stevens' Handbook of Experimental Psychology* (rev. ed.). New York: Wiley.

Hamm, R.M. (1985). Moment by moment variation in the cognitive activity of experts (Report No. 257). Boulder, CO: University of Colorado, Center for Research on Judgment and Policy.

Hamm, R.M., Clark, J.A., and Bursztajn, H. (1984). Psychiatrists' thorny judgments: Describing and improving decision making processes. *Medical Decision Making*, 4, 425–447.

Hammond, K.R. (1978). Toward increasing competence of thought in public policy formation. In K.R. Hammond (Ed.), *Judgment and Decision in Public Policy Formation*. Boulder, CO: Westview Press, pp. 11–32.

(1980). The integration of research in judgment and decision theory (Report # 226). Boulder: University of Colorado, Center for Research on Judgment and Policy.

(1981). Principles of organization in intuitive and analytical cognition (Report # 231). Boulder: University of Colorado, Center for Research on Judgment and Policy.

(1983). Teaching the new biology: Potential contributions from research in cognition. In C.P. Friedman and E.F. Purcell (Eds.), *The New Biology and Medical Education: Merging the Biological, Information, and Cognitive Sciences*. New York: Josiah Macy, Jr., Foundation, pp. 53–64.

(1986a). Generalization in operational contexts: What does it mean? Can it be done? *IEEE Transactions on Systems, Man, and Cybernetics*, SMC-16, 428–433.

(1986b). A theoretically based review of theory and research in judgment and decision making (Report # 260). Boulder: University of Colorado, Center for Research on Judgment and Policy.

Hammond, K.R., and Boyle, P. (1971). Quasi-rationality, quarrels, and new conceptions of feedback. *Bull. Br. Psychol. Soc.*, 24, 103–113.

Hammond, K.R., and Hamm, R.M. (1983). Thoughts on the acquisition of medical knowledge. In Charles P. Friedman and Elizabeth F. Purcell (Eds.), *The New Biology and Medical Education: Merging the Biological, Information, and Cognitive Sciences*. New York: Josiah Macy, Jr., Foundation, pp. 190–197.

Hammond, K.R., Hamm, R.M., Fisch, H.-U., and Joyce, C.R.B. (1982). Differential contributions of two forms of cognitive science to medical decision making. Paper presented to the Fourth Annual Meeting of the Society for Medical Decision Making, Boston, October 1982. Abstract in *Medical Decision Making*, 2, 358.

Hammond, K.R., Hamm, R.M., and Grassia, J.L. (1986). Generalizing over conditions by combining the multitrait-multimethod matrix and the representative design of experiments. *Psychological Bulletin*, 100, 257–269.

Hammond, K.R., Hamm, R.M., Grassia, J.L., and Pearson, T. (1987). Direct comparison of the efficacy and analytical cognition in expert judgment *IEEE Transactions on Systems, Man and Cybernetics*, SMC-17 (forthcoming).

Hammond, K.R., McClelland, G.H., and Mumpower, J. (1980). *Human Judgment and Decision Making*. New York: Hemisphere

Hare, H.A. (1902). *Practical Diagnosis: The Use of Symptoms and Physical Signs in the Diagnosis of Disease (Fifth Edition)*. Philadelphia: Lea Brothers and Co.

Hoffman, P.J. (1960). The paramorphic representation of clinical judgment. *Psychological Bulletin*, 57, 116–131.

Holt, R.R. (1970). Yet another look at clinical and statistical prediction: Or, is clinical psychology worthwhile? *American Psychologist*, 25, 337–349.

Howell, W.C. (1984). Task influences in the analytical-intuitive approach to decision making. Houston, TX: Rice University, Department of Psychology.

Johnson, P.E. (1982). Cognitive models of medical problem solving. In D.P. Connelly, E.S. Benson, M.D. Burke, and D. Fenderson (Eds.), *Clinical Decisions and Laboratory Use*. Minneapolis: Minnesota Press, pp. 39–51.

Kahneman, Daniel, Slovic, Paul, and Tversky, Amos (Eds.), *Judgment under Uncertainty: Heuristics and Biases*. Cambridge, UK: Cambridge University Press, 1982.

Kirwan, J.R., Chaput de Saintonge, D.M., Joyce, C.R.B., and Currey, H.L.F.

(1983). Clinical analysis: Practical application in rheumatoid arthritis. *Brit. J. of Rheumatology*, 22, 18–23.

Lusted, L.B. (1984). Uncertainty and indecision. *Medical Decision Making*, 4, 397–399.

Matchar, D.B., and Pauker, S.G. (1986) Transient ischemic attacks in a man with coronary artery disease: Two strategies neck and neck. *Medical Decision Making*, 6, 239–249.

Neame, R.L.B., Chir, M.B.B., Mitchell, K.R., Feletti, G.I., and McIntosh, J. (1985). Problem solving in undergraduate medical students. *Medical Decision Making*, 5, 311–324.

Newell, A., and Simon, H.A. (1972). *Human Problem Solving*. Englewood Cliffs, N.J.: Prentice-Hall.

Riegel, K.F. (1978) *Psychology Mon Amour: A Countertext*. Boston: Houghton-Mifflin.

(1979) *Foundations of Dialectical Psychology*. New York: Academic Press.

Rouse, William B., and Morris, Nancy M. On looking into the black box: Prospects and limits in the search for mental models. *Psychological Bulletin*, 1986, *100*, 349–363.

Rumelhart, D.E., McClelland, J.L., and the PDP Research Group (1986). *Parallel Distributed Processing: Explorations in the Microstructure of Cognition. Volume I: Foundations*. Cambridge, MA: MIT Press/Bradford Books.

Skinner, B.F. (1953). *Science and Human Behavior*. New York: Macmillan.

Smolensky, P. (1986). Information processing in dynamical systems: Foundations of Harmony Theory. Chapter 6 in D.E. Rumelhart, J.L. McClelland, and the PDP Research Group (Eds.), *Parallel Distributed Processing: Explorations in the Microstructure of Cognition. Volume I: Foundations*. Cambridge, MA: MIT Press/Bradford Books, pp. 194–281.

Weinstein, M.C., Fineberg, H.V., Elstein, A.S., Frazier, H.S., Neuhauser, D., Neutra, R.R., and McNeil, B.J. (1980). *Clinical Decision Analysis*. Philadelphia: W.B. Saunders Company.

Wigton, R.S., Hoellerich, V.L., and Patil, K. (1986). How physicians use clinical information in diagnosing pulmonary embolism: An application of conjoint analysis. *Medical Decision Making*, 6, 2–11.

PART 2

—————— ~ ——————

MODELLING THE CLINICIAN AND THE CLINICAL TASK

4

PSYCHOLOGY OF CLINICAL REASONING*

Arthur S. Elstein, Georges Bordage

The rapid growth of medical knowledge and sophisticated technology has introduced new health care interventions and contributed to more intricate clinical choices. Thus, the issue inevitably raised is, which of several possible interventions should be employed in a particular case? For example, should a malignant tumor be treated by drugs, surgery, or radiation, when available evidence indicates that each is only partially effective? Should two of the treatments be combined? If drug therapy is begun, can it ethically be discontinued if the patient fails to improve? How long should we wait? Who should decide? On what basis? A host of questions concerning *how clinical decisions are made* and *how they ought to be made* arise every time a moderately complex clinical problem is examined.

At the same time, the topics of judgment, problem solving, decision making, cognition, and reasoning have become active research areas in psychology. Psychologists have sought to apply both the tools and insights of this research to problems of individual and public health (Kaplan and Schwartz, 1975, 1977). Clinical reasoning has been among the topics explored. Clearly, all of us have a stake in understanding how clinicians reason about the problems with which they deal and how this reasoning might be improved. The first inquiry is descriptive, the second is normative or prescriptive.

Recent reviews indicate that the psychological research on these topics is steadily increasing (Shulman and Elstein, 1975; Slovic and Lichtenstein, 1971; Slovic, Fischhoff, and Lichtenstein, 1977). In this chapter we concentrate on two main approaches within the psychology of clinical reasoning. The *problem-solving approach* studies clinical reasoning from an information-processing standpoint (de Groot, 1965; Elstein, Shulman and Sprafka, 1978; Newell and Simon, 1972). The information-processing view of clinical reasoning aims to characterize the reasoning processes

* First published in Stone, G., Cohen, F., and Adler, N. (Eds.) *Health Psychology – A Handbook* (San Francisco: Jossey-Bass, 1979), 333–67 (333–49 only reproduced). © 1979 Jossey-Bass, Inc. Reprinted by permission.

by recording and analyzing the steps and thoughts of clinicians as they attempt to solve clinical problems. The goal is to describe the process associated with the particular task and to explain it in terms of basic psychological elements and principles. The *judgment approach* investigates the possibility of representing judgmental policy by means of correlational statistical models (Goldberg, 1970; Hammond and others, 1975; Hoffman, 1960).

The goal here is not to teach clinicians how to employ these approaches to improve their reasoning, although that outcome may occur in some small percentage of readers. Our intention is to acquaint the reader with two major approaches to the analysis of clinical reasoning and to facilitate direct contact with the research literature in this field. We shall provide the reader with the conceptual background needed to understand that literature and summarize some of the salient findings. The reader will then be able to understand, analyze, and react to research using either of these approaches.

INFORMATION PROCESSING

Bounded rationality

From the standpoint of the information-processing approach, the psychological principle basic to the understanding of clinical reasoning is the concept of bounded or limited rationality (Newell and Simon, 1972). This principle emphasizes that limits exist to the human capacity for rational thought that are *not* results of unconscious motives or psychodynamic conflicts. Because of our limited information-processing capabilities, we can do some things better than others and resort to certain strategies to help overcome our inherent limitations. In considering clinical reasoning, the most relevant limit is the relatively small capacity of working memory compared to the essentially infinite size of long-term memory. This means that, in a brief time, we cannot work efficiently with all we know about a problem or all the data that could be collected. Some common features of good and poor clinical reasoning are consequences of efforts to cope with this limitation. Given the limited size of working memory, one is literally required to process data serially, to select data carefully, to represent a clinical problem in simplified ways, and to work as rationally as possible within these simplified representations. These schematized portrayals of complex situations usually do not exhaust all the possibilities but they provide some initial formulations for the problem solver. Without them it would be very difficult to make progress on solving a clinical problem of any significant magnitude. While the principles used to simplify problems are often useful, they can nevertheless lead to certain errors.

Medical problem-solving

By representing the problem solver (the clinician) as a processor of information, "the goal of the information-processing psychologist is to define precisely the processes and states that a particular subject is using to solve a particular problem and to be able to list – for example, in the form of a computer program – the exact sequence of operations used" (Mayer, 1977, p. 133). Methodologically, the information-processing approach generally relies on direct observations of behavior combined with introspective reports to determine the thought processes used to solve a particular problem. The introspections may be obtained by having the problem solver think aloud while solving a problem or by videotaping the problem-solving session and then having the problem solver review and comment upon the performance.

A varied program of research on the psychology of medical reasoning was conducted by Elstein, Shulman, and Sprafka (1978). The core study was an in-depth descriptive analysis of the reasoning of a group of experienced internists as they performed on a number of medical and nonmedical problems. The medical problems were of varying degrees of fidelity to clinical reality. In one set, actors were trained to simulate patients, and the sequence and amount of data collection were controlled by each physician. At the other extreme, a set of paper problems was used in which both sequence and amount of data were controlled by the research team. These descriptive and comparative studies were augmented by a series of experimental investigations whose goal was to explore the role of several variables deemed to be important in medical problem solving. The use of thinking-aloud techniques and the acceptance of the problem solver's verbalizations as legitimate data place these investigations within the information-processing paradigm.

These investigators found that physicians engaged in diagnostic clinical reasoning commonly employ the strategy of generating and testing hypothetical solutions to the problem. A small set of hypotheses are generated very early in the clinical encounter, based on a very limited amount of data compared to what will eventually be collected. Often the chief complaint or the data obtained in the first few minutes of interaction with the patient are sufficient to establish this small set of working hypotheses. The clinician can then ask: "What findings would be observed if a particular hypothesis were true?" and the collection of data can be tailored to answer this question. The data collected can be used to reduce gradually the difference between the clinician's state of knowledge at any point and the knowledge needed to make a particular diagnosis.

There are four major components to this reasoning process:

1 *Cue acquisition.* Information is obtained by the clinicians by a variety
   of methods, including taking a history, performing a physical examination, or administering a battery of laboratory or psychological tests.
2 *Hypothesis generation.* Alternative problem formulations are
   retrieved from memory.
3 *Cue interpretation.* The data are interpreted in the light of the
   alternative hypotheses under consideration.
4 *Hypothesis evaluation.* The data are weighted and combined to
   determine if one of the diagnostic hypotheses already generated can be
   confirmed. If not, the problem must be recycled, generating new
   hypotheses and collecting additional data until verification is
   achieved.

This reasoning process transforms the ill-defined, open-ended problem
"What is wrong with the patient?" into a series of better-defined problems: "Could the abdominal pain be caused by acute appendicitis? or a
twisted ovarian cyst? or pelvic inflammatory disease? or ectopic pregnancy?" This set of alternatives makes matters more manageable. By
constructing a set of hypothesized end points, it becomes possible for the
clinician to work backwards from the diagnostic criteria of each hypothesis to the work-up to be conducted. The search for data is simplified
because only certain points will be addressed.

If a clinician proceeded purely by generating and testing hypotheses,
each work-up might be totally different from its predecessors, since the set
of problem formulations being evaluated would be different for each
patient. But there are routine components to most, if not all, clinical
work-ups. Routines are established partly as labor-saving devices. They
make it easier to perform clinical work by making it unnecessary to figure
out each time what will be done, thus reducing cognitive strain. Routines
have other purposes as well. A problem may be so common or so
important that a clinician may indeed wish to consider it for each patient,
so that components of the work-up intended to explore hypotheses
become routine. Routinely collected data may also suggest some
additional alternatives and are thus a hedge against prematurely restric-
ting the set of hypotheses being evaluated.

Hypothesis generation Hypotheses are retrieved from memory, using
very few cues to link up to the clinician's long-term memory store. The
number of hypotheses considered simultaneously in a work-up is limited,
usually around four or five. The number considered in a problem rarely
exceeds six or seven. However, effective capacity can be increased by
subsuming or nesting hypotheses or by substituting one for another in a
reformulation so that the total number of hypotheses under consideration
remains unchanged.

What principles are used to generate hypotheses? Elstein, Shulman and Sprafka (1978) found that considerations of disease incidence (frequency) were relatively more important than considerations of seriousness of disease in generating initial problem formulations. Consideration of underlying pathophysiological processes (for example, the mechanisms involved in producing jaundice in chronic progressive liver failure) was used relatively infrequently, a surprising result considering that knowledge of pathophysiology is thought to be one of the foundations of clinical medicine. It may be that the utilization of such knowledge by the experienced physician is so automatic that it is no longer in conscious awareness. Alternatively, it may be that hypotheses are generated more by consulting a network of associations in long-term memory that relate common findings to particular diseases or conditions. This network need not include much of the scientific rationale for the connections. That is, physicians could be accumulating information in the form of rough correlations between clinical findings and diseases, or conditional probabilities – statements of the probability of observing a particular finding given a particular disease. These correlations or conditional probabilities could omit statements of rationale or explanation – why a particular finding is associated with a certain condition. Such explanations would be more useful at a later stage of the diagnostic process, at the point of cue interpretation or treatment selection.

Two related strategies are used to generate most hypotheses: association from a cue or cluster of cues to a set of competing formulations and association from one formulation to additional competing formulations. The alternatives may be generated at one time based on the same set of cues or at several times using different clusters. Hypotheses are brought to mind either by a particular salient cue or by a combination of cues. As Barrows and Bennett (1972) noted in their study of neurologists, hypotheses seem to "pop" into the head of the clinician. From a psychological standpoint, strong links exist in memory between salient cues and certain hypotheses triggered by these cues.

The most salient hypotheses are identified as the most probable. But are they salient because they are subjectively probable? Or are they identified as being probable because they are experienced as vivid and salient possibilities? The work of Tversky and Kahneman (1973, 1974) on availability as a determinant of subjective probability suggests that the second explanation is likely. Errors in the subjective-probability assessments of clinicians have been found by Leaper and others (1972).

Another useful principle in generating diagnostic alternatives is to consider deliberately competing formulations. Once a hypothesis has been generated by association from a limited number of cues, the problem solver may direct attention to thinking about competitors for this hypothesis and toward acquiring data to evaluate hypotheses. Deliberately thinking of competing formulations so as to set up the problem in the form of multiple competing hypotheses is a problem-solving strategy widely utilized by experienced physicians, apparently because it eases the burden of processing negative information, since the information that is negative for one hypothesis is positive for another. This widely recommended strategy for inference (Chamberlain, 1965; Platt, 1964) can thus be understood as an adaptation to the bounded rationality of the human information processor.

Cue interpretation. Cues are interpreted by physicians on a three-point scale: as tending to *confirm* or *disconfirm* a hypothesis or as *noncontributory*. Judgments on this scale are made spontaneously by experienced physicians. The weighting scheme is roughly equivalent to a regression equation in which only the signs of the coefficients, not their magnitudes, are important (Dawes and Corrigan, 1974). (This matter is discussed further in the next section.) Some clinicians feel they use a five-point scale in this inference process, but what research has been done suggests there is little difference in the predictive power of the two systems. At any rate, a three-point scale and a five-point scale are both simplified ways of representing the diagnosticity of a cue that could be more formally represented by a correlation coefficient in the judgment model or by the ratio of the probability of observing this cue, given disease # 1, to the probability of observing it at all. Again, we see that the operations identified by information-processing research as those actually used in clinical reasoning are simplified approximations. The informal weighting scheme used by many clinicians is a simplified likelihood ratio that reduces the information-processing load.

Elstein, Shulman, and Sprafka (1978) found that thoroughness of cue acquisition and accuracy of cue interpretation in medicine were uncorrelated, and that diagnostic accuracy was related to both variables. Thus, inaccurate diagnosis may be due to either mistakes in data collection or in data interpretation. Further, errors in interpretation cannot necessarily be remedied by collecting additional data; indeed, the more data collected, the less likely it is that all will be used. In a related study, Gill and others (1973) reported that diagnostic error was due less to faulty data acquisition than to failure to manipulate large volumes of data correctly. However, practically any clinician can recall cases where mistakes were made because a particular item of information was omitted from the work-up. While in no way minimizing the importance of thoroughness, the point of the studies reviewed here is that greater thoroughness in acquiring data will not alone solve diagnostic problems. The data must be interpreted and integrated in the clinician's head; the difficulty of this task may be increased by adding more data, unless appropriate simplifying strategies are introduced.

Hypothesis evaluation. During a clinical work-up and especially at the conclusion of an extended sequence of data collection, the experienced clinician determines what diagnosis seems most likely *or* what actions should be taken next. In short, having interpreted individual cues or clusters of cues in terms of a set of hypotheses, the clinician must reach a diagnostic judgment. In many diagnostic problems, reasoning in this evaluation phase can be represented as a process of adding up the pros and cons for each alternative and choosing the one favored by the preponderance of the evidence. Often, the cons are ignored or discounted, as we shall see.

This simplification is another illustration of bounded rationality. We employ strategies that are satisfactory, not necessarily optimal, because to calculate the optimal strategy may be too complex a task without aids. Furthermore, the clinical work-up consists of a sequence of decisions, each made with only part of the data base. This serial data processing is, again, an adaptation to the limited size of working memory.

Potential problems of the clinical method

From the information-processing standpoint, clinical reasoning is a particular form of reasoning about a specific set of problems but is governed by some principles common to all thinking. In this section, some salient features of clinical reasoning will be related to more general information-processing principles. These principles serve to explain both why clinical reasoning is ordinarily conducted as described and why certain types of errors are more common than others.

Role of hypotheses in the reasoning process. Clinical diagnostic problems are characteristically solved by formulating a small number of alternative solutions and testing them. While it is possible to reformulate the problem as one moves along and to collect some data routinely, it is nonetheless the case that these preliminary formulations help to define an area within which a solution is sought, because data collection is always selective, especially in ambulatory settings. Early formulations are essential; nevertheless, they can be misleading. They may direct attention to irrelevant features of the problem, cause the clinician to engage in a search for inconsequential cues that would otherwise be ignored, or lead the clinician to refrain from a useful search for cues that would otherwise be collected.

Barrows and others (1977, 1978) found that the number of hypotheses generated was unrelated either to successful diagnostic outcome or to level of clinical experience. They suggested that the process of hypothesis generation and testing is so characteristic of human reasoning that it occurs without encouragement or training in adults. (A similar conclusion was reached by Elstein, Shulman, and Sprafka, 1978.) Nevertheless, the most prevalent cause of incorrect diagnosis in their studies was failure to generate and consider the relevant diagnostic hypothesis. Thus, the content of the set of hypotheses being considered is crucial and is influenced by experience and expectation.

It might be simpler if clinicians were steadfastly to discipline themselves not to generate early hypotheses at all and thus avoid the biases they create. For better or worse, however, it seems practically impossible to reason without hypotheses whenever the data base is as complex as it typically is in clinical problems. People are invariably trying to make sense out of their experience as it unfolds and are always generating hypotheses to explain their observations. With experienced clinicians, these early expectations are more helpful than deceptive. Experienced clinicians also try to consider several hypotheses constructed deliberately as alternatives to those immediately suggested by the problem. Since the number that can be considered effectively is limited, it is important to work with relevant alternatives. Sheer numbers will not substitute for relevance, and massive data processing is a poor substitute for thoughtful planning.

Overemphasizing positive findings.   The data in a clinical problem do not simply speak for themselves. Like all facts, they are filtered and interpreted through our expectations. The data best remembered tend to be those that fit the hypotheses generated. Where findings are distorted in recall or otherwise discounted, it is generally in the direction of making the facts more consistent with particular diagnostic pictures. The most common error in cue interpretation is to assign positive (confirmatory) weights to non-contributory findings (Elstein, Shulman, and Sprafka, 1978). Barrows and others (1977) reported that experienced physicians actively search for data to confirm hypotheses rather than to rule them out. Thus, negative findings tend to be de-emphasized. Similarly, Wallsten (1978) showed that clinical information collected in the latter portion of the work-up was systematically distorted to support prior opinions. Thus, early hypotheses tended to bias the interpretation of data collected later.

The discounting of disconfirming data is facilitated by the fact that clinical findings usually bear a probabilistic relationship to the underlying causes that produce them. As clinicians know only too well, very few signs or symptoms are pathognomonic of a particular disease. Many more are associated with several diseases, and diagnostic decisions are reached by weighing and combining evidence. One pitfall in clinical reasoning is to discount evidence that fails to confirm a favored hypothesis on the grounds that there is only a probabilistic relationship between evidence and hypotheses anyway and a perfect match is not be to be expected. This error is equivalent to over-emphasizing data affirming a hypothesis and slighting data that tend to disconfirm it.

An illustration of this pitfall is found in a classic study of clinical inference (Smedslund, 1963). A group of nurses were presented with a series of cases in which the presence or absence of a particular symptom was associated equally often with the presence or absence of a particular diagnosis. Each of the four possible combinations occurred 25 percent of the time in a series of brief case descriptions, so that the correlation between symptom and disease was zero. The nurses nonetheless concluded that the correlation was positive and could, of course, point to many instances in the series to support this erroneous conclusion. Equally numerous instances of a lack of association between symptom and disease were forgotten or neglected.

Excessive data collection. Clinical decision making depends on collecting relevant data, but sometimes it is not clear what is relevant. Clinical findings are often correlated with one another, since they are effects of an underlying common cause. In this circumstance, a number of cues are, in effect, redundant and can provide little additional information on logical or statistical grounds. The clinical decision could be made just as well by a formula that used fewer variables but weighted them properly. For example, one study of the use of a battery of twelve laboratory tests (Zieve, 1966) showed that most of the meaningful information could be accounted for by a formula for weighting and combining results on just four of these tests. Positive correlations between the tests accounted for the redundancy. Similarly, Neutra and Neff (1975) showed that a very satisfactory formula for predicting high-risk pregnancy did not need to use all the information collected on a questionnaire. When redundant data are collected, they are sometimes used erroneously to bolster confidence in the judgment or decision, although the accuracy of judgment can increase but little since no new information has been provided (Oskamp, 1965).

From the clinician's viewpoint, however, there is a rationale for collecting redundant information. It is recognized that many cues have low reliabilities. For example, the reliability of many cues in physical diagnosis is not terribly high (Koran, 1975). Hence, it is reasonable to check a finding twice. However, if cues are stable and have high reliabilities, repeat observations are redundant and unnecessary. This line of argument leads to three important questions: How accurately do clinicians discriminate reliable from unreliable cues? How accurately do clinicians estimate cue reliabilities? How well do they take these into account in planning sequences of data collection? Empirical work is much needed.

When the procedures for collecting redundant information are non-invasive and relatively inexpensive, such as taking a history or performing a physical examination, the decision maker may well be uninterested in a more efficient system for information processing, for the costs of developing and maintaining it may exceed foreseeable savings or gains. But if expensive or invasive procedures are involved, careful analysis of the inference process is warranted. For example, Neuhauser and Lewicki (1975) have shown that the clinical practice of obtaining six repetitions of a particular test for colon cancer adds very little diagnostic certainty over that provided by testing twice but substantially increases the cost. Excessive numbers of tests may be ordered for another reason: limitations on the human capacity for indirect inference. A problem solver often prefers to seek direct evidence of what could be logically deduced from the data already gathered, leading to collecting more data than would be needed by a more efficient information processor (Watson and Johnson-Laird, 1972). This is yet one more consequence of the bounded rationality of the human information-processing system.

Excessive data collection may impede the process of clinical inference by overloading the system's capacity. Accurate decision making depends upon both collecting and properly interpreting clinical data. The interpretive process can be adversely affected by collecting too much data, for the sheer volume of facts may impair the clinician's ability to sort out and focus upon the relevant variables. Formal analytic techniques, or even simply drawing a decision tree or flow chart, can help to focus attention on the information that is truly relevant to the decision at hand (Sisson, Schoomaker, and Ross, 1976).

Computer simulation and modeling

Akin to the information-processing paradigm is the field of computer representations of psychological processes. De Groot (1966) described machine simulations as an integral part of the approach, although at that time few such realizations existed. Within the information-processing context, computer simulations are used to test out a particular theory of clinical reasoning (Bordage and others, 1977). Using analyses from Elstein, Shulman, and Sprafka (1978), the characteristic features of the clinical diagnostician have been formalized into a set of computer programs (Vinsonhaler, Wagner, and Elstein, 1977). By varying parameters in both the clinician and the task environment, the problem-solving behavior of the physician is reproduced and studied. This set of computer programs provides ways of writing computer representations of fundamental properties of both the task environment and the problem solver.

Although this first type of computer usage is intended to simulate a given psychological theory of reasoning, the computer can also be used to generate computer models of clinical reasoning processes with the aim of building a theory. In the first case, the computer simulation follows and is built from the psychological theory, whereas in the latter the computer modeling precedes and helps generate the theory. This second approach constitutes the domain of artificial intelligence (AI). The work of Myers and Pople (1977) in internal medicine and of Shortliffe (1976) in infectious diseases are two examples of the use of AI methodology in diagnostic medicine. The elaboration of heuristic strategies and the role of natural language memory structures in clinical reasoning are current avenues of psychological research where computer modeling is likely to be fruitfully employed (Epstein and Kaplan, 1977; Schoolman and Bernstein, 1978).

Information processing as a research strategy

The information-processing approach to research on clinical reasoning has several strengths. First, it depends heavily on direct observation and analysis of clinical performance, even when simulated patients or problems are employed. While a psychological theory is undoubtedly employed to interpret the clinician's performance, the theory and method exercise less control over the type of data collected than is true of the judgment approach. The researcher is thus less likely to generalize from a tightly controlled but somewhat artificial research setting to the world of clinical reality. The materials used in the research resemble closely the types of situations clinicians actually deal with, particularly when compared to the tasks typically used in the more quantitatively rigorous research pursued within the other framework. For this reason, the rationale and research findings are communicated relatively easily to clinicians. Lastly, the conceptual framework used to analyze the data is closely related to the information-processing view of cognition now receiving so much attention. Research on clinical reasoning conducted from this standpoint connects naturally and directly with the active research areas of problem solving and memory. For those psychologists interested in theoretical coherence, this is a powerful reinforcement.

But the method has drawbacks too. Because the situations studied typically require a great deal of time, it is often possible to sample the subject's performance on only a limited number of problems. The use of more highly restricted task environments would make it possible to collect and analyze more instances of clinical reasoning within a given time. Since one of the major findings of research in clinical problem solving is that the strategies selected by the clinician are highly case related, concentrating on a small set of problems is a threat to generalizability at the same time that the detailed analysis of particular problems is one of the virtues of this approach. In addition, the information-processing approach yields a set of guidelines or heuristics for improving clinical reasoning, but the evidence that applying these systematically will indeed improve clinical judgment is not yet compelling. An information-processing analysis yields descriptions, understanding, and explanation of complex sequences of behavior, but these may not be the most efficient way to improve the output. Other research avenues that deliberately compare human performance to mathematical models may have greater potential in this regard.

JUDGMENT

Clinical judgment

The central questions asked within the judgment paradigm are: How do clinicians use and weigh the information given to them to make a judgment about some criterion event, such as a diagnosis or treatment? How consistent are the judgments across judges and across similar situations? Finally, how accurate are the judgments in comparison to a criterion?

The dichotomy between the judge (person) and the criterion event (environment) led Hammond and his co-workers to elaborate a conceptual framework for judgmental studies based on Brunswik's lens model (Brunswik, 1955; Hammond, 1955, 1975, 1977; Hammond and Adelman, 1976; Hammond and others, 1975). The lens model, depicted in Figure 1, uses the analogy of a convex lens to illustrate the relation between *a judge's perception* or estimate (Y_s) and the *object of perception*

Figure 1   The lens model

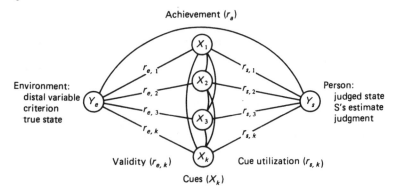

Achievement (r_a)

Environment:
distal variable
criterion
true state

Person:
judged state
S's estimate
judgment

Validity ($r_{e,\,k}$)   Cue utilization ($r_{s,\,k}$)

Cues (X_k)

or criterion (Y_e), as mediated by a set of cues $(X_{1,k})$. The cues are related probabilistically to both the judgment and the object. Thus, "judgment is a cognitive process similar to inductive inference, in which the person draws a conclusion, or an inference, Y_s, about something, Y_e, which he cannot see (or otherwise directly perceive), on the basis of data, X_k, which he can see (or otherwise directly perceive). In other words, judgments are made from palpable events and circumstances" (Hammond, 1975, p. 73). The arc, r_a, linking Y_s and Y_e, indicates the degree to which the person's judgment (Y_s) was correct (overall judgmental accuracy); that is, the extent to which the judgment made coincides with the actual event to be judged. The lens model can be used, for example, to depict a clinician examining a patient with a certain number of clinical findings $(X_k =$ symptoms, signs), such as headache and elevated blood pressure, and making a judgment (Y_s) concerning the patient's diagnosis (Y_e), such as hypertension or tension headache. Furthermore, the correlation r_a will indicate diagnostic accuracy over a series of cases (the hit rate).

Hoffman (1960), in a classic paper, suggested the use of a linear model (multiple regression equations) as a representation of clinical judges. He emphasized that the model was a *paramorphic* representation of the clinicians' policy and was to be interpreted as performing like the judges and not as describing actual information-processing strategies (Shulman and Elstein, 1975). The elements of the model include: the information given (cues, findings, attributes), their relative importance (weights), and their functional relationships (the combination rules). In the linear model, judgments are formulated as a simple weighted sum of the values of the information available. The weighted additive model can be mathematically represented as: $Y_s = C_o + w_1X_1 + w_2X_2 \ldots w_kX_k$, where Y_s represents the judgment, X the k different pieces of information available, w the relative weights, and C_o a constant.

In this approach, the investigator presents information in the form of separate cues to the judge, whose task it is to respond with a numerical or categorical classification (Cook and Stewart, 1975; Einhorn, 1974b). A regression equation is computed using these judgments as the dependent variable, and the equation is said to have captured the judge's policy (Hoffman, 1960; Slovic and Lichtenstein, 1971). For example, Moore and others (1974) asked six clinical endocrinologists to choose one of three treatments for an overactive thyroid on the basis of five pieces of clinical information. The use of the five findings was captured by a multiple regression equation in which the weights reflected each clinician's relative use of the available information. As is typical in studies of this type, analysis of the relative weights showed that the clinicians effectively used fewer than the five items in making their judgments. Overall, they tended to ignore laboratory data and concentrated on medical history. Thus, the clinicians were selective and did not use all the information given. The study implies either that the clinicians should be trained to attend more to laboratory data or that costs could be cut by omitting unused laboratory tests.

Policy capturing has been applied to a wide range of situations including: the interpretation of Minnesota Multiphasic Personality Inventory (MMPI) profiles (Goldberg, 1965, 1969; Kleinmuntz, 1963, 1968; Wiggins and Hoffman, 1968) and of X-ray films (Slovic, Rorer, and Hoffman, 1971); the work of admissions committees (Dawes, 1971, 1977; Goldberg, 1977) and police departments (Hammond and Adelman, 1976); and a variety of judgments in pathology (Einhorn, 1974a), pharmacology (Hammond and Joyce, 1975), and nursing (Zedeck and Kafry, 1977).

Goldberg (1970) showed that the same regression equations used to describe a set of judgments can also generate a set of predictions that will be more accurate than the judges' unaided predictions of the same series. The use of the equation to improve judgment is termed "bootstrapping." For example, Goldberg used the regression equations that represented the judgments of twenty-nine clinical psychologists in distinguishing psychotic from neurotic patients, on the basis of their MMPI profiles, to generate predictions of undiagnosed patients. He concluded that "linear regression models of clinical judges can be more accurate diagnostic predictors than are the humans who are modeled" and that "the composite judgment of all twenty-nine clinicians, which was more accurate than that of the typical individual judge, was not improved by the modeling procedure" (1970, p. 430).

Besides the previously described correlation between true and judged states (r_a), three additional correlations are used in a lens model analysis. The second correlation, R_e (see Figure 2), indicates how well the underlying reality can be predicted by the best possible weighted linear

Figure 2 The lens model (expanded version)

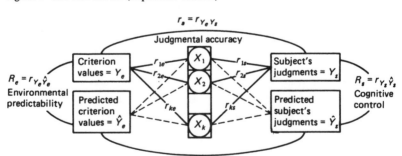

combination of the available cues. R_e measures the predictability or uncertainty of the environment (criterion) that is being judged. A third correlation, R_s, indicates how well a set of judgments can be predicted by a weighted linear combination of cue values and thus captures the judge's policy: Hammond and Summers (1972) identified this term as "cognitive control," the extent to which a subject controls the utilization of his knowledge. Knowledge of the environment, the fourth component, is represented by the correlation G between the regression predictions of reality and of the judgments. These four correlations are related (under a linear assumption) in a formula known as the lens model equation: $r_a = GR_eR_s$. The formula states that judgmental accuracy is limited first by the degree to which the task is predictable, R_e. Beyond that, accuracy is determined by knowledge of the properties of the task, G, and by cognitive control over the utilization of that knowledge, R_s. Furthermore, knowledge and cognitive control are statistically independent. Thus, to improve judgments one may either increase knowledge of the task or increase the consistency with which existing knowledge is used (Hammond and Summers, 1972).

A number of controversial issues are raised by this research paradigm. We shall consider three of these: clinical versus statistical prediction, linear versus configural models, and unit versus differential cue weighting.

Clinical versus statistical prediction

Clinical refers to any artful or intuitive means used by clinicians in reaching a diagnostic or therapeutic decision. *Statistical* (or actuarial) refers to the use of any formal quantitative techniques or formulas, such as regression equations, for these same clinical tasks. The controversy regarding the merits of these two approaches includes discussions of the role and the accuracy of statistical predictions in clinical psychology (Elstein, 1976; Hoffman, 1960; Holt, 1958; Meehl, 1954). Moreover, it raises yet another fundamental issue regarding the aims of research on judgment, namely whether it should be descriptive (Kleinmuntz, 1969) or prescriptive (Goldberg, 1970). Gough (1962, p. 527) characterized the controversy in the following terms: "By its proponents the statistical method has been described as operational, objective, reliable, sound, and verifiable, whereas by its opponents it has been called atomistic, pedantic, artificial, static, and pseudoscientific. The clinical approach, on the other hand, has been called dynamic, meaningful, deep, genuine, and sophisticated by its adherents, but by its opponents vague, hazy, subjective, unscientific, and verbalistic." Goldberg (1968, 1970), Sawyer (1966), and Einhorn (1972), among others, explored optimal blends of clinical and actuarial processing. These typically involve using clinical methods to gather preliminary information or to make subtle observations, and actuarial methods to combine the data for final decisions – hence, Einhorn's apt phrase, "expert measurement and mechanical combination" (1972).

A contemporary version of this controversy centers currently around the issue of "case uniqueness" (Dawes, 1977; Einhorn and Schacht, 1977). What is the trade-off between consistently using a judgmental rule with a fixed number of cues (as obtained through a policy-capturing procedure) and the deliberate consideration of an unexpected cue that is salient but not universally distributed? Whereas clinicians may feel short-changed by using a simplified regression equation, researchers praise its accuracy and prefer to ignore incidental cues. In his study of graduate admissions committees, Dawes (1977) argued that rule-generated procedures (actuarial) are superior to case-by-case procedures (clinical). In reviewing the merits of the approach, Dawes (1977, p. 90) held that it "probably predicts graduate success better than does clinical judgment ... it is fair and just in that it treats everyone alike ... it supplies potential candidates with knowledge of how they are to be evaluated, it makes us publicly accountable for our decisions, and finally ... it saves a great deal of time and effort."

Linear versus configural models

This debate focuses on the form of the rules for combining data. Is the linear model an adequate representation of the judgmental process? Along with the linear model, Hoffman (1960) had also proposed a configural model that would include interaction terms to account for the possibility that a particular judge interprets one item of information as contingent upon a second: see $r_{x_i x_k}$, in Figure 1. Subsequently, such researchers as Goldberg (1968, 1971), Hoffman (1968), and Einhorn (1970, 1972) proposed a variety of nonlinear models. In general, however, the addition of configural terms to the linear model (for example, exponential components) has failed to improve its accuracy as assessed by the proportion of variance in human judges' performance accounted for by the statistical representation (Goldberg, 1971; Dawes and Corrigan, 1974). Although clinical judges insist that they are using cues configurally, the simple linear model continues to represent judgments adequately. As previously stated, the judgment approach is paramorphic and does not intend to represent isomorphically the judge's mental process.

Unit versus differential cue weighting

How important is the calculation of exact weights to be assigned to each cue? Dawes and Corrigan (1974) and Schmidt (1971) found that by randomly assigning weights of the same sign or by assigning equal weights, the resulting linear model still did as well as (or better than) the original "captured" weights in predicting criterion values (Y_e on the left-hand side of the lens model). Dawes and Corrigan further investigated the use of unit weights (that is, $+ 1$ and $- 1$) and found that the unit weights did extremely well in predicting the criterion. They concluded that "decision makers (insofar as they are behaving appropriately) are paramorphically well represented by linear models . . . The whole trick is to decide what variables to look at and then to know how to add" (1974, p. 104). Accordingly, exact specification of differential weights does not appear to be critical. However, Schmitt and Levine (1977, p. 28) recently suggested that "much interesting and important research can be done on subjective weights. This conclusion is based on the fact that there are several statistical weights, and a convincing rationale for the use of one over another is unavailable." Recent research (Molidor, 1978) has shown that differential weighting models (both statistical and subjective) account for more variance on the right-hand side of the lens model than do the unit weighting models. Furthermore, additional differences were found depending on how the weighting models were computed. A unit-weighting model using raw scores yielded poorer predictions of actual judgments than did a unit-weighting model using standard scores.

The judgment paradigm intends to be both *descriptive* and *prescriptive*. It describes clinical judgments by means of multiple regression equations or similar formulas. It prescribes how to improve judgment when it points to the improvements achieved by use of a formula instead of human judgment. Studies of judgment are thus helpful to practicing clinicians in that they can explicitly describe and prescribe utilization of clinical information already available.

REFERENCES

Barrows, H.S., and Bennett, K. "Experimental Studies on the Diagnostic (Problem Solving) Skill of the Neurologist: Their Implications for Neurological Training." *Archives of Neurology*, 1972, 26, 273–277.

Barrows, H.S., Feightner, J.W., Neufeld, V.R., and Norman, G.R. "Analysis of the Clinical Methods of Medical Students and Physicians." School of Medicine, Hamilton, Ontario: McMaster University, 1978.

Barrows, H.S., Norman, G.R., Neufeld, V.R., and Feightner, J.W. "Studies of the Clinical Reasoning Process of Medical Students and Physicians." Proceedings of the Sixteenth Annual Conference on Research in Medical Education. Washington: Association of American Medical Colleges, 1977.

Bordage, G., Elstein, A.S., Vinsonhaler, J., and Wagner, C. "Computer-Aided and Computer-Simulated Medical Diagnosis." Proceedings of the First IEEE Symposium on Computer Application in Medical Care. Washington, D.C., 1977, 204–210.

Brunswik, E. "Representative Design and Probabilistic Theory in a Functional Psychology." *Psychological Review*, 1955, 62, 193–217.

Chamberlain, T.C. "The Method of Multiple Working Hypotheses." *Science*, 1965, 148, 754–759 (originally published 1890).

Cook, R.L., and Stewart, T.R. "A Comparison of Seven Methods of Obtaining Subjective Descriptions of Judgmental Policy." *Organizational Behavior and Human Performance*, 1975, 13, 31–45.

Dawes, R.M. "A Case Study of Graduate Admissions: Application of Three Principles of Human Decision Making." *American Psychologist*, 1971, 26, 180–188.

"Case-by-Case versus Rule-Generated Procedures for the Allocation of Scarce Resources." In M.F. Kaplan and S. Schwartz (Eds.). *Human Judgment and Decision Processes in Applied Settings*. New York: Academic Press, 1977, 83–94.

Dawes, R.M., and Corrigan, B. "Linear Models in Decision Making." *Psychological Bulletin*, 1974, 81, 95–106.

de Groot, A.D. *Thought and Choice in Chess*. The Hague: Mouton, 1965.

"Perception and Memory versus Thought: Some Old Ideas and Recent Findings." In B. Kleinmuntz (Ed.). *Problem Solving: Research, Method and Theory*. New York: Wiley, 1966.

Einhorn, H.J. "The Use of Nonlinear, Noncompensatory Models in Decision Making." *Psychological Bulletin*, 1970, 73, 221–230.

"Expert Measurement and Mechanical Combination." *Organizational Behavior and Human Performance*, 1972, 7, 86–106.

"Expert Judgment: Some Necessary Conditions and an Example." *Journal of Applied Psychology*, 1974a, 59, 562–571.

"Cue Definition and Residual Judgment." *Organizational Behavior and Human Performance*, 1974b, 12, 30–49.

Einhorn, H.J. and Schacht, S. "Decisions Based on Fallible Clinical Judgment." In M.F. Kaplan and S. Schwartz (Eds.). *Human Judgment and Decision Processes in Applied Settings*. New York: Academic Press, 1977, 125–144.

Elstein, A.S. "Clinical Judgment: Psychological Research and Medical Practice." *Science*, 1976, 194, 696–700.

Elstein, A.S., Shulman, L.S., and Sprafka, S.A. *Medical Problem Solving: An Analysis of Clinical Reasoning*. Cambridge: Harvard University Press, 1978.

Epstein, M.N., and Kaplan, E.B. "Criteria for Clinical Decision Making." In W. Schneider and A.L. Sagvall-Hein (Eds.). *Computational Linguistics in Medicine*. New York: North Holland, 1977.

Gill, P.W., Leaper, D.J., Guillou, P.J., Staniland, J.R., Horrocks, J.C., and de Dombal, F.T. "Observer Variation in Clinical Diagnosis – a Computer-Aided Assessment of Its Magnitude and Importance in 552 Patients with Abdominal Pain." *Methods of Information in Medicine*. 1973, 12, 108–113.

Goldberg, L.R. "Diagnosticians versus Diagnostic Signs: The Diagnosis of Psychosis versus Neurosis from the MMPI." *Psychological Monographs*, 1965, 79 (9, Whole No. 602).

"Simple Models or Simple Processes? Some Research on Clinical Judgments." *American Psychologist*, 1968, 23, 483–496.

"The Search for Configural Relationships in Personality Assessment: The Diagnosis of Psychosis versus Neurosis from the MMPI." *Multivariate Behavioral Research*, 1969, 4, 523–536.

"Man versus Model of Man: A Rationale, Plus Some Evidence for a Method of Improving on Clinical Inferences." *Psychological Bulletin*, 1970, 73, ·422–432.

"Five Models of Clinical Judgment: An Empirical Comparison Between Linear and Non-linear Representations of the Human Inference Process." *Organizational Behavior and Human Performance*, 1971, 6, 458–479.

"Admission to the Ph.D. Program in the Department of Psychology at the University of Oregon." *American Psychologist*, 1977, 32, 663–668.

Gough, H.G. "Clinical versus Statistical Prediction in Psychology." In L. Postman (Ed.). *Psychology in the Making*. New York: Knopf, 1962, 526–584.

Hammond, K.R. "Probabilistic Functioning and the Clinical Method." *Psychological Review*, 1955, 62, 255–262.

"Social Judgment Theory: Its Use in the Study of Psychoactive Drugs." In K.R. Hammond and C.R.B. Joyce (Eds.). *Psychoactive Drugs and Social Judgment: Theory and Research*. New York: Wiley, 1975, 69–105.

"Social Judgment Theory: Application in Policy Formation." In M.F. Kaplan and S. Schwartz (Eds.). *Human Judgment and Decision Processes in Applied Settings*. New York: Academic Press, 1977, 1–29.

Hammond, K.R., and Adelman, L. "Science, Values, and Human Judgment." *Science*, 1976, 194, 389–396.

Hammond, K.R., and Joyce, C.R.B. *Psychoactive Drugs and Social Judgment: Theory and Research*. New York: Wiley, 1975.

Hammond, K.R., Stewart, T.R., Brehmer, B., and Steinmann, D.D. "Social Judgment Theory." In M.F. Kaplan and S. Schwartz (Eds.). *Human Judgment and Decision Processes*. New York: Academic Press, 1975, 271–312.

Hammond, K.R., and Summers, D.A. "Cognitive Control." *Psychological Review*, 1972, 79, 58–67.

Hoffman, P.J. "The Paramorphic Representation of Clinical Judgment." *Psychological Bulletin*, 1960, 57, 116–131.

"Cue-Consistency and Configurality in Human Judgment." In B. Kleinmuntz (Ed.). *Formal Representation of Human Judgment*. New York: Wiley, 1968, 53–90.

Holt, R.R. "Clinical and Statistical Prediction: A Reformulation and Some New Data." *Journal of Abnormal and Social Psychology*, 1958, 56, 1–12.

Kaplan, M.F., and Schwartz, S. (Eds.). *Human Judgment and Decision Processes*. New York: Academic Press, 1975.

Human Judgment and Decision Processes in Applied Settings. New York: Academic Press, 1977.

Kleinmuntz, B. "MMPI Decision Rules for the Identification of College Maladjustment: A Digital Computer Approach." *Psychological Monographs*, 1963, 77 (14, Whole No. 577).

"The Processing of Clinical Information by Man and Machine." In B. Kleinmuntz (Ed.). *Formal Representation of Human Judgment*, New York: Wiley, 1968, 149–186.

Clinical Information Processing by Computer, New York: Holt, 1969.

Koran, L.M. "The Reliability of Clinical Methods, Data and Judgments." *New England Journal of Medicine*, 1975, *293*, 642–646 and 695–701.

Leaper, D.J., Horrocks, J.C., Staniland, J.R., and de Dombal, F.T. "Computer-Assisted Diagnosis of Abdominal Pain Using 'Estimates' Provided by Clinicians." *British Medical Journal*, 1972, *2*, 350–354.

Mayer, R.E. *Thinking and Problem Solving: An Introduction to Human Cognition and Learning*. Glenview, Illinois: Scott, Foresman, 1977.

Meehl, P.E. *Clinical versus Statistical Prediction*. Minneapolis: University of Minnesota Press, 1954.

Molidor, J.B. "The Use of Objective and Subjective Weights to Model a Medical School Admissions Task." Unpublished doctoral dissertation, Michigan State University, 1978.

Moore, M.F., Aitchison, J., Parker, L.S., and Taylor, T.R. "Use of Information in Thyrotoxicosis Treatment Allocation." *Methods of Information in Medicine*, 1974, *13*, 83–92.

Myers, J.D., and Pople, H.E. "Internist: A Consultative Diagnostic Program in Internal Medicine." Proceedings of the First IEEE Symposium on Computer Application in Medical Care, Washington, D.C., 1977.

Neuhauser, D., and Lewicki, A.M. "What Do We Gain From the Sixth Stool Guaiac?" *New England Journal of Medicine*, 1975, *293*, 226–228.

Neutra, R., and Neff, R. "Fetal Death in Eclampsia: II The Effect of Non-Therapeutic Factors." *British Journal of Obstetrics and Gynecology*, 1975, *82*, 390–396.

Newell, A., and Simon, H.A. *Human Problem Solving*, Englewood Cliffs, N.J.: Prentice-Hall, 1972.

Oskamp, S. "Overconfidence in Case-Study Judgments." *Journal of Consulting Psychology*, 1965, *29*, 261–265.

Platt, J.R. "Strong Inference." *Science*, 1964, *146*, 347–352.

Sawyer, J. "Measurement and Prediction: Clinical and Statistical." *Psychological Bulletin*, 1966, *66*, 178–200.

Schmidt, F.L. "The Relevant Efficiency of Regression in Simple Unit Predictor Weights in Applied Differential Psychology." *Educational and Psychological Measurement*, 1971, *31*, 699–714.

Schmitt, N., and Levine, R.L. "Statistical and Subjective Weights some Problems and Proposals." *Organizational Behavior and Human Performance*, 1977, *20*, 15–30.

Schoolman, H.M., and Bernstein, L.M. "Computer Use in Diagnosis, Prognosis and Therapy." *Science*, 1978, *200*, 926–931.

Shortliffe, E.H. *Computer-Based Medical Consultations: MYCIN*. New York: American Elsevier Publ. Co., 1976.

Shulman, L.S., and Elstein, A.S. "Studies of Problem Solving, Judgment and Decision Making: Implications for Educational Research." In F.N. Kerlinger (Ed.). *Review of Research in Education*. Itasca, Illinois: Peacock, 1975, *3*, 3–42.

Sisson, J.C., Schoomaker, E.B., and Ross, J.C. "Clinical Decision Analyses – The Hazard of Using Additional Data." *Journal of the American Medical Association*, 1976, *236*, 1259–1263.

Slovic, P., Fischhoff, B., and Lichtenstein, S. "Behavioral Decision Theory." *Annual Review of Psychology*, 1977, 28, 1–39.

Slovic, P., and Lichtenstein, S. "Comparison of Bayesian and Regression Approaches to the Study of Information Processing in Judgment." *Organizational Behavior and Human Performance*, 1971, 6, 649–744.

Slovic, P., Rorer, L.C., and Hoffman, P.J. "Analyzing Use of Diagnostic Signs." *Investigative Radiology*, 1971, 6, 18–26.

Smedslund, J. "The Concept of Correlation in Adults." *Scandinavian Journal of Psychology*, 1963, 4, 165–173.

Tversky, A., and Kahneman, D. "Availability: A Heuristic for Judging Frequency and Probability." *Cognitive Psychology*, 1973, 5, 207–332.

"Judgment Under Uncertainty: Heuristics and Biases." *Science*, 1974, *185*, 1124–1131.

Vinsonhaler, J., Wagner, C., and Elstein, A.S. "The Inquiry Theory: An Information-Processing Approach to Clinical Problem Solving." In Shires and Wolf (Eds.). *MEDINFO, 1977: Proceedings of the Second World Conference on Medical Informatics*. New York: North Holland, 1977, 157–160.

Wallsten, T.S. "Three Biases in the Cognitive Processing of Diagnostic Information." Unpublished paper. Psychometric Laboratory, Chapel Hill, N.C.: University of North Carolina, 1978.

Watson, P.C., and Johnson-Laird, P.N. *Psychology of Reasoning: Structure and Content*. Cambridge, Mass.: Harvard University Press, 1972.

Wiggins, N., and Hoffman, P.J. "Three Models of Clinical Judgment." *Journal of Abnormal Psychology*, 1968, 73, 70–77.

Zedeck, S., and Kafry, D. "Capturing Rater Policies for Processing Evaluation Data." *Organizational Behavior and Human Performance*, 1977, *13*, 269–294.

Zieve, L. "Misinterpretation and Abuse of Laboratory Tests by Clinicians." *Annals of the New York Acad. Science*, 1966, *134*, 563–572.

5

———— ~ ————

HOW PHYSICIANS USE CLINICAL INFORMATION IN DIAGNOSING PULMONARY EMBOLISM: AN APPLICATION OF CONJOINT ANALYSIS*

Robert S. Wigton, Vincent L. Hoellerich, Kashinath D. Patil

For many diseases, the medical literature may be unclear or contradictory regarding the optimal use of clinical findings in making the diagnosis. This is particularly true where a definitive test is either lacking or frequently not performed. Little is known about what diagnostic strategies physicians adopt when there is no clear guidance about the best use of diagnostic information. Does clinical experience provide sufficient learning that the majority of physicians develop accurate diagnostic strategies, or do individual physicians adopt idiosyncratic diagnostic strategies with little similarity to one another? To examine this question, we studied how physicians use clinical information in diagnosing pulmonary embolism.

If arteriography is not performed, the diagnosis of pulmonary embolism on clinical grounds can be very difficult. There are no standard diagnostic criteria, and some of the most useful findings, such as clinically evident thrombophlebitis or an unequivocally positive lung scan, are not present in the majority of cases. Other more common manifestations such as dyspnea, tachypnea and tachycardia are, unfortunately, not very specific for pulmonary embolism,[10] and their diagnostic usefulness is controversial. Laboratory findings previously thought to be of major diagnostic importance, such as the "diagnostic triad" of aspartate aminotransferase (SGOT), serum bilirubin, and lactic dehydrogenase (LDH), have not held up on clinical testing.

Since the literature holds no general agreement about how clinical findings should be used in this diagnosis, we investigated what diagnostic strategies experienced physicians have developed in the face of such uncertainty. In particular, we wondered how the diagnostic strategy of

* First published in *Medical Decision Making*, 6 (1986), 2–11. © 1986 Society for Medical Decision Making. Reprinted by permission.

experienced physicians would differ from that of less experienced house officers and students.

If greater experience causes physicians to converge on an optimal diagnostic strategy, then the use of important clinical information by different physicians should become similar as they obtain more experience. That is, they should learn what information is most important and how to use it. It has been shown, however, that even experienced physicians may use clinical information quite differently from one another in making a diagnosis. In a study of how radiologists weight clinical information to diagnose stomach cancer, Slovic *et al.* found that physicians differed in their use of clinical signs and that the idiosyncratic use of signs accounted in part for the variation in their judgments.[24] On the other hand, we could find no studies that examined whether experience changed the degree of similarity of different physicians' diagnostic strategies.

In addition, we wished to measure how closely the weighting of clinical information by expert and novice diagnosticians matched the optimal weighting of the same items as determined by multivariate analysis of actual clinical cases. Furthermore, since the use of clinical information should improve with experience, it would be reasonable to expect that the variables accounting for the most variance in the decisions of experienced physicians would correspond to those accounting for the most variance in real cases of suspected pulmonary embolism. We hypothesized that this correspondence would also be better for experienced physicians than for medical students since they would have the benefit of clinical experience with the disease.

Finally, we wished to determine whether physicians weight clinical information differently when making a diagnosis than when making a decision about therapy. Appropriate treatment for pulmonary embolism is anticoagulant therapy; however, anticoagulation is also appropriate for treatment of deep vein thrombosis, regardless of whether pulmonary embolus is suspected. Therefore, the signs and symptoms of deep vein thrombosis (which are also important in diagnosing pulmonary embolus) should account for more of the variance and have a greater weight in the decision to begin treatment than in the decision regarding diagnosis.

MATERIALS AND METHODS

To address these questions we used a decompositional model: the diagnostic situation was simulated using written case descriptions in which clinical information was varied systematically. Physicians' weighting of the clinical variables was inferred from their responses to case vignettes. Because it seemed particularly suitable to this type of study, we used conjoint analysis, a method used extensively in marketing to determine the impact of product attributes. It uses a fractional factorial design and thus was useful in limiting the number of vignettes that must be evaluated by each participant.

Lens model concept

In order to characterize physicians' diagnostic use of clinical information and to compare that with actual clinical cases, we used the Brunswik lens[12] as a conceptual model. This model (Fig. 1) views judgment as a simultaneous assessment of many different items of information (cues). On the right side of the lens the relative importance (weight) of each item to the resulting judgment is deduced from the relationship between the presence of that item and the judgment made. The overall model portrays cues (x_1–x_4) in the center of the lens, relating with different weights to real outcomes on the left side of the lens and to judgments, with a different set of weights, on the right.

For example, in the diagnosis of pulmonary embolus, the outcome of actual cases (i.e., whether or not the patient had a pulmonary embolus) is related mathematically to the weight of cues, such as chest pain, dyspnea, heart rate and lung scan results. These weights are represented in the diagram by the thickness of the line connecting the cue to the outcome on the left side of the lens. On the right side of the lens, the judge's diagnoses can be related to the same cues and a different set of weights derived. The accuracy of the judge's assessment can be represented by the correlation (r_a) between the judge's decisions and the true state (whether or not the patient actually had a pulmonary embolus).

Figure 1 Brunswik's lens model (see text for discussion)

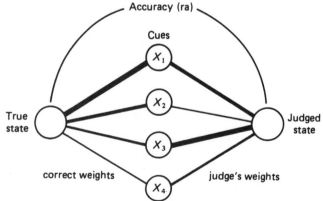

Conjoint analysis

Although we used the lens model as a conceptual basis, the procedures utilized were those of conjoint analysis as developed by Green and Rao.[8] The additive conjoint model[15] is a special case of conjoint measurement and is analogous to the absence of interaction in analysis of variance. Nonmetric outcome information can be dealt with using a monotone transformation to minimize a badness-of-fit measure (Kruskal's "Stress").[14] Originally used to examine consumer weightings of product attributes based on their preference ranking of profiles, conjoint analysis has come to be used with a variety of outcome measures and other methods of analysis, including ordinary least-squares regression.[9]

If regression approaches to the analysis of variance are used, a specific analysis of underlying assumptions of linearity and interaction terms can be made. Using this study as an example, with each clinical variable at three different levels a dummy-variable analysis can be performed according to the following model for two clinical factors:

$$u(x) = b_0 + b_1(x_{11}) + b_2(x_{12}) + b_3(x_{13})$$

$$+ b_4(x_{21}) + b_5(x_{22}) + b_6(x_{23}) + e$$

where e is the error term and $b_1, b_2, b_3 \ldots b_6$ are the coefficients for each of levels (1, 2, 3) for each clinical factor (1, 2). b_0 is the utility when all factors are at the first level. The contribution of each factor at a given level to the overall utility (e.g., $b_1(x_{12})$) is referred to in conjoint analysis as the part worth. In the dummy variable analysis, since $x = 1$ or $x = 0$, the part worth is equal to the coefficient, b.

A typical application of conjoint analysis asks the respondent to evaluate a series of profiles about a product or service within which the attributes of the product are varied, often using a nominal scale (e.g., Ford, Chrysler, GM) according to an orthogonal array.

Because the number of attributes may be irreducibly large, fractional factorial designs have been used to limit the number of profiles required. To accommodate several attributes with different numbers of levels within the same design, a variety of fractional factorial designs have been adopted.[7] When used with a fractional factorial design and scaled outcome measures, the conjoint analysis design resembles other multiattribute utility models such as Holistic Orthogonal Parameter Estimation (HOPE),[1] particularly in the use of differences between marginal means for estimation of weights.

Advantages of conjoint analysis   Use of a balanced orthogonal fractional factorial design in conjoint analysis allows investigators to use more than two factor levels and sufficient factors to make case vignettes realistic without requiring an unusable number of stimulus cases. For example, use of a full design in the current study of pulmonary embolus (seven clinical factors at three levels each) would have required 3^7 or 6,561 cases. Since most respondents required 20–30 minutes to evaluate 27 cases, larger number of cases would not have been practical for this study. The contribution of interactions among correlated factors has been examined[6] and many of the fractional factorial designs allow analysis to two-factor interactions.[7]

Presentation of the results of conjoint analysis includes the relative utility of each variable at each of its component levels (part worth). From this display, one can determine the linearity of the response and whether, in the case of ordered variables, there is a plateau or threshold in the response curve. This type of display can be derived from other methods as well (e.g., dummy variable regression or analysis of variance using a full design).

Another advantage of conjoint analysis is that if monotone transformation is not employed, the computation of weights can be done rapidly. At the time of this study, we had been developing an interactive computer feedback system that captured diagnostic weighting.[25] The speed of computation for conjoint analysis on a microcomputer (10–15 seconds) was much preferable to the 1–3 minutes required for multiple regression analysis.

Applications of conjoint analysis to medical topics

Orkin and Greenhow used conjoint analysis to study how faculty members weighted observed characteristics of anesthesiology residents in judging their clinical competence,[20] and later Clarke and Wigton examined how surgeons use information about residency candidates to select residents.[4] Richardson and colleagues examined the medical and social factors that contribute to the decision to refer high-risk obstetric patients to specialists,[22] and Wigton and colleagues used conjoint analysis to feed back to students the weighting of clinical information they used in learning to diagnose urinary tract infection.[25] Thus, in medical areas, conjoint analysis has been used more as a tool for capturing decision strategies than for preference or utility assessment per se. However, the study reported in this paper appears to be the first application of conjoint analysis to the study of diagnostic strategies used by experienced physicians.

Participants in the current study

Participants were selected to represent physicians at three levels of experience. Nineteen third-year medical students with six months of clinical experience or less represented a novice group: they had studied pulmonary embolism in classes but had little or no clinical experience with it. Twenty-three internal medicine residents represented an intermediate group: all had encountered cases where pulmonary embolus was considered in the differential diagnosis, but few had seen more than one or two cases. Thirteen faculty members comprised the experienced group. There were seven general internists, three cardiologists, and three gastroenterologists. All had at least five years of clinical experience and all were active clinicians, spending at least six months per year attending on inpatient services.

Study design and selection of variables

Each participant was asked to review 27 simulated cases. The presence and severity of eight clinical variables were varied systematically from case to case and the weighting given each variable was derived from analysis of the responses.

The eight clinical variables were selected from review of the literature and from review of cases by pulmonary and general medicine consultants with the goal of including all essential variables. The variables selected were age, chest pain, dyspnea (shortness of breath), heart rate, respiratory rate, examination of the legs, P_{O_2} (partial pressure of oxygen in arterial blood), and the results of the lung scan. Each variable was expressed at one of three levels of abnormality: o = no abnormality, 1 = intermediate or equivocal abnormality, 2 = serious, definite abnormality.

Where they could be determined from the literature, levels were defined to approximate intervals of equal importance relative to the diagnosis of pulmonary embolus. For example, the levels for the lung scan variable (Table 1) were chosen so that level o was a negative scan, level 1 represented a scan of medium likelihood (50 percent) and level 2, a highly positive scan (94 to 100 percent) as determined in clinical studies.[3,17] The wording for each level was intended to minimize confusion about the degree of abnormality. For example, the lung scan variable included both a description of the findings and an interpretation of the findings for each level: "normal" for level o, "possible" embolus for level 1, and "probable" embolus for level 2. Continuous variables such as the P_{O_2} were varied randomly within a defined range for each level. For example, at its lowest level, P_{O_2} was a randomly selected value between 50 and 55 mm Hg.

We used a fractional factorial design[21] which allowed measurement of all main effects with 27 cases and three levels. Thus, there were 27 cases with each variable at one of three levels of abnormality. For example, in the case illustrated in Table 2 the patient has chest pain and dyspnea at level 1, while heart rate is at level 2.

The cases were described on separate sheets of paper in the form of a

Table 1 *Examples of the three levels of abnormality for two of the variables (Lung scan, P_{O_2}) used in constructing the simulated cases*

Level[a]	Lung scan	P_{O_2}
0	$\dot{V}/\dot{Q}$ scan is normal	90–95 mm Hg
1	Perfusion scan shows multiple segmental defects *Impression:* possible pulmonary embolus	70–75 mm Hg
2	Perfusion scan shows multiple segmental defects not seen on ventilation scan *Impression:* probable pulmonary embolus	50–55 mm Hg

[a] 0 = no abnormality; 1 = intermediate or equivocal abnormality; 2 = definite or serious abnormality.

Table 2 *Example of a simulated case[a]*

A 20-year-old patient was admitted to the hospital
The medical history included:
  some dyspnea
  some chest discomfort
The physical examination showed:
  heart rate = 108/min
  respiratory rate = 17/min
  examination of legs: normal
P_{O_2} = 93 mm Hg
Perfusion scan shows multiple defects
Impression: possible pulmonary embolus
  1. Pulmonary embolus? (yes/no)
  2. What do you think is the likelihood that this patient has a pulmonary embolus?
    (0% to 100%)

[a] In this case, the variable "lung scan" is at level 1 (intermediate abnormality) and P_{O_2} is at level 0 (no abnormality).

deck and presented to participants in random order. The physicians were asked, first, whether they thought the patient described in the case actually had a pulmonary embolus; second, to estimate the likelihood that the patient had a pulmonary embolus (0–100 percent); and finally, whether they would begin anticoagulant therapy on the basis of the information presented.

Comparison with actual cases

In order to compare the participants' use of the clinical variables with how these same variables relate to the outcomes of actual cases, weights for the same eight variables were derived using stepwise multiple regression from records of 102 patients from another study.[13] These patients all had pulmonary arteriography for suspected pulmonary embolus during the period 1976–1981 at one of the three Omaha hospitals: the University of Nebraska Hospital (26 cases), Bishop Clarkson Memorial Hospital (33 cases), and the Omaha Veterans Administration Hospital (25 cases). Thirty-three percent of patients had positive arteriograms.

Data analysis

Data analysis used the programs of the SPSS (Statistical Package for the Social Sciences)[19] and SAS (Statistical Analysis System).[23] Discriminant analysis was performed for dichotomous outcome variables and used the SPSS program DISCRIMINANT. For the continuous outcome variable, dummy variable regression, multiple linear regression, and analysis of variance were used. Weights in the conjoint analysis were estimated from marginal means analyzed by variable level. The difference in variance explained between stepwise linear regression using each of the eight variables without modification and dummy variable regression was used to estimate the nonlinearity of the responses to the respective variable levels.

RESULTS

The effects of the three levels of each clinical variable on the estimated likelihood of pulmonary embolism are shown in Figure 2, the part worth for each variable. The lung scan results were given the greatest weight, followed by the findings on leg examination, P_{O_2}, and dyspnea. Three of

Figure 2 Utilities, expressed as average likelihood of pulmonary embolus for the three levels of abnormality (0, 1, 2) for the eight variables used in the simulated cases

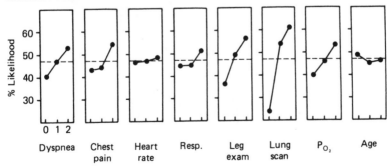

the variables (dyspnea, leg examination and P_{O_2}) appeared to have a linear relationship with the outcome. This observation was borne out in dummy variable analysis where there was no increase in variance explained (r^2) with separate analysis of each level using dummy variables.

The middle level for lung scan was used by the physicians as though it were much closer to the unequivocally positive scan in the upper level, although the literature indicates that the scan described represents a probability closer to 50 percent, compared with the near certainty of the upper level description. For the lung scan, the r^2 increased from 0.23 to 0.27 when analyzed as dummy variables, suggesting a small loss of power when a linear relationship is assumed.

Both chest pain and respiratory rate appear to show a threshold effect; there was little change in likelihood from the lowest to the middle level, but a change occurred from the middle to the highest. For example, the change in respiratory rate from the lowest level (average = 14/min) to the middle level (average = 19/min) had little effect on the outcome, while the change to the highest level (average = 24/min) produced an increase. This is consistent with recent clinical data relating respiratory rate to underlying pulmonary dysfunction.[5] In the dummy variable regression, only the upper level of each of these variables was statistically significant.

The part-worth display also indicates the direction of the relationship between each variable and the likelihood of diagnosis. All of the variables had a positive relationship except age, which did not reach significance in

Figure 3 Diagnostic use of lung scan results. Results of conjoint analysis for four groups of participants with different amounts of clinical experience: junior medical students (M-3), $n = 15$; first-year house officers (HO1), $n = 10$; third-year house officers (HO3), $n = 8$; and faculty members, $n = 12$. For comparison purposes, the plots of the part worth for the lung scan results are adjusted to show the deviation due to each level from the average estimated probability for each group. The percentage of total weight for each variable is determined by dividing the weight for that variable by the sum of the absolute values of the weights for all variables

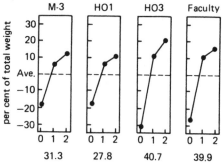

any of the analyses. The weight for each variable can be determined on these figures by measurement of the range of the values produced in going from the lowest level of a variable to the highest.

Each variable was analyzed for physicians at different levels of training. The results for the lung scan (Fig. 3) illustrate that the pattern were similar for all groups. Third-year house officers and faculty gave greater weight to the lung scan, as demonstrated in the greater change in mean probability from the lowest to the highest level. They also assigned a larger percentage of their total weighting to that variable. These differences in weighting observed for this variable were statistically significant, whereas the means of individual weights were not (see below). The shapes of the function were similar for all four groups in that the middle level (segmental defects on perfusion scan) produced a mean estimate much closer to the upper level (mismatched segmental defects on ventilation/perfusion scan) than to the lower (normal scan). The literature indicates that the actual likelihoods associated with these three descriptions are 0, 0.49 to 0.50, and 0.94 to 1.0 for levels 0, 1, and 2 respectively.[3,17]

We analyzed factor weighting for each participant using regression analysis and discriminant analysis for the continuous and bivariate outcomes, respectively. Analysis of the standardized (beta) weights for each participant for the lung scan variable (Fig. 4) indicates considerable variation in weighting among individuals. This variation was so great that the weights assigned lung scan results by faculty members varied from no weight at all to greater weight than that of all other variables combined.

Figure 4 Beta weights for each participant for the variable, "lung scan results." Participants are grouped according to level of training. The differences in mean weights for the four groups are not statistically significant (one-way ANOVA)

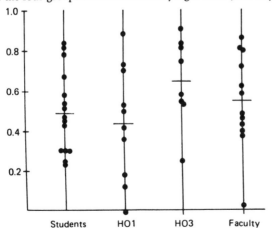

Table 3 *Relative weight and variance explained (r^2) for each clinical variable, analyzed by level of training*

Clinical variable	Students weight	r^2	HO1[a] weight	r^2	HO3[b] weight	r^2	Faculty weight	r^2	All participants weight	r^2
Dyspnea	20.1	0.08	10.9	0.02	6.7	0.01	9.2	0.02	12.6	0.03
Chest pain	12.9	0.03	8.8	0.02	9.6	0.02	9.7	0.02	10.4	0.02
Heart rate	0.3	0.00	5.8	0.01	2.2	0.00	1.9	0.00	2.5	0.00
Respiratory rate	1.1	0.00	9.6	0.02	7.8	0.01	5.0	0.00	5.4	0.01
Leg examination	22.2	0.09	18.2	0.07	19.3	0.09	18.0	0.06	19.0	0.07
Lung scan	31.3	0.19	27.8	0.16	40.7	0.41	39.9	0.29	34.7	0.23
P_{O_2}	9.8	0.02	15.4	0.05	6.0	0.01	15.9	0.05	13.2	0.03
Age	2.3	0.00	3.6	0.00	7.6	0.01	0.6	0.00	2.4	0.00
Total r^2		0.41		0.34		0.57		0.43		0.40

[a] First-year house officers.
[b] Third-year house officers.

Although the mean of weights was higher for the third-year house officers, no statistically significant difference was found (analysis of variance).

Relative weights given each clinical variable were analyzed by groups according to amount of prior training and experience. Table 3 includes the variance accounted for by that variable. Although lung scan results were most heavily weighted and accounted for nearly half or more of the variance explained in each group, some variables were differently weighted by the groups. For example, students gave a higher proportion of weight than other groups to dyspnea, and the lung scan results accounted for 70 percent of the variance in the house officer responses. The total variance explained was higher for the third-year house officers, suggesting they may have been more in agreement within the group on diagnostic use of the variables.

The overall r^2 for all participants was 0.40. Since the unexplained variance could be due to several factors, including lack of agreement on the best clinical strategy, inattention to the vignettes, inconsistency in individuals' answers and nonlinear relationships, we investigated some of these possibilities.

To examine the variance due to nonlinearity, we compared the overall r^2 from multiple linear regression (0.40) with that resulting from dummy variable analysis (0.44). This indicated that only a small part of the unexplained variance was due to the assumption of linear relationship.

To determine whether individuals were consistent in their use of variables over the 27 cases, we analyzed each individual's responses separately. The average r^2 for all individuals was 0.70. To examine consistency for the two questions with "yes" or "no" responses, the decision rule derived by discriminant analysis was used to predict the answers for the 27 cases from which it was derived. The predicted answers were correct 90 percent of the time.

Since roughly half of the unexplained variance appeared to be due to differences in individual strategies, we examined which variables were given the highest weight by individuals. Forty percent gave the greatest weight to variables other than the lung scan (16 percent to leg examination; 11 percent to P_{O_2}). On the average, the most heavily weighted variable accounted for 54 percent of the total variance explained for that individual.

To test the reproducibility of the weights determined for one individual on repeated measurements, three participants completed multiple sets of cases. Figure 5 shows the beta weights on four of the eight variables for one individual taking six different sets of 27 cases each. The different sets of cases were based on six different configurations of the factorial design and did not use the same vignettes. Thus, 162 different cases were administered in six sets on separate occasions more than a week apart.

Similar relatively close clusterings of the beta weights were found for all three participants.

To examine whether physicians used clinical information differently when making a diagnosis rather than deciding about therapy, we analyzed the weights from the responses to the three separate questions asked about each vignette: 1) "Is this a pulmonary embolus (yes or no)?", 2) "What do you think is the likelihood that this patient has a pulmonary embolus? (0 to 100 percent)", and 3) "Would you start heparin in this case?"

The results, shown in Table 4, indicate that weights derived from the two diagnostic questions are very similar but that the information about the leg examination was used quite differently in deciding therapy. The leg examination was given the largest weight and lung scan results the second largest weight in deciding about heparin therapy.

Weights derived from the physician's likelihood estimates were then compared, using the same variables, with weights derived from analysis of 102 actual cases of patients who had undergone angiography to diagnose pulmonary embolism (Table 5). It should be noted that the clinical setting

Figure 5 Beta weights for one student who evaluated six different sets of 27 cases with one- to two-week intervals between the six successive evaluation sessions

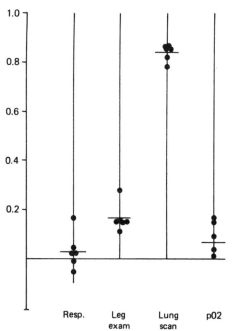

Table 4 *Relative weight given by all participants to each of the eight clinical factors in answering three questions*[a]

	Question asked		
	PE?[a] (Yes/No)	Likelihood of PE[b] (%)	Start treatment?[c] (Yes/No)
Dyspnea	12.16	12.56	7.78
Chest pain	9.79	10.38	6.38
Heart rate	1.68	2.50	7.62
Respiratory rate	3.78	5.35	5.29
Leg examination	20.42	19.01	35.63
Lung scan	35.11	34.65	27.84
P_{O_2}	12.87	13.16	8.85
Age	4.20	2.38	0.63

[a] Is this a pulmonary embolus (PE) (yes or no)?
[b] What do you think is the likelihood that this patient has a pulmonary embolus? (0 to 100%).
[c] Would you start heparin in this case?

of the actual cases was somewhat different from those in the simulations: all of the actual patients had been selected to undergo arteriography, whereas no such selection was implied in the simulations.

The weights used by physicians differed in many respects from those derived from the actual cases. Heart rate, which accounted for almost none of the variation on the simulated cases, was the most heavily weighted in the actual cases. Lung scan results were relatively important in the actual cases, but none of the remaining variables accounted for more than a small amount of variance in the actual cases. The total variance accounted for by the eight variables in the actual cases was only 20 percent. Other clinical variables were tested on the actual cases, but the only additional useful predictors were risk factors present in the patient history such as a history of cancer or recent surgical procedures.

DISCUSSION

In order to investigate what diagnostic strategies physicians adopt when the literature is unclear about the correct use of clinical information, we examined how physicians weighted eight items of clinical information in diagnosing pulmonary embolus. Analysis of diagnostic weighting by groups in different stages of training showed a high degree of similarity among the groups in how they approached the diagnosis. The results of the lung scan were the most heavily weighted, followed by the examination of the legs (for thrombophlebitis). Students gave more importance to

Table 5 *Comparison of weights derived from physician diagnosis of pulmonary embolus in simulated cases with weights derived from actual cases diagnosed by arteriography*

	Simulated cases		Actual cases ($n = 102$)	
	Relative weight	Change in r^2	Relative weight	Change in r^2
Dyspnea	12.6	0.03	2.1	0.00
Chest pain	10.4	0.02	9.8	0.01
Heart rate	2.5	0.00	31.2	0.12
Respiratory rate	5.4	0.01	11.1	0.01
Leg examination	19.0	0.07	11.1	0.01
Lung scan	34.6	0.23	23.1	0.04
P_{O_2}	13.2	0.03	5.4	0.00
Age	2.4	0.00	6.1	0.00
Total r^2		0.40		0.20

dyspnea than did the other groups, perhaps because they were less aware of the frequency with which this symptom is present in other conditions. Third-year house officers as a group relied the most heavily on the lung scan findings.

Although analysis by groups showed similar variable weighting, analysis of individual strategies revealed a high degree of variation. Lung scan results, which accounted for the majority of the explained variance overall, was given the highest weight by only 60 percent of participants. Clinical findings such as the P_{O_2}, the lung scan results, and the results of leg examinations were weighted most heavily by some and completely ignored by others. Similar variation in diagnostic strategies was found in the earlier studies by Slovic *et al.* on how radiologists diagnose gastric cancer.[24]

We investigated the hypothesis that physicians, as they obtain more clinical experience, develop strategies more similar to those of each other. This hypothesis was based on the assumption that increased knowledge and feedback from experience with actual cases would lead experienced physicians closer to an optimal strategy. One indicator of more homogeneous strategies would be an increase in the variance explained (r^2) in the pooled group responses by the linear equation derived through regression analysis. The variance explained in the faculty responses ($r^2 = 0.43$) was similar, however, to that for the students ($r^2 = 0.41$). The largest variance explained was in the third-year house officers, who might be expected to have the most homogeneous strategies since they had been training together for nearly three years.

There are problems, however, with the use of the variance explained as a measure of homogeneity of weighting, since the variance could have been decreased by several other factors. For example, poor attention to the vignettes, nonlinear variables, or irrelevance of the factors to the outcome could all reduce the r^2.

However, we investigated the possibility of nonlinearity with dummy variable analysis and found only a small improvement in variance when linearity was not assumed. We also examined the consistency of individual answers by analysis of the variance explained in each 27-case set and found that the average r^2 was 0.70, suggesting that only half of the unexplained variance may be due to variation in strategy. Also, the average r^2 of 0.70, together with the results of discriminant analysis, suggests that inattention was not a major problem.

Why are the individual physicians' strategies not more similar? It is easy to understand why students would show a high degree of variation, but faculty members with over 12 years of additional experience and training might be expected to show more homogeneity. One explanation may be that the medical literature is too confusing regarding how clinical findings should be used in making this diagnosis. There is abundant information about the relative frequency of positive findings (sensitivity) from sources such as the urokinase study,[18] but this information is of limited value if the specificity or the predictive value of the finding is not known. Few studies provide any help with these questions. In addition, there are no studies which define the optimal relative weighting of findings when they appear in combination as they do in actual situations. In describing verbally to the authors how they diagnose pulmonary embolism, faculty participants showed variation in interpretations and choices of major findings similar to that found by the conjoint analysis.

Despite the confusion in the medical literature, why are the strategies not more similar to one another in the more experienced clinicians (faculty members, senior residents) than they are in the students? Should not the experience with actual cases bring faculty closer to the correct weighting of variables and thus, closer to one another in their clinical strategies? One possibility is that the task is simply too complex for the weighting of multiple variables to be effectively influenced over time in a regular way by the results of cases encountered in practice. McDonald has concluded[16] that many diagnostic errors occur as a result of man's inherent limitations as a data processor. He suggests that computer-based protocols will be necessary to improve on clinicians' inconsistent use of diagnostic information.

Another explanation for the failure to find increasing uniformity with more experience is that cases of pulmonary embolus in which the outcomes are clearly known may occur infrequently in an individual physician's experience. Thus, the clinician might learn the true outcome so rarely that there would be no effective feedback. A third possibility is that making the correct diagnosis in the case of possible pulmonary embolus may not be important as long as the index of suspicion is high enough that anticoagulants are begun. If true, the consequences of misdiagnosis would be small and errors would not receive the attention they might otherwise receive.

Finally, it could be that the variables selected do not account for sufficient variation in the diagnosis. Thus, major differences in weighting of these variables would be unlikely to consistently affect diagnostic accuracy. That all of the most important variables identified in the literature were included in the study argues against this possibility. On the other hand, the failure of these eight variables to account for more than 20 percent of variance in 102 actual cases argues in its favor. It will be important to conduct further studies of diagnostic variation, with particular attention to those diagnoses where accurate multivariate predictors for the diagnosis can be defined in actual cases.

In comparing physician and student weights with those derived from actual cases, there was not a high degree of correspondence. Although the lung scan results were important in both situations, the heart rate, which accounted for the most variance in the actual cases, was used hardly at all in the simulated cases. The differences may be due to the differences in the patient populations considered. The simulated cases describe unselected patients suspected of having pulmonary embolism, while the actual cases were all those of patients who had arteriography, a subset that may differ in presentation, severity of illness, chronicity and type of disease present in those without pulmonary embolism. The usefulness of clinical findings can depend on the specific conditions present in the patients who do not have the disease in question, and thus selection of patients who had arteriography may introduce a "work-up" bias, where signs and symptoms common in patients being considered for the disease are undervalued because of their presence in patients without the disease for whom the diagnosis is being considered.

In many conditions, treatment will have been begun when the diagnosis was far from certain. In addition, clinical information may be used in different ways when considering treatment and when making a diagnosis. In this case we felt that the findings suggesting thrombophlebitis would be more important in making the decision to initiate heparin therapy than they would be in making the diagnosis of pulmonary embolus, since thrombophlebitis per se would be an indication for anticoagulation. Analysis of factor weighting in all groups showed this effect strongly, with the leg examination assuming the position of most heavily weighted variable in the question of whether to begin therapy. This difference between diagnostic and therapeutic information use should be considered in analyses of clinical strategies.

It is important to ask whether the simulated cases reliably captured the weighting of the participants. The observations suggest that all the determinations are consistent for a given participant. When three individuals completed six different series of 27 cases each, the weighting calculated for each variable changed little from series to series. Second, when individual strategies are analyzed, the average variance explained (for the continuous outcome variable) was 70 percent, suggesting consistency in individual response. Third, again in analysis of individual case sets, the decision rules derived from each participant's responses to the yes/no questions were able to predict the diagnoses given by that person an average of 90 percent of the time, again arguing for the consistency of information utilization in working through the cases.

It has been estimated that there have been more than a thousand applications of conjoint analysis in business and marketing.[2] Conjoint analysis has only recently been applied to medical topics[4,20,22,25] but is well suited to the study of diagnostic and therapeutic strategies in medical decision making. Depending on the application, the computations may be less complex than traditional multivariate methods. It is particularly well suited to models where a relatively large number of variables need to be included with some at a nominal level. The traditional display of part worth permits inspection for weight and linearity of responses, for threshold behavior, and is particularly useful where one is unable to predict the relationship of the different variable levels to each other.

Case vignettes using a factorial design have several advantages for studying diagnostic strategies. They are constructed so that the participant must decide which of several factors is most important to the diagnosis, a situation that may occur only occasionally in the cases encountered in practice. They are convenient and easy to administer.

On the other hand, there are significant problems with the representation of real-life variables in paper cases. Some variables, particularly numerical measurements such as vital signs, rates, or laboratory values, are probably communicated effectively to the subjects. Other types of information such as observations ("the patient appears toxic") may lack the influence or force they have in real life. In addition participants may not give the same quality of attention to a written vignette that they would to a real-life situation. Thus, further research is needed to determine whether the weighting used in these vignettes corresponds to weighting used in clinical situations.

If, on further study, the wide variation in diagnostic weighting proves to be a major source of variation in diagnostic accuracy, what could be done to produce more consistent weighting? Hammond[11] studied the learning of a somewhat more complex weighting task. He found that when he provided students with a graphic analysis of how they weighted each item, they learned to predict the answers far more effectively than when provided only outcome feedback. If these findings hold true for medical diagnosis, then this may provide a way to teach diagnostic skills far more effectively than present methods. We are currently investigating an interactive system using a microcomputer to present cases, analyze responses, and show students how their diagnostic weighting differed from that of experts in the field.[25]

In summary, we found that conjoint analysis can be used to reliably characterize how physicians weight clinical information in reaching a diagnosis in simulated cases of pulmonary embolism. Individual physicians and medical students varied widely in how they used clinical findings. There was no difference between groups at different levels of training either in the average weighting of each variable or in the degree of variation within the group. These results indicate a considerable variability in diagnostic information use which does not appear to decrease with increasing clinical experience. More study is needed to determine whether this degree of variation is true for other diagnostic entities, and what the consequences are in terms of diagnostic accuracy.

REFERENCES

1 Barron, F.H., Person, H.B.: Assessment of multiplicative functions via holistic judgments. *Organizational Behav. Hum. Performance* 24:147–166, 1979
2 Cattin, P., Wittink, D.R.: Commercial use of conjoint analysis: a survey. *J. Marketing* 46:44–53, 1982
3 Cheely, R., McCartney, W.H., Perry, J.R. *et al.*: The role of non-invasive tests versus pulmonary angiography in the diagnosis of pulmonary embolism. *Am. J. Med.* 70:17–22, 1981
4 Clarke, J.R., Wigston, R.S.: Development of an objective rating system for residency applications. *Surgery* 96:302–306, 1984
5 Gravelyn, T.R., Weg, J.G.: Respiratory rate as an indicator of acute airway dysfunction. *JAMA* 244:1123–1125, 1980
6 Green, P.E.: On the analysis of interactions in marketing research data. *J. Marketing Res.* 10:10–420, 1973
7 Green, P.E., Carroll, J.D., Carmone, F.J.: Some new types of fractional factorial designs for marketing experiments. *Res. Marketing* 1:99–122, 1978
8 Green, P.E., Rao, V.R.: Conjoint measurement for quantifying judgmental data. *J. Marketing Res.* 8:355–363, 1971
9 Green, P.E., Srinivasan, V.: Conjoint analysis in consumer research: issues and outlook. *J. Consumer Res.* 5:103–123, 1978
10 Guidotti, T.L., Fries, L.F., Bell, W.R. *et al.*: Accuracy of screening for pulmonary embolism in the emergency room. *Respiration* 37:309–317, 1979

11 Hammond, K.R.: Computer graphics as an aid to learning. *Science* 172:903–908, 1971

12 Hammond, K.R., Hursch, C.J., Todd, F.J.: Analyzing the components of clinical inference. *Psychol. Rev.* 71:438–456, 1964

13 Hoellerich, J.L., Wigton, R.S., Patil, K.D.: Use of clinical signs and symptoms in the diagnosis of pulmonary embolism (abstr.). *Clin. Res.* 20:644A

14 Kruskal, J.B.: Analysis of factorial experiments by estimating monotone transformations of the data. *J. Roy. Statistical Soc. Series B* 27:251–263, 1965

15 Luce, R.D., Tukey, J.W.: Simultaneous conjoint measurement: a new type of fundamental measurement. *J. Math. Psych.* 1:1–27, 1964

16 McDonald, C.J.: Protocol-based computer reminders, the quality of care and the non-perfectability of man. *N. Engl. J. Med.* 295:1351–55, 1976

17 McNeil, B.J.: A diagnostic strategy using ventilation-perfusion studies in patients suspect for pulmonary embolism. *J. Nucl. Med.* 17:613–617, 1976

18 National Cooperative Study. The urokinase pulmonary embolism trial. *Circulation* 47 suppl. 2: 1–108, 1973

19 Nie, N.H., Hull, C.H., Jenkins, C.G. *et al.*: *Statistical Package for the Social Sciences.* New York, McGraw-Hill, 1975, pp. 434–467

20 Orkin, F.K., Greenhow, D.E.: A study of decision making. *Anesthesiology* 48:267–271, 1978

21 Plackett, R.L., Burman, J.P.: The design of optimum multifactorial experiments. *Biometrika* 33:305–325, 1946

22 Richardson, D.K., Gabbe, S.G., Wind, Y.: Decision analysis of high-risk patient referral. *Obstet. Gynecol.* 63:496–501, 1984

23 SAS Institute Inc.: *SAS User's guide: Statistics*, 1982 edition. Cary, NC, SAS Institute Inc., 1982, p. 584

24 Slovic, P. Rorer, L.G., Hoffman, P.J.: Analyzing the use of diagnostic signs. *Invest. Radiol.* 6:18–26, 1971

25 Wigton, R.S., Patil, K.D., Hoellerich, V.L.: Enhanced learning of clinical diagnosis through computer graphics feed back of diagnostic weighting. Proceedings of the 23rd Annual Conference on Research in Medical Education, 1984, pp. 111–116

6

~

YOU CAN'T SYSTEMATIZE HUMAN JUDGMENT: DYSLEXIA*

Robyn M. Dawes

Friends tell me that important human judgment is often ineffable, unsystematic, and intuitive.

I agree. And it is, therefore, often bad.

Friends tell me that decisions that are effable, systematic, and explicit are dehumanized decisions.

I agree. But they are "dehumanized" only for the decision maker, and I am concerned with the consequences for the people affected by the decisions. Bad decisions are dehumanizing for them.

Friends tell me that judgments about people must be holistic, because people can be understood and appreciated only as integrated, indivisible entities.

I agree, if the characteristic of the person to be judged is a gestalt (such as beauty). If it is not (for instance, academic or work potential), then a holistic judgment is simply a delusion.

Friends tell me that they are good judges – particularly of people – when they make holistic, ineffable, intuitive, and unsystematic judgments.

I agree only that they think they are good judges. Most well-adjusted people believe that they make good decisions; judgmental successes are remembered more readily than are judgmental failures, and the role of extraneous factors is more readily appreciated in accounting for failures than for successes.

Friends tell me that effable and systematic decisions might be computerized, thereby bringing us closer to 1984 and the establishment of a Kafkaesque bureaucracy. I agree that 1984 is four years away. The essence of a Kafkaesque bureaucracy, however, is not that it has rules; rather it is that it appears to have coherent or humane rules but does not. ("What must I do to get out of the hospital?" "You know the answer to that." Or, "Your comprehensive homeowners policy covered your house only on its present foundations; but the mud slide moved it two inches off its foundation before totally demolishing it . . .") And computers can be

* First published in *New Directions for Methodology of Social and Behavioral Science*, 4 (1980), 67–78. © Jossey-Bass, Inc. 1980. Reprinted by permission.

used either for or against people; for example, I have yet to hear anyone complain about the airlines' use of computers – which makes booking, connecting, and rerouting pleasant and efficient. Or complain about the use of computers in successfully irradiating tumours.

The central thesis of this chapter is that in a wide variety of psychological contexts, systematic decisions based on a few explicable and defensible principles are superior to intuitive decisions – because they work better, because they are not subject to conscious or unconscious biases on the part of the decision maker, because they can be explicated and debated, and because their basis can be understood by those most affected by them.

DECISIONS ABOUT ADMISSION

The major decision I will discuss is that of admitting students to academic institutions. First, I will present descriptions about how it is actually done; second, I will present theory and research evidence indicating how it might be done better; third, I will discuss the ethical implications of doing it better – including those for affirmative action programs; finally I will recount how graduate students are chosen at the University of Oregon.

How are such decisions usually made? Two articles appeared in the spring of 1979 describing undergraduate admissions procedures at two leading universities, Brown and Duke. I will excerpt these in a non-random, biased, and unsystematic manner in order to show how such decisions are typically made.

A session at Brown*

On a rainy Sunday morning in March, Brown Admissions Director Jim Rogers and three members of the admissions committee contemplate a fat computer printout. It measures, in code, the credentials of the 11,421 high school seniors who have applied to Brown. Next to each applicant's name, a long string of numbers and cryptic abbreviations shows college board scores, class rank, grade-point average, and a preliminary rating for academic promise and personal quality [?] on a scale of 1 to 6. Other symbols reveal more: "LEG 1" is a legacy, the son of a Brown alumnus. "M1" is a black; "M8" a Chicano. "50" means the Brown football coach is interested, "70" that Brown's development office has marked the candidate's parents as potential benefactors.

The committee passes around a thick application folder from "Mary." "Whoops," says Rogers. "A 'Pinocchio'!" In Brown admissions jargon, that means her guidance counselor has checked off boxes rating her

---

* Thomas, 1979, pp. 51–52. Reprinted by permission from *Time*, the Weekly Newsmagazine; © Time Inc., 1979.

excellent for academic ability but only good or average for humor, imagination, and character. On the printed recommendation form, the low checks stick out from the high ones like a long, thin nose. A Pinocchio is often fatal. "A rating of average usually means the guidance counselor thinks there is something seriously wrong," explains the Admissions Officer Paulo de Oliveira. Mary's interview with a Brown alumnus was also lukewarm, and worse, she has written a "jock essay" (a very short one). Rogers scrawls a Z, the code for rejection, on her folder.

The next morning the admissions committee scans applications from a small rural high school in the Southwest. It is searching for prized specimens known as "neat small-town kids." Amy is near the top of her class, with mid-500 verbals, high-600 math and science. She is also poor, white, and "geo" – she would add to the geographic and economic diversity that saves Brown from becoming a postgraduate New England prep school. While just over 20 percent of the New York State applicants will get in, almost 40 percent will be admitted from Region 7 – Oklahoma, Texas, Arkansas, and Louisiana. Amy's high school loves her, and she wants to study engineering. Brown badly wants engineering students; unfortunately, Amy spells engineering wrong. "Dyslexia," says Jimmy Wrenn, a linguistics professor. After some debate, the committee puts her on the waiting list.

A session at Duke*

It is a sunlit Thursday morning, and around a long wooden table a college admissions committee squints at thick books of computer printouts and argues about a black high school senior with much promise but bad grades.

One of twelve children from a Detroit ghetto family, he wants to attend Duke University here, but his case perplexes admissions officials. Although they want to admit more blacks, this young man ranks in the bottom fifth of his class, and his scores are just average on the Scholastic Aptitude Test, which is said to measure college potential. "He's scary," mutters Edward Lingenheld, Duke's admissions director. Yet the Massachusetts prep school that the student is attending on an affirmative-action scholarship is one of the best private schools in the country. It backs him strongly, saying his character and leadership ability are outstanding.

After a few minutes of sharp debate, the committee, swayed mainly by the school's praise, decides to accept him. He is one of more than 6,800 high school seniors who want to get into Duke's freshman class next fall. Only 1,000 will make it.

---

* Reprinted by permission of Anthony Ramirez, *Cream of the Crop*, © Dow Jones & Co., Inc., 1979, all rights reserved.

Watching the admissions committee's deliberations here at Duke for a few days shows the shifting and sorting that lands some students in the college of their choice, and leaves others – often with almost identical grades and test scores – rejected.

The admissions marathon begins in early December, when the first applications trickle in. In all, the staff must ponder more than 8,000 applications (counting an extra 1,200 for the engineering and nursing schools), most of them in about nine weeks. Even with the hiring of seven part-timers (mostly faculty wives) to evaluate applications, each permanent staffer must study thoroughly as many as fifty applications a day.

The fatigue is evident. "I want to know if I goofed," says David Belton, an admissions staffer, asking advice from other staffers about a candidate. He says he had only two hours' sleep when he read the applicant's folder. (The candidate, after review, stays rejected.)

A major quality the committee look for is "spark."

One student, typical of many, seems to lack it. The son of a prosperous Harvard graduate, he is trying to decide where he's going in life. For "anticipated career" and "anticipated major" he has checked "undecided." Gifted in mathematics (a 790 on a math section of the S.A.T.), he is only a B student overall.

The committee considers his extracurricular activities lackluster. He is a stamp collector, a Boy Scout, and a Sunday school teacher, who also plays the piano and guitar and sings. On Duke's scale, his grades and extracurricular activities rank him a "D/D."

Nevertheless, an admissions staffer includes a note in the student's folder: "Bad Soph year but super scores. I really like him. Fine student – admit if possible."

His high school also recommends him "with enthusiasm," but an admissions staffer who interviewed him notes his "lethargic demeanor." David Miller, another staffer, says his admission would be "tantamount to saying scores can get you in."

The student writes, "Years from now, all the pressure of this decision will probably seem funny. But right now it seems very important to get it all sorted out. I will be relieved when the work and the waiting are over and commitment has been made, for better or worse."

The committee rejects him.

As I learned when selecting graduate students at the University of Oregon, such selection procedures are exciting, fun. Few things beat the combination of exhilaration and exhaustion felt by those in a compatible group faced with a demanding mission. The atmosphere in admissions committees is often that of a benign war room; crucial decisions are made about others' lives, but no one gets killed. It is not, however, so much fun for the Pinocchios of this world – or for those of us who cannot spell too well.

CLINICAL VERSUS STATISTICAL PREDICTION

Does it work? That is, are decisions made in this manner more efficacious than those made by a dull and systematic statistical integration of the predictive information at hand? This question has been studied extensively by psychologists and others interested in such outcomes as college success (Sarbin, 1943), graduate school success (Dawes, 1971), parole violation (Burgess, 1941), and psychiatric diagnosis (Goldberg, 1965). In all these studies, the same basic information presented to a clinician or clinicians asked to make an intuitive ("clinical") prediction was also used in a statistical model predicting that same outcome. This information usually consisted of test scores or biographical facts, but occasionally included observer ratings of specific attributes as well. In 1954, Meehl published an influential book in which he summarized approximately twenty such studies comparing the clinical integration method with the statistical one. In all studies, the statistical method did better, or the two methods tied. In most of these studies, the statistical method of choice was a regression equation – that is, a simple weighted average of the appropriately coded information where the weights are chosen in such a way as to maximize predictability. (The usual criterion of evaluating the models was the multiple correlation coefficient computed between predicted and obtained outcomes; in all cases, these correlation coefficients were computed on a "cross-validation sample," one independent of that from which the weights were obtained.)

Approximately ten years later, Sawyer (1966) reviewed a total of forty-five studies comparing clinical and statistical prediction. There was again *no* study in which a clinical combination method was superior to what Sawyer termed a "mechanical" (statistical) one, and in a majority of studies, the statistical prediction was superior. Unlike Meehl, Sawyer did not limit his review to situations where the clinical judge had information identical to that on which the statistical model was based, and he even included two studies (Bloom and Brundage, 1947; Schiedt, 1936) where the clinical judge had access to *more* information (an interview) and yet did *worse*. (The near total lack of validity of unstructured interviews as predictive techniques is documented and discussed in an article by Kelley in 1954, one that has to my knowledge gone unchallenged since.)

Nothing published in the standard journals after Sawyer's review has demonstrated that a context exists in which clinical prediction is superior. On the other hand, the number of contexts in which statistical prediction has been shown to be superior has grown consistently (Dawes, 1979) –

some of the more interesting being prediction of longevity of patients with Hodgkins Disease (Einhorn, 1972) and prediction of business failures (Libby, 1976).

Why do regression equations do so well compared to clinical judgment? First, it should be pointed out that neither method does as well as many people would like (comparisons typically being among multiple correlation coefficients ranging from .25 to .60). That has led many critics to dismiss the superiority of the statistical predictions on the grounds that "twice nothing is nothing" (letter from a dean quoted in Dawes, 1976a, pp. 6–7). But as I have argued elsewhere (Dawes, 1979) such criticisms are based on the assumption that the criteria to be predicted *should* be highly predictable, and there is no basis for such an assumption other than the reassuring hope that life is in fact predictable. (It is not.) Nor is there reason to believe that other experts making clinical predictions would do better than did those studied – although the argument that the wrong clinicians were used persists among many of my colleagues, who modestly maintain that *really* well-trained and insightful clinicians like themselves would not be subject to the biases, pitfalls, or incapacities of others.

So the regression equations do well compared to clinical judgment – perhaps as well as can be expected. The reason is that, in the contexts studied, each variable used in the prediction can easily be coded to have a *conditionally monotonic* relationship to the criterion. That is, higher values on each predictor are associated with higher values on the criterion irrespective of the values on the other predictors. For example, students with higher undergraduate grade point averages (GPA's) have a higher probability of success in graduate school than do those with lower GPA's; students with higher Graduate Record Examination scores (GRE's) have a higher probability of success than do those with lower GRE's, and there is no "crossed" ("disordinal") interaction that leads the GPA probability of success prediction to reverse direction at certain levels of GRE scores, or *vice versa*. Given that "more is better" – that is, given conditional monotonicity in the predictive situation – *regression equations do an extremely good job of making the prediction.* Dawes and Corrigan (1974) have summarized empirical, simulation, and mathematical studies all demonstrating the general principle that even when the best prediction of the criterion is not a weighted average of prediction variables, this average obtained from constructing a regression equation yields predictions that are excellent approximations to the best ones – provided only that the relationship is conditionally monotonic. So the regression equations work.

Even if a variable does not have a monotonic relationship with the criterion, in most contexts it is possible to rescale it so that it does. For example, if we were evaluating applicants for jobs in which too much intelligence were as detrimental as too little (such as custodian), then we could easily define a new variable termed "intellectual mediocrity" that would be assessed in terms of distance from an ideal level of mediocre capacity. All such "single peaked" functions can easily be converted to monotonic ones by defining desirability as distance from the peak (ideal level). (The reader is invited to think for a moment about variables that might be useful in predicting such phenomena as academic success, heart attacks, job success, longevity, or bankruptcy – to see how most are conditionally monotonic to begin with, and how the remainder can easily be made so.) In fact, almost all psychological, medical, or financial variables we use to predict outcomes of interest are monotone, or single peaked, and do not interact. No matter how much some of us may wish to get around it, it is better to be smarter, stronger, and more beautiful – have blood pressure nearer to 120/80, be closer to age 29, and be moderately aggressive.

Why are clinical judges not so good at the information integration process? Studies from experimental psychology have shown that people are very poor at integrating information from different dimensions if these are inherently noncomparable – as, for example, are a grade point average and a test score. There is even evidence that people cannot keep two distinct "analyzable" dimensions in mind at the same time (Shepard, 1964), especially if they are asked to make judgments in which information about one of these two dimensions may be missing (Slovic and MacPhillamy, 1974). If the cognitive processes of admissions committee members are not different qualitatively from those of experimental subjects, then it is not surprising that such judges do not integrate information well.

But clinical judges are important. The statistical model may integrate the information in an optimal manner, but it is always the individual (judge, clinician) who chooses the variables. Moreover, it is the human judge who knows the directional relationship between the predictor variables and the criterion of interest, or who can code the variables in such a way that they have a clear directional relationship. And it is precisely in situations where the predictor variables are good and where they have a monotonic relationship with the criterion that regression equations work well.

Weighting the variables The admissions committee or single clinical judge often does not have a regression equation available. The determination of the optimal weights used in such an equation requires a careful study of a large number of individual cases sampled from the population of people or objects to be judged – or the estimation of the weights may be severely in error. If such a study is impossible, can nothing be done other than to fall back on inferior clinical intuition in lieu of a superior but nonexistent regression equation? The answer is no. In the last five years, there has been a resurgence of interest in the degree to which weights that are not optimal may yield results close to the optimal ones. Dawes and Corrigan (1974) showed that weights *randomly* chosen – but in the right direction – yield results that are close to those that are obtained from optimal weights. (In those studies, all variables were made statistically comparable by standardizing them.) Moreover, in five judgment contexts, the outcomes obtained from pseudo-regression equations devised from such weights on the average outperformed clinical judges making the same predictions. Finally, Dawes and Corrigan showed that unit weights (+1 if the variable has a positive relationship with the criterion, −1 otherwise) did better on the average than did random weights, and did *much* better than did the clinical judges. Dawes and Corrigan concluded that (1974, p. 195) "the whole trick is to know what variables to look at and then to know how to add."

Later, the degree to which changes in predictions are affected by changes in weights (provided changes in signs are not involved) has been investigated by Edwards (1978), Einhorn and Hogarth (1975), Gardiner and Edwards (1975), Green (1977), Wainer (1976), and Wainer and Thissen (1976). These investigators have all reached the same conclusion: the changes in prediction are affected very little – not enough to make any difference in most applied situations.

Implementation of the Dawes-Corrigan trick of using experts to select the variables and then simply adding their values appears to "dehumanize" prediction situations – particularly those in which people are being selected or rejected. People are reduced to "mere numbers," and the allocation of scarce social resources is made on the basis of these numbers. So, even if such a procedure works better than does clinical judgment, should we not discard it? Is it not "horribly unfair to reject people without even interviewing them?" as I overheard one rejected applicant to Santa Barbara complain at the Los Angeles Renaissance Fair last summer. "How can they possibly tell what I'm like?"

The answer is that they cannot – nor could they with an interview (or a Rorschach test). The selection system is meant to do the *best possible* job for allocating scarce positions in graduate school; it will make mistakes (just as clinical judgment does), but fewer. Some people who will be rejected without an interview *will* have more potential than some of those accepted without one, but the research indicates that interviews will not discover which ones. Moreover, performance on an interview is *not* as meritorious a characteristic as a mere number like an undergraduate record – which represents work over three and a half years in a minimum of thirty-six classes. The rejected applicant who complained implied that she would rather be judged on the basis of a half hour talk under unusual circumstances (she is trying to impress an interviewer of unknown predilections and biases) than be judged on her past history of work and accomplishment. Unless that history is deficient, she might opt for the mere number; at the very least, if she wished each individual social decision to be made as if it were a general policy (Rawls, 1958) she would do so. (For a discussion of the ethics of allocating scarce resources on the basis of a systematic weighting of a few predictive and meritorious variables, see Dawes, 1977.)

I do not mean to imply that interviews are never useful. First, a structured interview or situation is of use if it taps a behavior that is important in the situation for which the interviewee is being considered; for example, job applicants for academic positions are routinely asked to give a talk about their work; the clarity, charm, and enthusiasm with which they can lecture – in particular about their own work – are important factors in determining how highly they will be evaluated in an academic position were they to obtain one. (I am not arguing that it is moral or socially productive that university professors be evaluated on such factors – just that they are.) Second, an unstructured interview may allow the interviewer to assess how he or she responds to the interviewee. Affective responses in particular are often formed precipitously and cannot be explained by a *conscious* weighting of components (Zajonc, 1980; Posner, personal communication). If it is important to assess such reactions – for instance, if the interviewee is applying to be a secretary of the interviewer – then clearly an interview is appropriate. But in the situations described in this chapter, the interview is neither structured to contain a sample of relevant work, nor is it conducted by a person who will have a close supervisory relationship to the applicant. The systematic combination of relevant predictors is superior.

Discrimination? Does this select-and-average-relevant-variables system tend to exclude minority applicants? Not unless it is implemented stupidly. It is true that minority applicants tend to score lower than majority ones on most selection variables. But that only demonstrates the *need* for affirmative action. It certainly does not demonstrate that such applicants are dumber in any biological sense, nor that the *tests* are somehow biased against minority group members. The reason for these conclusions is that the tests do exactly what they were constructed to do – assess potential for performance in a predominantly white middle class culture, and there is no such thing as aptitude independent of experience (certain naive ideas about mental functioning being different from all other functioning notwithstanding). Since on the whole minority applicants have less experience in this culture than do majority group applicants, their aptitude scores are lower.

What to do? Consistent with the approach advocated in this chapter, I would simply add a factor with an explicit score for minority group status. This factor would be sufficiently large to guarantee that *on the average* (not as part of a quota for each year) the desired proportion of minority group members would be selected. Only the most qualified majority students who would otherwise be admitted would be rejected. Moreover, the predictability of the selection criteria would be affected very little (Dawes, 1976b), even if the minority group applicants did as poorly on the whole on the criterion behavior as on the standard selection variables. (A similar approach was first proposed by Darlington, 1971).

Is that legal? In the Bakke decision (McCormack, 1978), Justice Powell – who held the pivotal vote – stated that ethnic origin may be a factor in admissions to academic institutions. But there appear to be three qualifications. First, the "purpose" must be to have a representative student body rather than to affect society. (I guess I just cannot think like a lawyer; to me, identical outcomes imply the same policy.) Second, he implied – although he did not state – that an ethnic origin factor must be one of many, such as ability to play left guard. Third, he prohibited "doctoring" test scores for ethnic origin, although the ethnicity factor may be added later. (Again, believing that the sum of sums is equal to the sum of sums, I fail to see the distinction between first adding something to a test score and then amalgamating the result with other things – as opposed to amalgamating the test score with other things and then adding an ethnicity factor.) The answer to the question at the beginning of this paragraph is: Maybe.

How would the type of procedure advocated here be implemented? Recently, Goldberg (1977) has described the admissions procedure for evaluating students who have applied to the graduate program in psychology at the University of Oregon. First, each applicant's past record and aptitude test scores are amalgamated in a simple additive combination:

$$GPA + \frac{V + Q}{200}$$

where GPA is the undergraduate grade point average, and V and Q are raw scores on the verbal and quantitative parts of the GRE respectively. Note that this formula is *compensatory*; applicants with mediocre records may score high if they show evidence of outstanding aptitude, and vice versa. (In fact, even the verbal and quantitative parts of the GRE are compensatory.)

Majority applicants who score below 9.7 are rejected. Past research (Dawes, 1971) has shown that such applicants stand no chance of being admitted even when purely intuitive decisions are made. The use of this formula – and its publication – saves both heartache for students who have no chance of being admitted, and faculty time and guilt in rejecting huge numbers of such applicants.

Finally, only the majority students passing the 9.7 cut and all minority students are considered on a case-by-case basis. Here, letters of recommendation are important, but unfortunately no way of coding them to make them comparable has yet been devised. What the reviewers look for is concrete evidence of accomplishment (such as independent research projects). Unfortunately, in my view, the reviewers also look for "fit" between the student's interests and theirs. (It seems pretty silly to me for Duke to reject a 17-year-old applicant partly because he is honestly "undecided" about his major. In fact, one could argue that many applicants who have decided on a career at age 17 are suffering from "premature closure" of the intellect – or premature maturity in general. Similarly, college seniors who claim to know the interests they wish to pursue in psychology for the next forty-five years may well include those with the least inquiring and flexible minds. Ditto for those rated as "mature" by the letter writers. That is all speculation. No studies. In the absence of any evidence that such interest variables are predictive – and they are certainly not meritorious – I would ignore them.)

This procedure is dry, unexciting, "peripheralistic," routinized (hence effable), and communicable. Basically, Oregon weights three factors: how well the applicant has done in the past, how intelligent he or she appears to be on the basis of a standardized test, and what independent work he or she has done of the type that will be expected in graduate school and beyond. The Oregon psychologists do not claim to understand applicants in their entirety; in fact, they do not even claim to have "spark" detectors in their heads. Perhaps they are less able than are the admissions officers elsewhere who search for spark. Or perhaps, being familiar with the literature on the poor track records of such clinical judgments, the Oregon psychologists are merely a bit more modest. At any rate, the applicants to Oregon are chosen on the basis of what they *do*, not on the basis of how they impress. *And they know how they will be chosen.* While the type of approach used at Oregon has been decried by some psychologists (Holt, 1978) as failing to be "centralist" and "dynamic" (and everyone knows that the center is better than the periphery, and that dynamism is better than stagnation), it has two rather compelling things going for it. (1) It judges people on the basis of what they do (and how else should people be judged?) (2) It works.

REFERENCES

Bloom, R.F., and Brundage, E.G. "Prediction of Success in Elementary Schools for Enlisted Personnel." In D.B. Stuit (Ed.), *Personal Research and Test Develop-*

ment in the Bureau of Naval Personnel. Princeton, N.J.: Princeton University Press, 1947.

Burgess, E.W. "An Experiment in the Standardization of the Case-Study Method." *Sociometry*, 1941, 4, 329–348.

Darlington, R.B. "Another Look at Cultural Fairness." *Journal of Educational Measurement*, 1971, 3 (2), 71–82.

Dawes, R.M. "A Case Study of Graduate Admissions: Application of Three Principles of Human Decision-Making." *American Psychologist*, 1971, 26, 181–188.

"Shallow Psychology." In J. Carroll and J. Payne (Eds.), *Cognition and Social Behavior.* Hillsdale, N.J.: Erlbaum, 1976a.

"Multivariate Selection of Students in a Racist Society: A Systematically Unfair Approach." In M. Zelany (Ed.), *Multiple Criteria Decision Making: Kyoto 1975.* New York: Springer Verlag, 1976b.

"Case-by-Case Versus Rule-Generated Procedures for the Allocation of Scarce Resources." In M.F. Kaplan and S. Schwartz (Eds.), *Human Judgment and Decision Processes: Applications in an Applied Setting.* New York: Springer Verlag, 1977.

"The Robust Beauty of Improper Linear Models." *American Psychologist*, 1979, 34, 571–582.

Dawes, R.M., and Corrigan, B. "Linear Models in Decision Making." *Psychological Bulletin*, 1974, 81, 95–106.

Edwards, W.M. 'Technology for Director Dubious: Evaluation and Discussion in Public Contexts." In K.R. Hammond (Ed.), *Judgment and Decision in Public Policy Formation.* Boulder, Colo.: Westview Press, 1978.

Einhorn, H.J. "Expert Measurement and Mechanical Combination." *Organizational Behavior and Human Performance*, 1972, 7, 86–106.

Einhorn, H.J., and Hogarth, R.M. "Unit Weighting Schemes for Decision Making." *Organizational Behavior and Human Performance*, 1975, 13, 171–192.

Gardiner, P.C., and Edwards, W. "Public Values: Multiattribute–Utility Measurement for Social Decision Making." In M.F. Kaplan and S. Schwartz (Eds.), *Human Judgment and Decision Processes.* New York: Academic Press, 1975.

Goldberg, L.R. "Diagnostician Versus Diagnostic Signs: The Diagnosis of Psychosis Versus Neurosis from the MMPI." *Psychological Monographs*, 1965, 79 (9, whole No. 602).

"Admissions to the Ph.D. Program in the Department of Psychology." *American Psychologist*, 1977, 32, 663–668.

Green, B.F., Jr. "Parameter Sensitivity in Multivariate Methods." *Multivariate Behavioral Research*, 1977, 12, 263–287.

Holt, R.R. *Methods in Clinical Psychology.* Vol. 2: *Prediction and Research.* New York: Plenum Press, 1978.

Kelley, E.L. "Evaluation of the Interview as a Selection Technique." In *Proceedings of the 1953 International Conference on Testing Problems.* Princeton, N.J.: Educational Testing Service, 1954.

Libby, R. "Man Versus Model of Man: Some Conflicting Evidence." *Organizational Behavior and Human Performance*, 1976, 16, 1–12.

McCormack, W. "The Bakke Decision: Implications for Higher Education Admissions." A report of the ACE-AALS Committee on Education, American Council on Education, Association of American Law Schools, 1978.

Meehl, P.E. *Clinical Versus Statistical Prediction: A Theoretical Analysis and Review of the Literature*. Minneapolis: University of Minnesota Press, 1954.

Ramirez, A. "Cream of the Crop?" *The Wall Street Journal*, April 6, 1979, 193 (68), p. 1.

Rawls, J. "Justice as Fairness." *Philosophical Review*, 1958, 67, 164–194.

Sarbin, T.R. "A Contribution to the Study of Actuarial and Individual Methods of Prediction." *American Journal of Sociology*, 1943, 48, 593–602.

Sawyer, J. "Measurement *and* Prediction, Clinical *and* Statistical." *Psychological Bulletin*, 1966, 66, 178–200.

Schiedt, R. "*Ein Breitag zum Problem der Rückfallsprognose*." (Doctoral dissertation.) Munich: Müncher Zeitungs Verlag, 1936.

Shepard, R.N. "On Subjectively Optimal Selection Among Multi-Attribute Alternatives." In M.W. Shelley, and G.L. Bryan (Eds.), *Human Judgments and Optimality*. New York: Wiley, 1964.

Slovic, P., and MacPhillamy, D.J. "Dimensional Commensurability and Cue Utilization in Comparative Judgment." *Organizational Behavior and Human Performance*, 1974, 11, 172–194.

Thomas, E. "Choosing the Class of '83." *Time*, April 9, 1979, pp. 51–52.

Wainer, H. "Estimating Coefficients in Linear Models: It Don't Make No Nevermind." *Psychological Bulletin*, 1976, 83, 312–3;17.

Wainer, H., and Thissen, D. "Three Steps Toward Robust Regression." *Psychometrica*, 1976, 41, 9–34.

Zajonc, R.B. "Feeling and Thinking: Preferences Need No Inferences." *American Psychologist*, 1980, 35, 151–175.

7

---~---

FACTORS INFLUENCING THE USE OF A DECISION RULE IN A PROBABILISTIC TASK*

Hal R. Arkes, Robyn M. Dawes, Caryn Christensen

A number of researchers have drawn rather pessimistic conclusions concerning the human's ability to make accurate judgments in a wide variety of tasks. Such tasks include assessing the lethality of various disasters (Lichtenstein, Slovic, Fischhoff, Layman, & Combs, 1978), judging the extent of covariation between two events (Arkes & Harkness, 1983), predicting the success of prospective graduate students (Dawes, 1971), assessing the severity of Hodgkin's disease (Einhorn, 1972), and judging the quality of journal articles (Mahoney, 1977).

Perhaps as a result of the difficulty people have in making accurate judgments, decision aids and algorithms have been developed to help the decision maker in arriving at a sound conclusion. For example, every psychological test contains a set of procedures or instructions for interpreting or scoring test results.

Yet such aids are often ignored. For example, Goldberg (1968) devised a very simple unit weighted linear formula for using the Minnesota Multiphasic Personality Inventory (MMPI) to distinguish neurotics from psychotics with 70 percent accuracy. The fact that 70 percent is better than any group of clinicians has done on the same task has apparently not deterred clinical practitioners from eschewing the formula in favor of intuition based on "experience" (with little systematic feedback). Or consider projective tests. Because their reliability and validity is at best dubious, a nonpractitioner might believe that standardized scoring procedures would be rigidly followed in order to realize every possible iota of their putative validity. On the contrary, Wade and Baker (1977) report that only 18.5 percent of the clinicians they surveyed used standardized procedures, while 81.5 percent used personalized ("creative") procedures.

One reason why standardized scoring rules and decision aids may be shunned is that they are blatantly imperfect. The Goldberg formula has a hit rate of 70 percent. The clinicians surveyed by Wade and Baker

* First published in *Organizational Behavior and Human Decision Processes*, 37 (1986), 93–110. © 1986 Academic Press, Inc. Reprinted by permission.

apparently thought they could do better using their own scoring rules. Dawes (1979) suggests that in predicting outcomes important to us we want to be able to account for *all* of the variance (even when giving lip service to the vicissitudes of life). If we use a standardized procedure, we know we cannot predict everything. A performance of less than 100 percent still leaves "room for improvement" – particularly according to those whose background or training leads them to believe that they have special expertise. Perhaps many people are convinced that with more insight or effort improvement will surely occur.

When they abandon standard procedures, however, judges use cues inconsistently (Dawes & Corrigan, 1974). In contrast, statistical formulas, algorithms, etc., use cues perfectly consistently. Given a particular MMPI profile, for example, the Goldberg formula always makes the same prediction. Not so the human judge. Hammond and Summers (1972) have shown that this lack of consistency necessarily must detract from judgment performance.

The main purpose of this paper is to examine conditions under which a decision aid is not used. We realize that decision aids may involve computer displays, iterative Bayesian procedures, and other sophisticated techniques (e.g., Adelman, Donnell, Phelps, & Patterson, 1982). However, in our two studies, our aid consists of a very simple and very helpful classification rule: if a stimulus has characteristic X, the probability is .70 (.75 in Experiment 2) that it belongs in category A; otherwise it has a probability of .70 (.75 in Experiment 2) of belonging to category B. Subjects are free to use or not use the decision rule as they see fit.

In both of our studies subjects were presented with multiple cues to which they could apply (or not apply) the decision aid. In Experiment 1, three of the groups of subjects were given outcome feedback after each trial. Subjects who used the decision rule would have had to tolerate feedback indicating that only 70 percent of their decisions were correct while 30 percent of their decisions were incorrect.

A number of researchers have found that outcome feedback generally results in *decreased* accuracy on probabilistic tasks (Hammond, Summers, & Deane, 1973; Schmitt, Coyle, & King, 1976). In their task which most closely approximated that used in our Experiment 1, Schmitt *et al.* found that the detrimental effect of feedback on accuracy was due to the substantially reduced levels of response consistency. Brehmer and Kuylenstierna (1978) attempted to reduce response inconsistency by telling subjects that the task was probabilistic and that therefore subjects should not expect to be correct on every trial. No matter how explicit the experimenter made the instructions, however, subjects' responses were not affected in any way.

The first experiment examined decision rule use and judgment accuracy on a judgment task akin to those attempted by the practitioner who has a viable rule available.

Our first variable consisted of four different instructional conditions. In all conditions subjects were given a rule that would result in a performance level of 70 percent. In the control group subjects were told that 70 percent is "about as well as people can do." In an innovate group subjects were encouraged to try to surpass this level of performance by using their keen perception. Our hypothesis was that this instruction would motivate our subjects to attempt to account for more outcome variance than the task allows, and hence be more inconsistent and "innovative" than subjects in the control group. The third group was our debiasing group. Subjects were warned that abandonment of the rule would drastically hurt performance. We hypothesized that this debiasing would result in increased rule usage and thus higher accuracy. Our fourth group was similar to the control group except that no outcome feedback was provided. As mentioned above, previous research has indicated that such lack of feedback enhances performance; if that finding is replicated here, performance and consistency in this condition can be used as a standard against which to compare the deleterious effects of feedback combined with our three instructional sets.

Another variable we manipulated was presence or absence of monetary incentives for accurate judgment. Our overall hypothesis is that the *more* motivated our judges are the *less* they will rely on a judgment rule. Hence we predicted that incentive would have the paradoxical effect of decreasing performance due to the decrease in consistency.

In order to test these predictions we designed a judgment task with which undergraduate subjects could become involved. We presented subjects with what was purportedly a small sample of a student's transcript. From the cues on this transcript (courses and grades), subjects had to judge whether or not that student had graduated with honors.

EXPERIMENT I

Method

Subjects   Two hundred twenty-six undergraduates received extra course credit for their participation in the experiment.

Stimulus materials   Forty slides each consisted of the names of three academic courses and a grade after the name of each course. The only grades used were A and B. The courses were randomly selected from a list of the five most advanced undergraduate courses in every department at the University of Oregon. Excluded from this list were courses with the

Table 1 *Chart shown to subjects during Experiment 1*

	Honors?	
Number of A's	Yes (%)	No (%)
0	19	81
1	39	61
2	62	38
3	79	21

word "honors" in the title, courses cross-listed in more than one department, and courses with nondescript titles such as "seminar." The 40 slides were divided into fourths such that each fourth had 0, 1, 2 or 3 A's, respectively, after the names of the three courses. The position of the lone A or B on a slide (when that occurred) was counterbalanced.

Procedure   A chart identical to Table 1 was in full view during the whole experiment. The following instructions were read to all subjects, with the exception of the no-feedback subjects, who were not read the italicized words:

Today I'm going to ask you to participate in a judgment task. I'm going to present you with some information about each of 40 members of the Ohio University class of 1981. What you have to do is look at the information concerning each student and judge whether or not that student graduated with honors. Remember, all of the 40 students graduated. We want you to judge which ones graduated with honors and which ones graduated without honors.

Here's how the task will work. I'll display a slide on the screen for student number 1. That slide will show the grades the student earned in three randomly selected courses during his or her senior year. For example, the first slide might read, Organic Chemistry – A, Social Psychology – B, American History – A. You are to judge whether or not this student graduated with honors. Please make your judgment by checking the appropriate box on your answer sheet. Then *I'll tell you whether the student on slide number 1 actually did or did not graduate with honors. After I've given you this feedback,* we'll go on to student number 2. There will be 40 such student slides.

To facilitate your judgments, we've compiled a chart based on a survey of the entire class of 1981. You can see that those who have no A's among the three randomly chosen courses are likely not to have graduated with honors. As the number of A's increases, the student is more likely to have been an honors graduate. For example, only 19 percent of the students with no A's among the three randomly chosen courses graduated with honors. In contrast, 79 percent of the students with all A's graduated with honors. In general, those who got no A's or 1 A in the three courses were not likely to have graduated with honors. Those who got 2 or 3 A's were likely to have graduated with honors. A rule you can therefore use is to guess "honors" when a student has 2 or 3 A's and guess "not honors" when a student has 0 or 1 A. In that way you'll get most of them right.

At this point the instructions for the groups diverged. The control group and no-feedback group were told:

There's one more thing you ought to know. If you use the rule based on the number of A's, you'll get about 70 percent correct on this task. That's about as well as people can do. Some people think that if they are really observant, they might do better. However, we haven't found evidence that people really can do much better than the 70 percent.

The innovate group was told:

There's one more thing you ought to know. I can tell you from our experience with this task that most people can't judge at a rate better than 70 percent correct on this task. However, we think that people who are extremely observant might be able to beat the 70 percent level. Give it a try.

The debiasing group was told:

There's one more thing you ought to know. I can tell you from our experience with this task that no one – not even experts – can judge at a rate better than 70 percent correct on this task. People who try to do better than 70 percent on this task actually do a lot worse. So just follow an obvious strategy that will allow you to get most of the answers right.

All subjects were given four practice trials. Subjects other than those in the no-feedback group received feedback after each practice trial. The experimenter then repeated the appropriate instructions that had pertained specifically to the control, innovate, debiasing, and no-feedback groups.

Each of these four groups was divided into three subgroups: no money, salary, and award. The no-money group received no special instructions. The salary group heard:

There's one final important piece of information. We'll pay each of you a dime for each correct answer you give. For instance, since there are 40 questions, you will receive a total of $4 if you answer all questions correctly. If you answer 20 of the 40 questions correctly, you will receive $2.

The award group heard instead:

There's one final important piece of information. We'll pay $5 to the person who gets the greatest number correct. If two or more of you tie, we'll randomly choose the winner from among those tied.

All groups except the no-feedback group were read the following paragraph, the no-feedback group receiving instead only the first three sentences of the paragraph:

Each slide will be shown for 10 s. At the end of 10 s I'll say "Mark." If you haven't marked the "honors" or "not honors" box already, you should do so immediately. A few seconds after I say "Mark," I'll tell you what the correct answer was. Be sure to put your answer down before I give you the correct answer.

The answer sheet contained two columns of 40 lines. One column was labeled "honors" and the other "not honors." Each slide was shown for 20 s. After the first 10 s, the experimenter said "Mark." Five seconds later the correct feedback was given ("honors" or "not honors") to all but the no-feedback subjects. Five seconds after that the slide tray was advanced.

The feedback was given almost precisely according to the scheme in Table 1. The actual percentages of honors feedback for the 0-, 1-, 2-, and 3-A groups were 20, 40, 60, and 80, respectively. The numbers in Table 1 were altered slightly from these real percentages so as to make the chart look more representative of a real survey. Within each slide type (0, 1, 2, or 3 A's) the order of the feedback was random, given the constraint of the frequency of "honors" and "not honors" feedback within each type.

Given this procedure, the subjects who followed the rule (guess "honors" if 2 or 3 A's; guess "not honors" otherwise) would judge correctly 70 percent of the time. Subjects who ignore the rule would judge correctly only 50 percent of the time. Due to the randomization and counterbalancing procedures we employed, use of the rule was the *only* way (other than sheer luck) to perform well on this task.

No-money, salary, and award subjects within the control group numbered 22, 18, and 16; within the innovate group they numbered 20, 17, and 21; within the debiasing group they numbered 18, 20 and 17; within the no-feedback group they numbered 22, 19, and 16. Subjects were run in small groups (8–12 per group) in an otherwise empty classroom.

Results

A 3 (Incentive: none, salary, award) × 4 (Group: control, innovate, debias, no feedback) analysis of variance was performed on the number of correct judgments. The incentive main effect was significant, $F(2,214) = 5.89$, as was the group main effect, $F(3,214) = 6.92$, both p's $< .01$, both $MS_e = 6.50$. The interaction did not approach significance. Figure 1 presents these data.

We used an a priori contrast (Myers, 1972, p. 362) to compare the no-money group with the two incentive groups: the two types of incentive resulted in *fewer* correct judgments than did no incentive ($p < .01$).

We also contrasted the debiasing group with the control and innovate groups: the debiasing group judged significantly more accurately ($p < .01$). Encouragement to abandon the rule led to performance indistinguishable from that of the control group. Finally, the performance of the no-feedback group was comparable to that of the debiasing group and significantly better than that of the control group ($p < .01$). To summarize these results of the instructional variable, the debiasing instructions and the omission of feedback were effective in raising performance.

Our hypothesized reason for the relatively higher accuracy in the no-money and debiasing groups was that subjects in such groups would more consistently use the rule. We hypothesized that highly motivated and "innovative" subjects would be more likely to abandon whatever hypothesis they were using after judging incorrectly on a given trial. We tested this hypothesis directly by examining each subject's pattern of judgments.

Suppose a subject sees a stimulus with two A's and a B, guesses "honors," and is then told that "not honors" was the correct judgment. Four stimuli later the subject sees another instance of two A's and a B. A subject who again guesses "honors" has maintained his or her (probably correct) hypothesis despite the prior negative feedback. We simply counted the number of times each subject kept his or her hypothesis on the next instance of a stimulus given an error on the prior instance of that type of stimulus. We hypothesized that the higher accuracy of the debias and no-incentive groups was due to their greater tendency to maintain hypotheses despite occasional instances of negative feedback.

Figure 1 Number of correct judgments as a function of instructions and incentive. △, Control; ×, debias; □, innovate; ⊠, no feedback

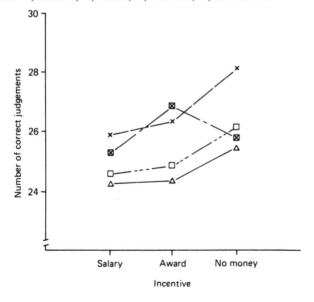

For every subject we calculated the proportion of error trials which were followed by hypothesis maintenance. This dependent variable was entered into a 3×4 analysis of variance analogous to the prior analysis. As was the case in that analysis, the group factor was significant, $F(3,214) = 3.56, p < .02, MS_e = 305.69$. An a priori contrast revealed that the debias group maintained their hypotheses significantly more often than the control and innovate groups ($p < .025$). The no-feedback group also maintained their hypotheses more often than did the control and innovate groups ($p < .025$). Unlike the results of the prior analysis of variance, the incentive main effect only approached significance, $F(2,214) = 2.22, p = .11, MS_e = 305.69$. Figure 2 depicts these data.

Discussion

In most concept formation (Bruner, Goodnow, & Austin, 1956) and problem-solving tasks, a win–stay, lose–shift strategy is eminently rational. If what you are doing led to a wrong answer, change what you are doing. If what you are doing worked, continue to do it. In a probabilistic task, however, the lose–shift strategy will be counterproductive if it is used after every error. This is due to the fact that in a probabilistic task, even the best strategy will result in some errors. If an

Figure 2 Hypothesis maintenance after error trials as a function of instructions and incentive. △, Control; ×, debias; □, innovate; ⊠, no feedback

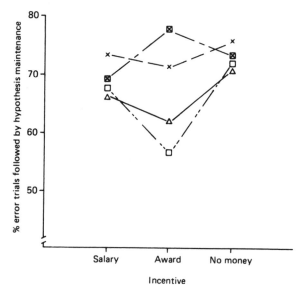

error results in the abandonment of the optimal strategy, then perform-ance will necessarily suffer. Experiment 1 has shown that those who are not given an incentive for good judgment are less likely to shift strategies and therefore will have higher performance.

Despite the fact that the salary and award groups both have a financial incentive, they do have a potential difference in their optimal strategy. A subject in the award group might decide to abandon the rule if he or she felt that everyone else would use the rule. Since only the best judge will receive the $5 award for best performance, use of the rule would not enable one to surpass the performance of those who might also be assumed to be using it. For example, in duplicate bridge tournaments, where the incentive is to do *better* than players at other tables, declarers will violate standard safe rules for making contracts in order to have a chance of an overtrick.

Such reasoning would not apply to the salary group. They receive more money for more correct judgments, irrespective of anyone else's perform-ance. There is no good reason to abandon the rule in this case. Yet both incentive groups do so. In a probabilistic task, enthusiastic adherence to a lose–shift strategy is detrimental. One must be tolerant of occasional errors in such a task. Apparently highly motivated subjects are less likely to be patient with such errors.

A second important finding is that the innovate and control groups performed equivalently. This leads us to conclude that control group subjects, informed of the decision rule and its efficacy, use it as little as those explicitly told to find a better strategy. The debiasing group subjects, warned of the negative consequences of forsaking the rule, used it to a significantly greater extent than the other two groups.

The superiority of the no-feedback group over the control group is consistent with previous research indicating that outcome feedback results in decreased accuracy on probabilistic tasks (Hammond *et al.*, 1973; Schmitt *et al.*, 1976). The relatively high performance of the no-feedback was comparable to that of the debias group. Furthermore, subjects in both the debias and no-feedback groups maintained their hypotheses more than subjects in the control group did. In light of the similar performance of the no-feedback and debias groups, we hypo-thesize that the debiasing instructions may have led subjects to disregard the negative outcome feedback, thus promoting their toleration of the errors that are a necessary feature of a probabilistic task.

Because our judgment rule stated what the proportion of honors graduates was for each number of A grades, the rule thereby provided base rate information. A large amount of research has been conducted during the last decade in order to determine if and when subjects would use base rate information in their predictions and judgments. Early research (Kahneman & Tversky, 1973) emphasized the underutilization of base rate information. In their most widely cited experiment, Kahneman and Tversky (1973) presented people with a brief description of Tom W. Some subjects were told that Tom's description was randomly drawn from descriptions of 100 people, 70 of whom were lawyers and 30 of whom were engineers. Other subjects were told that the 100 people were composed of 30 lawyers and 70 engineers. Both groups gave estimates of 50 percent as the probability that Tom was an engineer (median estimates). Thus the groups did not fully use the base rate information (70:30, 30:70) in arriving at their estimate.

Subsequent researchers have documented a number of factors which appear to foster the use of base rates. First, the base rate is used more when it appears to bear a causal relation to the individual case (e.g. Ajzen, 1977). For example, the proportion of blue and green cabs in a city does not appear to influence subjects' judgments about the color of a reckless taxi as much as does the proportion of blue and green cabs involved in accidents in that city (Bar-Hillel, 1980). Second, Manis, Dovalina, Avis, and Cardoze (1980) suggest that when a subject has to make a discrete prediction ("Is she a Democrat or Republican?"), the base rate will be used more than when a continuous response measure is employed ("What is the probability from 0.0 to 1.0 that she is a Democrat?"). Third, when no individual case information is presented, subjects will use base rates in categorizing the individual case (Kahneman & Tversky, 1973). Fourth, when subjects are assured that the individual case or cases are a representative sample, base rates are used more than when no such assurances are given (Hansen & Donoghue, 1977; Wells & Harvey, 1977). Fifth, when subjects are asked to adopt a "judgment orientation," base rates are used more than when a "clinical orientation" is induced (Zukier & Pepitone, 1984).

In all of these studies an independent variable is manipulated and its influence on base rate utilization is assessed. However, our research differs from these traditional base rate studies in one very significant way: we *explicitly tell* the subjects precisely how effective the use of the base rate will be. In our research the base rate is bluntly advanced as a helpful decision rule which will aid the subject in performing the judgment task; subjects are informed on the percentage of correct answers that they will attain if they use the base rate in a particular way. Thus our research differed from prior base rate studies in that any benefit of base rate usage did not have to be discovered by our subjects.

EXPERIMENT 2

That incentive caused a decrease in judgment performance was a paradoxical result found in Experiment 1. In Experiment 2 we attempted to demonstrate another paradoxical result: expertise can result in poorer judgment performance.

The task used in Experiment 2 differed in an important respect from that used in Experiment 1. In the first experiment the only valid basis for judging "honors" or "not honors" was the number of A's. Due to counterbalancing and randomization procedures, no other cue was related in any systematic way with the to-be-predicted event – graduation with or without honors. Thus subjects could not successfully use any real-world knowledge base to improve their task performance. In Experiment 2 we used a realistic baseball judgment task. Subjects well informed about baseball would have a substantial knowledge base to bring to bear upon the task. A reasonable assumption might be that this knowledge would necessarily be an asset on a baseball judgment task.

However, expertise has been shown to be a detriment in some memory tasks (e.g., Arkes & Freedman, 1984; Arkes & Harkness, 1980; Chase & Simon, 1973). In study 1 of Arkes and Harkness (1980), for example, speech therapists who correctly made a diagnosis of Down's syndrome later falsely recognized Down's syndrome symptoms that were not present in the original symptom set. Therapists unable to make the initial diagnosis showed significantly more accurate recognition performance.

In the present study we examined the willingness to use a decision rule. Those who consider themselves experts might deem such an aid to be quite unnecessary for themselves. This would be a manifestation of what Dawes (1976) has called "cognitive conceit." Those who do not consider themselves experts might choose to use the aid, thereby surpassing the judgment performance of the experts.

Method

Subjects   Forty-two undergraduates received course credit for their participation in the experiment.

Stimulus materials   The first 33 items of the baseball questionnaire used by Arkes and Freedman (1984) were used in this study. These questions dealt with rules and terminology of baseball. These items were used to assess knowledge of baseball.

The judgment task involved choosing which one of three possible players won the "Most Valuable Player" Award in the National League each year from 1940 to 1961, excluding those few years in which pitchers won the award. For each year subjects saw a list of three players' names with four pieces of information after each name: the player's batting average, number of home runs, and number of runs batted in for that year, and the position in the standings that his team finished. For each year we listed completely accurate information for the award winner and two other players who had outstanding performances that year. The order of the listing of the three players was random within each year.

Procedure   All subjects were tested in one large group. First the 33-item baseball quiz was administered to the students. Twelve minutes were allowed for its completion. The judgment task followed immediately. The following instructions were read:

> We are interested in the way you make difficult judgments. In order to investigate this topic, we want you to judge which of three people won the Most Valuable Player Award in the National League from 1940 to 1961. For each year we will present you with the names of three players. One of them really did win the award. The other two did not win it. Beside each player's name we will present four pieces of information to help you make your decision. These pieces of information are
> a   The person's batting average that year,
> b   The number of home runs the person hit that year,
> c   The number of runs batted in that year,
> d   What position the player's team finished that year.
> (One means the player's team finished in first place, 2 means second place, etc.)

An example was provided at this time using the 1974 baseball season statistics for Steve Garvey, Mike Schmidt, and Johnny Bench.

> Before you begin the real list, we ought to explain why we've included where a player's team finished that year. If two players had good years, but one was on a first-place team while the other was on the third-place team, the player on the first-place team was *very* likely to have won the award. In general, being on a team that finished "high up" in the standings is a huge advantage in winning the Most Valuable Player Award. In fact, if you choose for each year the player whose team finished highest in the standings about 75 percent of your choices will be correct.

> OK. For each year circle the name of the player who you think won the award.

It should be noted that the rule was accurately described. Use of the rule would result in a correct judgment rate of 74 percent. It should also be noted that there was nothing artificial or deceptive in this judgment task. The four pieces of information we provided concerning each player's offensive performance and team standing are indeed the major factors determining the winner of the Most Valuable Player Award (for all candidates who are not pitchers).

With one exception, for each year we listed three players whose teams finished in three different places in the standings. The exception was 1959. We inadvertently listed two players who both played for the second-place Milwaukee Braves. Since the award winner that year, Ernie Banks, played for the fifth-place Cubs, subjects who attempted to follow the rule by choosing either Brave would be scored equivalently; in either case their judgment would be incorrect.

Twelve minutes were allowed for the judgment task, at the completion of which subjects were asked to estimate how many correct judgments they had made. Subjects were told that 19 correct was the maximum, since that was the number of questions. They were told that 6 was the minimum, since random guesses would result in about one-third of the 19 being correct. Subjects were finally asked to what extent their judgments were influenced by the rule, "Choose the player whose team finished highest in the standings." Subjects used a 7-point scale anchored by *I never used that rule* (1) to *I always used that rule* (7).

Results

We wanted to compare the judgment performance of those who know a great deal about baseball to those who know only a moderate amount. We did not want to generalize our results to those who were ignorant about baseball, since those completely unfamiliar with a topic are generally not called upon to render judgments in that area. Therefore we excluded the data of 14 subjects who answered more than 75 percent of the 33 questionnaire items incorrectly. (These included foreign female subjects who knew absolutely nothing about baseball.) The remaining subjects were divided into the moderate-knowledge group (16 people who scored between 9 and 18 on the questionnaire) and the high-knowledge group (12 people who scored above 18).

The moderate-knowledge group significantly exceeded the high-knowledge group in number of correct judgments, 11.4 to 9.4, $t(26) = 2.42$, $p < .05$. (Both groups fell short of the 14 items they would have judged correctly had they consistently used the rule.) The moderate-knowledge group used the rule significantly more often, 4.7 to 3.7, $t(26) = 2.15$, $p < .05$. Despite the fact that the moderate-knowledge group had higher performance, they gave a lower estimated number of correct judgments than the other group, 10.7 to 11.8. The discrepancy between estimated number correct and actual number correct differed significantly between the groups, $t = 2.70$, $p < .02$. The moderate-knowledge group was slightly underconfident (estimated correct minus actual correct = −0.62), while the high-knowledge group was seriously overconfident (estimated correct minus actual correct = 2.42). Table 2 contains a matrix depicting the correlations between these variables.

Discussion

One of the dangers of overconfidence is that one feels that no assistance is needed. If one assumes that his or her judgment is quite good, decision aids would be entirely superfluous. Indeed, in Experiment 2 the more

Table 2 *Intercorrelations between variables of Experiment 2*

Variables	(1)	(2)	(3)	(4)	(5)
Quiz score (1)	1.00				
Correct judgments (2)	−.40*	1.00			
Estimated correct					
judgments (3)	.32*	.08	1.00		
Extent of rule use (4)	−.47**	.58**	−.37*	1.00	
Estimated minus actual					
corr. judgments (5)	.53**	−.64**	.71**	−.69**	1.00

knowledgeable subjects were less likely to use the rule, which resulted in inferior performance.

While their study did not use subjects of differing knowledge levels in a particular domain, Dollinger and Riger (1984) did obtain results that are related to ours. Dollinger and Riger (1984) asked subjects to watch videotapes of robbery "suspects" responding in a word-association task. The word associations were the critical cues in differentiating guilty suspects from innocent ones, and subjects who used these cues were successful in making the differentiation. Other subjects apparently chose to use a complex combination of word associations, tone of voice, facial expression, and other characteristics of the suspect to arrive at their judgment. These subjects performed more poorly on the judgment task. We hypothesize that an analogous result occurred in our study. The moderate-knowledge subjects were not confident. They therefore accepted the assistance provided by the decision rule and consequently performed well. The high-knowledge subjects were relatively confident. They therefore used the rule less, instead weighing the merits of home run superiority versus batting average superiority, etc. Their reliance on such characteristics resulted in relatively poor performance.

GENERAL DISCUSSION

The results of these two studies suggest three factors which influence the likelihood that a decision rule will be used in a probabilistic task. In Experiment 1 we learned that incentive for high performance resulted in less use of the decision rule whether the incentive was given for each correct judgment or for the best performance among a group of judges. Also in Experiment 1 we learned that warning subjects of the counter-productive results of abandoning the rule caused the subjects to use the rule more. In fact, the warning enabled subjects to overcome the usually deleterious effects of outcome feedback in a probabilistic task. Finally, we learned in Experiment 2 that those with expertise (or those who judged themselves to have expertise) were less likely to use a decision rule than those with less expertise. By choosing not to use the rule, such "experts" performed worse but had higher confidence in their performance than the nonexperts.

The first factor, incentives for good performance, actually resulted in poorer performance. Since the use of the decision rule was the *only* way (other than lucky guessing) to achieve good performance, poorer performance by both incentive groups necessitates the conclusion that incentives resulted in less use of the decision rule. Very few studies have demonstrated the detrimental influence of incentives on current task performance. (See B. Schwartz, 1982, for an example.) Probabilistic tasks represent a special case in which such a result is the rule rather than the exception. In a probabilistic task subjects who are using the best strategy must be willing to tolerate errors without resorting to a strategy shift. Subjects receiving incentives for good performance apparently find it difficult to maintain their strategy while making the incorrect choices which are endemic to any probabilistic task. This would explain why accuracy and hypothesis maintenance were highest when incentives were not given.

The other independent variable used in Experiment 1 – instructions – has also been investigated in previous probabilistic learning experiments. In a comprehensive review article, Myers (1976) concluded that it is virtually impossible to convince subjects to adhere rigidly to the optimal strategy. In prior research neither instructions nor incentives have been effective in causing a majority of subjects to follow the optimal strategy on every trial. We found that the threat of poorer performance if the decision rule were abandoned was effective in eliciting significantly better adherence to the optimal strategy. In fact, the no-incentive–debias group made an average of 28.2 correct responses out of 40, which is very close to the 28 correct responses that would have been achieved had the rule been followed on every trial.

The factors we examined in our two studies are present in a large number of important decision-making contexts. For example, due to their long period of training clinical psychologists are presumed to have considerable expertise. They receive substantial monetary incentives. And finally, creative or innovative use of diagnostic signs is apparently not at all discouraged (Little & Schneidman, 1959). Therefore decision aids are rather unlikely to be used (Wade & Baker, 1977).

The medical diagnosis situation provides another example. Both high incentive and expertise are present. Numerous articles and letters in the medical literature contain evidence that many physicians are wary of algorithms and computer-assisted diagnoses because such assistance takes the "art" out of clinical judgment. (See W.B. Schwartz, 1979, and

Komaroff, 1982, for a summary of such concerns.) Many physicians would rather use personal decision rules instead of boring algorithms. A report by deDombal, Leaper, Horrocks, Staniland, and McCann (1974) illustrates this point. During an 18-month period the authors used a computer-based diagnosis system which surpassed physicians in diagnostic accuracy. During the course of this research after each physician made a diagnosis, he or she was informed of the computer's diagnosis. The diagnostic accuracy of the physicians gradually rose toward that of the computer during the 18-month period. The authors attributed this improvement in part to the "discipline" forced upon the physicians, the constraint of carefully collecting patient information, the "constant emphasis on reliability of clinical data collected, and the rapid 'feedback' from the computer," which may have promoted learning. When the computer system was terminated, the physicians very quickly reverted to their previous lower level of diagnostic accuracy. Apparently discipline and reliability fell victim to creativity and inconsistency.

Note that in both the psychological and medical diagnosis scenarios described above, there exist well-meaning diagnosticians with high motivation, high expertise, and few constraints on innovative tendencies. These are the conditions under which decision aids are less likely to be used – to the detriment of those being served.

REFERENCES

Adelman, L., Donnell, M.L., Phelps, R.H., & Patterson, J.F. (1982). An iterative Bayesian decision aid: Toward improving the user-aid and user-organization interfaces. *IEEE Transactions on Systems, Man, and Cybernetics*, 12, 733–743.
Ajzen, I. (1977). Intuitive theories of events and effects of base-rate information on prediction. *Journal of Personality and Social Psychology*, 35, 303–314.
Arkes, H.R., & Freedman, M.R. (1984). A demonstration of the costs and benefits of expertise in recognition memory. *Memory & Cognition*, 12, 84–89
Arkes, H.R., & Harkness, A.R. (1980). The effect of making a diagnosis on subsequent recognition of symptoms. *Journal of Experimental Psychology: Human Learning and Memory*, 6, 568–575.
(1983). Estimates of contingency between two dichotomous variables. *Journal of Experimental Psychology: General*, 112, 117–135.
Bar-Hillel, M. (1980). The base-rate fallacy in probability judgments. *Acta Psychologica*, 44, 211–233.
Brehmer, B., & Kuylenstierna, J. (1978). Task information and performance in probabilistic inference tasks. *Organizational Behavior and Human Performance*, 22, 445–464.
Bruner, J.S., Goodnow, J.J., & Austin, G.A. (1956). *A study of thinking*. New York: Wiley.

Chase, W.G., & Simon, H.A. (1973). Perception in chess. *Cognitive Psychology*, 4, 55–81.

Dawes, R.M. (1971). A case study of graduate admissions: Application of three principles of human decision making. *American Psychologist*, 26, 180–188.

(1976). Shallow psychology. In J.S. Carroll & J.W. Payne (Eds.), *Cognition and social behavior*. Hillsdale, NJ: Erlbaum.

(1979). The robust beauty of improper linear models in decision making. *American Psychologist*, 34, 571–582.

Dawes, R.M., & Corrigan, B. (1974). Linear models in decision making. *Psychological Bulletin*, 81, 95–106.

deDombal, F.T., Leaper, D.J., Horrocks, J.C., Staniland, J.R., & McCann, A.P. (1974). Human and computer-aided diagnosis of abdominal pain: Further report with emphasis on performance of clinicians. *British Medical Journal*, 1, 376–380.

Dollinger, S.J., & Riger, A.L. (1984). On penetrating the "mask": The role of sagacity and acumen in a word-association/clinical-judgment task. *Journal of Personality and Social Psychology*, 46, 145–152.

Einhorn, H.J. (1972). Expert measurement and mechanical combination. *Organizational Behavior and Human Performance*, 7, 86–106.

Goldberg, L.R. (1968). Simple models or simple processes? Some research on clinical judgments. *American Psychologist*, 23, 483–496.

Hammond, K.R., & Summers, D.A. (1972). Cognitive control. *Psychological Review*, 79, 58–67.

Hammond, K.R., Summers, D.A., & Deane, D.H. (1973). Negative effects of outcome feedback in multiple cue probability learning experiments. *Organizational Behavior and Human Performance*, 9, 30–34.

Hansen, R.D., & Donoghue, J.M. (1977). The power of consensus: Information derived from one's own behavior. *Journal of Personality and Social Psychology*, 35, 294–302.

Kahneman, D., & Tversky, A. (1973). On the psychology of prediction. *Psychological Review*, 80, 237–251.

Komaroff, A.L. (1982). Algorithms and the "art" of medicine. *American Journal of Public Health*, 72, 10–12.

Lichtenstein, S., Slovic, P., Fischhoff, B., Layman, M., & Combs, B. (1978). Judged frequency of lethal events. *Journal of Experimental Psychology: Human Learning and Memory*, 4, 551–578.

Little, K.B., & Schneidman, E.S. (1959). Congruencies among interpretations of psychological test and anamnestic data. *Psychological Monographs*, 73 (6, Whole No. 476).

Mahoney, M.J. (1977). Publication prejudices. An experimental study of confirmatory bias in the peer review system. *Cognitive Therapy and Research*, 1, 161–175.

Manis, M., Dovalina, I., Avis, N.E., & Cardoze, S. (1980). Base rates can affect individual predictions. *Journal of Personality and Social Psychology*, 38, 231–248.

Myers, J.L. (1972). *Fundamentals of experimental design* (2nd ed.). Boston: Allyn & Bacon.

(1976). Probability learning and sequence learning. In W.K. Estes (Ed.), *Handbook of learning and cognitive processes* (Vol. 6). Hillsdale, NJ: Erlbaum.

Schmitt, N., Coyle, B.W., & King, L. (1976). Feedback and task predictability as determinants of performance in multiple cue probability learning tasks. *Organizational Behavior and Human Performance*, 16, 388–402.

Schwartz, B. (1982). Reinforcement-induced behavioral stereotypy: How not to teach people to discover rules. *Journal of Experimental Psychology: General*, 111, 23–59.

Schwartz, W.B. (1979). Decision analysis: A look at the chief complaints. *New England Journal of Medicine*, 300, 556–559.

Wade, T.C., & Baker, T.B. (1977). Opinions and use of psychological tests: A survey of clinical psychologists. *American Psychologist*, 32, 874–882.

Wells, G.L., & Harvey, J.H. (1977). Do people use consensus information in making causal attributions? *Journal of Personality and Social Psychology*, 35, 279–293.

Zukier, H., & Pepitone, A. (1984). Social roles and strategies in prediction: Some determinants of the use of base-rate information. *Journal of Personality and Social Psychology*, 47, 349–360.

8

ACCEPTING ERROR TO MAKE LESS ERROR*

Hillel J. Einhorn

On a recent program of *Wall Street Week*, the eminent economist Milton Friedman was being interviewed by Louis Rukeyser. Mr Rukeyser, who is a cynic about clinical and statistical prediction, asked Friedman what he would do about the Federal Reserve Board, which has been an object of Friedman's criticism for many years. Without missing a beat, Friedman replied, "I would get rid of them." After expressing surprise, Rukeyser asked, "What would you use to replace them?" "A computer," responded Mr Friedman. He then went on to explain that the money supply should be set by using a simple rule that is consistently applied. This would, he argued, provide for more stability and certainty in determining economic policy.

Whatever the merits of his argument, I feel confident (i.e., probability = .999) that the idea of replacing the Federal Reserve Board by a computer algorithm will seem absurd and dangerous to most people. Be that as it may, the point of this example is to illustrate that the clinical versus statistical prediction controversy is enduring and general. Not only is the controversy alive and well in economics, but the rapid growth in computer use will spread the conflict to new fields and intensify the battle where it already exists.

The purpose of this article is to understand why the controversy exists and persists. In what follows, I argue that the clinical and statistical approaches rest on quite different philosophical assumptions about the nature of error and the appropriate level of accuracy to be expected in prediction. To examine these issues, a case is made for each approach. Thereafter, a decision analysis is introduced to examine the costs and benefits of subscribing to each position.

THE CLINICAL APPROACH

Clinicians are determinists in their diagnostic activities. That is, symptoms, signs, and the like are viewed as manifestations of underlying causal

* First published in *Journal of Personality Assessment*, 50 (1986), 387–95. © 1986 Society of Personality Assessment, Inc. Reprinted by permission.

processes that can be known in principle. Because much clinical reasoning involves diagnosis or backward inference (i.e., making inferences from effects to prior causes), the clinician, like the historian, has much latitude (or degrees of freedom) in reconstructing the past to make the present seem most likely (a kind of maximum likelihood approach, if you will). However, when engaging in prediction or forward inference, one is soon confronted with discrepancies between predicted and actual outcomes. Such discrepancies are often surprising, especially if the explanation for past behavior provides a coherent account of the facts. One is reminded of the unpleasant surprise that awaits the modeler who fits the data with many parameters only to find that the model cannot predict new cases. Thus, it is often the case that the power of post hoc explanation is matched by the paucity of predictive validity.

Given the fluency of causal reasoning, it is not difficult to construct reasons for why discrepancies in prediction occur. Indeed, in hindsight, it seems as if the outcomes could not have been otherwise (see Fischhoff, 1975, on "hindsight bias" as a form of creeping determinism). However, to what degree can (should) prediction errors be explained? It is at this point that the clinical and statistical approaches diverge, with the divergence having much to do with the meaning and significance of "random error."

Although the concept of randomness is complex and difficult to define (Lopes, 1982), it suggests an irreducible unpredictability and disorder of outcomes. The basic question then becomes: How much of behavior is random and how much is systematic? The answer depends on what is meant by randomness. For example, consider the random walk theory of stock market prices. Although most people have not heard of this theory, many have first hand experience with its implications. Do stock prices follow a random walk? To date, the market remains difficult to predict (many have tried unsuccessfully). However, does that mean that it is impossible to do so? Imagine that there is a seven-way interaction that predicts price·changes, but no one has yet induced it from the mass of complex and noisy data that is available. If there is hidden systematicity, one's gamble in searching for a predictive rule may pay off. On the other hand, such an interaction may not exist, despite the fact that there are "experts" selling advice on what stocks to buy (are they simply selling "snake oil"?). Thus, if prediction error is due to our lack of knowledge and if randomness is only a label for our current ignorance, there are at least two reactions. The first is characteristic of the clinical approach; it says that the goal of perfect predictability, although difficult to attain, is not impossible. Moreover, this goal may be useful in itself because it can motivate the search for improved predictability via increased understanding of the causal texture of the environment (Tolman & Brunswik, 1935).

The second reaction is characteristic of the statistical approach and emphasizes the possibility of a futile search for a Holy Grail. This is considered in greater detail later.

The importance of causal understanding, which is essential to the clinical approach, has other implications. Although the controversy between the clinical and statistical approaches centers on prediction, has too much attention been given to prediction per se? To illustrate, consider the following scenario:

Imagine that you lived several thousand years ago and belonged to a tribe of methodologically sophisticated cave-dwellers. Your methodological sophistication is such that you have available to you all present day means of the methodological arsenal – details of the principles of deductive logic, probability theory, access to computational equipment, etc. However, your level of substantive knowledge lags several thousand years behind your methodological sophistication. In particular, you have little knowledge about physics, chemistry or biology. In recent years, your tribe has noted an alarming decrease in its birth-rate. Furthermore, the tribe's statistician estimates that unless the trend is shortly reversed, extinction is a real possibility. The tribe's chief has accordingly launched an urgent project to determine the cause of birth. You are a member of the project team and have been assured that all means, including various forms of experimentation with human subjects, will be permitted to resolve this crucial issue. (Einhorn & Hogarth, 1982, p. 23)

The foregoing story illustrates the following points. First, the goal of prediction is to provide guidance for taking action. Therefore, prediction is intimately tied to decision making and should be evaluated within this context. Indeed, one might find small consolation in being able to predict accurately when the tribe will become extinct. Second, when decisions are based on predictions, the determination of forecast accuracy is problematic because outcomes are a function of predictions and actions (Einhorn & Hogarth, 1978). For example, if the president takes strong antirecession measures based on predictions of an economic slow-down, how is one to evaluate the accuracy of the forecast? Consider the outcome of no recession. This could result from an incorrect forecast and a useless action or from an accurate forecast and a highly effective action. Similarly, a recession could indicate an accurate forecast with an ineffective action or an inaccurate forecast with an action that causes the malady it is intended to prevent. Some actions are taken to counteract the prediction of undesirable events, but other actions cause the very outcomes that are predicted. For example:

People in a small town hear a rumor that the banks are about to fail. They think that if this forecast is accurate, they had better withdraw their money as soon as possible. Accordingly, they go to the banks to close their accounts (those sceptical of the forecast see many people withdrawing money and either take this as a sign that the rumor is true or foresee the consequences of waiting too long, thus joining the crowd in either case). By the end of the day the banks have failed, thereby confirming the rumor. (Einhorn & Hogarth, 1982, p. 24)

Note that awareness of such self-fulfilling prophecies is often low and can lead to overconfidence in predictions that are of low or even zero accuracy (see Einhorn, 1980; Einhorn & Hogarth, 1978).

Third, in order to understand the relations between predictions, actions, and outcomes, one needs a causal model of the process. In this regard, the clinical approach, with its emphasis on diagnosis and causal understanding, is important. Moreover, the role of clinical judgment in the development of models and the determination of relevant variables has been sadly neglected. Consider the following conclusion from the literature on clinical versus statistical prediction stated by Dawes and Corrigan (1974): "the whole trick is to decide what variables to look at and then to know how to add" (p. 105). Assuming we can add, how do we decide what variables to look at? Such decisions must rest on some implicit or explicit theory of the phenomenon that allows one to distinguish relevant from irrelevant factors. Therefore, prediction depends on backward inference, which involves both the forming of hypotheses to interpret the past and the choosing of relevant from irrelevant variables in that interpretation.

THE STATISTICAL APPROACH

Although the clinical approach rests on the worthy and optimistic goal of perfect predictability, it is a goal that can have negative consequences, which are noted later. The statistical approach, on the other hand, accepts error. This acceptance can occur in several ways. First, one may believe that the world is inherently uncertain. In this case, probabilistic knowledge is the best we can hope for, and random error cannot be reduced by greater knowledge. Second, one can maintain determinism at the level of the physical world but believe that our knowledge of that world will always be fragmentary and hence uncertain. In this case, randomness is due to ignorance, but the goal of perfect predictability is abandoned as being too unrealistic. Third, the use of any equation or algorithm, with its limited number of variables and mechanical combining rule, can never capture the richness and full complexity of the phenomenon it is meant to predict (recall Meehl's discussion of "broken leg cues," 1954, p. 25). Thus, models are simplifications of reality that must lead to errors in prediction (cf. Chapanis, 1961).

Let us now consider how the acceptance of error can lead to less error. To do so, recall the research on probability learning done several years ago (e.g., Edwards, 1956; Estes, 1962). In these studies, either a red or green light is illuminated on each of a number of trials, and subjects are asked to predict which light will go on. If the prediction is correct, subjects are given a cash payoff; if the prediction is wrong, there is no payoff. However, unbeknownst to the subject, the lights are programmed to go on according to a binomial process with a given proportion of red and green (e.g., 60 percent red and 40 percent green). Thus, the process is random, although subjects do not know this. The major result of these experiments is something called "probability matching"; that is, subjects respond to the lights in the same proportion as they occur. For example, in the aforementioned case, subjects predict red 60 percent of the time and green 40 percent. The expected payoff for such a strategy can be calculated as follows: Because the subject predicts red on 60 percent of the trials and red occurs on 60 percent, the subject will be correct (and receive the payoff) on 36 percent of the trials. Similarly for green; the subject predicts green on 40 percent of the trials, and green occurs on 40 percent. Hence, 16 percent of the trials will be correctly predicted. Therefore, over both predictions, subjects will be correct on 36 percent + 16 percent = 52 percent of the trials. Now consider how well subjects would do by using a simple rule that said: Always predict the most likely color. Note that such a strategy accepts error; however, it also leads to 60 percent correct predictions (i.e., I always say red, and red occurs 60 percent of the time). Inasmuch as 60 percent is greater than 52 percent, subjects would make more money if they accepted error and consistently used a simple rule. Indeed, such a rule maximizes their wealth in this situation. However, most are trying to predict perfectly and are engaged in a futile attempt to see patterns in the data that are diagnostic of the (nonexistent) rule that they believe determines the onset of the lights. (The analogy to the stock market is noted without further comment.)

Another example of accepting error to make less error comes from the work on equal or unit weights in linear models (Dawes & Corrigan, 1974; Einhorn & Hogarth, 1975). Many people are surprised that equally weighted linear regression models can outpredict models with "optimal" weights on new cases. The reason for the surprise is that we often believe that the weights for the variables are not equal. Thus, the use of equal weights deliberately introduces error into the model. However, there is a benefit from such a procedure, namely that equal weighting protects one against a reversal of the relative weighting of the variables on the basis of poor data. Thus, if X_1 and X_2 have a true relative weighting of 2:1, equal weights protect one from data showing that the weight for X_2 is larger than that for X_1. Therefore, if data are of sufficiently poor quality, seeking error can lead to less error in prediction.

Although the idea of trade-offs among errors may be new to some, there are several more mundane advantages of the statistical approach that nonetheless deserve mention. First, the statistical approach demands that empirical evidence, rather than authority, be the deciding factor in determining the predictive accuracy of any device. Hence, the statistical approach is egalitarian: It trusts no one and takes little on faith. In fact, Armstrong's (1978) notion of a "seer-sucker theory of prediction" seems to capture the attitude of the statistical approach to all undocumented claims of expertise. The theory has only one axiom: For every seer there is a sucker. A second issue concerns inconsistency in judgment due to fatigue, boredom, memory and attentional limitations, and so on. Such inconsistency is not generally useful. Indeed, if someone has a valid rule that is applied inconsistently, predictive accuracy will suffer. However, clinical judgment can be improved by techniques such as "bootstrapping," in which a model of the clinical thought processes predicts more accurately than the person from whom the model was developed (Goldberg, 1970). Such models have been developed in many fields, and the results are encouraging (see Camerer, 1981, for a review and theoretical discussion).

A DECISION ANALYSIS

I have tried to make a case for both the clinical and statistical approaches, and the question naturally arises: Which is better? Such a naive question deserves an answer like: It depends. This section considers some of the factors upon which it depends.

To begin, consider Figure 1, which shows a decision matrix with choices as rows and states of the world as columns. For the sake of simplicity, only two choices and states are shown. First, consider the choice alternatives: One can decide that a phenomenon of interest is systematic and thus capable of being predicted, or one can decide that the phenomenon is random and not predictable. Now consider the possible states of nature. The phenomenon is systematic in the first column, whereas it is random in the second. The intersection of rows and columns

Figure 1 Decision matrix for comparing the clinical and statistical approaches

States of nature

		Systematic	Random
Choices	Syst.	Hit	Myth, magic, illusions of control
	Random	Lost opportunities, illusions of no control	Hit

results in four possible outcomes: the "hits," shown in the diagonal, and the errors, shown in the off-diagonal. Note that there are two kinds of errors. If one decides that a phenomenon is systematic when it is random, the error that results is manifest in myths, magic, superstitions, and illusions of control (Langer, 1975). This error is most likely to characterize the clinical approach, which seeks causal explanations for all behavior. Moreover, there are numerous examples of this type of error, which have been discussed in the behavioral decision theory literature (for a review, see Einhorn & Hogarth, 1981; Nisbett & Ross, 1980).

Let us now consider the other error, which is more likely to characterize the statistical approach. This error results in lost opportunities and illusions of the lack of control. For example, consider the state of knowledge of the movement of heavenly bodies after Copernicus but before Kepler. The Copernican revolution put the sun at the center of the solar system with the planets revolving in circular orbits. This model of planetary motion gives reasonably accurate predictions. However, we know that the orbits are not circular; they are elliptical, and errors in prediction occurred. If probabilism were around during the time of Copernicus, one might have explained planetary motion as consisting of circular orbits plus a random error term. Such a probabilistic model would explain most of the variance, but it would represent a lost opportunity to understand more clearly the true nature of the phenomenon. Of course, successes in seeking to explain all the variance of behavior are dramatic. However, dramatic failures also exist. Recall Einstein's famous statement that, "God does not play dice with the world." His unsuccessful attempts to disprove quantum theory illustrate the difficulty of abandoning the goal of perfect predictability.

What conclusions can be drawn from the foregoing analysis? First, the choice between the clinical and statistical approach in any given situation will depend on:

1 One's beliefs regarding the probabilities of the states of nature. I have considered only two states, but there are many states representing various levels of systematicity and error. Hence, one's prior probabilities over the various states will greatly affect the choice of strategy.
2 The relative costs of the two types of errors. For example, to what degree is superstition an appropriate price to pay for not missing an opportunity to predict more accurately?
3 The relative payoffs for the hits/correct choices.

Hence, the choice between the clinical and statistical approaches can be seen as a special case of decision making under uncertainty; each has its associated risks and potential benefits. At the least, this conceptualization demonstrates why the controversy will never be resolved. Researchers will "place their bets" differently, whether the field be personality theory or particle physics.

CONCLUSION

The clinical versus statistical controversy represents a basic conflict about the predictability of behavior. The evidence is clear and convincing that the statistical approach does a better job of forecasting, but the clinical approach is not without its virtues. Indeed, I tend to think of the clinical approach as a high risk strategy; that is, the chance of being able to predict all the variance of behavior (or even a substantial amount) is very low, but the payoff is correspondingly high. On the other hand, the acceptance of error to make less error is likely to be a safer and more accurate strategy over a wide range of practical situations. Thus, the statistical approach leads to better performance on the average. In my view, this is a compelling argument for its use.

REFERENCES

Armstrong, J.S. (1978). *Long-range forecasting: From crystal ball to computer.* New York: Wiley.
Camerer, C. (1981). General conditions for the success of bootstrapping models. *Organizational Behavior and Human Performance, 27,* 411–422.
Chapanis, A. (1961). Men, machines, and models. *American Psychologist, 16,* 113–131.
Dawes, R.M., & Corrigan, B. (1974). Linear models in decision making. *Psychological Bulletin, 81,* 95–106.
Edwards, W. (1956). Reward probability, amount, and information as determiners of sequential two-alternative decisions. *Journal of Experimental Psychology, 52,* 177–188.
Einhorn, H.J. (1980). Learning from experience and suboptimal rules in decision making. In T.S. Wallsten (Ed.), *Cognitive processes in choice and decision behavior* (pp. 66–80). Hillsdale, NJ: Lawrence Erlbaum Associates, Inc.
Einhorn, H.J., & Hogarth, R.M. (1975). Unit weighting schemes for decision making. *Organizational Behavior and Human Performance, 13,* 171–192.
Confidence in judgment: Persistence of the illusion of validity. *Psychological Review, 85,* 395–416.
Behavioral decision theory: Processes of judgment and choice. *Annual Review of Psychology, 32,* 53–88.
Prediction, diagnosis, and causal thinking in forecasting. *Journal of Forecasting, 1,* 23–36.
Estes, W.K. (1962). Learning theory. *Annual Review of Psychology, 13,* 107–144.
Fischhoff, B. (1975). Hindsight≠foresight: The effect of outcome knowledge on judgment under uncertainty. *Journal of Experimental Psychology: Human Perception and Performance, 1,* 288–299.

Goldberg, L.R. (1970). Man versus model of man: A rationale, plus some evidence, for a method of improving on clinical inferences. *Psychological Bulletin, 73*, 422–432.

Langer, E.J. (1975). The illusion of control. *Journal of Personality and Social Psychology, 32*, 311–328.

Lopes, L.L. (1982). Doing the impossible: A note on induction and the experience of randomness. *Journal of Experimental Psychology: Human Learning and Memory, 8*, 626–636.

Meehl, P.E. (1954). *Clinical versus statistical prediction: A theoretical analysis and review of the literature.* Minneapolis: University of Minnesota Press.

Nisbett, R.E., & Ross, L.D. (1980). *Human inference: Strategies and shortcomings of social judgment.* Englewood Cliffs, NJ: Prentice-Hall.

Tolman, E.C., & Brunswik, E. (1935). The organism and the causal texture of the environment. *Psychological Review, 42*, 43–77.

9

COMPUTER-AIDED DIAGNOSIS OF ACUTE ABDOMINAL PAIN: THE BRITISH EXPERIENCE*

F.T. de Dombal

This presentation reviews the U.K. experience of computer-aided diagnosis of acute abdominal pain – which now relates to over 30,000 cases seen in more than 10 hospitals during a 13 year period. Following a discussion of the philosophy, construction and mode of usage of the systems employed results of this experience are presented. Computer-aided diagnosis in this area has been shown to be feasible and (if correctly utilised) leads to improvements in patient care, diagnosis, and decision making by the doctors involved. In this context, the computer is simply one element of an integrated package reaffirming the importance of traditional clinical medicine.

The United Kingdom has probably amassed a greater experience of computer-aided diagnosis – performed in real-time and involving real-life patients – than anywhere else in the world. As regards acute abdominal pain for example, experiments with computer-aided diagnosis began as long ago as 1969; and in the intervening 14 years have involved over 30,000 patients. This experience has allowed some conclusions to be drawn and the ensuing paragraphs present some of the experience – in order to describe the philosophy behind the U.K. experiments and also to draw some general conclusions from work carried out in a number of centres.

MATERIAL AND METHODS

At the outset it is worth discussing the overall philosophy of the U.K. experiments with computer-aided diagnosis in the area of acute abdominal pain. In common with many other workers, those involved in these experiments have been profoundly influenced by the work of Lusted (1968),[1] who has aptly commented that talk of "computers diagnosing illness" or "doing diagnosis" – or of computers removing from the doctor the responsibility for making medical decisions was simply not helpful at that present time. U.K. research therefore opted for an alternative solution

* First published in *Revue d'Épidémiologie et de Santé Publique*, 32 (1984) 50–6. © 1984 Masson, Editeur s.a. Reprinted by permission.

and an alternative role for the computer – one in which the computer would aid diagnosis, both in the sense of acting as an extra "special investigation" and also in an educational sense (rather than subsuming the doctor's traditional role). This basic decision regarding the role of the computer has had a profound influence upon the design of U.K. systems.

The overall aim amongst U.K. research workers has thus been to create a kind of "package" in which the computer is merely a part. In this "package" (which is as much educational as computational) the doctor first collects information from the patient in the form of a *structured case history*. An example of such a data collection form is shown in Figure 1. This data collection form is that used in the current multicentre study.

Two points should be noted in connection with the use of this form. First it is an extremely precise form – designed from practical experience by over 100 surgeons to reflect the information which they themselves consider desirable to collect from each patient with acute abdominal pain. Moreover in this context it is noteworthy that each of the terms on the form – such as rebound tenderness or guarding – has been *carefully defined in advance* by the same surgical team – and the form thus has an extremely important effect per se in guiding the inexperienced surgeon towards a surgical "lingua franca".

But perhaps even more important and more significant in connection with the computer is the location of the space for the computer's diagnostic prediction – placed (where it should be according to this philosophy!) among the other "special investigations" – to be consulted only *after* a preliminary diagnostic prediction has been made by the doctor in charge of the case.

As regards the mathematical model used by the computer, the kind of philosophical background outlined above makes it desirable (though not mandatory!) to utilise some kind of probabilistic model in which the computer offers odds, and guidance, rather than conclusions. In practice, most U.K. work has utilised a model derived from the theorem of the Reverend Thomas Bayes (1763).[2] This theorem is well-described elsewhere[1] but it may be worth pointing out at this juncture that Bayes Theorem was preferred to other philosophical approaches and models (such as "knowledge engineering" which has recently become popular) for two main reasons.

First, Bayes Theorem fits rather appropriately into the philosophical framework of the U.K. experiments. If the doctor orders a blood test performed, he receives in return a series of numbers on a sheet of paper which he then interprets – discarding the numbers as being "misleading" if this seems to be appropriate in the circumstances of the case in question.

Most doctors find it easier to over-rule a probabilistic suggestion from the computer than a suggestion which has the appearance of emanating from a computer "consultant". Many doctors (in practice) find this reassuring!

Moreover, it must also be stressed that the studies so far carried out in the realms of "artificial intelligence" in no way represent a large scale real-life trial of the systems in question. For these reasons – faute de mieux – Bayes Theorem has been preferred as the basis of most U.K. experiments in the area of acute abdominal pain.

Finally, in recent years, a major controversy has arisen concerning the *source of the data* to be utilised by the computer as a basis for its diagnostic prediction. Some workers have suggested that it is necessary to approach "experts" and obtain from them a series of "guesstimates" as to such matters as conditional probability (the proportion say of patients with acute appendicitis who have rebound tenderness). Studies in the U.K. have however very clearly indicated that such "guesstimates" of probability are highly suspect. U.K. studies (to be described) have thus utilised not the "guesstimates" of "experts" but observed findings in large scale prior studies of the area in question. Early studies in the years around 1970 utilised a "database" of information concerning 600 patients from the West Riding of Yorkshire (Table 1). Later studies have made use of a much expanded database of information collated from over 20 centres by the Research Committee of the World Organisation of Gastroenterology.[3]

Little needs to be added concerning the hardware and software of the U.K. systems. The use of Bayesian probability, and databases which are little more than (Table 1) matrices of relatively modest size, has meant in turn that most U.K. systems have been implemented upon microcomputer systems such as the ubiquitous PET and APPLE.

Sample case   We may envisage a sample case presenting to a U.K. hospital with ·acute abdominal pain for which computer assistance in diagnosis is desired. In this instance the sequence of events occurs as follows:

Step 1. First the doctor collects a routine structured case history from the patient. An interview and an examination are carried out along predetermined lines using the special proforma provided for this purpose (Fig. 1).

Step 2. These data are next entered into a small desk-top micro-computer. For this purpose a simple coding system may be used. Actually in most U.K. systems the data collection sheet (Fig. 1) is of the "no carbon required" type and automatically generates a copy which has been *pre-coded* to assist data entry into the computer.

Abdominal Pain Chart

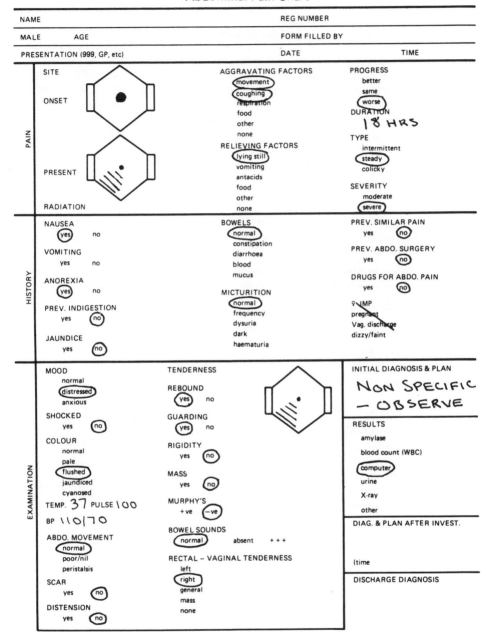

Figure 1 Sample of structured data collection form as used currently in the U.K. national trial of computer-aided diagnosis for patients with acute abdominal pain

Step 3. The computer compares the "new" patient's data (via a Bayesian analysis) with details of 6,000 other similar patients.

Step 4. From this comparison a diagnostic prediction is generated (Fig. 2). This prediction is made available to the doctor, who may compare the computer's diagnostic prediction with his own. If these differ, additional routines may be called upon. For example, the doctor may ask the computer to explain its prediction – by indicating the symptoms and signs which most help to discriminate between the computer's diagnostic prediction and that of the doctor.

Step 5. The final diagnosis (and decision) is left where it should be – in the hands of the doctor.

Figure 2 Computer printout resulting from analysis (see text) of case data in Figure 1. Note doctors diagnosis (non specific) does not agree with computer prediction

```
COMPUTER-AIDED DIAGNOSIS PROGRAM

ACUTE ABDOMINAL PAIN

This is an experimental programme to help you make accurate diagnoses.
CLINICAL JUDGEMENT MUST ALWAYS TAKE PRECEDENCE


COMPUTER user is : M CHAN  (Project/Research Assistant)
DATA from         : S.H.O.

Patient's Reg.No : 123456
Date             : 21/07/83  at 1130 hrs.


SYMPTOMS

    MALE
    AGE10-19
    PAIN ONSET CENTRAL
    PAIN NOW PLO
    AGGRAV BY MOVT
    AGGRAV BY COUGH
    RELIEF-LYING
    GETTING WORSE          CLINICIANS PREDICTION    : NON SPECIFIC
    PAIN 12-24 HRS
    STEADY NOW             INVESTIGATIONS           : NONE
    SEVERE
    NAUSEA
    VOMITING
    ANOREXIA               INITIAL PLAN - <H&E>     : OBSERVE/REVIEW
    NO PREV INDIGESTION
    NO JAUNDICE
    BOWELS NORMAL          COMPUTER PREDICTION
    MICTURITION NORMAL
    NO PREV SIMILAR PAIN
    NO PREV ABD SURGERY                          0%              100%
    NOT TAKING DRUGS
                          APPENDICITIS     |

EXAMINATION               DIVERTICULAR DIS |

    DISTRESSED            PERFORATED ULCER |
    FLUSHED
    REDO.MVT.NORMAL       NON-SPECIFIC PAIN |
    NO SCARS
    NO DISTENSION         CHOLECYSTITIS    |
    TENDER FLQ
    REBOUND               BOWEL OBSTRUCTION |
    GUARDING
    NO RIGIDITY           PANCREATITIS     |
    NO SWELLINGS
    MURPHY -'E            RENAL COLIC      |
    NORMAL BOWEL SOUNDS
    TENDER RT FR          DYSPEPSIA        |
```

Table 1 Sample of database of clinical information about patients with acute abdominal pain fed into computer system prior to commencing computer-aided diagnostic studies.

Patient characteristics	Diagnosis[a]						
	Appendicitis (100)	Diverticular disease (100)	Perforated peptic ulcer (100)	Non-specific abdominal pain (100)	Cholecystitis (100)	Small bowel obstruction (50)	Pancreatitis (50)
Sex							
Male	51	38	79	33	27	54	48
Female	49	62	21	67	73	46	52
Age							
0–9	19	0	0	20	0	2	0
10–19	31	0	2	34	1	4	2
20–29	22	1	10	16	8	6	4
30–39	10	3	27	8	19	14	16
40–49	6	12	30	8	31	22	28
50–59	5	26	17	7	22	24	22
60–69	4	32	9	4	12	18	20
70 +	3	26	5	3	7	12	8
Site of pain at onset							
Right upper quadrant	1	0	8	3	45	2	6
Left upper quadrant	0	2	5	1	1	2	6
Right lower quadrant	23	1	1	28	3	2	0
Left lower quadrant	1	44	0	4	0	2	0
Upper half	4	1	46	9	27	18	62
Lower half	11	25	1	10	1	14	0
Right half	9	1	8	5	13	2	2
Left half	1	13	2	3	0	2	2
Central	44	7	8	29	6	44	12
General	6	6	20	8	3	12	10
Nil	1	1	1	1	1	1	1

[a] In brackets: number of patients for each diagnostic group.

F.T. de Dombal

Table 2 *Comparison of clinicians and computer's diagnostic accuracy in unselected, prospective, consecutive, series of 552 patients*[a]

Category of clinicians	Correct diagnosis %
Admitting doctors	42
House surgeons[b]	71
Registrar[c]	79
Senior clinician[d]	82
Computer-aided system	91

[a]Series of patients from the Professorial Surgical Unit, Leeds, January 1971–August 1972.
[b]Physicians with less than 6 months experience.
[c]Physicians with between 1–2 yrs surgical experience.
[d]Over 5 yrs surgical experience.

RESULTS

Initial studies

Initial studies carried out in Leeds (de Dombal *et al.* 1972)[4] concerned a total of 552 patients admitted to the Professorial Surgical Unit of the General Infirmary at Leeds. The results of these studies (Table 2) are of some importance, *for these results were almost universally misunderstood.* For example, the accuracy of the computer (91 percent) was held by some to be an indication of the computer's superior ability – but in reality it was irrelevant (other than as an indication of what CAN be achieved in this area). Similarly the accuracy of the admitting surgeon in the Accident & Emergency Department (42 percent) was held to be poor – but subsequent studies in the U.K. and elsewhere have indicated that this value is about average for the prediction of the hospital doctor in this situation. Finally, and most important of all, the figures for the house surgeon and registrar (71 percent and 79 percent) were held to be probably about average – whereas in fact these figures were about 20 percent above those to be expected of doctors at this stage of their training.

Only when this latter realisation has emerged – that doctors in contact with the package (that is the computer, the data collection forms, and the feedback from both) had improved their own diagnostic performance – did the true potential value of the system emerge.

Subsequent studies

Subsequent studies set out to explore this prospect – that discipline and clarification of terminology, coupled with the feedback from the com-

Table 3 *Change in diagnostic accuracy and decision-making during computer-aided decision – support studies*

	Area					
	Leeds (5,000 cases)		Airedale (1,500 cases)		Edinburgh (2,500 cases)	
	B[a]	A[a]	B	A	B	A
Percent diagnostic accuracy at initial clinical contact	45	63	54	65	55	77
Percent perforation rate for acute appendicitis	36	< 10	27	13	25	< 10
Percent negative laparotomy	24	10	22	16	18	10
Percent patients not kept in hospital for 24 hrs[b]	20	40	16	25	19	34

[a]B: Before system introduced; A: after system introduced.
[b]Hospital bednights saved (per annum): Leeds > 500; Airedale > 400; Edinburgh > 400.

puter, might improve the *doctor's* own performance. Initial studies (de Dombal *et al.* 1974)[5] showed that doctors in contact with the system improved both their diagnostic *and* their decision-making performance.

Between 1974 and 1982 a number of studies have been carried out in the U.K. By far the most important of these have been the studies carried out at three hospitals in the U.K., The General Infirmary at Leeds, Airedale District Hospital, Yorkshire and Bangour District General Hospital in Scotland. The results from these three hospitals are summarised in Table 3.[6]

Particularly noteworthy in these data are two points. First there has been a broad congruence of the results – that is to say the results at each of these three widely disparate hospitals have been rather similar. Second the results shown in the table have been maintained in each hospital over a period of years – for some 7–8 years minimum. Indeed for all three hospitals together the 1982 data (the latest available) compare rather favourably with those from the earliest years in the study. This latter point is particularly important. It is quite simple to design a system which will effect temporary improvements in performance. Indeed the mere knowledge that performance is being monitored tends to improve it. Nonetheless it is singularly difficult to maintain such an improvement over the period of several years.

Finally it should be noted that improvements in diagnostic and decision making performance have given rise to a number of savings in hospital resources in each of the hospitals concerned. In these days of cash limits and strained resources such savings are doubly welcome. Moreover it should be noted that such savings in hospital resources have been achieved without detriment to the patient.

Current studies

Because of these results, and the potential which they convey, a further trial of the system outlined has begun in the U.K. In this trial (which commenced on August 1, 1982) a total of nine hospitals have attempted to duplicate the results shown in earlier trials in Leeds, Airedale and Bangour and also attempted to quantify more precisely the impact (if any) upon the health care practices and delivery in the hospitals involved. During the initial stages of the trial (although detailed results must await more definitive analysis) preliminary indications suggest that most of the hospitals concerned have managed to achieve similar results. [The final results and evaluation, confirming this picture, are reported in 7.]

CONCLUSIONS

From these studies in the U.K. certain tentative conclusions emerge:

1   Computer assistance for the doctor involved in diagnosing acute abdominal pain is feasible. It can be provided in real time with relatively simple computing facilities.

2   Such usage is most appropriate if the computer is viewed as an extra test (like an X Ray or blood test) rather than as a "Consultant".

3   In such a mode of use the utilisation of the computer will inevitably be patchy. X Rays and blood tests are not expected to be used in every patient but *at need* – and this should be the modus operandi of the computer.

4   When used in this fashion, experience in the U.K. indicates that such usage results in improvements in both diagnostic and decision-making performance on the part of clinicians.

5   These improvements are maintained over a period of several years and result in substantial savings in hospital resource utilisation.

6   Undoubtedly the reasons for these improvements are multi-factorial. For example they depend crucially upon the careful predefinition of terminology to be used and careful data collection by doctors using the system. So called "regional variations" in presentation of cases have usually been shown to be due to variations in terminology or lack of precision in data collection rather than true variations in disease presentation.

7   Perhaps the most valuable contribution of the computer has been the stimulus it has given to the whole question of data collection in this area. Suddenly – for a variety of reasons not unassociated with

computer – the humble symptom is back in fashion. As Professor Card aptly has remarked we may thus be witnessing the renaissance of classical medicine. And if the computer *is* of assistance in this process then (bearing in mind the decline in bulk of the modern micro-computer) it will have been worth its weight in gold!

REFERENCES

1 Lusted, L.B.: *Introduction to Medical Decision Making.* Springfield, Ill, Thomas, 1968.
2 Bayes, T.: An essay towards solving a problem in the doctrine of chances. *Philos. Trans R. Soc. Lond (Biol.)*, 1973, *53*, 370.
3 Bouchier, I.A.D., de Dombal, F.T.: Studies co-ordinated for the Research Committee of the Organisation Mondiale de Gastroenterologie. *Scand. J. Gastroenterol.*, 1979, *14*, Supplement 56.
4 De Dombal, F.T., Leaper, D.J., Staniland, J.R., Horrocks, Jane C., McCann, A.P.: Computer-aided diagnosis of acute abdominal pain. *Br. Med. J.*, 1972, 2, 9–13.
5 De Dombal, F.T., Leaper, D.J., Horrocks, Jane C., Staniland, J.R., McCann, A.P.: Human and computer-aided diagnosis of abdominal pain: Further report with emphasis on performance of clinicians. *Br. Med. J.*, 1974, 1, 376–380.
6 De Dombal, F.T.: Computers and the surgeon – a matter of decision. In: Nyhus, L.M., ed. *Surgery Annual 1979.* Vol. 11, 33–57.
7 Adams, I.D., Chan, M., Clifford, P.C., *et al.* Computer aided diagnosis of acute abdominal pain: a multi-centre study. *British Medical Journal*, 1986, *293*, 800–804.

IO

————— ~ —————

THE ART OF DIAGNOSIS: SOLVING THE CLINICOPATHOLOGICAL EXERCISE*

David M. Eddy, Charles H. Clanton

Clinicopathological conferences (Cpcs) such as those reported in the *Journal* are a regular activity in many hospitals. They are the offspring of the case method of teaching instituted at the Harvard Law School in the 1870s and introduced to the Massachusetts General Hospital in 1910 by Dr Richard Cabot. Drs Castleman and Dudley have explained the purpose of the CPC as "an exercise in deductive reasoning. . . . It is less important to pinpoint the correct diagnosis than to present a logical and instructive analysis of the pertinent conditions involved."[1]

This paper describes the mental strategies or heuristics that many physicians appear to use when they solve the diagnostic problems presented in Cpcs.

THE PROBLEM

The formulation of a differential diagnosis is one of the most important and intellectually challenging aspects of medical reasoning. When a clinician encounters a patient, the clinician faces a vast amount of information: the patient's lifelong personal and medical history; the patient's report of the current medical problem; and the results of numerous examinations, procedures, and tests. In addition to this information the clinician must have a tremendous amount of knowledge about health and disease. Somehow, seasoned clinicians are able to sort their way through the details, clear the confusion, and make the diagnosis.

Ideally, to select the most probable diagnosis, a physician needs to calculate and compare the probabilities of various diseases that could have caused the patient's signs and symptoms. The complexity of this task is demonstrated by a brief examination of the elements of an analytic solution.

Let us write the probability that a disease caused a specific set of signs

* First published in *The New England Journal of Medicine*, Vol. 306 (1982), 1263–8.
© 1982 New England Journal of Medicine. Reprinted by permission.

and symptoms as P(disease|findings). (The symbol "|" is read as "given.")
To select the most likely diagnosis one must estimate this probability for
all the possible diseases, taking into account all the signs and symptoms
present in the case. The most direct way to do this is with Bayes' formula,
which in its simplest form can be written:

$$P(disease|findings) = \frac{P(findings|disease) \times P(disease)}{P(findings)}$$

The difficulty of the diagnostic task can be appreciated by considering
each component of this formula.

P(disease|findings)

We are trying to estimate the probability that a patient has a disease, given
the presence of a particular set of signs and symptoms. Medical knowledge, however, is not usually collected, reported, or learned in this form.
Rather, we learn the signs and symptoms that occur with each disease, and
most medical knowledge is organized according to disease. Somehow
physicians must use this information to estimate P(disease|findings). This
is calculated from the right-hand side of the equation.

P(findings|disease)

Knowing the signs and symptoms that typically occur with particular
diseases gives us some information about the numerator of the equation,
but to estimate the actual probability of a particular set of signs and
symptoms, given a particular disease, we must do considerably more
work. First of all, although any good textbook or article will list the signs
and symptoms that occur with a disease, few indicate in any more than a
general way the probability that each sign or symptoms occurs with the
disease. For example, one might know that a malignant breast mass is
"typically" nodular, firm, painless, and fixed to adjacent structures. In a
detailed description one might even read that a malignant breast mass is
"usually nodular, almost always firm, occasionally . . ." and so forth. But
to use Bayes' formula one would need to know the actual frequency with
which each of the signs occurs: "A malignant breast mass is firm in
90 percent of cases, nodular 70 percent of the time . . ., and painful in
only 5 percent of cases."

Even with this information, the calculation is not simple. It is not
enough to know the frequency of a single symptom in a particular disease.
We must assess the probability that the symptom in question will occur,
given that a long list of other symptoms are present or absent – e.g.,
P(cough and headache and . . . |disease). For example, we may know the

probability of fever in a patient with shigella, but what we would need to know is the probability of fever in a patient with shigella who has nausea and headache but no vomiting, dehydration, or abdominal pain and only minimal diarrhea. This example involved seven findings; in a typical CPC there may be hundreds.

P(disease)

Suppose we have succeeded in obtaining accurate estimates of P(findings|disease) for the particular disease in question. To proceed we now need to know the underlying frequency of the disease in the population. The medical profession's reluctance to deal with probabilities of this type is indicated in the clinical maxims "statistics are for dead men" and "the patient is a case of one." One textbook of diagnosis actually states:

Statistical methods can only be applied to a population of thousands. The individual either has a rare disease or doesn't have it; the relative incidence of two diseases is *completely irrelevant* to the problem of making his diagnosis.[2]

Even if a clinician did intend to include information about the underlying frequency of the disease, human beings would still be notoriously poor at dealing with differences in small probabilities. For example we distinguish poorly between a chance of one in 10,000 and one in 1,000 or even one in 100. Unfortunately, the frequency of many diseases is in this range, and the seemingly unimportant differences (all are "rare") can swing the odds of one diagnosis as compared with another by a factor of 10 or 100.

P(findings)

To estimate the denominator of the right-hand side of the equation, we must consider the probability that a patient's signs and symptoms could have been caused by any of the potential diseases. This probability must be calculated for each disease in the manner just described, and all the probabilities must be added together. That is, for every possible disease we must calculate P(findings|disease) × P(disease). In addition to involving all the problems presented in the preceding paragraphs, this task is further complicated by the sheer number of diseases that must be considered. The calculation is simplified somewhat by the fact that the less likely the disease, the less important it is to include it in the formula, but in complicated cases we can still be left with dozens if not scores of diseases.

Thus, we do not have good information about any one of the component probabilities of the formula, and even if we did, the sheer size of the equation would eliminate any chance of solving it in our heads. Even the simplest of Bayesian problems, such as interpreting the results of a single laboratory test with a known sensitivity and specificity, are beyond our intuition.[3,4] In the CPC we may be dealing with hundreds of signs and symptoms and scores of possible diseases.

In summary, a physician faces three main obstacles in solving a CPC: the amount of information to be considered, the need to interpret signs and symptoms even though medical knowledge is learned primarily by disease, and the need to manipulate probabilities. These obstacles make it exceedingly unlikely that the reasoning process used by physicians to perform complicated diagnoses resembles Bayes' theorem as presented in our equation.

METHODS

Somehow both clinicians and students manage to solve CPCs with remarkable success.[5] To learn how they do it we examined 50 case reports published in the *Journal* in 1974 and 1979. Our method was informal in the tradition of observational sociology. The information available to the discussant was reported in the case presentations. In the analysis of the case, the discussants revealed how that information was used. Some left a clear trail of their reasoning; more often the trail was obscure. In no case did a discussant explicitly describe the process used to make the diagnosis, and only occasionally did it appear that the discussants were conscious of a general pattern in their reasoning. From this study emerged a general model that seems to capture the most common pattern of reasoning used by most clinicians most of the time. Perhaps more important, in the cases in which the elements of this model were not observed, no other pattern could be found.

We have not attempted to quantitate the patterns observed. The purpose of this paper is the same as the purpose of the CPC itself – to stimulate thinking about the diagnostic reasoning process; it is not to quantitate what is inherently a subjective process, to force all clinicians into a common mode, or to establish a general theory of human thinking.

THE MODEL

Our study suggests that the following six steps are used to arrive at a clinical diagnosis: aggregation of elementary findings, selection of a "pivot" (or pathognomonic finding), generation of a cause list, pruning of the cause list, selection of the diagnosis, and validation of the diagnosis.

Aggregation of the findings

We define an elementary finding as any single piece of information about the case. A history of productive cough and rales heard on pulmonary auscultation during the initial physical examination are two examples of elementary findings. In a typical CPC the discussant is presented with hundreds of elementary findings. It is clearly impossible for any person to process this amount of information at one time, and the first task must be to reduce the size of the problem. A physician does this by combining sets of elementary findings into what we will call aggregate findings. Given a patient who presents with extreme polyuria, nocturia, polydipsia, and a urinary specific gravity below 1.003 in the absence of exogenous vasopressin, a discussant aggregated these four elementary findings into the aggregate finding of diabetes insipidus.[6] From this point on, a discussant can use the single aggregate finding in place of the elementary findings. In this way, the information contained in hundreds of elementary findings can be captured in relatively few aggregate findings.

The results of aggregation first appear when the discussant summarizes the case. This apparently innocuous opening crystallizes one of the most important cognitive steps taken to arrive at a differential diagnosis; the summary reveals how the discussant has consolidated most of the elementary findings and condensed the case into a manageable form. For example, a 1500-word description of a case with more than 200 elementary findings was captured in the following set of elementary and aggregate findings:

This 60-year-old woman with a history of heavy smoking had respiratory failure 10 days after the onset of symptoms of a respiratory-tract infection. Severe hypoxia was associated with a dry cough and patchy bilateral pulmonary infiltrates and was followed by obtundation, clinical and laboratory evidence of a coagulopathy and additional organ-system complications.[7]

Aggregation takes advantage of the fact that there is a hierarchical structure to the facts of the case. By focusing on higher and higher levels of abstraction through aggregation, the physician captures the important features of the case with fewer and fewer labels. Even though aggregation is most prominent in the review of the case, further aggregation can occur later in the discussion, and aggregate findings may be further consolidated.

The goal of aggregation, like the goal of diagnostic reasoning, is to find an explanation or cause of a set of findings. Aggregation differs from diagnosis, however, in that relatively few elementary findings are involved; they are closely related to one another and easily identifiable as belonging to a single group, and they can be analyzed apart from the rest of the patient's problems. Furthermore, they usually involve a clinical pattern for which a definite and unambiguous explanation will be apparent to the expert diagnostician. Hence, the recognition of a pattern of findings is sufficient for aggregation, whereas diagnosis often requires the more extensive reasoning mechanisms typical of the CPC.

After aggregation, the physician has a more difficult task. The aggregates and remaining elementary findings can be explained by some diagnosis or combination of diagnoses, but how is the discussant to select which diseases should be considered? As Dr Cabot has said:

To throw open the mind's door and allow *all* disease to enter into consideration each time that we are called to a bedside is foolish in the attempt, and impossible in the performance.[8]

Selection of a pivot

In very rare cases, there is a pathognomonic finding – one that can occur only with a single condition. Lacking this, the discussant must move from a list of findings to a list of causes for those findings. At first glance, it might appear that the discussant should try to identify conditions that could explain, or at least be consistent with, all the aggregate findings. This would be a monumental cognitive task, however, and our discussants used a far simpler and more efficient heuristic device. Most commonly, each discussant selected one or possibly two findings, focused on it, and temporarily ignored all the other findings. We call this the selection of a pivot.

One of the most striking features of the radiologic findings is the prominence of the central pulmonary arteries, which brings up a differential diagnosis that merits consideration.[9]

Why should a hepatic artery rupture in a [27-year-old] person?[8]

The selection of a pivot greatly simplifes the problem, for instead of trying to remember and analyze all the aggregate findings of the case, the physician need only think about one – one that the physician has personally chosen. The powerful role of pivots in the diagnostic process is reflected in the fact that, although most medical knowledge may be stored according to disease, certain rather common findings receive separate attention (e.g., a coin lesion in the lung, protein-urias, and abdominal pain). When possible, these are the signs or symptoms chosen as pivots.

Generation of a cause list

After selecting a pivot, the discussant temporarily ignores all the other details of the case and concentrates on compiling a list of diseases that could have caused the pivot. This is a relatively simple task, equivalent to listing the differential diagnosis of an uncomplicated sign or symptom that the discussant knows well. For example, one discussant selected a pulmonary density on an x-ray film as a pivot, and went on to say:

The differential diagnosis involves consideration of five categories of pulmonary densities – those of traumatic origin, congenital lesions, tumours, malignant or benign, areas of infarction and infections.[10]

The pivot is a bridge across which the physician can move from a list of signs, symptoms, and aggregate findings to the realm of possible diagnoses. This solves the problem that most clinical knowledge is stored according to disease rather than findings. With use of a single pivot, the discussant's memory is not stressed by the need to explain all the aggregate findings. This heuristic device also obviates the need for explicit probabilistic reasoning; the discussant is not concerned with the probability of any disease on the list, only with the fact that it could have caused the pivot. Since new diseases are rarely added to the cause list, the pivot should be central to the case and should be a powerful stimulus for evoking a differential diagnosis.

Pruning the cause list

The next step is to inspect the diseases on the cause list one at a time and measure them against the findings of the case, noting both the presence and absence of critical findings. Because only the pivot has been used to construct the cause list, most of its diseases will not be plausible explanations of the case. In the case with the pulmonary density, a congenital lesion was included in the cause list because of the pivot selected, but then it was immediately excluded:

I shall rule out traumatic and congenital lesions on the basis of the history and the normal x-ray films a short time before this illness.[10]

Usually, most of the diseases can be rapidly excluded, as in the following excerpts from a single case:

. . there are no data to support the diagnosis of histoplasmosis. . . .
. . . the radiographic picture is compatible with a varicella-zoster pneumonia, but I shall exclude that diagnosis because. . . .
. . . I shall rely on [the results of a test] in ruling out disease due to the cytomegalovirus. . . .
. . . bronchiolo-alveolar-cell carcinoma . . . is a distinct possibility. . . .[11]

If the likelihood of a disease falls below some threshold of credibility it is rejected; otherwise it is retained on the list to ensure that the true cause is not eliminated. If this process filters out all but one disease, the discussant's job is nearly done. If more than one disease remains, this pruned cause list is a tentative differential diagnosis of the case.

The burden of the pruning task on the memory is relatively small. The physician focuses on one possible diagnosis at a time, comparing one by one the patient's findings with the signs and symptoms that characterize the diseases, again taking advantage of the fact that most medical knowledge is stored according to disease. The problem of assessing probabilities is also bypassed in this step. In pruning the cause list the discussant begins the search for the most probable diagnosis. But rather than try to estimate the probability that the patient has a particular disease, the physician merely has to determine whether the pattern of findings in the case could have been caused by the disease under consideration. This is a comparison rather than a calculation, and it uses knowledge of the characteristics of diseases instead of requiring estimation of the probabilities of a disease, given the findings.

Any diagnosis excluded at this point is unlikely to be recovered later,[12] therefore, it is dangerous to set too low a threshold for rejecting a diagnosis.

Selection of the clinical diagnosis

In a clinical setting, if physicians are seriously entertaining more than one diagnosis, they can usually order additional tests or procedures to distinguish among the remaining possibilities. In the CPC, however, the discussant has the more complicated task of analyzing mentally the list of diseases in the differential diagnosis to select the most likely diagnosis. Again, most discussants use a heuristic approach to shrink the list without ever having to estimate the probability of any disease. They take the diseases two at a time and compare the ability of each to explain the case. The diagnosis with the characteristic features that most closely match the patient's findings is retained, whereas the other is eliminated.

. . the most difficult distinction is between a solitary pyogenic abscess . . . and an amebic abscess. . . .[13]
. . . the enlarging lymph nodes and spleen suggest the diagnosis of lymphoma and not leukemia.[14]
It is possible for alveolar proteinosis to present in this way. . . . However, the radiologic findings of a mixed pattern lead me to the diagnosis of bronchiolo-alveolar-cell carcinoma.[11]

If one disease seems much more likely than the other, the less likely one may be dropped from further considerations. If both explain the case almost equally well, they may both be retained. This process continues through all the diseases on the list. At the end of this series of comparisons, the list has usually been whittled down, and a final differential diagnosis established. Few claims are made about the true probability of a diagnosis or the relative probability of two diagnoses. If no diagnosis is much more likely than any other, the choice of a preferred diagnosis is often quite arbitrary.

If I had to pick one, instinct would tell me to choose ascariasis, and science would tell me to choose filiariasis.[10]

Interestingly, the heuristic device of comparing diseases two at a time is theoretically correct. If one always chooses the more likely of two diseases in these comparisons, the winner will inevitably be the most probable disease. The beauty and power of this approach is that it allows selection of the most probable disease without requiring estimation of a single probability. The discussant chooses the best candidate from dozens of diseases without ever having to think about more than two at a time. And each comparison is performed by matching the characteristics of diseases, which is the way most medical information is learned.

Validation of the clinical diagnosis

The previous two steps excluded unlikely candidates from the cause list, which was generated by examining only one of the patient's findings – the pivot. Now the discussant must consider whether the final diagnosis can explain all the findings of the case. Since the clinical diagnosis has been derived solely from the pivot, it is possible that some findings may remain unexplained. This final step provides a review of the selected diagnosis for completeness. As one discussant put it,

Before accepting that diagnosis I must ask two questions. Are there atypical features or discordant facts? Should other diagnoses be considered?[15]

Occasionally the final diagnosis cannot comfortably explain all the important findings. The discussant may then repeat the entire process, using one of the unexplained findings as a new pivot to identify a second or third diagnosis. When no unexplained finding has the characteristics of a satisfactory pivot, a valiant attempt may be made to dismiss the objectionable findings.

. . lack of [abdominal] pain by no means excludes the possibility of a dissecting aneurysm . . . The importance is that asymptomatic dissection does occur. . . .

The events during laparotomy . . . are puzzling but do not contradict the diagnosis of a dissecting aneurysm.[16]

Discussion

The diagnostic process in general[17,18] and the CPC in particular[19] have been described previously. This study highlights the complexity of the problem, the difficulties of a direct probabilistic analysis, and the power of the specific heuristic devices used by discussants.

It is impossible to state precisely the extent to which the diagnostic methods displayed in CPCs are used in practice. The CPC is an artificial forum. Cases are chosen not by nature but by pathologists. Discussants know this and have good reason to believe that both they and the cases have been chosen for specific reasons. The discussant's access to information is limited. Having had no contact with the patient, the discussant lacks the clues provided by that contact. The discussant has no opportunity to observe the case over time, to order additional tests, to discuss the case with colleagues, or simply to wait. The case presentation has been filtered by biased comrades. Finally, physicians in practice rarely have to explain their reasoning on a stage.

However, the CPC is not so contrived that it is without value. It is similar in many ways to conferences, rounds, consultations, and other situations in which a physician is asked to give advice on the basis of a case presentation. Furthermore, it closely resembles the reasoning process used under more ordinary circumstances. The CPC freezes a moment in the diagnosis of an extremely complicated case. It suspends the progress of the disease and the flow of information and asks the clinician to come to a diagnosis. This might tell us little about how a physician's understanding of a case changes with time, but it can tell us a great deal about how the existing information is processed and a tentative diagnosis is constructed at any particular time. Whenever physicians make clinical decisions, they must digest the information available at that time. The CPC is an enlarged snapshot of this moment.

The need to assess one's knowledge of a case and draw a tentative conclusion is not artificial. Real diagnostic problems can present all the obstacles encountered in the CPC. Somehow these obstacles must be overcome. There is no doubt that a direct analytical solution such as Bayes' formula is beyond the capacity of the unaided human mind, and the heuristics uncovered in this study of CPCs may well be used on the wards.

Even so, CPCs differ from the typical diagnostic problems of practice in two ways. The first is that most problems are far simpler and easier to solve, yielding to little more than aggregation. The patient presents with the classic findings of one or two conditions, and the diagnosis is evident. Manipulation of a cause list is needed only when the aggregation process still leaves many other findings in a confusing picture.

The second difference concerns the use of information about the underlying frequency of a disease. In the CPC the underlying frequency of a disease is of almost no consequence since the cases are selected. Although the maxims quoted earlier in this paper suggest skepticism about this type of information in actual practice, other maxims suggest its value: "When you hear hoofbeats, think of horses not of zebras" and "Follow Sutton's law; go where the money is." If the prior probability of a condition were included in the diagnostic model described in this paper, it would affect the fifth step – the selection of a final diagnosis from the pruned cause list. In this step a discussant matches the pattern of signs and symptoms characteristic of the two diseases against the signs and symptoms presented by the patient. In a more realistic setting, physicians should also let the underlying frequency of a disease affect their sense of the chance that the disease caused the patient's condition.

The purpose of the CPC is to challenge the discussant and to educate the audience about the methods of diagnostic reasoning. To do this well the cases selected for analysis should have certain characteristics. First of all, they must be complicated. If they are too simple, the diagnosis can be made by aggregation alone, and the rest of the discussion becomes a lecture, which may be worthwhile but does not teach diagnostic reasoning. Secondly, the diagnosis should be feasible and reasonable. Thirdly, the discussant should be considered correct if he chooses the diagnosis that is deemed most probable, given the available information, whether or not the choice was the actual diagnosis. After all, if the discussant does not select the most probable diagnosis, he will be wrong the majority of the time. CPCs with these characteristics are excellent windows through which to study diagnostic reasoning.

REFERENCES

1 Castleman, B., Dudley, H.R., Clinicopathological conferences of the Massachusetts General Hospital: selected medical cases. Boston: Little, Brown, 1960.
2 DeGowin, E.L., DeGowin, R.L. *Bedside diagnostic examination.* 2nd ed. London: Macmillan, 1969.
3 Eddy, D.M. Probabilistic reasoning in clinical medicine: problems and opportunities. In: Kahneman, D., Slovic, P., Tversky, A., eds. *Judgement under uncertainty: heuristics and biases.* New York: Cambridge University Press, 1982.
4 Casscells, W., Schoenberger, A., Graboys, T. Interpretation by physicians of clinical laboratory results. *N. Eng. J. Med.* 1978; 299:999–1001.
5 Orlowski, J.P. Are the Case Records obsolete? *N. Engl. J. Med.* 1980; 302:1207–8.

6 Case Records of the Massachusetts General Hospital (Case 41–1974). *N. Engl. J. Med.* 1974; 291:837–43.

7 Case Records of the Massachusetts General Hospital (Case 6–1979). *N. Engl. J. Med.* 1979; 300:301–9.

8 Cabot, R.C. Differential diagnosis presented through an analysis of 383 cases. Philadelphia: W.B. Saunders, 1911.

9 Case Records of the Massachusetts General Hospital (Case 3–1974). *N. Engl. J. Med.* 1974; 290:216–23.

10 Case Records of the Massachusetts General Hospital (Case 13–1979). *N. Engl. J. Med.* 1979; 300:723–9.

11 Case Records of the Massachusetts General Hospital (Case 34–1974. *N. Engl. J. Med.* 1974; 291:464–9.

12 Ledley, R.S., Lusted, L.B. Reasoning foundations of medical diagnosis. *Science.* 1959; 130:9–21.

13 Case Records of the Massachusetts General Hospital (Case 37–1974). *N. Engl. J. Med.* 1974; 291:617–23.

14 Case Records of the Massachusetts General Hospital (Case 11–1979). *N. Engl. J. Med.* 1979; 300:610–7.

15 Case Records of the Massachusetts General Hospital (Case 12–1979). *N. Engl. J. Med.* 1979; 300:664–8.

16 Case Records of the Massachusetts General Hospital (Case 32–1974). *N. Engl. J. Med.* 1974; 291:350–7.

17 Harvey, A.M., Johns, R.S., Owens, A.H., Jr., Ross, R.S., eds. *Principles and practice of medicine.* 18th ed. New York: Appleton-Century-Crofts, 1972.

18 Elstein, A.S., Shulman, L.S., Sprafka, S.A. *Medical problem solving: an analysis of clinical reasoning.* Cambridge, Mass.: Harvard University Press, 1978.

19 Eddy, D.M. Medical diagnosis: a descriptive model. In: Proceedings of the International Conference on Cybernetics and Society, September 1975. New York: Institute of Electrical and Electronics Engineers, 1975.

I I

~

TOWARD A THEORY OF
CLINICAL EXPERTISE*

Jerome P. Kassirer, Benjamin J. Kuipers, G. Anthony Gorry

Sound clinical decisions depend upon the integration of a variety of facts regarding a patient's condition with an extensive store of medical knowledge. As a result of scientific and technologic advances, the knowledge that underlies the practice of clinical medicine has expanded at a rapid rate. But the intellectual challenges of clinical practice are still formidable, and little is known about the mental processes that enable physicians to make the diverse and difficult decisions required in the clinical setting. The intellectual abilities that form the basis of clinical expertise seem to many to be mysterious, collectively constituting the cognitive skills or wisdom of which physicians are most proud but about which they have little explicit understanding.

An experimental method that has proved valuable in the study of a variety of mental abilities can shed some light upon the ways in which clinicians think about clinical problems and how they decide which actions to take. With methods from cognitive psychology, data on clinical reasoning gleaned from analysis of transcripts (*protocols*) of verbalized problem-solving ("thinking aloud") behavior are used to detect individual components of the reasoning process. The framework for organizing and integrating these components is provided by computer science, particularly by work done in *artificial intelligence*, the branch of computer science concerned with the structure of intelligent systems, whether human or computer. The *cognitive theory* (that is, the hypotheses about the elements of the reasoning process and how they interact) is expressed as a computer program that, when executed, produces simulated behavior that can be compared with that observed in physicians.

In this report, we consider how this experimental method can be used to elucidate aspects of clinical problem-solving. Because of the complexity of problem-solving behavior evoked in the clinical setting, the method must be used carefully, and in certain instances improvements in experimental techniques are needed. But the potential benefits in medicine of a deeper

* First published in *American Journal of Medicine*, 73 (1982) 251–9. © American Journal of Medicine. Reprinted by permission.

understanding of the clinical cognitive process are great. We believe that with the development of this experimental method, the study of clinical cognition will become an important research endeavor for the medical community.

COLLECTING DATA ON CLINICAL PROBLEM-SOLVING

Prescriptive problem-solving approaches such as decision analysis avoid the question of how clinical decisions are actually made and instead specify how they ought to be made.[1-8] Decision analysis is most useful to the clinician in situations in which a choice must be made between a few clearly defined courses of action. Although some experienced physicians see in decision analysis more precise versions of the principles they follow in making such choices, even those skilled in applying the method believe that the quantification required may distort clinical problems.[9-12] Then, too, because alternative actions may be unclear, because so many options seem possible, or because data are missing, some clinical problems cannot be easily cast in the formal mold of decision analysis. Therefore, while productive work on decision analysis and related formalisms goes on, the search for sound strategies to solve less well-structured clinical problems continues.

One natural source of such strategies is physicians with a high degree of clinical competence. Investigations of expert behavior are not new to medicine. Through the years, reflective physicians have attempted to cast some light upon the judgmental processes that are so important to clinical wisdom.[13-19] This kind of "thinking about thinking" has its limitations, however, because recollections about past problems and the ways in which they were solved are frequently recast by memory in unnoticed or even unknown ways.[20-22] Further, when clinicians combine the particular findings regarding an individual patient with their knowledge of the manifestations of diseases, they may select problem-solving strategies that are useful only in a particular medical situation.[23] They may also manifest individual cognitive styles that further affect these reasoning strategies.[24] Differences in style among experts make it extremely difficult to identify common patterns of thought solely from instrospections. Thus, important aspects of clinical problem-solving probably remain inaccessible to introspection, as we know to be true for certain processes involved in perception and memory.[25] Although "predigested" data originating from introspection are a continuing source of important clues, an improved understanding of clinical cognition is apt to require a more scientific approach. In our view, the foundation of this approach is the careful observations of physicians who solve clinical problems.

Such studies of physicians can be carried out using methods for gathering data that range from multiple-choice tests to videotaped simulations of patient encounters. The degree of correspondence between the experimental setting and actual clinical encounter, the *fidelity*, is one important dimension in the design of these experiments, and the range of responses permitted the subject is another dimension. The clinical setting has been simulated in a simple manner by "pencil and paper" presentations of problems and in more complex ways by computer interaction. In some of these studies, the physician was allowed a considerable latitude of responses while attempting to solve the problem, but in most cases the subject's actions were restricted to a limited set. In one such study of limited fidelity, subjects requested patient information from a computer simulation of abdominal pain.[26] In another study, subjects selected cards containing patient data from an array of labeled packets.[27] Such experiments are easy to administer and to score, but the restrictions on the expression by the subject are likely to obscure the complex thought processes that the experiments are intended to reveal. Thus, both the fidelity of the setting and the expressive range of the data are low. Although such highly focused experiments may be appropriate once our understanding of clinical problem-solving is advanced enough to support hypotheses that allow specific, conflicting predictions,[28] we are only just approaching the point at which we can formulate such hypotheses.

PROTOCOL ANALYSIS

Clinical problem-solving requires a store of medical knowledge and reasoning processes with which to apply that knowledge to a given patient. Initial studies suggest that medical knowledge and medical reasoning are intimately intertwined. Support for the idea that expertise is critically dependent on a complement of knowledge is derived from a study of chess masters. Such experts do not recall a randomly arranged chess board any better than novices do, but when confronted with a position that·could occur in a real game, they typically reproduce the board exactly.[29,30] The perception of the chess board by masters, then, is greatly determined by their knowledge of plausible patterns of the chess pieces. It seems likely that chess moves and strategies are also linked to these patterns. In our study of subspecialists in internal medicine, problem-solving skills diminished notably when the subjects were confronted with problems outside their subspeciality areas.[24] Similarly, Elstein *et al.*[23] found great differences in the problem-solving behavior of nonspeciality physicians in regard to clinical problems in neurology, gastroenterology, and hematology. These results suggest that, as in chess, problem-solving strategies in medicine are probably closely linked to knowledge of the medical problem in question. The process of acquiring expertise in chess appears to consist of learning approximately 50,000 configurations and their significance.[29] Perhaps physicians also must learn thousands of "configurations" of findings in order to perform as experts. When expertise has been studied in other fields,[31] the extent and organization of knowledge in long-term memory also seem important. These observations reduce the plausibility that expertise in medicine will be found to derive from a single, general-purpose problem-solving method.

The formulation of theories that account for the role of medical knowledge in medical expertise requires that data collected on the behavior of physicians be sufficiently rich in order to reflect the complexity of that knowledge and its use. For this reason, in a recent study, we focused on the analysis of recorded and transcribed protocols of expert physicians who were asked to "think aloud" while solving a complex clinical problem.[24,32] The findings of an actual patient with analgesic nephropathy complicated by acute pyelonephritis, renal insufficiency, and metabolic acidosis were simulated by a physican totally familiar with the patient's clinical and laboratory data. The physician-subjects studied were given the patient's age, sex, and chief complaints, and were then required to elicit further information. Subjects were not restricted in their questioning but were asked to describe their reasoning process as they requested, obtained, and interpreted the clinical data. Verbatim transcripts of these sessions served as the source of data for the analysis of clinical problem-solving. These data consisted of statements indicating the physicians' current focus of attention, the diagnostic hypotheses under consideration, and the relation of the clinical findings to those hypotheses.

In an analogous experiment, Elstein *et al.*[23] made videotapes of the interaction between physician-subjects and actors trained to play the part of real patients with a variety of diseases. The physicians were asked to discuss their thoughts about the cases during natural breaks in the interviews, such as between taking a history and conducting a physical examination. The subjects also reviewed the videotapes of their diagnostic sessions and described what they thought were the mental processes responsible for their questions.

The analysis of protocols from such studies requires much care. First, as anyone knows who has solved a problem while explaining it to someone else, the mere act of speaking changes the underlying thought processes.[22] But it is unlikely that thinking without speaking is entirely different from thinking while speaking, and presumably understanding the latter will help us understand the former, even if additional factors affect speechless thought. Second, because no person can be expected to verbalize every thought, certain intermediate states of the reasoning process will be omitted. Although individual utterances can be interpreted unambiguously, omissions make it difficult (or perhaps impossible) to reconstruct the underlying process in its entirety.[25] Third, and perhaps most important, subjects often make inaccurate or misleading inferences about their own thought processes. Observations about previous thought processes are particularly subject to retrospective biases, because judgments are significantly influenced by knowledge of outcomes.[20–22,33] In a comprehensive review of social psychology experiments on introspective reports, it was observed that "subjects are sometimes (1) unaware of the existence of a stimulus that importantly influenced a response, (2) unaware of the existence of the response, and (3) unaware that the stimulus had affected the response."[20] The retrospective report of the reasoning processes of a subject is strongly affected by his own concepts of the mechanisms of his mind, so a careful analysis of a protocol must therefore exclude statements that could be considered introspections. As Newell and Simon[34] point out: "Retrospective accounts leave much more opportunity for the subject to mix current knowledge with past knowledge, making reliable inference from the protocol difficult. Nor, in the thinking-aloud protocol, is the subject asked to theorize about his own behavior – only to report the information and intentions that are within his current sphere of conscious awareness. All theorizing about the causes and consequences of the subject's knowledge state is carried out and validated by the experimenters, not by the subject."

Applying this criterion to the experiments of Elstein *et al.*,[23] we are led to question the role of "stimulated recall" of previous thought processes by the physician-subjects while they watched videotapes of their earlier encounters with the simulated patient. Statements obtained from subjects

Figure 1 In this excerpt from a protocol [24, p. 247], the experimenter (E) is acting as a source of data about the patient. The physician-subject (S) takes the initiative in seeking information. This excerpt illustrates the rapidity with which experienced clinicians generate hypotheses concerning the patient (italicized below). The specificity of these hypotheses is noteworthy in view of the small number of facts available about the patient

E: This is a 57-year old woman who is admitted to the hospital with the chief complaint of nausea, vomiting, abdominal pain, and frequency of urination.

S: First, I'm going to ask some questions about the character of her urinary stream because I'm in thinking terms of *infection in her lower urinary tract*. Did this patient notice any blood in her urine?

E: No she didn't.

S: That she didn't have gross hematuria makes me turn away from one possibility – that she might have *passed a stone in association with infection*. She might have had a hemorrhegic cystitis but that makes it unlikely, just at first cut. You said she had frequency – did she have pain on urination? I'm asking that in terms of also *inflammation of the bladder*.

E: She did complain of some burning on urination.

S: Now again continuing along the infection line, I'm going to ask whether she had a fever just in terms of *generalized infection*.

during breaks in the patient encounter are likely to mix useful reports of hypotheses currently entertained with biased retrospective theorizing about what took place during the problem-solving episode. The investigators attempted to validate the conclusions reached from retrospective observations by comparing them with the protocols. While this validation may avoid most errors, it is questionable whether retrospective observations are worth collecting at all, at least under careful experimental conditions. Since such observations must be validated, they cannot support hypotheses by themselves, and their function is to suggest hypotheses that might not have been evident from other data. Even if this is a valid rationale, the justification for the elaborate experimental setting is uncertain. Videotapes may stimulate insights, but thoughtful introspection by experienced clinicians may be just as useful. Although we agree in general with the findings of the study by Elstein *et al.*,[23] we believe that an experimental design that relies heavily on retrospective observation is potentially flawed.

The analysis of protocols requires, in addition to extraordinary patience, extensive knowledge of the problem being addressed by the subject. The participation of experienced clinicians appears to be a necessary part of this analysis. For example, we have encountered instances in which an ambiguous statement could be clarified, or a tentative analysis rejected, only by a reader who was deeply familiar with the typical thought and language patterns of physicians.

The data gathered from protocols are not recast into preselected categories as in conventional experimental approaches. The case against trying to categorize statements from verbal data has been made in a convincing fashion by Newell and Simon: "Language is a device for encoding information. To recode it into another language that preserves all the meaning is hardly to encode it at all. To recode it into another language with substantial loss of meaning throws away the very data we hope to obtain by recording protocols."[34] Thus, it is tedious but not difficult for experts familiar with the medical concepts involved in a problem to analyze a protocol. However, it is difficult for them to state precisely how the analysis should be done. In the study by Elstein *et al.*,[23] even those skilled in the analysis of transcripts were unable to devise rules that would reliably discriminate between questions seeking routine information and questions that were hypothesis-driven, even though the distinction seemed intuitively clear. So there is a need for more adequate methods of analyzing data in the form of verbal protocols. We believe as do others[22] that these methods must be based on a deeper understanding of several cognitive processes – the process by which introspections are verbalized and the process by which general knowledge is applied to solve specific problems.

COGNITIVE SIMULATION

To construct a theory of clinical cognition that includes concepts pertinent to clinical problem-solving (e.g., generating, confirming, and refuting diagnostic hypotheses, and assessing the coherence and adequacy of diagnostic categorization),[23,24] we need a substantial number of well-defined concepts for "thinking about thinking." Computer science may provide such a basis. The past two decades of research in artificial intelligence have produced precise descriptions of a number of reasoning and problem-solving strategies that can be used as models in the analysis of protocols.

The idea of mechanical simulation of the mind can be traced back to ancient mythology,[35] but the use of the computer as a laboratory for cognitive simulation dates back to 1956 when Newell and Simon modeled human behavior in proving theorems in propositional logic with a computer program called the Logic Theory Machine.[36] These investigators and their colleagues at Carnegie–Mellon University have worked extensively on human problem-solving by analyzing verbal transcripts and implementing computer models of the resulting theories.[34] Other cognitive psychologists have used data structures drawn from computer science to simulate certain behavioral properties of human memory.[37] Working computer simulations also have been produced for theories of certain aspects of human abilities such as vision[38] and language.[39]

Consider an example of protocol analysis leading to a corresponding computational model of an aspect of clinical problem-solving. One feature of clinical cognition already studied in some depth is the process of taking the history of the present illness.[23,24,40-44] These experiments provide evidence that the questions asked by a physician taking the

Figure 2 In this protocol excerpt, the subject has been asked to justify and explain his diagnosis of nephrotic syndrome after being given a case summary. This excerpt illustrates a strategy of enumerating the features associated with nephrotic syndrome in general (lines 2, 4, 8, 9, 11) as an index to the corresponding findings for this particular case (lines 3, 5–7, 10, 12).

2:1   OK. The nephrotic syndrome by definition is
2:2   a state where a patient with a hypoalbuminemia
2:3   which we see evident by her serum albumin of 2 g percent.
2:4   Hypercholesterolemia is quite often found.
2:5   The cholesterol here is only mildly elevated
2:6   so it is not very abnormal,
2:7   but on the other hand it would not necessarily go against it.
2:8   Often in the urine in the sediment,
2:9   in addition to finding large amounts of protein
2:10 which we see here
2:11 we find fatty casts or maltese crosses under the microscope.
2:12 My assumption would be that the patient probably does have fat in the urine.

history of the present illness are prompted by specific hypotheses that are prompted in turn by patient data. These hypotheses suggest confirming, disconfirming, or differential diagnosis questions to the physician. As the surviving hypotheses provide a better and better fit to the available evidence, the physician carries out a detailed process of matching the features of the disease hypotheses with the patient idea.

To investigate this behavior in detail, we first collected a verbatim transcript of a physician-subject taking the history of the present illness. Figure 1 shows a clinician associating highly specific hypotheses with the first few facts provided about the patient. In the slightly different context of explaining the facts of a particular case, we see in Figure 2 a clear example of matching the features of a hypothesized disease with the corresponding features of the patient.

In our study of the problem-solving behavior of expert clinicians, we used protocols such as these to identify a number of strategies for evoking, evaluating, differentiating, refuting, and confirming disease hypotheses.[24]

Figure 3 A typical "frame." Information about a disease, a physiologic state, etc., is stored in the computer in the form of a "frame" within the long-term memory. Included in the typical frame, as shown here for nephrotic syndrome, are descriptions of typical findings, numerical factors to be used in scoring, and links to other frames (e.g., "may-be-caused-by," "may-be-complicated-by"). There are also rules for excluding ("must-not-have") and satisfying ("is-sufficient") the fit of the frame to the case at hand (40, p. 988).

Name: Nephrotic syndrome
Is a type of: Clinical state
Finding: Low serum albumin concentration
Finding: Heavy proteinuria
Finding: > 5 g/24 hours proteinuria
Finding: Massive, symmetrical edema
Finding: Either facial or periorbital and symmetrical edema
Finding: High-serum cholesterol concentration
Finding: Urine lipids present
Must not have: Proteinuria absent
Is sufficient: Both massive edema and
> 5 g/24 hours of proteinuria
Major scoring:
  Serum albumin concentration
    Low: 1.0
    High: − 1.0
  Proteinuria:
    > 5 g/24 hours: 1.0
    Heavy: 0.5
    Either absent or light: − 1.0
  Edema:
    Massive and symmetrical: 1.0
    Not masssive but symmetrical: 0.3
    Erythematous: − 0.2
    Assymetrical: − 0.5
    Absent: − 1.0

Minor scoring:
  Serum cholesterol concentration:
    High: 1.0
    Not high: − 1.0
  Urine lipids:
    Present: 1.0
    Absent: − 0.5
May-be-caused-by:
  Acute glomerulonephritis
  Chronic glomerulonephritis
  Nephrotoxic drugs
  Insect bite
  Idiopathic nephrotic syndrome
  Systemic lupus erythematosus
  Diabetes mellitus
May-be-complicated-by:
  Hypovolemia
  Cellulitis
May-be-cause-of:
  Sodium retention
Differential diagnosis:
  If neck veins elevated
    consider: constrictive pericarditis
  If ascites present
    consider: cirrhosis
  If pulmonary emboli present
    consider: renal vein thrombosis

Once a segment of a protocol is recognized as an instance of one of the methods – for example, an instance of matching of findings and hypotheses – it becomes possible to make a correspondence between individual statements in the transcript and steps in a computer simulation of the problem-solving method. Pauker *et al.*[40] designed and implemented the "Present Illness Program" to simulate the hypothesis-directed process of taking the history of the present illness. This computer program embodies not only the strategies identified in protocol analysis, but also a representation of the medical knowledge apparently used by the physician. For the program to simulate even a fragment of a protocol, it needs an extensive collection of medical facts that are intricately associated with one another.[40] A small sample of the program's medical knowledge is shown in Figure 3. The figure does not, of course, convey the interconnections of these facts with others as they are represented in the computer program.

The result of running the Present Illness Program is a dialogue between the computer and the user, in which the program's questions are determined by the disease hypotheses it is entertaining at any given time. In the dialogue in Figure 4, the program pursues useful information in a way that is similar to that observed in an experienced physician. This dialogue

Figure 4 Initial portion of a representative "present illness" dialogue (40, p. 983). The questions were asked by the computer and the responses (preceded by ⪢) are those of the user. The presenting evidence evokes a small set of hypotheses, which then determine the selection of questions, giving the dialogue its focused quality.

Presenting problem: A young man with massive pedal edema.

1A.	Is pedal edema, which is massive,			1G.	Is it,	
	1. For days?				1. Painful?	
	2. For weeks?				2. Not painful?	⪢ 2
	3. For months?			2.	Is there dyspnea?	⪢ No
	4. For years?		⪢ 1	3.	Is there heavy alcohol consumption?	⪢ No
1B.	Is it,			3A.	Is alcohol consumption	
	1. First time?				1. None?	
	2. Infrequent?				2. Rare?	
	3. Occasional?				3. Social?	⪢ 3
	4. Frequent?		⪢ 1	4.	Is there jaundice?	⪢ No
1C.	Is it,			5.	Was there proteinuria in the past?	⪢ Unknown
	1. Without temporal pattern?			5A.	Is there large policy life insurance?	⪢ No
	2. Worse in morning?			5A1.	Is life insurance,	
	3. Worse in evening?		⪢ 3		1. None?	
1D.	Is it,				2. Unable-to-obtain?	
	1. Symmetrical?				3. Small-policy?	⪢ 3
	2. Asymmetrical?		⪢ 1	5B.	Is there served in armed forces?	⪢ Yes
IE.	Is it,			6.	Is there varicose veins?	⪢ No
	1. Pitting?			7.	Was there edema in the past?	⪢ No
	2. Non-pitting?		⪢ 1	8.	Is there edema in the past?	⪢ No
1F.	Is it,			8A.	Is there . . .	
	1. Erythematous?					
	2. Not erythematous?		⪢ 2			

provides qualitative evidence of the similarity between the behavior of the program and the clinicians.

It is impossible to overestimate the importance of implementing a working version of such a program. The initial qualitative impressions extracted from the transcript are greatly refined and deepened by the requirement of designing a working program: each step of the reasoning process must be specified in such detail that it can be performed by the computer. Once the program is running, its behavior can be compared with the behavior observed in physician-subjects, and additional modifications of the program can be made.

A working simulation of a cognitive theory shows that the theory has passed an important hurdle: it is sufficient to explain the observed behavior. The simulation alluded to previously is too fragmentary to prove that clinical cognition can be simulated. Along with other cognitive simulations, however, it suggests that hypotheses concerning the thought process of physicians can be precisely represented as computer programs and that the predictions needed for testing the hypotheses can be generated by running the program as a simulation of the physician. This approach is being applied productively to medical problems such as congenital heart disease, sepsis, glaucoma, and others.[41,44–46] Once different theories are found that are also sufficient to explain the same behavior, standard methods of scientific hypothesis testing can be applied to discriminate between them.

The use of computer simulation in the study of clinical cognition has been simplified in recent years by improved technology for representing knowledge in computer systems.[47–49] The increasing power and decreasing cost of computer hardware make it possible to develop programs and corresponding theories that rely on large collections of knowledge or large numbers of small procedures.[50] In the past, such theories were rejected as being too "messy" and awkward to comprehend or to test. Substantial advances in theories of learning, languages, and common sense reasoning have also contributed to this effort. These developments are derived principally from work in artificial intelligence.

There are great advantages to the use of the computer as a "psychological laboratory." The programmer of a computer simulation is forced to confront each design issue that stands in the way of working computer programs. By contrast, an English-language description of a theory may remain incomplete and ambiguous in many subtle and unrecognized ways. Naturally, the computer simulation resembles the human being only to a certain level of detail and the underlying theory may make no claim about how the human being performs certain primitive operations. No one, for example, claims that the brain is programmed in any known computer language. Nonetheless, we can trace the sequence of actions that the program takes in response to test cases. These *action sequences* are the predictions of the theory as it applies to the specific situation represented by the test case. By comparing these predictions with the actual behavior, it is possible to uncover inadequacies that allow the theory to be refined (or "debugged"), just as a computer program is perfected by a similar process. The experiment reported recently by Johnson and his colleagues[45] illustrates the careful application of this method. These investigators compared the sequences in which diagnostic hypotheses were evoked, on the one hand, by physician-subjects and on the other by a computer program designed to simulate expert diagnosis of congenital heart disease. The remarkable similarity found in the sequences strongly supports the validity of the problem-solving theory.

The existence of a computer program that solves a medical problem does not prove that its method is the one physicians use to solve the same problem. However, a successful detailed simulation by the computer program of aspects of the physicians' problem-solving behavior increases our confidence in the theory underlying the program.

SIGNIFICANCE

The success of current educational practices in producing competent physicians is evidence that apprenticeship sharpens and extends clinical judgment. However, problem-solving techniques are usually transmitted implicitly, with the expectation that the student will assimilate them by mimicking the observable practices of experts at work. In a sense, the student is expected to "pick up the game" after instruction in only the rules, and without didactic exposure to the tactics and strategies that enhance the chance of winning. We believe that students would profit from pedagogic techniques designed to teach the problem-solving methods used by experts in clinical reasoning, but first these problem-solving methods must be elucidated. The experimental approach discussed here should help in identifying and clarifying these methods. A better understanding of clinical decision-making could also have a positive effect on the practice of medicine by enabling the physician to examine, articulate, and criticize his reasoning, thereby avoiding certain pitfalls and biases that normally affect decision-making in the face of uncertainty.[51] Finally, knowledge of the reasoning strategies of expert clinicians could prove exceptionally useful in the development of computer programs to assist in clinical decision-making

REFERENCES

1 Raiffa, H.: *Decision analysis: introductory lectures on choices under uncertainty.* Reading, MA: Addison-Wesley, 1968.

2 Schwartz, W.B., Gorry, G.A., Kassirer, J.P., Essig, A.: Decision analysis and clinical judgment. *Am. J. Med.* 1973; 55: 459.

3 Pauker, S.P., Pauker, S.G.: Prenatal diagnosis: a directive approach to genetic counseling using decision analysis. *Yale J. Biol. Med.* 1977; 50: 275.

4 Safran, C., Desforges, J.G., Tsichlis, P.N., Bluming, A.Z.: Decision analysis to evaluate lymphangiography in the management of patients with Hodgkin's disease. *N. Engl. J. Med.* 1977; 296: 1088.

5 Pauker, S.G., Kassirer, J.P.: Therapeutic decision making a cost-benefit analysis. *N. Engl. J. Med.* 1975; 293: 229.

6 Pauker, S.G., Kassirer, J.P.: The threshold approach to clinical decision making. *N. Engl. J. Med..* 1980; 302: 1109.

7 McNeil, B.J., Hessel, S.J., Branch, W.T., Bjork, L., Adelstein, S.J.: Measures of clinical efficacy. III. The value of the lungscan in the evaluation of young patients with pleuritic chest pain. *J. Nucl. Med.* 1976; 17: 163.

8 Emerson, P.A., Teather, D., Handley, A.J.: The application of decision theory to the prevention of deep venous thrombosis following myocardial infarction. *Q. J. Med.* 1974; 43: 380.

9 Feinstein, A.R.: Clinical biostatistics XXXIX: the haze of Bayes, the aerial palaces of decision analysis, and the computerized Ouija board. *Clin. Pharmacol. Ther.* 1977; 21: 482.

10 Ransohoff, D.F., Feinstein, A.R.: Is decision analysis useful in clinical medicine? *Yale J. Biol. Med.* 1976; 49: 165.

11 Ingelfinger, F.J.: Decision in medicine. *N. Engl. J. Med.* 1975; 293: 254.

12 Schwartz, W.B.: Decision analysis. A look at the chief complaints. *N. Engl. J. Med.* 1979; 300: 556.

13 Feinstein, A.R.: An analysis of diagnostic reasoning. I. The domains and disorders of clinical macrobiology. *Yale J. Biol. Med.* 1973; 46: 212.

14 Morgan, W.L. Jr., Engel, G.L.: *The clinical approach to the patient.* Philadelphia: W.B. Saunders, 1969.

15 MacLeon, J.G., ed.: *Clinicial examination.* New York: Churchill-Livingstone, 1976.

16 Wulff, H.R.: *Rational diagnosis and treatment.* Oxford: Blackwell Scientific Publications, 1976.

17 Enelow, A.J., Swisher, S.N.: *Interviewing and patient care.* New York: Oxford University Press, 1972.

18 Judge, R.D., Zuidema, G.D. (eds): *Methods of clinical examination; a physiologic approach.* 3rd ed. Boston: Little, Brown, 1974.

19 Feinstein, A.R.: *Clinical judgment.* New York: R.E. Krieger, 1967.

20 Nisbett, R.E., Wilson, T.D.: Telling more than we can know: verbal reports on mental processes. *Psychol. Rev.* 1977; 84: 231.

21 Wood, G.: The knew-it-all-along effect. *J. Exp. Psychol.* [Hum. Percept.] 1978; 4: 345.

22 Ericsson, K.A., Simon, H.A.: Verbal reports as data. *Psychol. Rev.* 1980; 87: 215.

23 Elstein, A.S., Shulman, L.S., Sprafka, S.A.: *Medical problem solving: an analysis of clinical reasoning.* Cambridge, MA: Harvard University Press, 1978.

24 Kassirer, J.P., Gorry, G.A.: Clinical problem solving: a behavioral analysis. *Ann. Intern. Med.* 1978; 89: 245.

25 Lindsay, P.H., Norman, D.A.: *Human information processing: an introduction to psychology.* New York: Academic Press, 1972.

26 De Dombal, F.T., Horrocks, J.C., Staniland, J.R., Gill, P.W.: Simulation of clinical diagnosis: a comparative study. *Br. Med. J.* 1971; 2: 575.

27 Rimoldi, H.J.A.: The test of diagnostic skills. *J. Med. Educ.* 1961; 36: 73.

28 Popper, K.: *The logic of scientific discovery,* 3rd ed. London: Hutchinson, 1972.

29 Chase, W.G., Simon, H.A.: The mind's eye in chess. In: Chase, W.G. (ed.) *Visual information processing.* New York: Academic Press, 1973.

30 de Groot, A.D.: *Thought and choice in chess.* The Hague: Mouton, 1965.

31 Larkin, J., McDermott, J., Simon, D.P., Simon, H.A.: Expert and novice performance in solving physics problems. *Science* 1980; 208: 1335.

32 Miller, P.B.: *Strategy selection in medical diagnosis.* Cambridge, MA: Massachusetts Institute of Technology, Project MAC Technical Report 153, 1975.

33 Fischhoff, B: Hindsight≠foresight: the effect of outcome knowledge on judgment under uncertainty. *J. Exp. Psychol.* [*Hum. Percept.*] 1975; 1: 288.

34 Newell, A., Simon, H.A.: *Human problem solving.* Englewood Cliffs, NJ: Prentice-Hall, 1972; 184, 166.

35 McCorduck, P.: *Machines who think.* San Francisco: W.H. Freeman, 1979.

36 Newell, A., Simon, H.A.: The Logic Theory Machine: a complex information processing system. *IRE Trans. Inf. Theory* 1956; IT-2: 61.

37 Anderson, J.R., Bower, G.: *Human associative memory,* 2nd ed. Washington, DC: Hemisphere Publishing, 1974.

38 Marr, D., Nishihara, H.K.: Visual information processing: artificial intelligence and the sensorium of sight. *Technol. Rev.* 1978; 81: 28.

39 Marcus, M.: *A theory of syntactic recognition of natural language.* Cambridge, MA: MIT Press, 1980.

40 Pauker, S.G., Gorry, G.A., Kassirer, J.P., Schwartz, W.B.: Towards the simulation of clinical cognition: taking a present illness by computer. *Am. J. Med.* 1976; 60: 981.

41 Pople, H.E. Jr., Myers, J.D., Millar, R.A.: DIALOG: a model of diagnostic logic for internal medicine. Proceedings of the Fourth International Conference on Artificial Intelligence, 1975.

42 Pople, H.E. Jr.: The formation of composite hypotheses in diagnostic problem solving: an exercise in synthetic reasoning. Proceedings of the Sixth International Joint Conference on Artificial Intelligence. Available from Carnegie–Mellon University, Pittsburgh, PA, 1977.

43 Rubin, A.D.: Hypothesis formation and evaluation in medical diagnosis. Cambridge, MA: MIT, Artificial Intelligence Laboratory Technical Report 316.

44 Shortliffe, E.H.: *Computer-based medical consultation; MYCIN.* New York: Elsevier–North Holland, 1976.

45 Johnson, P.E., Barreto, A., Hassebrock, F. *et al.:* Expertise and error in diagnostic reasoning. *Cognitive Science* 1981; 5: 235.

46 Weiss, S.M., Kulikowski, C.A., Amarel, S., Safir, A.: A model-based method for computer-aided medical decision-making. *Artif. Intell.* 1978; II: 145.

47 Minsky, M.: A framework for representing knowledge. In: Winston, P.H., ed. *The psychology of computer vision.* New York: McGraw-Hill, 1975.

48 Waterman, D.A., Hayes-Roth, F.: *Pattern-directed inference systems.* New York: Academic Press, 1978.

49 Findler, N.V. (ed.): *Associate networks: the representation and use of knowledge of computers.* New York: Academic Press, 1979.

50 Winston, P.H.: *Artificial Intelligence.* Reading, MA: Addison-Wesley, 1977.

51 Tversky, A., Kahneman, D.: Judgment under uncertainty; heuristics and biases. *Science* 1974; 185: 1124.

12

~

FORMAL AND KNOWLEDGE-BASED METHODS IN DECISION TECHNOLOGY*

John Fox

INTRODUCTION

Many types of computer system can be used to help make decisions. Business, professional, public, and personal decisions can all be supported by data-processing techniques. Databases can provide information for stock-control decisions; statistical packages can identify significant situations or trends for public policy; accounting programs may help to plan personal spending, and so on. However I am not concerned here with data-processing techniques which simply inform decision-makers, but with a more complete decision technology. Decision technology goes beyond data processing – it embodies a theory of what decisions are and methods for taking them.

Most decision concepts, and strategies for decision-making, have formal roots in mathematics, notably probability theory. In recent years a new kind of system has emerged which is informal and often non-mathematical. These are "knowledge-based" or "expert" systems. This paper assesses the contribution of expert systems to the understanding of decision-making and the development of decision technology.

The focus of the paper is medicine, because medicine is almost certainly the largest, non-military area of application for both traditional and knowledge-based decision technologies. It therefore provides us with a relatively secure base to carry out an assessment of the state of the field. However the concepts discussed are applicable to other fields of decision-making. The paper gives an overview of knowledge-based techniques, an assessment of their contribution to decision technology, and some proposals for a knowledge-based framework for decision-making.

WHAT ARE KNOWLEDGE-BASED SYSTEMS AND EXPERT SYSTEMS?

Knowledge-based systems come from artificial intelligence (AI). They are computer programs which use knowledge of a subject, task, user (or even

* First published in *Acta Psychologica* 56 (1984), 303–31. © 1984 Elsevier Science Publishers B.V. (North-Holland). Reprinted by permission.

Table 1 *An example of a consultation using the ICRF terminal care system. The user has indicated that the patient is suffering from dyspnoea or breathlessness. (User input follow the ** prompts, all other lines were typed by the system.) The user entered UNK in response to question 7 to indicate that the answer is unknown. A feature of many systems is that only questions relevant to the current problem are asked, so consultations are only as long as is necessary. Other consultations may be longer and more comprehensive.*

PATIENT-1

---

1) Name:
** FRED SMITH
2) What problems are troubling Fred Smith?
** DYSPNOEA
3) What is the severity of the dyspnoea?
** MILD
4) Does Fred Smith have bronchospasm?
** YES
5) Is Fred Smith taking any medication?
** NO
6) Does Fred Smith have a pleural effusion?
** NO
7) Does Fred Smith have anaemia?
** UNK
8) Does Fred Smith have a mediastinal tumour?
** NO

Advice for DYSPNOEA
    Steroids are the most effective treatment for bronchospasm (the long-term effects are not important in terminal patients).
    Investigate the possibility of anaemia if its correction would improve Fred Smith's personal or family life.

General Advice for DYSPNOEA
    Oxygen is not recommended (because it does not usually ease the dyspnoea of terminal patients).

---

knowledge about themselves) to do something. This may be interpreting typed language; interpreting speech or visual images; controlling a robot or a production line; advising on decisions or solving problems. We speak of "knowledge" rather than "information" or "data" in order to emphasise that the aim is for knowledge to be stored explicitly rather than represented implicitly in abstract representations like numbers or computer algorithms. How and why we aim to do this will be dealt with later. Expert systems are knowledge-based systems with two special features. First, they are primarily concerned with making decisions – as opposed to seeing, hearing etc. Second, they are interactive computer systems – not autonomous robots or process controllers.

Table 2 *The explanation facility of EMYCIN, a package designed at Stanford University for developing expert systems like that in Table 1. The user was puzzled when asked if his patient has dyspepsia (indigestion), so instead of answering immediately he entered the command WHY. The second WHY produced an explanation at the next higher level in the logical process.*

---

7) Does Fred Smith have dyspepsia?
** WHY
[i.e.   WHY is it important to determine whether PATIENT-1 has dyspepsia?]
[1.0]   This will aid in determining whether PATIENT-1 is suspected of having a peptic ulcer.
If
[1.1]   1) Fred Smith has dyspepsia, or
         2) Fred Smith has evidence of gastro-intestinal haemorrhage
then
    it is definite (1.0) that Fred Smith is suspected of having a peptic ulcer
[RULE020]
    [back to question 7 . . .]
** WHY
[i.e.   WHY is it important to determine whether PATIENT-1 is suspected of having a peptic ulcer?]
[2.0]   . . . in order to determine the recommendations for pain.
    It has already been established that
[2.1]   an anti-inflammatory drug should be recommended for Fred Smith, and
[2.2]   oral drugs are suitable for Fred Smith
    Therefore, if
[2.3]   Fred Smith is not suspected of having a peptic ulcer
then
    it is definite (1.0) that the following is one of the
       recommendations for pain: Aspirin orally
    [RULE079]
    [back to question 7 . . .]
** NO

At present most expert systems are consultants. The user supplies problem information and the system asks questions and makes suggestions or decisions. In medicine the systems may suggest likely diagnoses, choice of tests, treatments etc. A short consultation with a knowledge-based system for advising on the management of terminal patients is given in Table 1. This expert system is being developed by P. Alvey and the author at the Imperial Cancer Research Fund's laboratories. Expert systems gain particular appeal when they can provide explanations. If a doctor is unhappy about the recommended decisions, or about questions the system has asked, an explanation of the system's reasoning can be requested, and a judgment made about its validity. Table 2 illustrates an explanation facility.

Table 3 *Examples of how knowledge can be represented as facts and rules. (a) Many facts can be represented as relationships (underlined) between objects. (b) Facts are not always true; it is sometimes necessary to hedge the fact by adding a measure of certainty (underlined). This may be numerical, as in the first example, when the certainty value may be exploited with Bayesian procedures in making inferences. If linguistic, or "covert" representations of certainty are used, as in the last two examples, then it will be necessary to define methods for revising and combining certainties in linguistic or logical ways. There are no generally agreed methods for these operations. (c) A rule in the EMYCIN style, which shows how the underlying logic can be presented in a readable way. The rules can also have a value attached to them when an inference cannot be made with certainty: the example here is a certain inference.*

(a)	duodenal-ulcer <u>is-a-kind-of</u> peptic-ulcer
	duodenum <u>is-a-part-of</u> gi-system
	ulceration <u>is-a-cause-of</u> bleeding

(b)	gastric-cancer is-associated-with weight loss <u>(.7)</u>
	Cholecystitis is-associated-with severe-pain <u>(usually)</u>
	oesophagitis is-<u>usually</u>-associated-with reflux

(c)	If: (1) An anti-inflammatory drug should be recommended for the patient,
	(2) Oral drugs are suitable for the patient, and
	(3) The patient is not suspected of having a peptic ulcer
	Then: It is definite (1.0) that the following is one of the recommendations for pain:
	Aspirin orally

The structure of expert systems

Terminology isn't settled yet but the structure of an expert system is simple. It has three essential parts, the triptych of data, knowledge base and shell. The parts are essential in the same way that a reference signal, a comparator and a feedback loop are essential to a control system; they are not always distinct, particularly if other components have been added, but functionally they are certainly there. Fig. 1 illustrates the triptych, along with some of the jargon of the field. Knowledge is commonly represented in the form of facts and rules, as illustrated in Table 3.

There are two main ways in which shells use knowledge to solve problems. In the "data-driven" method the available data are examined and all the rules which are applicable are operated. Any conclusions which are made by these rules contribute to the fund of data and may in turn allow other rules to operate. The cycle may be repeated many times until eventually a definite diagnosis or a firm recommendation is reached.

The other method, the "goal-driven" approach, starts at the opposite end of the logical process. It identifies the conclusions it needs to establish, its goals, and examines the rules to see which ones contribute directly to these goals. Then by looking at the "If . . ." part of the rules it identifies the data required to make these conclusions. The missing data are then filled in by treating them as new "sub-goals", or by asking the user. As in the data-driven method this cycle may be repeated many times, and may require many generations of sub-goals before the system obtains all necessary data to make or refute its main goal.

It is currently popular to represent knowledge as rules and facts but it can be expressed in other ways. For example it can be implemented as networks of elementary relationships – semantic nets – or more highly structured collections of interrelated material – frames. (Conventional programs can be included in a knowledge base and while sometimes necessary it is a retrograde step, as we shall see shortly.) The shell may interpret the data by logical deduction, or by more informal methods such as fuzzy reasoning, depending on the rules and facts in the knowledge base and the primitive functions which are available. The outcomes of such processes include inferences, and signals which trigger operations like asking the user for further symptom information. We shall see examples of all these ideas later.

If the facts and rules are comprehensive they contain all the information that is required to make any decision; all the shell does is control the timely retrieval of relevant facts and rules. It is widely agreed that quite unsophisticated algorithms are sufficient for providing this control. In principle data-driven or goal-driven techniques are sufficient for all the logical steps. The power of the system comes from the contents of the knowledge base not from sophisticated features of the shell.

Figure 1 The expert system triptych of a "shell" which uses "knowledge" to interpret "data"

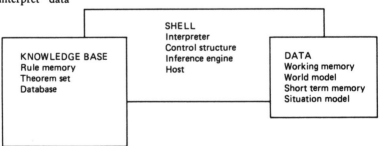

Relationship to traditional systems

The triptych is not unique to expert systems. Conventional decision aids, such as statistical diagnosis systems, may also be thought of as having three elements.

The most commonly used probabilistic technique for diagnosis uses estimates of how often particular symptoms and signs occur in groups of patients with particular diseases. Assume there are two equally likely diseases, A and B. If a symptom occurs more often in A than in B, for example, then a patient who has the symptom is more likely to be suffering from A than B. Bayes' rule for the calculation of probabilities gives a way of combining the evidence from many symptoms and signs; in theory it can be used to distinguish any number of conditions.

Tim de Dombal has carried out the most complete and careful studies of the use of Bayes' rule in computer assisted diagnosis to date (e.g., de Dombal 1979). In reviewing his work on computer assistance in the diagnosis of acute abdominal pain he analyses the problems in detail, and provides objective measurements of the impact of his system in a number of centres. The contribution of the system to increases in diagnostic accuracy (rising from around 70% to around 90%) and reduction in appendix perforation rates (from 24 percent to 11 percent) and negative laparotomy rates (from 36 percent to 14 percent) is of great significance.

Another sort of choice that regularly has to be made is the choice between alternative investigations. An extension of Bayesian theory lets us estimate the expected amount of information that will be provided by each of the alternative tests. This can be done because information is technically defined as something that reduces uncertainty, our uncertainty about something being inversely related to its probability. Lindley (1956) showed one way of calculating the likely information yield of a procedure by looking at each candidate investigation and determining the uncertainty that would still be present after a negative outcome and a positive outcome, weighting each with the overall probability of each outcome for each diagnosis that is possible, and summing the values to give a total expected uncertainty. Subtracting the prior uncertainty gives a measure of the expected information provided by the investigation.

Decision theory provides important extensions to these basic probabilistic concepts. In particular it is necessary to incorporate values and costs into decision-making, and the theory shows how to distinguish the probability element of a decision from its utility. One test may be more informative or reliable than another, but it may be so costly in money or in patient distress that it should be rejected in favor of the less reliable test, at least in the first instance. An operation for a life-threatening condition might be a complete success, a failure, or a partial success leaving the patient confined to bed. The theory shows how to formalise part of the process of weighing up the consequences of the alternatives. Spiegelhalter and Smith (1981) give an extensive review of the techniques available for decisions of this type.

All these approaches can be viewed as having a triptych structure; an interpreter (some mathematical formula) is used to analyse data (symptoms, candidate investigations) by reference to a body of information about probabilities or utilities.

Knowledge-based systems radically extend these concepts, because they let us get away from the purely abstract representations of mathematics and allow the computer to deal with the meaning of concepts to some extent. For example, a table of conditional probabilities represents the frequencies with which events co-occur, like the frequency of co-occurrence of diseases and symptoms. These numbers represent a *relationship* between the symptoms and diseases, but in an abstract form. They say nothing about what a symptom is, what a disease is, whether "measles" is a symptom or a disease, or whether a symptom is caused by a disease or just statistically associated with it. Each number records the *scale* of a relationship but not its *sense*.

In knowledge-based systems we try to represent knowledge in a way that preserves the natural sense as well as the scale of relationships. One way of doing this is by storing the relationships as explicit facts (Table 3 (a)). If the relationship is not clear-cut we may quantify it with numbers or in some other way (Table 3 (b)).

The potential to exploit the sense of relationships as well as the strength gives expert systems their potential for intelligibility. In addition it is a rich source of inferences. For example, knowledge of causal relationships may let us account for observations or suggest new hypotheses (duodenal ulcers cause bleeding but not vice versa). "Inheritance" of properties among members of classes can lead to valuable generalisations (duodenal and gastric ulcers inherit generic properties of ulcers). Logical constraints can be used for planning (a drug which may exacerbate one of the patient's problems is undesirable). Furthermore many processes need to be described over time (events can be described as before, after, during, simultaneous etc.). In many fields, even those as imprecise as medicine, the qualitative element is usually at least as important as the quantitative one and needs to be reflected in our decision-making techniques.

This process of making knowledge explicit does not stop here in the static or "declarative" part of the knowledge base. In expert systems it is often extended into the "procedural" parts of the system, primarily by including rules like that in Table 3 (c) in the knowledge base. Rules describe actions within the general format "IF this THEN do that".

Another way of viewing rules is to see them as exploiting the logical relationship of implication; the conditions are logical premises and when they are true then the action is to draw a conclusion.

When we define rules we are applying the idea of explication again. This time we are making logical fragments of reasoning explicit, and the reasoning of the computer becomes more like that of a doctor. It also yields the potential for accountability – we can see how a conclusion is arrived at, and judge it critically.

The three-part structure can facilitate communication with the user as well as calculation. All user input can go into the working data memory, not just input data and inferences but also queries from the user like "what is aspirin?" or "why did you recommend drug X instead of drug Y?" (Fox *et al.* 1983). Simple messages can be interpreted by parts of the knowledge base specialised for that purpose; facts about parts of speech, grammar rules, special programs for parsing and of course knowledge about the application itself. This is a radical idea which only becomes practical with knowledge over and above, though not independent of, the knowledge required to do the decision-making task.

Examples of medical expert systems

The first medical expert system was MYCIN, developed by Shortliffe and colleagues at Stanford University (Shortliffe 1976). MYCIN gives advice on bacterial infections and their treatment. This program first showed the practical value of many features now associated with expert system; use of knowledge derived from experts in the form of rules; rule-based explanation techniques; goal driven control; imprecise reasoning with measures of belief. EMYCIN (Empty MYCIN) was subsequently developed by Van Melle (1980); EMYCIN is an expert system shell with all MYCIN's features but without any rules which commit it to a particular application. EMYCIN has been used for a number of other applications, including the terminal care advisor illustrated in Tables 1 and 2.

Other medical expert systems use other AI methods. CASNET (Causal ASsociation NETwork) from Rutgers University was developed for the problem of diagnosing and treating the eye condition glaucoma. CASNET differs from MYCIN in its emphasis on causal modelling of the disease and less emphasis on explanation. For example in glaucoma the increase of pressure in the fluid inside the eye can lead to permanent damage. The CASNET system contains knowledge of such facts and can build a model of the disease process in the individual patient using the causal information in conjunction with probabilistic data (Weiss *et al.* 1978). A model of this type can help in the prediction of the future course of the disease and seems a natural form of reasoning for the clinician who uses the

Table 4 *Summary of a number of medical expert systems including evaluation data where these are available. Evaluation = evaluation criterion; performance – result of evaluation; status – whether in use, under development or whether project completed; site – where the work was done.*

Expert system shell	Evaluation	Results	Status	Site
MYCIN (recommends therapy for bacterial infections)	EMYCIN Agreement with experts	55/80	Complete	Stanford
INTERNIST (general diagnosis in internal medicine)	Informal routine cases Accuracy – hard cases	Modest 18/20	Complete	Pittsburgh Pittsburgh
CASNET (diagnosis and treatment of glaucoma)	EXPERT Agreement with experts	Same	Complete	Rutgers
PUFF (interpretation of respiration data)	EMYCIN Agreement with experts	90%	In use	Stanford
Diagnosis of dyspepsia from symptoms	PSYCO Objective accuracy	72%	Complete	Sheffield
	PSYCO Comparison with Bayes	Equal	Complete	Sheffield
Management of terminal illness	EMYCIN Informal assessment		Devel.	ICRF
Diagnosis from leukaemia sample data	EMYCIN Agreement with expert	75%	Devel.	ICRF
Oncocin (formulation of cancer chemotherapy protocols)	Under development		Devel.	Stanford

system. As with MYCIN an expert system shell, EXPERT, has been developed.

The INTERNIST-1 system (Pople 1982) interprets clinical information in internal medicine. Internist is striking because of the scale of the system; over a number of years it has been developed to the point where it can assist with the diagnosis of about 600 diseases in internal medicine. An interesting though rudimentary feature of INTERNIST is that it can choose between several different strategies for carrying out differential diagnoses. Different hypothesis-testing strategies which have often been observed in human behaviour (e.g. Fox 1980) are built into the program. INTERNIST will investigate subjects which verify, eliminate or discriminate among its hypotheses depending upon the number of hypotheses under consideration.

VM (Ventilator Manager) is designed for the intensive care unit; it is able to interpret the clinical significance of signals from equipment used to monitor and assist a patient's respiration. VM can summarise the patient's condition and make recommendations about adjustments. PUFF was an EMYCIN system for diagnosing respiratory conditions which has been recoded in Basic and is now in routine use at Pacific Medical Center (Aikins *et al.* 1982). The MYCIN group is now working on a new system, Oncocin, to assist with the management of cancer chemotherapy protocols. Oncocin is used regularly in the clinic, though on an experimental basis. The system for advising on the management of terminal patients, and one for interpreting blood sample data in a leukaemia laboratory, have been developed with EMYCIN at the Imperial Cancer Research Fund. PSYCO, a system originally developed for psychological simulation, was applied to the diagnosis of dyspepsia, and evaluated favourably using objective diagnostic data (Fox *et al.* 1980). The performance and development status of these systems is summarised in Table 4. More discussion and evaluation information, including non-medical expert systems, is given by Duda and Shortliffe (1983). Some general reviews of expert systems are Stefik *et al.* (1982); Davis (1982); and Michie (1983).

THE CASE FOR KNOWLEDGE-BASED SYSTEMS

The performance of expert systems is encouraging, but as yet few have been introduced into clinical practice or a full clinical trial carried out. Furthermore the published figures are really no better than those which have been obtained using traditional methods for diagnosis (de Dombal 1979). Therefore, what is the case for a knowledge-based decision technology which is not well understood, as against formal methods which are?

The argument seems to run like this: statistical decision technology has been on the verge of a practical breakthrough for twenty years. Weaknesses in human decision-making have been amply demonstrated and the power of formal decision-making techniques has often been shown – but except in a few specialised areas the practical adoption of the techniques has been disappointing. Why? Knowledge-based approaches may have brought some of the reasons into focus.

First there is the problem of compiling quantitative databases for mathematical systems. Subjective and objective methods have been tried but neither are entirely satisfactory – because decision-makers find it difficult to express their practical knowledge in quantitative terms, while actuarial estimation of probabilities and other parameters is laborious and costly. Second, formal decision procedures are relatively unintelligible to the user, and they have no natural mechanisms for ensuring accountability of decision-making. Finally formalisation tends to impose an artificially simple model of the decision; essentially selection of the item with maximum probability or utility from among a fixed set of alternatives.

Knowledge-based techniques let us attack these problems in a new way. Using languages which can express facts and inference rules we can represent an experienced decision-maker's knowledge qualitatively, informally and naturally. This holds the promise of developing knowledge bases quickly using the knowledge of human experts. Furthermore the representation of experts' knowledge as facts and rules makes the procedures relatively intelligible and facilitates the provision of explanations. This helps knowledge bases to be built and refined progressively, and in practical use the systems are more understandable and accountable to the user. Also the relational nature of the knowledge base assists automatic, logic-based consistency checking and quality control. Finally, as was hinted at in INTERNIST, and will be elaborated later, we can represent a variety of decision-making strategies in the knowledge base that more closely reflect the strategies of the human decision-maker.

It seems, then, that these methods might solve, or at least radically reduce, current problems in decision technology; but of course things are rarely this clear cut. Let us look at the claims in more detail.

Claim 1: Rules are a natural representation for expert knowledge

It is said that direct representation of knowledge as facts and IF . . . THEN . . . rules allows experts to specify expert systems directly, in a natural way, and to locate missing or incorrect material which causes the systems to misbehave.

Practical experience is consistent with the claim that rules are quite a natural way to express knowledge of complex domains. Domain experts can develop substantial systems without specialised AI knowledge (though it helps). Using EMYCIN the ICRF terminal care advisor and leukaemia diagnosis system were taken to a sufficiently advanced stage to be demonstrable in four and two months respectively. The terminal care system currently contains about 200 rules (Alvey 1983) and the leukaemia system about 70 (Myers *et al.* 1983). The authors of the first system is a surgeon, the second a leukaemia research worker.

Expert systems are not always implemented directly by an expert in the field of application. If the expert has no computing skill then collaboration with a "knowledge engineer" may be needed. This introduces the problem of establishing good communication between the computer professional and the expert who is to provide the knowledge for the system. The problem of eliciting knowledge from the expert in the form of rules and facts is not as hard as trying to formulate the knowledge in formal or algorithmic terms. Nevertheless it can be a slow hit-and-miss process.

Representing human knowledge as rules seems justified on theoretical as well as practical grounds. Newell and Simon (1972) first suggested using production rules to simulate human problem-solving. Since then many studies have shown that rule-based programs can model human thinking. The methods can also be used to model decision-making and diagnosis (Fox 1980, 1981).

However it cannot be claimed that human knowledge is exclusively rule-based; perception and imagery are important in decision-making and are not easily described in this way. Furthermore it would be dangerous to assume that when experts can articulate their experience in rule form they do so without error or distortion. It is well established that experts' estimates of probabilities can deviate systematically from objective estimates. The same could be true of qualitative judgments. Recent work has suggested that in tasks with a non-obvious structure, skill at verbalising task knowledge is poorly or even negatively correlated with skill at actually doing the task (Broadbent *et al.* 1983; Berry and Broadbent 1983). The debate about the accuracy of introspection (Nisbett and Wilson 1977) also raises serious doubts about the reliability of subjective reporting of knowledge. Nevertheless, as we have seen, it is possible to build successful systems based on individual experience. Whether this is only possible when the tasks have a simple structure, or whether programming and executing the rules facilitates debugging remains to be established.

Claim 2: Expert systems can be developed incrementally

Typically, the development of an expert system involves a large number of small design cycles; add a rule, run the system and check its behaviour, add or improve a rule and so on. This progressive, empirical refinement is possible for a number of reasons. First the rule base is modular; each rule deals with a small, independent fragment of the domain. Second, because the knowledge is separated from the control mechanisms the addition of new rules doesn't create new "bugs" as is so typical with conventional programs. (This is because each new rule should be logically independent of older rules. Also, since the program statements are a set of rules whose execution is determined by events, not a preprogrammed sequence of steps, there is no sequencing requirement that can be violated by additional rules.)

However the overall picture may be less clear cut. Myers *et al.* (1983) report developing an expert system for leukaemia diagnosis; they examined the effects of gradually adding rules to the knowledge base. Although performance improved with greater knowledge some of the increased rate of correct diagnosis was obtained at a cost in overdiagnosis (increased false alarms) on a prospective patient series. This is what one might expect from the statistical view in terms overfitting a model to data. Knowledge engineering techniques alone do not overcome such classical problems.

The claim that rules are independent should not be overstated. True independence of rules is only achieved when the system relies primarily on recognition of patterns rather than searching or transforming data. Some tasks which require highly controlled operations (e.g., exhaustive search through data trees, iteration over arrays) are clumsy to implement with rule-based techniques. Indeed some expert system packages compromise and provide extensive facilities for programming with rules, which means the rules cannot be regarded as purely logical statements; this can produce difficulties in developing knowledge bases (Alvey 1983). Finally there is a lot of current interest in using "meta-rules" in knowledge bases. Meta-rules control the application of other rules. It is not known how meta-rules interact, or whether their use will introduce problems for incremental development of rule-based systems.

Claim 3: Rules facilitate logic-based quality control of software

The rules of an expert system are really formulas in logic. They can therefore be checked for logical consistency. EMYCIN is able to carry out simple checks on the consistency of the expert's rules (e.g., rules with the same premises should not lead to inconsistent conclusions), and work in logic-programming and program specification languages is likely to provide a variety of more powerful features in the future.

However, there are two areas where new ideas are needed. First, a major practical problem for expert systems can be that they are incomplete, not inconsistent. They simply don't know enough about the application. Although it is possible to estimate uncertainty (in the probability sense) when all possible events are known, it is not at present possible to estimate ignorance, i.e. what one doesn't know. Secondly, there is a whole subject of meaning and semantics. A rule may be superficially consistent, but it can still be an incorrect or even meaningless rule for the domain. With present techniques of knowledge acquisition and limited processing of meaning this situation is unlikely to improve much in the short-term.

Claim 4: Expert systems are intelligible and accountable

Perhaps the most interesting and potent idea introduced by expert systems is that of explanation. Rule-based systems have the capacity to explain aspects of what they are doing, and how they came to certain conclusions. If the user wants to know why the system is asking a question, for example, the rule which led to the question can be translated into English. Explanation of a conclusion is given by reporting the rules which led to the conclusion. MYCIN pioneered the practical use of the idea and all EMYCIN based systems have it automatically.

These techniques are valuable but insufficient. They are limited to explanations at the rule level and are incapable of giving, say, summaries of their reasoning or describing the decision-making strategies underlying their reasoning. This last observation is a telling one because it is not simply a weakness in current explanation techniques but a weakness of expert system technology. In my view *expert systems do not have a decision-making strategy*. What they have is a mechanism for proving things logically – data-driven or goal-driven inference – plus some probabilistic mechanisms to deal with cases where inferences cannot be made with certainty. The idea that computer programs can explain themselves is a radical one that should be adopted throughout decision technology, but we need more techniques. General explanation techniques for decision technology may not emerge until we have a knowledge-based theory of decision-making.

Research has so far failed to provide a knowledge-based decision theory in other important respects. First no new solution to the problem of how values and costs may be incorporated into the decision process has been offered. To my knowledge no expert system has any facilities at all for this. Second, because the systems draw upon empirical knowledge of contingencies, rather than any axiomatic theory, there is no basis for evaluating the optimality of the decision process. All that is currently possible is to carry out empirical evaluation of their practical performance (Duda and Shortliffe 1983) or comparisons with formal techniques (Fox *et al.* 1980).

To summarise, expert systems use rules to interpret data and make suggestions about decisions. Rules and facts are relatively easy to compile into intelligible knowledge bases, incrementally, from expert experience. They facilitate consistency checks and simple explanation because the knowledge is explicit rather than implicit in an algorithm. However, expert systems do not yet exemplify a theory of decision-making which is comparably explicit. The decision-making components (data and goal driven inference and probability calculation) are algorithms embedded in the shell, not parts of the knowledge base. This limits intelligibility and flexibility. The rest of the paper explores the possibility of an explicit decision theory and what such a theory might provide.

TOWARDS A KNOWLEDGE-BASED DECISION THEORY

Decisions are traditionally seen as choices. The choices may be between different diagnoses, when we usually use some form of probability and select on the basis of maximum likelihood or maximum belief. Alternatively we may be choosing tests or investigations, in which case we may try to maximise information yield, or we are choosing treatments and try to maximise expected utility. These approaches have great strength. They reduce decisions to forms which are tractable within axiomatic models like Bayes' rule, information theory, or subjective expected utility theory.

But there are weaknesses. Usually practical decision problems are not simple and may not be axiomatisable (though that involves deep issues). Practical decisions usually involve tasks of different types; almost any medical decision about how to treat a patient will involve many steps. Some are relatively easy to define – what is wrong with the patient, what is the best way of finding out, what would be the most cost-effective treatment and so on. Other parts may be harder to analyse – is the patient ill? how may we plan a treatment regime to cover for possible contingencies? Traditional decision models are completely general; any decision can be cast as one of choosing between a finite set of alternatives, but the theory isn't complete. For instance:

1 No available theory says how a complex decision should be broken into its component tasks, so the framing of decisions remains intuitive, e.g., does "diagnosis" require sequential steps (information gathering followed by probabilistic classification, say) or is it a repetitive, hypothesise-and-test procedure?

2 There is no theory to tell us how to select a decision procedure that is appropriate for each component task, e.g., is "diagnosis" a probability maximisation task? or is it a problem in resource utilisation?

The simple but crucial point is that we need to be able to make decisions about decisions. For example if we had a library of decision models we could calculate some measure of goodness of fit between the decision as presented and the models in the library, and then use the method which best fits the situation. As far as I am aware this has not been done within a traditional framework. I am inclined to doubt that it can be done. When decision procedures are cast as mathematical functions or as computer algorithms they become executable but not analysable. Bayes' rule can be used to calculate numbers, but not to calculate its own appropriateness. In short, to use the jargon of artificial intelligence, decision theory needs a "meta theory". Knowledge-based concepts could provide such a theory.

An old idea in artificial intelligence is that there is no distinction between programs and data – programs can be the data of other programs. We see this in a simple form in the rules of expert systems:

IF   the patient has spots, and
           the patient has a temperature   (1)
THEN   the diagnosis may be measles

The rule has both "procedural" and "declarative" readings. We can execute it as a program – to make an inference about a diagnosis from symptoms – or we can examine its contents to see if it fits the current decision problem. The rule fits if we are trying to make a diagnosis but not if we are trying to select a treatment. We can extend this idea a little towards the meta-level:

IF   the number of possible diagnoses is small
                                     (2)
THEN   use a differential diagnosis procedure

IF   the number of possible diagnoses is large
                                     (3)
THEN   try to eliminate some possibilities

These rules say how to choose between simple decision strategies. By making the procedures explicit in the knowledge base, rather than being embedded inaccessibly in an algorithm that can only be executed, we acquire great power. We can even make decisions about how to decide how to select appropriate decision procedures, and so on. This last ability allows us to move towards a meta-theory which is independent of applications – as the following example illustrates:

IF   the cost of making the wrong decision is high, and
           the cost of delaying a decision is low   (4)
THEN   choose an exhaustive information gathering procedure

A model of the decision

It has been remarked that for a system to qualify as decision technology it must (a) embody some concept of what a decision is, and (b) have mechanisms for implementing specific decisions within the general framework. Since any process can be modelled as a function that maps from a domain of definition to a range of values, decision processes can be regarded as functions for mapping contingencies onto choices. In general the functions may exploit rules, facts, mathematical operators, or combinations of other decision functions. Taking a "diagnosis" example, a simple structure emerges (the braces { } are the usual indicator for sets):

NAME   Medical diagnosis
Domain   {symptom}
Range   {disease}   (5)
Function   {diagnosis rule}

The next step is to provide information about the decision elements which allow us to make decisions. In this case we need to define symptoms, disease and the diagnosis rules:

symptom   spots, temperature, swollen-glands
disease   measles, mumps
diagnosis-rule (IF symptom = spots, and
                     symptom = temperature
                  THEN disease = measles),   (6)
                  (IF symptom = swollen-glands, and
                  _   symptom = temperature
                  THEN disease = mumps)

None of this information needs to be explicitly available; it could be embedded in a decision-making algorithm. However by making all the knowledge explicit higher-level decisions are easier to express. For example, in the INTERNIST system, criteria based on the number of current hypotheses are used to select different investigation strategies; they can be written as rules ("count" is a primitive function which counts data elements matching a data template supplied to it as a parameter; in this case it returns the number of hypotheses which are current):

NAME   differential diagnosis strategy
Domain   {hypothesis}
Range   {decision-strategy}
Function   {strategy-rule}
decision-strategy verify, eliminate, discriminate
strategy-rule   (IF count(hypothesis X) = 1
                       THEN decision-strategy = verify),   (7)
                    (IF count(hypothesis X) > 1, and
                        count(hypothesis X) < 5
                       THEN decision-strategy = discriminate).
                    (IF count(hypothesis X) > = 5
                       THEN decision-strategy = eliminate)

Ordinary decision procedures, such as Bayes' rule, can also be represented. The operator *, for combining prior and conditional probabilities, is assumed to be a primitive; the range and domain of the function are recorded explicitly as facts.

NAME	Bayes	
Domain	{prior probability},	
	{conditional probability}	
Range	{posterior probability}	(8)
Function	prior probability * conditional probability	
prior probability	positive-real-number from unit-interval	
posterior probability	positive-real-number from unit-interval	

The formulation is sufficiently general to provide a limited framework for cost-benefit decisions. One approach would be to incorporate a cost-benefit calculation procedure in the same way the probabilistic procedure was represented in the last example. A second method would be to include qualitative selection rules like rule 4 above, but referring to specific actions (investigations or treatments) rather than general strategies.

Simple decision processes, like finding out whether a symptom is present, are straightforward ("ask-user" is treated as a primitive operator):

NAME	Find symptom	
Domain	{symptom}	
Range	present, absent	(9)
Function	ask-user {symptom}	

Another useful aspect of having decision-making methods made explicit in a knowledge base is that alternative methods can be provided in case one should fail. For example, some conditions can be inferred from other conditions; only if there is insufficient information to make a determination will it be necessary to ask the user. An example of this comes from terminal care and the treatment of dysphagia (difficulty in swallowing). If it is known that the patient has a hernia it is probable that the base of the oesophagus will be constricted, leading to the difficulty. If no such judgement can be established with the available data then the computer will have to ask the user for information to establish the dysphagia's cause:

NAME	Cause of dysphagia	
Domain	{gi-symptoms} {gi-signs}	
Range	{cause-of-dysphagia}	(10)
Function	(If gi-sign is hiatus-hernia	
	THEN cause-of-dysphagia may-be oesophageal-	
	stricture, etc.) OR ask-user	

Table 5 *The leukaemia analysis is treated as a structure containing decisions about test results, the blood "cell-lineage" and "cell-type", and leukaemia type. In each decision there is a function which maps values from the decision domain to values in the decision range. Domain and range values may be specified explicitly, or by means of features which define sets, indicated by braces, { }. The decision function may exploit rules (which may draw upon facts), mathematical operators, or a combination of simpler decisions.*

NAME	LEUKAEMIA SAMPLE ANALYSIS
Domain	{lab-test}, {clinical-diagnosis}
Range	{leukaemia-type}
Function	first-test-battery, then diagnosis, then further-tests, then diagnosis
NAME	leukaemia type
Domain	{cell-lineage}, {cell-type}
Range	{leukaemia-type}
Function	{diagnosis-rule}
diagnosis-rule	(IF cell-type is null-cell, and cell-lineage is acute-lymphoblastic-leukaemia THEN leukaemia-type is null-all, IF cell-type is common-cell, and cell-lineage is acute-lymphoblastic-leukaemia THEN leukaemia-type is common-all, etc)
NAME	further-tests
Domain	{leukaemia-type}
Range	{further-test}
Function	IF leukaemia-type maybe b-cell THEN further-test is kappa/lambda, IF leukaemia-type maybe t-cell THEN further-test is {t-cell subsets}
further-test	kappa/lambda, . . . {t-cell subsets}
t-cell subsets	OKT1, . . . OKT6, OKT8, OKT11A
NAME	cell-lineage
Domain	{first-test-battery}
Range	{cell-lineage}
Function	IF Tdt is positive, and age-group is child THEN cell-lineage is acute-lymphoblastic-leukaemia, . . .
cell-lineage	all, cell, . . . burkitt-cells
NAME	cell-type
Domain	{first-test-battery}
Range	{cell type}
Function	IF HLA-DR is positive THEN cell-type is-not t-cell, . . .
cell-type	t-cell, b-cell, . . . myeloid
NAME	lab-test
Domain	Tdt, mouse-rosettes, . . . Smlg, E-rosettes
Range	positive, negative
Function	IF Tdt > 20 THEN Tdt is positive, IF Tdt = < 20 THEN Tdt is negative, . . .

We can now see how a complex decision may be represented. The example taken is the problem of managing the laboratory analysis of blood samples for leukaemia diagnosis. This is a task which involves several steps and many tests on the blood cells. Not all tests are carried out in the first battery; some are selected on the basis of diagnoses suspected from the first results. The structure of the analysis is illustrated schematically in Figure 2. Table 5 gives a knowledge representation for this function tree.

Judgement and policies

Expert systems have shown that the explicit use of knowledge in the form of rules and facts can give considerable competence in specialised fields. They also represent an important step towards systems which are intelligible and accountable. Is the framework presented here applicable to less specialised decision-making?

Consider the work of the medical general practitioner (GP), a decision-maker and manager with a daunting range of work. Brooke (1983) summarises some of the ways in which GP decision-making differs from the decision-making of specialists. He notes the wide range of problems that are presented to the GP, their ill-defined character, the greater range of information the GP has about the patient's background, and the requirement that information be integrated over time, sometimes a lifetime. He shows also the heterogeneity of decision types; some are diagnosis related, some management related, problem related, family related and so on.

Consider the patient who repeatedly visits his doctor complaining of vague indigestion, but who is known to have distressing family problems. The GP will not necessarily see his task as formulating an exact "diagnosis". Often he will simply decide upon an action; to recommend antacids or counselling, or to refer the patient, or deliberately postpone a decision. There are at least two levels of decision-making here, the classic one of deciding the diagnosis (when appropriate) and also a higher level

Figure 2 Function tree for leukaemia sample analysis. The overall decision is treated as a number of simpler decisions; analyse the results from an initial battery of tests; form a provisional diagnosis; select additional tests to confirm any suspected diagnoses; reconsider the diagnosis. The details of the structure are given in Table 5

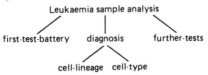

Table 6 *Decisions are viewed as complex functions which link situations with possible conclusions or actions. These functions can then be viewed as networks of possible decisions. The decisions in Fig. 3 are formulated, hypothetically, as a number of IF . . . THEN . . . decision rules. Rules 1 and 2 and others in the decision "possible causes of dyspepsia" are for interpreting a patient's history. Rule 3 is a meta-rule for deciding when to attempt a differential diagnosis on the basis that if a possible cause could be treated by the GP then a diagnosis should be attempted, otherwise an option would be to refer the patient. Rule 4 is an example of a diagnosis rule, which helps to discriminate between gastric and duodenal ulcers.*

NAME	possible cause of dyspepsia
Domain	{gi-history}, {gi-signs}
Range	peptic-ulcer, gastric-cancer, gall-stones, . . . functional
Function	

             (IF age is elderly, and   (1)
                weight-loss is present, and
                weight-loss is recent
             THEN dyspepsia could-be-caused-by gastric-cancer,
             IF   pain is present   (2)
                pain is-at right-hypochondrium, and
                pain has-severity severe, or
                pain has-pattern occasional-attacks
             THEN dyspepsia could-be-caused-by cholecystitis, . . . etc)

NAME	attempt a differential diagnosis of dyspepsia
Domain	{possible-causes-of-dyspepsia}
Range	differential-diagnosis-of-dyspepsia
Function	

             (IF dyspepsia could-be-caused-by Condition, and   (3)
               Condition is-a locally-treatable-condition
             THEN decide differential-diagnosis-of dyspepsia, . . . etc)
             OR decide referral

NAME	differential diagnosis of dyspepsia
Domain	{possible-causes-of-dyspepsia}
Range	duodenal-ulcer, gastric-ulcer, gastric-cancer, . . . gall-stones
Function	

             (IF dyspepsia could-be-caused-by peptic-ulcer, and   (4)
               dyspepsia is-aggravated-by food, and
               dyspepsia is-immediately-after meals
             THEN gastric-ulcer is-a-probable-cause-of dyspepsia . . . etc)

judgment – that of deciding whether to attempt a diagnosis at all or to take some other action, such as arranging referral to a specialist.

Both these types of decision, and the criteria by which they are made, should be made explicit. Once they are made explicit we can discuss and validate them, and perhaps exploit them in an expert system. The management of indigestion and the problem of referring patients sheds light on how this may be done.

The management of indigestion (dyspepsia) might be represented diagrammatically as the function tree in Fig. 3. This illustrates one view of the management of a patient. If the "possible-cause" rules suggest that an organic condition may be responsible for the indigestion then the decision may be taken to attempt a differential diagnosis, by attempting to establish facts which will discriminate, verify or eliminate the various alternatives. Each of these decisions can now be formulated as explicit functions, illustrated in Table 6.

If we can formulate complex decisions in this way an interesting possibility presents itself, one which is at the core of a general practitioner's work. In rule 3 of Table 6 we are not just stating a special-case rule about dyspepsia but one that embodies a deeper principle of wider relevance; the rule could be generalised to cover many other circumstances. The principle is "if any problem may be caused by an organic condition, and the condition can be treated by a GP, then it is appropriate to attempt a differential diagnosis".

Similar policy rules can be formulated for other general classes of decision. Contingencies may arise which indicate that action should be postponed, or that a patient should be referred, or that no action should be taken. Brooke suggests that the GP has a "cognitive map" of these

Figure 3 An illustrative view of part of the decision network of dyspepsia. Particular patterns in the history suggest possible organic causes. If it is decided to attempt a differential diagnosis then various types of rules can be used to distinguish, verify or eliminate alternative diagnoses

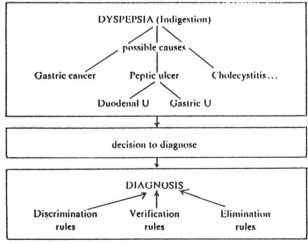

decisions. We might represent a cognitive map of the major classes of GP decisions as a network, as in Fig. 4. Many, perhaps all of the criteria for the decisions in Fig. 4 can be represented in terms of rules. They may represent a GP's subjective – even personal – policies. However, in order to formulate such policies, to make the logic clear so that a computer can follow them, we need to extend the rule machinery a little.

Most of the rules that have been presented formally refer to particular symptoms, signs, etc. which are significant for specific medical decisions. Rules for general policies and principles will have to cover many situations, including many which may not have been foreseen in detail by the system designers. One kind of general rule is obtained by substituting variables for some or all of the objects mentioned in the rule, while leaving the relationship terms constant.

For example, consider "the referral decision" which we might characterise as "the problem of referring all and only those patients who should be referred" (to another doctor). A possible referral policy, covering some easily recognisable situations, is formulated in Table 7 as an explicit set of three rules containing variables.

The validity of decision policies

Not all doctors will agree with the rules in this policy. However, the very fact that they are intelligible enough to be questioned is a considerable strength. The policy can be examined from three points of view.

1 Is the policy consistent? As we saw earlier, although rules may use familiar terms they are, from a formal standpoint, logical formulas which are sufficiently simple that some kinds of logical consistency can be checked.
2 Does the policy cover enough situations: is it complete? We can never be sure that a policy is complete and covers all possible contingencies, but

Figure 4 Many types of decision made by GPs are general, "policy" decisions which subsume particular decisions for particular medical problems. These policy decisions can be viewed as a network of interconnected decisions, in which the conditions under which particular decisions are made can be described by "meta"-rules.

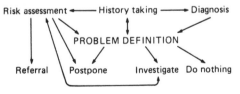

Table 7 *Policy decisions can also be formulated as rules. However the rules are not "special-case rules" and do not refer explicitly to particular diseases, patients etc. They include variables (underlined) which refer to classes of things rather than particular things.*

NAME	referral
Domain	{patients}, {problems}, {diseases}
Range	{patients}, {specialists}
Function	
	IF Patient is-suspected-of Disease, and (5)
	Disease is-a-kind-of progressive-disease, and
	Specialist is-a-specialist-in Disease
	THEN Patient should-be-referred-to Specialist
	IF Problem is-a-problem-for Patient, and (6)
	Problem could-be-caused-by Disease, and
	Disease is-a-kind-of life-threatening-condition, and
	Patient is-anxious-about Disease, and
	Specialist is-a-specialist-in Disease
	THEN Patient should-be-referred-to Specialist
	IF Problem is-a-problem-for Patient, and (7)
	Problem is-a-long-standing-problem, and
	Problem is-inconvenient-for Patient, and
	Specialist is-a-specialist-in Disease
	THEN Patient should-be-referred-to Specialist

sometimes we can detect if it is incomplete. If a policy is just a special sort of decision function which relates contingencies to actions then, once the range of possible contingencies, or the domain of possible actions has been specified, it is possible to see if the rules of the policy fail to mention any of the contingencies or actions.

3 Does the policy prescribe the correct actions in all circumstances? This is the hardest question of all, though it is not new. Mathematical decision theorists tried to capture "rational" policies for treatment selection, resource utilisation, etc. by combining measures of outcome likelihood with estimates of utility, using many procedures. However rules seem to express our intuitions about desirable policies more naturally than mathematics. Rules allow us to express arbitrary concepts and relationships, not just numerical ones. Rules, furthermore, appear to be a common way of expressing written policies, as in legislation and regulations, which suggests they are a preferred medium for communicating our intuitions. For a GP the validity of a policy (for referral, say) is the extent to which the outcomes prescribed by the policy agree with his intuitions (about whether a patient should be referred). Many problems are intrinsically subjective in this way: often there is no other practical standard.

Of course an individual's intuition may be controversial and we may prefer to obtain a consensus rather than assume that any one individual's intuitions are "correct". Forming a consensus about policy, however, depends upon a community being able to discuss its decision options in a common language. Once again the key is the intelligibility that rules seem to offer as a language for expressing decision criteria.

SUMMARY

Some of the concepts underlying expert systems have been described, and claims made for them have been assessed. Expert systems may make a major contribution to decision technology, primarily through their emphasis on the explicit representation of knowledge. If knowledge is represented abstractly, as in numerical decision-analysis, penalties may be incurred in terms of the intelligibility of the decision aids, and the imposition of unnatural and inflexible decision models on their users. However, expert systems research has concentrated on implementation problems, such as how to represent qualitative concepts in the computer and how to combine logical and probabilistic inference methods; there has been little attempt to create a knowledge-based theory of decision-making comparable to the established concepts of statistical decision theory.

The spirit of a knowledge-based decision theory is that we try to avoid, or at least postpone, the use of formal, abstract representations of knowledge for decision-making. We try to make the criteria of decisions explicit in the rules we use and the facts those rules exploit. By making an expert's knowledge of rules and facts explicit, decision-technology becomes more intelligible and more accountable. In formulating decision functions we may also reveal problematic elements of the decision process which need to be dealt with as decisions in their own right, and may require their own idiosyncratic decision procedures. However these benefits are obtained by trading qualitative richness for quantitative precision. In some cases there will be insufficient knowledge to make a clear decision on qualitative grounds alone, so provision may be made for the use of complementary quantitative methods.

Decisions can be represented explicitly in a knowledge-base as function trees or networks. This is a general framework for decision-theory. It permits use of rule-based reasoning, or mathematical decision functions if needed. Specific, domain decisions can be described, as can general policies, and decisions about how to approach other decisions. An explicit function tree confers several advantages. Functions can be heterogeneous and more closely reflect human understanding of different decision tasks. They can be stored in libraries and selected when they match new decision problems. Existing explanation mechanisms can be used with the rules in the knowledge base, and in addition the function tree provides a higher-level structure from which to explain the principles or justifications behind a decision strategy.

REFERENCES

Aikins, J. *et al.*, 1982. PUFF: an expert system for interpretation of pulmonary function data, HPP-82-13. Computer Science Dept., Stanford University, CA.

Alvey, P., 1983. The problems in designing a medical expert system. Proceedings of Expert Systems 83. Churchill College, Cambridge, pp. 30–42. (Imperial Cancer Research Fund, Biomedical Computing Unit Report.)

Berry, D.C. and D.E. Broadbent, 1983. On the relationship between task performance and verbal knowledge. Dept. of Experimental Psychology, Oxford University.

Broadbent, D.E., P. Fitzgerald and M.H.P. Broadbent, 1983. Implicit and explicit judgement in the control of complex systems. Dept. of Experimental Psychology, Oxford University.

Brooke, J.B., 1983. "Decision = patient with problem + doctor with problem: a consideration of general practice decision making". In: Proceedings of Workshop of Decision Making in General Practice, Holme-Pierrepont, Nottingham.

Davis, R., 1982. Expert systems: where are we and where do we go from here? *Artificial Intelligence Magazine* 3(2), 3–22.

De Dombal, F.T., 1979. Computers and the surgeon – a matter of decision. *Surgery Annual* 11, 33–57.

Duda, R.O. and E.H. Shortliffe, 1983. Expert systems research. *Science* 220, 261–8.

Fox, J., 1980. Making decisions under the influence of memory. *Psychological Review* 87(2), 190–211.

Fox, J., 1981. Medical diagnosis: inference, recall and a theory of skill. Unpublished manuscript.

Fox, J., P. Alvey and C.D. Myers, 1983. Decision technology and man–machine interaction: the PROPS package. Proceedings of Expert Systems 83, Churchill College, Cambridge, pp. 30–42. (Imperial Cancer Research Fund, Biomedical Computing Unit Report.)

Fox, J., D.C. Barber and K.D. Bardhan, 1980. Alternatives to Bayes: a quantitative comparison with rule-based diagnosis. *Methods of Information in Medicine* 19(4), 210–215.

Lindley, D.V., 1956. On a measure of the information provided by an experiment. *Annals of Mathematical Statistics* 27, 986–1005.

Michie, D. (ed.), 1983. *Readings in expert systems*. London: Gordon and Breach.

Myers, C.D., J. Fox, S.M. Pegram and M.F. Greaves, 1983. Knowledge acquisition for expert systems: experience using EMYCIN for leukaemia diagnosis. Proceedings of Expert Systems 83, Churchill College, Cambridge, pp. 227–293. (Imperial Cancer Research Fund, Biomedical Computing Unit Report.)

252   *J. Fox*

Newell, A. and H.A. Simon, 1972. *Human problem-solving.* Englewood Cliffs, NJ: Prentice-Hall.

Nisbett, R.E. and T.D. Wilson, 1977. Telling more than we can know: verbal reports on mental processes. *Psychological Review* 84, 231–259.

Pople, H., 1982. "INTERNIST-1". In: P. Szolovits (ed.). *Artificial intelligence in medicine.* Boulder, CO: Westview Press.

Shortliffe, E.H., 1976. *Computer-based medical consultations: MYCIN.* New York: Elsevier.

Spiegelhalter, D.J. and A.F.M. Smith, 1981. "Decision analysis and clinical decision". In: R. Coppi and P. Bithell (eds.). *Perspectives in medical statistics.* London: Academic Press.

Stefik, M., J. Aikins, R. Balzer, J. Benoit, L. Birnbaum, F. Hayes-Roth and E. Sacerdoti, 1982. The organisation of expert systems: a prescriptive tutorial. *Artificial Intelligence* 18(2), 135–174.

Van Melle, W., 1980. A domain independent system that aids in constructing knowledge based consultation programs, HPP-80-11. Computer Science Dept., Stanford University, CA, June.

Weiss, S.M., C.A. Kulikowski, S. Amarel and A. Satin, 1978. A model-based method for computer aided medical decision-making. *Artificial Intelligence* 1, 145–172.

PART 3

~

THE DECISION ANALYTIC APPROACH TO
CLINICAL DECISIONS

DECISION ANALYSIS

13

— ~ —

CLINICAL DECISIONMAKING*

Peter Doubilet, Barbara J. McNeil

As the potential benefits, risks, and monetary costs, of medical interventions have escalated, the choices made by today's physician have a far greater impact on the individual patient, and collectively on society, than ever before. At the same time, the expanding diagnostic and therapeutic armamentarium has, for many clinical problems, made the selection of a correct strategy more complex by increasing the number of available options. Thus, it has become both more important and more difficult for the physician to make decisions wisely.

These factors have stimulated research efforts of three types: descriptive studies that examine how physicians actually make decisions; artificial intelligence approaches that attempt to encode, in a computer program, the kinds of inference steps used by physicians in reaching diagnostic or therapeutic decisions; and prescriptive, analytic studies that combine data mathematically and determine the optimal strategy (with respect to a specific criterion) in a particular clinical situation. We consider only the latter in this article. Studies that fall into this category employ a variety of techniques, which we will refer to collectively as decision analysis[1,2] (using the term in its broadest sense). These techniques can be used to select among available options in an individual patient or can be applied to a group of patients who share a given set of characteristics.

Decision analysis is most applicable to clinical questions that cannot be answered by appealing directly to the results of a clinical trial or to a large data base. This can occur because no trial has been carried out or because the patient in question differs substantially from the populations in existing sources of data. Consider the decision between coronary artery bypass surgery and medical management in each of the following patients: a middle-aged man with three-vessel coronary disease (3VD) and chronic lymphocytic leukemia (or other chronic disease that may shorten his life-span); a 75-year-old woman with 3VD; and a 65-year-old woman with two-vessel disease, whose life-style is sufficiently impaired by her

* First published in *Medical Care*, 23 (1985), 648–62. © 1985 Lippincott/Harper & Row. Reprinted by permission.

angina that she considers each year spent in her current state to have only one half the value of a normal (pain-free) year. She would, for example, prefer 6 pain-free years to 10 years in her current state. All of these decisions need data from several sources, including age- and sex-specific annual mortality rates in the general population and excess annual mortality rates associated with three-vessel disease and with chronic lymphocytic leukemia. For the decision in the third patient, information is also needed concerning the likelihood of pain relief with surgical and medical therapy.

In situations such as these, analytic approaches to decisionmaking can synthesize many pieces of diverse data and thereby be a useful adjunct to clinical judgment. Information may be derived from a variety of sources, including clinical studies, data bases, and experts' subjective estimates. Further, the patient's attitudes and values can be incorporated into the analysis.

The analytic approach to decisionmaking involves a number of steps, each of which poses its own set of problems to the clinical decision analyst. These steps are:

1 Construct a mathematic model of the decision problem (this is commonly done using a decision tree, which displays the available decision options, or strategies, and the possible consequences of each).
2 Assign probabilities to uncertain events.
3 Assign values (utilities) to each potential outcome.

The expected utility of each strategy is then computed; the strategy with the highest expected utility is the optimal one. A fourth step, known as sensitivity analysis, should then be carried out:

4 Systematically alter the initial assumptions (made in steps 1–3) to determine how sensitive the optimal strategy is to their variation within a reasonable range.

In this article, we discuss the current status of work in each of these four areas, briefly reviewing some of the major contributions that have been made. Our focus is on methodology, not on applications to specific clinical problems. We also examine the obstacles that remain and indicate possible directions for future research.

MODELLING THE DECISION PROBLEM

Conventional approach

The first step in an analytic approach to a clinical decision is precisely defining the problem: specifying the patient (or group of patients) to whom the analysis is directed, the alternative strategies being considered, and the criterion by which the choice among these alternatives is to be made. We restrict our attention to analyses in which the criterion involves optimizing the expected value of a single parameter (e.g., maximizing life expectancy or minimizing expected monetary cost) or of a combination of two or more such parameters. Once so defined, the clinical decision problem can be represented, or modelled, using a decision tree.

We illustrate this process via the decision whether or not to operate on a patient with suspected acute appendicitis (modified from Pauker and Kassirer[3]). We assume that: 1) The patient has either acute appendicitis or gastroenteritis; 2) There are two alternative strategies: "operate now" or "observe, and operate only if the patient's condition worsens"; and 3) The criterion is maximizing the short-term (1-month) survival rate. Under these restrictions, the decision tree in Figure 1 models the decision problem. Square nodes (□) indicate decision points (or mandated actions if followed by only one branch), and circular nodes (○) indicate chance occurrences. The decision tree serves several functions. First, it visually displays the clinical problem and the strategies under consideration. Second, it keeps track of the probability and utility data that must be obtained. Third, it indicates the way in which the data are to be combined mathematically; for each strategy, multiplying the values along each branch and then summing over all branches.

The tree in Figure 1 is, of course, an oversimplified model of the actual decision problem. Factors other than mortality that may influence the clinical decision, including nonfatal complications of appendicitis and/or surgery, are not considered. Further, other disease states that can produce

Figure 1 Decision tree for suspected acute appendicitis

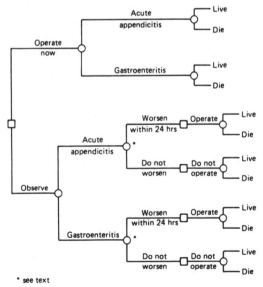

* see text

right-sided abdominal pain, such as cholecystitis and diverticulitis, are ignored. A more complete analysis might consider a variety of strategies that involve diagnostic tests for these diseases, such as ultrasonography, hepatobiliary scanning, or barium enema, performed at initial presentation or after a clinical observation period.

The above discussion reflects a tension between two competing objectives that frequently arises in decision analytic approaches to clinical problems: including enough detail to be medically relevant, but keeping the model from becoming unmanageably large. Developments over the last several years have pushed back the boundary of what is "manageable." These are of two types: computer programs that assist in the construction of decision trees and that carry out the required computations, and the introduction of more sophisticated modelling techniques into the medical arena.

Several microcomputer programs[4,5] aimed primarily at medical users take advantage of the fact that decision trees typically contain multiple repeating subunits, or subtrees. For example, even the simple tree in Figure 1 contains six copies of the two-branch "live–die" subtree, and two copies of the subtree following the nodes labelled with an asterisk in Figure 1. (Note that a subtree always has the same structure, but that the probabilities and utilities assigned to its branches may vary depending on the location of the subtree within the entire tree.) By allowing the user to define subtrees that can be recalled multiple times, the computer can save considerable time in the construction of large trees.

Other available time-saving features include a technique for efficient construction of certain trees that contain near-identical subunits, via the use of "Boolean nodes,"[4] and mechanisms that allow a single tree to be reused multiple times (with different data). The latter is achieved by allowing probabilities and utilities to be entered not only as constants (e.g., probability of acute appendicitis=0.6 in a given patient), but also as variables or mathematic expressions.

Modelling techniques for time-dependent decisions

Conventional decision analysis, with or without computer assistance, is often an unwieldy tool for decisions that depend on the occurrence and timing of future events ("time-dependent" problems). Attempts to model such problems tend to result in trees that are too large for practical use. Sophisticated techniques for time-dependent problems, including Markov analysis[6,7] and variants, have therefore been imported into the medical arena.

We illustrate the limitations of conventional decision analysis for time-dependent problems and outline the Markov approach, using the following clinical example: the decision whether to perform carotid endarterectomy on an 80-year-old woman who has a stenotic lesion in one of her carotid arteries but has not suffered an irreversible cerebrovascular accident (stroke). The goal is to maximize the length of time the woman can expect to remain alive without, or with at most a minor, stroke. Unlike the appendicitis decision, the decisionmaker must consider not only whether, but also when, adverse outcomes occur: a major stroke, or death, 5 years hence must be distinguished from the same event occurring 6 months from now. The endarterectomy decision can be modelled by a decision tree such as that in Figure 2, in which the patient's condition is "observed" every 6 months. (Shortening the "observation period" would increase the accuracy of the analysis, at the expense of enlarging the tree.) The decision tree grows exponentially with the number of time periods considered. Even with computer assistance, the tree becomes unacceptably large if one wishes to compare the two strategies over a 10-year follow-up period.

The endarterectomy decision can instead be modelled as a Markov process if we make the following assumption: the probability that a patient in a given state at the beginning of a time period changes to any

Figure 2 Decision tree for carotid endarterectomy. AL, alive without stroke; MI, alive with minor stroke; MJ, alive with major stroke; DE, dead

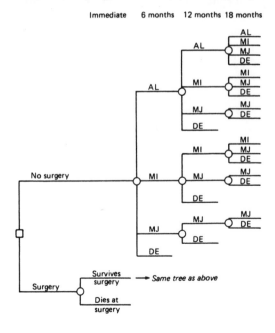

other state by the end of that time period does not depend on that patient's states prior to the time period in question. (For example, all patients who have suffered a minor stroke (and no worse) by 5 years are assumed to have the same chance of suffering a major stroke over the next 6 months, regardless of when their minor stroke occurred.) We can then model the problem by a modified decision tree (Fig. 3), in which two or more arrows can terminate at the same point. This tree remains of manageable size, no longer growing exponentially over time. More important, the relevant probabilities and utilities can be expressed compactly in the form of matrices and vectors, and computation of expected utilities is achieved by means of elementary matrix operations (e.g., matrix multiplication) that are performed easily by computer. The Markov approach is discussed in detail elsewhere.[6,7]

Not all time-dependent clinical decisions can be easily modelled as Markov processes. In particular, such models apply only to problems in which the probabilities of future events depend solely on the patient's present state, and not on past states. This condition fails to apply in at least one important class of clinical problems: decisions involving the optimal use of repeated diagnostic tests (e.g., screening for breast cancer using a schedule of physical examinations and/or mammograms). Because diagnostic tests are imperfect (i.e., can be falsely positive or negative), a patient's history of prior test results, not merely the most recent results, affects his or her likelihood of having the disease in question. Eddy has developed a modified Markov approach that applies to this class of problems.[8] He computes the probabilities of transitions among states, taking into account both current and prior test results, based on several types of data, including disease incidence rate, rate of disease progression

Figure 3 "Markov decision tree' for carotid endarterectomy. AL, alive without stroke; MI, alive with minor stroke; MJ, alive with major stroke; DE, dead

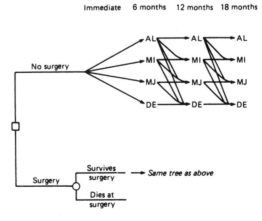

over time, test sensitivity as a function of disease state, and effectiveness of available therapy as a function of disease state at time of detection. The major application of his approach has been a cost-effectiveness analysis of screening for a variety of cancers in the general population. The technique, however, can be applied to a broad spectrum of clinical problems that involve the use of diagnostic tests.

Future directions and research needs

Further work is still needed to allow accurate and efficient modelling of other classes of problems that are difficult to approach using conventional decision analysis but for which, unlike time-dependent problems, successful alternatives have not yet been developed. Prominent among these are decisions involving the sequential use of diagnostic tests, each of which can take on several possible values. In such settings, the number of possible strategies can be very large. Consider, for example, the use of computed tomography (CT) and ultrasound (US) in the diagnosis and management of suspected pancreatic cancer. Assume that each test can take on five possible values – definitely normal, probably normal, possibly abnormal, probably abnormal, definitely abnormal – and that two management options – operate and do not operate – are available. One possible strategy is: "do CT; operate if it is definitely abnormal, and do nothing further if it is definitely or probably normal; otherwise, do US, followed by surgery if the CT was probably abnormal and the US is at least possibly abnormal, or if the CT was possibly abnormal and the US is definitely abnormal." This is only 1 of 388 strategies that can be defined. (In fact, many more are available if repeat use of CT or US is allowed.) The number of possible strategies increases rapidly with an increase in the number of tests, test results, or management options. A decision tree including all possible strategies and their consequences would be unmanageably large. While developments such as Boolean nodes and Markov processes can allow the possible outcomes of each strategy to be compactly represented, there is no such mechanism to deal with an overabundance of strategies. A solution to this problem – via a computer program that can generate and evaluate all strategies, a closed-form analytic method, or an approximation technique that efficiently locates a strategy of near-maximum expected utility – would expand the range of questions to which decision analysis can be applied.

PROBABILITIES

Physicians are constantly faced with uncertainty: a particular patient with right lower quadrant pain may or may not have appendicitis; a negative stress test in a patient with chest pain may be a true or false negative; an

80-year-old woman subjected to carotid endarterectomy may or may not survive the operating procedure. The clinical decision analyst faces the same uncertainties and must respond by assigning a quantitative estimate, or probability value, to each. Such probability estimates can be obtained objectively, based on a collection of data, or subjectively, based on an expert's informed judgment. We will treat these two approaches separately.

Objectively determined probabilities

The principle underlying objective probability assessment is that the probability of an event equals the frequency with which it occurs in a population. In the medical setting, the first step in estimating a probability objectively is, therefore, to find a collection of data about an appropriate group of patients, in which the final outcome state (e.g., specific diagnosis, treatment success, or failure) of each is recorded. Such data may involve large (if possible) or small numbers of patients. The latter is often necessary, as illustrated by a recent analysis of the management of suspected Herpes simplex encephalitis.[9] The probability of survival without severe neurologic sequelae in untreated patients with this disease was estimated on the basis of a study in which two of seven untreated patients survived without severe sequelae to be 29 percent.

Large-scale medical data bases, when available, are obviously preferable. Not only do they yield estimates that are more reliable, but a well-designed data base will also allow probability estimation tailored to specific characteristics of the individual. This can be done if the data base records each patient's final outcome state together with information concerning relevant clinical or laboratory features (indicants) that are, or may be, associated with the outcome. For example, a data base that records the angiographic findings of a group of patients who undergo coronary angiography should – to be useful at predicting the probability of significant coronary disease in future individuals – record each patient's age, sex, presence or absence (and type) of chest pain, blood pressure, and other coronary risk factors. Some of the common approaches to analyzing such data bases in medicine are reviewed.

The most direct way to estimate probability from a data base is to determine how frequently the event in question occurs among the subset of patients in the data base who are similar to the individual at hand. Suppose, for example, one sought the probability of significant coronary artery disease in a middle-aged man with atypical angina who is a cigarette smoker with normal blood pressure, serum cholesterol of 180 mg/dl, and no history of diabetes. Using a coronary disease data base of the type outlined in the previous paragraph (e.g., see reference 10), one could determine the frequency of coronary disease among patients whose features are similar to the person described above.

This direct approach is useful only if the number of indicants is small or the number of patients in the data base is large. Otherwise, an individual's set of indicants may be represented in the data base by so few patients that no reliable estimate may be obtained. This problem results from the inefficiency of the direct approach: it ignores data about patients in the data base who share some, but not all, indicants with the individual at hand. Other approaches to data-base analysis, more efficient in their use of data than the direct approach, have been used. All, however, involve assumptions that may or may not be valid in any particular application.

One such approach assumes that the indicants are conditionally independent: that within any outcome state, the probability of any combination of indicants equals the product of the probabilities of the individual indicants. The probability that a particular patient falls into a given outcome state is then computed by applying Bayes' theorem sequentially. At each step the probability is revised to take into account the presence or absence (or the numeric value) of an indicant; this process is continued until all indicants have been considered. Examples of this approach in medicine include the differential diagnosis of acute abdominal pain based on clinical symptoms and signs,[11] diagnosis of renal cyst versus tumor versus normal variant based on excretory urographic findings,[12] and predicting the likelihood of coronary artery disease based on the results of noninvasive diagnostic tests.[13] The technique is statistically robust in that data concerning all patients are included at each step. Its danger is that it can lead to incorrect results in a clinical setting in which the indicants are not conditionally independent.

When there are only two outcome states, linear discriminant analysis[14] is another approach that is more efficient than direct probability assessment from a data base. Its use is theoretically valid only when the indicants satisfy a number of requirements, such as possessing normal probability distributions. In practice, however, it is often used with indicants that are binary (o if absent, 1 if present) or that otherwise fail to conform to normal distributions. This technique, in brief, consists of the following: Each indicant is assigned a weight; based on these, any patient (in or out of the data base) can be assigned a discriminant score equal to the weighted sum of his or her indicant values (i.e., for each indicant, the patient's indicant value is multiplied by that indicant's weight, and these are all added together to produce a score). The weights are chosen in such a way that, when all patients in the data base are considered, the scores in one outcome state are as far apart as possible from the scores in the other outcome state. The discriminant score of a new individual (i.e., one not in the data base) can be used to predict the group to which that person belongs by selecting a cutoff score; patients with scores above the cutoff are assigned to one state, and those below the cutoff are assigned to the other state. Where to place the cutoff depends on two factors – the consequences of errors (false-positive and false-negative) and the prevalence of each outcome state. Alternatively, and more important in the context of decision analysis, a discriminant score can be converted into a probability. Examples of discriminant analysis used in this way involve the diagnosis of pigmented versus cholesterol stones on the basis of their characteristics on an oral cholecystogram[15] and the estimation of neonatal death rates based on risk factors such as maternal age and toxemia.[16]

Another statistical technique that can be used to compute probabilities in the two-outcome situation is logistic regression analysis.[17] The probability P that a patient falls into a particular outcome state (e.g., that the patient has the disease in question) is computed by the formula

$$P = e^A/(1 + e^A)$$

where A is a weighted sum of the patient's indicant values. The indicant weights, which differ from those in the linear discriminant function, are obtained using a process known as maximum likelihood estimation. While conceptually similar, the logistic approach has a number of advantages over linear discriminant analysis when used for probability estimation because it is more direct and involves the estimation of fewer parameters. It makes fewer assumptions about the structure of the data (e.g., it allows binary and other non-normally distributed indicants), and hence can be applied to a wider variety of data bases. Examples of its use in medicine include determining the probability of coronary artery disease[18] and acute ischemic heart disease[19] based on demographic and clinical characteristics and that of infection following hysterectomy, based on age, type of operation, and other risk factors.[20]

Since chance nodes in a decision tree may have more than two branches, it is often necessary for the decision analyst to determine the probability that a patient belongs to any one of several outcome states. The technique of polychotomous logistic regression can be used to compute these probabilities based on a set of indicants; it is related to but more complex than the simple logistic approach used in the binary situation. Because few statistical software packages can handle the polychotomous case and those few have technical limitations and require time-consuming, costly computations, Wijesinha *et al.*[21] have developed a method for performing polychotomous logistic regression as a series of simple logistic regressions. This method has been used in three situations in diagnostic radiology: to predict, based on symptoms, signs, and laboratory data, the outcome (i.e., diagnosis) of computed tomography,[21] upper gastrointestinal series,[22] and excretory urography.[23]

Several general issues must be raised in a discussion of objective probability assessment from data bases. First, before any approach to estimating probabilities is accepted, it must be validated on a data set different from that used to generate it. (It is possible, of course, to split a single data base into two parts for this purpose.) Failure to do so may lead to spurious results, since the data collection on which the predictive formula is based may include chance (as opposed to real) associations between groups of indicants and outcomes. Second, any prediction from a data base implicitly assumes that the distribution of disease (or other outcome) states in the data base is identical to that in the population to which the predictive algorithm is being applied. If the distributions of outcome states differ, Bayes' theorem must be used to adjust the probability estimates.[24] Finally, even after correction for such differences, predictions based on one population may not be transferable to another.[25-27] This can occur because of differences in disease severity, definitions of indicants and outcome measures, therapy, and other factors. It is therefore essential to verify the applicability of a predictive algorithm to any new population.

Subjective probabilities

Problems associated with collecting large enough and specific enough data bases for objective probability assessment have emphasized the potential value of subjective estimation of probabilities. To be useful, subjective probabilities must be well calibrated to truth. (A person would be poorly calibrated if the actual frequency of an event in a large group of patients differs considerably from the subjectively estimated probability of its recurrence.)

Unfortunately, a considerable body of research suggests that people in general, and physicians in particular, perform poorly at the task of predicting probabilities.[28] Most studies have shown a strong tendency to overestimate the likelihood of an event occurring. This was shown dramatically in physicians' estimates of the probability of pneumonia[29] and skull fracture.[30] In each study, physicians assigned probability values to patients suspected of having the diagnosis in question, and radiographic confirmation was then obtained. Calibration for predicting pneumonia was so poor that among patients assigned the highest confidence level (approximately 88 percent), the proportion who actually had pneumonia was less than 20 percent. In the second study, among 19 patients estimated to have a 50 percent probability of skull fracture, only 1 (5.3 percent) actually had a fracture. In other studies, people have been shown to specify too narrow a confidence range about their best probability estimate[31,32] and to be too conservative in altering probability estimates when provided with additional information.[33]

The work of Tversky and Kahneman[34] suggests that poor performance at estimating probabilities is due, at least in part, to the application of certain heuristic rules of reasoning that lead to systematic errors (or biases). For example, the availability heuristic causes individuals to judge an event more probable if instances of its occurrence are more easily recalled. The representativeness heuristic leads individuals to estimate the probability of event A belonging to class B based on the extent to which A resembles B. This heuristic can lead one to underestimate the effect of the prior, or base-rate, probability, when estimating conditional probabilities. In a medical setting, it can cause physicians to overestimate the likelihood of combinations of symptoms occurring in diseased patients.[35]

Future directions and research needs

Statistical techniques for the analysis of data bases are well developed. There are, however, a limited number of large-scale, unbiased, medical data bases to which such techniques can be applied. The reasons for this will have to be dealt with if the situation is to be changed. First, collecting and maintaining an accurate data base is an expensive, time-consuming task. Second, inter-institutional collaboration is often required to assure sufficiently large sample sizes, especially for uncommon diseases or events. An investigator may be less willing to contribute time to be part of a communal data base than to be in possession of his or her own data base. Third, many current data collections are of limited value because of inappropriate entry criteria. For example, some have used the performance of a particular diagnostic test as an entry point; unless all patients suspected of having the disease in question have such a test, the data set is biased for most applications.

All decision analyses and attempts to evaluate the impact of new diagnostic and therapeutic technologies require accurate probabilities defining the relevant clinical situation. Improved clinical decisionmaking requires more and better data bases and better-calibrated subjective probability assessors. Thus it is essential that:

1 Encouragement (in terms of financial and academic support) be given for the creation of large, unbiased, clinically useful data bases related to important contemporary problems.

2 Research be done in the area of cognitive processes to better understand the mechanisms that lead to systematic errors in the estimation of probabilities and thus to train individuals to avoid these pitfalls.

UTILITIES

Assigning utility values to the terminal branches (final outcome states) of a decision tree is often the most difficult and controversial aspect of an analysis, especially if it involves probing the attitudes of the decision-maker. The latter is avoided in two situations: when there are only two final outcome states (e.g., dead versus alive, cured versus uncured) or when the outcomes can be measured in terms of a natural underlying scale (e.g., years of survival or monetary cost). In these cases, the criterion of maximizing expected utility takes on a concrete meaning: maximizing the probability of the preferred outcome in the first case, and maximizing a quantity such as life expectancy or monetary savings in the second.

Several types of utility measures do involve attitudes, or value judg-ments. These include: 1) relative value scales, commonly ranging from 0 for the worst outcome to 1 (or 100) for the best, used when there are more than two final outcome states and no natural underlying scale; 2) transformations of a natural underlying scale that take into account attitudes toward risk, used for decisionmakers who are risk-averse (those who would, for example, prefer a sure 10 years of survival to a 50–50 chance between 20 years and immediate death) or for decisionmakers who are risk-seeking;[2] and 3) multiattribute utility functions that combine several aspects (e.g., length of life, quality of life, monetary cost) of each outcome, in a way that reflects the decisionmaker's attitude toward the trade-offs among them.[36] In the last category, linear combinations of attribute values are often used, as in the case of cost–benefit analyses.[2] Multiplicative combinations, typified by quality-adjusted life expect-ancy,[37] have been used in other settings. More complex multiattribute utility functions[38] have had limited use so far in medical decision analyses.

Utility assessment in the above situations is achieved via the standard gamble (or lottery) and time-trade-off methods.[1] The assessor is asked questions such as "Which would you prefer: living with major compli-cations, on the one hand, or a 90 percent chance of living normally and a 10 percent chance of immediate death, on the other?" or "Would you prefer 20 years with normal speech or 25 years with the 'esophageal' speech that follows laryngectomy?"[39]

Many decision analyses in the medical literature involve binary or natural utility scales, because of the complex – and often controversial – issues associated with the use and assessment of value judgments. If attitudes are to be incorporated into a decision analysis, a central question is: "Whose attitudes?" Judgments concerning the relative importance of length and quality of life should, ideally, be made by the patient. However, the patient may not fully comprehend events that he or she has not yet experienced, or may be unwilling or unable to deal with hypothetic gambles concerning life, death, and morbidity. Judgments involving trade-offs between health and money present even more difficult prob-lems. Here, potential answers to "Whose attitudes?" include the patient, physician, third-party payor, or "society." The willingness of each to expend resources for a given health benefit might vary considerably from group to group. The explicit consideration of such trade-offs also leads to difficult ethical issues concerning appropriate levels of health care for young versus old,[40] rich versus poor, and insured versus uninsured. (We do not claim that such issues should be ignored, but merely that their controversial nature has led many decision analysts – or journal editors – to avoid them.)

Investigation into the process of eliciting preferences has produced results that further complicate the incorporation of value judgements into decision analysis. In one study, utilities assigned using the standard gamble technique were found to be influenced by the choice of extreme outcomes, indicating internal inconsistencies in the subjects' assessments.[41] Further, it has been shown that changes in the way a choice is presented, without altering its substantive nature, can lead to major shifts of preference (the "framing" effect).[42] For example, when data summarizing the results of surgery and radiation therapy were presented to groups of patients, physicians, and business students, the attractiveness of surgery in each group was substantially greater when the choice was framed in terms of probability of living rather than probability of dying.[43] Changing the frame can even result in a shift from risk-aversion to risk-seeking.[42]

Future directions and research needs

Outcome measures such as life expectancy and monetary cost are most accurate when estimated from high-quality, unbiased data bases. This again underscores the need to encourage and support their creation.

The wide range of individual preferences indicates the importance of incorporating these values into the decisionmaking process. In view of the demonstrated difficulties in eliciting coherent value judgments, much work remains to be done before this objective can be reliably achieved. This work will be hampered by the fact that preferences, unlike subjective probabilities, cannot be validated externally. At the least, methods of eliciting preferences that yield reproducible and internally consistent responses must be devised.

SENSITIVITY ANALYSIS

As discussed in the two previous sections, probability and utility data required for medical decision analyses are often uncertain or unreliable. Objective estimates must often be based on small numbers of patients, outdated or biased data bases, or studies whose patients differ from the individual or group to whom the decision analysis is being applied. Subjective estimates may be afflicted by a variety of biases and inconsistencies. Physicians are therefore unlikely to be influenced by a decision analysis whose result is contrary to their clinical judgment unless the analyst provides an argument that addresses the uncertainty in data estimates in the tree. That is, once the expected utilities of all strategies have been computed, the analyst must address the question: "Taking into account the uncertainty in data used in the analysis, how confident should one be in its conclusions?"

Conventional sensitivity analysis

Traditional sensitivity analyses have dealt with uncertain data by varying one or more of the probability or utility estimates from baseline values and by then observing the effect on the choice of strategy.[2] If a single strategy has the highest expected utility over a reasonable range of estimates, then it can be recommended with confidence (provided that the decision tree itself is an adequate model of the clinical problem). On the other hand, if the optimal strategy is sensitive to variation of baseline estimates, then the results must be viewed with caution and further data collection considered.

This approach has several limitations. It is cumbersome when more than two or three quantities are allowed to vary simultaneously, and the results of a multiple-way analysis cannot readily be presented. Even a three-way sensitivity analysis, using families of curves on a graph,[44] may be difficult for a mathematically unsophisticated reader to follow. This restriction to no more than three-way analysis is a major drawback for most clinically relevant trees: if a tree has, for example, 50 probabilities and utilities, then the results of a three-way analysis are conditional upon the validity of the estimates selected for the remaining 47 quantities. Thus, conventional sensitivity analysis is most useful when there is only a small number of parameters with uncertain values.

Probabilistic sensitivity analysis

When there are numerous unreliable data estimates, a recently described[45] probabilistic approach to sensitivity analysis that allows uncertainty in all parameters to be considered simultaneously can be used. Each probability and utility in the decision tree is assumed to be a variable quantity with a range of possible values having an associated distribution function. The expected utility of each decision option is a sum of products of these probabilities and utilities; it is thus a variable quality whose distribution function depends on those of the individual probabilities and utilities.

Calculating precisely the distributions of expected utilities is impossible unless the decision tree is very simple (and usually unrealistic). Instead, a

Monte Carlo approach is used; that is, each probability and utility is randomly assigned a value from its distribution, and the expected utility of each option is computed. This process is repeated many times, and the frequency that each strategy is optimal is noted. This frequency gives a measure of the confidence with which an optimal strategy can be selected. If no single strategy is optimal in a large fraction of the runs, then too much uncertainty exists to rely confidently on the results of the analysis. Conversely, if one strategy has the highest expected utility in a large majority (e.g. 95 percent) of the runs, then, – barring systematic errors in the model or the data – that strategy can be selected confidently as the optimal one.

One can also record the frequency that each strategy "buys" or "costs" a specified amount of utility. A strategy "buys" a given amount of utility if its expected utility is at least this amount greater than that of all other strategies. It "costs" a given amount of utility if its expected utility is at least this amount less than that of any other strategy. These frequencies can be of value when the magnitude of the difference in expected utility is important (e.g., if there is an amount below which differences are considered clinically unimportant).

While probabilistic sensitivity analysis is easily described, there are a number of impediments to its implementation as a decision-analytic tool: specifying distribution functions about all parameters can be a difficult and time-consuming task; probabilities simulated from any chance node must sum to one, a constraint not easily satisfied at nodes with more than two branches; and correlation among parameters, if present, must be accounted for in the simulation process. We have recently addressed these issues and provided practical, though approximate, solutions[46] to each. Our approach to simplifying the construction of distribution functions, for example, is to assume that each can be approximated by a parametric distribution. The logistic–normal distribution, for example, is a convenient and mathematically tractable model for probabilities, as well as for utilities that are measured on a bounded (e.g., zero to one) scale. Based on our formulas, each distribution function can be specified by two values of the probability or utility: the mean and the upper or lower bound of its 95 percent (or other) confidence range.

Future directions and research needs

Probabilistic sensitivity analysis, unlike the conventional variety, permits the analyst to make a summary statement concerning the certainty that the strategy selected is in fact optimal. This technique may therefore ease the communication between analyst and physician. Computer implementation of the technique, via an interactive program that carries out all computations (including construction of parametric distribution functions) would be an important step toward realizing this potential.

In addition, basic research is still needed to answer several outstanding questions. Given a decision tree and a set of distribution functions for all probabilities and utilities, how many simulation runs should be carried out? Are there families of distribution functions, other than the logistic–normal, that can be used conveniently? If so, how dependent are the results of a probabilistic sensitivity analysis on the choice of parametric family? How can physicians be trained to be better subjective estimators of extreme, as well as mean, values of probabilities and utilities? Perhaps most important, what is the relationship between certainty in the result, as determined by probabilistic sensitivity analysis, and magnitude of difference in expected utility? That is, in which of the two following situations should the physician be more influenced by the results of a decision analysis: 1) the optimal strategy has an expected utility only slightly greater than its closest competitor, but is found to be 95 percent certain to be best; or 2) the optimal strategy's expected utility is considerably greater, but it is only 55 percent certain to be best.

EPILOGUE

Over the last 10–15 years, decision analysis has achieved increasing visibility in the medical literature. Applications to a wide variety of clinical problems have appeared, including: coronary artery bypass surgery versus medical management for documented coronary artery disease;[47,48] diagnosis and treatment of renovascular hypertension;[48] prenatal diagnosis of Down's syndrome and other conditions diagnosable by amniocentesis;[50] treatment of gastric cancer;[51] management of suspected streptococcal pharyngitis[52] and Herpes simplex encephalitis;[9,53] screening for cancer in asymptomatic individuals;[8] use of Hepatitis B vaccine;[54] diagnostic evaluation of jaundice;[55] and prophylactic cholecystectomy versus expectant management of silent gallstones.[56]

On a substantive level, however, the impact of decision analysis in medicine has remained small. While some analyses have clearly influenced medicine practice – notably the analyses of cancer screening, which led to the current American Cancer Society guidelines,[57] and of renovascular hypertension, which has contributed to the declining use of the hypertensive urogram – most have not. Further, physicians still perform poorly at basic analytic tasks, such as probability revision following a diagnostic test,[58,59] and commonly confuse the sensitivity and specificity of a test with its predictive value.[60]

Technical advances, more and better data bases, and deeper understanding of cognitive processes will, as discussed in previous sections,

make decision analysis a more powerful tool. Other potential developments, such as computer-based decision tree libraries and computerized
medical records, could speed the construction of trees and the collection
of data. But the potential role of decision analysis will not be fully realized
until another obstacle is overcome: the lack of understanding and
misconceptions that most physicians have of decision analysis.[61] One
important misconception concerns the notion of validation in decision
analysis. Most statements, or hypotheses, in other areas of medicine can
be tested empirically, and it is often assumed that this approach should be
applied to decision analyses. There are several reasons why this is not the
case, as we illustrate using the analysis of silent gallstone management.[56]
In that study, a Markov analysis concluded that expectant management
yields an additional 4–18 days of life expectancy when compared with
prophylactic cholecystectomy in men aged 30–50 years. Comparing this
conclusion with the consensus (if it exists) of experts in the field would not
help to determine which of expert judgment or decision analysis is
superior. A randomized controlled trial with sufficient statistical power to
detect (or reject) a difference as small as 18 days of life expectancy would
require very large numbers of patients followed over several decades, and
its results would be meaningless unless medical and surgical therapies
remained unchanged in efficacy and risk over that period. (The problem of
statistical power is not unique to this example, since analyses of many
clinical problems yield small differences in expected utilities.[62]) Further,
such a trial would be of no value to today's patients, whose management
must be based on the best data that is currently available. To this end, if
the Markov model of silent gallstones includes all relevant factors and
uses best available data, it follows on mathematical grounds (not requiring empiric verification) that the analysis yields the best possible current
estimate of life expectancy. (If one believes the model to be incomplete or
better data to exist, this would not be a condemnation of decision
analysis; instead, one should reconstruct the model or alter the data.)
Thus, acceptance of the conclusion of a decision analysis must rely not on
empiric validation, but instead on the belief that the model is sufficiently
complete and the data are the best available.

   Another related, commonly held, misconception is that decision analysis is of little value unless reliable data are available. This objection fails to
recognize that any means of reaching a decision, including intuitive
approaches, such as clinical judgment, is limited by the quality of
available data. Decision analysis is not more severely affected than is
clinical judgment when good data are lacking; the former is merely more
vulnerable to criticism because its explicit nature lays bare all assumptions. In fact, sensitivity analysis allows the decision analyst to deal better
with uncertain data than can decisionmakers whose assumptions are

implicit. (The above argument notwithstanding, a decision analyst will spend his or her time more effectively in attacking problems for which reasonable data exist and which apply to large numbers of patients.)

Physician education is, therefore, crucial to the future role of decision analysis in medicine. Development of courses must be financially supported and academically rewarded. Education at all levels is important, but exposure of medical students to decision analysis is likely to have the greatest impact, since these individuals are at a formative time in their training and may be able to apply quantitative skills, recently learned in college. To be successful, courses must go beyond teaching "number-crunching" skills, such as folding back decision trees and applying Bayes' theorem; they must deal with the fundamental concepts of decision-making under conditions of uncertainty. Such courses might influence the way in which physicians approach clinical problems. Even if not, they would enable physicians critically to evaluate applications of decision analysis, to incorporate the results of these analyses into decisions involving their patients, and to identify areas in which a formal analysis could augment clinical judgment.

REFERENCES

1 Raiffa, H. *Decision analysis: introductory lectures on choices under uncertainty*. Reading, MA: Addison-Wesley, 1968.

2 Weinstein, M.C., Fineberg, H.V., Elstein, A.S., et al. *Clinical decision analysis*. Philadelphia: W.B. Saunders, 1980.

3 Pauker, S.G., Kassirer, J.P. Therapeutic decision making: a cost-benefit analysis. *N. Engl. J. Med.* 1975; 293:229.

4 Lau, J., Kassirer, J.P., Pauker, S.G. DECISION MAKER 3.0: Improved decision analysis by personal computer. *Med. Decis. Making* 1983; 3:39.

5 Silverstein, M.D. A clinical decision analysis program for the Apple computer. *Med. Decis. Making* 1983; 3:29.

6 Kemeny, J.G., Snell, J.L. *Finite Markov chains*. New York: Springer–Verlag, 1976.

7 Beck, J.R., Pauker, S.G. The Markov process in medical prognosis. *Med. Decis. Making* 1983; 3:419.

8 Eddy, D.M. *Screening for cancer: theory, analysis, and design*. Englewood Cliffs, NJ: Prentice–Hall, 1980.

9 Barza, M., Pauker, S.G. The decision to biopsy, treat, or wait in suspected Herpes virus encephalitis. *Ann. Intern. Med.* 1980; 92:641.

10 The principle investigators of CASS and their associates: the National Heart, Lung, and Blood Institute Coronary Artery Surgery Study. *Circulation* 1981; 63:11.

11 Horrocks, J.C., McCann, A.P., Staniland, J.R., et al. Computer-aided diagnosis: description of an adaptable system, and operational experience with 2034 cases. *Br. Med. J.* 1972; 2:5.

12 Fryback, D.G., Thornbury, J.R. Evaluation of a computerized Bayesian model for diagnosis of renal cyst vs. tumor vs. normal variant from excretory urogram information. *Invest. Radiol.* 1976; 11:102.

13 Diamond, G.A., Forrester, J.S. Analysis of probability as an aid in the clinical diagnosis of coronary artery disease. *N. Engl. J. Med.* 1979; 300:1350.

14 Armitage, P. *Statistical methods in medical research.* Oxford: Blackwell Scientific Publications, 1971.

15 Dolgin, S.M., Schwartz, J.S., Kressel, H.Y., *et al.* Identification of patients with cholesterol or pigment gallstones by discriminant analysis of radiographic features. *N. Engl. J. Med.* 1981; 304:808.

16 Neutra, R.P., Feinberg, S.E., Greenland, S., *et al.* Effect of fetal monitoring on neonatal death rates. *N. Engl. J. Med.* 1978; 299:324.

17 Cox, D.R. *The analysis of binary data.* London: Methuen, 1970.

18 Pryor, D.B., Harrell, F.E., Lee, K.L., *et al.* Estimating the likelihood of significant coronary artery disease. *Am. J. Med.* 1983; 75:771.

19 Pozen, M.W., D'Agostino, R.B., Mitchell, J.B., *et al.* The usefulness of a predictive instrument to reduce inappropriate admissions to the coronary care unit. *Ann. Intern. Med.* 1980; 92:238.

20 Shapiro, M., Munoz, A., Tager, I.B., *et al.* Risk factors for infection at the operative site after abdominal or vaginal hysterectomy. *N. Engl. J. Med.* 1982; 307:1661.

21 Wijesinha, A., Begg, C.B., Funkenstein, H.H., *et al.* Methodology for the differential diagnosis of a complex data set: a case study using data from routine CT scan examinations. *Med. Decis. Making* 1983; 2:133.

22 McNeil, B.J., Wijesinha, A., Bynum, T.E., *et al.* Selection criteria for upper gastrointestinal examinations: attempts at improvement. *Radiology* 1984; 150:311.

23 Doubilet, P., McNeil, B.J., Van Houten, F.X., *et al.* Excretory urography in current practice: evidence against overutilization. *Radiology* 1985; 154: 607.

24 McNeil, B.J., Hanley, J.A. Statistical approaches to clinical predictions. *N. Engl. J. Med.* 1981; 304:1292.

25 Fischl, M.A., Pitchenik, A., Gardner, L.B. An index predicting relapse and need for hospitalization in patients with acute bronchial asthma. *N. Engl. J. Med.* 1981; 305:783.

26 Rose, C.C., Murphy, J.G., Schwartz, J.S. Performance of an index predicting the response of patients with acute bronchial asthma to intensive emergency department treatment. *N. Engl. J. Med.* 1984; 310:573.

27 Centor, R.M., Yarbrough, B., Wood, J.P. Inability to predict relapse in acute asthma. *N. Engl. J. Med.* 1984; 310:577.

28 Lichtenstein, S., Fischhoff, B., Phillips, L.D. Calibration of probabilities: the state of the art to 1980. In: Kahneman, D., Slovic, P., Tversky, A., eds. *Judgment under uncertainty: heuristics and biases.* Cambridge: Cambridge University Press, 1982; 306–334.

29 Christensen–Szalanski, J.J.J., Bushyhead, J.B. Physicians' use of probabilistic information in a real clinical setting. *J. Exp. Psychol* [Hum Percept] 1981; 7:928.

30 DeSmet, A.A., Fryback, D.G., Thornbury, J.R. A second look at the utility of radiographic skull examinations for trauma. *Am. J. Roentgenol* 1979; 132:95.

31 Stael von Holstein, C.–A.S. Two techniques for assessment of subjective probability distributions: an experimental study. *Acta Psychol* 1971; 35:478.

32 Lichtenstein, S., Fischhoff, B. Training for calibration. *Organizational Behavior and Human Performance.* 1980; 26:149.

33 Phillips, L.D., Edwards, W. Conservatism in a simple probability inference task. *J. Exp. Psychol.* 1966; 72:346.

34 Tversky, A., Kahneman, D. Judgment under uncertainty: heuristics and biases. *Science* 1974; 185:1124.

35 Tversky, A., Kahneman, D. Extensional versus intuitive reasoning: the conjunctive fallacy in probability judgement. *Psychol. Rev.* 1983; 90:293.

36 Keeney, R.L., Raiffa, H. *Decisions with multiple objectives: preferences and value tradeoffs.* New York: John Wiley & Sons, 1976.

37 Weinstein, M.C., Stason, W.B. Foundations of cost-effectiveness analysis for health and medical practices. *N. Engl. J. Med.* 1977; 296:716.

38 Fryback, D.G., Keeney, R.L. Constructing a complex judgmental model: an index of trauma severity. *Mgt. Sci.* 1983; 29:869.

39 McNeil, B.J., Weischelbaum, R., Pauker, S.G. Speech and survival: tradeoffs between quality and quantity of life in laryngeal cancer. *N. Engl. J. Med.* 1981; 305:982.

40 Avorn, J. Benefit and cost analysis in geriatric cases: turning age discrimination into health policy. *N. Engl. J. Med.* 1984; 310:1294.

41 Llewellyn–Thomas, H., Sutherland, H.J., Tibshirani, R., et al. The measurement of patients' values in medicine. *Med. Decis. Making* 1982; 2:449.

42 Tversky, A., Kahneman, D. The framing of decisions and the psychology of choice. *Science* 1981; 211:453.

43 McNeil, B.J., Pauker, S.G., Sox, H.C., et al. On the elicitation of preferences for alternative therapies. *N. Engl. J. Med.* 1982; 306:1259.

44 Plante, D.A., Pauker, S.G. Enterococcal endocarditis and penicillin allergy. *Med. Decis. Making* 1983; 3:81.

45 Pass, T.M., Goldstein, L.P. A computerized aid for medical cost-effectiveness analysis. *Med. Decis. Making* 1981; 1:465.

46 Doubilet, P., Begg, C.B., Weinstein, M.C., et al. Probabilistic sensitivity analysis using Monte Carlo simulation: a practical approach. *Med. Decis. Making* 1985; 5, 157–77.

47 Pauker, S.G. Coronary artery surgery: the use of decision analysis. *Ann. Intern. Med.* 1976; 85:8.

48 Pliskin, J.S., Stason, W.B., Weinstein, M.C., et al. Coronary artery bypass graft surgery: clinical decision-making and cost-effectiveness. *Med. Decis. Making* 1981; 1:10.

49 McNeil, B.J., Varady, P.D., Burrows, B.A., et al. Measures of clinical efficacy. I. Cost-effectiveness calculations in the diagnosis and treatment of renovascular disease. *N. Engl. J. Med.* 1975; 293:216.

50 Pauker, S.P., Pauker, S.G. Prenatal diagnosis: a directive approach to genetic counseling using decision analysis. *Yale J. Med. Biol.* 1977; 50:275.

51 Doubilet, P., McNeil, B.J. Treatment choice in gastric carcinoma: a decision-analytic approach. *Med. Decis. Making* 1982; 2:261.

52 Tompkins, R.K., Burnes, D.C., Cable, W.E. An analysis of the cost-effectiveness of pharyngitis management and acute rheumatic fever prevention. *Ann. Intern. Med.* 1977; 84:481.

53 Braun, P. The clinical management of suspected Herpes virus encephalitis: a decision-analytic view. *Am. J. Med.* 1980; 69:895.

54 Mulley, A.G., Silverstein, M.D., Dienstang, J.L. Indications for use of hepatitis B vaccine, based on cost-effectiveness analysis. *N. Engl. J. Med.* 1982; 307:644.

55 Richter, J.M., Silverstein, M.D., Schapiro, R. Suspected obstructive jaundice: a decision analysis of diagnostic strategies. *Ann. Intern. Med.* 1983; 99:46.

56 Ransohoff, D.F., Gracie, W.A., Wolfenson, L.B., *et al.* Prophylactcic cholecystectomy or expectant management of silent gallstones. *Ann. Intern. Med.* 1983; 99:199.

57 American Cancer Society Report on the cancer-related checkup. *CA* 1980; 30:194.

58 Casscells, W., Schoenberger, A., Grayboys, T.B. Interpretation by physicians of clinical laboratory results. *N. Engl. J. Med.* 1978; 299:999.

59 Berwick, D.M., Fineberg, H.V., Weinstein, M.C. When doctors meet numbers. *Am. J. Med.* 1981: 71:991.

60 Eddy, D.M. Probabilistic reasoning in medicine: problems and opportunities. In: Kahneman, D., Slovic, P., Tversky, A., eds. *Judgment under uncertainty: heuristics and biases.* Cambridge: Cambridge University Press, 1982; 249–257.

61 Schwartz, W.B. Decision analysis: a look at the chief complaints. *N. Engl. J. Med.* 1979; 300:556.

62 Kassirer, J.P., Pauker, S.G. The toss-up. *N. Engl. J. Med.* 1981; 305:1467.

14

RECURRENT DEEP VENOUS THROMBOSIS IN PREGNANCY: ANALYSIS OF THE RISKS AND BENEFITS OF ANTICOAGULATION*

Karen Klein, Stephen G. Pauker

CASE DESCRIPTION

EW, a 25-year-old woman who was three months pregnant and in good health, developed pain and swelling of her left thigh. A venogram revealed a complete cutoff at the level of the popliteal vein – no deep veins were opacified above that level. Although the diagnosis of recurrent deep venous thrombophlebitis (DVT) was made, she desired to carry the pregnancy to term. Full dose intravenous heparin therapy resulted in a good clinical response. Past medical history revealed a single prior episode of deep venous thrombophlebitis, which occurred approximately two years ago following a sprain of her left ankle.

The significant risk of pulmonary embolus in this patient was taken to be a strong indication for long-term anticoagulant therapy. Unfortunately, the administration of either warfarin or heparin during pregnancy poses significant risk to the fetus. This dilemma prompted a request for consultation with the Division of Clinical Decision Making.

THE PROBLEM STATED

This decision can be considered in two stages. First, the clinician must decide whether or not to administer anticoagulant therapy. The possibility of pulmonary embolus with its associated mortality argues for the use of anticoagulants; the risk of fetal complications argues against their use. Second, if long-term outpatient anticoagulant therapy is to be employed, the physician must choose between warfarin and subcutaneous heparin. Warfarin carries a significant risk of both perinatal mortality and fetal abnormalities, but has established efficacy in treating thrombophlebitis. On the other hand, heparin therapy is associated with increased perinatal mortality but not with fetal abnormalities. The efficacy of *subcutaneous* heparin is open to question; nevertheless, heparin might be

* First published in *Medical Decision Making*, 1 (1981), 181–202. © 1981 Birkhauser Boston, Inc. Reprinted by permission.

the preferred drug for a family that places a high burden value on the birth of an abnormal infant. It is difficult to balance the benefit of avoiding fetal abnormalities against uncertain efficacy without quantitative analysis. In this clinical decision conference, we provide a framework for selecting the most appropriate management option, considering the parents' attitudes towards unfavorable outcomes for both mother and fetus as well as the physician's assessment of drug efficacy.

SUMMARY OF AVAILABLE DATA

Incidence of pulmonary embolism   Thromboembolic disease is a known complication of pregnancy. Furthermore, a history of DVT is a risk factor for the development of the disease during pregnancy.[1] The incidence of pulmonary embolism in pregnant patients with DVT has been reported over a wide range, but is generally considered high enough to warrant intervention.[1] Baskin, Murray, and Harris report an incidence of 9–12 percent,[1] whereas Henderson, Lund, and Crasman report an incidence of 16–27 percent[2] and Villesanta estimates 19 percent.[3] In four studies between 1946 and 1960, the overall incidence of pulmonary embolism in patients with DVT was approximately 30 percent.[4] Aaro and Juergens[5] evaluated 32,337 pregnant women and found only 47 with evidence of DVT during or after pregnancy. They identified 13 women with pulmonary embolism, but only five had a prior history of DVT. Thus the incidence of pulmonary embolism in this study was 5/47, or 11 percent, however, the criteria for diagnosis were not stated in that report. Thus, in the face of DVT, many clinicians not only recommend anticoagulation during pregnancy, but also suggest prevention of pregnancy in patients with prior history of pulmonary embolism.[2]

Mortality of pulmonary embolism   Villesanta reports the mortality from pulmonary embolism to be 28 percent.[3] In a review of five studies, four reported a mortality rate of untreated pulmonary embolism ranging from 30–38 percent, although one study reported only an 18–25 percent mortality rate.[6,7] In Crane's study of 391 patients treated with heparin, 30 went on to pulmonary embolism, 4 of these fatal (13.3 percent).[8] However, Crane also quotes a study of Jorpes, where seven out of twenty-eight patients with pulmonary embolism (25 percent) died while on IV heparin therapy.

Efficacy of anticoagulation   The efficacy of anticoagulation can be defined as the difference between the expected and observed number of emboli, divided by the expected number. Thus an efficacy of zero suggests no effect while 100 percent efficacy implies the elimination of emboli.

The efficacy of warfarin in the prevention of recurrent thromboembolic disease is well documented. A review of warfarin therapy for thromboembolism quotes ten studies with efficacies of 75–100 percent, and one study with an efficacy of 52 percent.[9] In patients with deep vein thrombosis treated with intravenous heparin followed by oral warfarin, the incidence of pulmonary embolism was less than 5 percent.[4] If compared to the incidence of approximately 25 percent in untreated patients, the calculated efficacy is 80 percent. In his review, Crane reports similar efficacy. A study published in 1949 reported an efficacy of 78 percent, and a 1948 study identified three cases of pulmonary embolism in 96 treated patients with deep vein thrombosis, an efficacy of 87 percent.[8]

Since 1966 there have been over 30 controlled studies, involving a total of more than 2,000 patients, which have investigated the efficacy of low dose subcutaneous heparin in the prevention of deep vein thrombosis and pulmonary embolism.[9,10,11] The majority of these studies have involved elective surgical patients. The results have shown that perioperative low dose heparin is effective in preventing thromboembolic disease in patients over forty years of age who undergo elective abdominothoracic surgery.[8,9,10,12] Efficacy generally varied between 60 percent and 80 percent, with one study demonstrating 52 percent and one 100 percent.[4,8,9,13–16] Results have been less promising in patients undergoing hip or prostate surgery.[9,11,17] In a double blind study where low dose heparin was used for one week in patients undergoing elective surgery of the abdomen, thorax, or lower extremities, thromboembolic disease was reduced by 75 percent. (Thromboembolism was present in 16 of 653 untreated and 4 of 643 treated patients.[13]) Similarly, in a prospective randomized trial involving 2,075 controls and 2,045 patients treated with low dose heparin for an eight-day perioperative period, the incidence of pulmonary embolism was reduced from 1.9 percent to 0.49 percent, an efficacy of 75 percent.[15] A study that used both pulmonary embolism and deep venous thrombosis as end points found low dose heparin to have an efficacy of 66 percent.[14] A more recent study found a 22 percent incidence of thromboembolism in controls compared to a 4 percent incidence in patients treated with low dose heparin – an efficacy of 82 percent.[16]

Little information is available, however, on the use of low dose heparin during pregnancy. Furthermore, since requirements for heparin increase in late pregnancy, laboratory parameters of heparin effect must be closely monitored in these patients.[11] In a series of 22 pregnant women with a history of deep vein thrombosis who received outpatient low dose subcutaneous heparin therapy, deep vein thrombosis recurred in two cases; there were no cases of pulmonary embolism.[18]

Two studies comparing warfarin to low dose heparin have shown warfarin to provide greater protection. In one, nine of 35 patients (26 percent) treated with low dose heparin had recurrent deep vein thrombosis, compared to none of 33 patients treated with warfarin.[19] Unfortunately, this study did not examine the issue of pulmonary embolism, and it specifically excluded pregnant women. In another study of patients with a history of severe recurrent thromboembolic disease, no significant difference in efficacy was found between warfarin and heparin when used for six months.[20] However, the overall incidence of recurrence was 29 percent in the heparin-treated groups and 38 percent in the warfarin-treated groups, unchanged from the incidence in untreated patients.

Thus, although low dose heparin has been proved effective in certain patients undergoing elective surgical procedures, there is as yet no specific information about its efficacy in preventing pulmonary embolism during pregnancy.

Incidence and mortality of bleeding secondary to anticoagulation   Anticoagulant therapy carries a relatively small risk of either fatal or nonfatal bleeding. The reported incidence of significant bleeds varies from 2 percent–4 percent in seven studies.[8,15,21,22] The mortality from bleeding has been estimated between 0 percent–0.5 percent.[4,8,21,22,23] One study found a 5 percent mortality rate in patients with major bleeding; however, three deaths occurred in 4 patients who were over 60 years of age and had concurrent medical problems.[22]

Incidence of fetal complications   There have been a number of isolated reports on the effects of anticoagulants on the fetus.[21,24–27] Warfarin embryopathy, a syndrome consisting of nasal hypoplasia and stippled epiphyses, has been associated with exposure to that drug in the first trimester.[28] Exposure in the second and third trimesters is associated with a 13 percent risk of perinatal death and a 10 percent risk of fetal abnormalities involving the eye and the central nervous system, as well as with significant developmental delay.[28] In an extensive review of 418 pregnancies exposed to warfarin and 135 pregnancies exposed to heparin, heparin used during the second and third trimesters was associated with a 20 percent risk of perinatal death, but essentially no increased risk of significant fetal abnormalities (0.7 percent).[28]

Although earlier reports quote perinatal mortality rates as high as 18.4 percent with warfarin, it is now felt that such high complication rates were due to excessive doses of warfarin and its use close to term.[29] The current practice of discontinuing warfarin by the 36th week of gestation (and administering heparin if necessary) has eliminated such increased mortality.

ANALYSIS OF THE DECISION

Assumptions In analyzing this decision, we shall make the following assumptions:

1 There is a chance that this woman will develop a pulmonary embolus from her deep vein thrombophlebitis, and that chance can be expressed as a probability. Similarly the chance of death as a consequence of pulmonary embolism can also be quantified.

2 Long-term anticoagulant therapy will decrease the likelihood of developing pulmonary embolism, and that chance can be expressed as the efficacy of the drug. The chance of death after the occurrence of a pulmonary embolus will, however, not be altered by anticoagulant therapy.

3 If this patient is not initially given anticoagulants and develops pulmonary embolism and survives the episode, the physician could, in theory, either start anticoagulant therapy at that time or continue with the original management plan. However, we shall assume that, in this situation, anticoagulants would be administered to decrease the chance of further pulmonary embolism.

4 All patients receiving anticoagulants are at risk for bleeding which may be either fatal or nonfatal.

5 If the woman dies unexpectedly during pregnancy, there is no chance of salvaging the infant. If the woman survives, she will deliver an infant who is either alive and well, alive and abnormal, or dead. We have not considered unfavorable fetal outcomes from causes other than anticoagulants. We have assumed that aside from the risks associated with DVT and anticoagulation, this woman's chance of having a normal, healthy infant are the same as that of any woman in the general population.

6 The birth of a normal infant is the best possible outcome.

7 Death of the mother is the worst possible outcome. (Although certain patients might be more willing to accept their own death than the death of or a significant abnormality in their infant, for the purpose of our analysis we shall assume the loss of the mother to be the outcome with the lowest utility.)

8 Fetal death or anticoagulant-related abnormalities are outcomes of intermediate value.

STRUCTURE OF THE ANALYSIS

The decision trees shown in Figures 1 and 2 summarize the structure of this analysis. In Figure 1, the square decision node at the extreme left denotes the choice to anticoagulate or not to anticoagulate. The identical structure will be used to evaluate both warfarin and low dose heparin therapy by using data (efficacy, risks) appropriate for each drug. The chance events which follow each management option are denoted by circular nodes. Without anticoagulation there is a certain probability (P) of developing a pulmonary embolus. The probability of *not* developing a pulmonary embolus is therefore (1−P). This latter branch results in the best outcome, i.e., both mother and infant are alive and well. If pulmonary embolism occurs, it may be fatal (probability FPE) resulting in the worst outcome, i.e., death of both mother and fetus. If the woman survives the pulmonary embolus (probability 1−FPE), anticoagulants will be administered.

The structure of the anticoagulation branch of the decision tree is similar to that of the no-anticoagulation branch, except that the probability of pulmonary embolus is lower because of the efficacy of this management option, denoted as E. When efficacy is perfect (E=1), the

Figure 1 Decision tree demonstrating the alternative options of anticoagulation and no anticoagulation. Branches relate to events concerning the maternal aspect of the problem

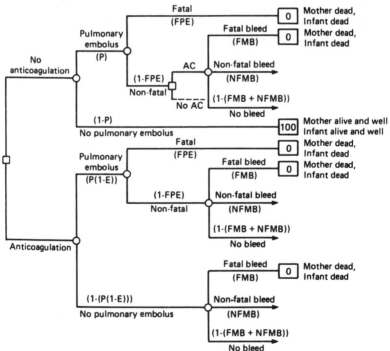

incidence of pulmonary embolus is zero. When anticoagulation has no efficacy (E=o), the incidence of pulmonary embolus remains P. Thus, the probability of pulmonary embolus on anticoagulation is P(1−E). The probability of no pulmonary embolus on anticoagulation is, of course, 1−(P(1−E)).

Figure 1 also shows the *maternal* complications of anticoagulant therapy. The mother can suffer a fatal bleeding episode (probability FMB), resulting in the death of both mother and infant. On the other hand, the mother may survive, having suffered a nonfatal bleeding episode (probability NFMB) or having had no complications of anticoagulants (probability 1−(FMB+NFMB)).

For all situations in which the mother survives, the possible *fetal* outcomes after anticoagulation are summarized in Figure 2. Anticoagulant fetopathy may develop (probability ACF) or may not occur (probability 1−ACF). In certain circumstances, it may be important to define anticoagulant fetopathy in greater detail, distinguishing between fetal death (probability FD) and fetal abnormality (probability 1−FD).

ASSIGNMENT OF THE PROBABILITIES

Table 1 summarizes the symbols used to denote the probabilities of all chance events and the baseline values of those probabilities. The incidence of pulmonary embolism in untreated pregnant women with DVT varies from 12 percent–30 percent; we shall assume a baseline value of 20 percent. Mortality of pulmonary embolism is consistently around 30 percent. In this setting, the efficacy of warfarin is at least 75 percent, but the efficacy of low dose heparin is unclear. Initially, we shall assume its

Figure 2 Sub-tree illustrating fetal aspects of the problem

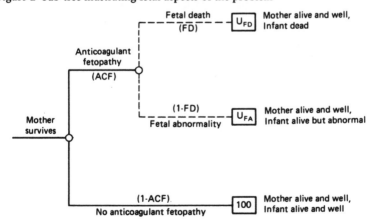

Table 1 *Probabilities of chance events*

Event	Symbol	Baseline value
Anticoagulant fetopathy	ACF	0.2
Efficacy of anticoagulation	E	0.75
Fetal death, given fetopathy	FD	0.55–1.0[a]
Fatal maternal bleed	FMB	0.00015[b]
Fatality, given pulmonary embolus	FPE	0.3
Non-fatal maternal bleed	NFMB	0.2985[b]
Pulmonary embolus (without therapy)	P	0.2

[a] For warfarin 0.55; for heparin 1.0.
[b] Total probability of maternal bleeding is 0.03; of these, 0.5% are fatal.

efficacy is also 75 percent. Note that an efficacy for both therapies of 75 percent reduces the probability of pulmonary embolus from 20 percent to 5 percent.

Based on the firm data about the rate of fatal and nonfatal bleeding secondary to anticoagulation, we shall assume the overall rate of bleeding to be 3 percent and the probability of death after a bleed to be 0.5, resulting in a 0.0015 probability of a fatal maternal bleed.

Finally, we shall assume a value of 20 percent for the incidence of anticoagulant fetopathy. Since warfarin results in a 13 percent mortality rate and a 10 percent risk of abnormality, fetal death accounts for 55 percent of warfarin-related fetopathy, and fetal abnormalities account for 45 percent. In contrast, heparin does not result in malformations; rather, the entire risk is due to fetal death. Thus, for heparin the probability of fetal death is 1.0.

ASSIGNMENT OF UTILITIES

In our initial analysis, we shall ignore the morbidity of nonfatal maternal bleeds, since in the broad utility structure of the analysis such consequences will cause only minor changes in the utility. Thus, there are four possible outcomes in this analysis, as listed in Table 2. A utility of 100 has been assigned to the most favorable outcome, both mother and infant alive and well. The least favorable outcome, both mother and infant dead, has been assigned a utility of zero. Between these extremes, the outcomes, mother well, infant dead, and mother well, infant abnormal, must be assigned utilities that reflect the parents' attitudes and desires.

Although a number of methods can be used to determine a patient's attitudes towards alternative outcomes, we have chosen the lottery approach. Each of the remaining outcomes (mother well, infant abnormal, and mother well, infant dead) is addressed separately. Let us first

Table 2 *Utilities of outcomes*

Outcome		Utility[a]
Mother	Infant	
Well	Well	100
Well	Abnormal	U_{FA}
Well	Dead	U_{FD}
Dead	Dead	0

[a] Under some circumstances, the symbol U_F is used to denote the expected utility of anticoagulant "fetopathy" without distinguishing between abnormal and dead infants.

consider the outcome mother well, infant dead. The symbol U_{FD} will be used to denote this utility. The patient (or in this case, the prospective parents) can be presented with two options, one a certain outcome and the other a gamble. The certain option describes the outcome to be assigned a utility (mother well, infant dead), whereas the gamble is between the best (mother and infant well) and the worst (mother and infant dead) possible outcomes. For various probabilities of the gamble resulting in the worst outcome, the patient is asked to choose between the gamble and the certain (but intermediate) outcome. The probability at which the patient is indifferent between the gamble and the certain outcome can be used to assign a utility to the intermediate outcome state.

The lottery technique is illustrated in Figure 3. In this schematic presentation, the intermediate outcome is called "fetopathy" and will be assigned a utility denoted as U_F. In practice, one of the two outcomes, infant abnormal, or infant dead, would be substituted for "fetopathy present." The balance in Figure 3a represents the two options – certain fetopathy versus a gamble between the best and the worst outcomes where the probability of the worst outcome is α. The patient is asked to consider a series of balances, each with a different value of α, and to indicate the value of α for which the two options are equally bad, i.e., the value of α at which the balance just balances. For low values of α, the gamble will probably be preferred, whereas for high values of α certain fetopathy will likely be preferred to the substantial risk of maternal death.

The indifference point is shown as a decision tree on the right side of Figure 3. At the indifference value of α the expected utilities of the two options will be equal. The expected value of the upper branch of the decision node will be $(1-\alpha) \times 100$ plus $\alpha \times 0$, or $100 (1-\alpha)$; the expected value of the lower branch is simply U_F. If α_1 denotes the indifference value of α, then $U_F = 100 (1-\alpha_1)$. For example, if the indifference point occurs when α equals 0.1 (i.e., at a 10 percent risk of maternal death), then U_F equals $100 (1-0.1)$, or 90.

This method can be used to assess the parents' utility value for losing their infant, and can then be reapplied to assess their utility for giving birth to an abnormal infant. Furthermore, it allows parental attitudes toward both maternal and infant outcomes to be considered within the same analysis. Since this technique closely reflects the actual clinical dilemma, it is particularly useful in this type of management problem. Note that we have made no assumptions about the relative value of fetal death versus fetal abnormality. For some parents, U_{FD} would exceed U_{FA}; for others, U_{FD} would be less than U_{FA}; for still others they would be equally bad outcomes.

Since this patient was being treated in a hospital in New Hampshire, we did not have the opportunity to meet with the patient and to assess her attitudes toward various fetal outcomes. We were only advised that she wished to keep the pregnancy. We therefore kept the utility of fetopathy (U_F) as a variable for subsequent sensitivity analysis so that any attitudes can be considered. Nevertheless, for the sake of a concrete example, let us assume that $U_{FD}=U_{FA}=U_F=90$; in other words, assume that $\alpha_1=0.1$.

CALCULATING THE EXPECTED VALUES

Once probabilities and utilities are assigned to each outcome, the expected utility can be calculated for each management option – treating with anticoagulants or refraining from use of anticoagulants. For chance nodes, utilities at the end of each branch are multiplied by their corres-

Figure 3 The lottery method for utility assessment – (a) Balance of certain option versus standard gamble. (b) Decision tree

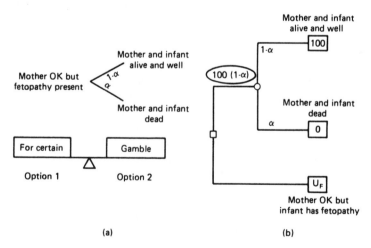

(a)   (b)

ponding probabilities and the results are added together. By folding back the tree in this manner from right to left, we arrive at the expected utility for each branch of the decision node. The management option with the higher expected utility is the preferred choice.

Using baseline values for the probabilities (Table 1) and assuming that the utility of fetopathy is 90, we find that the expected utility of anticoagulation is 96.52 and the expected utility of withholding anticoagulation is 93.72. Thus, under the baseline assumptions, anticoagulation would be the preferred plan. Since we have made a number of assumptions, it becomes important to see if changes in any of those assumptions could alter the decision.

SENSITIVITY ANALYSIS

Decision analysis is an aid to making decisions under conditions of uncertainty. Since many explicit assumptions must be made during any analysis, it is important to see if the decision is altered when reasonable variations in the data are considered. In a one-way sensitivity analysis we

Figure 4 One-way sensitivity analysis – Examining the effect of the probability of pulmonary embolus on the expected value of anticoagulation versus no anticoagulation

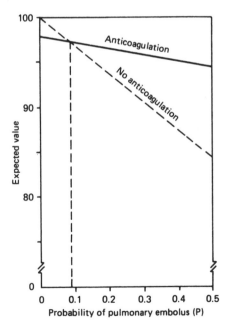

vary only one parameter at a time, keeping the remaining variables constant. If changing a probability or a utility alters the apparent best choice, we say the decision is "sensitive" to such changes. The point at which the decision changes from one choice to the other is called the "threshold" value for that variable. Initially, we shall perform several one-way sensitivity analyses before proceeding to examination of the effect of varying two and then three variables simultaneously. Such sensitivity analyses are often more clearly understood when expressed graphically.

One-way sensitivity analyses In Figure 4, we examine the effect of varying the probability of pulmonary embolus, keeping the remaining variables constant at their baseline values. The solid line shows the expected utility of anticoagulation as a function of the probability of pulmonary embolus; the dotted line represents the expected utility of withholding anticoagulation. In our original analysis, the probability of pulmonary embolus was assumed to be 20 percent. The graph again demonstrates that at that probability, anticoagulation is preferred, with an expected value of 96.5 as compared to an expected value of 93.7 for

Figure 5 One-way sensitivity analysis – Examining the effect of the efficacy of anticoagulation on the expected value of anticoagulation versus no anticoagulation

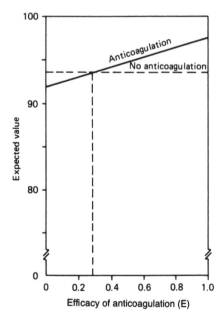

withholding anticoagulants. The figure demonstrates that anticoagulation remains the preferred management option as long as the probability of pulmonary embolus is greater than 8.4 percent.

In Figure 5 we examine the impact of variations in the efficacy of anticoagulation. Anticoagulation remains the preferred choice unless its efficacy is less than 27 percent. This is a particularly pertinent threshold since the efficacy of low dose heparin for the prevention of pulmonary emboli during pregnancy is uncertain. If, as some studies suggest, the efficacy is similar to that of warfarin (75 percent), then anticoagulation would be appropriate. However, if the efficacy is only 20 percent or 25 percent, this analysis suggests that withholding anticoagulants would be more appropriate for this couple. This issue will be dealt with more fully with a three-way sensitivity analysis that includes the utility of infant outcomes as well as the efficacy of therapy.

Figure 6 summarizes the effect of the utility of anticoagulant fetopathy in a one-way sensitivity analysis. Anticoagulation is preferred only if fetopathy (fatal and/or nonfatal) has a utility greater than 74. If the parents felt the burden of fetopathy to be greater (i.e., its utility to be lower) than this threshold, perhaps approaching that of maternal death, the preferred plan would be to refrain from anticoagulation.

Available data locates mortality from pulmonary embolus consistently

Figure 6 One-way sensitivity analysis – Examining the effect of the utility of anticoagulation fetopathy on the expected value of anticoagulation versus no anticoagulation

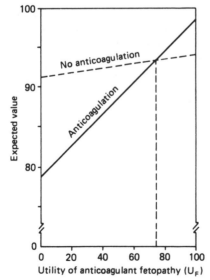

above 25 percent. Sensitivity analysis revealed that anticoagulation would remain the preferred management option unless the mortality rate was below 11.7 percent. Sensitivity analyses were performed on the probability of a fatal bleed during anticoagulant therapy. The decision was insensitive to this variable within the bounds of clinically relevant probabilities, i.e., unless the probability of a fatal hemorrhage exceeded 25 percent.

The decision was also found to be insensitive to variations in utilities for a nonfatal maternal bleed. Since we assigned a value of 100 to the outcome, mother alive and well, we may represent the morbidity of nonfatal bleed as 100×M, where M is some number between 0 and 1. Even if the probability of a bleed were 10 percent, the decision remains in favor of anticoagulation as long as the utility assigned to a nonfatal bleed is greater than 66 percent of that assigned to the best outcome.

A final one-way analysis (Figure 7b) demonstrates that the threshold value for the probability of anticoagulant fetopathy is 53 percent. Given other baseline estimates, one would tolerate a 53 percent incidence of fetopathy before choosing to *not* anticoagulate this pregnant patient with DVT.

The results of these various one-way sensitivity analyses are summarized in Table 3. The threshold value for each of the first four parameters in that table is sufficiently far from reasonable expected variations to

Figure 7 Series of one-way sensitivity analyses – Examining the effect of the probability of anticoagulant fetopathy on the expected value of anticoagulation versus no anticoagulation for different values of the probability of pulmonary embolus

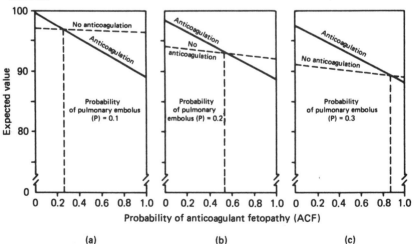

Table 3 *One-way sensitivity analysis*

Parameter	Symbol	Baseline value	Threshold value
Probability of anticoagulant fetopathy	ACF	0.2	0.53
Efficacy of anticoagulation	E	0.75	0.27
Probability of fatal maternal bleed	FMB	0.0015	0.25
Probability of fatality given pulmonary embolus	FPE	0.3	0.117
Probability of pulmonary embolus	P	0.2	0.084
Utility of fetopathy	U_F	90	74

make it fairly clear that the decision is insensitive to such variations. In contrast, the baseline value for the probability of pulmonary embolus is less than 2½ times the threshold value. Therefore, we shall examine the joint effect of varying both that parameter and the "softest" baseline probability, the probability of anticoagulant fetopathy. Rather than proceeding directly to a two-way sensitivity analysis, let us perform a series of one-way analyses, as shown in Figure 7. Figure 7a shows the effect of lowering the probability of pulmonary embolus to 10 percent. The expected utilities of both anticoagulation and no anticoagulation increase for all probabilities of anticoagulant fetopathy, but the effect is more marked on the no-anticoagulation option. Thus, the acceptable threshold risk of fetopathy is lower (24 percent, versus 53 percent in Figure 7b). Conversely, if the probability of pulmonary embolus were higher (i.e., 30 percent as in Figure 7c), an 87 percent probability of fetopathy would be tolerable before anticoagulation would be judged inappropriate.

Two-way sensitivity analyses   In the remaining sensitivity analyses, we shall examine the impact of variations in the utilities of various types of fetopathy on the optimal decision. We shall be considering the joint effects of several variables as we perform both two-way and three-way sensitivity analyses.

First, let us consider the interaction between the efficacy of anticoagulation and the burden of anticoagulant fetopathy. Figure 8a summarizes this two-way sensitivity analysis. The efficacy of therapy is plotted along the horizontal axis, and the utility of fetopathy along the vertical axis. The line dividing the graph into two areas (*Anticoagulation* and *No Anticoagulation*) represents the threshold values for these variables. Each point on this line corresponds to a value of E and a value of U_F which result in equal expected utilities for the two management options. Any combination of efficacy and burden defines a unique point on the graph. If the point lies in the shaded area, then anticoagulation is the better choice; if the point lies in the unshaded area, then it would be better to withhold anticoagulation. The baseline estimates of 75 percent drug efficacy and fetopathy utility of 90 place the decision firmly in the area marked *Anticoagulation*. If a utility of 90 is maintained, but the efficacy of therapy is thought to be only 20 percent, the point now falls below the line and therefore in the area designated *No Anticoagulation*. One can also see that even if the efficacy of the drug were 100 percent, its use would not be indicated unless the utility of fetopathy were greater than 65.

Figure 8b shows the effect of variations in the probability of pulmonary embolus in untreated patients with deep venous thrombosis. Each line summarizes a set of threshold calculations. As can be seen in the figure, a decrease in the probability of pulmonary embolism results in a corresponding decrease in the set of conditions for which anticoagulation would be preferable. For a given probability of pulmonary embolus, one would require either a certain minimal utility of fetopathy or a minimal efficacy of anticoagulation in order to decide to treat. For instance, if the probability of pulmonary embolism were 0.3 and the efficacy of anti-

Figure 8 (a) Two-way sensitivity analysis – Examining the effect of the efficacy of anticoagulation versus the utility of anticoagulant fetopathy on the decision. (b) Three-way sensitivity analysis – For different probabilities of pulmonary embolus

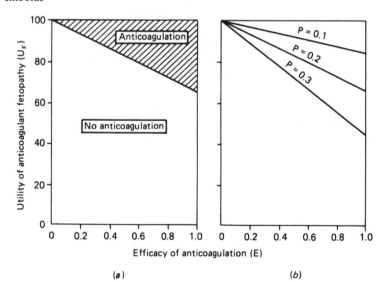

coagulation were 100 percent, utility of fetopathy need only be greater than 43 to prefer *Anticoagulation*. In contrast, if the probability of pulmonary embolus were only 10 percent, the threshold utility for a drug with perfect efficacy rises to 83.6.

If the drug under consideration is warfarin, then the efficacy of anticoagulation is well established (75 percent) but both fetal death and fetal malformation can occur. In that case, it becomes important to examine the tradeoff between the woman's attitude toward these two different bad fetal outcomes. Using the lottery method, the physician can obtain utilities for both infant outcomes and can plot them on the graph. Such a two-way sensitivity analysis is summarized in Figure 9. Again, every combination of U_{FD} and U_{FA} specifies a unique point. If that point falls within the shaded area, then warfarin therapy is to be preferred; otherwise, anticoagulation should be withheld. Such a graph allows the physician to take parental attitudes into account when deciding on therapy. For example, whereas our assumed utilities for fetal death and abnormality (both 90) are squarely within the warfarin region, utilities of 50 would imply that warfarin should be withheld, and utilities of 74 would fall on the threshold.

In contrast, if the drug under consideration were low-dose heparin, then fetal abnormalities would not be a major issue, whereas drug efficacy would be. In this case, the tradeoff would be between the utility of fetal death and the efficacy of therapy, as summarized in Figure 10. The

Figure 9 Two-way sensitivity analysis – examining the effect of the utility of fetal death versus the utility of fetal abnormality on the decision to use warfarin versus no anticoagulation

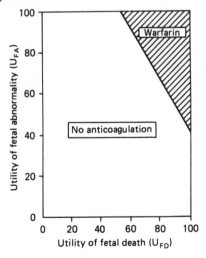

requisite threshold efficacy rises sharply with decreases in the utility of
fetal death (i.e., increases in the burden of that outcome). If efficacy were
perfect, the utility of fetal death would still have to exceed 65. If the
efficacy were 75 percent (which is to say that heparin is as effective as
warfarin), therapy would be indicated if the utility of fetal death were
greater than 74. If heparin efficacy were only 25 percent, the utility of fetal
death would have to exceed 90 for treatment to be preferred.

   The previous sensitivity analyses (Figures 4–10) have demonstrated
that anticoagulation is by and large preferable to no anticoagulation,
within reasonable clinical estimates of the probabilities of pulmonary
embolus, anticoagulant fetopathy, and maternal anticoagulant complications. What becomes the crucial question, then, is how to choose one
drug over the other. The decision is dependent on the interaction between
the physician's estimate of the efficacy of low dose heparin and the
parents' attitudes towards the possibilities of fetal death or abnormality.
In Figure 11, we present a three-way analysis which balances the efficacy
of heparin therapy with parental attitudes. We assume that the efficacy of
warfarin is fixed at 75 percent. The graph is divided into a region in which
warfarin therapy is preferred and one in which heparin therapy is better.
Utilities of fetal death and fetal abnormality are specified on the horizontal and vertical axes. The physician chooses the threshold line between

Figure 10 Two-way sensitivity analysis – examining the effect of the utility of
fetal death versus the efficacy of anticoagulation with low dose heparin on the
decision to use heparin versus no anticoagulation

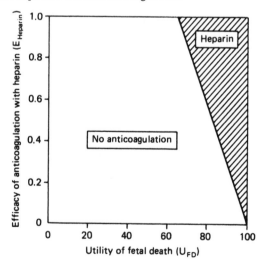

warfarin and heparin by specifying an estimate of heparin efficacy. If the burdens of the two types of fetopathy are equal, and if the efficacy of heparin equals that of warfarin (75 percent), then the two alternatives would be equivalent. If fetal death is less severe a burden than fetal abnormality (i.e., if U_{FD} exceeds U_{FA}, then the balance swings toward heparin; if U_{FA} exceeds U_{FD}, then the balance swings toward warfarin. Finally, all the other things being equal, decreases in the efficacy of heparin (with warfarin efficacy held constant) will enlarge the region in which warfarin is to be preferred.

COMMENTS

Current medical practice suggests that the treatment of deep venous thrombosis in pregnancy should include the long-term use of anti-coagulants. Heparin is recommended during the first trimester, followed by warfarin until the 36th week of gestation. Thereafter, heparin is reintroduced while warfarin is withdrawn, to minimize the risk of fetal and maternal hemorrhage during labor and delivery. Although the high risk of warfarin embryopathy is avoided by this regimen, it nevertheless still places the family at risk for unfavorable infant outcomes. With this analysis we have attempted to illustrate how parental attitudes towards

Figure 11 Three-way sensitivity analysis – examining the effect of the utility of fetal death versus the utility of fetal abnormality on the decision to use warfarin versus heparin, using varying efficacies of heparin

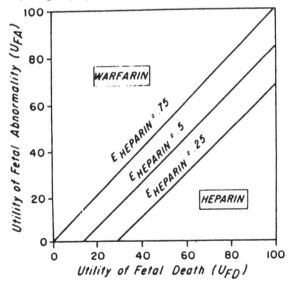

the loss of an infant or the birth of an abnormal child might affect the therapeutic decision for a pregnant woman at risk for pulmonary embolism.

Decisions involving pregnancy can be particularly difficult because the costs and benefits may differ for mother and fetus. Although decision analysis has been applied to perinatal issues,[30] it remains difficult to examine the interaction between maternal and fetal outcomes. Quantitative analysis with patient-derived utility assessment offers a model for balancing the risk of maternal death against the risks of unfavorable fetal or infant outcomes. Furthermore, the physician's estimate of the efficacy of low dose heparin will play a particularly important role if the birth of a significantly abnormal infant is especially undesirable for a given parent.

REFERENCES

1 Baskin, H.F., Murray, J.M., Harris, R.E.: Low-dose heparin for prevention of thromboembolic disease in pregnancy. *Am. J. Obstet. Gynecol.* 129:590–591, 1977

2 Henderson, S.R., Lund, C.J., Crasman, W.T.: Antepartum pulmonary embolism. *Am. J. Obstet. Gynecol.* 112:476–486, 1972

3 Handin, R.I.: Thromboembolic complications of pregnancy and oral contraceptives. *Prog. in Cardiovasc. Dis.* XVI:395–405, 1974

4 Adar, R., Salzman, E.W.: Treatment of thrombosis of veins of the lower extremities. *N. Engl. J. Med.* 292:348–350, 1975

5 Aaro, L.A., Juergens, J.L.: Thrombophlebitis associated with pregnancy. *Am. J. Obstet. Gynecol.* 109:1128–1136, 1871

6 Dalen, J.E., Alpert, J.S.: Natural history of pulmonary embolism. *Prog. in Cardiovasc. Dis.* XVII:257–270, 1975.

7 Sharma, G.V.R.K., Sasahara, A.A.: Diagnosis and treatment of pulmonary embolism. *Med. Clin. North. Am.* 63:239–250, 1979.

8 Crane, C.: Deep venous thrombosis and pulmonary embolism. *N. Engl. J. Med.* 257:147–157, 1957.

9 Gallus, A.S., Hirsh, J.: Prevention of venous thromboembolism. *Seminars in Thromb and Hemost* 2:232–290, 1976.

10 Moser, K.M.: State of the art – pulmonary embolism. *Am. Rev. Respir. Dis.* 115:829–852, 1977.

11 Wessler, S., Gitel, S.N.: Low-dose heparin. Is the risk worth the benefit? *Am. Heart J.* 98:94–101, 1979.

12 Sherry, S.: Low dose heparin prophylaxis for postoperative venous thromboembolism. *N. Engl. J. Med.* 293:300–302, 1975.

13 Kiil, J., Kiil, J., Axelsen, F., Andersen, D.: Prophylaxis against postoperative pulmonary embolus and deep-vein thrombosis by low-dose heparin. *Lancet*: 1115–1116, 1978.

14 Lahnborg, G., Bergstrom, K., Friman, L., Lagergren, H.: Effect of low-dose

heparin on incidence of postoperative pulmonary embolism detected by photoscanning. *Lancet*:329–331, 1974.

15 Kakkar, V.V., Corrigan, T.P., Fossard, D.P., *et al.*: Prevention of fatal postoperative pulmonary embolism by low doses of heparin. *Lancet*:45–51, 1975.

16 Negus, D., Cox, S.J., Friedgood, A., Peel, A.L.G.: Ultra-low dose intravenous heparin in the prevention of postoperative deep vein thrombosis. *Lancet*: 891–894, 1980.

17 Harris, W.H., *et al.*: Comparison of warfarin, low-molecular-weight dextran, aspirin, and subcutaneous heparin in prevention of venous thromboembolism folllowing total hip replacement. *J. Bone Joint Surg.* 56-A:1552–1562, 1974.

18 Spearing, G., Fraser, I., Turner, G., Dixon, G.: Long-term self-administered subcutaneous heparin in pregnancy. *Br. Med. J.*:1457–1458, 1978.

19 Kull, R., *et al.*: Warfarin sodium versus low dose heparin in the long term treatment of venous thrombosis. *N. Engl. J. Med.* 301:855–858, 1979.

20 Bynum, L.J., Wilson, J.E.: Low dose heparin therapy in the long-term management of venous thromboembolism. *Am. J. Med.* 67:553–556, 1979.

21 Bloomfield, D.K.: Fetal deaths and malformations associated with the use of coumadin derivatives in pregnancy. *Am. J. Obstet. Gynecol.* 107:883–888, 1970.

22 Coon, W.W., Willis, P.W.: Hemorrhagic complications of anticoagulant therapy. *Arch. Int. Med.* 133:386–392, 1974.

23 Davis, R.J.: Letter. *Ann. Intern. Med.* 88:713, 1978.

24 Pettifor, J.M., Benson, R.: Congenital malformations association with the administration of oral anticoagulants during pregnancy. *J. Pediatr.* 86:459–462, 1975.

25 Hirsh, K., Cade, J.F., Gallus, A.S.: Fetal effects of coumadin administered during pregnancy. *Blood* 36:623–627, 1970.

26 Kerber, I.J., Warr, O.S., Richardson, C.: Pregnancy in a patient with a prosthetic mitral value associated with a fetal anomaly attributed to warfarin sodium. *JAMA* 203:223–225, 1968.

27 Hirsh, J., Cade, J.F., Gallus, A.S.: Anticoagulants in pregnancy. A review of indications and complications. *Am. Heart J.* 83:301–305, 1972.

28 Hall, J.G., Pauli, R.M., Wilson, K.M.: Maternal and fetal sequelae of anticoagulation during pregnancy. *Am. J. Med.* 68:122–140, 1980.

29 Merrill, L.K., VerBurg, D.J.: The choice of long-term anticoagulants for the pregnant patient. *Obstet. Gynecol.* 47:711–714, 1976.

30 Shy, K.K., LoGerfo, J.P., Karp, L.E.: Evaluation of elective repeat cesarean section as a standard of care. An application of decision analysis. *Am. J. Obstet. Gynecol.* 139:123–129, 1981.

15

COMPARISON OF PHYSICIANS' DECISIONS
REGARDING ESTROGEN REPLACEMENT
THERAPY FOR MENOPAUSAL WOMEN AND
DECISIONS DERIVED FROM A DECISION
ANALYTIC MODEL*

*Arthur S. Elstein, Gerald B. Holzman, Michael M. Ravitch,
William A. Metheny, Margaret M. Holmes, Ruth B. Hoppe,
Marilyn L. Rothert, David R. Rovner*

Decision analysis[1-6] is a formal analytic framework that is increasingly being applied to the problem of selecting an action in clinical situations in which the optimal choice is not intuitively clear or the judgments of competent physicians differ. These situations often involve complex combinations of uncertainty, values, risks, and benefits, precisely where human judgment may encounter difficulty in reaching an optimal solution[7-9] and where a decision aid may be useful. The techniques and principles of clinical decision analysis constitute a family of tools for the logical analysis of such complex clinical situations. Selecting a management plan is accomplished by a detailed analysis of the available alternatives and their potential consequences, the criterion for selection being the maximization of expected utility, a quantitative measure of preference. Clinical decision analysis has been applied to a variety of medical problems to determine how to treat or work-up a specific patient,[10,11] to analyze management alternatives for certain problems,[12-14] and to assess the value of diagnostic tests.[15,16]

In the analysis by Weinstein[17] of risks and benefits of estrogen replacement therapy, probabilities of outcomes contingent on treatment were obtained from the published literature. The sources of probability estimates were specifically noted as was the extent to which they were explicitly based upon published reports or had to be extrapolated from available data. The analysis demonstrated perhaps unintentionally, how difficult it is to reconcile conflicting reports that were conducted in different settings with different populations and with use of a variety of methods. Policy formulation from this complex and confusing literature

* First published in *American Journal of Medicine*, 80 (1986), 246–58. © 1986 Technical Publishing. Reprinted by permission.

must be particularly difficult for practicing physicians who, in general, lack the knowledge of statistics and research design necessary to evaluate and aggregate the studies.

We have applied a decision analytic model to the problem of estrogen replacement therapy for menopausal women, a situation in which a range of clinical opinions can be elicited. Using a series of written case descriptions, we compared the decisions reached by experienced physicians with recommended actions derived from an expected utility model constructed for each clinician. The model incorporated into a standard decision tree each physician's estimates of the relevant probabilities and utilities. The research was designed to answer three questions:

1   How consistent are the observed decisions with the recommendations of the decision analytic model? Stated slightly differently, how well does expected utility theory describe choice behavior in this situation?

2   To what degree can documented differences in prescribing practices be explained in terms of different beliefs about the risks and benefits of estrogen replacement?

3   How dependent are the results on the method of utility assessment employed?

Various opinions have been expressed in the literature about the indications and contraindications for estrogen use.[18–22] Even where consensus about the risks and benefits exists, there is disagreement about the importance of one compared with another and hence about the appropriate extent of use.

Fractures associated with osteoporosis are a major health problem in elderly women. Vertebral fractures have been observed in 25 percent of white women over age 60.[23,24] Hip fracture occurs in 20 percent of women reaching age 90, with mortality estimates ranging from 17 to 50 percent within three months of the injury.[23,25–27] Hip fracture in elderly women has been implicated in 50,000 deaths per year at an annual cost of $2 billion.[18] Although the role and effectiveness of estrogen in delaying or preventing osteoporosis have been the subject of some debate, epidemiologic data suggest that long-term estrogen therapy is associated with a substantial reduction in risk of fractures,[18] perhaps as much as 50 to 60 percent.[28]

Estrogen has been associated with an increased risk of the development of endometrial cancer. It is estimated that the risk is from 0.0007[18] to 0.001[29] per year in women who do not take estrogen, increasing from three- to eight-fold or more if estrogen is used.[17,30] Research also indicates that progesterone prescribed cyclically with estrogen reduces the risk to about the level without estrogen therapy or perhaps less.[31,32] Other potential risks have been documented or suspected,[19] including abnormal glucose tolerance, cancer of the breast, cholelithiasis, and thromboembolic disease. Exogenous estrogen had been noted to increase morbidity and mortality following myocardial disease,[33] but more recently it has been associated with a decrease in cardiac mortality[29] and in fact mortality in general.[34] Part of the difficulty in judging the appropriateness of estrogen therapy arises from the lag between the onset of menopause and the occurrence of significant outcomes other than relief of symptoms. Both endometrial cancer and fractures associated with osteoporosis are delayed outcomes, most likely to occur 10 or more years after menopause. Hence, discounting future risks and benefits to present value is unnecessary.

In earlier research in this area,[35] physicians' judgments regarding the appropriateness of estrogen replacement therapy were studied in a series of brief written cases that systematically incorporated four variables: risk of endometrial cancer, severity of vasomotor symptoms, risk of fractures associated with osteoporosis, and current treatment status. Decisions to prescribe depended mainly on endometrial cancer risk and vasomotor symptom severity, whereas fracture risk and treatment status were of negligible importance. These decisions were used as the point of comparison for the decision analytic study reported herein.

METHODS

The subjects, all paid volunteers, were 50 community physicians practicing in mid-Michigan cities, 25 gynecologists and 25 family physicians. More detail about the composition of the sample is available.[35] Each physician was mailed a questionnaire that included a series of 12 case descriptions of postmenopausal women about age 50. Each case provided information on three factors: endometrial cancer risk (three levels: standard, moderate, high), vasomotor symptom severity (two levels: standard, high), and osteoporosis risk (two levels: standard, high). Thus, the cases represented all possible combinations of factor levels in a 3 by 2 by 2 design. None of the patients was currently receiving estrogen therapy or had ever been.

For each case, respondents marked a 10 cm line to indicate the likelihood of prescribing estrogen for that patient. They were to assume that they were prescribing their usual steroid formulations. The scale was anchored at one end by "Virtually certain I would *not* prescribe" and at the other end by "Virtually certain I would prescribe." For example, a mark of 6.5 cm was interpreted as a 65 percent probability that the physician would prescribe estrogen for that patient. To relate the judgments to decision analysis, responses were classified in three decision categories: probability judgments below 0.40 were classified as "Do not prescribe;" those between 0.40 and 0.60 inclusive were classified as "Undecided;" those above 0.60 were classified as "Prescribe."

A multiattribute decision analytic model was formulated that conceptualized five possible treatment regimens and three major categories of treatment outcomes. The treatment regimens were: no estrogen treatment, estrogen alone for up to three years, estrogen with progesterone for up to three years, estrogen alone for five or more years, estrogen with progesterone for five or more years. The categories were: vasomotor symptoms, endometrial cancer, and hip fractures associated with osteoporosis. Four possible outcomes were formulated for each category to cover the spectrum of severity and degree of disability (Appendix A).

Figure 1 Decision tree for estrogen replacement therapy. T_1=no treatment; T_2=estrogen only for up to three years; T_3=estrogen and progesterone for up to three years; T_4=estrogen only for five or more years; T_5=estrogen and progesterone for five or more years

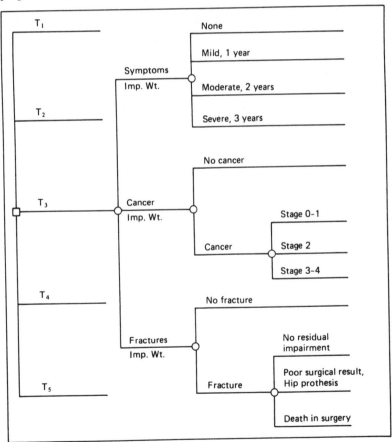

Table 1 *Subjective probability of the development of endometrial cancer in 25 years conditional on cancer risk level and treatment regimen*

Risk level	T_1 Mean	SD	T_2 Mean	SD	T_3 Mean	SD	T_4 Mean	SD	T_5 Mean	SD
High	0.07	0.08	0.13	0.15	0.07	0.10	0.16	0.17	0.09	0.14
Moderate	0.04	0.04	0.08	0.10	0.05	0.07	0.09	0.10	0.05	0.08
Standard	0.02	0.02	0.03	0.05	0.02	0.03	0.04	0.05	0.03	0.05

T_1 = no treatment; T_2 = estrogen only for up to three years; T_3 = estrogen and progesterone for up to three years; T_4 = estrogen only for five or more years; T_5 = estrogen and progesterone for five or more years.

Table 2 *Subjective probability of detecting endometrial pathologic condition at various stages, contingent on treatment status*

Stage	Treated Mean	SD	Range	Not treated Mean	SD	Range
Atypical adenomatous hyperplasia	0.60	0.29	0.01–0.96	0.43	0.29	0.00–0.98
I	0.24	0.21	0.02–0.85	0.27	0.18	0.01–0.90
II	0.09	0.08	0.00–0.35	0.14	0.10	0.00–0.40
III	0.05	0.07	0.00–0.35	0.10	0.11	0.00–0.55
IV	0.02	0.03	0.00–0.14	0.06	0.06	0.00–0.20

A section of the questionnaire was also used to elicit the subjective probabilities needed for the decision analytic model. These included:

1 Probabilities of various levels of symptom relief (severity and duration) in patients with standard and severe vasomotor symptoms treated or not treated with estrogen.

2 Probability of hip fracture occurring in patients with standard and high osteoporosis risk treated or not treated with estrogen.

3 Probabilities of specific outcomes if fractures were to occur in patients treated or not treated with estrogen.

4 Probability of the development of endometrial cancer for patients at three different risk levels (standard, moderate, high) under each of five treatment plans.

5 Probabilities of endometrial pathologic condition being detected at specific stages if it were to develop in patients at different cancer risk levels, with or without replacement estrogen treatment.

After the questionnaire had been completed, individual interviews were conducted to assess utilities for specific outcomes within each category (fracture, cancer, or symptoms) and importance weights for the categories. Utilities were assessed twice, first by category scaling[36] and then by lottery technique.[1,37] The physicians were asked to estimate the preferences most of their patients would have for the outcomes. Edwards'[38] simplified multiattribute rating technique was used to elicit importance weights. Further details of the assessment procedures are provided in Appendix B.

A partial decision tree for this analysis is shown in Figure 1. T_1 to T_5 are the five treatment options already mentioned. A complete tree would show branching identical to that displayed for T_3 following each regimen.

Since estrogen can be prescribed for varying lengths of time, it was necessary to define when a patient would be considered treated. With regard to relief of vasomotor symptoms, any regimen with estrogen was counted as treatment, since all four would be effective. With respect to osteoporosis and prevention of fractures, only the two regimens giving estrogen for five or more years were defined as treatment, since most reports advocating estrogen for this purpose indicate that long-term use (certainly more than five years) is required to produce the desired effect. For endometrial cancer, the five regimens were considered separately, since both duration of estrogen treatment and use of progesterone affect the risks.

Estimates of the relevant parameters provided by each physician were inserted into the tree structure. For any respondent, importance weights and utilities were evaluations of outcomes constant across treatments or levels of risk. The estimated probabilities, however, did vary according to risk factors and treatment strategy. For each physician, the expected utility was then calculated for five treatment regimens for each of 12 patients, once using utilities derived from category scaling (obtained from 50 physicians) and again using utilities derived from standard gambles (n=49). A difference in expected utility of 0.1 or more between treatments was interpreted as favoring the alternative with the greater expected utility; smaller differences were considered too close to call, a toss-up.[39]

One-way sensitivity analyses were performed to determine the extent to which estimates of probabilities and importance weights would have to be adjusted to equate the expected utility of treatment and no treatment.

RESULTS

Beliefs and attitudes: risks and benefits

The category of cancer outcomes was ranked first in importance by 34 of 50 physicians; the symptom category was ranked first by 16. None ranked fractures as the most important category. The means of the importance weights were: endometrial cancer 0.52; symptoms 0.30; and fractures 0.18.

Table 1 displays the mean subjective probabilities of the development of endometrial cancer over a 25-year period (from age 50 to 75) for patients at different risk levels under different treatment regimens. The estimated risk was doubled for short-term estrogen use (up to three years) and was slightly higher with prolonged estrogen use. For each risk group, combining progesterone with estrogen lowered the mean probability of the development of endometrial cancer to about the incidence expected with no treatment. It was generally thought that if an endometrial pathologic condition were to develop, it would usually be detected earlier among treated than among untreated patients (Table 1).

Figure 2 shows cumulative probability distributions of the mean proportion of patients expected to experience relief of symptoms within four time intervals, depending on treatment and severity of symptoms. Estrogen replacement therapy was expected to reduce the severity and duration of vasomotor symptoms greatly for all patients. When treatment was held constant, severe symptoms were expected to be more persistent than standard symptoms.

Patients judged to be at standard risk for osteoporosis were estimated to have a mean probability of 9 percent (±10 percent) for the development of a serious fracture (such as hip fracture) in a 25-year interval (Table 3). This risk was reduced to 5 percent (±8 percent) if patients were treated for five or more years with estrogen. For patients at high risk for the development of osteoporosis, the mean likelihood of serious fractures in

Figure 2 Menopausal symptom relief as a function of symptom severity and treatment status. Cumulative distributions of mean probabilities of symptom relief over time. □=severe symptoms, untreated; △=severe symptoms, treated; ○=standard symptoms, untreated; ■=standard symptoms, treated

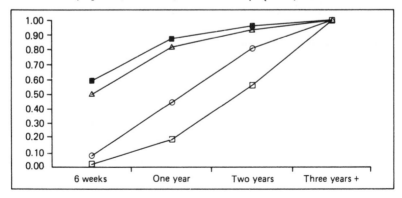

Table 3 *Probability of fractures associated with osteoporosis over 25 years, contingent on osteoporosis risk level and treatment regimen*

| | Treatment status[a] | | | |
| | Not treated | | Treated | |
Risk level	Mean	SD	Mean	SD
Standard	0.09	0.10	0.05	0.08
High	0.23	0.18	0.11	0.12

[a] Treatment means replacement estrogen for at least 5 years.

the same interval was 23 percent ($\pm$18 percent) with no therapy, but dropped to 11 percent ($\pm$12 percent) with estrogen therapy (Table 3). Thus, estrogen is believed to reduce the probability of fractures by about half regardless of the patient's osteoporosis risk level, again consistent with published literature.[28]

Estrogen therapy was also believed to improve surgical results of patients who fractured a hip. Table 4 shows that the estimated surgical mortality following fracture was about the same with or without estrogen therapy, but probability of good surgical results was somewhat enhanced for those who had received hormone therapy.

Means, standard deviations, and ranges of utilities for specific outcomes are shown in Table 5. Four outcomes were defined within each category. The best outcome was arbitrarily assigned a utility of 1.0 and the worst a utility of 0. (This method of utility assessment may make it appear that two or three years of severe vasomotor symptoms are worse than a stage 2 endometrial cancer. But we shall show that even if symptoms are discounted entirely, the thrust of the decision analysis is unchanged.) The only disagreement about the ranking of outcomes occurred for fracture outcomes: five of 50 physicians believed that most patients would prefer perioperative death to chronic pain and disability due to osteoporotic fractures even if relieved a few years later by a prosthesis. Thus, the average utility of perioperative death was slightly greater than 0.00. With the lottery method, a few physicians indicated that it was simply not worth risking the worst outcome, so that both intermediate states were valued at 1.00, equivalent to the best outcome. One physician declined to provide any estimates using lotteries, insisting that he could not put himself in a patient's place regarding choices among outcomes, but found category scaling acceptable. In general, the values of intermediate outcomes were slightly higher when elicited by lottery than by category scaling.

Table 4 *Probability of specific fracture outcomes, given a hip fracture while treated or untreated*

	Treatment status[a]			
	Untreated		Treated	
Outcomes	Mean	SD	Mean	SD
Good surgical result	0.51	0.21	0.65	0.16
Poor surgical result	0.38	0.18	0.26	0.14
Fracture-related death	0.10	0.13	0.09	0.11

[a] Treatment means replacement estrogen for at least 5 years.

Expected utilities

Mean expected utilities derived from the lottery method are shown in Table 6. For every case, the mean expected utility of any estrogen regimen (T_2 to T_5) was always greater than the mean expected utility of no therapy. The expected utility of treating five years or more (T_4 or T_5) was slightly greater than for treating three years or less (T_2 or T_3). The mean expected utility of estrogen and progesterone combined (T_3 or T_5) was slightly greater than the mean expected utility of estrogen alone (T_2 or T_4). Mean lottery expected utilities were generally slightly higher than those obtained with category scaling, but the recommendations of the decision analysis were about the same with either method.

A cross-tabulation comparing prescribing decisions observed in the cases with those recommended by the decision analysis is shown in Table 7. The large number of decision analytic toss-ups results from the criterion used: any two strategies were considered equivalent if the difference between their expected utilities was less than 0.10. If the toss-up band were narrowed, most of these instances would fall into the "treat" category. About one third of the observed decisions were to prescribe (202) whereas more than half (337) were against treatment. Only 49 observed decisions were in the toss-up range, indicating that physicians tended to act decisively in these cases. The decision analysis, on the other hand, did not identify a single instance in which it would be preferable not to treat if the belief structure of any physician were systematically inserted into the model.

Sensitivity analysis

Sensitivity analysis was used to determine the values that model parameters must assume for "no estrogen" to be equivalent in expected utility

Table 5 *Utilities for cancer, symptom, and fracture outcome states assessed by lottery and category scaling*

State	Cancer		Symptom		Fracture	
	Lottery	Category scaling (n = 50)	Lottery	Category scaling (n = 50)	Lottery	Category scaling (n = 50)
I	1.000	1.000	1.000	1.000	1.000	1.000
II						
Mean	0.915	0.780	0.823	0.759	0.849	0.713
SD	0.137	0.174	0.190	0.177	0.168	0.191
Range	0.150–1.0	0.100–0.990	0.200–1.0	0.050–0.950	0.150–1.0	0.200–0.900
III						
Mean	0.749	0.414	0.596	0.384	0.592	0.261
SD	0.241	0.220	0.230	0.192	0.322	0.191
Range	0.050–1.0	0.020–0.930	0.130–1.0	0.020–0.830	0.0–1.0	0.0–0.750
IV						
Mean	0.000	0.000	0.000	0.000	0.054[a]	0.023[a]
SD					0.174	0.084
Range					0–0.750	0.0–0.500

[a] Five physicians believed that most patients would prefer perioperative death to chronic pain and disability.

Table 6 *Mean expected utilities of five treatment regimens for 12 cases*

	Cue level			Regimens[a]				
Case	Cancer risk	Fracture risk	Symptom severity	T_1	T_2	T_3	T_4	T_5
1	Standard	Standard	Standard	0.874	0.955	0.957	0.957	0.959
2	Standard	Standard	High	0.806	0.942	0.943	0.944	0.945
3	Standard	High	Standard	0.865	0.947	0.948	0.954	0.956
4	Standard	High	High	0.797	0.938	0.935	0.940	0.942
5	Moderate	Standard	Standard	0.871	0.952	0.954	0.954	0.957
6	Moderate	Standard	High	0.803	0.938	0.941	0.940	0.943
7	Moderate	High	Standard	0.862	0.943	0.946	0.950	0.954
8	Moderate	High	High	0.794	0.930	0.932	0.937	0.940
9	High	Standard	Standard	0.866	0.948	0.952	0.947	0.953
10	High	Standard	High	0.798	0.934	0.938	0.934	0.939
11	High	High	Standard	0.857	0.939	0.944	0.944	0.950
12	High	High	High	0.790	0.925	0.930	0.930	0.936

[a] See Table 1 for definition of abbreviations.

Table 7 *Cross-tabulation of observed prescribing decisions and recommendations of decision analytic model*

	Decision analysis		
	Treat	Toss-up	Do not treat	
Observed decisions				
Treat	97	105	0	202
Toss-up	23	26	0	49
Do not treat	113	224	0	337
	233	355	0	588

Data obtained from 49 physicians.

to "estrogen and progesterone for five or more years." For Cases 1, 9, and 12 that span the risk spectrum in our series (Table 6), probabilities, importance weights, and utilities were varied systematically one at a time to see how much these parameters could vary before the expected utility of no treatment would be equal to the expected utility of estrogen and progesterone for five years or more. To simplify this analysis, mean values of the relevant parameters were used throughout instead of carrying it out for each physician.

If all parameter estimates except probability of the development of endometrial cancer with estrogen and progesterone for five or more years are held constant, then the two plans have equal expected utilities only if that probability is 0.68 for Case 1, 0.76 for Case 9, and 1.13 for Case 12. The first two probabilities are eight to 10 times any reported in the literature and the third is mathematically impossible. If all parameters are held constant except the probabilities of early and late detection of endometrial cancer for patients receiving estrogen and progesterone for five or more years, the probability of early detection would have to drop to zero and the probability of late detection would have to rise to 0.95 or more for the expected utility of not treating to be equivalent to treating. These probabilities are outside the most pessimistic estimates of any of our physician subjects or of any reported study.

The sensitivity analysis disclosed that the importance weight for cancer outcomes would need to be 0.99 or greater in all three cases to equate the two strategies. In effect, then, the expected utilities of the two regimens would be equal only if the benefits of symptom relief and reducing fractures associated with osteoporosis are completely excluded from the model. Thus, the utilities shown in Table 5 have no bearing on the outcome. The model is driven by the probabilities of cancer versus the probabilities of fracture outcomes.

Our respondents believed that incidents of cancer were more likely to be detected at an early stage if patients were receiving estrogen replacement therapy than if they were not, probably because patients being treated would be more regularly screened for cancer. Improving early detection of cancer in patients not receiving estrogen replacement therapy might be thought to substantially alter the results of the decision analysis. Therefore, for Cases 1, 9, and 12 in Table 6, the mean estimates of probabilities and utilities were inserted into the decision analysis formula to determine the expected utility of "no estrogen" treatment, assuming that early detection in each of these patients was the same as if they had been receiving estrogen therapy. For Case 1 (standard levels of cancer risk, symptom severity, and fracture risk), the expected utility under these conditions of "no estrogen" treatment would be 0.875. For Case 9 (high cancer risk, standard symptom severity and fracture risk), the expected utility of not treating with estrogen was 0.868, and for Case 12 (all three risk factors high), the expected utility would be 0.793. Clearly, the slight improvement in the expected utility for "no estrogen" treatment does not substantially improve the argument against estrogen therapy.

The mathematic reason for this rather small improvement lies in the physicians' estimates of the probability that cancer will occur, given the patient's risk level and the recommended treatment, compared with their estimates of the probabilities of fractures, specific fracture outcomes, and symptom relief contingent on patient's risk factors and treatment regimens. Because the probabilities involved are all fairly large for fractures and symptoms, their effects show up in the first decimal place of the computed expected utility. For endometrial cancer, the probabilities are relatively smaller, and therefore the computation of expected utility changes only in the second or third decimal place.

In summary, even if patients not receiving estrogen were examined as regularly as patients receiving estrogen, and if early detection rates are assumed to be identical in both groups, this would not substantially alter the argument of the decision analysis that the expected utility of treatment with estrogen and progesterone is at least equivalent to and usually better than for no treatment.

Finally, to take the most extreme utility assessment possible that would favor no treatment, the utility of all fracture outcomes except death was set at 1.00, and death was set at 0.0; for symptom relief, utility of any duration except the worst (three years) was set at 1.0; and for cancer outcomes, no cancer was set at 1.0, whereas the utility of any other outcome was set at 0.0. Even under this stringent test, the expected utility of treating with estrogen and progesterone for five or more years exceeded the expected utility of no treatment for all three cases. The sensitivity analysis thus demonstrated that the recommendations of the decision analysis were robust across any plausible estimate of the probabilities of the development or detection of endometrial cancer, the importance weights, or the utilities.

Experimental design

The purposes of this investigation were to investigate (1) the relation of well-documented differences in prescribing practices to differences in beliefs about the risks and benefits of estrogen replacement therapy, and (2) the consistency of observed decisions with the recommendations of a decision analytic model employing the criterion of maximizing expected utility. The set of cases used in this study was constructed so that all possible combinations of factors were represented once. This design facilitated certain statistical analyses but it also created a set unrepresentative of clinical practice in certain crucial respects. In particular, high risks for cancer and osteoporosis were both overrepresented in the series. This structure, however, does not impinge on the research aims, since we have compared observed decisions in these cases with the outcomes of decision analysis applied to the same risk structure.

Decision analysis is explicit and quantitative. In this study, for example, some possible risks and benefits of estrogen replacement were explicitly excluded from consideration on the grounds that they were either not well established in fact or were such rare events, compared with the frequencies of the three outcomes explicitly included, that they could not affect the decision to any significant degree. This assumption can be questioned and tested by constructing additional branches for the decision tree, re-estimating the importance weights, obtaining additional subjective probabilities and utilities for the outcomes on the new branches, and then recalculating expected utilities.

Risk aversion

A person who declines a particular gamble in favor of a certain outcome of lesser value is said to be averse to the risk implied in the gamble. For example, preferring $40 for sure in favor of a coin toss to win $100 or $0 demonstrates aversion to risk. In clinical terms, risk aversion makes intermediate health care outcomes more attractive and increases the distance between them and the least desirable outcome, because people will settle for less in order to avoid gambling with death. In this study, higher values of intermediate outcomes were elicited by lotteries than by category scaling (Table 5). Since the lotteries involve an element of risk and category scaling does not, the findings appear to reflect a moderate amount of risk aversion, as is commonly found in clinical decision analyses.[40]

Discrepancy between behavior and the model

Decision analysis provides a divide-and-conquer strategy to cope with complex, difficult situations. The approach rests on the assumption that better results can be achieved in these instances by analyzing a problem into components, structuring these into a decision tree as a logical framework, and then obtaining or estimating the probabilities and values needed to fill in the tree. Answers to difficult problems are therefore sought by first obtaining answers or estimates to more easily answered questions and then combining these components by the technique of averaging out and folding back. Recommendations derived in this way will be consistent with the stated values and beliefs of the decision-maker who provided them, even if they seem contraintuitive.

The decision tree employed in this study was the same for all physicians and for all cases; it was individualized by incorporating each physician's estimates of the risks and benefits of five different treatment regimens. These risks and benefits were formally defined in quantitative terms as subjective probabilities, utilities, and importance weights. The great virtue of this model is that these estimates can be combined by a logical rule to determine, for each physician and for each case, the strategy with the greatest expected utility. The results summarized in Table 7 show clearly that the model is not a good fit to the observed decisions. The clinicians studied did not prescribe for most patients (a finding consistent with the decline in estrogen-prescribing that has been noted elsewhere). The model recommended therapy for more patients than physicians were inclined to treat and never recommended no treatment. It may be concluded that the model emphasized different criteria than appear to have been employed in intuitive clinical decision-making and that the beliefs and attitudes obtained by eliciting subjective probabilities, utilities, and importance weights were not systematically related to the prescribing judgments made on the written cases.

What features of the expected utility model and of human clinical judgment can account for this discrepancy? Our earlier research[35] showed that physicians placed considerable emphasis on the risk of endometrial cancer in their observed judgments. In this study, the sensitivity analysis demonstrated that this risk plays little part in the decision analytic model. Formal calculations indicated that estrogen therapy will not substantially decrease expected utility in the cancer dimension because very poor outcomes are so rare, but therapy will have very powerful effects on increasing expected utility with respect to relieving symptoms and reducing osteoporosis risk. To refrain from prescribing in the face of these beliefs means that the physicians are, in effect, giving more weight to avoiding cancer outcomes than they believe even the patients would give. The sensitivity analysis also shows that the gains in osteoporosis risk reduction believed to be achievable by estrogen replacement therapy are so great that no plausible importance weight for cancer can make "no treatment" the optimal action.

One possible explanation for this situation is that the subjective probabilities provided by the physicians for the analysis are substantially in error, since they are unaccustomed to expressing their views in this fashion, whereas their practice habits reflect a more accurate understanding of the risks and benefits. In fact, however, those subjective estimates that can be meaningfully compared with published data are remarkably similar to the published figures. On the whole, the estimates of the panel reflected a grasp of the range of figures in the published medical literature, so their behavior cannot be attributed to erroneous knowledge about the various risks. The physicians' beliefs about the efficacy of estrogen therapy in the prevention of fractures (Table 3) indicate that they did not withhold estrogen because it was believed to be ineffective in reducing the incidence of osteoporosis.

It appears to have been particularly difficult for the panel to incorporate into their observed decision-making another feature of their beliefs and opinions that the model takes into account systematically. Table 2 shows that the subjective probability of early detection of cancer, when favorable outcomes are more likely, is greater when patients are receiving estrogen. Presumably, this benefit of treatment accrues because of regular follow-up when the endometrium may be periodically sampled, as recommended by several authorities.[18,30,33] The decision analysis thus implies that even patients with a high cancer risk (e.g., Case 9, Table 6) ought to be treated because, paradoxically, the very act that may increase risk for the patient, namely estrogen therapy, may also decrease that risk by facilitating early detection. Intuitive clinical judgment appeared to have had difficulty putting into perspective the gains to be achieved by early detection whereas the decision analysis incorporated them systematically.

It might be argued that the cases were too brief and did not provide the physicians with the information needed to make affirmative treatment decisions. On this view, the decision "not to treat" might be understood as deferring treatment pending the results of additional laboratory studies. In fact, high and moderate cancer risks in these cases were defined by historical information and physical findings. Although these risk levels could be better defined by additional laboratory studies, this shift (even if it were to occur) could not affect the overall trend of the data, because physicians tended to treat only patients with severe symptoms and standard cancer risk, ignoring osteoporosis risk. The model suggests that osteoporosis risk reduction should contribute more to the decision and that the physicians on the whole were underprescribing. This tendency was not confined to patients with high or moderate cancer risk.

The results also illustrate the principle that acquiring new knowledge does not necessarily change performance. Practice habits persist even though the knowledge and beliefs that were their underlying rationale have changed. The clinical literature of the late 70s focused on the association between estrogen and endometrial carcinoma.[41,42] The literature of the 80s has emphasized more the problem of osteoporosis and the role of estrogen in its prevention.[28,43–50]

Psychologic studies of judgment and decision-making have repeatedly shown that it is difficult for human judgment to reach optimal decisions in complex, multivariate environments.[51] Further, in situations with multiple objectives in which it is unclear how to take all of them into account, actual decision behavior often follows the course of action implied by the most important objective because such choices are more easily justified.[52] The behavior observed in this series of cases is consistent with this principle, although suboptimal with respect to the criterion of expected utility. The observed decisions were consistent with the wish to avoid undesirable consequences in the most important dimensions, even though these decisions tended to increase risks on a less important attribute. In effect, a very small risk of cancer looms very large psychologically, larger in fact than the respondents' stated intentions. This overweighting of small probabilities is a feature of prospect theory.[53]

We should also consider the possibility that unfavorable outcomes attributable to personal action may be judged as worse than equally unfavorable outcomes due to inaction. In thinking about prescribing estrogen, physicians may view themselves as potentially causing cancer and then invoke the ancient axiom, "First of all, do no harm," as justification. The difficulty with this strategy, of course is that not prescribing may also prove to be harmful. Yet there seems to be a clear psychologic distinction between hazards caused by human action and those that "just happen." Determining fault is a central part of every accident analysis. Decision theory, on the other hand, evaluates outcomes prospectively and independently of the actions that produce them, and thus implies that effects are to be judged independently of causes. However, since the determination of responsibility for a bad outcome and the search for causes seem to be inherent in human reasoning about risks and hazards, decision theory may not be an adequate descriptive theory where issues of responsibility and regret are concerned.[54,55]

In summary, our study suggests that the practice habits of the clinicians studied, as mirrored in their responses to a series of 12 written cases, are inconsistent with a decision analytic model incorporating their own beliefs and values for several reasons:

1 Lag between changes in knowledge and opinion on the one hand and practice patterns on the other.
2 Difficulty in combining multiple competing factors into a decision that maximizes the expected utility criterion. In particular, the gains believed by our panel to be achievable by early detection are largely neglected in their clinical judgments, and very small probabilities are over-weighted.
3 Perceptions of responsibility and blame and anticipation of regret.

Implications

This study has implications both for medical practice regarding estrogen therapy for the menopause and for the application of decision analysis to other clinical problems.

In regard to the first topic, our results suggest that at the very least, physicians ought to carefully reexamine their practice patterns in the light of their beliefs and opinions. Withholding treatment may be inconsistent with the clinician's own beliefs about the risks and benefits of estrogen therapy and may be guided by the understandable wish to avoid causing rare but very undesirable outcomes at the price of exposing patients to far more likely, but somewhat less undesirable, hazards. Some risk is unavoidable in this situation, and careful thought must be given to the magnitude of each kind of risk and obtainable benefit. The decision analysis shows that vasomotor symptom relief is not the issue and that even if estrogen did not relieve these symptoms, it would still be desirable because of the decline in fracture risk. Moreover, several physicians stated that they would personally give more weight to osteoporosis prophylaxis than they thought their patients would. Now, if treatment is preferred according to a model that overweights cancer risk, then it must be even more strongly preferred if additional weight is given to preventing osteoporosis.

As far as clinical applications of decision analysis are concerned, our point is more complex. Decision analysis has been recommended as a procedure to select the optimal action on the grounds that decision theory is an explicit logical approach to decision-making under uncertainty. This study joins several others[53,56,57] in showing that departures from the principles of normative decision theory are a regular feature of human decision-making, even among experts. The theory does not describe decision-making but rather prescribes how decisions ought to be made. It should not be too surprising, then, if decision analysis occasionally yields results that are contraintuitive, even if every single component of the analysis is faultless. Two problems then arise: First, what sort of explanation would be needed for an analysis to be convincing? Obviously, appeals to rationality or intuition will not be persuasive because the conclusion will often "feel" wrong even if it is logically coherent. Furthermore, quantitative analysis of the situation is not the method used in intuitive clinical judgment,[58,59] and so needs some explanation. And as we have seen, the decision analytic representation is not a replica of the clinician's thought process,[60] although it may model the clinician's objectives.

Second, if intuitive clinical decisions do not conform to the recommendations of a formal analysis for a particular situation, how can we decide whether human judgment is suboptimal in that instance or whether the model has been inadequately formulated? The standard view for some time has been that human judgment is easily susceptible to errors of the kind discussed herein.[51,56,61] It may well be argued, however, that human judgment is influenced by aspects of the task that are excluded by the expected utility model but ought to be included: for example, the attribution of responsibility and anticipation of regret. Lopes,[57] for instance, points out that the expected utility model presupposes a long-term view of the problem. In this view, persons should follow the tenets of the value expected in a very large number of trials. Most persons, however, take the short-term view in that they consider the value to be expected most frequently. Often these two are not the same, as shown in the famous St. Petersburg paradox. These meta-analytic questions will continue to occupy and perplex researchers in the field of clinical decision-making for some time.

APPENDIX A

Outcome scenarios

Fractures

1 Twenty-five years of good health followed by an acute myocardial infarction and death during sleep at age 75.
2 Fifteen years of good health (age 65). Fracture of right femoral neck at age 65. Repaired surgically. Hospitalized one week. Four weeks of convalescence. Minimal discomfort or lack of mobility for the next 10 years. Sudden death due to an acute myocardial infarction during sleep at age 75.
3 Fifteen years of good health. Fracture of right femoral neck at age 65. Poor surgical result necessitating use of walker for six months. Over next two and a half years, patient has moderate pain poorly controlled by aspirin, acetaminophen, or propoxyphene hydrochloride. Has trouble walking up and down stairs; notices increased pain when standing. Thus is not able to do much

shopping. At age 68, patient undergoes surgery for implantation of a prosthetic hip joint. After three months' recuperation, patient is able to resume normal activities. She walks with a cane, which restricts her activities during the winter. Occasional minor pain in her other hip joint and in her lower back is relieved by a brief rest and aspirin. The patient is otherwise in good health from age 69 to 75. She dies in her sleep of an acute myocardial infarction at age 75.

4 Fifteen years of good health (age 65). Fracture of the right femoral neck at age 65. Patient dies during surgery from an embolus at age 65.

Menopausal symptoms

1 Twenty-five years of good health followed by an acute myocardial infarction and death during sleep at age 75.

2 Five to six hot flashes per day starting two months before the actual menopause and lasting one year. No change in sleeping habits, headaches, etc. Lives for 24 years in good health. Dies in sleep at age 75 from an acute myocardial infarction.

3 For six months prior to the actual menopause, the patient experiences hot flashes. These increase in number and severity so that six months after the menopause they are at peak severity. At this time, the patient has 10 to 20 hot flashes per 24 hours. She wakes up in the middle of the night at least once with sweats. She is mildly depressed but still maintains her activities as a housewife and is able to take care of her two-bedroom home. These symptoms remain severe for six months and then begin to subside. She has hot flashes for a total of two years. Her health is otherwise good. She lives to age 75, dying in her sleep with an acute myocardial infarction.

4 For nine months prior to the actual menopause, the patient experiences hot flashes, which number about 10 to 20 per 24 hours. The hot flashes increase in number, severity, and length so that nine months after the menopause they are at their worst. At this time, they number 50 to 60 per 24 hours and may last several minutes. They interfere with sleep to the point at which the patient is constantly tired and unable to perform adequately simple chores required of a housewife maintaining a two-bedroom household. Gradually the hot flashes diminish so that the patient experiences none three years after her menopause. During the early menopause, however, she is extremely depressed and consults her doctor frequently because of an almost constant headache. No organic problems are found and the woman dies in her sleep of an acute myocardial infarction at age 75.

Endometrial cancer

1 Twenty-five years of good health followed by an acute myocardial infarction and death during sleep at age 75.

2 Fifteen years of good health (age 65) followed by postmenopausal spotting. A dilation and curettage is performed and a diagnosis of grade 1, stage I adenocarcinoma of the endometrium is made. The patient undergoes total

abdominal hysterectomy with bilateral salpingo-oophorectomy. She is hospitalized seven days, convalesces six weeks, and has no further trouble. She dies of an acute myocardial infarction during her sleep at age 75.

3 Fifteen years of good health followed by one week of post-menopausal bleeding. A dilation and curettage is performed and a diagnosis of grade 2, stage II adenocarcinoma of the endometrium is made. The patient undergoes four weeks of whole-pelvic radiation therapy (4,000 rads), during which time she has nausea, vomiting, and diarrhea. One week later, the patient receives intrauterine cesium, which remains in place for 72 hours. Four weeks later, the patient undergoes total abdominal hysterectomy with bilateral salpingo-oophorectomy. She is hospitalized for seven days and convalesces for six weeks. Three years later (age 68), the woman has vaginal bleeding. A small vaginal cuff recurrence is noted. The patient receives intralesional radium needle therapy, and treatment with megestrol acetate is begun. Within one month, she resumes her normal life and lives in good health. She dies in her sleep at age 75 due to an acute myocardial infarction.

4 Fourteen years of good health followed by three weeks of postmenopausal bleeding. At age 65, a dilation and curettage is performed and the diagnosis of grade 3 adenocarcinoma of the endometrium is made. This is believed to be a stage IV lesion because of filling defects noted on liver scanning. The patient undergoes six weeks of whole-pelvic radiation (5,000 rads) and begins to receive bi-weekly injections of high-dose progesterone. Throughout radiation therapy, the patient is nauseated and vomits. She feels ill and finds it hard to function. She loses a total of 30 pounds, going from five feet five inches and 140 pounds to 110 pounds. Two months after radiation, the patient still feels poorly, and bloody diarrhea develops. This is not adequately controlled medically. The woman feels weaker and continues to lose weight. Eleven months after the diagnosis, pulmonary metastases develop. At this time, chemotherapy with doxorubicin hydrochloride and cyclophosphamide is begun. Again the patient has severe nausea and vomiting. Alopecia develops. One month later at age 65, she is dead. During her last month of life, she experiences increasing respiratory difficulty.

APPENDIX B

Procedures for assessing utilities and importance weights

In category scaling, descriptions of four outcomes within each outcome category were presented on 4 by 6 index cards; a time-line on each card graphically indicated periods of healthy life, illness, or disability, and age at death. The physician marked a scale to show the relative preference patients generally would have for the four outcomes. The least desirable was arbitrarily rated 0, the most desirable 100, and the intermediate outcomes were located at points on the scale consistent with their relative desirability.

In assessment of utilities using lotteries, a cardboard roulette wheel was used to vary the probabilities of best and worst outcomes. The task was to find the probability distribution for the gamble such that most patients would judge it and an intermediate outcome equally attractive. For each outcome category, the most desirable and least desirable outcomes were presented initially as a 50:50 gamble. These probabilities were adjusted by successive approximations to the point at which the physician could not be sure whether most patients would prefer the gamble or the certain intermediate outcome. At this indifference point, the expected value of the gamble and the value of the intermediate outcome are equal, so the utility of the intermediate outcome has been determined by reference to the lottery.[1]

To assess importance weights, the physicians were asked to estimate how concerned, on the average, their patients would be about vasomotor symptoms, endometrial cancer, and fractures associated with osteoporosis, assuming they knew any outcome within a category was possible but did not know how likely each was. First, the respondent ranked the attributes from least to most important, and a weight of 10 was arbitrarily assigned to the least important. Then the respondent judged on a ratio scale how many more times patients would be concerned about the other two. The three numbers obtained were rescaled to sum to 1.00 by dividing each by the sum of the three.

Expected utility (*EU*) for each treatment was calculated by multiplying the utilities of outcomes within each category by their probabilities and the relevant importance weight and adding the three components. The computation of expected utilities can be expressed algebraically by the following formula:

$$EU(T_t|SL_x, CL_y, FL_z) = IW_s\left[\sum_{s=1}^{4} P(S_s|T_t, SL_x)U(S_s)\right]$$

$$+ IW_c\left[P(C-|T_t, CL_y)U(C-)\right.$$

$$\left. + P(C+|T_t, CL_y)\sum_{c=1}^{3} P(C+, T_t)U(C_c)\right]$$

$$+ IW_f\left[P(F-|T_t, FL_z(U(F-) + P(F+|T_t, FL_z)\sum_{f=1}^{3} P(F_t|F+, T_t)U(F_f)\right]$$

where T_t=a specific treatment (1 to 5); SL_x=level of vasomotor symptom severity; CL_y=level of endometrial cancer risk; FL_z=level of fracture risk; IW=importance weight for the indicated category (s=symptoms, c=cancer, f=fractures); P=probability; S_s=specific symptom outcome; U=utility; C_c=specific cancer outcome; F_f=specific fracture outcome; $C+$=endometrial pathologic condition develops; $C-$=no endometrial pathologic condition; $F+$=hip fracture occurs; $F-$=no hip fracture.

REFERENCES

1 Weinstein, M.C., Fineberg, H.V., Elstein, A.S., *et al.: Clinical decision analysis.* Philadelphia: W.B. Saunders, 1980.
2 Pauker, S.G., Kassirer J.P.: Clinical application of decision analysis: a detailed illustration. *Semin. Nucl. Med.* 1978; 8:324–335.

3 Pauker, S.G., Kassirer, J.P.: The threshold approach to clinical decision making. *N. Engl. J. Med.* 1980; 302: 1109–1117.
4 Schwartz, W.B.: Decision analysis: a look at the chief complaints. *N. Engl. J. Med.* 1979; 300:556–559.
5 Politser, P.: Decision analysis and clinical judgment. *Med. Decis. Making* 1981; 1:361–389.
6 Spiegelhalter, D.J., Smith A.F.M.: Decision analysis and clinical decisions. In: Coppi, R., Bithell, P., eds. *Perspectives in medical statistics*. London: Academic Press, 1981; 103–131.
7 Slovic, P., Lichtenstein, S.: Comparison of Bayesian and regression approaches to the study of information processing in judgment. *Organizational Behavior and Human Performance* 1971; 6:649–744.
8 Elstein, A.S., Bordage, G.: Psychology of clinical reasoning. In: Stone, G., Cohen, F., Adler, N., eds. *Health psychology*. San Francisco: Jossey-Bass, 1979; 333–367.
9 Hogarth, R.M.: *Judgment and choice*. New York: Wiley, 1980.
10 Lau, J., Levey, A.S., Kassirer, J.P., Pauker, S.G.: Idiopathic nephrotic syndrome in a 53-year-old woman: is a kidney biopsy necessary? *Med. Decis. Making* 1982; 2:497–519.
11 Doubilet, P., McNeil, B.J.: Treatment choice in gastric carcinoma: a decision-analytic approach. *Med. Decis. Making* 1982; 2:261–274.
12 Koprowski, C., Cebul, R.: Comparing surgical and non-surgical approaches to the management of patients with transient ischemic attacks (submitted for publication).
13 Iansek, R., Elstein, A.S., Balla, J.I.: Application of decision analysis to management of cerebral arteriovenous malformation. *Lancet* 1983; 1:1132–1135.
14 Shy, K.K., LoGerfo, J.P., Karp, L.E.: Evaluation of elective repeat cesarean section as a standard of care: an application of decision analysis. *Am. J. Obstet. Gynecol.* 1981; 139:123–29.
15 McNeil, B.J., Adelstein, S.J.: Determining the value of diagnostic and screening tests. *J. Nucl. Med.* 1976; 17:439–448.
16 Galen, R.S., Gambino, S.R.: *Beyond normality: the predictive value and efficiency of medical diagnoses*. New York: Wiley, 1975.
17 Weinstein, M.C.: Estrogen use in postmenopausal women: costs, risks and benefits. *N. Engl. J. Med.* 1980; 303:308–316.
18 Hammond, C.B., Maxson, W.S.: Current status of estrogen therapy for the menopause. *Fertil. Steril.* 1982; 37:5–25.
19 Jones, H.W., Jones, G.S.: *Novak's textbook of gynecology*, 10th ed. Baltimore: Williams & Wilkins, 1981.
20 Speroff, L., Glass, R.H., Kase, N.G.: *Clinical gynecologic endocrinology and infertility*, 3rd ed. Baltimore: Williams & Wilkins, 1983.
21 Speroff, L.: Editor's formulation. *Semin. Reprod. Endocrinol.* 1983; 1:75–77.
22 Antunes, C.M.F., Stolley, P.D., Rosenshein, N.B., et al.: Endometrial cancer and estrogen use. *N. Engl. J. Med.* 1979; 300:9–13.
23 Alffram, P.H.: An epidemiologic study of cervical and intertrochanteric fractures of the femur in an urban population. *Acta Orthop. Scand.* 1964; 65 (suppl): 1–109.

24 Urist, M.R.: Observations bearing on the problem of osteoporosis. In: Rodah, K., Nicholson, J.R., Brown, E.M., Jr., eds. *Bone as a tissue*. New York: McGraw-Hill, 1960; 18–45.

25 Heaney, R.P.: Estrogens and postmenopausal osteoporosis. *Clin. Obstet. Gynecol.* 1976; 19:791–803.

26 Brenner, P.F., Mishell, D.R., Jr.: Menopause. In: Mishell, D.R., Davajan, V., eds. *Reproductive endocrinology, infertility and contraception*. Philadelphia: F.A. Davis, 1979; 161–187.

27 Worley, R.J.: Age, estrogen, and bone density. *Clin. Obstet. Gynecol.* 1981; 24:203–218.

28 Weiss, N.S., Ure, C.L., Ballard, J.H., Williams, A.R., Daling, J.R.: Decreased risk of fractures of the hip and lower forearm with postmenopausal use of estrogen. *N. Engl. J. Med.* 1980; 303:1195–1198.

29 Council on Scientific Affairs, American Medical Association: Estrogen replacement in the menopause. *JAMA* 1983; 249:359–361.

30 Judd, H.L., Cleary, R.E., Creasman, W.T., *et al.*; Estrogen replacement theory. *J. Obstet. Gynecol.* 1981; 58:267–275.

31 Holzman, G.B.: Menopause and perimenopause problems. In: Hale, R.W., Krieger, J.A., eds. *Concise textbook of gynecology*. New Hyde Park, New York: Medical Examination Publishing, 1983; 321–332.

32 Weinstein, M.C., Schiff, I.: Cost-effectiveness of hormone replacement therapy in the menopause. *Obstet. Gynecol. Survey* 1983; 38:445–455.

33 Coronary Drug Project Research Group: The Coronary Drug Project: findings leading to discontinuation of the 2.5 milligrams per day estrogen group. *JAMA* 1973; 226:652–657.

34 Bush, T.L., Cowan, C.D., Barrett-Connor, E., *et al.*: Estrogen use and all-cause mortality. *JAMA* 1983; 249:903–906.

35 Holzman, G.B., Ravitch, M.M., Metheny, W., *et al.*: Judgments about estrogen replacement therapy for menopausal women. *Obstet. Gynecol.* 1984; 63:303–311.

36 Torrance, G.W.: Social preferences for health states: an empirical evaluation of three measurement techniques. *Socio-Econ. Plan Sci.* 1976; 10:129–136.

37 Raiffa, H.: *Decision analysis: introductory lectures on choices under uncertainty*. Reading, Maryland: Addison-Wesley, 1968.

38 Edwards, W.: How to use multiattribute utility measurement for social decisionmaking. *IEEE Transactions on Systems, Man, and Cybernetics* 1977; 7:326–340.

39 Kassirer, J.P., Pauker, S.G.: The toss-up. *N. Engl. J. Med.* 1981; 305:1467–1469.

40 McNeil, B.J., Weichselbaum, R., Pauker, S.G.: Fallacy of five-year survival in lung cancer. *N. Engl. J. Med.* 1978; 299: 1397–1401.

41 Ziel, H.K., Finkel, W.D.: Increased risk of endometrial carcinoma among users of conjugated estrogens. *N. Engl. J. Med.* 1975; 293:1167–1170.

42 Smith, D.C., Prentice, R., Thompson, D.J., *et al.*: Association of exogenous estrogen and endometrial carcinoma. *N. Engl. J. Med.* 1975; 293:1164–1167.

43 Lindsay, R., Hart, D.M., MacLean, A., *et al.*: Bone response to termination of oestrogen treatment. *Lancet* 1978; I:1325–1327.

44 Nachtigall, L.E., Nachtigall, R.H., Nachtigall, R.D., *et al.*: Estrogen

replacement therapy I: a 10-year prospective study in the relationship to osteoporosis. *Obstet. Gynecol.* 1979; 53: 277–281.

45 Hammond, C.B., Jelovsek, F.R., Lee, K.L., *et al.*: Effects of long-term estrogen replacement therapy I. Metabolic effects. *Am. J. Obstet. Gynecol.* 1979; 133:525–536.

46 Hutchinson, T.A., Polansky, S.M., Feinstein, A.R.: Post-menopausal oestrogens protect against fractures of hip and distal radius: a case-control study. *Lancet* 1979; II: 705–709.

47 Johnson, R.E., Specht, E.E.: The risk of hip fracture in postmenopausal females with and without estrogen drug exposure. *Am. J. Public Health* 1981; 71:138–144.

48 Paganini-Hill, A., Ross, R.K., Gerkins, V.R., *et al.*: Menopausal estrogen therapy and hip fractures. *Ann. Intern. Med.* 1981; 95:28–31.

49 Krieger, N., Kelsey, J.L., Holford, T.R., *et al.*: An epidemiologic study of hip fracture in postmenopausal women. *Am. J. Epidemiol.* 1982; 116:141–148.

50 Gambrell, R.D.: The menopause: benefits and risks of estrogen-progesterone replacement therapy. *Fertil. Steril.* 1982; 37:457–474.

51 Nisbett, R.E., Ross, L.: *Human inference: strategies and shortcomings of social judgment.* Englewood Cliffs, New Jersey: Prentice-Hall, 1980.

52 Slovic, P.: Choice between equally valued alternatives. *J. Exp. Psychol.* [*Hum Percept*] 1975; 1:280–287.

53 Tversky, A., Kahneman, D.: The framing of decisions and the psychology of choice. *Science* 1981; 211:453–458.

54 Schoemaker, P.J.H.: *Experiments on decisions under risk: the expected utility hypothesis.* Boston: Martinus Nijhoff, 1980.

55 Bell, D.E.: Regret in decision making under uncertainty. *Operations Research* 1982; 30:961–981.

56 Kahneman, D., Slovic, P., Tversky, A., eds. *Judgment Under Uncertainty: Heuristics and Biases.* New York: Cambridge University Press, 1982.

57 Lopes, L.L.: Decision making in the short run. *J. Exp. Psycho.* [*Hum Learn Mem*] 1981; 7:377–385.

58 Eddy, D.M., Clanton, C.H.: The art of diagnosis: solving the clinico-pathological exercise. *N. Engl. J. Med.* 1982; 306:1263–1268.

59 Elstein, A.S., Shulman, L.S., Sprafka, S.A.: *Medical problem solving: an analysis of clinical reasoning.* Cambridge: Harvard University Press, 1978.

60 Duda, R.O., Shortliffe, E.H.: Expert systems research. *Science* 1983; 220:261–268.

61 Einhorn, H.J., Hogarth, R.M.: Behavioral decision theory: processes of judgment and choice. *Annu. Rev. Psychol.* 1981; 32:52–88.

16

_____ ~ _____

HYPOTHESIS EVALUATION FROM A BAYESIAN PERSPECTIVE*

Baruch Fischhoff, Ruth Beyth-Marom

Hypothesis evaluation is a crucial intellectual activity. Not surprisingly, it is also a focus of psychological research. A variety of methods have been applied to understand how people gather and interpret information in order to evaluate hypotheses. Either implicitly or explicitly, some theory of how people _should_ evaluate hypotheses provides the conceptual framework for studies of how they _do_ evaluate them. Such a prescriptive theory provides a set of articulated terms for describing tasks and a definition of appropriate behavior against which actual performance can be compared. The theory might even be descriptively valid at a certain level if people are found to follow its dictates, either due to natural predilections or because they have been trained to do so. Even when behavior is suboptimal, some psychological insight may be obtained by asking whether that behavior may be described as a systematic deviation from the theory. Reference to a normative theory can also identify performance deficits that need to be understood and rectified.

One general and popular normative scheme is Bayesian inference, a set of procedures based upon Bayes' theorem and the subjectivist interpretation of probability. These procedures show how to (a) identify the data sources that are most useful for discriminating between competing hypotheses, (b) assess the implications of an observed datum _vis-à-vis_ the truth of competing hypotheses, (c) aggregate the implications of different data into an overall appraisal of the relative likelihood of those hypotheses being correct, and (d) use that appraisal to select the course of action that seem best in light of available evidence. Excellent detailed expositions of the scheme may be found in Edwards, Lindman, and Savage (1963), Lindley (1965), Novick and Jackson (1974), and Phillips (1973).

The present article presents a simple version of Bayesian inference. From this scheme, it derives a taxonomy of logically possible deviations

* First published in _Psychological Review_, 90 (1983), 239–60. © 1983 American Psychological Association. Reprinted by permission of the publisher and author.

and identifies potential biases for which positive evidence is lacking – raising the question of whether it was an opportunity to observe sub-optimal behavior that researchers missed or an opportunity to exhibit suboptimal behavior that subjects "missed." The theory is complete in the sense that it treats all of the basic issues that arise in Bayesian inference and that must be faced when one assesses the optimality of behavior. It is incomplete in that it does not show how the theory can be adapted to model all possible situations. For example, all of the hypotheses we consider here are discrete, both for simplicity's sake and because the studies we cite have used discrete hypotheses. The treatment of continuous hypotheses (e.g., "Today's mean temperature is x") is considered by Edwards *et al.* (1963) and others.

THEORY

Definition of probability

From the Bayesian perspective, knowledge is represented in terms of statements or hypotheses, H_i, each of which is characterized by a subjective probability, $P(H_i)$, representing one's confidence in its truth (DeFinetti, 1976). For example, one might be .75 confident that it will snow tomorrow. Such probabilities are subjective in the sense that individuals with different knowledge (or beliefs) may legitimately assess $P(H_i)$ quite differently. The term *assess* is used rather than *estimate* to emphasize that a probability expresses one's own feelings rather than an appraisal of a property of the physical world. Thus, there is no "right" probability value for a particular statement. Even if a very low probability proves to be associated with a true statement, one cannot be sure that it was not an accurate reflection of the assessor's (apparently erroneous) store of knowledge.

The constraints on subjective probabilities emerge when one considers sets of assessments. Formally speaking, a set of probabilities should be orderly or *coherent* in the sense of following the probability axioms (Kyburg & Smokler, 1980; Savage, 1954).[1] For example, $P(H) + P(\bar{H})$ should total 1.0.

Updating

Additional derivations from the probability axioms lead to Bayes' theorem, which governs the way in which one's beliefs in hypotheses should be updated in the light of new information. In its simplest form, the theorem treats the implications of an observation that produces the datum (D) for determining whether a hypothesis (H) is true, relative to its complement, $\bar{H}$. In such cases, Bayes' theorem states that

$$\frac{P(H/D)}{P(\bar{H}/D)} = \frac{P(D/H)}{P(D/\bar{H})} \cdot \frac{P(H)}{P(\bar{H})}. \tag{1}$$

Reading from the right, the three terms in this formula are (a) the prior odds that H (and not $\bar{H}$) is true in the light of all that is known before the receipt of D, (b) the likelihood ratio, representing the information value of D with respect to the truth of H, and (c) the posterior odds that H is true in the light of all that is known after the receipt of D. Equation 1 could also be applied to any pair of competing hypotheses, A and B (with A replacing H and B replacing $\bar{H}$).

Although the subjectivist interpretation of probability is controversial, Bayes' theorem generally is not. The axioms from which it is derived are common to most interpretations of probability. Bayesians have more frequent recourse to the theorem because the subjectivist position enables them to incorporate prior beliefs explicitly in their inferential processes.[2]

Likelihood ratios

If the probability of observing D given that H is true is different from the probability of observing D when H is not true, then the likelihood ratio is different from 1 and the posterior odds are different from the prior odds. That is, the odds favoring H have become smaller or greater as a result of having observed D. Such a datum is considered to be informative or *diagnostic*. Its degree of diagnosticity can be expressed in terms of how different the likelihood ratio is from 1. Clearly, diagnosticity depends upon the hypotheses being tested. A datum that distinguishes one hypotheses from its complement may be completely uninformative about another pair of hypotheses. Data do not answer all questions equally well.

The value of the likelihood ratio is independent of the value of the prior odds. One could in principle observe a datum strongly supporting a hypothesis that is initially very unlikely. If that happened, one's posterior odds favoring H might still be very low, although not as low as they were before. There is also no necessary relationship between the values of the numerator and the denominator of the likelihood ratio. A datum might strongly favor H even if it is very unlikely given the truth of H. Similarly, observing a datum that is a necessary concomitant of H, that is, $P(D/H) \approx 1$, may be uninformative if it is also a necessary concomitant of $\bar{H}$.

Action

The apparatus of Bayesian inference also provides tools for converting one's beliefs in hypotheses into guides to action. In simplest terms, these tools translate the cost associated with erroneously acting as though a

Table 1 *Potential sources of bias in Bayesian hypothesis evaluation*

Task	Potential bias	Special cases
Hypothesis formation	Untestable	Ambiguity, complexity, evidence unobservable
	Nonpartition	Nonexclusive, nonexhaustive
Assessing component probabilities	Misrepresentation	Strategic responses, nonproper scoring rules
	Incoherence	Noncomplementarity, disorganized knowledge
	Miscalibration	Overconfidence
	Nonconformity	Reliance on availability or representativeness
	Objectivism	—
Assessing prior odds	Poor survey of background	Incomplete, selective
	Failure to assess	Base-rate fallacy
Assessing likelihood ratio	Failure to assess	Noncausal, "knew-it-all-along"
	Distortion by prior beliefs	Preconceptions, lack of convergence
	Neglect of alternative hypotheses	Pseudodiagnosticity, inertia, cold readings
Aggregation	Wrong rule	Averaging, conservatism?
	Misapplying right rule	Computational error, conservatism?
Information search	Failure to search	Premature conviction
	Nondiagnostic questions	Tradition, habit
	Inefficient search	Failure to ask potentially falsifying questions
	Unrepresentative sampling	—
Action	Incomplete analysis	Neglecting consequences, unstable values
	Forgetting critical value	Confusing actual and effective certitude

hypothesis is true and the cost of erroneously acting as though a hypothesis is false into a *critical ratio*. If the posterior odds favoring *H* are above this value, then one is better off acting as though *H* is true; if they are below the value, then one is better off acting as though *H* is false.

The value of the critical ratio depends, of course, on the particular kinds of action that are contemplated and the outcomes that are associated with them. Where one's posterior odds stand *vis-à-vis* the critical ratio depends on both one's prior odds and the evidence that has subsequently been received. Two individuals who had agreed on the costs of the different errors and on the meaning of the different data might still act differently, if they had different prior odds. On the other hand, if the cumulative weight of the new evidence was sufficient, they might act in the same way, despite having initially had quite discrepant beliefs – for example, if the evidence carried them from prior odds of 1:10 and 1:1 to posterior odds of 100:1 and 1,000:1, respectively.

When it is possible to collect more data, additional Bayesian procedures can help identify the most useful source (Raiffa, 1968). Such *value-of-information* analyses evaluate the expected impact of each possible observation on the expected utility of the actions one can take. They can also tell when the cost of further observation is greater than its expected benefit.

WAYS TO STRAY

Bayesian inference, like other normative schemes, regards only those who adhere to its every detail as behaving optimally. Conversely, every component of the scheme offers some opportunity for suboptimality. This section catalogues possible pitfalls. For the normative minded, these possibilities might be seen as defining Bayesian inference negatively by pointing to behavior that is inconsistent with it.

For the descriptive minded, these logical possibilities suggest judgmental biases that might be observed in empirical studies. If observed in situations in which people are properly instructed and motivated to respond correctly, such deviations can be theoretically informative because they seem to reflect deep-seated judgmental processes. From a practical standpoint, such deviations suggest opportunities for constructive interventions that might lead to better inferences and subsequently, to better decisions based on those inferences. These interventions might include training, the use of decision aids, or the replacement of intuition by formalized procedures (Edwards, 1968; Fischhoff, 1982; Kahneman & Tversky, 1979).

These potential biases are presented in Table 1. The left-hand column shows the task in which the problem could arise; the center column describes the possible biases; and the right-hand column points to phenomena reported in the literature that we have interpreted as special cases of these biases, which are described in detail in the following section.

Hypothesis formation

For hypothesis evaluation to begin, there must be hypotheses to evaluate. Indeed, because the diagnostic impact of data is defined only in the context of particular hypotheses, there is no systematic way that data can even be collected without such a context. In the absence of any hypotheses, the collection of data is merely idle stockpiling. Although it is a logical possibility, it does not seem to be a troublesome or common bias. In practice, even the most ambling data collection may be guided by a vague idea of the hypotheses that the collector might be asked to evaluate. Or, it may be conducted for exploratory purposes, with the goal of generating, rather than evaluating, hypotheses. If the collector's goal is to see something that fortuitously stimulates a creative insight, then the Bayesian model, or any other formal model, can offer little guidance or reprobation.

A more serious threat than the absence of hypotheses to evaluate is the possession of hypotheses that cannot be evaluated. One route to formulating hypotheses that cannot be evaluated lies through ambiguity, either intentional or inadvertent. To take a popular example, astrology columns offer hypotheses about what consequences follow what acts (e.g., "You will be better off avoiding risky enterprises"). Yet these acts and consequences are so vaguely defined that it is unclear whether what eventually happens supports the hypothesis. A more sophisticated form of ambiguity can be found in the probabilistic risk analyses used to generate detailed hypotheses about the operation of technical systems (e.g., "Toxins can be released to the atmosphere only if the following events occur"; Green & Bourne, 1972; U.S. Nuclear Regulatory Commission, Note 1). Although actual operating experience should afford an opportunity to evaluate these hypotheses, it may be unclear whether the specific events that are observed are subsumed by the generic events described in the analysis. For example, investigators disagreed over whether the fire at the Browns Ferry Nuclear Power Plant in 1975 was included among the then-definitive analysis of reactor operation (U.S. Nuclear Regulatory Commission, Note 2, Note 3).

Complexity offers a second route to formulating hypotheses that cannot be evaluated. Hypotheses that are set out clearly may have such great detail that no datum provides a clear message. For example, political advisors may escape charges of having predicted events incorrectly by noting that every last detail of their advice was not followed ("Had they only listened to me and done X and Y as well, then everything would have been all right").[3] O'Leary, Coplin, Shapiro, and Dean (1974) found that among practitioners of international relations (i.e., those working for business or government) theories are of "such complexity that no single quantitative work could even begin to test their validity" (p. 228). Indeed, some historians argue that the accounts of events that they produce are not hypotheses at all but attempts to integrate available knowledge into a coherent whole. In this light, a valid explanation accommodates all facts, leaving none to test it. This attitude toward hypotheses has its own strengths and weaknesses (Fischhoff, 1980).

Because it considers the relative support that evidence provides to competing hypotheses, the Bayesian scheme requires not only the individual hypotheses but also the set of hypotheses to be well formulated. In effect, those hypotheses must partition some space of possibilities.[4] Computationally, problems arise with nonexclusive hypotheses, which render the message of evidence ambiguous.

Whereas achieving mutually exclusive hypotheses requires precision of formulation, securing an exhaustive set of hypotheses often requires the exercise of imagination. Technically, it is easy to make a set exhaustive by defining it in terms of H and $\bar{H}$, by declaring the hypotheses that one has thought of to be the only ones of interest, or by adding a hypothesis consisting of "all other possibilities," a role that $\bar{H}$ may fill. Although such specification is adequate for some purposes, wherever the alternatives to H are poorly defined, it is hard to evaluate $P(D/\bar{H})$ and, hence, the implications of D for H. Whenever the set of alternatives is incomplete, major surprises are possible. The difficulties of exhaustive enumeration are often exploited by mystery writers who unearth a neglected hypothesis that tidily accounts for available evidence. Both for generating hypotheses and for evaluating $P(D/\text{all other possibilities})$, an important skill is estimating the completeness of the set of already listed hypotheses. Evidence suggests that people tend to exaggerate the completeness of hypothesis sets (Fischhoff, Slovic, & Lichtenstein, 1978; Mehle, Gettys, Manning, Baca & Fisher, 1981).

A final problem is that even well-formulated hypotheses may be wrong for the actions contemplated. The acid test of relevance is whether perfect information about the hypothesis (i.e., knowing whether it is true or false) would make any difference to one's actions. For example, if ethical principles proscribe incarcerating juveniles with adults, then hypotheses about the effect of prison on delinquents have no consequences for criminal policy. If their support for military spending depends upon the relative strength of the pro- and anti-arms lobbies, then legislators need not choose among competing hypotheses regarding Soviet intentions. The pejorative label for such impractical hypotheses is "academic."

More charitably, they are "hypotheses relevant to possible future actions."

Assessing component probabilities

To find a place in the Bayesian model, one's beliefs must be translated into subjective probabilities of the form appearing in the model. Any difficulties in assessing such component probabilities would impair hypothesis evaluation. As mentioned, the Bayesian perspective holds probabilities to be subjective expressions, reflecting the assessor's beliefs. Accepting the subjectivist position does not, however, mean accepting any probability as an appropriate assessment of someone's state of belief. There are a number of ways in which the assessment of probabilities can go wrong.

One possible problem is lack of candor. People may misstate their beliefs, perhaps to give a response that is expected of them, perhaps to avoid admitting that an unpleasant event is likely to happen, or perhaps to achieve some strategic advantage by misrepresenting how much they know or what they believe. When the truth of statements can eventually be ascertained, the use of proper scoring rules should encourage candor (Murphy, 1972). These rules reward people as a function of both their stated beliefs and the (eventually revealed) state of the world in such a way that the probability with the highest expected value is the one expressing one's true belief. Whether these rules prove effective in practice is a moot point (Lichtenstein, Fischhoff, & Phillips, 1982; von Winterfeldt & Edwards, 1982). Where they do not prove effective or where they cannot even be applied because the truth will not be known or because no reward system is possible, other means of assuring candor are needed.

The crucial assessment problem from the subjectivist perspective is lack of coherence, failure of one's assessments to follow the probability axioms. Violations may be due to a poor job of reviewing one's knowledge. For example, $P(H)$ and $P(\bar{H})$ may not equal 1 when the two hypotheses are not evaluated simultaneously – and concentration on each evokes a different subset of one's knowledge. It is also possible that the beliefs themselves are not well thought through. In that case, working harder on probability assessment may lead to even more incoherent probabilities by revealing the underlying inconsistencies. Here, the structure of belief requires refinement (Lindley, Tversky, & Brown, 1979).

Another symptom of poor assessment is *miscalibration*, failure of one's confidence to correspond to reality. If a hypothesis with a prior probability of .2 eventually is found to be true, the initial assessment is dubious. However, it may be an accurate summary of the assessor's knowledge at that moment. Recurrent association of high prior probabilities with hypotheses that prove to be false should be cause for serious concern. Calibration formalizes this reliance on the eventually accepted truth of hypotheses for validating probability assessments. Specifically, for the well-calibrated assessor, probability judgments of XX are associated with true hypotheses XX percent of the time. Empirical studies of calibration have shown that probabilities are related, but are not identical, to proportions of correct hypotheses. The most common deviation is overconfidence – for example, being only 80 percent correct when 1.00 confident (Lichtenstein, Fischhoff, & Phillips, 1982).[5] As with incoherence, miscalibration may be traced to people's assessment procedures or to the knowledge base that they rely on.

A third symptom is *nonconformity*, producing a probability that differs from that of "expert" assessors for no apparent reason. The existence of such consensus is most likely when there is a statistical data base upon which to base probability assessments (e.g., public health records of mortality). In this restricted realm, the distinction between subjective and objective probabilities becomes blurred, as subjectivists would typically act as though they concur with the relative-frequency interpretation of probability, which objectivists consider to be the only meaningful one. Subjectivists would, however, never concede that frequency counts are a completely objective measure of probability, arguing that judgment is needed to establish the equivalence and independence of the set of trials from which the count was extracted and to extrapolate that frequency to future events.

Another way to look at bias is in terms of the process by which assessments are produced. There is reason for concern whenever the assessors have followed procedures that are inconsistent with the rules of statistical inference and are unaware of those inconsistencies. Two well-known deviations are reliance on the availability and representativeness heuristics when making probability assessments (Kahneman, Slovic, & Tversky, 1982; Tversky & Kahneman, 1974). Users of the former judge an event to be likely to the extent that examplars are easy to recall or imagine; users of the latter judge an event to be likely to the extent that it represents the salient features of the process that might produce it. Although both rules can provide good service, they can also lead the user astray in predictable ways. For example, reliance on availability induces overestimation of unusually salient events (e.g., the probability of dying from flashy, hence overreported, causes such as tornadoes and homicide; Lichtenstein, Slovic, Fischhoff, Layman, & Combs, 1978).

A final process problem is the refusal to consider anything but relative frequency data when one assesses probabilities. Although subjectivists acknowledge the potential relevance of such data, they will not be bound to them. Indeed, a key selling point of Bayesian inference is its ability to accommodate diverse kinds of data. One can, for example, assess probabilities for a meaningful shrug or an off-hand comment as well as for a bead drawn from an urn or for a 40-subject experiment. The only difference is that as one moves from beads to shrugs, it becomes increasingly difficult to attest to the reasonableness of a particular assessment. An assessor who failed to seek useful and available nonfrequency evidence would, from a Bayesian perspective, be foolish. An individual who ignored nonfrequency evidence that was already on hand would be biased.[6]

Assessing the prior

Prior beliefs are captured by the ratio of the probabilities of the competing hypotheses prior to the collection of further evidence. As a result, the difficulties of assessing prior beliefs are by and large the sum of the difficulties of formulating hypotheses and assessing component probabilities, as already discussed. There seem, however, to be at least two additional (and incompatible) problems that may affect this particular stage of the assessment process.

One such problem is not treating the component probabilities equally. An extreme form of inequality is neglecting one of the hypotheses. When people act as though a hypothesis that is most probably true is absolutely true, they have effectively neglected its complement. In that case, hypothesis evaluation never begins, because one hypothesis is treated as fact. Even when both hypotheses are considered, one may be given deferential treatment. Skeptics, for example, may give undue weight to evidence that contradicts a favored hypothesis; they have a warm spot in their hearts for complements. On the other hand, Koriat, Lichtenstein, and Fischhoff (1980) found favoritism for initially favored hypotheses: Subjects who were asked to determine the relative likelihood of two possible answers to a question seemed to search primarily for supporting evidence.[7] Such directed search may serve legitimate purposes, for example, seeing if any case at all can be made for, or against, a particular hypothesis. However, it may be very difficult to estimate and to correct for the bias that it induces in the resultant sample of evidence. Indeed, it is the failure to realize the biases in the samples produced by the availability heuristic that makes it a potentially dangerous judgment rule.

These difficulties vanish in the presence of another bias that has attracted considerable attention of late: neglecting the base rate (Kahneman & Tversky, 1973). The *base-rate fallacy* refers to the tendency to allow one's posterior beliefs to be dominated by the information that one extracts from the additional datum, D, to the neglect of the prior beliefs, expressing what typically has been observed. The several recent reviews of this literature (Bar-Hillel, 1980; Bar-Hillel & Fischhoff, 1981; Borgida & Brekke, 1981) may be summarized as indicating that people rely most heavily on whatever information seems most relevant to the task at hand. Thus, for example, when testing a pair of hypotheses such as "John is a lawyer/John is an engineer," even weak diagnostic information relating directly to John may dominate base-rate information reporting the overall prevalence of the two professions. Base-rate information is used, however, if it can be linked more directly to the inference or if the case-specific information is palpably worthless.

The evidence for the base-rate fallacy comes primarily from studies in which base-rate information was presented, yet neglected. As such, the fallacy can be viewed as a problem of aggregation, which we treat two sections below. It is discussed here because the failure to use explicitly presented base rates strongly suggests that they will not be spontaneously sought or assessed. This suspicion is confirmed, for example, by Lyon and Slovic's (1976) finding that, when asked directly, one half of their subjects did not believe that base rates were relevant to their judgments.[8]

Assessing the likelihood ratio

In principle, people can ignore the likelihood just as well as the base rate, allowing one to speak of the "likelihood-ratio fallacy" whenever people fail even to consider the likelihood ratio for a pertinent datum. This may happen, for example, when the datum provides merely circumstantial evidence (Einhorn & Hogarth, 1982), when it cannot be woven into a causal account involving the hypothesis (Tversky & Kahneman, 1980), or when it reports a nonoccurrence. A classic example of the latter is Sherlock Holmes's observation (Doyle, 1974) that his colleague, Inspector Gregory, had not considered the significance of a dog failing to bark when an intruder approached.

Failure to assess the likelihood ratio of received evidence may also be encouraged by hindsight bias, underestimating the informativeness of new data (Fischhoff, 1975, 1982). The feeling that one knew all along that D was true might make the calculation of D's likelihood ratio seem unnecessary. Denying that D has anything to add does not, however, mean that it will not have any impact – only that one will be unaware of that impact. At the same time as people deny its contribution, new information can change their thinking in ways that they cannot appreciate or undo (Fischhoff, 1977; Sue, Smith, & Caldwell, 1973). These unintended influences may or may not be those that would follow from a deliberative analysis.

When judges do assess the likelihood ratio, the sequencing of that operation may expose it to the influence of the preceding operations. In particular, the interpretation of new evidence may be affected by previous beliefs, thereby subverting the independence of the likelihood ratio and prior. Nisbett and Ross (1980) offer an impressive catalog of ways in which people can interpret and reinterpret new information so as to render it consistent with their prior beliefs. So great is people's ability to exploit the ambiguities in evidence to the advantage of their preconceptions and to discount inconsistent evidence, that erroneous beliefs can persevere long after they should have been abandoned.[9]

Such biased interpretation of evidence also thwarts the effective convergence of belief that should follow use of Bayesian inference. However discrepant the initial position of two individuals, their posterior beliefs should converge for practical purposes, providing they observe a sufficiently large set of diagnostic data about whose interpretation they agree. The ability to interpret a datum as supporting contradictory hypotheses means that convergence may never occur. Whatever data the two observers see, they become more convinced of their respective prior beliefs.

When people choose to evaluate evidence, they must compare two conditional probabilities, $P(D/H)$ and $P(D/\bar{H})$. Such comparison is essential because there is no necessary relationship between these two components of the likelihood ratio. A variety of studies suggest, however, that people consider only the numerator. That is, they are interested in how consistent the evidence is with the hypothesis they are testing, $P(D/H)$ and fail to consider its consistency with the alternative hypothesis, $P(D/\bar{H})$. As a result, the size of $P(D/H)$ determines D's support for H. Users of this strategy act as though they assume that the two conditional probabilities are inversely related, although, in principle, both may be high or low. A datum with a low $P(D/H)$ may provide strong evidence of H if $P(D/\bar{H})$ is even lower; a datum for which $P(D/H)$ is high may reveal nothing if $P(D/\bar{H})$ is equally high.

Four examples should give some flavor of the variety of guises within which incomplete appraisal of the likelihood ratio may emerge:

1 Doherty, Mynatt, Tweney, and Schiavo (1979) presented subjects with six species of data, D_i and allowed them to inquire about the values of 6 of the 12 conditional probabilities: $P(D_1/H)$, $P(D_1/\bar{H})$, ... $P(D_6/H)$, $P(D_6/\bar{H})$. Few subjects requested any of the pairs of conditional probabilities [e.g., $P(D_3/H)$ and $P(D_3/\bar{H})$] needed to compute likelihood ratios. The authors labeled this tendency to pick but one member of each pair, *pseudodiagnosticity*. The probabilities that subjects did solicit were primarily those, $P(D/H_i)$, involving the hypothesis, H, that a preceding manipulation had made appear more likely. The authors called this tendency *confirmatory bias* (a term to which we will return).

2 Troutman and Shanteau (1977) had subjects draw beads from a box which contained either 70 red, 30 white, and 50 blue beads or 30 red, 70 white, and 50 blue beads and infer the probability that the box was predominantly white (W). Drawing two blue beads reduced subjects' confidence in their initially favored hypothesis (W), even though that observation is equally unlikely under either hypothesis: $P(D/R) = P(D/W) = .11$. Thus, subjects considered only $P(D/H)$ for their favored hypothesis.

3 In a similar experiment, without the blue beads, Pitz, Downing, and Reinhold (1967) found that subjects who were fairly confident that the box was predominantly red would increase their confidence in that hypothesis after observing a white. Subjects apparently felt that they should see an occasional white, neglecting the fact that that event was still more likely if the box being used was predominantly white. Pitz *et al.* called this failure of inconsistent evidence to slow the increase of confidence in H an *inertia effect*. The inappropriate increase in faith in H here contrasts with the inappropriate decrease in it in a study by Troutman and Shanteau (1977). We would trace these two opposite effects to the same underlying cause, neglecting $P(D/\bar{H})$.

4 A favorite ploy of magicians, mentalists, and pseudopsychics who claim to read other people's minds is to provide universally valid personality descriptions (Forer, 1949; Hyman, 1977) that apply to almost everyone, although this is not transparently so. These operators trust their listeners to assess P (this description/my mind is being read) and not P (this description/my mind is not being read).

A final threat to the validity of assessed likelihood ratios comes from the fact that the probabilities involved all concern conditional events. This added complexity seems to complicate probability assessment, with people forgetting the conditioning event, reversing the roles of the two events, or just feeling confused (Eddy, 1982; Moskowitz & Sarin, in press).

Aggregation

Assuming that judges have attended to and assessed all components of the Bayesian model, they must still combine them to arrive at posterior odds. The two logically possible sources of error here are (a) using the wrong aggregation rule, for example, averaging, rather than multiplying, the likelihood ratio and prior odds, and (b) using the right rule, but applying it inappropriately, for example, making a computational error. Establishing whether either or both of these potential biases actually occurs was a focus of early research into intuitive Bayesian inference (reviewed by Slovic & Lichtenstein, 1971).

Most of these early studies used the un-Bayesian strategy of creating inferential tasks in which the experimenter could claim to know the correct subjective probability for all participants. This was done by using highly artificial stimuli for which all reasonable observers should have the same subjective probability. For example, subjects might be shown a series of poker chips and be asked to evaluate the hypotheses: They are being drawn from a bookbag with 70 percent blue chips and 30 percent red chips/they are being drawn from a bag with 70 percent red chips and 30 percent blue chips. The predominant result of this research was that subjects' confidence in the apparently correct hypothesis did not increase as quickly as the accumulating evidence indicated that it should.

A lively debate ensued over whether this poor performance, called *conservatism*, reflected failure to appreciate how diagnostic the evidence was, called *misperception*, or failure to combine those diagnosticity assessments according to Bayes' rule, *misaggregation*. Aside from its theoretical interest, this dispute had considerable practical importance. If people can assess component probabilities but cannot combine them, then person–machine systems may be able to relieve them of the mechanical computations. Moreover, the system could incorporate an elicitation scheme that kept users from ever forgetting any component probabilities. However, if people are the only source of probabilities and they cannot assess them very well, then the machine may be just spinning its discs (Edwards, 1962).

Although the source of this conservatism was never determined, the hypotheses that were raised reflect the problems that could interfere with aggregation. Examples, details of which may be found in Slovic and Lichtenstein (1971) are (a) anchoring – people stay stuck to their previous estimates, (b) response bias – reluctance to give extreme responses pushes answers toward the center of the response range, (c) ceiling effect – fear of "using up" the probability scale makes people hedge their responses, (d) nonlinearity – although a given D should produce the same ratio of posterior odds to prior odds whenever it is received, people may try instead to make the differences between prior and posterior probability of H constant, and (e) response mode – probability assessments may be less optimal responses than the odds (or log odds) assessments for the same task; despite their formal equivalence, one response mode may be a more natural way for people to assess and express their knowledge about a particular problem.

In the end, this line of research was quietly abandoned without establishing the relative roles of these different factors. This cessation of activity seems to be partly due to the discovery of the base-rate fallacy, which represents the antithesis of conservatism and other phenomena that led researchers to conclusions such as the following: "It may not be unreasonable to assume that . . . the probability estimation task is too unfamiliar and complex to be meaningful" (Pitz, Downing, & Reinhold, 1967, p. 392). "Evidence to date seems to indicate that subjects are processing information in ways fundamentally different from Bayesian . . . models" (Slovic & Lichtenstein, 1971, p. 728). "In his evaluation of evidence, man is apparently not a conservative Bayesian; he is not Bayesian at all" (Kahneman & Tversky, 1973, p. 450).

Information search

Obviously, Bayesian updating requires the collection of additional information beyond what was incorporated in the prior odds. Whether collection is contemplated at all should depend on whether one's a priori confidence in the truth of the hypothesis is adequate for deciding what to do and on the possibilities for additional data to change one's mind. When one would like to know more, the specific data collected should depend on the opportunities presented.

These opportunities can be conceptualized as questions that can elicit a set of possible answers, or D_i, each of which carries a message regarding the truth of the hypotheses. All other things being equal (e.g., the cost of asking), the most valuable questions are those that are expected to produce the most diagnostic answers. Conversely, one should never ask questions all of whose possible answers have likelihood ratios of 1. Such questions should change neither one's beliefs regarding the truth of the hypotheses nor one's choice of action based on those beliefs. Value-of-information analysis includes a variety of schemes for deciding how much one should spend for information in general and how to devise the most efficient sampling strategies. It considers such factors as the cost of asking, the consequences of the possible decisions, the a priori probability of receiving different possible answers, and the likelihood ratios associated with those answers (Brown, Kahr, & Peterson, 1974; Raiffa, 1968).

Why might someone disregard these considerations and ask questions whose answers cannot be diagnostic? Tradition is one possible reason. A datum may always have been collected, without serious analysis of what has been learned from it. Official forms and graduate school applications might be two familiar loci for nondiagnostic questions. These traditions may spawn or be spawned by beliefs about the kinds of evidence that are inherently more valuable. In various circles, secret, quantitative, or introspective information might have this special status of always meriting inquiry (Fischer, 1970). Misdirected search may occur also when people's task changes and they fail to realize that the questions that helped to evaluate the old hypotheses are no longer as effective in evaluating the new ones. For example, a psychiatric social worker who moved from private practice to a large public agency might require a whole new set of question-asking skills.

The factors leading to pointless questions can, in less extreme form, lead to inefficient ones – questions that provide some information, yet less than the maximum possible. These search problems may be aggravated by difficulties with other aspects of the inferential process. Value-of-information analysis requires a *preposterior* analysis, in which one anticipates what one will believe and what one will do if various possible data are observed. If people have difficulty assessing likelihood ratios for actual data, then they are unlikely to assess them properly for hypothetical data. A further obstacle to appraising the expected value of possible questions is the very hypotheticality of the questions. When seen "in the flesh," information may have more or less impact than it was expected to have, in which case it is not clear whether to trust the actual or the anticipated impact (Fischhoff, Slovic, & Lichtenstein, 1979).

A noteworthy form of inefficiency is ignoring the opportunity to ask potentially falsifying questions, ones whose answers have a reasonable chance of effectively ruling out some hypothesis (e.g., a physician failing to order a test that could eliminate the possibility of a particular disease). What constitutes a "reasonable chance" depends on the usual value-of-information analysis factors (e.g., the prior probability of the disease, the importance of its detection, the cost of the test).

An obvious danger in information search is inadvertently selecting an unrepresentative set of evidence and arriving at erroneous beliefs. When a proper sampling frame is available (e.g., for the Census), one can describe a variety of specific violations of representative sampling (Kish, 1965). If those biases can be characterized, then it is possible, in principle, to correct for them (Bar-Hillel, 1979). Such situations may, however, be relatively rare with Bayesian inference, where information can come from a variety of sources and in a variety of forms. Good sense then becomes the only guide to drawing and interpreting samples. As the history of scientific progress shows, it may take a fortuitous, if unpleasant, surprise to reveal an unintended bias in sampled information.[10]

Action

Bayesian inference is embedded in statistical decision theory. Its output, posterior odds, summarizes beliefs in a way that facilitates selecting the optimal course of action. Similarly, knowledge of the possible actions and their associated consequences is essential in determining what information to gather. Two Bayesian judges who contemplated different actions, or evaluated their consequences differently, might justifiably formulate different hypotheses and collect different data even though they agree on the interpretation of all possible data.

Many of the difficulties that frustrate attempts to take prudent action on the basis of available knowledge, are not unique to Bayesian inference. These include not having well-articulated values (i.e., not knowing what one wants), failing to think through all the consequences of different actions, and allowing one's preferences to be manipulated by the way in which problems are presented (Fischhoff, Slovic, & Lichtenstein, 1980; Rokeach, 1973; Tversky & Kahneman, 1981).

With other familiar problems, the Bayesian framework may offer an illuminating nomenclature and even some assistance. For example, people may forget that rejecting one option always means accepting another (if only the inaction option) that may prove even less attractive if it is examined. Conversely, accepting any option can mean forgoing others because there are not enough resources to go around. When evaluating an option, one must consider the *opportunity costs* of doing without the net benefits that would be gained by adopting other options (Vaupel & Graham, 1981). The Bayesian framework forces one to consider at least two options.

As mentioned earlier, the critical ratio provides a threshold for translating posterior odds into action: If they are above that threshold, act as though H were true; if they are below it, act as though $\bar{H}$ were true. The ratio is set by considering the consequences of being right and of being wrong in either case. Thus, it is the Bayesian way to relate uncertain knowledge to concrete actions by showing which action seems to be in one's best interest. In evaluating these actions, it is important to remember that (a) in the presence of uncertainty, the best action may not lead to the best outcome, (b) people must act on the basis of what they themselves believe at the time of decision, not what others believe or subsequently learn (Fischhoff, 1975), and (c) when uncertainty is great, there may be little difference in the apparent attractiveness of competing actions (von Winterfeldt & Edwards, 1982).

One danger in embedding inference in a decision-making framework is that it may encourage people to confuse "acting as though H is true" with "believing that H is true." Decision makers who confuse the two may not attend to signals indicating that their best guess about H was wrong and requires revision (Gärdenfors & Sahlin, 1982). Scientists who confuse the two may forget the uncertainties that they themselves acknowledged before offering a best-guess interpretation of experimental results.

COMPLICATIONS

In this presentation, the interpretation of a datum is complete once one has compared the two conditional probabilities comprising the likelihood ratio. Such appraisal assumes that the datum is taken at face value. More sophisticated Bayesian models are available for situations in which that assumption seems dubious and the interpretation of data depends upon contextual factors. Two such elaborations deal with *source credibility* and *conditional independence*. These complications also point to the need for care in making claims of biased, or non-Bayesian, inferences.

Source credibility

Every datum comes from some source. Knowing that source may, in principle, have quite diverse effects on the datum's interpretation. In common parlance one speaks about sources that have unusual or limited credibility as well as those that may attempt to mislead or may have been misled themselves. On the basis of detailed modeling of the informational properties of evidentiary situations that may arise in the courtroom, Schum (1980, 1981) has shown how source credibility information may reduce, enhance, or even reverse the diagnostic impact of a particular datum. The subtlety of Schum's models suggests both the difficulty of applying Bayesian inference properly and the pitfalls awaiting those trying to rely on intuition. Without understanding the impact of source credibility information, it is hard to know how it is or how it should be interpreted.

A common task in judgment research requires participants to decide whether a target individual belongs to Category A or Category B on the basis of a brief description and some base-rate information. These descriptions vary along dimensions such as the internal consistency of the information they contain and the ratio of relevant to irrelevant information. Typically, investigators have considered only the informational content of these messages when analyzing the impact that these variations should have and do have on behavior. In principle, however, each shift in content could signal a different level of credibility. If subjects are sensitive to these signals, they may choose to respond in ways that are at odds with those dictated by the informational content – and be justified in doing so.

For example, Manis, Dovalina, Avis, and Cardoze (1980), as well as Ginosar and Trope (1980), varied the consistency of the information in a description. With consistent profiles, all information that pointed toward any category pointed toward the same category; with inconsistent profiles, such diagnostic bits pointed in both directions. Subjects relied less on inconsistent information. This might reflect sensitivity to its apparently lower diagnosticity, or it might reflect doubt about its overall credibility. If one doubts that inconsistent people exist (Cooper, 1981), one may discount sources that have produced descriptions showing inconsistency. Both responses could be justified normatively and would lead to similar judgments. However, they suggest different psychological processes. The latter interpretation would mean that this is a situation in which people do understand the need to regress predictions based on unreliable information (Kahneman & Tversky, 1973).

In situations where the content of a message provides a cue regarding its validity, failure to consider that message may lead investigators to mistake sensitivity for bias. For example, in an experimental study of manuscript reviewing, Mahoney (1977) berated his scientist subjects for being more hospitable towards a fictitious study when its reported result confirmed the dominant hypothesis in their field than when it disconfirmed it. This differential receptiveness could reflect the stodginess and prejudices of normal science (Kuhn, 1962), which refuses to relinquish its pet beliefs. However, it could also reflect a belief that investigators who report disconfirming results tend to use inferior research methods (e.g., small samples leading to more spurious results), to commit common mistakes in experimental design, or, simply, to be charlatans. Mahoney himself might set a double standard if he were told that a study did or did not confirm the existence of telekinesis.

These reinterpretations are, of course, entirely speculative. To discipline them by fact, one needs to discover (a) how subjects structure the problem (e.g., their worries about source credibility) and (b) how they appraise the different components of the inferential model that they are using. For either describing or evaluating behavior, one must establish both what people believe and what they try to do with those beliefs (see also Wetzel, 1982).

Conditional independence

The most general way of thinking about contextual effects is as an interaction between the meaning of two or more data. That is, one datum, D_i, creates a context that affects the interpretation of another datum, D_j. In Bayesian terms, such interactions are said to reflect *conditional nonindependence* because the conditional probability $P(D_j/H)$ is not necessarily equal to $P(D_j/H, D_i)$. As a result, one cannot compute the cumulative impact of a set of data simply by multiplying their respective likelihood ratios.

Source-credibility problems may be viewed as a special case of conditional nonindependence: Information about the source affects interpretation of the message. Conversely, the message may affect one's view of the credibility of the source. Conditional nonindependence is also the grounds for configural judgment, the focus of many studies of clinical diagnosis (Goldberg, 1968; Slovic & Lichtenstein, 1971). For the configural judge, the meaning of a particular cue depends upon the status of others (e.g., "That tone of voice suggests 'not suicidal' to me unless I know that it was spoken at midday"). The research record shows that, although clinicians claim to interpret cues configurally, firm evidence of configural judgment is hard to find. This discrepancy may reflect the insensitivity of the research tool, the inaccuracy of the clinicians' introspections about their own judgmental processes, or their failure to use their configural strategies consistently (Dawes, 1979; Slovic & Lichtenstein, 1971).

In studies of clinical diagnosis, both the relationships between cues and people's judgments of those relationships are modeled, typically by linear regression equations. Configural relations are represented in those equations by interaction terms. In the Bayesian model, conditional nonindependence is treated by assessing joint conditional probabilities that consider interrelated data simultaneously. Considering the subtleties of Schum's analyses of source-credibility problems, it is very difficult to model these relationships either in the world or in people's judgments. Indeed, this very complexity may mean that sets of interrelated data defy explicit normative modeling, leaving them the province of judgment (Navon, 1981).

For the expert analyst of evidence, this leads to the frustrating situation of having to take a best guess at what the data mean knowing that their mutual implications have not been understood. Because such complications are common, those frustrations will also be common. Although lay judges may face conditional nonindependence equally often, they may not always take account of it. Perhaps it is the norm to take evidence at face value unless some alarm is sounded by the evidence itself or by the source presenting it. If that is the case, then simple Bayesian models may prove as effective for hypothesis evaluation behavior as simple regression models proved for clinical judgment. As with the regression models, these Bayesian models could be interpreted literally or as "paramorphic models" capturing stimulus–response relationships without claiming to describe the underlying cognitive processes (Hoffman, 1960).

Limits

Just as there are practical limits to the informational complexities that can be treated adequately within the Bayesian framework, so there are value considerations that are best recognized and left alone. People are not always just acquiring knowledge for the sake of optimizing their actions. Some pursuits that are not sensibly accommodated in the Bayesian framework can lead to deliberately non-Bayesian behavior. For example, people may deliberately act suboptimally in the short run when they are pursuing long-run goals such as "maintaining social relations (e.g., preserving and cultivating information sources), gaining and sustaining recognition (e.g., exuding confidence where accountability is low), and being accepted (e.g., by passing up smart solutions that make one appear out of step)" (Fischhoff, 1981, p. 902). Thus, people may ask non-diagnostic questions in order to keep the conversation going, and they may pass up diagnostic ones because asking them seems untoward.

With sufficient ingenuity, such behavior could probably be translated into Bayesian terms so as to show that it is not just purposeful, but also optimal – in the sense of having the highest expected value of any course of action. Thus, for example, asking a question could be treated as an act that has consequences other than the cost of asking it and the information that it produces. These consequences might include the possible penalty of being censured for impertinence or the chance of producing a completely unexpected result leading to the creation of new hypotheses. Practically speaking, anticipating and analyzing such considerations would be very difficult. Theoretically speaking, the attempt to do so might have a very ad hoc character, as though the investigator were groping for causes that might conceivably shape people's hypothesis evaluation. To be useful, these interpretations must walk a tightrope between giving people too little credit and giving them too much. At the former extreme, any behavior for which the investigator finds no ready Bayesian expression reflects cognitive incompetence. At the other extreme, people do whatever is right for them, and the observer's task is to determine what it is that they have managed to optimize (Cohen [and commentary], 1981; Fischhoff, Goitein, & Shapira, 1982; Hogarth, 1981).

Neither our understanding of people nor our ability to help them is served by uncritically assuming either that there is no way for them to justify behavior that seems suboptimal to us or that there is a hidden method to any apparent madness that they exhibit.

NOTES

1 The demand of coherence is what differentiates DeMorgan's "pure subjective" interpretation of probability – as whatever people actually believe – from DeFinetti's personalistic interpretation of probability as rational belief (see Kyburg & Smokler, 1980).

2 Although beyond the scope of the present article, discussion of cases in which Bayes' theorem might not be the most useful way of updating beliefs may be found in Diaconis and Zabell (1982), Good (1950), and Jeffrey (1965, 1968). One troublesome situation is receiving information that changes one's whole system of beliefs [and not just $P(H)$].

3 A topical example may be found in the runaway inflation that has followed the linking of incomes and loans to the cost-of-living index in several countries. Although his economic theories predicted the opposite result, Milton Friedman has denied that this unhappy experience constitutes evidence against his

theories because the countries involved did not implement the indexation exactly as he prescribed. Even more troubling for the status of his theories about the economy is that further thought (perhaps stimulated by this irrelevant experience) has led him to conclude that his earlier derivation was wrong and that, in fact, indexation encourages inflation under some conditions ("How Indexation Builds In Inflation," 1979).

4 In the case of multiple hypotheses, the posterior probability $P(H_i/D) = P(D/H_i) P(H_i)/\Sigma P(D/H_i) P(H_i)$. A diagnostic datum is then one for which $P(D/H_i) \neq \Sigma P(D/H_i) P(H_i)$.

5 Those who interpret subjective probabilities in terms of intuitively appropriate betting odds would never say 1.00 because that would mean willingness to bet everything on the truth of the hypothesis involved. In that light, the only reasonable interpretation of 1.00 is as "nearly 1.00" or "above .995 and rounded upward."

6 One difficulty that the Bayesian approach avoids is vagueness in expressing beliefs. People often disagree considerably about the interpretation of verbal expressions of likelihood (e.g., "probably true"). Moreover, the same individual may use a term differently in different contexts (Beyth-Marom, 1982; Reyna, 1981). The Bayesian approach requires explicitness.

7 One might argue that the collection of diverse pieces of existing evidence should not be considered the *assessment of a base rate*, a term that should be reserved for aggregating statistical data (e.g., 70% of previous cases have supported *H*). Following that argument would lead one to the Laplacian assumption that all hypotheses are equally likely a priori except in the presence of statistical data to the contrary. In that case, the problems discussed in the text would be relegated to the section on assessing likelihood ratios associated with the diverse data. A further argument holds that even statistical data were separate pieces until they were aggregated – meaning that their aggregation required the use of likelihood ratios. At this extreme, a priori odds would always be equal to 1.

8 Ascribing neglect to subjects requires confidence that the investigator knows what base rates really are relevant on the basis of what subjects have been told. Although this determination is relatively clear in most experiments, it can be quite difficult in real-life problems.

9 The undue influence of prior information in this context is in sharp contrast to the neglect of prior information observed with the base-rate fallacy. One difference between the two cases is that in the former case the prior beliefs are actually posterior odds that subjects had generated by actively weighing previous evidence. In many base-rate fallacy studies, the prior beliefs were only a statistical summary reporting what someone else had typically observed. A second difference is that the perseverating prior beliefs were more specific than the neglected ones, fitting Bar-Hillel's (1980) account.

10 Deliberately unrepresentative sampling seems to be another possible bias to be included in this section. However, we feel that such biases are better conceptualized as problems of data interpretation than as problems of sampling.

REFERENCE NOTES

1 U.S. Nuclear Regulatory Commission. *Fault tree handbook* (NUREG-0492). Washington, D.C.: Author, 1981.
2 U.S. Regulatory Commission. *Reactor safety study: An assessment of accident risks in U.S. commercial nuclear power plants* (WASH-1400, NUREG-75/014). Washington, D.C.: Author, 1975.
3 U.S. Regulatory Commission. *Risk assessment review group report to the U.S. Nuclear Regulatory Commission* (NUREG/CR-0400). Washington, D.C.: Author, 1978.

REFERENCES

Bar-Hillel, M. The role of sample size in sample evaluation. *Organizational Behavior and Human Performance*, 1979, 24, 245–257.
The base-rate fallacy in probability judgments. *Acta Psychologica*, 1980, 44, 211–233.
Bar-Hillel, M., & Fischhoff, B. When do base rates affect predictions? *Journal of Personality and Social Psychology*, 1981, 41, 671–680.
Beyth-Marom, R. How probable is probable? Numerical translation of verbal probability expressions. *Journal of Forecasting*, 1982, 1, 257–269.
Borgida, E., & Brekke, N. The base-rate fallacy in attribution and prediction. In J. H. Harvey, W. J. Ickes, & R. F. Kidd (Eds.), *New directions in attribution research* (Vol. 3). Hillsdale, N.J.: Erlbaum, 1981.
Brown, R. V., Kahr, A. S., & Peterson, C. *Decision analysis for the manager.* New York: Holt, Rinehart & Winston, 1974.
Cohen, J. Can human irrationality be experimentally demonstrated? *The Behavioral and Brain Sciences*, 1981, 4, 317–370.
Cooper, W. H. Ubiquitous halo. *Psychological Bulletin*, 1981, 90, 218–244.
Dawes, R. M. The robust beauty of improper linear models in decision making. *American Psychologist*, 1979, 34, 571–582.
DeFinetti, B. Probability: Beware of falsifications! *Scientia*, 1976, 3, 283–303.
Diaconis, P., & Zabell, S. L. Updating subjective probability. *Journal of the American Statistical Association*, 1982, 77, 822–829.
Doherty, M. E., Mynatt, C. R., Tweney, R. D., & Schiavo, M. D. Pseudodiagnosticity. *Acta Psychologica*, 1979, 43, 111–121.
Doyle, A. C. *The memoirs of Sherlock Holmes.* London: Murray & Cape, 1974. (Originally published 1893.)
Eddy, D. M. Probabilistic reasoning in clinical medicine: Problems and opportunities. In D. Kahneman, P. Slovic, & A. Tversky (Eds.), *Judgment under uncertainty: Heuristics and biases.* New York: Cambridge University Press, 1982.
Edwards, W. Dynamic decision theory and probabilistic information processing. *Human Factors*, 1962, 4, 59–73.
Conservatism in human information processing. In B. Kleinmuntz (Ed.), *Formal representation of human judgment.* New York: Wiley, 1968.

Edwards, W., Lindman, H., & Savage, L. J. Bayesian statistical inference for psychological research. *Psychological Review*, 1963, 70, 193–242.

Einhorn, H. J., & Hogarth, R. M. Prediction, diagnosis and causal thinking in forecasting. *Journal of Forecasting*, 1982, 1, 23–36.

Fischer, D. H. *Historians' fallacies*. New York: Harper & Row, 1970.

Fischhoff, B. Hindsight≠foresight: The effect of outcome knowledge on judgment under uncertainty. *Journal of Experimental Psychology: Human Perception and Performance*, 1975, 1, 288–299.

Perceived informativeness of facts. *Journal of Experimental Psychology: Human Perception and Performance*, 1977, 3, 349–358.

For those condemned to study the past: Reflections on historical judgment. In R. A. Shweder & D. W. Fiske (Eds.), *New directions for methodology of behavior science: Fallible judgment in behavioral research*. San Francisco: Jossey-Bass, 1980.

Inferential interference (Review of *Human inference: Strategies and shortcomings of social judgment*, by R. Nisbett & L. Ross). *Contemporary Psychology*, 1981, 26, 901–903.

Debiasing. In D. Kahneman, P. Slovic, & A. Tversky, (Eds.), *Judgment under uncertainty: Heuristics and biases*. New York: Cambridge University Press, 1982.

Fischhoff, B., Goitein, B., & Shapira, Z. The experienced utility of expected utility approaches. In N. Feather (Ed.), *Expectancy, incentive and action*. Hillsdale, N.J.: Erlbaum, 1982.

Fischhoff, B., Slovic, P., & Lichtenstein, S. Fault trees: Sensitivity of estimated failure probabilities to problem representation. *Journal of Experimental Psychology: Human Perception and Performance*, 1978, 4, 330–344.

Subjective sensitivity analysis. *Organizational Behavior and Human Performance*, 1979, 23, 339–359.

Knowing what you want: Measuring labile values. In T. Wallsten (Ed.), *Cognitive processes in choice and decision behavior*. Hillsdale, N.J.: Erlbaum, 1980.

Forer, B. The fallacy of personal validation: A classroom demonstration of gullibility. *Journal of Abnormal and Social Psychology*, 1949, 44, 118–123.

Gärdenfors, P., & Sahlin, N.-E. Unreliable probabilities, risk taking, and decision making. *Synthese*, 1982, 53, 361–386.

Ginosar, Z., & Trope, Y. The effects of base rates and individuating information on judgments about another person. *Journal of Experimental Social Psychology*, 1980, 16, 228–242.

Goldberg, L. R. Simple models or simple processes? Some research in clinical judgment. *American Psychologist*, 1968, 23, 486–496.

Good, I. J. *Probability and the weighting of evidence*. New York: Hafner, 1950.

Green, A. E., & Bourne, A. J. *Reliability technology*. New York: Wiley Interscience, 1972.

Hoffman, P. J. The paramorphic representation of clinical judgment. *Psychological Bulletin*, 1960, 47, 116–131.

Hogarth, R. M. Beyond discrete biases: Functional and dysfunctional aspects of judgmental heuristics. *Psychological Bulletin*, 1981, 90, 191–217.

How indexation builds in inflation. *Business Week*, November 12, 1979, pp. 114–116.

Hyman, R., Cold reading. *Zetetic* (The Skeptical Inquirer), 1977, 1(2), 18–37.

Jeffrey, R. *The logic of decision*. New York: McGraw-Hill, 1965.

Probable knowledge. In I. Lakatos (Ed.), *The problem of inductive logic*. Amsterdam: North-Holland, 1968.

Kahneman, D., & Tversky, A. On the psychology of prediction. *Psychological Review*, 1973, 80, 237–251.

Intuitive predictions: Biases and corrective procedures. *TIMS Studies in Management Science*, 1979, 12, 313–327.

Kahneman, D., Slovic, P. & Tversky, A. (Eds.), *Judgment under uncertainty: Heuristics and biases*. New York: Cambridge University Press, 1982.

Kish, L. *Survey sampling*. New York: Wiley, 1965.

Koriat, A., Lichtenstein, S., & Fischhoff, B. Reasons for confidence. *Journal of Experimental Psychology: Human Learning and Memory*, 1980, 6, 107–118.

Kuhn, T. *Structure of scientific revolutions*. Princeton, N.J.: Princeton University Press, 1962.

Kyburg, H. E., & Smokler, H. E. (Eds.), *Studies in subjective probability*. Huntington, New York: Krieger, 1980.

Lichtenstein, S., Fischhoff, B., & Phillips, L. D. Calibration of probabilities: The state of the art to 1980. In D. Kahneman, P. Slovic, & A. Tversky (Eds.), *Judgment under uncertainty: Heuristics and biases*. New York: Cambridge University Press, 1982.

Lichtenstein, S., Slovic, P., Fischhoff, B., Layman, M., & Combs, B. Judged frequency of lethal events. *Journal of Experimental Psychology: Human Learning and Memory*, 1978, 4, 551–578.

Lindley, D. V. *Introduction to probability and statistics from a Bayesian viewpoint*. Cambridge, England: Cambridge University Press, 1965.

Lindley, D. V., Tversky, A., & Brown, R. V. On the reconciliation of probability assessments. *Journal of the Royal Statistical Society* (Series A), 1979, 142, Pt. 2, 146–180.

Lyon, D., & Slovic, P. Dominance of accuracy information and neglect of base rates in probability estimation. *Acta Psychologica*, 1976, 40, 287–298.

Mahoney, M. J. Publication prejudices. *Cognitive Therapy and Research*, 1977, 1, 161–175.

Manis, M., Dovalina, I., Avis, N. E., & Cardoze, S. Base rates can affect individual predictions. *Journal of Personality and Social Psychology*, 1980, 38, 231–240.

Mehle, T., Gettys, C. V., Manning, C., Baca, S., & Fisher, S. The availability explanation of excessive plausibility assessments. *Acta Psychologica*, 1981, 49, 127–140.

Moskowitz, H., Sarin, R. K. Improving the consistency of conditional probability assessments for forecasting and decision making. *Management Science*, 1983, 29, 735–49.

Murphy, A. H. Scalar and vector partitions of the probability score: Two-stage situation. *Journal of Applied Meteorology*, 1972, 11, 273–282.

Navon, D. Statistical and metastatistical considerations in analysing the desirability of human Bayesian conservatism. *British Journal of Mathematical & Statistical Psychology*, 1981, *34*, 205–212.

Nisbett, R., & Ross, L. *Human inference: Strategies and shortcomings of social judgment*. Englewood Cliffs, N.J.: Prentice-Hall, 1980.

Novick, M. R., & Jackson, P. E. *Statistical methods for educational and psychological research*. New York: McGraw-Hill, 1974.

O'Leary, M. K., Coplin, W. D., Shapiro, H. B., & Dean, D. The quest for relevance. *International Studies Quarterly*, 1974, *18*, 211–237.

Phillips, L. D. *Bayesian statistics for social scientists*. London: Nelson, 1973.

Pitz, G. F., Downing, L., & Reinhold, H. Sequential effects in the revision of subjective probabilities. *Canadian Journal of Psychology*, 1967, *21*, 381–393.

Raiffa, H. *Decision analysis*. Reading, Mass.: Addison-Wesley, 1968.

Reyna, V. F. The language of possibility and probability: Effects of negation on meaning. *Memory and Cognition*, 1981, *9*, 642–650.

Rokeach, M. *The nature of human values*. New York: Free Press, 1973.

Savage, L. J. *The foundations of statistics*. New York: Wiley, 1954.

Schlaifer, R. *Analysis of decisions under uncertainty*. New York: McGraw-Hill, 1969.

Schum, D. Current developments in research on cascaded inference processes. In T. Wallsten (Ed.), *Cognitive processes in choice and decision behavior*. Hillsdale, N.J.: Erlbaum, 1980.

Sorting out the effects of witness sensitivity and response criterion placement upon the inferential value of testimonial evidence. *Organizational Behavior and Human Performance*, 1981, *27*, 153–196.

Slovic, P., & Lichtenstein, S. Comparison of Bayesian and regression approaches to the study of information processing in judgment. *Organizational Behavior and Human Performance*, 1971, *6*, 649–744.

Sue, S., Smith, R. E., & Caldwell, C. Effects of inadmissible evidence on the decision of simulated jurors: A moral dilemma. *Journal of Applied Social Psychology*, 1973, *3*, 345–353.

Troutman, C. M., & Shanteau, J. Inferences based on nondiagnostic information. *Organizational Behavior and Human Performance*, 1977, *19*, 43–55.

Tversky, A., & Kahneman, D. Judgment under uncertainty: Heuristics and biases. *Science*, 1974, *185*, 1124–1131.

Causal schemas in judgments under uncertainty. In M. Fishbein (Ed.), *Progress in social psychology*. Hillsdale, N.J.: Erlbaum, 1980.

The framing of decisions and the rationality of choice. *Science*, 1981, *211*, 453–458.

Vaupel, J., & Graham, J. Eggs in your bier. *The Public Interest*, 1981, *61*, 3–17.

Wetzel, C. G. Self-serving biases in attribution: A Bayesian analysis. *Journal of Personality & Social Psychology*, 1982, *43*, 197–209.

von Winterfeldt, D., & Edwards, W. Costs and payoffs in perceptual research. *Psychological Bulletin*, 1982, *91*, 609–622.

~

17

DIFFERENTIAL DIAGNOSIS AND THE COMPETING-HYPOTHESES HEURISTIC: A PRACTICAL APPROACH TO JUDGMENT UNDER UNCERTAINTY AND BAYESIAN PROBABILITY*

Fredric M. Wolf, Larry D. Gruppen, John E. Billi

The medical community is becoming increasingly aware of the growing complexity involved in clinical decision making.[1] The level of understanding and sophistication necessary to diagnose, treat, and manage medical problems increases concomitantly with the increase in new diagnostic and therapeutic procedures. Moreover, it is well recognized that there is a great deal of uncertainty inherent in clinical information, in the interpretation of laboratory data, in the relationship between clinical findings and disease, and in the effects of various therapies.[1] It is also known that physicians, like most people, often do not manage uncertainty very well and may be prone to making certain errors that may affect the quality of clinical care.[2]

Over the past decade, a number of studies have examined the strategies (i.e., heuristics) and processes by which physicians solve medical problems. A number of these studies have taken a descriptive approach by trying to clarify the steps and methods that clinicians generally use in problem-solving situation.[2,3] The picture of clinical problem solving that emerges from these studies is that of a physician with limited capacity for processing information who is try to make sense of a problem situation typified by a large amount of both complexly interrelated information and uncertainty regarding the correct diagnosis. One model that describes the physician's problem-solving efforts has three components: (1) an early formulation of a small number (three to five) of hypotheses (disease candidates) based on clinical data initially available in conjunction with the physician's prior experience and knowledge, (2) subsequent pursuit of more clinical data to confirm or reject these hypotheses, and (3) selection of a final hypothesis after a critical level of confirmation has been reached.[2,7]

In contrast to the *descriptive* approaches taken by some of the studies in

* First published in *Journal of the American Medical Association*, 253 (1985), 2858–62.
© 1985 American Medical Association. Reprinted by permission.

medical problem solving, other researchers have focused on a *prescriptive* approach in an attempt to determine the correct or optimal method that ought to be used in making a particular clinical decision.[8] Normal human decision making often is inconsistent with solutions derived from a prescriptive (or normative) approach. Such shortcomings in human judgment include a bias toward positive and confirming evidence, primacy effects of initial information, premature closure on a hypothesis, inability to deal properly with probabilities, diagnostic conservatism, and others.[9-14] These shortcomings have provided the impetus for the development of a wide range of possible corrective strategies.

One prominent prescriptive model is based on Bayes' theorem, which provides a rational, normative means of formulating a differential diagnosis and selecting a most probable diagnosis. Bayes' theorem has been applied to clinical practice and research in a variety of settings. These applications have included guidance on therapeutic decisions in patients with an uncertain diagnosis, assistance in analyzing the cost effectiveness and risk-benefit ratio for medical procedures, and insight into the meaning of such test performance characteristics as false-negative rate.[15-19] Bayes' theorem can be used in its mathematical form when estimates of the likelihood of a disease for relevant groups of individuals and the sensitivity and specificity of diagnostic tests are available. (The sensitivity of a diagnostic test is the ratio of the number of true-positive test results to the total number of patients with the disease [false-negatives plus true-positives]. Specificity of a test is the ratio of true-negative test results to patients without the disease [true-negatives plus false-positives].) While it often is burdensome to perform the mathematical calculations associated with Bayes' theorem, the development of computer programs to manage this task makes it increasingly possible to use the theorem as a supplement to clinical judgment.[20,21] Even without performing the calculations, Bayes' theorem can aid in patient management by assisting the clinician in deciding the relevance of specific additional data. This can guide test selection, which is increasingly important in light of rising medical costs.

Notwithstanding these contributions, the use of Bayes' theorem as a normative guide for decision making has come under attack from a variety of directions. Some of the most frequent criticisms have focused on the large amount of specific information required for its use, the difficulty in generating hypotheses from signs and symptoms (since medical knowledge is taught primarily by disease), the documented inability of human beings to manipulate probabilities in their heads, and the unavailability of prior probability estimates (such as prevalence or incidence rates for relevant patient subgroups).[2,11,22,23] Harris[24] has pointed out the additional difficulty created by the paucity of available information concerning the sensitivities and specificities of commonly used laboratory tests, information that is needed to use Bayesian or any other decision-analysis approach. Bayes' theorem also has been criticized for its inability to conveniently allow for the hypotheses of multiple diseases in the same patient or for the nonindependence of symptoms within one disease. Although attempts to extend Bayes' theorem to avoid these oversimplifications are currently under investigation, they are not as yet ready for clinical use.[21]

In spite of these criticisms, the underlying logic of Bayes' theorem is still valid and useful even when knowledge of the precise probabilities is not available.[17] Increasingly, apparently simple and efficient heuristics suggested by Eddy and Clanton[2] and Elstein *et al.*[3] can be incorporated within a Bayesian framework. An understanding of the logic underlying the Bayesian framework per se may be more helpful in improving systematic diagnostic problem solving than the manipulation of probabilities. In order to explain this reasoning, it is necessary first to review briefly Bayes' theorem. In its simplest form, the theorem may be written as follows:

$$P(\text{disease}|\text{findings}) = [P(\text{findings}|\text{disease}) \times P(\text{disease})]/P(\text{findings}) \quad (1)$$

The probability that a patient has a particular disease, given the presence of a set of particular symptoms and signs ($P[\text{disease}|\text{findings}]$) is the Bayesian, conditional, posterior probability of interest. In order to determine this probability, the calculations on the right side of the equation must be made. The numerator is the product of the probability of having this particular set of findings, given the presence of the disease being considered ($P[\text{findings}|\text{disease}]$) and the probability of having the disease ($P[\text{disease}]$) in the relevant patient population. $P(\text{disease})$ also is referred to as the prior probability or base rate, or in medicine the prevalance of the disease. The numerator then is divided by P (findings), which is the sum of $P(\text{findings}|\text{disease}) \times P(\text{disease})$ for each potential disease being considered as a part of the differential diagnosis. In the simplest case, where only two diseases (D) constitute the differential diagnosis and only one symptom (S) is being considered, Bayes' theorem may be written as follows:

$$P(D_1|S) = [P(S|D_1) \times P(D_1)]/\{[P(S|D_1) \times P(D_1)] + [P(S|D_2) \times P(D_2)]\} \quad (2)$$

The subscripts indicate whether we are examining the first or second disease. If $P(D_1|S) > .50$, then the probability that the patient has disease 1 is greater than the probability of his having disease 2. If $P(D_1|S) < .50$, then disease 2 is more likely. If $P(D_1|S) = .50$, then both diseases are equally likely. While not used in this way in the present study, disease 2 could be considered to be "not disease 1," that is, it could be any other disease or no disease at all. As can be readily seen, using Bayes' theorem becomes a complex task even in this simplest form with only two disease possibilities. Most medical cases are not limited by even this simplicity.

While it is understandable that Eddy and Clanton,[2] Harris,[24] and others are skeptical of the practical value of a Bayesian approach to medical decision making, there is an inherent element of logical reasoning built into Bayes' theorem that may prove helpful even without the necessity of calculating any probability values. If we examine the denominator on the right side of formula 2, we see that any given symptom (S in this illustration) must be examined across all the diseases being entertained in the differential diagnosis (D_1 and D_2 in this illustration). Elstein et al.[3] have defined the competing-hypotheses heuristic as the consideration of each piece of information (e.g., symptom) with respect to all hypotheses under consideration before a diagnostic judgment is made. Wolf[25] pointed out the relationship between the competing-hypotheses heuristic and Bayes' theorem, as the information necessary to use the competing-hypotheses heuristic is also the information required to solve the denominator in Bayes' theorem in formula 2 above. Individuals are unable to compare the diagnosticity of the datum of each disease if they do not select additional diagnostic information (data) pertaining to the likelihood of the first datum, given each of the other plausible diseases in the differential diagnosis. Other data selections, e.g., additional symptoms pertaining to the first plausible disease category under consideration, cannot be used to solve Bayes' theorem to arrive at the correct probability of having the disease given the symptom. In the context of Eddy and Clanton's decision-making model, this heuristic could be used by evaluating the one or two pivotal findings of a patient's case across each disease in the "possible cause list." By evaluating each competing-disease hypothesis in light of the pivotal finding, the physician could make more effective use of the available information and would be less likely to close prematurely on a single diagnostic hypothesis. The physician also would be directed toward the systematic collection of more useful information, be it sign, symptom, or laboratory result.

In spite of the value of the competing-hypothesis heuristic, Kern and Doherty[26] and Wolf[25] have shown that most medical students prefer to select symptomatic information that is incompatible with the competing-hypotheses heuristic and the logic of Bayes' theorem. Instead of evaluating one symptom across multiple diseases, many medical students seek information about several symptoms for a single disease. The degree to which *physicians* employ the competing-hypotheses heuristic currently is not known and is addressed for the first time in this study, to the best of our knowledge. The implications of selecting diagnostic information consistent with the heuristic also is examined by analyzing the effects of optimal datum selection on diagnostic accuracy.

METHODS

Description of the instrument

The instrument used in the present study was adapted from those developed by Kern and Doherty[26] and modified by Wolf.[25] The questions were designed to capture the simplest application of Bayes' theorem to medical diagnosis. Subjects were asked to decide which of two diagnoses was more likely, given information concerning one symptom. The optimal solution based on the competing-hypotheses heuristic is to consider the probability of each disease, given the same symptom, with the disease with the higher probability being the more likely diagnosis. In order to assess house officers behavior in selecting the optimal information (datum), a 2 × 2 matrix yielding four pieces of information was provided for each of three separate simulated patient situations. An illustration of this type of problem is provided in the Figure. In each case, house officers were told that the patient had two symptoms, and they were initially provided with one datum regarding the percentage (i.e., probability) of people with disease A that have a particular symptom. In the first situation, information was provided that 66 percent of those people who have contracted disease A have had a fever. Subjects were then given the choice of selecting either the percentage of patients with disease B that have the same symptom (fever, the optimal choice), or data regarding the prevalence of a different symptom (rash), in disease A or disease B. These were selected by removing one of the three opaque stickers that cover the alternative data choices. Subjects were not given the correct answers to any of the problems. In cases 1 and 2, subjects were informed that about an equal number of people suffer from disease A as from disease B (that is, the prior probabilities or base rates for diseases A and B are equal). In case 3, subjects were informed that about twice as many people suffer from disease A as from disease B (i.e. unequal base rates). In all cases, the competing-hypotheses heuristic dictates that the same symptom must be evaluated in relation to the rival plausible disease(s) before the most probable diagnosis can be determined.

The Table summarizes the actual datum given for each case and the probability values available for selection by the subjects. In case 1, the symptom rash is not diagnostically helpful because it does not provide the information needed to solve the equation for Bayes' theorem. Moreover, the probability of having a rash is the same (62 percent) for both diseases A and B. The probability of having a fever and disease B (84 percent), however, is greater than the probability of having a fever and disease A (66 percent). Thus, the most likely diagnosis in this example is disease B. It is likely that subjects selecting information regarding a rash for either diseases A or B would not believe that disease B is the more probable of the two diseases: only those subjects selecting information regarding fever for disease B would be likely to correctly select it as the more probable disease. As can be seen in the Table, the location of the initial datum provided to subjects was varied for the three cases. This minimized the possibility of a response bias effect.

Subjects and data collection

The 89 subjects in the study were new first-year house officers at the University of Michigan Medical Center, Ann Arbor, who participated in an optional orientation course. The house officers represented a variety of fields of planned medical specialization and accurately reflected the distribution of medical specialities at the university. Approximately 92 percent of all the first-year house officers in the course completed the questionnaire.

RESULTS

Individual cases

An analysis of the distribution of choices over the three possible pieces of data for each of the three problems indicated that these subjects are not making random choices on any one case ($\chi^2 = 14.03$, 25.21, and 39.15, respectively, all $P < .01$). Most choices for each case clustered either around the datum that, relative to the provided datum, corresponded to the same symptom and the alternative disease (the optimal choice) or

	Disease A	Disease B
Fever	66%	●
No fever	34%	
Rash		
No rash	●	●

About an equal number of people
suffer from each disease

Problem: which one additional piece of information do you want to select?

	% of Patients*	
Percentage of patients in relevant population with specific symptoms given the presence of two diseases (A and B)	Disease A	Disease B
Case 1 (diseases A and B are equally likely, i.e. equal base rates)		
Fever	66 (given)	84
Rash	62	62
Case 2 (equal base rates)		
Cough	24	43
Leg pains	31	58 (given)
Case 3 (disease A twice as likely as disease B, i.e. unequal base rates)		
Dizziness	45	55
Blurred vision	15 (given	72

* Percentages in the table indicate the probability (P) of the presence of a symptom (S) given a particular disease (D) in Bayes' theorem, e.g., $P(S|D_A)$. In case 1 $P(S_{fever}|D_A) = .66$

around the datum that corresponded to the same disease and the alternative symptom. The subjects tended not to select the datum on the diagonal from the given information, that is, the datum for the alternative disease and the alternative symptom.

Patterns across cases

In a additional analysis, the subjects were classified according to their total number of correct data selections across all three cases. This analysis examined the consistency of data selection within each individual subject. With three problems, there were four possible groupings of subjects' patterns of data selection. The distribution of subjects in these four groups was significantly different from chance ($\chi^2 = 9.62$, $P < .05$). About 14 percent of the subjects consistently selected the nonoptimal data, and one third made only one right datum selection. About 29 percent selected correctly on two of the problems, while 24 percent were consistently correct. In other words, the majority of the subjects chose correctly on one or two problems; relatively few were consistently wrong, while an intermediate number were consistently correct.

Relation between data selection and choice of diagnosis

Across all three cases, approximately 97 percent of the subjects selecting optimum data also chose the most likely diagnosis according to Bayes' theorem; only 53 percent of the subjects selecting nonoptimum data chose the most likely diagnosis. Because the diagnostic choice was limited to only two diseases in each of these cases, disease A or B, it was expected that 50 percent of the subjects would select the most likely diagnosis on the basis of chance alone.

COMMENT

Only a minority (24 percent) of house officers selected optimal symptomatic data consistent with the competing-hypotheses heuristic and Bayes' theorem across all three patient cases. Evaluating symptoms in relation to only one disease does not by itself address the specificity of those symptoms for that disease. A nonspecific symptom frequently may be present in more than one disease. Failing to evaluate a symptom across all potential diagnostic hypotheses may result in a false-positive (or negative) error because the frequency of the symptom in a second disease actually may be greater (or lower) than in the first disease. This may be true even when the frequency of the symptom is extremely high (or low) in the first disease. The failure to request and evaluate symptomatic data across competing diseases has been termed "pseudodiagnosticity."[26]

Because medical education is presented in a disease-oriented manner, it is likely that much of actual clinical diagnostic reasoning is approached from a "within" hypothesis perspective in which the clinician determines the most likely diagnosis by how well the actual case fits a prototypical case for the disease under consideration. Clinicians who make diagnostic judgments solely based on the clusters of clinical findings associated with a particular disease most likely would not make comparisons consistent with the competing-hypotheses heuristic and Bayes' theorem.

Interestingly, most house officers (62 percent) selected the optimal datum in only one (33 percent) or two (29 percent) of the three cases. This might suggest a case-specific pattern of reasoning rather than a preset strategy used across all cases. Asking subjects to explain why they select certain data and not others might provide insight into the mental strategies being used. The pattern of results for each of the three cases was in general similar even though different base rates and conditional probabilities (in the cells of the matrices) were provided to house officers before they made their datum selections. A more systematic study of the effect on datum selection of (1) differences in magnitude of the conditional probabilities provided in the matrix, (2) differences between relatively abstract, artificial problems and more real problems with actual diseases provided instead of diseases A and B, and (3) differences between subjects with different levels of medical training and sophistication is currently in progress. Related research questions that remain for future investigation include the effect on datum selection of (1) the absence of a symptom, (2) a normal finding, and (3) more complex clinical cases where patients have multiple symptoms/findings and/or multiple diseases.

Results in the present study illustrated the link between data selection and selection of a diagnosis, as almost all (97 percent) of the house officers selecting the optimal data chose the most probable diagnosis specified by Bayes' theorem; only a chance number (53 percent) of house officers selecting nonoptimal data chose this diagnosis. While this is a previously undocumented finding, to the best of our knowledge, it is not surprising given the fact that selection of a diagnosis is virtually determined by the information the physician seeks and has available at the time. It should be kept in mind, however, that the most probable diagnosis on the basis of one symptom may not be most likely when all data are considered. Moreover, the most likely diagnosis still may not be the correct diagnosis. Thus, this approach is suggested to complement rather than replace sound clinical judgment.

It has been demonstrated in another study that the use of this heuristic can be learned easily. After a brief educational intervention in a study reported by Wolf,[25] 95 percent and 87 percent of the medical students studied made the optimal datum selections for two new cases, one with equal and the other with unequal base rates. It is likely that house officers also could be trained to use this heuristic especially if emphasis was placed not on calculating the actual Bayesian probabilities, but on systematically evaluating each symptom in relation to each plausible disease in the differential diagnosis.

Eddy and Clanton[2] described a six-step general model that seems to capture the most common pattern of reasoning used by most clinicians most of the time when solving the diagnostic problems of 50 clinico-pathological conferences published in the *New England Journal of Medicine*. These steps included (1) aggregation of groups of findings into patterns, (2) selection of a "pivot" or key finding, (3) generation of a cause list, (4) pruning of the cause list, (5) selection of a diagnosis, and (6) validation of the diagnosis. In cases where they were unable to identify these elements, they were unable to identify any other pattern. While they pointed out that Bayes' theorem theoretically should govern the formulation of a differential diagnosis and the most probable diagnosis, they recognized that a variety of "obstacles make it exceedingly unlikely that the reasoning process used by physicians to perform complicated diagnoses resembles Bayes' theorem."[2] We suggest that clinical decision making might profit by evaluating the pivotal finding (Eddy and Clanton's[2] pivot heuristic) across all competing plausible diseases (Elstein and colleagues'[3] competing-hypotheses heuristic) to arrive at the most likely diagnosis. Furthermore, Eddy and Clanton suggested a practical approach in which the clinician performs this comparative evaluation by beginning with the two most probable diseases and proceeding in a sequential pairwise fashion down the list of other possible diagnoses. In this way, the competing diseases can be eliminated one at a time. Because Eddy and Clanton identified this strategy but did not give it a name, we suggest labeling this the "pairwise" heuristic.

The first and most useful step in the application of Bayes' theorem to clinical situations is to learn to differentiate optimal (useful) from nonoptimal (useless or misleading) data. Selection of optimal data may in itself assist the clinician in arriving at the most probable diagnosis even without performing the mathematical calculations involved in the use of Bayes' theorem. It is in this sense that probability and decision analysis may find a useful place in clinical reasoning. While this study and others[25,26] have provided evidence of the less than optimal use of the competing-hypotheses heuristic in simulated cases, the degree to which practicing physicians select optimal information in real patient encounters remains as yet undetermined.

REFERENCES

1 Ziporyn, T.: Medical decision making: Analyzing options in the face of uncertainty. *JAMA* 1983; 249:2133–2142.
2 Eddy, D.M., Clanton, C.H.: The art of diagnosis: Solving the clinicopathological exercise. *N. Engl. J. Med.* 1982; 306:1263–1268.
3 Elstein, A.S., Shulman, L.S., Sprafka, S.A. *et al.*: *Medical Problem Solving: An Analysis of Clinical Reasoning*. Cambridge, Mass., Harvard University Press, 1978.
4 Elstein, A.S., Bordage, G.: Psychology of clinical reasoning, in Stone, G.C., Cohen, F., Adler, N.E. *et al.* (eds): *Health Psychology: A Handbook*, San Francisco, Jossey-Bass Inc., 1979.
5 Elstein, A.S., Rovner, D.R., Holzman, G.B. *et al.*: Psychological approaches to medical decision making. *Am. Behav. Sci.* 1982; 25:557–584.
6 Johnson, P.E., Duran, A.S., Hassebruck, F. *et al.*: Expertise and error in diagnostic reasoning. *Cognitive Sci.* 1981; 5:235–283.
7 Vu, N.V.: Describing, teaching, and predicting medical problem-solving: A review. *Eval. Health Prof.* 1980; 3:435–459.
8 Pauker, S.G.: Prescriptive approaches to medical decision making. *Am. Behav. Sci.* 1982; 25:507–522.
9 Arkes, H.R.: Impediments to accurate clinical judgment and possible ways to minimize their impact. *J. Consult. Clin. Psychol.* 1981; 49:323–330.

10 Einhorn, H.J., Hogarth, R.M.: Behavioral decision theory: Processes of judgment and choice. *Annu. Rev. Psychol.* 1981; 32:53–88.

11 Tversky, A., Kahneman, D.: Judgment under uncertainty: Heuristics and biases. *Science* 1974; 195:1124–1131.

12 Kozielecki, J.: A model for diagnostic problem solving. *Acta Psychol.* 1972; 36:370–380.

13 Nisbett, R., Ross, L.: *Human Inference: Strategies and Shortcomings of Social Judgment,* Englewood Cliffs, N.J., Prentice-Hall Inc., 1980.

14 Eraker, S.A., Politser, P.: How decisions are reached: Physician and patient. *Ann. Intern. Med.* 1982; 97:262–268.

15 Rifkin, R.D., Hood, W.B.: Bayesian analysis of electrocardiographic exercise stress testing. *N. Engl. J. Med.* 1977; 297:681–686.

16 Diamond, G.A., Forrester, J.S.: Analysis of probability as an aid in the clinical diagnosis of coronary-artery disease. *N. Engl. J. Med.* 1979; 300:1350–1358.

17 Jones, R.B.: Bayes' theorem, the exercise ECG, and coronary artery disease. *JAMA* 1979; 242:1067–1068.

18 Pauker, S.G., Kassirer, J.P.: Therapeutic decision-making: A cost-benefit analysis. *N. Engl. J. Med.* 1975; 293:229–234.

19 Pauker, S.G., Kassirer, J.P.: The threshold approach to clinical decision-making. *N. Engl. J. Med.* 1980; 302:1109–1117.

20 Diamond, G.A.: Bayes' theorem: A practical aid to clinical judgment for diagnosis of coronary-artery disease. *Practical Cardiol.* 1984; 10:47–77.

21 Ziporyn, T.: Computer-assisted medical decision-making: Interest growing. *JAMA* 1982; 248:913–918.

22 Feinstein, A.R.: The haze of Bayes, the aerial palaces of decision analysis, and the computerized Ouija board. *Clin. Pharmacol. Ther.* 1977; 21:482–496.

23 Bursztajn, H., Feinbloom, R.I., Hamm, R.M. *et al.*: *Medical Choices, Medical Chances: How Patients, Families, and Physicians Can Cope With Uncertainty.* New York, Delacorte Press, 1981.

24 Harris, J.M.: The hazards of bedside Bayes. *JAMA* 1981; 246:2602–2605.

25 Wolf, F.M.: Increasing the use of the competing hypotheses heuristic in clinical decision-making, in Herschmen, A. (ed.): *Abstracts of Papers of the 149th National Meeting.* Washington, D.C., American Association for the Advancement of Science, 1983, p. 127.

26 Kern, L., Doherty, M.E.: "Pseudodiagnosticity" in an idealized medical problem-solving environment. *J. Med. Educ.* 1982; 57:100–104.

18

~

PHYSICIANS' USE OF PROBABILISTIC INFORMATION IN A REAL CLINICAL SETTING*

Jay J.J. Christensen-Szalanski, James B. Bushyhead

Past researchers have identified biased heuristics that people use when processing probabilistic information in a laboratory setting (Fischhoff, 1975; Kahneman & Tversky, 1972; Lichtenstein, Fischhoff, & Phillips, 1977; Tversky & Kahneman, 1974). These biases are commonly assumed to be inherent in a person's information-processing abilities. However, articles by Slovic on stockbrokers (1969), Murphy and Winkler on weather forecasters (1974), Ebbesen and Konečni on court judges (1975), and Phelps and Shanteau on livestock judges (1978) have suggested that experts in a real-life setting are often not subject to the same cognitive limitations found in laboratory studies. This investigation studied a group of physicians managing possible pneumonia patients in an outpatient clinic. It examined their methods of using probabilistic information when estimating a patient's probability of pneumonia and a symptom's diagnostic value.

GENERAL METHOD

Participants

Nine physicians participated in this study. Each physician was either board-eligible or board-certified in internal or adolescent medicine. Board-eligible physicians have completed specialized training beyond medical school. Board-certified physicians are board-eligible and have passed a national certification board examination.

Procedure

Clinical information available to physicians.   To standardize the type of information obtained from different patients over the course of the study, research assistants used a checklist to collect a standard medical history

* First published in *Journal of Experimental Psychology: Human Perception and Performance*, 7 (1981), 928–35. © 1981 American Psychological Association Inc. Reprinted by permission of the publisher and author.

from each patient. The physicians then completed the checklist to obtain the predefined physical examination and reviewed the historical data, supplementing it with their own questions when they saw fit. The physicians examined 1,531 first-time patients with a cough of less than 1 mo. duration at the walk-in clinic at Brooke Army Medical Center in San Antonio, Texas. The majority of patients were either retired military personnel, their dependents, or dependents of active service members. Each patient was examined by only one physician.

Assignment of pneumonia probability. After completing the history and physical examination, physicians were required to estimate the probability that the patient had pneumonia. Probability estimates were made on a scale that ranged from 0 (certain that the patient does not have pneumonia) to 100 (certain that the patient does have pneumonia) for all patients in the study. Because the patients could have diseases other than pneumonia, an assigned probability of pneumonia of $p = .00$ does not necessarily imply that the physician was certain that the patient was well. It could also mean that the physician was certain that the patient had a disease other than pneumonia. Probability estimates were made without knowledge of chest X-ray results.

Assignment of pneumonia status. Because most physicians consider the chest X-ray to be the definitive test for pneumonia, chest X-rays were taken of all patients in the study. Radiologists then examined each patient's X-ray and decided whether the patient had pneumonia. The radiologist made the diagnosis without knowledge of the patient's history and physical findings (except that all patients had an acute cough) or the examining physician's probability estimates.

EXPERIMENT I

Validity of probability estimates

Although the physician's ability to estimate probability may be important for correct patient management (Elstein, Shulman, & Sprafka, 1978; Christensen-Szalanski & Bushyhead, Note 1), there are no published studies that report on the validity of physicians' probability estimates. "Degree of calibration" is a frequently used measure of validity in the psychological and meteorological literature (Lichtenstein & Fischhoff, 1977; Lichtenstein, *et al.*, 1977; Murphy & Winkler, 1974): It indicates the ability to evaluate a *set* of probability estimates. A physician would be considered to be "perfectly calibrated" if he or she assigned a pneumonia probability of N to patients of whom $N\%$ really did have pneumonia.

Lichtenstein *et al.* (1977) have reviewed the experimental calibration literature. They found that people normally either overestimate how much they know or overestimate how often an event will occur. However, participants in the studies they reviewed were usually required to answer two-alternative multiple choice questions and indicate their confidence in the selected alternative. (E.g., What is absinthe? (a) a liqueur; (b) a precious stone.) Participants in this task probably judged the cost of selecting alternative (a) and being wrong as equal to the cost of selecting alternative (b) and being wrong; The payoff matrix was the same regardless of the alternative they selected (Lichtenstein *et al.*, 1977). Physicians in a clinical setting might be using a different payoff matrix – one that assigns a greater cost to a false negative diagnosis than to a false positive diagnosis (Scheff, 1963).

This study reports on physician's degree of calibration when judging a patient's probability of pneumonia and the payoff matrix associated with the physicians' decision to assign a pneumonia diagnosis.

Method

Obtaining a calibration curve. The calibration curve was constructed by the common process of first grouping (across physicians) the probability estimates into probability ranges to ensure stability of the calibration estimates (Lichtenstein & Fischhoff, 1977). Six ranges were used for this study (0%, 1%–20%, 21%–40%, 41%–60%, 61%—80%, 81%–100%). The mean assigned probability for each range was plotted against the percentage of radiographically diagnosed pneumonia cases within each range to yield the calibration curve.

Obtaining personal outcome values. Several months after all the patients were examined, physicians received a questionnaire that listed the possible outcomes for the pneumonia diagnosis decision: (a) Assign a pneumonia diagnosis to a patient who does have pneumonia. (b) Assign a pneumonia diagnosis to a patient who does not have pneumonia. (c) Assign a nonpneumonia diagnosis to a patient who does have pneumonia. (d) Assign a nonpneumonia diagnosis to a patient who does not have pneumonia. Physicians were asked to assign a value rating for each outcome using a balanced scale that ranged from − 50 (worst thing I could do) to + 50 (best thing I could do). All questionnaires were completed anonymously and sent to the experimenter by mail. One physician who was transferred to another Army base before the questionnaire was sent left no forwarding address. Therefore, the value data are based on eight physicians' responses.

Results

Physicians' calibration.   Previous research on the physicians participating in this study (Christensen-Szalanski & Bushyhead, Note 1) showed that their subjective probability estimate of a patient having pneumonia was significantly correlated with their decision to give a patient a diagnostic chest X-ray ($r = .99$, $p < .05$) and to assign a pneumonia diagnosis ($r = .99$, $p < .05$). This suggests that physicians have internally valid probability estimates. The present study however, suggests that physicians' probability estimates are not externally valid. The observed physicians' calibration is compared with perfect calibration in Figure 1. A binomial test was used to compare the percentage of diagnosed pneumonia cases for each probability range to the percentage expected for perfect calibration. For each probability range greater than zero, the observed number of pneumonia diagnoses was significantly less than that expected if physicians were perfectly calibrated ($p < .001$). Thus, physicians expressed an overestimation bias when assigning the probability that a patient had pneumonia.

Payoff matrix of pneumonia diagnosis decision.   The physicians' mean values reported for the possible outcomes of a pneumonia diagnosis decision are shown in Figure 2. Two Wilcoxon signed rank tests were used to compare the values assigned to the different outcomes for each physician. There was no difference between the physicians' values for a

Figure 1   Relationship between physicians' subjective probability of pneumonia and the actual probability of pneumonia

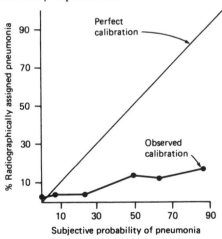

correct pneumonia diagnosis and a correct nonpneumonia diagnosis ($T = 13, z = 1.43, p > .15$). Nor was there a difference between the values for an incorrect pneumonia diagnosis and an incorrect nonpneumonia diagnosis ($T = 17, z = .14, p > .80$). These data suggest that in this setting the payoff matrix was the same for the two diagnoses. By implication, the overestimation bias is cognitive and not motivational.

EXPERIMENT 2

Base rate information and the absence of a cue

Medical schools teach students the frequency of symptoms or test results, given a particular disease. In practice, however, the opposite relationship is more important: How frequent is the disease, given a symptom or test result? For example, suppose the physician was informed of the following hypothetical relationship: Ninety percent of all patients who have pneumonia have chills. Ninety percent of all patients who do not have pneumonia do not have chills.

A patient with chills entering the physician's office does not necessarily have a 90 percent chance of having pneumonia. Suppose 70 percent of the patients who visit a certain clinic have pneumonia. A physician seeing patients in that setting should be more than 95 percent certain that a patient with chills has pneumonia. However, if only .1 percent of the patients who visit another clinic have pneumonia, a physician seeing patients in the second clinic setting should recognize that there is not a 95 percent chance but less than a 1 percent chance that a patient with chills has pneumonia.

The symptom, patient, and physician are identical in the two settings.

Figure 2 Physicians' mean values for outcomes of pneumonia diagnosis (Pn Dx) decision

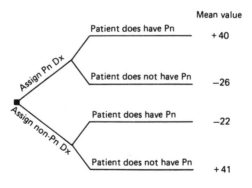

Table 1 *Hypothetical relationship between chills and pneumonia*

	A. Prior $P(\text{Pn}) = (a + b)/N$			B. Prior $P(\text{Pn}) = .70^a$			C. Prior $P(\text{Pn}) = .001^b$		
	Chills			Chills			Chills		
Chills	Present	Absent	Total	Present	Absent	Total	Present	Absent	Total
Present	a	b	$a + b$	6,300	700	7,000	9	1	10
Absent	c	d	$c + d$	300	2,700	3,000	999	8,991	9,990
Total	$a + c$	$b + d$	N	6,600	3,400	10,000	1,008	8,992	10,000

Prior probability of pneumonia is (A) unspecified, (B) equal to $p = .70$, and (C) equal to $p = .001$.
^{a} $P(\text{Pn}|\text{Chills present}) = a/(a + c) = 6300/6600 = .955$.
^{b} $P(\text{Pn}|\text{Chills present}) = a/(a + c) = 9/1008 = .009$.

The difference in the posterior probabilities is caused by the different prior probabilities or base rates of pneumonia in the two patient populations. This result can be explained by using Bayes' Theorem as given below (also see Table 1):

$$\frac{P(\text{Pn}|\text{Chills})}{P(\text{No Pn}|\text{Chills})} = \frac{P(\text{Chills}|\text{Pn})}{P(\text{Chills}|\text{No Pn})} \times \frac{P(\text{Pn})}{P(\text{No Pn})}. \qquad (1)$$

These calculations can be simplified if we substitute a, b, c, d, and N from Table 1(A) into the equation where a, b, c, and d correspond to the number of patients in each cell and N corresponds to the total number of patients in the study population.

$$\frac{P(\text{Pn}|\text{Chills})}{P(\text{No Pn}|\text{Chills})} = \frac{\dfrac{a}{a + b}}{\dfrac{c}{c + d}} \times \frac{\dfrac{a + b}{N}}{\dfrac{c + d}{N}}, \qquad (2)$$

and therefore:

$$P(\text{Pn}|\text{Chills}) = \frac{a}{a + c}. \qquad (3)$$

The quantity $a/(a + c)$ is the posterior probability that a patient with chills ·has pneumonia. This quantity is referred to in the medical literature as the predictive value of chills for identifying pneumonia. Table 1(B) and (C) shows the calculations for the predictive value of chills for the two prior probabilities of pneumonia given in the above examples.

Although it is important that the physician be sensitive to the base rate or prevalence of a disease to use diagnostic information correctly, recent psychological research suggests that people in general, including trained statisticians, ignore base-rate probabilities when presented with diagnostic information if they rely on intuition rather than calculation (Bar-Hillel, 1980; Hammerton, 1973; Lyon & Slovic, 1976; Tversky & Kahneman, 1974). Participants in these laboratory studies were assumed to be unable to use base-rate information because of the posterior probability estimates they made in response to pencil-and paper word problems that presented the base-rate information in a very explicit quantitative format. This study examined physicians' ability to estimate posterior probabilities and the predictive value of information when the physicians must obtain the pneumonia base-rate information from *their experience* in a clinical setting.

This study also examined the physicians' ability to estimate the predictive value of an "absent symptom," since the absence of a symptom also can be helpful in assigning a diagnosis. Past psychological research has suggested that people do not efficiently process the "absence of cues" (Bourne & Guy, 1968; Hovland & Weiss, 1953; Nahinsky & Slaymaker, 1970). Thus we expected that physicians would not be able to use the absence of symptoms as efficiently as the presence of symptoms.

Method

Present and absent symptoms.   The 117 symptoms that were present in at least 1% of the patient population were considered to be cues that were available to the physician.

Actual predictive value of the information.   For each of the 117 symptoms a 2 × 2 contingency table, similar to Table 1(A) was constructed relating the presence of the symptom with the presence of radiographically diagnosed pneumonia. Using these contingency tables, the predictive value of the presence of each symptom (i.e., $P(\text{Pn}|\text{Symptom Present})$) was determined by calculating the ratio $a/(a + c)$. The predictive value of the absence of each symptom (i.e., $P(\text{Pn}|\text{Symptom Absent})$) was determined by calculating the ratio $b/(b + d)$.

Physicians' estimate of the predictive value of the information.   The physician's estimate of the predictive value of the presence of a symptom was determined by calculating the mean probability of pneumonia assigned to patients with that symptom. Conversely, the physicans' estimate of the predictive value of the absence of a symptom was determined by calculating the mean probability of pneumonia assigned to patients without that symptom.

Results

Physicians' sensitivity to the predictive value of symptoms when present. For each symptom, the physicians' estimate of the predictive value of the observation of a "present" symptom was plotted against the actual predictive value of the symptom when present (see Figure 3). Figure 3 reveals the relatively poor predictive value of any single symptom at identifying pneumonia. This is largely a result of the low prior probability of pneumonia in the present clinical setting (3 cases per 100 patients). A least squared regression line of a symptom's actual predictive value on its estimated predictive value is also shown in Figure 3. The significantly positive slope, $s_b = .106$, $t(115) = 7.61$, $p < .001$, suggests that physicians may be sensitive to relative differences in the predictive value of symptoms when present. A slope of less than 1.0, $t(115) = 1.79$, $p = .08$, however, implies that this sensitivity may not be perfect. The constant in the regression equation is also significantly greater than 0, $s_c = .463$, $t(115) = 12.6$, $p < .001$.

Physicians' sensitivity to the predictive value of symptoms when absent. The physicians' estimate of the predictive value of the observation of an "absent symptom" was plotted against the actual predictive

Figure 3 Relationship between actual predictive value (Pr) of symptoms when present and physicians' estimated predictive value

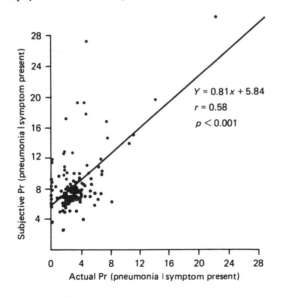

$Y = 0.81x + 5.84$
$r = 0.58$
$p < 0.001$

Subjective Pr (pneumonia I symptom present)

Actual Pr (pneumonia I symptom present)

value of the symptom when absent (see Figure 4). The results are similar to the analysis of physicians' use of the predictive value of abnormal findings: Analysis yields a regression coefficient significantly greater than 0, $s_b = .077$, $t(115) = 5.44$, $p < .001$, and less than 1.0, $t(115) = 7.57$, $p < .001$, and a constant term significantly greater than 0, $s_c = .203$, $t(115) = 25.6$, $p < .001$.

The obtained regression coefficient for the physicians' sensitivity to absent symptoms was smaller than that for present symptoms. This result agrees with the previously cited experimental research that decision makers can not process the absence of cues as efficiently as the presence of cues. There are two reasons, however, why the difference in the obtained regression coefficients in the present study may be artificial. First, an examination of Figure 4 reveals that the absent symptom regression is "weighted down" by a single outlier corresponding to rhinnorea (or runny nose), the presence of which may be more suggestive of a common cold than of pneumonia. If this single outlier is eliminated from the regression calculations, the resulting regression equation is $Y = .71X + 4.45$ ($r = 0.60$, $p < .001$). The new regression coefficient for the absent-symptom equation is nearly identical to that for the present-symptom equation, $s_{b_1 - b_2} = .600$, $t(113) = .16$, $p > .80$. Second, even without eliminating any outliers, a t-test comparison of the two original regression coefficients fails to detect any significant difference, $s_{b_1 - b_2} = .458$, $t(113) = .85$, $p < .40$. Thus, physicians in this study appear

Figure 4 Relationship between actual predictive value (Pr) of symptoms when absent and physicians' estimated predictive value

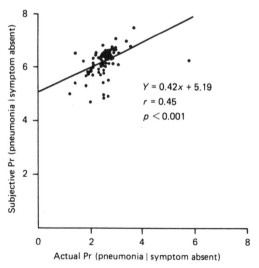

$Y = 0.42x + 5.19$
$r = 0.45$
$p < 0.001$

Subjective Pr (pneumonia | symptom absent)

Actual Pr (pneumonia | symptom absent)

to use the absence of a clinical finding as efficiently as the presence of a clinical finding when estimating the predictive value of the finding.

This study analyzed a decision maker's ability to make judgments in a real-life setting that posed problems of genuine value for the decision maker. Decision makers in this setting might be expected to process information differently from participants in some laboratory settings because the decision makers, as experts, are more experienced with the stimuli and tasks and thus may be better able to avoid cognitive limitations (Slovic, 1969) or because more valuable, real-life problems motivate the decision maker to devote more time and energy to using more accurate problem-solving strategies (Beach & Mitchell, 1978; Christensen-Szalanski, 1978, 1980). Given this expectation, several observations of these two experiments merit further discussion.

Overestimation of pneumonia probability

The payoff matrix for various kinds of correct and incorrect diagnoses can not account for the overestimation of pneumonia probability. Although it is possible that the questionnaire did not reflect the value matrix that physicians use when estimating pneumonia probability, the estimation of probabilities theoretically should not depend upon the payoff matrix. Utility theory presupposes that the assignment of probabilities and values to the outcomes of a decision are independent processes: Only the actual decision is dependent upon the value matrix (Raiffa, 1968). Even if physicians did consider it better to assign a pneumonia diagnosis to a nonpneumonia patient than vice versa, they should not be motivated to over-estimate the probability of pneumonia. Instead they should over-assign a pneumonia diagnosis because the payoff matrix dictates a lower threshold probability (Swets, 1964) for the assignment of a pneumonia diagnosis.

Since the decision maker expresses the overestimation bias in a setting that should encourage the use of accurate information-processing strategies, it is unlikely that this bias is a result of the decision maker using inaccurate strategies. Interestingly, the two regression analyses of Experiment 2, with slopes less than 1.0 and constants greater than zero, imply that physicians underestimate the relative differences in the predictive values of the symptoms, but when processing the information they add a relatively large positive constant, which results in over-estimation of a symptom's diagnostic value. The limited range of the results in Figures 3 and 4 makes the interpretation of these regression analyses difficult to generalize. However, perhaps in the present setting the constant that contributes to the overestimation is the physicians' perception that a person entering a clinic is sick until shown to be well.

Use of the absence of information

In the present study, physicians appeared to be equally sensitive to relative changes in the predictive value of the presence and the absence of clinical findings. It is possible that physicians were using a more accurate strategy to process the absence of a cue than the usually untrained participants of psychology experiments. Another possible explanation for these results, however, is that the physicians' judgment was aided by the procedure of this study.

Hulse, Deese, and Egeth (1975, p. 269) reported that helping people to attend to the absence of cues can increase their use of the information. The procedure in this study required physicians to fill in a predefined checklist of signs and symptoms when examining patients. By using this checklist to guide their examination of the patients, physicians were required to attend to symptoms that were absent as well as to those present. Perhaps it was this increased attention that aided the physicians to use the absent-cue information. This interpretation is inconsistent with a study by de Dombal, Leaper, Horrocks, Staniland, and McCann (1974) that suggests that physicians' performance when examining patients with abdominal pain can be improved by the use of a checklist.

The design and results of the present study do not support one of these explanations over another, since the realism of the study reduced the experimenters' control of the presence of correlated symptoms. For example, if the absence of symptom X always occurred with the presence of important symptom Y, perhaps physicians' apparent "use" of the absent symptom was simply an artifact due to this correlation. A more controlled experiment is needed to support these results before a checklist of symptoms can be recommended as an aid to the physician's judgment process.

Use of base-rate information

Since base-rate information is necessary to calculate predictive value, the significant positive correlation between a symptom's actual predictive value for pneumonia and that obtained from the physician's estimate of a patient's probability of pneumonia suggests that physicians do use base-rate information. These results may not be surprising to any one who has heard his or her physician say, "You probably have ———. There's a lot of that going around now." Such a statement implies the use of base-rate information. The results of the present study, however contradict earlier conclusions that people cannot use base-rate information.

A possible explanation for this contradiction may be that the previously reported psychology studies, which tested the participants' ability to use base-rate information when presented in quantitative word problems, did not test ability to use base-rate information obtained *from experience.* Although physicians in the present study appeared to use base-rate information, comparably trained physicians were unable to use base-rate information when it was presented quantitatively in a pencil-and-paper problem (Casscells, Schoenberger, & Graboys, 1978). The experience of a 3 percent base rate is more salient and thus may be easier for physicians to intuitively incorporate into their judgment processes than reading a sentence that states the base-rate is 3 percent. Additionally, several studies have suggested that the salience of the base-rate information can mediate the participant's ability to use the information: (a) Presenting only base-rate information in the word problem (Kahneman & Tversky, 1973); (b) making the base-rate information causally related to the problem outcome (Tversky & Kahneman, 1980); and (c) repeatedly presenting to a participant copies of a specific word problem that are identical except for the base-rate (Fischhoff, Slovic & Lichtenstein, 1979) all improved the participant's ability to use base-rate information.

CONCLUSION

The present study examined physicians' decision making in a real clinical setting. Physicians overestimated the patient's probability of pneumonia but were sensitive to relative differences in the predictive value of symptoms when present and absent, and appeared to use base-rate information correctly when making clinical judgments.

The realism of the study reduced the experimenters' control over the presence of correlated symptoms and the frequency of the pneumonia base-rate and therefore limits the strength of these conclusions. Nevertheless, this study also identified several unanswered research questions: (a) Do physicians underestimate the predictive value of a clinical finding but overestimate a patient's probability of pneumonia because of a perception that people entering a clinic are ill until proven well? (b) Can information processing be improved by using a checklist of symptoms when examining patients? (c) Can the experience of base-rate information enable a decision maker to use base-rate information? Although experimental settings may be needed to answer these questions, the results of the present study reaffirm the need for caution in generalizing from the laboratory setting to real-life decisions without investigating the real-life setting.

REFERENCE NOTE

1 Christensen-Szalanski, J. J. J., & Bushyhead, J. B. *Decision analysis as a model of physician decision making* (Tech. Rep. 79–45). Department of Health Services Research, U.S. Public Health Service Hospital, Seattle, Washington, August 1979. (Submitted for publication.)

REFERENCES

Bar-Hillel, M. The base rate fallacy in probability judgments. *Acta Psychologica*, 1980, 44, 211–233.

Beach, L. R., & Mitchell, T. R. A contingency model for the selection of decision strategies. *Academy Management Review*, 1978, 3, 439–449.

Bourne, L. E., Jr., & Guy, D. E. Learning conceptual rules: II. The role of positive and negative instances. *Journal of Experimental Psychology*, 1968, 77, 488–494.

Casscells, B. S., Schoenberger, A., & Graboys, T. B. Interpretation by physicians of clinical laboratory results. *New England Journal of Medicine*, 1978, 299, 999–1000.

Christensen-Szalanski, J. J. J. Problem solving stategies: A selection mechanism, some implications, and some data. *Organizational Behavior and Human Performance*, 1978, 22, 307–323.

A further examination of the selection of problem solving strategies: The effects of deadlines and analytic aptitudes. *Organizational Behavior and Human Performance*, 1980, 25, 107–122.

de Dombal, F. T., Leaper, D.J., Horrocks, J.C., Staniland, J.R., & McCann, A.P. Human and computer-aided diagnosis of abdominal pain: Further report with emphasis on performance of clinicians. *British Medical Journal*, 1974, 1, 376–380.

Ebbesen, E. B. & Konečni, V. J. Decision making and information integration in the courts: The setting of bail. *Journal of Personality and Social Psychology*, 1975, 32, 805–821.

Elstein, A. S., Shulman, L. S., & Sprafka, S. A. *Medical problem solving: An analysis of clinical reasoning*. Cambridge, Mass.: Harvard University Press, 1978.

Fischhoff, B., Hindsight≠foresight: The effect of outcome knowledge on judgment under uncertainty. *Journal of Experimental Psychology: Human Perception and Performance*, 1, 288–299.

Fischhoff, B., Slovic, P., & Lichtenstein, S. Subjective sensitivity analysis. *Organizational Behavior and Human Performance*, 1979, 23, 339–359.

Hammerton, M. A case of radical probability estimation. *Journal of Experimental Psychology*, 1973, 101, 242–254.

Hovland, C. I., & Weiss, W. Transmission of information concerning concepts through positive and negative instances. *Journal of Experimental Psychology*, 1953, 43, 175–182.

Hulse, S. H., Deese, J., & Egeth, H. *The psychology of learning* (4th ed.). New York: McGraw-Hill, 1975.

Kahneman, D., & Tversky, A. Subjective probability: A judgment of representativeness. *Cognitive Psychology*, 1972, *3*, 430–454.

On the psychology of prediction. *Psychology Review*, 1973, *80*, 237–251.

Lichtenstein, S. & Fischhoff, B. Do those who know more also know more about how much they know? The calibration of probability judgments. *Organizational Behavior and Human Performance*, 1977, *20*, 159–183.

Lichtenstein, S., Fischhoff, B., & Phillips, L. D. Calibration of probabilities: The state of the art. In H. Jungemann & D. deZeeuw (Eds.), *Decision making and change in human affairs*. Amsterdam: D. Reidel, 1977.

Lyon, D., & Slovic, P. Dominance of accuracy information and neglect of base rates in probability estimation. *Acta Psychologica*, 1976, *40*, 287–298.

Murphy, A. H., & Winkler, R. L. Subjective probability forecasting experiments in meteorology: Some preliminary results. *Bulletin of the American Meteorological Society*, 1974, *55*, 1206–1216.

Nahinsky, I. D., & Slaymaker, F. L. Use of negative instances in conjunctive concept identification. *Journal of Experimental Psychology*, 1970, *84*, 64–84.

Phelps, R. H., & Shanteau, J. Livestock judges: How much information can an expert use? *Organizational Behavior and Human Performance*, 1978, *21*, 209–219.

Raiffa, H. *Decision analysis: Introductory lectures on choices under uncertainty*. Reading, Mass.: Addison-Wesley, 1968.

Scheff, T. J. Decision rules and types of error, and their consequences in medical diagnosis. *Behavioral Science*, 1963, *8*, 97–107.

Slovic, P. Analyzing the expert judge: A descriptive study of a stockbroker's decision process. *Journal of Applied Psychology*, 1969, *53*, 255–263.

Swets, J. A. (Ed.). *Signal detection and recognition by human observers*. New York: Wiley, 1964.

Tversky, A., & Kahneman, D. Judgment under uncertainty: Heuristics and biases. *Science*, 1974, *185*, 1124–1131.

Causal schemata in judgment under uncertainty. In M. Fishbein (Ed.), *Progress in social psychology*. Hillsdale, N.J.: Erlbaum, 1980.

19

HINDSIGHT BIAS AMONG PHYSICIANS WEIGHING THE LIKELIHOOD OF DIAGNOSES*

Hal R. Arkes, Paul D. Saville, Robert L. Wortmann, Allan R. Harkness

Those who know an event has occurred may claim that had they been asked to predict the event in advance, they would have been very likely to do so. In fact, people with hindsight knowledge do assign higher probability estimates to an event than those who must predict the event without the advantage of that knowledge (Fischhoff, 1975). This effect is known as hindsight bias.

The impact of the hindsight bias has been previously demonstrated in studies employing historical events and psychotherapy case histories (Fischhoff, 1975), facts of general knowledge (Wood, 1978), and the outcome of scientific experiments (Slovic & Fischhoff, 1977). The current experiment sought to extend the empirical data base to medical diagnosis. This interest reflects a trend toward the examination of the medical diagnostic process as a cognitive task in which established cognitive phenomenon should be experimentally demonstrable (Arkes & Harkness, 1980).

METHOD

Subjects

Seventy-five MDs participated in the study. Each was either a house officer or a member of the teaching faculty at the Medical College of Wisconsin. The participants were divided into five groups of 15 each.

Stimulus material

Physicians in the "foresight" group were presented with an actual case history of a frequently encountered clinical problem. The information presented permitted consideration of four possible diagnoses, since no symptom excluded, or was limited to, any one diagnosis. The material presented to the physicians in this group was as follows:

* First published in *Journal of Applied Psychology*, 66 (1981), 252–4. © 1981 American Psychological Association, Inc. Reprinted by permission of the publisher and author.

This is a case history. We would like you to read this and then decide what the probability is that you would have assigned to each of four possible diseases had you been making the diagnosis. Assign a probability to each diagnosis, making sure the probabilities add to 100 percent.

A 37-year-old male bartender had been well until he developed increasing pain in his left knee, which became hot and swollen. A few days later, pain, swelling, and heat developed in his left wrist and right knee. Examination revealed swelling, heat, and effusion in both knees and left wrist. There were no deformities. His liver was enlarged 2 cm below the costal margin. CBC was normal. ESR was 30 mm (westergren). Latex test was neg. SMA 12 was not back yet. Hb_sAg was not back yet. Joint fluid contains 20,000 WBC; 80% polys: viscosity low. There were excess pus cells in urine. Fever was 100° F.

Now, please assign to each of the four possible diagnoses the probability you think you would have assigned. Be sure the probabilities sum to 100 percent.

———— Reiter's syndrome (incomplete)
———— Post streptococcal arthritis in an adult (rheumatic fever)
———— Gout
———— Serum hepatitis in pre-icteric phase

There were also four hindsight groups, each receiving the same information as the foresight group with the exception of a different first sentence. The four first sentences were: This is a case history of Reiter's syndrome (incomplete); this is a case history of poststreptococcal arthritis in an adult (rheumatic fever); this is a case history of gout; this is a case history of serum hepatitis in pre-icteric phase. Note that the second sentence for all hindsight subjects constituted a request for their individual, independent assessment of the patient.

Procedure

Sixty-nine physicians were given one of the questionnaires at group meetings. Six others were handed the questionnaires individually. No names or other identifying marks were requested, thus assuring anonymity.

RESULTS

The mean probability assigned to each diagnosis by each group is presented in Table 1. Comparisons between each hindsight group and the corresponding foresight estimate are indicated. Two rows do not sum to 100 because one physician in each of these rows made a small arithmetic error resulting in the estimates adding to a number other than 100. The data were nevertheless included.

Table 1 *Mean probabilities assigned to each diagnosis*

Group	N	Outcome provided	Reiter's	Post-streptococcal arthritis	Gout	Hepatitis
				Outcome evaluated		
Foresight	15	None	43.9	11.1	29.0	15.7[a]
Hindsight	15	Reiter's	39.2 (7)	15.2	24.7	20.9
Hindsight	15	Post-streptococcal arthritis	36.7	31.0 (11)	10.0	22.3
Hindsight	15	Gout	38.6	10.3	34.9 (7)	16.1[b]
Hindsight	15	Hepatitis	34.8	16.0	12.2	37.7[a] (13)

All probabilities are multiplied by 100. The numbers in parentheses indicate the number of physicians whose probability estimate for that particular diagnosis exceeded the corresponding foresight estimate.
[a] Row does not sum to 100.0 due to arithmetic error by one subject.
[b] Row does not sum to 100.0 due to rounding error.

Since parametric statistics involve the estimation of the parameter μ, and since the mean probability for a given diagnosis within a hindsight group is constrained by the other estimates in that group, nonparametric statistics were used. Thirty-eight out of 60 hindsight subjects gave higher probability estimates to the known-to-have-occurred diagnosis than the corresponding probability estimate obtained from the foresight group ($p < .02$, sign test). For each hindsight group we independently examined the number of physicians who gave a higher hindsight probability estimate to the known-to-have-occurred diagnosis than the estimate for that diagnosis generated by the foresight group. In the poststreptococcal arthritis hindsight group, 11 of 15 physicians ($p < .0625$), and in the serum hepatitis hindsight group, 13 of 15 physicians ($p < .005$), gave higher estimates than the corresponding foresight estimates. For each of the two hindsight groups corresponding to the diagnoses rated most likely by the foresight group (Reiter's and gout), only 7 of 15 physicians assigned higher hindsight probabilities than the foresight group had assigned.

DISCUSSION

The primary result was that the physicians exhibited the hindsight bias. However, the bias was restricted to the two diagnoses assigned the lowest probability estimates by the foresight group. For these diagnoses, the hindsight groups claimed they were two to three times as likely to make the diagnosis as the foresight group. This result replicates the findings of

Fischhoff (1977) and Wood (1978) who found that the hindsight bias is strongest for those events initially judged to be least plausible.

This study, like most prior related investigations in the psychological literature, used written material as the subject matter. The question remains whether the results of this study would generalize to actual clinical situations. Elstein, Shulman, and Sprafka (1978) have shown that studies employing "high-fidelity" simultations (professional actors "having" symptoms) gave very similar results to "low-fidelity" simulations (written descriptions of symptoms). This result, plus the fact that a case history from an actual patient was employed, leads us to feel confident in the validity of the results of this study.

The power of the hindsight bias may perhaps be best appreciated by considering an important difference between the present investigation and prior work by Fischhoff (1975). In Fischhoff's study, the stimulus material included historical events and psychotherapy case histories. For example, foresight subjects were given background information about the warring factions in the British–Gurka struggle and were asked to assign probabilities to various outcomes, such as a British victory or a Gurka victory. Hindsight subjects, who were given this background information plus a purported outcome, would have in general *no* prior knowledge with which to evaluate either the likelihood of the outcome or the influence of esoteric background information on the British (or Gurka) victory. The subject was making the judgment from a position of virtually complete ignorance, therefore rendering himself or herself susceptible to bias. The situation in the present experiment is different. The physicians have a great deal of knowledge about the likelihood of various diseases and about the relation between the given symptoms and diseases. Compared to Fischhoff's subjects, the physicians are far better equipped to make an informed decision. Yet even from this relatively advantageous position, the physicians are still susceptible to bias in their judgments. This suggests to us that the hindsight bias is extremely compelling, even though it is limited to less probable diagnoses.

The demonstration of hindsight bias among practicing physicians has several important implications. The presence of the bias suggests that individuals in this study tried to make sense out of what they knew had happened rather than analyzing the available data independently. This is the situation faced by a physician who is asked to see a patient in consultation and render a second opinion or assume care for a patient previously managed by another physician. The hindsight bias would result in second opinions corroborating first opinions. In short, diagnostic accuracy may be compromised by knowledge of previous diagnoses.

Knowledge of the hindsight bias also has important implications for medical education. Most clinical and medical education occurs in a practical setting. Students work with groups of physicians who have the primary responsibility for diagnosis and patient care. If the students have continuous access to patients' diagnoses, they are likely to become overconfident in assessing their own diagnostic accuracy and may not appreciate the initial difficulty of making the diagnosis they subsequently review. This sort of retrospective analysis is probably not optimal given the compelling nature of the hindsight bias.

REFERENCES

Arkes, H. R., & Harkness, A. R. The effect of making a diagnosis on subsequent recognition of symptoms. *Journal of Experimental Psychology: Human Learning and Memory,* 1980, 6, 568–575.
Elstein, A. S., Shulman, A. S., & Sprafka, S. A. *Medical problem solving: An analysis of clinical reasoning.* Cambridge, Mass.: Harvard University Press, 1978.
Fischhoff, B. Hindsight≠foresight; The effect of outcome knowledge on judgment under uncertainty. *Journal of Experimental Psychology: Human Perception and Performance,* 1975, 1, 288–299.
   Perceived informativeness of facts. *Journal of Experimental Psychology: Human Perception and Performance,* 1977, 3, 349–358.
Slovic, P., & Fischhoff, B. On the psychology of experimental surprises. *Journal of Experimental Psychology: Human Perception and Performance,* 1977, 3, 544–551.
Wood, G. The knew-it-all-along effect. *Journal of Experimental Psychology: Human Perception and Performance,* 1978, 4, 345–353.

20

~

HOW DECISIONS ARE REACHED: PHYSICIAN AND PATIENT*

Stephen A. Eraker, Peter Politser

How can physicians consider patient preferences in reaching medical decisions? Few empirical findings are available to guide the physician. A number of investigators have found that people generally want to be informed about potential risks.[1–7] Patient participation in medical decisions appears to be increasing, possibly as a result of public dissatisfaction with the medical profession or due to basic questioning of physician autonomy and expertise.[8–15] A recent review [12] concludes that because of the uncertainties associated with most medical decisions, physicians who assume complete autonomy for medical decisions put themselves in a very difficult ethical position. As medical decisions become technically more complex and are associated with greater costs to the patient, physicians have been increasingly motivated to incorporate patient preferences in these critical decisions.[16–19]

Certainly these factors are more relevant in some situations than in others. Clinical decisions that are particularly ambiguous are characterized by uncertainty and the need to make value judgments about what risks are worth taking. Is the risk of operative mortality from coronary artery bypass grafting justified by the possibility of an improved length or quality of life? The optimal decision for a skilled laborer whose angina precludes physical work might be coronary artery surgery, whereas the optimal decision for the sedentary office clerk might be medical management. Because of patient preferences, the best decision for one patient need not be the same as that for another nearly identical patient.

The question of how value judgments should be incorporated in decisions is a difficult one. Although it is the patient who must live with the results of a decision, many patients believe that the physician who regularly treats many conditions never experienced by the patient is best able to understand the possible outcomes and to ascertain what risks are

---

* First published in *Annals of Internal Medicine*, 97 (1982), 262—8. © 1982 American College of Physicians. Reprinted by permission.

worth taking. Some family physicians who have known patients for many years may be in a good position to estimate their patient's preferences informally. There are also situations in which the physician clearly cannot rely on direct statements of patient preference. In the case where the patient's mental state is either impaired or questionable, this may be impractical. The preferences of an agitated patient may be difficult to ascertain, those of a schizophrenic patient may be difficult to understand, and those of a comatose patient may be impossible to ascertain (except as expressed through relatives). Also, the physician may feel that it is improper to be overly explicit about a subject as sensitive as trade-offs between life and disability. The physician may not want to arouse the patient's concern over a hypothetical state that is extremely unlikely. Because of this, some patients may be most comfortable in placing complete faith in the judgment of the physician. However, it may sometimes be wise to question whether physicians are too willing to accept this responsibility. Sometimes it may simply be emotionally easier and less time-consuming to paternalistically make therapeutic recommendations. This approach may not always serve the patient's best interests.

Most physicians would probably agree about the importance of considering all significant aspects of alternative therapies with patient preferences in mind. However, even when patients can discuss their wishes, the course of action may be unclear. For example, how can physicians evaluate critical trade-offs such as benefit and risk or quality and quantity of life? One proposed solution has been to use a quantitative method called decision analysis to measure patient preferences and to use these values to reach a decision.

DECISION ANALYSIS

Decision analysis offers a precise quantitative method for patients to express their views about the acceptability of the various risks and benefits of diagnostic and therapeutic interventions.[20–22] Advocates have claimed that decision analysis enhances effective decision making by providing for logical, systematic analysis and by prescribing a course of action that will conform most fully to the decision maker's own goals, expectations, and values.[23–26] Decision analysis is considered by some to be particularly useful in major medical decisions when health outcomes are unique and unfamiliar and there is ample time available for deliberation before action. Recent reviews have shown numerous medical applications of decision analysis, although most involved hypothetical situations.[27–29]

The basis for decision analysis is the theory of expected utility.[30] This theory derives from a set of principles that are thought to satisfy criteria for rational choices, that is, the choices a person should make. A consequence of the theory is that these choices can be represented by quantitative measurements of the value of the various outcomes to that person. ("Value" is sometimes distinguished from the "utility" of an outcome, depending on the method of assessment;[32] we will not make such a distinction in this paper.) For example, the value of a drug in treating headaches might be expressed as the duration of pain relief. The expected utility of an outcome would then be obtained by multiplying the duration of relief by its probability of occurrence. According to the theory, when faced with a choice, a person will prefer the outcome that offers the highest expected utility.[20–22,31,32]

Several studies have evaluated patient preferences on the benefits and risk of alternative therapies. McNeil and associates[33] have used an expected utility approach to study the attitudes of patients with lung cancer toward the risks of therapy. Risk-aversive patients valued life during the next few months much more than a gamble for longer life. The implication of an expected utility analysis[15] that some patients with operable lung cancer would choose radiation therapy over surgery, even though surgery offers a higher probability for long-term survival. Radiation therapy appears more attractive to some patients because it avoids any short-term operative risk. McNeil and associates[34] recently investigated attitudes of healthy volunteers with hypothetical carcinoma of the larynx to ascertain preferences for longevity and voice preservation. To maintain their voices, according to measurements of their values, approximately 20% of volunteers should choose radiation instead of surgery.

Krischer[35] assessed value judgments from physicians and families of children with cleft lip and palate. He found differences in values affecting the desirability of treatment. Pauker[24] considered hypothetical preference for medical and surgical therapy for coronary artery disease in light of severity. Coronary bypass surgery would be theoretically preferred by most patients with disabling angina but not by asymptotic patients. In all of these examples decision analysis offered a convenient means for patients to express their views about the acceptability of various risks and restrictions of life style. These studies are considered to represent the state of the art of applied decision analysis and show that a consideration of patient preferences could potentially have an important effect on therapeutic decisions. The studies indicated that patient values could be articulated within an analytic framework oriented to practical decision making, and could be combined with physician judgment about outcome probabilities to yield shared decisions. Whether it would be wise to do this is another question.

Decision analysis claims a number of advantages and is said to be explicit, quantitative, and prescriptive.[20] Decision analysis is explicit in that it forces the decision maker to structure the decision problem and break it into its components. This procedure may help foster completeness and avoid the potentially detrimental simplifications of the unaided decision maker. Decision analysis is intended to maintain the essential ingredients and ensure that they are used in a manner logically consistent with the decision maker's basic preferences.[36]

Within the decision analysis framework, one can identify the location, extent, and importance of any areas of disagreement, and ascertain if any such disagreements have a significant impact on the indicated decision. For example, a patient and physician might disagree about the importance of a 2-week convalescence after an elective cholecystectomy. Furthermore, any changes in the circumstances bearing on a decision problem can be incorporated into the existing analysis by changing values and by adding or altering the scope of the problem.

Another potential advantage derives from the fact that decision analysis is quantitative. The decision maker must specify the probabilities and be precise about the values placed on outcomes. Decision analysis does not replace physicians with arithmetic or change the role of clinical judgment in decision making. Rather, it aids skilled physicians by providing them with mathematical techniques to support, supplement, and ensure the internal consistency of their judgments. Also, there is considerable depth to the thinking and logic underlying quality decision analysis. Although it is argued that decision analysis oversimplifies the situation, it may provide a complete evaluation of complex problems that would be difficult to achieve with clinical judgment alone.

Decision analysis may, therefore be a valuable aid to physicians. How strictly the results of such an analysis should be followed, however, has been subject to considerable controversy.[25,32] Although the results of these analyses may provide useful information, most research on decisions has involved hypothetical situations. There may be questions as to when the recommendations should actually be followed. Indeed, a number of such questions arise when one reviews the psychological literature on how people actually make decisions. It is precisely at this point that a body of psychological research, sometimes referred to as behavioral decision theory, has fundamentally challenged the validity of applied decision analysis. The implications of this challenge for the practicing physician concerned with patient participation in medical decisions are not trivial.

BEHAVIORAL DECISION THEORY

Behavioral decision theory is a body of research and theory about how people actually think and use information in making decisions. Gross discrepancies have been noted between expected behavior according to prescriptive models of decision analysis and the actual descriptive behavior of decision makers.[36-42] This body of research should be distinguished from studies of social-psychological factors affecting decisions. Such factors are included in models that predict compliance with preventive health recommendations or therapeutic regimens.[43,50] One such model, the Health Belief Model, contains the concepts of utility and probability and is conceptually consistent with decision analysis.[45] This model does not, however, fully explain the topic of our subsequent discussion: why many people do not make choices consistent with the principles of decision analysis.[51]

One issue often mentioned in behavioral decision theory concerns problems with decision analysis due to the unfamiliarity of the outcomes. Patients and physicians are most likely to have clear values on medical outcomes that are familiar, simple, and directly experienced.[52] Many medical decisions, however, take us into new situations for which we have never considered our preferences, for example, coronary artery surgery. Whether or not decision analysis is used, the outcomes may be unfamiliar, but legitimate concerns have been expressed about the wisdom of attempting to quantify values in these situations.

Furthermore, decision analysis assumes that people have reasonably well-defined preferences. Methods used to ascertain patient or physician values are said to be neutral tools that translate subjective values into quantitative expression.[52] We all recognize, however, that both physicians and patients at times have difficulty knowing what they want. In this circumstance, the way the physician asks the patient what he or she wants may become major forces in shaping the values expressed. Physicians can induce random error by confusing the patients, systematic error by hinting at the "correct" response, or unduly extreme judgments by requiring patients to express their wishes with more clarity and coherence than warranted.[52] Also, relative subtle changes in the formulation or framing of choice problems have been found to cause significant shifts of preference between options.[42]

Additional problems with decision analysis involve probability reasoning. A great deal of effort has been devoted to understanding how people perceive and use probabilities of uncertain events. This research indicates that people often make substantial errors in judging probabilities or making predictions.[36,40-42,53] Some of these have been attributed to the use of judgmental heuristics or over-simplification strategies that make complex tasks more simple. Although these strategies may sometimes lead to appropriate decisions, they do not always and may introduce serious biases into the decision process by affecting interpretation of both values and probabilities. Although not an exhaustive listing, biases that may be significant to the physician concerned about considering patient preferences in medical decision making include: risks involving gains and losses, the framing effect, the certainty effect, sunk costs, regret, availability, vividness, and anchoring and adjustment.

RISK INVOLVING GAINS AND LOSSES

Contrasting attitudes involving gains and losses have been shown in various problems.[42,54] These attitudes raise concern about value-assessment methods, even when they do not directly violate decision analytic principles. Patient preferences for hypothetical choices between drug therapies for severe headaches, hypertension, and chest pain were recently examined by Eraker and Sox.[55] To characterize attitudes to various therapeutic situations, a questionnaire was used that depicted scenarios involving choices between alternative drug treatments.

The scenarios described well-recognized drug effects. However, the duration of these effects and the probability of their occurrence were assigned hypothetical values. Patterns of patient preference in drug therapy decisions with uncertain outcomes were characterized by analyzing choices of therapy. In each scenario, the patient chose between two drugs with equivalent effects, one having two possible outcomes occurring by chance ("uncertain outcome") and the other drug having a single outcome ("certain outcome"). When outcomes were described as gains, most patients were averse to risk. Significantly more patients chose a certain and intermediate number of hours of pain relief rather than taking a chance on an uncertain outcome of equal expected value that involved either no effect or a very large favorable effect. For example, assume that a patient faced a choice between a drug that provided 1 hour of pain relief versus a drug that would give 2 hours of relief if it worked, but had only a 50% chance of working. Most patients would prefer the 1 hour of pain relief for certain, even though the expected number of hours of pain relief for the uncertain outcome (50% × 2 hours of pain relief = 1 hour of pain relief) was the same. When the outcomes were described as losses, most patients were willing to take a risk. Given the choice between many hours of nausea with a chance at experiencing no adverse reaction, and an equally valued certain and intermediate adverse drug effect, more patients preferred the former risk. No significant differences were found between patients who actually suffered from the ailments described and patients who did not.

The principal conclusion of Eraker and Sox[55] is that patients' attitudes towards risk may differ in different therapeutic situations and depend on how information is presented to them. For example, a patient with leukemia may prefer to take a drug that is almost certain to provide an intermediate extension of life rather than take a drug that might provide a greater extension of life but might not work at all. If a physician were discussing the choice of two alternative therapeutic drugs, there could be an emphasis on comparing their favorable effects or comparing their adverse effects. Emphasizing the therapeutic effects of the two drugs might lead the patient to a different decision than if the adverse effects were compared.

Another implication of the patient preference work of Eraker and Sox[55] concerns the dilemma of how far physicians should look into the future when portraying possible outcomes of treatment to the patient. The portrayal of future possible outcomes may have a significant effect on patient preferences. For example, if a particular analgesic has a 50 percent chance of not giving significant pain relief to a patient on a given day, the patient may not be very impressed with the possible benefits. However, if the success of the drug is variable across repeated administrations, the probability of some effect during the next week may be much greater. That is, over a week of repeated administration the chance of significant pain relief might be 80%. If we present information based on repeated days of therapy as opposed to discussing the therapeutic results for a single day, patient preferences may change considerably.

THE FRAMING EFFECT

In one study, respondents were asked to estimate the risks of an unnamed oral contraceptive described in two package inserts distributed by the manufacturer, one designed for doctors and one for patients.[56] Readers of the patients' form thought that the risk of death from blood clots was 5.1 times as great for users as for non-users. Readers of the doctors' form thought that the risk was "only" 2.5 times as great. By contrast, readers of the patients' form estimated a much lower overall death rate of 1 in 40,000 compared with 1 in 2,000 for readers of the doctors' form. The risk of death seemed greater in the doctors' form by one measure and less by another almost identical measure. The reason for this discrepancy involves framing or presentation of the information. The patients' version gave a number of representative death and morbidity rates, showing that an absolute value of risk that seemed relatively high was actually an order of magnitude smaller. It appears that different numerical values may be attached to the same information, depending on the framing of the information.[42]

THE CERTAINTY EFFECT

It is often possible to frame protective health action in either certain or uncertain form. In the following hypothetical illustration, a 60-year-old white woman with Hodgkin's disease for the past 5 years is told that pneumococcal vaccine would provide full protection against the specific risk of pneumococcal pneumonia. She decides to receive the pneumococcal vaccine. Three years later she is again advised to receive the vaccine but told that it would provide partial protection against either bacterial or viral pneumonia. She decides not to receive the immunization. A given behavior may appear more attractive when it is presented as an elimination of a specific risk, pneumococcal pneumonia, than when it is described as a general reduction of risk from bacterial or viral pneumonia.

The "certainty effect" indicates that a reduction of probability of an outcome by a constant factor has more impact when the outcome was initially certain than when it was merely probable.[40,42] Tversky and Kahneman[42] found that in a question dealing with a hypothetical epidemic, most respondents preferred an 80 percent chance to lose 100 lives to a sure loss of 75 lives. Respondents also preferred a 10 percent chance to lose 75 lives to an 8 percent chance of losing 100 lives. That is, a reduction of the probabilities by a constant factor of one-tenth completely changed people's preferences. As indicated by Tversky and Kahneman,[42] this violated a fundamental axiom of expected utility theory, the theory used in decision analyses. The certainty effect shows that outcomes perceived with certainty are overweighted relative to uncertain outcomes. The contrast between the reduction and elimination of risk indicates how the manipulation of certainty can influence preferences.

The certainty effect may be relevant to the interpretation of many decision analyses, such as the study by McNeil and associates[33] involving patients with lung cancer. Here a hypothetical situation was examined in which patients considered a choice between surviving for 25 years and dying immediately. The patient was asked to specify the period of certain survival he would consider equivalent to that gamble. The results of many patients disclosed an underlying tendency to prefer certain survival for a number of years. This result has been interpreted as risk aversion, that people prefer a guaranteed moderately good outcome over a gamble on either a very good or a very poor result. For such a risk-averse patient, the utility of "living for 2 years" for certain is greater than the utility of an even chance at "living for 4 years" and "immediate or perioperative death." The finding of risk aversion, however, could have been due to an underlying preference for certainty not explainable in the context of expected utility theory. The use of decision analyses based on expected utility theory to make treatment recommendations might not reflect the patient's true preferences for longevity. We are not implying that McNeil and associates did anything unusual in their analysis and do not mean to discount their contribution. The methods used in their study are well established and often recommended by decision analysts. However, as McNeil and associates[33] themselves carefully observed, physicians desiring to incorporate patient preferences by using expected utility theory should proceed cautiously. The potentially serious problems with the measurement of preferences noted here give added reason for such caution. People frequently exhibit patterns of preference that appear incompatible with expected utility theory.[40,42]

SUNK COSTS

Economic theory implies that historical or sunk costs should be irrelevant to the consumer. Consider the following example from Thaler:[57] "A man joins a tennis club and pays a $300 yearly membership fee. After 2 weeks of playing he develops a tennis elbow. He continues to play (in pain) saying "I don't want to waste the $300.'" Suppose that the man says he would not have played if given a free membership, which would be a different situation than having paid for it. The willingness to continue playing in pain would be an example of a change in preference due to sunk costs.

Behavioral decision research has found that sunk costs, in this case the $300, are important in decision making. It has been shown that as people lose, they often do not adjust the reference point from which they evaluate their losses. Subsequently they may take bets that would be normally unacceptable. This is supported by the observation that bets on long shots are most popular on the last race of the day. Bettors apparently have not adapted to their losses and are trying to make up for them.[42,57] Physicians also may need to consider the contribution of sunk costs in considering preferences of their patients. If physicians were to point out such biases to their patients, this could be a step toward modifying behavior that is not in the patients' best interests.

REGRET

Patients with very minor symptoms not needing medical attention often visit the physician. Physicians find this difficult to understand. A partial explanation may be provided by psychological research on preference, specifically the regret phenomenon. This is illustrated by the following example of a 45-year-old man who smokes, with a cough for the past 2 weeks. He must decide whether to spend $20 to see the physician. Most patients and physicians find decisions involving trade-offs between health care and money to be very distasteful.[57] A high-deductible health insurance policy forces persons to make such decisions, often at considerable psychic costs. If the decision is made not to see the physican, there will surely be regret if the cough continues or the patient is later found to have lung cancer. Regret may loom so large that the visit and roentgenogram will be sought even for very small probabilities of disease.

Regret could also cause patients to minimize involvement in the decision making process. For example, suppose the patient has lung cancer, and the choice must be made between lobectomy and radiation therapy. Assuming that each procedure has the same probability of success, it has been argued that a rational patient would not want to know that a choice existed.[57] Based on a desire to avoid regret for having made or even contributed to the "wrong" decision, there is an incentive to let the physician choose. The assumption is that the physician knows the patient well and thus can do a good job of reflecting the patient's preferences. Unfortunately, there is scant empirical data describing patient preferences and almost no data on the ability of physicians to infer them. Although some paternalistic physicians may be more comfortable not involving the patient, it is significant that this ethically requires the physician to bear most and possibly all of the responsibility costs for unfortunate medical outcomes.[57]

AVAILABILITY

Availability refers to the tendency for people to judge the likelihood of an event by the ease with which relevant instances can be recalled.[58] For instance, a 72-year-old white man with untreated severe hypertension presented in the emergency room complaining of blurred vision. After documenting the presence of papilledema, the physician informs the patient that he needs to be admitted in order to treat his malignant hypertension. The patient refuses to be admitted, stating that his 74-year-old brother had recently died in the hospital.

When physicians discuss the sensitive issue of longevity with patients, it is important to be aware that availability is not unduly biasing the discussion. Availability suggests that judgments will be influenced by both direct experience with death of friends and relatives, as well as by indirect exposure through movies, books, television, and newspaper.[59]

VIVIDNESS

The vividness of some health related experiences may also influence patient preferences in medical decisions.[41] A 55-year-old white woman notices a lump in her right breast. She avoids mentioning this to her family as well as her physician because her mother died many years ago of painful, metastatic breast cancer.

Research indicates that very significant information may have little effect on decisions, merely because it is pallid. By contrast, concrete, emotionally stimulating data will have a disproportionate effect on decisions.[60] One study[59] indicates that the frequency of occurrence of dramatic events such as cancer, homicide, or multiple-death catastrophes are overestimated because of the disproportionately greater publicity. In contrast, unremarkable or less dramatic events such as asthma, diabetes, and emphysema are underestimated. In addition to possibly showing the availability bias, this study shows that even the relatively intelligent persons in this study did not have valid perceptions about the frequency of hazardous events to which they might be exposed. Physicians who involve patients in the decision making process should be aware of the potential impact of biases introduced by availability and vividness, which make the patient's true preferences more difficult to ascertain.

ANCHORING AND ADJUSTMENT

In anchoring, a natural starting point is used as a first approximation or anchor for the judgment.[37] The anchor is then adjusted to accommodate the implications of additional information. Often the adjustment is smaller than it should be considering the importance of new information. In one study, subjects were asked to judge the lethality of various potential causes of death such as influenza, hypertension, diabetes, heart attacks, and cancer.[61] One of four formally equivalent formats was used to judge lethality (such as, for each afflicted person who dies, how many survive? For each 100,000 persons afflicted, how many will die?) The judgments indicated a dramatic effect of framing on expressed risk perceptions. For example, when people estimated the lethality rate for influenza directly, their mean response was 393 deaths per 100,000 cases. When told that 80,000,000 people catch influenza in a normal year and asked to estimate the number who die, the respondents' mean estimated death rate was only six per 100,000 cases. Anchoring on the larger number changed the estimated rate by a factor of more than 60. Similar discrepancies occurred with other causes of death and hazards. These imply that physicians should exercise extreme care in presenting information. Although much more research is needed to ascertain what methods of presentation are better than others, the studies mentioned here should help make physicians aware of the potential dangers of using a single particular method.

DISCUSSION

The preceding review has discussed how physicians can consider patient preferences in reaching medical decisions. Although decision analysis is a means for encouraging patient participation in clinical decision making, it is based on hypothetical situations. A large body of empirically based research in behavioral decision theory indicates that there are many potential biases and distortions that could affect any recommendation based exclusively on decision analysis. Although not meant to be an exhaustive list, significant factors include: distortions in risks involving gains and losses, the framing effect, the certainty effect, sunk costs, regret, availability, vividness, and anchoring and adjustment. Some of these biases, such as the certainty effect, may cause direct violations of the principles on which decision analysis is based. Others, however, are only potential sources of bias in the measures of probability and value.

Many of these problems are not unique to decision analysis and may affect social-psychological approaches to patient behavior and decision making as well.[43–50] Also, they are likely to affect the way patients make decisions intuitively. The same body of behavioral decision research that suggests criticisms of decision analysis also suggests that our intuitive decision-making capacities may be severely limited.[27,42,51] In fact, it has been argued that informal decision making may be even more likely to be affected by these biases and distortions.[28] Moreover, these biases may be harder to detect. People apparently can have great difficulty in storing and processing large amounts of information simultaneously without distorting it or leaving out important parts. Although decision analysis does not provide easy or unambiguous answers, it can focus attention on the right issues. It may help people to more adequately comprehend complex problems by breaking them down into smaller, more understandable events. Accordingly, patients may be aided by decision analysis despite the potential biases.

It is even possible that physician judgment could be helped by these techniques. Some literature suggests that physicians may be vulnerable to certain biases and omissions.[27,62–66] There is legitimate controversy over this issue, which has been reviewed in detail by Politser.[27] However, the current evidence provides reason for concern and motivates further research.

It is uncertain what the physician should do in advance of the needed research. Should we accept the limitations of intuitive judgment or should we use decision analysis when possible, even if it may introduce certain biases? To obtain a more definitive answer to these questions, it will be important to ascertain whether estimates of probabilities and values are subject to predictable biases. These biases, if recognized, might be eliminated by alternative presentations of information or by numerical corrections in the measurements. We believe decision analysis can sometimes be a useful tool for both patient and physician if applied with caution. Although decision analysis undoubtedly will have a role in medical decisions and the allocation of scarce medical resources, it is still in an early stage of development and many problems need to be resolved before we can reap its full benefits. With or without this technologic aid, if physicians are to better serve the patient's best interests they must understand the way patients perceive and evaluate medical risks and benefits. From research thus far, this seems to depend heavily on the way the information is presented. We hope the discussion of common biases of decision making will help physicians to better understand patient preferences. In critical decisions of great consequences to the patient, whether decision analysis is used formally or not, this enhanced understanding could be a major contribution to quality of patient care.

REFERENCES

1 Alfidi, R.J. Informed consent: a study of patient reaction. *JAMA*, 1971;216:1325–9.
2 Weinstein, N.D. Seeking reassuring or threatening information about environmental cancer. *J. Behav. Med.* 1979;2:125–39.
3 Schwartz, E.D. The use of a checklist in obtaining informed consent for treatment with medication. *Hosp. Community Psychiatry.* 1978;29:97–100.
4 Roling, G.T., Pressgrove, L.W., Keeffe, E.B., Raffin, S.B. An appraisal of patients' reactions to "informed consent" for peroral endoscopy. *Gastrointest. Endosc.* 1977;24:69–70.
5 Bergler, J.H., Pennington, A.C., Metcalfe, M., Fries, E. Informed consent: how much does the patient understand? *Clin. Pharmacol. Ther.* 1980;27:435–40.
6 Joubert, P., Lasagna, L. Commentary: patient package inserts: 1. Nature, notions, and needs. *Clin. Pharmacol. Ther.* 1975;18:507–13.
7 Morris, L.A., Mazis, M., Gordon, E. A survey of the effects of oral contraceptive patient information. *JAMA.* 1977;238:2504–8.
8 Reinhard, E.H. Medicine and the crisis in confidence. *Pharos.* 1974;37:117–23.
9 Chapman, C.B. Doctors and their autonomy: past events and future prospects. *Science.* 1978;200:851–6.
10 Haug, M.R., Lavin, B. Public challenge of physician authority. *Med. Care.* 1979;17:844–58.
11 Brody, D.S. Feedback from patients as a means of teaching the nontechnological aspects of medical care. *J. Med. Educ.* 1980;55:34–41.
12 Brody, D.S. The patient's role in clinical decision-making. *Ann. Intern. Med.* 1980;93:718–22.
13 Tancredi, L.R., Barsky, A.J. Technology and health care decision making – conceptualizing the process for societal informed consent. *Med. Care.* 1974;12:845–59.
14 Pellegrino, E.D. Medical ethics, education, and the physician's image [Editorial]. *JAMA.* 1976;235:1043–4.
15 Slack, W.V. The patient's right to decide. *Lancet.* 1977;2:240.
16 Becker, E.L. Finite resources and medical triage. *Am. J. Med.* 1979;66:549–50.
17 Turnbull, A.D., Carlon, G., Baron, R., Sichel, W., Young, C., Howland, W.

The inverse relationship between cost and survival in the critically ill cancer patient. *Crit. Care Med.* 1979;7:20–3.

18 Childress, J.F. Rationing of medical treatment. In: Reich, W.T. ed. *Encyclopedia of Bioethics.* New York: Macmillan Publishing Co.; 1979; 1414–9.

19 Zook, C.J., Moore, F.D. High-cost users of medical care. *N. Engl. J. Med.* 1980;302:996–1002.

20 Weinstein, M.C., Fineberg, H.V., Elstein, A.S. *et al. Clinical Decision Analysis.* Philadelphia: W.B. Saunders Company: 1980.

21 Raiffa, H. *Decision Analysis: Introductory Lectures on Choices under Uncertainty.* Reading, Massachusetts: Addison-Wesley; 1968.

22 Howard, R.A. The foundations of decision analysis. *IEEE Trans. Systems Sci. Cybernetics.* 1968;SSC-4(3):211–9.

23 Schwartz, W.B., Gorry, G.A., Kassirer, J.P., Essig, A. Decision analysis and clinical judgment. *Am. J. Med.* 1973;55:459–72.

24 Pauker, S.G. Coronary artery surgery: the use of decision analysis. *Ann. Intern. Med.* 1976;85:8–18.

25 Howard, R. An assessment of decision analysis. *Operations Research.* 1980;28:4–27.

26 Eraker, S.A., Sasse, L. The serum digoxin test and digoxin toxicity: a bayesian approach to decision making. *Circulation.* 1981;64:409–20.

27 Politser, P.E. Decision analysis and clinical judgment: a reevaluation. *Med. Decision Making.* 1981;1:361–89.

28 Krischer, J.P. An annotated bibliography of decision analytic applications to health care. *Operations Research.* 1980;28:97–113.

29 Albert, D.A. Decision theory in medicine: a review and critique. *Milbank Mem. Fund Q.* 1978;56:362–401.

30 Von Neumann, J., Morgenstern, O. *Theory of Games and Economic Behavior.* Princeton, New Jersey: Princeton University Press; 1947.

31 McNeil, B.J., Keeler, E., Adelstein, S.J. Primer on certain elements of medical decision making. *N. Engl. J. Med.* 1975;293:211–5.

32 Keeney, R.L., Raiffa, H. *Decisions with Multiple Objectives: Preferences and Value Tradeoffs.* New York: John Wiley & Sons, Inc.; 1976.

33 McNeil, B.J., Weichselbaum, R., Pauker, S.G. Fallacy of the five-year survival in lung cancer. *N. Engl. J. Med.* 1978;299:1397–401.

34 McNeil, B.J., Weichselbaum, R., Pauker, S.G. Speech and survival: Tradeoffs between quality and quantity of life in laryngeal cancer. *N. Engl. J. Med.* 1981;305:982–7.

35 Krischer, J.P. The mathematics of cleft lip and palate treatment evaluation: measuring the desirability of treatment outcomes. *Cleft Palate J.* 1976;13:165–80.

36 Slovic, P. Toward understanding and improving decisions. In: Howell, W.C., Fleishman, E.A., eds. *Human Performance and Productivity. Vol. 2. Information Processing and Decision Making.* Hillsdale, New Jersey: Erlbaum Associates; 1982.

37 Tversky, A., Kahneman, D. Judgment under uncertainty: heuristics and biases. *Science.* 1974;185:1124–31.

38 Slovic, P., Fischhoff, B., Lichtenstein, S. Cognitive process and societal risk

taking. In: Carroll, J., Payne, J. eds. *Cognition and Social Behavior*. Hillsdale, New Jersey: Erlbaum Associates; 1976.

39 Slovic, P., Fischhoff, B., Lichtenstein, S. Behavioral decision theory. *Annu. Rev. Psychol.* 1977;28:1–39.

40 Kahneman, D., Tversky, A. Prospect theory: an analysis of decision under risk. *Econometrica.* 1979;47:263–91.

41 Nisbett, R., Ross, L. *Human Inference: Strategies and Shortcomings of Social Judgment*. Englewood Cliffs, New Jersey: Prentice-Hall; 1980.

42 Tversky, A., Kahneman, D. The framing of decisions and the psychology of choice. *Science.* 1981;211:453–8.

43 Cummings, K.M., Becker, M.H., Maile, M.C. Bringing the models together: an empirical approach to combining variables used to explain health actions. *J. Behav. Med.* 1980;3:123–45.

44 Rosenstock, I.M. Why people use health services. *Milbank Mem. Fund Q.* 1966;44:94–124.

45 Becker, M.H., ed. *The Health Belief Model and Personal Health Behavior*. Thorofare, New Jersey: Charles B. Slack, Inc.; 1974.

46 Kirscht, J.P. The health belief model and illness behavior. *Health Educ. Monogr.* 1974;2:60–81.

47 Becker, M.H., Haefner, D.P., Kasl, S.V., Kirscht, J.P., Maiman, L.A., Rosenstock, I.M. Selected psychosocial models and correlates of individual health-related behaviors. *Med. Care.* 1977;15(suppl. 5): 27–46.

48 Kirscht, J.D., Rosenstock, I.M. Patients' problems in following the recommendation of health experts. In: Stone, G., Cohen, F., Adler, N. eds. *Health Psychology*. New York: Jossey-Bass, Inc.; 1979:189–214.

49 Becker, M.H., Maiman, L.A. Patient compliance. In: Melmon, K.L., ed. *Drug Therapies: Concepts for Physicians*. New York: Elsevier/North Holland Inc.: 1981:65–79.

50 Lewin, K. *Resolving Social Conflicts*. New York: Harper and Brothers; 1948.

51 Cohen, L.J. On the psychology of prediction: whose is the fallacy? *Cognitition.* 1979;7:385–407.

52 Fischhoff, B., Slovic, P., Lichtenstein, S. Knowing what you want: measuring labile values. In: Wallsten, T.S., ed. *Cognitive Processes in Choice and Decision Behavior*. Hillsdale, New Jersey: Erlbaum Associates; 1980:117–41.

53 Einhorn, H.J., Hogarth, R.M. Behavioral decision theory: process of judgment and choice. *Annu. Rev. Psychol.* 1981;32:53–88.

54 Fishburn, P.C., Kochenberger, G.A. Two-piece Von Neumann-Morgenstern utility functions. *Decision Sciences.* 1979;10:503–18.

55 Eraker, S.A., Sox, H.C. Assessment of patients' preferences for therapeutic outcomes. *Med. Dec. Making.* 1981;1:29–39.

56 Fischhoff, B. *Informing People About the Risks of Oral Contraceptives*. Eugene, Oregon: Decision Research; 1980. (Decision Research Report 80–3).

57 Thaler, R. Toward a positive theory of consumer choice. *J. Econ. Behav. Organization.* 1980;1:39–60.

58 Tversky, A., Kahneman, D. Availability: a heuristic for judging frequency and probability. *Cognitive Psychol.* 1973;5:207–32.

59 Lichtenstein, S., Slovic, P., Fischhoff, B., Layman, M., Combs, B. Judged frequency of lethal events. *Exp. Psychol. Hum. Learn.* 1978;4:551–78.

60 Nisbett, R., Borgida, E., Crandall, R., Reed, H. Popular induction: information is not necessarily informative. In: Carroll, J., Payne, J. eds. *Cognition and Social Behavior*. Hillsdale, New Jersey: Erlbaum Associates; 1976:113–33.

61 Fischhoff, B., MacGregor, D. *Judged Lethality*. Eugene, Oregon: Decision Research: 1980. (Decision Research Report 80-4).

62 Elstein, A.S. Clinical judgement: psychological research and medical practice. *Science.* 1976;194:696–700.

63 Detmer, D.E., Fryback, D.G. and Gassner, K. Heuristics and biases in medical decision-making. *J Med Educ.* 1978;53:682–3

64 Politser, P.E. Reliability, decision rules and the value of repeated tests. *Med Dec Making.* 1982;2:47–69

65 Politser, P.E. Computer-based consultation for repeated diagnostic tests. In: O'Neill, J.T., ed. *Proceedings of the Fourth Annual Symposium on Computer Applications in Medical Care*. Washington, D.C.: IEEE; 1980.

66 Politser, P.E. *The Evaluation of Repeated Medical Tests: Logical and Statistical Considerations* [Dissertation]. Ann Arbor: University of Michigan. 1982. 222 pp.

21

~

THE MEASUREMENT OF PATIENTS' VALUES
IN MEDICINE*

*H. Llewellyn-Thomas, H.J. Sutherland, R. Tibshirani,
A. Ciampi, J.E. Till, N.F. Boyd*

INTRODUCTION

Judgments about the value of life in various states of health underlie many
if not all clinical decisions. For example, what risk of operative death
should a patient with malignant disease take in order to obtain a chance of
cure? What probable benefit from a drug justifies the risk of a disabling
side effect? Does the usefulness of the information derived from an
investigation outweigh the risk that must be taken in order to obtain it? To
answer these and other similar questions that arise every day in clinical
practice, two types of information are required. Not only is medical
information about the likelihood of various outcomes necessary, but
information about the relative values of the alternate outcomes is also
needed, and these values must be incorporated into the decision-making
process.

Although the values and experience of the physician are likely to
influence medical decisions, it is the patient's values that require particular
attention, especially in circumstances where treatment alternatives
involve trade-offs between the duration and the quality of life. Incorporation of patients' values into the decision-making process would be
simplified if these values could be made explicit, directly measured, and
quantitatively expressed, but despite the central importance of value
judgments to much medical decision making there is little information
available about how values should be measured, or about the factors that
influence their measurements.

Several methods exist for eliciting value judgments,[1-4] but the technique developed by Von Neumann and Morgenstern and known as the
"standard gamble"[4] is widely regarded as the reference method for
measuring values for health.[2-5] It has a well-established axiomatic basis
and a conceptual framework suitable for assessing attitudes toward
decision making under conditions of risk.

* First published in *Medical Decision Making*, 2 (1982), 449–62. © Birkhäuser Boston, Inc.
Reprinted by permission.

The standard gamble is best known to those concerned with utility and decision theory in economic analysis, but it is not restricted in its domain and has been used to obtain value judgments about different states of health, as well as to assess the attitudes of individual patients toward risk.[2,6,7]

When the standard gamble is used to measure an individual's value (or utility) for a health state, the procedure usually begins with presenting a written description of the health state (a scenario) to the individual whose opinion is being sought (the rater). After reading the scenario, the rater is asked to imagine a hypothetical situation in which he or she is confronted with a choice. The options available are to continue living in the state of health described in the scenario, or to take a gamble. The gamble, which might be expressed as taking a medication or having an operation, has two possible outcomes. The "best" outcome is usually the immediate restoration of perfect health, and the "worst" outcome is immediate death. This choice is illustrated in Figure 1 for a health state Y whose value is being sought. X and Z are the outcomes of the gamble – perfect health and death, respectively. The last step in the standard gamble is to systematically vary the probability (p) of attaining the best outcome of the gamble (state X) until a point is reached at which the rater is indifferent between continued life in state Y and taking the gamble. This value (p) is referred to as the rater's "indifference probability." The utility or value of state Y is then determined with the formula:[8]

$$U_y = (p)(U_x) + (1 - p)(U_z),$$

where U_x and U_z indicate, respectively, the utilities or values of states X and Z. When the "best" outcome of the gamble is perfect health, U_x is arbitrarily set at 1.0, and when death is the "worst" outcome, U_z is arbitrarily set at 0. With these outcomes, $U_y = p$.

If a rater perceives health state Y as particularly undesirable, his indifference probability will decrease – that is, he will be prepared to take

Figure 1   The choice in the standard gamble

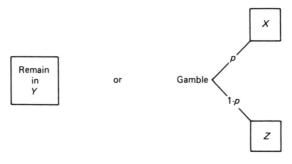

a greater risk to try to escape state *Y* – and therefore the utility for health state *Y* is low. On the other hand, if the rater considers health state *Y* as relatively tolerable, his indifference probability will increase – that is, he will be unwilling to take much risk in the gamble – and therefore the utility for health state *Y* is high.

The conceptual framework of the gamble does allow the substitution of outcomes other than perfect health and death in the gamble. When such substitutions are made the utilities for the substituted outcomes must be known, and could be determined by earlier gambles in which the values of these states were assessed against the outcomes of perfect health ($U = 1.0$) and death ($U = 0$). According to expected utility theory, the utility a rater assigns to a particular health state should not be influenced by the alternative outcomes offered in the gamble; a rater will adjust his indifference probability to allow for these alterations in the utility of the gamble outcomes.

We undertook this study to examine the influence of several factors on the measurement of utilities for different states of health. This paper is concerned with only one of these, the potential influence of different outcomes in the standard gamble. If the standard gamble is internally consistent we would expect to find that the utilities for different states of health would remain the same when other health states are substituted for perfect health and death as outcomes in the gamble. The effects of other factors on the process of measurement will be reported elsewhere.

METHODS

The general design of the study was to describe a series of health states in the form of written scenarios, to present these scenarios to a group of patients who served as raters, and to seek their opinions about the relative values of these health states. The patients first ranked the health states in descending order of preference, then utilities for the states were obtained using the standard gamble in three different ways.

Health states and scenarios. Interviews were conducted with patients being treated for a variety of malignant diseases. Twelve patients with a wide range of functional disability were selected, and written descriptions of their functional status and symptoms were presented according to two formats, examples of which are shown in Table 1. In Scenario Style 1, the dimensions of age, mobility, physical activity, social activity, and principal symptom or problem were described in the manner developed by Bush.[9] In Scenario Style 2, similar information was presented, but in a narrative format and written in the first person. A further systematic difference between the two scenario styles was that in Style 2 all symptoms or problems described by the patient were listed, whereas only the most prominent of these was mentioned in Style 1.

After pretesting, we selected five of the 12 sets of scenarios that provided the widest attainable spread of utilities as measured by the standard gamble.

Table 1 *Scenario styles*

Case E

Style 1

Age: 40–64 employee/housekeeper

Mobility: traveled freely

Physical activity: walked freely

Social activity: performed major but limited in other activities

Symptom/problem: general tiredness, weakness, or weight loss

Style 2

I am in the age range 40–64 years. I am able to work. Over the past year I have noticed a feeling of tiredness, and I have lost 20 pounds in weight. I have little energy, and I am unable to keep up with my usual routine. I have made an effort to walk to work, but I have let the house and hobbies "slide." I am sleeping poorly. I am maintaining my present weight.

Case A

Style 1

Age: 40–64 employee/housekeeper

Mobility: traveled freely

Physical activity: walked freely

Social activity: did not perform major but performed self care activities

Symptom/problem: pain in chest, stomach, side, back, or hips

Style 2

I am in the age range 40–64 years. I am unable to work. I am tired and sleep poorly due to discomfort in my back and arm. I am worried about my health and finances. I am able to drive my car, and I make an effort to work about my neighborhood.

Case D

Style 1

Age: 40–64 employee/housekeeper

Mobility: traveled with difficulty

Physical activity: walked with limitations

Social activity: did not perform major but performed self care activities

Symptom/problem: general tiredness, weakness, or weight loss

Style 2

I am in the age range 40–64 years. I have been tired and weak and unable to work. I have lost 15 pounds in weight. I walk slowly, and travel outside the house is difficult. Much of the day I am alone, lying down in my bedroom. Social contact with my friends is reduced.

Case C

Style 1

Age: 40–64 employee/housekeeper

Mobility: in house

Physical activity: walked with limitations

Social activity: did not perform major but performed self care activities

Symptom/problem: sick or upset stomach, vomiting, or diarrhea (watery bowel movements)

Style 2

I am in the age range 40–64 years. I live alone and am confined to my home. During the past six months I have lost 35 pounds in weight. I am only able to eat small amounts of food at present and I vomit occasionally. I am tired and weak and walk with the aid of a walker. I require assistance to get into and out of the bathtub. Social contact with my friends and family is infrequent.

Table 1 *continued*

Case B	
Style 1	**Style 2**
Age: 40–64 employee/housekeeper	I am in the age range 40–64 years. Although I worked until recently, I am presently hospitalized and on complete bed rest. A nurse bathes, dresses, and feeds me. I am confused about time and place and have some memory loss. I have vomited and am only able to take clear fluids by mouth. I am dehydrated (lack water) and receive fluids by vein (IV therapy). I am incontinent (unable to control my bowels and bladder) and presently have a catheter (tube into the bladder). I have low back pain.
Mobility: in hospital	
Physical activity: in bed	
Social activity: required assistance with self care	
Symptom/problem: trouble learning, remembering, or thinking clearly	

Patient raters. The raters in this study were 64 outpatients receiving radiotherapy for the treatment of malignant disease. Patients were selected if they appeared well enough to participate in the study and were available on a second occasion four to seven days after the first contact. Altogether, 80 patients were approached for the study. Because of language difficulties, impaired hearing or sight, or poor general health, 14 were considered unsuitable. Of the 66 patients who entered the study, two withdrew after the first interview because of deterioration in their health. No patient elected to withdraw because of difficulties encountered with the study.

The standard gamble was administered in this study by two interviewers (the authors HS and HLT), both registered nurses with extensive experience in eliciting preference judgments about health states. Rehearsing and testing were carried out before the study to ensure that the interviewers administered the standard gamble in a similar way and obtained similar results.

Measurement procedures. To illustrate the approach to identifying indifference probabilities, raters were first given a brief series of hypothetical exercises with the standard gamble, using monetary outcomes. They were then given the five health states, described in Scenario Style 1 or 2. The sequence in which the five health states were given to each rater and the style of scenarios used were both randomly determined. Raters were asked to rank the scenarios in descending order of preference. Perfect health and death, states that were subsequently used in the standard gamble itself, were not included in this ranking task. For the purposes of this study it was assumed that perfect health represented the highest attainable health state, and death the worst, and that all other health states occupied intermediate positions.

Table 2 *Examples of alternative outcomes of the standard gamble according to health state and method*

		Outcomes of gamble					
	Rank order	Method 1		Method 2		Method 3	
	of health states	Best	Worst	Best	Worst	Best	Worst
Most	E	Health	Death	Health	Death	Health	A
Preferred	A	Health	Death	E	Death	Health	D
	D	Health	Death	A	Death	Health	C
Least	C	Health	Death	D	Death	Health	B
Preferred	B	Health	Death	C	Death	Health	Death

After arranging the states in rank order, utilities were obtained for each state from each rater, using the standard gamble in the three ways described in Table 2. The three methods used are distinguished by the alternative outcomes for the gamble. In the first method, the "worst" outcome of the gamble was death, which was arbitrarily assigned the utility 0, while the "best" outcome of the gamble was perfect health, as defined by the World Health Organization (i.e., a state of complete physical, mental, and social well-being, not merely the absence of disease or infirmity), which was arbitrarily assigned the utility 1.0. The two outcomes of perfect health and death were the same for each of the five health states for which utilities were measured in the first method. Utilities obtained for the health states by this method became "reference utilities" for the remaining two methods.

In the second method, the "worst" outcome of the gamble was again death for all states, but the "best" outcome was determined by the rank order earlier assigned to the states by the rater. Thus, if Scenario E had been ranked first, the sequence of assessments in the second method began with judging Scenario E against the gamble outcomes of perfect health and death; then, if Scenario A had been ranked second after Scenario E, the gamble outcomes for assessing Scenario A were Scenario E and death. This process of systematically replacing the "best" gamble outcome with health states of sequentially decreasing value continued down the rank order of scenarios.

In the third method, the "best" outcome of the gamble was perfect health for all states, and the "worst" outcome was determined by the original rank order of the states assigned by the rater. Thus, if Scenario B had been ranked last, the sequence of assessments in the third method began with judging Scenario B against a gamble in which death and health were the outcomes; then, if Scenario C had been ranked immediately above Scenario B, the gamble outcomes were Scenario B and perfect health. This systematic substitution of health states for gamble outcome continued up the rank order of scenarios.

After completion of these procedures, the process was repeated with the same raters, and administered by the same interviewer, after an interval of four to seven days. The only change introduced on the second occasion was that the five scenarios were presented in the style to which the patient rater had not been exposed in the first part of the study.

The expected utility equation was used to compute the utilities assigned to each scenario by each of the three standard gamble methods. In computing the utilities generated by the second and third methods, the utilities assigned to the health states when they were employed as gamble outcomes were those obtained from the first or "reference" method.

RESULTS

Characteristics of the raters. The raters were aged 20 to 77, and the mean age was 55. There were 28 male and 36 female raters.

Rank ordering of the scenarios. Because of the process used to develop and select the scenarios employed in this study, we expected and obtained a high level of agreement about the order in which the scenarios would be ranked in order of preference. Fifty-four (84 percent) of the 64 raters ranked the five states described in the descending order E, A, D, C, and B. These 54 raters also ranked the scenarios in the same order on both interviews. Of the remaining ten raters, nine ranked the scenarios in the same E, A, D, C, B order in one of the two interviews. Differences in rank order in the other interviews generally involved only two cases of intermediate levels of health. One rater ranked the scenarios uniquely in the two interviews. When computing the utilities generated by the second and third methods, the rank order of the scenarios used for any given rater was always the order provided by that rater at that same interview.

Utilities obtained for the scenarios by the standard gamble. Figure 2 shows the mean utilities obtained from the 64 raters for each of the five scenarios described in Style 1, according to each of the three methods in which the standard gamble was administered. Figure 3 shows the mean utilities obtained according to the way in which the standard gamble was administered for the five scenarios, with the health states described in Style 2. In both figures, the mean utilities are plotted in descending rank order.

To make statistical comparisons between the mean utilities obtained for each scenario by these three methods, we adopted the mean utility obtained by the first method, in which the outcomes of the gamble were perfect health and death, as a reference with which to compare the mean utilities obtained by the other two methods. Statistical comparisons of mean values were made with the paired t-test, and the contrasts that achieved statistical significance are indicated in Figures 2 and 3.

The replications of the gamble that were built into the study were always separated by four different gambles, but gave virtually identical results. For Scenario E, the most preferred health state described, the outcomes of perfect health and death were offered in the gamble in both the first and second methods, and identical mean values were obtained on each occasion. Similarly, for the least desirable health state, Scenario B, the outcomes of perfect health and death were offered in the gamble in the first and third methods, and again similar mean values were obtained on each occasion.

As Figures 2 and 3 show, similar mean utilities were obtained with the first method (the reference gamble that had perfect health and death as the

Figure 2   Mean utilities for Style 1 scenarios, obtained by three standard gamble methods.
□ = standard gamble method 1 (perfect health and death as outcomes)
○ = standard gamble method 2 (death and other health states as outcomes)
● = standard gamble method 3 (perfect health and other health states as outcomes)
Statistical significance is indicated for paired t-tests of differences between method 1 results and results obtained with methods 2 and 3

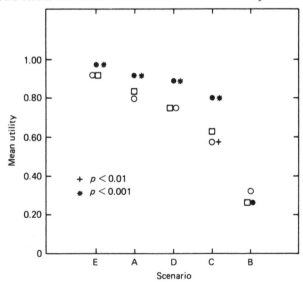

outcomes) and with the second method (in which the endpoint of perfect health was replaced in the gamble by the scenarios in descending order of preference). The two methods gave statistically significant differences in utilities for only one scenario in Style 1 and for two scenarios in Style 2.

However, mean utility values were substantially altered in the third method of administering the standard gamble, in which the outcome of death was replaced by the other health states in ascending order of preference. For each of the four health states for which this substitution was made, the mean utility was systematically different from that obtained with the other two methods used to administer the gamble. With both scenario styles, all four mean utilities were statistically higher than those obtained with the reference gamble.

These changes in attitude toward the health state according to the standard gamble method used to assess the state are illustrated in Table 3 for a single rater and one health state. The results shown are those obtained for one rater assessing the health state described in Scenario C,

Figure 3 Mean utilities for Style 2 scenarios, obtained by three standard gamble methods.
□ = standard gamble method 1 (perfect health and death as outcomes)
○ = standard gamble method 2 (death and other health states as outcomes)
● = standard gamble method 3 (perfect health and other health states as outcomes)
Statistical significance is indicated for paired *t*-tests of differences between method 1 results and results obtained with methods 2 and 3.

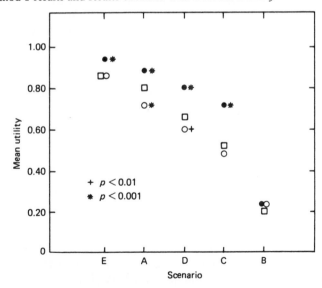

Table 3 *Examples of results of standard gamble according to method, for one rater and one health state*

Gamble method[a]	Health state assessed	Gamble outcomes[b]	p^c	UC^d
1	C	Perfect health (1.0) Death (0.0)	0.65	0.65
2	C	Scenario D (0.85) Death (0.0)	0.75	0.64
3	C	Perfect Health (1.0) Scenario B (0.45)	0.80	0.89

[a] See Methods for description.
[b] Utilities for outcomes in parentheses.
[c] p = Indifference probability for gamble.
[d] UC = Utility measured for health state C.

according to each of the three methods. In the first method, the probability at which this rater became indifferent between continued life in the state described in the scenario and the alternative outcomes offered in the gamble was 0.65; the utility of the health state described was thus also 0.65.

In the second method, the successful outcome of the gamble was the attainment of the state of health described in Scenario D, whose utility for this rater had previously been determined by the first method to be 0.85. The probability of success at which this rater was indifferent between continued life as described in Scenario C and the gamble with outcomes of life in Scenario D or death was 0.75. Thus, the utility of health state C as assessed by this method was approximately 0.65:

$$U_c = (0.75)(0.85) + (0.25)(0.00) = 0.64$$

In the third method, where death was replaced by Scenario B, the indifference probability was 0.80. The utility of Scenario B for this rater had previously been determined by the first method to be 0.45. Therefore, the utility of health state C as assessed by this method was substantially higher than the value obtained by the other two methods:

$$U_c = (0.80)(1.0) + (0.20)(0.45) = 0.89$$

Additional analyses.   As mentioned in the Introduction, the results reported here are part of a more extensive investigation of factors that might influence utility measurement, and those results will be reported in a subsequent paper. Scenario style did significantly influence the utility for health states. In particular, scenarios presented in Style 2 were consistently assigned lower utilities than were scenarios presented in Style 1; possibly health states described in the narrative format of Style 2 are more vividly imagined by raters.

Factors that did not significantly influence the utility included the interviewer, the sequence in which the patient was presented with the different scenario styles, and the patient's self-assessment of his own state of health, using a 10 cm linear analogue scale with the endpoints "Death" and "Perfect Health."[10,11] Further analyses were carried out to determine whether the significant differences between utilities obtained with Methods 1 and 3 could be explained by any of these factors.

Separate analyses were carried out for each scenario style. For each scenario in which Method 3 generated utilities significantly different from those elicited with Method 1, multiple regression was used to describe the values of the dependent variable (the differences in utilities) in terms of the explanatory variables of interviewer, style sequence, and self-assessed level of health.[12] For each scenario, in both styles of presentation, the results indicated that the effects of these variables could not reduce the magnitude and statistical significance of the systematic change in measured utility noted in the third method of administering the standard gamble.

DISCUSSION

These results show that the values obtained from a group of raters for a series of health states, using the standard gamble as the method of measurement, are strongly influenced by characteristics of the "failure" outcome of the gamble. Although the possibility of death as an outcome of the gamble might intuitively be expected to influence the raters' judgments, it should be noted that raters did not behave in such a way as to suggest that the avoidance of the possibility of death was an overriding consideration. On the contrary, raters were prepared to bear a greater risk (i.e., accept a lower probability of success) in the gamble when death was the "worst" outcome.

Notwithstanding the complexity of the standard gamble as a method of measurement, difficulties in administering and understanding the method are unlikely to explain the results that we have obtained. This group of raters gave highly reproducible results in the replicate gambles involving two of the five health states in each of the two interviews, and the systematic influence of the presence or absence of death as an outcome was seen for both styles of scenario and on two occasions separated by several days. Furthermore, when the results obtained from the two groups of 32 raters seen by each interviewer were analyzed separately, very similar results were obtained in both groups.

Any bias introduced by the use of utilities for health states measured by the first method as reference utilities, in subsequent methods where these states were used as outcomes in the gamble, also appears unlikely to explain our findings. Any such bias would be expected to influence all utilities assessed with other health states replacing perfect health or death as outcomes in the gamble, and not only those in which death was replaced.

The observation that individuals confronted with choices do not behave in the manner expected under the prescriptive rules of decision theory is not novel. Kahneman and Tversky have shown that choices for probabilistically identical outcomes are systematically influenced by whether the choice is framed in terms of its possible losses or gains. These authors found that raters generally behaved in a manner that was risk-averse when choices were framed in terms of their potential gains, and were risk-seeking when choices were framed in terms of their possible losses. Tversky and Kahneman use "prospect theory," which proposes that numerically equivalent gains or losses are not perceived as representing equivalent changes in value, to explain this behavior.[13,14] If the use of the standard gamble as a method for evaluating health states rests upon a valid assumption – that those health states occupy positions on an interval value scale – then prospect theory may be applicable to our observations.

If the raters in our study perceived gambles with death as a possible outcome as being framed in terms of "losses," and gambles without death as an outcome as being framed in terms of "gains," then the systematic changes noted in their preferences according to the presence or absence of death as a possible outcome are similar to the behavior observed by Kahneman and Tversky. However, our study was not designed to investigate this phenomenon, and the raters were not presented with choices in a manner that allows any firm conclusions to be drawn about the possible effects of "framing."

A further possible explanation for our results is that some of the health states described were perceived, at some point in time, as being worse than death. For example, a short period of time spent in a particular health state might be preferred to immediate death, but the contemplation (albeit hypothetical) of an entire lifetime spent in that state may eventually result in a shift in preferences; immediate death becomes preferable to a lifetime in the state described in the scenario. The measured utility of states of ill health is known to decline with increasing time spent in those states,[15] and if the utility of a state is initially low when assessed against immediate death, a further decline in utility with increasing time may ultimately render the state less desirable than death. In our results, the utilities most influenced by the substitution of other states for death in the standard gamble were those with low mean initial utilities as assessed in the reference gamble, an observation that is consistent with this suggestion.

On the other hand, as demonstrated in Table 3, an individual who had not given the "worst" scenario, Scenario B, an extremely low initial utility (0.45) still demonstrated increased risk aversion when this scenario appeared in the third method. The possible effects of the value for time on the gamble results could be examined further by explicitly stating the time spent in a health state in a manner analogous to that used by Torrance.[2]

In assessing individual preferences, a particular patient's values for different states of health should not be thought of as constant, but can be expected to vary according to the available alternatives. Thus, in some circumstances, patients with a given level of disability may be more willing to undergo a risky procedure involving the chance of death than one in which there is a possibility of failure that would result in increased disability. If attempts are to be made to assess an individual patient's values with the standard gamble in the context of a clinical decision, it would seem reasonable to include death as an outcome in the standard gamble where this is a possible outcome of the clinical situation under consideration, but to omit death where this is not a possibility, and to substitute the worst possible alternative clinical outcome.

Our results also have implications for the incorporation of values or weights in the health states indices needed to compare the health of populations, to assess the efficacy of therapeutic or preventive programmes, or to make decisions about the allocation of health care resources.[8] These weighted indices require the assessment of the utilities of groups of individuals for different states of health, and underlying this scaling of preferences is the fundamental assumption that health is a continuum with death as its lower boundary.[6] However, the assumption that health is a continuum is inconsistent with our observation that the relationship between different states of health, as assessed by the standard gamble, is strongly influenced by the alternatives offered in the standard gamble.

The finding that patients' measured preferences for health states are not consistent with the axioms of expected utility theory does not in any way diminish the importance of these preferences or reduce the need to incorporate them into clinical decisions. However, it seems clear that a greater understanding of the complex factors that influence choices made by patients faced with decisions about their health will be needed before the formal measurement of patients' values can be usefully added to other aspects of assessments.

REFERENCES

1 Patrick, D.L., Bush, J.W., Chen, M.M.: Methods for measuring levels of well-being for a health state index. *Health Serv. Res.* 8:228–245, 1973

2 Torrance, G.W.: Social preferences for health states. An empirical evaluation of three measurement techniques. *Socioecon. Plann. Sci.* 10:129–136, 1976

3 Culyer, A.J.: *Measuring Health. Lessons for Ontario.* Toronto: University of Toronto Press, 1978

4 Von Neumann, J., Morgenstern, D.: *The Theory of Games and Economic Behavior* (3rd ed.). New York: John Wiley, 1953

5 Weinstein, M.C., Fineberg, H.V.: *Clinical Decision Analysis.* Philadelphia: W.B. Saunders, 1980

6 McNeil, B.J., Weichselbaum, R., Pauker, S.G.: Fallacy of the 5 year survival rate in lung cancer. *N. Engl. J. Med.* 299:1397–1401, 1979

7 Wolfson, A.: *A Health Index for Ontario.* Toronto: Ministry of Treasury and Intergovernmental Affairs, 1974

8 Torrance, G.W., Thomas, W.H., Sackett, D.L.: A utility maximization model for evaluation of health care programmes. *Health Serv. Res.* 7:118–133, 1972

9 Patrick, D.L., Bush, J.W., Chen, M.M.: Towards an operational definition of health. *J. Health Soc. Behav.* 14:6–23, 1973

10 Bond, A., Lader, M.: The use of analogue scales in rating subjective feelings. *Br. J. Med. Psychol.* 47:211–218, 1974

11 Aitken, R.C.B.: Measurement of feelings using visual analogue scales. *Proc. R. Soc. Med.* 62:989–996, 1969

12 Morrison, D.F.: *Multivariate Statistical Methods* (2nd ed.). New York: McGraw-Hill, 1976

13 Tversky, A., Kahneman, D.: The framing of decisions and the psychology of choice. *Science* 211:453–458, 1981

14 Kahneman, D., Tversky, A.: Prospect theory. An analysis of decision under risk. *Econometrica* 47:263–291, 1979

15 Sackett, D.L., Torrance, G.W.: The utility of different health states as perceived by the general public. *J. Chronic Dis.* 31:697–704, 1978

16 Torrance, G.W.: Health status index models. A unified mathematical view. *Manage. Science* 22:990–1001, 1976

22

---- ~ ----

CLINICAL DECISION ANALYSIS*

Baruch Fischhoff

Enormous progress has been made in developing formal models and computational aids for decision analysis. Much has been learned about how to represent both exotic and routine decision problems and how to compile judgments of value and likelihoods into composite recommendations with accompanying sensitivity analyses.

When it comes time to apply these tools, however, decision analysts must more or less rely on their own wits. There is no codified body of knowledge telling them when to use formal models and when to rely on intuitive judgments, how to approach decision makers and how to coax from them their true problems, which elicitation methods to use and when to trust their results, which parameters should be subjected to sensitivity analysis and what range of alternative values should be used, how to make certain that the assumptions and conclusions of an analysis are understood and heeded, or when decision analysis is likely to improve the understanding of a decision problem and when it is not likely to be cost effective. Such knowledge as does exist regarding these topics is largely anecdotal. It is acquired by trial and error in the field, perhaps aided by apprenticeship with a veteran practitioner.[25]

In order for the application of decision analysis to progress as rapidly as its theoretical developments, a systematic basis is needed for these practical skills. We need to know what works where and how well in order to evaluate the work of experienced analysts and to guide the professional training of aspiring ones. Creating such a fund of knowledge will require both empirical and theoretical work, the former to validate our techniques and the assumptions underlying them, the latter to understand how, in principle, these tools relate to particular settings. In essence, the application of decision analysis must be transformed from a clinical art to a clinical science.

How does one structure this complex task? The approach adopted here is to examine the patterns that have emerged from a related profession

* First published in *Operations Research*, 28 (1980), 28–43. © 1980 Operations Research Society of America. Reprinted by permission.

undergoing a similar transformation. The profession that I have chosen is psychotherapy, the broad collection of theories and procedures designed to help people live their lives better. Like decision analysis, these approaches attempt to help clients understand their world, their desires and their options. They acknowledge that indecision and bad decisions are due at least in part to the complexity and constraints of the world in which their clients live and that a precondition for effective action is explicitly facing difficult issues, like uncertainties and motives. Although the clients of decision analysts, if not the analysts themselves, might back off from the analogy with psychotherapy, the similarities between these two helping professions seem sufficiently strong to hope that psychotherapy research might provide a preliminary organization of the topics decision analysis must face, as well as some germane substantive results.

The transformation of psychotherapy began some 50 years ago with therapists' realization that they could not satisfy either critics or their own critical sense with evidence like "my clients say it helps them" and "the theory makes intuitive sense to me." Nor were they comfortable with sending their students out into the world with a bag of tricks and the admonition to use them wisely. The tale of their attempts to systematize their realm is not one of unremitting progress. Like other scientific endeavors, it has produced its share of dead ends, misconceptualized issues and misleading results. From the present perspective, one can identify a number of issues that have proved to be both critical and fruitful for psychotherapy and might serve the same role for decision analysis. These are: (a) Does it work? (b) How valid are its assumptions and assessment procedures? (c) How can the personal skills of practitioners be improved? (d) What are the bases of resistance to treatment? (e) How is the effectiveness and appropriateness of the approach limited by the social, political, psychological and ideological world in which the client lives?

DOES IT WORK?

The ideal way to evaluate a technique is through a controlled experimental design. Potential clients would be randomly divided between two groups, one receiving the treatment of interest (decision analysis, psychotherapy), while the other receives no treatment at all or an alternative treatment. In a sophisticated design the alternative would be a placebo treatment, some form of advice that sounds useful but which should (from the perspective of decision analysis) have no systematic impact on decision-making effectiveness.

It is hard to imagine a situation in which such rigorous control would be possible. For example, both proprietary and ethical considerations might prohibit one from assigning clients to "decision analysis" and "other analysis" conditions. In such situations, evaluation might still be possible through the use of quasi-experimental designs in which statistical control substitutes for unobtainable experimental control.[6,28]

The fact that psychotherapy as a profession worries about evaluating itself is certainly to its credit. Failure to develop an evaluation methodology would have suggested that it had something to hide. However, the existence of a methodology and a commitment to its use does not guarantee the steady accumulation of wisdom. In articles reviewing research on the effectiveness of such diverse treatments as marathon encounter groups, sensitivity training, drug abuse reduction, marriage therapy, and behavior modification for juvenile delinquents, one finds a litany of methodological criticisms: lack of a control group, inappropriate control groups, impressionistic statistical analysis, biased data collection, lack of follow-up observations, failure to check observer reliability, unrepresentative samples, inappropriate outcome measures. Poor methodology often tends to produce results prejudiced against therapies whose efficacy is being tested. Sloppy research increases error variance (noise) and makes it hard to detect differences between groups.[23] While decision analysts may have little interest in the results of studies on marathon encounter groups, these *methodological* pitfalls are relevant to anyone interested in evaluating decision analysis.

Psychotherapy researchers have found specific effects that may mask the actual degree of success or failure encountered by a treatment:

a   The fact that practitioners have been trained in a method and claim to be carrying it out is no guarantee that they are. Assessing the fidelity of implementation is critical for knowing what is being evaluated.

b   A well-designed therapeutic program may fail because of the tenacity of the client's problem or unanticipated and uncontrollable changes in the client's world. Thus "good therapy" does not necessarily imply "good outcome."

c   Many people who apparently benefit from treatment would have improved anyway, due to changes in their life circumstances or outlook. Thus, "good outcome" does not necessarily imply "good therapy."

d   The success of some treatments may be less due to their substantive, theory-based message and manipulations than to the atmosphere they create. These "nonspecific treatment effects" include suggestion, reduced apprehension, increased self-confidence and heightened attention to the problem.

e   Unsubstantiated evaluations by practitioners are not to be trusted. Even dispassionate clinicians of high integrity may see treatment effects where statistical analysis shows random fluctuations,[16] a record of past success which is exaggerated,[13] or proven treatment programs where there are but folklore and bandwagon effects.[29]

f   Results can be biased by looking only for the positive effects a treatment produces and ignoring possible detrimental effects or by looking only for the negative effects.[27]

g   In some cases, defining a "good outcome" is far from trivial, for example, when one must weigh short-term and long-term well-being.

To draw a few of the possible parallels with decision analysis, some products labeled "decision analysis" really are not, and the craft should not be judged by their performance. The vicissitudes of life may "reward" well-analyzed decisions with unfortunate outcomes. Nor can it be presumed that everyone who seems to have done well after decision analysis would have floundered without it; good habits, luck and situational pressures would have "spontaneously" produced some good decisions. Decision analysis may help a decision maker simply because the analyst's deckside manner helps the decision maker focus attention and resources on the problem, and not because of the specific techniques used and their axiomatic justification. Although it is reassuring to hear clients say that our efforts help them, such claims are insufficient evidence. It may be obscurant to invoke unmeasurable benefits, like enhanced peace of mind or self-confidence, when we lack concrete proof of efficacy.

The possibility of treatments not being implemented as their designers intended raised a thorny problem for the evaluator. Obviously, it would be unfair to detract from decision analysis on the basis of crude, ineffectual analyses done by poorly trained individuals or under severe time constraints. Or would it? If the treatment "package" cannot be employed regularly by most practitioners, there is little point to it. If only a selected few can master the craft and the masters do little to monitor those acting in the craft's name, then its usefulness is limited. Its role is further limited if the experience is so unpleasant or expensive that few clients ever get the full treatment. A program with a relatively high drop-out rate but great success with those who complete it will not be highly regarded, particularly when one considers that people who stay in treatment are those most susceptible to persuasive messages of any kind.[3] Since all the resources (computer time, analyst fees, decision-makers' attention) needed for a full, proper decision analysis will seldom be available, a critical evaluation question becomes: Does decision analysis degrade gracefully? A partial analysis is obviously not as good as a full-blown one, but is it better than none at all?

No clear overview of the current state of decision analysis now exists. Such an overview could be achieved by reviewing a random sample of recent reports of decision analysis and subjecting them to questions like those in Table 1.

Table 1 *Criteria for analyzing analyses*

Are the assumptions of the analysts listed?
Are the assumptions of the clients listed (e.g., those implicit in the way the problem was formulated)?
Are any of these assumptions tested, or is supporting evidence from other sources cited?
Are probabilities used? If so, is any justification given for the particular procedure by which they are elicited?
Are probabilities or utilities measured in more than one way?
Are values elicited from more than one person?
Are sensitivity analyses conducted, for probabilities, for utilities, with more than one factor varying at once?
Are interactions between impacts considered?
Is more than one problem structure used as a cross check?
Are possible alternatives given by the client or created with the client?
Are gaps in scientific knowledge noted?
Is a bottom line figure given, and if so, how is it hedged?
Is the public involved, and if so, at what state?
Is there consideration of political feasibility or legal constraints?
Is there external criticism of the report, and if so, has the analysis been redone in its light?
Is there indication of when the analysis should be redone to consider possible changes of circumstances?
Is an attempt made to evaluate the analysis or to indicate how interested parties might do so on their own?
How much did the analysis cost?

If the reviewer has opinions about the quality of the analyses or the competence of the analysts, such judgments can be related to these criteria to see what good reports contain and what good analysts do.

Watson and Brown[37] have pioneered an alternative, reflexive evaluation strategy using decision analysis to analyze past decision analyses. Perhaps foretelling the difficulties awaiting such efforts, in two of the three case studies chosen by Watson and Brown,[36] the greatest benefits of the analyses seemed to come not from the decisions they recommended, but from their contribution to organizational processes (reduction of controversy and improvement of communication), considerations left out of Watson and Brown's formal model for the sake of simplicity.

HOW VALID ARE ITS ASSUMPTIONS AND ASSESSMENT PROCEDURES?

When technical difficulties preclude validating entire treatment programs, one may still be able to assess the validity of the theoretical assumptions upon which the programs are based and the effectiveness of their component techniques. Such research can also point to what the treatment's strengths are and how they can be improved. In the context of psychotherapy, the most valuable results have emerged from attempts to test previously unquestioned theoretical assumptions, e.g., stable personality traits exist; feedback facilitates learning; psychopathology is related to unconscious libidinal and aggressive wishes; self-awareness is necessary for improvement.

As might be expected, the divide-and-conquer approach to evaluation has appealed to students of decision analysis. Tests of whether people accept the normative assumptions upon which decision analysis is based have shown (with varying degrees of definitiveness) that people often do not wish to accept Savage's independence axiom,[32] that they occasionally want their judgments to be intransitive,[34] that there do not seem to be consistent individual differences in risk aversion,[42] and that verbally expressed preferences are not always consistent with those revealed in people's behavior.[30] Much less is known about the appropriateness of other assumptions: Are probability and utility judgments independent? Can we acceptably resolve inconsistencies in people's preferences due to theoretically irrelevant differences in elicitation procedure? Will people reply honestly to our questions about their values and, if not, can we spot their lies or "strategic responses?" Is it possible for the decision analyst to act as a neutral agent when eliciting judgments?[14]

The development of assessment procedures has long been a growth industry in psychotherapy. With the possibility of measuring every feasible personality and behavioral trait, psychologists produce over 3000 books, chapters and journal articles on assessment per year.[15] Unfortunately, there is no generally accepted characterization of the universe of traits and the relationship between seemingly similar traits (e.g., honesty and straightforwardness). As a result, it is difficult to know what conclusions to make from comparisons between studies.

By contrast, decision analysis is primarily interested in the assessment of two well-defined quantities, probabilities and utilities. Although the quantity of research here is perhaps 1/100 of that in personality assessment, the cumulative progress is probably greater. We know quite a lot about probabilities (e.g., they tend to reflect overconfidence although their validity depends heavily on context.[19]) Somewhat less is known about eliciting utilities, although studies[11,35] that compare a variety of methods using evaluative criteria drawn from the sophisticated methodology of psychometricians show great promise. Almost nothing is known about another topic which could be considered an assessment problem: determining the structure of a decision-maker's problem.

Psychometricians have discovered two threats to the generality of assessment procedures which should concern decision analysts. One is that the people's feelings about a particular object and the numbers they assign to those feelings can vary greatly with arbitrary features of the elicitation procedure, such as the order in which alternatives are presented, the heterogeneity of the set of alternatives, the contrast established between the first two alternatives, whether the response scale is bounded, and the respondents' preconceptions about how the numbers are supposed to be used.[14,26,27] The second threat is that it is not tests but responses which have validities and reliabilities. Thus, the adequacy of an elicitation procedure in one context with one particular set of individuals is not a guarantee of universal applicability.

Once we understand the flaws in our assumptions and procedures, we need an error theory to tell us what their cumulative impact is. As Fischer[11] notes, without an error theory, we cannot know to what extent violations of assumptions and lack of robustness in responses threaten the results of a decision analysis. Important steps toward developing such a theory (or theories) are:

a   Fischer's[11] work with multidimensional utility models;

b   von Winterfeldt and Edwards'[40] finding that with continuous decision options (e.g., invest X dollars) some inaccuracy in individual probability and utility assessments will not produce terribly suboptimal decisions;

c   Lichtenstein *et al.*'s[19] demonstration of how moderate miscalibration in probability assessment can substantially reduce expected utility with discrete decision options (e.g., operate/do not operate);

d   von Winterfeldt and Edwards'[4] identification of the ease with which dominated alternatives can be selected through improper problem modeling;

e   Aschenbrenner and Kasubek's[2] finding that two different, only partially overlapping, sets of attributes produced similar results in a multiattribute utility analysis;

f   Kastenberg, McKone and Okrent's[17] discovery of the extreme sensitivity of risk assessments to the treatment of outliers; and

g   Tihansky's[33] finding that errors in different estimates were positively correlated and, therefore, would not tend to cancel one another out.

These are but pieces of an error theory. Particularly useful additions would be guidelines to the way in which uncertainty from varying sources (people not knowing what they want, people being affected by choice of questioning procedure, people being confused by instructions, random error, etc.) is compounded. Until an adequate theory is developed, we will have to be very generous in performing sensitivity analyses for errors arising from judgmental sources.

HOW CAN CLINICAL SKILLS BE IMPROVED?

However powerful their measures and theories may be, clinicians realize that in the last analysis, they, themselves, are their own major tool. They must instill confidence in clients, choose the appropriate questioning procedures to elicit sensitive information, handle crises, understand what is not being said, avoid imposing their own values and perceptions, and cooperate in creating solutions. To this end, clinical psychologists undergo 3–4 years of supervised practice, psychiatrists spend 1–2 years in internship and psychoanalysts undergo psychoanalysis to be fully aware of how they see and interact with others.

Such training assumes that the finer points of the craft can be learned only in the clinic of a master. To expedite this training, many researchers are attempting to discover just what it is that makes masters. Since these studies consider the interaction between therapists and clients with serious personal problems, one should use caution in drawing inferences regarding the interactions between decision analysts and corporate executives or government officials. One result that seems likely to generalize from the psychotherapeutic context is the extent to which one individual can shape another's responses by such subtle measures as appreciative grunts and nonverbal communication (posture, facial expressions, etc.). One can readily imagine an analyst subtly pressuring a client to change a probability assessment to a value the analyst believes to be more acceptable (analyst seems displeased; client thinks, "well, you're the expert on probabilities. Maybe what I meant was . . .") or an analyst and client "agreeing" that the latter's preferences on different attributes are really independent, making the elicitation procedure considerably less arduous. Slovic and Tversky[32] showed how direct pressure can induce clients to accept axiomatic principles. Further possibilities for influencing judgments emerge when the analyst works with groups. For example, the fact that group discussions tend to polarize opinions[21] suggest that the analyst can exert some control over the group's decision by deciding if and when the group should meet. Plott and Levine[24] demonstrated the extent to which group decisions can be manipulated by varying the order in which issues are considered. These effects must be understood if the analyst is to restrain, control or exploit them.

In general, however, we have little concrete evidence regarding clinical skills in decision analysis and their improvement. One place to start would be a taxonomy of decision situations indicating which techniques to use where. Several such guides have been derived from formal properties of the decision situations.[9,18,22] Additional efforts might look at more subjective aspects: the public visibility of the issue at hand; how articulated people's values are; how much freedom the analyst and decision maker have to construct alternatives; and whether any evaluation of the analysis is planned. Such a guide should tell us, among other things: When, in order to avoid misplaced precision, should all resources be invested in problem structuring and none in attaching numbers? Can high-priced analysts be replaced by paraprofessionals? When is it advisable to acknowledge the poorly developed nature of people's preferences and the limits on their information-processing abilities and to sacrifice axiomatic rigor for less demanding procedures?[8] Psychological theories have been likened to box cameras which take pretty good pictures because they require subjects to be at a great distance, in the sun and immobile;[43] is the same true of decision analysis?

WHAT CAUSES RESISTANCE TO TREATMENT?

Resistance to treatment takes many forms, all threatening its success. The client may reject the approach because it is not expected to work, because its procedures (e.g., talking openly about sensitive matters) are threatening, because it is too expensive, because of objections to its underlying philosophy, or because of reluctance to admit that there is a problem. The client who accepts the approach may resist its recommendations because they require assuming too much responsibility for a situation, because it seems easier to stumble along than to undertake the needed action, or because the analysis mandates acknowledging one's own fallibility, desires and uncertainties.

Even if the client is willing and able to adopt the approach and its directives, treatment may fail when the times comes to implement it in a hostile, unaccepting world. Classic failures of this type have been encountered by the T-group (or organizational development) movement, which tries to improve communication in a work setting by involving some workers and managers in intensive group experiences stressing openness and sensitivity. All too often, however, the behavioral changes induced by the pressure of the group situation and the manipulation of the group leader vanish when group members return to their hierarchic work settings. Although one might argue that it is not the client but the client's world which is "sick" and in need of help, the result is still a frustrating failure likely to reinforce old, bad habits.

Variants of all these problems seem possible with decision analysis, particularly when it is first introduced into organizations accustomed to less rigorous methods. In such contexts, its greatest potential advantages may prove to be stumbling blocks. Decision analysis requires explicit statement of problems. This, however, may produce great discomfort. Its computational procedures greatly relieve the decision-maker's mental load; however, for those unfamiliar with its logic, its recommendations may appear to be the output of numerical mumbo-jumbo with no intuitive appeal. Unlike other procedures, its logic is axiomatically grounded;

however, for uninitiated superiors, subordinates, and constituents, abandoning the comfortable old maxims (e.g., "This is the way we've always done it") may come quite hard.

Resistance within the organization may come from people who feel that they have not been involved early enough and adequately enough in the analysis. Like staunch believers in due process by law, they may believe that the decision-making process is more important than its product. Others may resist because they do not like the resultant recommendations. To achieve their ends, they may fight hard and dirty, questioning every fact and assumption in the analysis and casting aspersions on the integrity of its analysts, however well the analysis is done and however much its conclusions are qualified.[4,7] Analysts who believe in their work may face an uncomfortable choice between orphaning their analyses and adopting an advocacy role for the analysis and, thereby, for the recommended alternative.

Some of these problems are due to the fact that decision analysis, some of the problems to which it is applied, and the very idea of analysis are new. As a result, the social forms needed to incorporate it are either missing or in a state of flux.[39] Westman,[38] for example, complains that the legal mandate given regulators entrusted with improving U.S. water quality precludes their adopting the most cost-effective methods. Often projects are held up so long and altered so extensively in legal and administrative proceedings that their accompanying analyses becomes antiquated. Majone[20] has argued persuasively that alternatives are almost never adopted as proposed; rather, they are subject to continuous negotiation and alteration by the parties concerned.

Acknowledgment of these difficulties might lead to redirection of decision analysis. Brown[5] proposes that analysts treat action options as events and directly assess the uncertainty surrounding the form in which they will be realized. The preferred alternative might turn out to be one with dominated consequences but a better chance of being implemented. Another response would be for analysts to decide that feasibility is both a relative and mutable thing and append to each alternative a discussion of how it is likely to be waylaid en route to implementation and what needs to be done to keep it maximally intact.

In the long run, though, the adaptation should be mutual, with society and its component entities realizing the need to accommodate formal procedures. Toward this end, the educational potential of each analysis should be exploited. Broad participation should be viewed as an opportunity, not a burden. In some ways, it may be more important to build the analytic capacity of a society or organization than to guarantee the adoption of particular, desirable alternatives.

HOW DO POLITICS, IDEOLOGY AND ETHICS IMPINGE UPON ANALYSIS?

Attempts to shape and direct others' lives cannot be value neutral. The practitioner who is "only trying to help" has at the least made the evaluation that there is a situation needing help. The practitioner who is "only trying to do what is best for the client" cannot avoid at least some subtle hints at what that "best" is. Even client-centered therapists, whose goal is to reflect and clarify their clients' own thoughts, are still promulgating the world view that people are responsible for their own predicaments and can extricate themselves if they understand themselves sufficiently well. Indeed, the very search for lasting solutions to problems implies that the client's universe has more orderliness than may be the case.

The ideological biases of many therapeutic interventions are familiar intellectual topics: the mechanistic image of people projected by behaviorism and its potential for control, the ethnocentrism of psychoanalysis, the narcissism of many contemporary therapies, the general tendency to treat clients as objects rather than colleagues in therapy, and the fatalism induced by approaches that teach people to accept their own life crises as inevitable.

Even when a therapy's philosophical basis is acceptable, it may be resisted because of ethical problems or political bias in the way it is used. Much opposition to behavior modification arose from its use in institutional settings (prisons, asylums) in which free, informed consent for treatment by the patient is impossible. A frequent problem for practitioners is determining who the true client is, the patient or someone else (e.g., a hospital administrator) interested in maintaining order. Other therapies have lost their credibility because therapists have become so dependent upon government and the politically powerful for their livelihood that they have lost the ability to make independent criticism, others because they can be afforded only the rich, still others because they seem to be applied mainly to coerce the poor.

At first blush, the image of people and society fostered by decision analysis seems to be a highly flattering one. With proper coaching, people are capable of understanding and expressing what they know and what they want. Acknowledging their own information-processing limitations, people will prefer to have their values and beliefs combined mechanically and then will accept the indicated course of action.

There may, however, be problems with this seemingly innocuous perspective. One is that it may create an illusion of analyzability for problems that are insoluble, contributing to the mystique of science and "technical fixes." Because it asks us about everything important, it may lead us to believe that we have and should have beliefs and opinions about everything. We may be forced, for the sake of answering the analyst, to create preferences that are only superficially understood. Forcing people to have (necessarily shallow) opinions about many things may be an excellent way to guarantee that they have articulated views about nothing. Persistent questioning about poorly formulated beliefs may lead to responses designed to make the elicitor happy and to overreliance on easily measured and justified standards like monetary values.

In the public domain, the very reasonableness of decision analysis is based upon a political-ideological assumption: that society is sufficiently cohesive that its problems can be resolved by reason and without struggle. Although this "get on with business" orientation will be pleasing to many, it will not satisfy all. For those who do not believe that society is in a fine-tuning stage, any technique that fails to mobilize public consciousness and involvement has little to recommend it.

Like therapy, if decision analysis is not biased at its core it can be biased in its application. For example, most applications to societal problems seem to foster the transfer of decision-making power to a technical elite by offering little opportunity for effective citizen participation.[31] Although this trend seems inevitable due to the highly technical nature of the issues studied, in principle it might be countered by a concerted effort by analysts to go beyond the narrow dictates of their analytical mandate. The theoretical problems of aggregating group opinions need not forestall efforts to elicit them. To take another example, most analyses ignore the issue of equitable distribution of good and bad consequences. Although this is not a necessary feature of decision analysis, repeated omission of equity considerations will suggest lack of interest in such issues, or even evasiveness, on the part of analysts and those who hire them.

When analytic resources are limited, the analyst must take cues from someone about how to restrict the alternatives and consequences considered. That someone is likely to be the one who commissioned the study. If commissioners come consistently from one sector of society and consistently prefer (or reject out of hand) particular kinds of solutions or consequences, a persistent bias may be produced. Such bias would also determine what issues are never analyzed and how results are presented. If the commissioners are public officials, there may be a predisposition toward reports that bury uncertainties and delicate assumptions in sophisticated technical machinations and masses of undigested data.[12]

Psychotherapy's response to charges of ideological bias has been fairly minimal, with the most dramatic proposals within the profession being to encourage truth-in-packaging (e.g., providing potential clients with a description of the assumptions and procedures of an approach). Its response to charges of improprieties in therapeutic interactions has been more extreme. Clinical psychologists, for example, have organized as a guild with rigorous standards for entry, state and national licensing, censure mechanisms (albeit not often used), external review of research proposals and papers, and a strict code of ethics. That code addresses issues like recognizing and acknowledging the limits to one's competence, protecting clients' confidentiality and policing one's colleagues.[1]

Whether a guild structure is needed or appropriate for decision analysis is a moot point. Certainly, all that calls itself decision analysis does not glitter. However, the costs of controlling incompetent analysts might be substantial, draining the efforts of qualified analysts, discrediting the profession by unrepresentative public quibbling and raising prices through restraint of trade. Perhaps more modest steps might be appropriate, if any are needed at all:

a Setting up a "public interest decision analysis group" similar to that set up by the largest accounting firms in the United States in order to "give accounting away,"

b Insisting that some fixed amount of funds (say, 10 percent) in all analysis contracts be allocated to independent external review,

c Establishing a professional norm of participating in voluntary review networks,

d Teaching students to conduct and document enough sensitivity analyses to satisfy a report's most skeptical critics, or

e Adopting informal guidelines like those proposed by Fairly[10] for experts called upon to assess probabilities of rare accidents.

Because it functions in the public domain, as well as in the private sector, decision analysis faces ethical dilemmas at least as challenging as those faced by psychotherapy. For example, the American Psychological Association's ethics committee[1] was unable to agree on how to revise their standards regarding confidentiality (leaving them unchanged from 1964) even without having to consider (as the decision analyst might) the additional problems of what to do with proprietary information or information that could cause public panic if released. Therapists may find themselves forced to treat a delinquent when they should be treating the family. Similarly, analysts may get well into a problem before realizing that the wrong problem has been attacked, or that the wrong information has been provided, or that they are being set up to produce an advocacy rather than an honest analysis. Therapists often face the problem of how to assure informed consent by psychologically incompetent clients, whereas analysts are often asked to pursue their craft on behalf of clients, perhaps a whole society, judged by someone to be technically incompetent.

CONCLUSION

The analyst's job is extremely difficult. Confronting the issues raised above will make it even more difficult. However, the fact that they can be explicitly identified is in some sense a tribute to the clarity and comprehensiveness of decision analysis and its potential for development. As a result, I believe that efforts to implement a research program exploring these problems in the context of decision analysis would be well rewarded. Some of these issues have obvious pecuniary importance for the long-term prosperity of the field and its practitioners (e.g., proving its effectiveness and buttressing its foundations). Others, like examining ideological and ethical questions, will be intellectually stimulating. Still others, though, will seem like exercises in validating what common sense knows to be true (e.g., that there is more to decision analysis than putting on a good act). However, study of even these issues may have merit, for common sense may be superficial or wrong, and may vary across individuals, as psychotherapy's concerted effort to test and refine common sense has shown. Furthermore, examining the obvious can help convince others that we are right, improve our confidence in (and willingness to act upon) our knowledge, and help us learn why we were right all along.

REFERENCES

1 American Psychological Association, "Revised Ethical Standards for Psychologists," *APA Monitor* 8, 22–23 (1977).
2 K. M. Aschenbrenner and W. Kasubek, "Convergence of Multiattribute Evaluations when Different Sets of Attributes Are Used," in *Decision Making and Change in Human Affairs*, H. Jungermann and G. deZeeuw (eds.), D. Reidel, Amsterdam, 1977.
3 A. Bandura, *Principles of Behavior Modification*, Holt, Rinehart & Winston, New York, 1969.
4 S. M. Barrager, B. R. Judd and D. W. North, "Decision Analysis of Energy Alternatives: A Comprehensive Framework for Decision Making," Stanford Research Institute, Palo Alto, Calif., 1976.
5 R. V. Brown, "Modeling Subsequent Acts for Decision Analysis," Decisions & Designs, Inc. (McLean, Va.) *DDI Technical Report 75-1*, 1975.
6 D. T. Campbell and J. C. Stanley, "Experimental and Quasi-Experimental Designs for Research in Teaching," in *Handbook of Research on Teaching*, N. L. Gage (ed.), Rand McNally, Chicago, 1966.
7 J. L. Creighton, "The Limitations and Constraints on Effective Citizen Participation," Address to the Interagency Council on Citizen Participation, Washington, D.C., Dec. 8, 1976.
8 W. Edwards, "How to Use Multi-attribute Utility Measurement for Social Decision Making", *IEEE Trans. Systems Man. Cybernet.* 7, 326–340 (1977).

9 S. V. Emelyanov and V. M. Ozernoi, "Decision Making in Multi-objective Problems: A Survey," *Problems of Control and Information Theory*, pp. 51–64 (1975).

10 W. B. Fairley, "Evaluating the 'Small' Probability of a Catastrophic Accident from the Marine Transportation of Liquefied Natural Gas," in *Statistics and Public Policy*, W. B. Fairley and F. Mosteller (eds.), Addison-Wesley, Reading, Mass., 1977.

11 G. W. Fischer, "Multidimensional Utility Models for Risky and Riskless Choice," *Organizational Behavior Human Performance* 17, 127–146 (1976).

12 B. Fischhoff, "Cost-Benefit Analysis and the Art of Motorcycle Maintenance", *Policy Sci.* 8, 177–202 (1977).

13 B. Fischhoff and R. Beyth, "I Knew It Would Happen": Remembered Probabilities of Once-Future Things, *Organizational Behavior Human Performance* 13, 1–16 (1975).

14 B. Fischhoff, P. Slovic and S. Lichtenstein, "Knowing What You Want: Measuring Labile Values," in *Cognitive Processes in Choice and Decision Behavior*, T. Wallsten (ed.), Erlbaum, Hillsdale, N.J., 1980.

15 L. R. Goldberg, "Objective Diagnostic Tests and Measures," *Ann. Rev. Psychol.* 25, 343–366 (1974).

16 R. R. Jones, M. Weinrott and R. S. Vaught, "Effects of Serial Dependency on the Agreement between Visual and Statistical Inference", *J. Appl. Behavior Anal.* 11, 277–283 (1978).

17 W. E. Kastenberg, T. E. McKone and D. Okrent, "On Risk Assessment in the Absence of Complete Data," *UCLA Report No. UCLA-ENG-7677*, July 1976.

18 R. Keeney and H. Raiffa, "A Critique of Formal Analysis in Public Decision Making," in *Analysis of Public Systems*, A. W. Drake, R. L. Keeney and P. M. Morse (eds.), MIT Press, Cambridge, Mass., 1972.

19 S. Lichtenstein, B. Fischhoff and L. D. Phillips, "Calibration of Probabilities: The State of the Art," in *Decision Making and Change in Human Affairs*, H. Jungermann and G. deZeeuw (eds.), D. Reidel, Amsterdam, 1977.

20 G. Majone, "Choice Among Policy Instruments for Pollution Control," *Policy Anal.* 7, 589–613 (1976).

21 D. G. Myers and H. Lamm, "The Polarizing Effect of Group Discussions," *Am. Sci.* 63, 297–303 (1975).

22 D. Pearce, "The Limits of Cost-Benefit Analysis as a Guide to Environmental Policy," *Kyklos* 29, 97–112 (1976).

23 R. Perloff, E. Perloff and E. Sussna, "Program Evaluation," *Ann. Rev. Psychol.* 27, 569–594 (1976).

24 C. R. Plott and M. E. Levine, "A Model of Agenda Influence on Committee Decisions," *Am. Econ. Rev.* 68, 146–160 (1978).

25 M. Polanyi, *Personal Knowledge*, Routledge & Kegan Paul, London, 1962.

26 E. C. Poulton, "The New Psychophysics: Six Models for Magnitude Estimation," *Psychol. Bull.* 69, 1–19 (1968).

27 E. C. Poulton, "Quantitative Subjective Judgments Are Almost Always Biased, Sometimes Completely Misleading," *Br. J. Psychol.* 68, 409–425 (1977).

28 H. W. Riecken and R. F. Boruch, *Social Experimentation: A Method for*

Planning and Evaluating Social Intervention, Academic Press, New York, 1974.

29 F. Schechtman, "Convention and Contemporary Approaches to Psychotherapy," *Am. Psychol.* **32**, 197–204 (1977).

30 H. Schuman and M. P. Johnson, "Attitudes and Behavior," *Ann. Rev. Sociol.* **40**, 161–207 (1976).

31 W. R. D. Sewell and T. O'Riordan, "The Culture of Participation in Environmental Decision Making," *Natural Resources J.* **16**, 1–21 (1976).

32 P. Slovic and A. Tversky, "Who Accepts Savage's Axiom?" *Behav. Sci.* **19**, 368–373 (1974).

33 D. Tihansky, "Confidence Assessment of Military Air Frame Cost Predictions," *Opns. Res.* **24**, 26–43 (1976).

34 A. Tversky, "Intransitivity of Preferences," *Psychol. Rev.* **76**, 31–48 (1969).

35 I. Vertinsky and E. Wong, "Eliciting Preferences and the Construction of Indifference Maps: A Comparative Empirical Evaluation of Two Measurement Methodologies," *Socio-Econ. Planning Sci.* **9**, 15–24 (1975).

36 S. R. Watson and R. V. Brown, "Issues in the Value of Decision Analysis". Decisions and Designs (McLean, Va.), *DDI Tech. Report 75–10*, 1975.

37 S. R. Watson, "The Valuation of Decision Analysis," *J. Roy. Statist. Soc. Ser. A* **141**, 69–78 (1978).

38 W. E. Westman, "Problems in Implementing U.S. Water Quality Goals," *Am. Sci.* **65**, 197–203 (1977).

39 A. F. Wichelman, "Administrative Agency Implementation of the NEPA of 1969: A Conceptual Framework for Explaining Differential Response," *Natural Resources J.* **16**, 263–300 (1976).

40 D. von Winterfeldt and W. Edwards, "Evaluation of Complex Stimuli Using Multi-attribute Utility Procedures," University of Michigan, Engineering Psychology Laboratory (Ann Arbor., Mich.), *Technical Report 011313-2-T*, 1973.

41 D. von Winterfeldt, "Error in Decision Analysis: How to Create the Possibility of Large Losses by Using Dominated Strategies," University of Southern California, Social Science Research Institute (Los Angeles, Ca.). *SSRI Research Report 75-4*, 1975.

42 G. N. Wright and L. D. Phillips, "Personality and Probabilistic Thinking," *Br. J. Psychol.*, **70**, 295–303 (1979).

43 R. B. Zuniga, "The Experimenting Society and Radical Social Reform," *Am. Psychol.* **30**, 99–115 (1975).

PART 4

~

THE CONTEXTS OF CLINICAL DECISIONS

23

~

RATIONING HOSPITAL CARE: LESSONS FROM BRITAIN*

William B. Schwartz, Henry J. Aaron

Resistance to the decades-long rise in the cost of hospital care in the United States is growing rapidly. In consequence, all physicians and patients soon may have to live with, and within, a system that limits expenditures. The process has, in fact, already begun. Fixed per diem reimbursement, reimbursements according to specific diagnosis, and overall revenue limits are currently being implemented by several states or by the federal government under Medicare. In addition, many businesses are pursuing cost containment though so-called preferred-provider organizations.

It is unclear how far our efforts to control hospital costs will go, but one thing is clear: If we go far enough some medical benefits will have to be withheld from at least some patients. Under such circumstances, key questions will arise. Who will decide whether a particular patient is entitled to treatment? What criteria will be used to make the choice? And how will we learn to live with the answers?

An indication – probably a good one – comes from Britain, which has had long experience with medical rationing and now spends half the amount per capita on hospital care that we do. Although there are differences between our two countries, our shared language and the common elements in our political and medical cultures make the British experience relevant to the United States. To be sure, the British experience cannot be taken as a literal forecast for the coming years in the United States. For example, it seems unlikely that Americans would accept rationing as willingly as have the British, who have had a special affection for the National Health Service since its creation just after World War II. Nevertheless, the British experiment has yielded the best data we are likely to find in advance of embarking on an intensive program to curb medical expenditures.

---

* First published in *The New England Journal of Medicine*, vol. 310 (1984), 52–6. © The New England Journal of Medicine. Reprinted by permission.

NATURE OF THE STUDY

To establish how the British allocate scarce funds among various techno-logical approaches and patients, we conducted many interviews with officials of the National Health Service and with physicians and other providers. The findings summarized here are a sampling drawn from a larger study.[1]

We first identified several technologies for close study, most of which were developed in the late 1960s or during the 1970s. These included the use of CT scanning, cancer chemotherapy, bone-marrow transplantation, long-term dialysis, treatment of hemophilia, intensive care, coronary-artery surgery, hip replacement, total parenteral nutrition, diagnostic X-ray examination, and radiotherapy. Because total British spending on medical care was rising slowly in this period, funds allocated to the newer techniques necessarily came at the expense of older ones.

To assess the degree to which a particular treatment is rationed in Britain, we used as an initial benchmark the quantity of service provided per capita in the United States. We recognize, of course, that an appreci-able number of Americans do not have adequate access to hospital services and that some hospitals lack facilities that their staffs would deem optimal for patient care. To this extent, our measure of "full service" is an underestimate. But if, as seems likely, some techniques are overused in the United States, they act as counter-balancing factors in our estimates. Physicians do disagree about the appropriateness of employing various technological approaches in particular cases, but in each instance in which British demand is below that in the United States we have found independent evidence that rationing is indeed occurring. Long waiting lists for hip replacements, the absence of CT scanners in many teaching hospitals, and a rate of coronary-artery surgery that is far below optimal indicate that resource constraints are a dominant feature of the British scene.

LIVING WITH LIMITS

Many factors influence how many resources are devoted to each form of medical technology. Among them are the age of the typical patient, the average cost per patient, the total number of eligible patients, and the "visibility" of the disease affecting them. The results of our study are summarized below.

Three kinds of treatment are provided at essentially the same level in Britain as in the United States: All patients with hemophilia obtain high-quality treatment, including adequate supplies of the required clot-ting factors; megavoltage radiotherapy appears to be readily available in

England to virtually all cancer patients who can benefit from it; and bone-marrow transplantation is performed at the same relative frequency as in the United States.

The other treatment methods are rationed. The British perform only half as many X-ray examinations per capita as do Americans, and they use only half as much film per examination. Furthermore, the overall rate of treatment of chronic renal failure in Britain is less than half that in the United States. Kidneys are transplanted at a comparable rate, but dialysis is carried out in Britain at a rate less than one third that in the United States. In addition, total parenteral nutrition is undertaken only about one fourth as often as in the United States, and Great Britain has only one sixth the CT-scanning capability of the United States. The British hospital system has only one fifth to one tenth the number of intensive-care beds, relative to population, that the United States has. Finally, the rate of coronary-artery surgery in Britain is only 10 per cent that in the United States.

Chemotherapy for cancer has, perhaps, an intermediate position between unrationed and rationed treatment methods. Chemotherapy for potentially curable tumors is administered at approximately the same rate as in the United States. On the other hand, tumors that are not highly responsive to chemotherapy are treated far less often.

To sustain acceptance of a health system that systematically denies many patients useful, even lifesaving, care is no easy task. Physicians, who are the principal gatekeepers of the system, must find ways to reconcile the economic limitations with their personal and professional values. Patients must either adjust to the restrictions of which they are aware or circumvent them; they may often, of course, be unaware of the medical possibilities.

The physician as gatekeeper

Explicit limitation of medical resources puts physicians in a position that many of them find awkward. Neither the training nor the ethics of medicine prepare most physicians to make the required decisions in economic terms. Therefore, whenever possible, British doctors recast a problem of resource scarcity into medical terms. They have developed standards of care that incorporate economic reality into medical judgments.

Rationalization   Physicians and other health-care personnel seek ways to make the denial of potentially beneficial care seem either routine or, for the particular patient, optimal. For example, an internist confronted with a patient beyond the prevailing, if unofficial, age at which one's chances of receiving dialysis become slight is likely to tell the patient and family that nothing of medical benefit can be done and that he or she will simply make the patient as comfortable as possible. A nephrologist with a patient for whom dialysis would be technically or socially difficult to manage[2] may well say that dialysis would be painful and burdensome. A resident alien from a poor country may be told that he or she should return home – where, as it happens, modern care is likely to be unavailable.

Likewise, relatively restrictive criteria for coronary-artery surgery are employed. By focusing on the class of cases in which coronary-artery surgery demonstrably increases survival rates or relieves anginal pain that is altogether disabling, surgeons can discount the benefit of the procedure for those whose pain is less severe.

Confronted with the need to allocate scarce services to the patients who would benefit most, many doctors alleviate their own discomfort by persuading themselves that some treatable patients would not benefit at all. But for the patient with renal failure who cannot receive dialysis, the person with persisting anginal pain who cannot qualify for surgery, or the patient whose head injuries are misdiagnosed for lack of a CT scanner, this view is unpersuasive even if the political judgment that resources must be constrained is correct.

It is clear that not all British doctors believe that they are providing all potentially beneficial care to their patients. Many realize that they are acting as society's agent in the rationing process. One consultant spoke of the process as follows:

The sense that I have is that there are many situations where resources are sufficiently short so that there must be decisions made as to who is treated. Given that circumstance, the physician, in order to live with himself and to sleep well at night, has to look at the arguments for not treating a patient. And there are always some – social, medical, whatever. In many instances he heightens, sharpens, or brings into focus the negative component in order to make himself and the patient comfortable about not going forward.

Although most British doctors would like to deploy more resources than are now available, they seem to recognize that their country is not rich enough to provide all the possible benefits of medical care. In responding to a question about whether he thought more beds in his hospital should be devoted to intensive care, a doctor in charge of the intensive-care unit of one of London's leading teaching hospitals summed up his views like this:

No. It has to be appropriate to the surroundings. Now, what we have by your standards is way short of the mark. It would be too small in America, but if you took this unit and put it down in the middle of Sri Lanka or India, it would stick out like a sore thumb. It would be an obscene waste of money.

Clinical freedom and resource constraints.   The British profess that all doctors in consultation with their patients should be entirely free to determine diagnoses and treatments and that their decisions should not be subjected to second guessing except in egregious situations, and then only by medical colleagues or the courts. This principle reflects the need for doctors to make dozens of choices a day quickly and decisively.

Under the rubric of clinical freedom, physicians can sometimes divert scarce resources to patients in whom they are interested, but by doing so they lower the quality or quantity of care available to others. Other doctors may intervene when they recognize that such a situation exists. The British system is almost optimally constructed to deal with the threats to budget limits posed by the abuse of clinical freedom because day-to-day budgetary decisions fall mainly to tenured physicians who are employed on salary. Because the participants have no direct financial interest in the allocation of the hospital's resources, debates about the budget are not shadowed by personal financial consequences. Budget negotiations are said to be marked by compromise and by trade-offs born of the recognition that the participants must spend all or most of their professional lives in each other's company.

For the most part, these debates concern questions of capacity and maintenance – what equipment to buy, what rehabilitations to seek, what staff to hire, what vacancies to leave unfilled – but normally not the medical practice of individual physicians. Problems in that area do occur, however. For example, the aggressive use of chemotherapeutic agents in one leading hospital and the introduction of total parenteral nutrition in another created serious budgetary problems. In each case, actions were taken by the senior staff that led to voluntary curbs by the physicians responsible for the excessive expenditures.

Short-circuiting delays A major consequence of limited resources in British hospital care is that familiar British phenomenon, the queue. Except in emergencies, care may be considerably delayed. For example, of the 556,000 patients awaiting surgery of all kinds in 1979, 31 percent had waited for more than one year. Cases classified as urgent represented 7 percent of those on the waiting list and nearly three fourths of those cases had been on the lists for more than one month.[3] The concerned physician can exploit several mechanisms to short-circuit the waiting period. The general practitioner who thinks that a patient should be seen by a consultant without a long delay knows that by telephoning the consultant he or she is more likely to get the patient seen than by writing a letter. If the physician wants even faster action, he or she can declare, perhaps with some exaggeration, that the patient is too sick to travel and must be seen at home. Domiciliary visits – house calls – are made promptly. The number of domiciliary visits increased about one third during the

1970s.[4] Although these short-circuiting mechanisms are useful in a few cases, British clinicians think they do little to break the constraints of the system.

The problem of saying no   Physicians often must refuse treatment to certain patients; the older patient who is a candidate for long-term dialysis is the prime example. Saying no to such a patient will always be difficult. Often in such a case the local internist either does not raise the possibility of dialysis or simply states that the treatment does not seem to be indicated. Because of the respect that most patients have for physicians, the doctor's recommendations are usually followed with little complaint. We were repeatedly told by physicians who have worked in both the United States and Britain that the readiness of the British patient to defer to the doctor's authority largely explains a willingness to forgo the various kinds of care that are in short supply.

The local physician's role as gatekeeper explains why dialysis centers rarely have to turn away patients. Older patients are not usually referred because the local physician is well aware that they could not be accommodated. The general practitioner or internist thus spares the nephrologist from having to say no, spares the patient and family a painful rejection, and avoids having to face the patient and relatives after rejection.

Safety valves for the patient

Charity   Charity plays a minor overall part in British medicine, but it is important in selected fields. A few major hospitals retain endowments from pre-National Health Service days. Selected forms of medical equipment, notable CT scanners, have been purchased largely with donations. Private funds have also been used to endow senior consultancies in selected fields, notably oncology.

Some lessons emerge from such gifts. First of all, donors are reported to be more willing to give equipment or a facility than to pay for its continued operation and maintenance. For this reason, gifts have often enticed or pressured authorities into changing their priorities. The gift of a CT scanner unaccompanied by funds for operation thus burdens the budget of the area in which it is located. The endowment of a professorial chair may entail complementary hiring of other support staff and a provision of beds to which the holder of the chair will have admitting privileges. Such expenses also usually fall to the National Health Service budget. Secondly, to the extent that health authorities anticipate gifts, they can divert resources to other uses. In that event, gifts do not change priorities but rather augment total health spending.

The private sector   The National Health Service has permitted its consultants to have part-time private practices, and National Health Service hospitals retain a few beds for paying patients. In addition, private hospitals in England and Wales had nearly 7000 beds in 1981.[5] By going to see National Health Service consultants privately, enterprising patients can usually avoid the queue for elective care and receive prompt attention. This strategy yields the largest dividend in the case of procedures such as hip replacement, for which the wait may be as long as several years.

Since the late 1970s the private sector has grown rapidly, to the point that some 5 percent of total expenditures on physicians and hospital care – notably, elective surgery and consultations – is now provided privately.[6] Thus, a patient facing a long wait for elective surgery in an aging National Health Service hospital may instead choose prompt treatment in a new private hospital where he can have such amenities as a private room. Moreover, the National Health Service provides backup protection against serious complications. If, for example, a major medical problem develops after hip surgery in a private facility, the patient will be transferred immediately.

The private sector is unlikely, however, to break through the fundamental limitations of rationing unless standards of care in National Health Service facilities decline seriously. In the first place, sophisticated care depends on equipment, laboratories, and skilled specialists and entails high overhead expenses. Such care is prohibitively costly unless the demand is high. Until and unless shortages in the National Health Service are pervasive enough to drive a substantial proportion of British patients to seek such services outside the public sector, private medicine will be unable to afford to offer high-quality tertiary care.

Likewise, insurance coverage for such care is unlikely to spread widely. People at low risk of needing elaborate and costly care are unlikely to pay premiums for private insurance to cover the costs of treatments, such as dialysis, that might only be available to them outside the system. But if only high-risk persons enroll, the insurance cannot profitably be underwritten. Thus, as a case in point, virtually no dialysis in Britain is performed outside the National Health Service.

"Working the system"   Although most British patients are said to take the word of their physician about a course of action (or nonaction), some will not passively accept a denial of care. First of all, a patient can ask his physician to arrange for a second opinion, which in most instances, we are told, is provided without protest. The emergency room may also provide direct access to specialized services for which the patient may previously have been deemed "unsuitable."

Alternatively, the patient may occasionally penetrate the referral barrier by going directly to the clinic of a particular specialist. One leading nephrologist indicated, for example, that a patient who sits down in the waiting room will probably be seen and a slot found for him or her in the dialysis program. A cancer expert at one of the leading British centers supported this point by emphasizing how difficult it is to refuse care to the patient who appears at the doorstep. The key to turning down the patient "is not to get eyeball to eyeball with him because if you do there is no way you can actually say no."

The level of assertive behavior by patients seeking care is manageable at present. But consultants express some fear that the regular system, in which the local physician determines referrals, could break down if too many patients came to emergency rooms and clinics from which they could not be turned away.

Exploiting geography   Shortages are worse in some places than others. For example, the waiting time for hip replacement varies widely across regions,[7] and patients face few administrative impediments if they wish to travel to areas where waiting periods are short. But few people do so, probably because of a reluctance to leave familiar surroundings and the emotional support provided by friends and relatives.

Why malpractice litigation doesn't mobilize resources

There is no reason, in principle, why malpractice suits could not be used to put pressure on the government to expand medical services. For example, in the case of a patient with a head injury that was mishandled for lack of a CT scan, both the physician and the local hospital authority could be sued. If costly awards against the government were to result, Parliament might find it cheaper to provide more CT scanners than to continue paying damages.

In practice, however, there are many impediments to bringing malpractice suits.[8] Litigation is costly. The plaintiff must pay his lawyer a predetermined fee to initiate a suit, rather than arrange a contingency fee. Should he lose, the plaintiff must also pay the defendant's costs – typically, even as of 1971, $7,500 to $25,000.[9] The Legal Aid Scheme entitles indigent plaintiffs to sue at government expense, but few qualify because "indigency" requires disposable income to be less than roughly $3,500 per year (Brooke Barnett, J.W.: personal communication). Thus, not surprisingly, the annual premium charged in 1982 by the Medical Defense Union, the largest and oldest of Britain's three malpractice insurers, was only about $250.[9] In the 25 years from 1947–1972, only 2809 malpractice claims were brought.[8] By contrast, more than $1\frac{1}{2}$ times as many claims on a per capita basis were closed in the United States during 1976 alone.[10]

Another sort of suit is possible under the National Health Services Act of 1977, which stipulates that "the Secretary of State is under a duty to provide services to such an extent that he considers necessary to meet all reasonable requirements."[11] Under this statute patients or doctors might bring an action requiring the central government to provide appropriate facilities, as they see it. So far, no such action has been initiated.

In summary, it seems clear that the acceptance of scarcity as a general feature of British society and affection for the National Health Service have all contributed to a widespread acceptance of the rationing process. Moreover, various safety valves have provided outlets for the most disaffected. It appears doubtful that citizens of the United States would accept such limits – or even less severe ones – as readily. If limits are set, however, we believe that they will stimulate responses in physicians and patients that will be similar in many respects to those we observed in Britain.

REFERENCES

1 Aaron, J.H., Schwartz, W.B. The painful prescription: rationing hospital care. Washington, D.C.: The Brookings Institution, 1984.

2 Medical Services Study Group of the Royal College of Physicians. Deaths from chronic renal failure under the age of 50. *Br. Med. J.* 1981; 283:283–6.

3 Department of Health and Social Security. Orthopaedic Services: waiting time for outpatient appointments and inpatient treatment: report of a Working Party to the Secretary of State for Social Services. London: Her Majesty's Stationery Office, 1981:4–5.

4 Dowie, R. National trends in domiciliary consultations. *Br. Med. J.* 1983; 286:819–22.

5 Questions in the Commons: private hospital beds. *Br. Med. J.* 1982; 284:520.

6 Hurst, J. The patterns of health care expenditures. National health expenditure. Sect. II. London: Department of Health and Social Services, August 1980: Table 7. (internal memorandum).

7 Office of Health Economics. Hip replacement and the National Health Service. Luton, England: White Crescent Press, 1982.

8 Appendix to the Report of the Secretary's Commission on Medical Malpractice, 1973: the malpractice problem in Great Britain. Washington, D.C.: Department of Health, Education, Welfare, January 16, 1973. (DHEW publication no. (OS)73-89):854–70.

9 Medical defense union annual report, 1982. London, England.

10 NAIC malpractice claims. Vol. 2. Milwaukee, Wis.: National Association of Insurance Commissioners, September 1980:119.

11 Office of Health Economics. Renal failure: a priority in health? Luton, England: White Crescent Press, 1978.

24

~

RESOURCE ALLOCATION DECISIONS IN HEALTH CARE: A ROLE FOR QUALITY OF LIFE ASSESSMENTS?*

Michael F. Drummond

INTRODUCTION

This paper discusses the relevance of quality of life measurement in clinical, epidemiological and economic research to resource allocation decisions in health care. The main aim is to offer guidance to clinical and economic evaluators undertaking studies and to health care decision makers who seek to use the results.

First, some background to the resource allocation problem in health care is given, outlining how resource allocation decisions are made and the concerns that have been expressed. Second, the contribution of health services research to improved decision making is discussed. The growing link between clinical and epidemiological research and methods of economic evaluation is described. Economic analyses that have incorporated quality of life assessments are reviewed. Third, current issues in the use of quality of life assessments in economic evaluation are discussed, including comments on whether one can advise on best practice and whether it is instructive to compare health care interventions in terms of their "cost per quality-adjusted life-year gained."

THE RESOURCE ALLOCATION PROBLEM IN HEALTH CARE

Resources for the provision of health care are *scarce*, in that there are not, and never will be, enough resources to satisfy human wants completely. Therefore, in choosing to use resources in one health care programme or treatment, the community forgoes the opportunity to use the same resources in another competing activity. Hence the economist's notion of *opportunity cost*; that is, the cost of using resources in one health care programme is the value of the benefits they would have generated in their best alternative use. For example, one might argue that the real cost of

* First published in *Journal of Chronic Diseases*, Vol. 40, No. 6 (1987) 605–16. © Pergamon Journals Ltd. Reprinted by permission.

expanded use of high technology diagnostic aids such as C-T scanning is not the money spent on equipment and staff, but the community care programmes that may have not been given funds to expand.

All countries, no matter what their stage of industrial development, need to make tough choices in the use of health care resources. The problems encountered in the decision process may, however, take different forms depending on how health care is financed and delivered. In a relatively decentralized or "liberal" system such as that in the United States, the problem may be rising health care expenditures, and considerable efforts may be directed towards cost containment measures. In a relatively centralized or "socialized" system such as that in the U.K., the problem may be trying to meet stated priorities in the face of an increasingly stretched budget which is fixed by the government. In all systems, the resource allocation problems are intensified by the rapid technological change in medicine which shows no sign of abating.[1,2]

An extra complication arises because there are essentially two co-existing resource allocation processes. On the one hand there are *planning decisions*, made on behalf of the community by health care jurisdictions. These decisions concern issues such as whether or not particular facilities should be provided, where they should be located, and whether particular public health programmes (such as screening or immunization schemes) should be funded. Occasionally planning decisions concern individual medical procedures, in so far as they may relate to whether or not a treatment is eligible for reimbursement by a health insurance plan.

The second resource allocation process involves *clinical decisions*, made by practitioners on behalf of individual patients. These have resource consequences too; in the U.K., it was estimated that each hospital doctor made decisions which committed resources worth in excess of £140,000 annually (or £500,000 in today's prices).[3] Although clinical decisions may be partially constrained by the facilities provided, in the main they are made without reference to those planning, managing or funding the health care system. This presents obvious problems for those trying to ensure a rational use of health care resources.

HEALTH SERVICES RESEARCH AND RESOURCE ALLOCATION
DECISIONS IN HEALTH CARE

In the face of the resource allocation problem outlined above, what can health services research contribute? This issue is discussed below, with particular emphasis on economic evaluation and its link to clinical and epidemiological research.

Clinical and epidemiological research

Clinical and epidemiological research, or at least the part concerned with assessing health care interventions, seeks to establish whether treatments or programmes do more good than harm.[4] It contributes to the resolution of the resource problem in health care to the extent that it provides evidence for the discontinuation of ineffective therapies, or evidence against the adoption of new drugs, devices or procedures that are no more effective than current practices. There are well-known difficulties in this research, such as the fact that many new medical technologies diffuse throughout the health care system before their effectiveness is adequately assessed. Also a lag sometimes exists between the time a research finding is published and when the necessary changes in clinical practice are made.[5] These problems have led some to prescribe guidelines for the clinical and economic evaluation of health technologies.[6]

However, more fundamentally, if one accepts the notion of scarcity, demonstration of a procedure's effectiveness is a necessary, but not sufficient, condition for its adoption. The benefits from applying the procedure must be compared with its cost (i.e. the benefits forgone). This is what economic evaluation seeks to accomplish.

Figure 1 Common forms of analysis

1. Cost-analysis: C_1, $C_1 + C_2$
2. Cost-effectiveness analysis (CEA): $(C_1 + C_2)/E$; $(C_1 - B_1)/E$; $(C_1 + C_2 - B_1 - B_2)/E$
3. Cost-utility analysis (CUA): $(C_1 + C_2)/U$; $(C_1 - B_1)/U$; $(C_1 + C_2 - B_1 - B_2)/U$
4. Cost-benefit analysis (CBA): $B_1 + B_2 - C_1 - C_2$; $(B_1 + B_2)/(C_1 + C_2)$

   Also sometimes includes consideration of C_3 and B_3

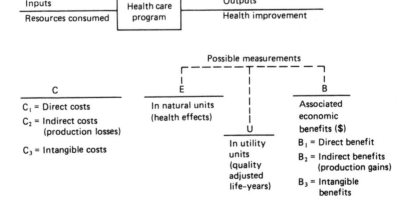

Economic evaluation

There are several forms of economic evaluation, but all forms compare the inputs to a health care programme with some combination of the outputs (See Fig. 1). The inputs include the direct costs to the health care sector and to patients and their families in providing care, the indirect costs (in production losses) arising when individuals are withdrawn from the workforce to be given therapy, and the intangible costs associated with therapy, such as pain and suffering.

The outputs of health care programmes can be assessed in many ways. First, they can be measured in the most convenient natural units such as "number of cases treated" or "number of years of life gained." The effects could also be measured in terms of improvements on a quality of life scale. An evaluation having health effects in the denominator would be termed a *cost-effectiveness analysis* although, as seen in Fig. 1, there are several possible formulations for the numerator.

Second, the outputs of health care programmes can be measured in quality-adjusted life-years (QALYs), where the life extension gained is adjusted by a series of "utility" weights reflecting the relative value of one health state compared to another. Utility, therefore, is a specific kind of quality of life measure which has gained prominence in economic evaluation in health care. An evaluation having utilities in the denominator would be called a *cost-utility analysis*.

Finally, the outputs can be measured in money terms. Some categories of economic benefit are easy to assess in this way, such as the savings in direct medical care costs resulting from improved health, or the production gains from earlier return to work. Other more intangible benefits, such as the value to patients or their families of feeling healthier, are obviously more difficult to express in money terms, although such measurements are sometimes attempted.[7,8]

The form of economic evaluation where outputs are measured in money terms, *cost-benefit analysis*, is potentially the broadest form since it allows a direct comparison of all costs with all benefits. In principle one could assess whether the benefits of a programme justify the costs, and whether it should be mounted. However, the intangible benefits are rarely estimated, and the analysis is often reduced to a comparison of items that can easily be expressed in money terms. Therefore, cost-benefit analysis *as practised* is often a more limited form of analysis than cost-effectiveness or cost-utility analysis, as seen from the formulations in Fig. 1.

The application of economic evaluation in health care has been extensively reviewed and several key methodological principles have emerged.[9-12] These have been summarized in the form of 10 questions to ask of any published study.[13] (See Fig. 2).) A detailed discussion of all the methodological points is beyond the scope of this paper. Three points are discussed below because they are particularly germane to the inclusion of quality of life measurements in economic evaluations.

1. *Valuation of outputs and the increased popularity of cost-utility analysis.* It was noted above that the forms of economic evaluation differ in how they assess the outputs of health programmes. Whereas the valuation of costs is relatively straightforward, though not without controversy, the valuation of the benefits of improved health, particularly the intangible benefits, has been a frequent source of debate. Economists argue that the theoretically correct approach would be to base valuation on the total amount that individuals are willing to pay for the health improvement. Some empirical studies have been mounted, most notably in the difficult area of valuation of human life.[8] Critics of this approach point to the great variability in the estimates obtained. They question whether individuals are knowledgeable enough to make sensible judgements, and point out that these valuations are not independent of the prevailing distribution of income.

It might be argued that the best way around the problem of valuation of health improvements is not to attempt it at all and to undertake more cost-effectiveness analyses. Such analyses can be useful, particularly where it can be assumed that the unit of output (e.g. the "successfully treated case") is "worth having," and where there is a single health improvement of interest, such as "years of life gained." Many analyses of life saving interventions have reported results in terms of cost per year of life gained, most notably chronic renal failure studies.[14]

Cost-effectiveness analysis can also be used where there are multiple effects, such as improvements in various aspects of the quality of life,

Figure 2 Ten questions to ask to a published study.
(Source: Department of Clinical Epidemiology and Biostatistics)[13]

1. Was a well defined question posed in answerable form?
2. Was a comprehensive description of the competing alternatives given (i.e. can you tell who did what to whom, where and how often)?
3. Was there evidence that the programs' effectiveness had been established?
4. Were all important and relevant costs and consequences for each alternative identified?
5. Were costs and consequences measured accurately in appropriate physical units (e.g. hours of nursing time, number of physician visits, days lost from work or years of life gained) prior to valuation?
6. Were costs and consequences valued credibly?
7. Were costs and consequences adjusted for differential timing?
8. Was an incremental analysis of costs and consequences of alternatives performed?
9. Was a sensitivity analysis performed?
10. Did the presentation and discussion of the results of the study include all issues of concern to users?

providing one treatment dominates the other in all respects. Otherwise there are problems in weighing improvements in one aspect of the quality of life against another. However, such analyses are inevitably limited because modern medicine is concerned with improving the quality, not quantity, of life. In addition, one may not want to make assumptions about whether particular programmes are worth having, and the priority that should be assigned to each. Also, it would be rare to find one treatment superior to another in all aspects of outcome. Finally, some interventions, such as cancer chemotherapy and neonatal intensive care for very-low-birth-weight infants, may involve a trade-off between extension of life and the quality of that life.

For these reasons there has been increased interest in cost-utility analysis, where *valuation* of health improvement is attempted, although not in money terms. The *relative* valuation of health states in "utilities" represents an interesting half-way house, where some objections to the methods economists use to solicit valuations from individuals can be aired in the constructive arena of multidisciplinary activity. The methods for obtaining utility values will not be described in detail here because they are discussed in another paper in this issue.[15] However, several cost-utility analyses are reviewed.

2. *Links between economic evaluation and clinical research*. The methodological principles outlined in Fig. 2 show that economic evaluation requires assessment of the medical effectiveness of the treatments or programmes being compared. The quality of medical evidence on which economic evaluations are based varies considerably. A typical, yet frustrating, approach is for the economic analyst to assemble various pieces of evidence from the literature. Culyer and Maynard found that although numerous trials of cimetidine (a new technology for the treatment of peptic ulcer disease) had been carried out, none provided a suitable foundation for their study.[16] The existing trials either evaluated inappropriate alternatives (such as a placebo which was unlikely to be administered in actual medical practice), were not well controlled, were too small, or included an inadequate range of measurements. For example, measurements in clinical trials are often confined to narrow assessments of medical "improvement" or "cure". They do not include broader assessments of the patient's functioning, such as the ability to return to work, which would be important in a subsequent economic analysis.

This would lead one to recommend that economic evaluation be more frequently undertaken alongside clinical trials, and that more of these trials incorporate quality of life assessments. A few trials do include an economic component. In a recently published review of economic evaluation, 88 out of 100 studies assessed alternative treatments or programmes.[12] Of these, 18 were conducted alongside randomized controlled clinical trials, and 30 were conducted alongside a prospective clinical study. Although the review cited was not based on a random sample from the literature, it was biased towards the more comprehensive and well conducted studies. Therefore, it is unlikely that the figures quoted give an underestimate of the extent to which economic analysis is based on good medical evidence.

The advantages of undertaking economic analysis in clinical trials have been discussed by Drummond and Stoddart.[17] One advantage is the potential improvements in methodology resulting from multidisciplinary working. Another is that since medical technologies often diffuse widely before their costs and benefits are fully evaluated, inclusion of economic analysis at the trial stage would give some chance of timely economic evidence being produced. However, the disadvantages of including economic analysis in clinical trials should not be minimized. Difficulties that have been highlighted are:

- the design and conduct of trials is already time-consuming, complex, and costly, without having to incorporate yet another dimension;
- economic expertise is often unavailable to those carrying out trials;
- many trials, particularly those of new drugs, are not directly concerned with eventual implementation of the therapy, but with assessing the new therapy's efficacy under ideal conditions when compared with a placebo;
- even those trials that assess the new therapy's effectiveness compared with existing practices when delivered to a defined population (management trials) might be conducted under such experimental conditions that costs and outcomes in regular service use could be different from those experienced during the trial,
- many trials show the new therapy to be either inefficacious or no more effective than the old, and it would be a waste of time to assess the economics of a regimen that would never be adopted;
- economics and medicine are uneasy bedfellows, and it might be better for clinical researchers to concentrate on establishing medical efficacy and effectiveness, leaving to health planners and politicians the question of whether a new therapy should be provided.[17]

Drummond and Stoddart suggest that some of these difficulties could be overcome by "phasing in" the economic analysis as more is known about the likely outcome of the clinical evaluation. In cost-utility analysis a key issue is whether the utility assessments need to be obtained as part of the clinical trial.

3. *Allowance for differential timing of costs and benefits.* A feature of many comparisons of health care interventions is that the costs and benefits occur at different points in time, for example a curative option

may yield benefits in improved health immediately, whereas the benefits of a preventive programme may be in the future. Similarly, treatments or programmes may differ in the time profiles of their resource outlays, some requiring significant capital expenditure immediately, others not. It is argued that, as individuals or as a community, we are not indifferent to the timing of costs and benefits, preferring to postpone the former and bring forward the latter. The most widely accepted method of incorporating this notion into economic evaluations is to *discount costs and benefits occurring in the future to present values.* This has the effect of giving less weight to future events. The discounting procedure must be applied to both costs and benefits or conflicting results are obtained.[18] The logic for, and mechanics of, discounting are discussed in more detail elsewhere.[19] The relevance of discounting to the debate about quality of life assessments in economic evaluations is that quality measured should be capable of being discounted if the time profile of outcomes differs among alternative interventions. The quality-adjusted life-year measure incorporates discounting, but other approaches to quality measurement might not.

Economic evaluations incorporating quality of life assessments

Three types of economic evaluation that incorporate quality of life assessments are found in the literature. The recent study of the economics of heart transplantation in the U.K. is an example of the first type. It uses quantity and quality of life as outcomes, but does not combine these data to derive a single index such as the quality-adjusted life-year.[20] In the study cited, Buxton *et al.* assessed survival post-transplant and the change in quality of life as measured by the Nottingham Health Profile. (This instrument measures quality of life along six dimensions: physical mobility, pain, sleep, energy, social isolation and emotional reactions.) Buxton *et al.* present the profile of measures but avoid the question of weighting improvements *between* the six dimensions. The instrument, however, does incorporate weightings *within* each dimension. It is well established in economics that *simple* scoring systems to reduce a profile of measures to a single index or score should be avoided. This is because the combination of various disabilities may be greater than the sum of the parts.[21] However, it is possible to find examples in the literature where, in the quest to find a single index to compare with costs, simple additions of disparate outcomes are made. For example, in evaluating alternative interventions to reduce perinatal mortality, Chapalain compares the costs with the sum of the deaths and cases of handicap avoided, implicitly weighting these equally.[22] Nevertheless, there may be occasions where the results obtained by simple

M. Drummond

scoring systems do not differ significantly from those obtained from more sophisticated approaches.[23]

The second type of economic evaluation that incorporates quality of life assessment uses a single index, usually the quality-adjusted life-year. But these studies do not undertake utility assessments on patients or other relevant respondents. An example is the study by Stason and Weinstein on options for hypertension screening and treatment.[24] Despite side effects, hypertension therapy may increase length of life and avert morbidity caused by strokes. Thus, an assumption was made about the quality of a year of life gained by hypertension therapy. It was assumed that a year with side effects was equivalent to 0.99 of a healthy year. This assessment was based on expert consensus and was not independently verified. The authors did test the sensitivity of their results to the assumption made, however, by reworking the analysis assuming that a year with side effects was equivalent to 0.98 of a healthy year. In this case study results changed as a consequence of the assumption made. Other examples of this approach are reported elsewhere.[25–28]

The third type of study is one which undertakes utility assessments as part of the economic evaluation. A good example is the study by Boyle *et al.* on neonatal intensive case for very-low-birth-weight infants.[29] The costs and consequences of setting up a regional neonatal intensive care programme were expressed in several ways, including the incremental cost per quality-adjusted life-year. The QALYs added by the programme were calculated using paediatricians' forecasts of lifetime outcomes for babies, and utility assessments of health states made by a random sample of parents of Hamilton (Ontario) schoolchildren. Another example of an economic evaluation incorporating utility assessments is that reported by Paterson on oral gold therapy for rheumatoid arthritis.[30] Sponsors of this study were keen to undertake utility assessments on arthritis patients, even though it may have been possible to combine data on the levels of pain and restriction of functioning with utility assessments obtained in previous studies.

Now that more economic evaluations of this type are being undertaken, many important issues are emerging, such as:

- Whose assessments of quality of life are relevant and how should these be obtained?
- Should one search for a generalizable quality of life measure and attempt to standardize methodology?
- Is it right to construct "league tables" of health care interventions in terms of cost per quality-adjusted life-year gained?

These issues will be discussed later in this paper. First, some general issues in the interpretation of study results for resource allocation decisions are reviewed.

Interpreting the results of analysis for decision making purposes

It was suggested above that there are two co-existing resource allocation processes in health care: planning decisions and clinical decisions. Key questions are: to which set of decisions does health services research (particularly economic evaluation) pertain, and how should the results of analysis be used? It might be argued that in clinical and epidemiological research using clinical trials, the situation is relatively straightforward. That is, the aim of clinical trials is to establish whether interventions are effective and whether results should be used by clinical practitioners in planning therapy for their patients. However, the ways in which trial results are used are probably more complex. For example, there may be crucial differences between the characteristics of patients in the trial and the clinical practitioner's own patients. In addition, there may be important differences between settings. Therefore, the trial results do not give a precise prescription for action. Trial results may also be used for planning decisions where evidence of effectiveness is being sought by funding agencies before reimbursements are allowed for a new drug or procedure. Therefore, clinical and epidemiological research applies to both sets of resource allocation decisions.

Similar issues arise in the interpretation of economic evaluation results. They are compounded by the fact that the analyses are broader in scope, including a consideration of costs as well as consequences. Most economists would argue that their analyses apply mainly to planning decisions; that is, decisions made on behalf of the community as a whole. This avoids the difficult ethical issue of considering costs in making clinical decisions.

The link between analysis and some planning decisions is relatively clear. For example, in an evaluation of vaccination strategies against pneumococcal pneumonia, Willems *et al.* were able to discuss the cost per QALY gained by vaccinating different age groups and the mechanisms by which funding might be made available to encourage vaccination of the elderly.[26] However, they point out that there are other considerations in health care decision making, such as equity or fairness in the distribution of health care resources. Such factors should be considered alongside cost per QALY when interpreting study results.

Neonatal intensive care has extra complexities. It was found that the cost per QALY gained varied by birthweight group (Canadian $3200 for babies weighing between 1000 and 1499 g, but $22,400 for babies weighing between 500 and 999 g.[29] The authors take the view that their study relates to planning decisions and state:

The findings of our study have several potential applications. Countries or regions with insufficient present capacity to provide intensive care for all very-low-birth-weight infants may wish to give priority to infants in the group weighing 1000 to

1499 g at birth. Societies with undeveloped facilities for the intensive care of very-low-birth-weight infants may choose to develop first the capacity to provide neonatal intensive care for infants weighing 1000 to 1499 g. Clearly, the rationing of neonatal intensive care – i.e. its preferential provision to those most likely to benefit or those from whom society is most likely to benefit – raises important ethical questions that require discussion.

The difficulty in relating analysis to resource allocation decisions in this case arises from the fact that the facilities for providing neonatal intensive care to the two birthweight groups are largely indistinguishable. Therefore, such rationing can only take place through clinical decisions. It might be argued that in making planning decisions about the size of neonatal units, tougher choices are imposed on clinicians if the planned capacity only accommodates the expected number of babies weighting 1000 g and over. In situations where it is possible to develop prognostic indicators, the way forward may be to explore costs and QALYs in relation to these. Nonetheless, the relationship between economic evaluation results and resource allocation decisions at the planning or clinical level can be quite complex.

KEY ISSUES IN THE USE OF QUALITY OF LIFE ASSESSMENTS IN ECONOMIC EVALUATION

Three key issues identified earlier having to do with the use of quality of life assessments in economic evaluation are discussed below.
- Whose assessments of quality of life are relevant and how should these be obtained?
- Should one search for a generalizable quality of life measure?
- Is it right to construct "league tables" of health care interventions in terms of cost per quality-adjusted life-year gained?

Whose assessments of quality of life are relevant and how should these be obtained?

It might be argued that where economic analysis seeks to inform planning decisions (the majority of cases), the relevant values are those of the general public or their elected representatives. This does not mean that utility measurements on patients are irrelevant to economic evaluations. Those charged with making decisions on behalf of the community may have an interest in how patients value the improvements in quality of life brought about by therapy, especially because the decision makers may have little experience of the illness concerned. For clinical decision-making purposes, the patient's assessments are important. Therefore, measurements of the patient's quality of life should continue to be the main focus in clinical trials, although for economic evaluation utility assessments from the general public will also be required.

An interesting area for investigation is whether patients' utility assessments and the treatment decisions they would make differ significantly from those of doctors. Most investigators have found no difference by age or sex, or among different groups; namely, the general public, physicians, nurses, patients.[31–33]

However, a few investigators have found small differences.[32] Williams notes that one study with 70 respondents in the U.K. included 10 doctors, all of whom appeared to have a greater aversion to disability and distress than the population at large; they overvalued reductions in disability and distress compared with the rest of the population.[28]

A related issue is whether economic analysis should obtain estimates of utilities during the course of a study, or whether these can be obtained by a quick and inexpensive consensus-forming exercise. It is worthwhile to note that economic evaluation, in contrast to the controlled clinical trial, often uses point estimates for variables and does not estimate these in a way that enables confidence intervals to be constructed. Some variables, such as the discount rate, are not observable in the same way as clinical outcomes. The general method used by economic analysts to cope with uncertainty is to ascertain how sensitive study results are to changes in the value assumed for the variable concerned. If the results *are* sensitive, effort needs to be made to seek a more accurate estimate.

In principle, the same logic should apply to utility estimates. Compared to other variables such as *number* of years of life gained, the values assumed for utility of health states might have little impact on the results. It is interesting to note that in the health status index developed in the U.K. by Kind *et al.* (which was used by Williams in his study of coronary artery bypass grafting) 18 of the 29 health states have a utility value of 0.90 or greater.[34,28] For respondents to assign a value lower than this, they would have to be confined to a wheelchair or be suffering severe distress, and have their choice of work or performance at work severely limited (see Table 1). The question then becomes what proportion of therapies impact on health states outside the range (on this index) 0.9–1.0? If quality improvements really are being sought within such a small range, it is likely that changes in length of life will dominate in the analysis. This may be an artifact of the particular index cited, however, for Torrance reports utility values over a much wider range.[15] Nevertheless, it would be prudent for those contemplating quality of life measurement within the context of an economic evaluation to consult the range of utility values in the literature to ascertain whether study results are likely to be sensitive to small changes in these values.

Finally, if it is decided that utility measurements should be part of the

Table 1 *Valuation matrix for 70 respondents*

		Distress rating			
	Disability rating	A. No distress	B. Mild	C. Moderate	D. Severe
I	No disability	1.000	0.995	0.990	0.967
II	Slight social disability	0.990	0.986	0.973	0.932
III	Severe social disability and/or slight physical impairment	0.980	0.972	0.956	0.912
IV	Physical ability severely limited (e.g. light housework only)	0.964	0.956	0.942	0.870
V	Unable to take paid employment or education, largely housebound	0.946	0.935	0.900	0.700
VI	Confined to chair or wheelchair	0.875	0.845	0.680	0.000
VII	Confined to bed	0.677	0.564	0.000	− 1.486
VIII	Unconscious	− 1.028	**	**	**

Healthy = 1.0; Dead = 0.0
*Source: Kind *et al.* (1982).
**Not applicable.

economic evaluation, do such measurements need to be linked to a clinical trial? The benefits of broadening traditional clinical measures to include quality of life assessments, and of undertaking economic analysis alongside clinical trials, have been discussed. Another advantage of undertaking utility assessments during the trial would be the ease of access to patients. If assessments were being made for the clinical evaluation, the extra cost of undertaking utility assessments for economic evaluation may be small. However, two points are worth noting.

First, the values of patients might not be relevant to planning decisions. Therefore, estimation of utility values can be seen as a separate exercise. Second, Thompson and Cohen have pointed out that, in contrast to other assessments of quality of life, estimation of utility values may be unpleasant for the respondent.[35] Therefore, the application of these methods as part of a research study raises ethical issues. However, it should be noted that issues raised in the estimation of utility values, namely tradeoffs between different health outcomes, should be part of the interaction between doctor and patient concerning the choice of therapy.

Should one search for a generalizable quality of life measure?

There are several dimensions to this question. The first issue, which applies to clinical and economic evaluation, is whether one should attempt to devise a standard instrument which can be used for a range of populations. This instrument would facilitate comparisons between health care interventions across many fields. The main message from the clinical literature appears to be that whereas general measures do facilitate comparisons, they may be unable to detect small, but clinically important, differences. The desired course of action might be for clinical trials to use at least one specific and one general measure.[36]

In economic evaluation the issue of generalizability centres around use of the quality-adjusted life-year measure. This index provides a common unit account which enables comparisons to be made across a wide range of programmes. It also incorporates discounting. Even if economic studies used other standard quality of life scales similar to those used in clinical evaluations, comparisons would be limited. The team undertaking the heart transplant study in the U.K. debated the advantages and disadvantages of using a standard (clinical) quality of life measure or utilities.[20,23] They used the Nottingham Health Profile, which did not cause any major difficulties, since the majority of patients improved on all of the six dimensions post-transplant. Therefore, there were no problems of comparing improvement on one dimension with deterioration on another. This may have become an issue if comparisons had been made with another intervention, unless one intervention were to dominate the other on all six dimensions.

Advantages claimed for the profile approach were that it had the potential to show subtle changes in the patient's health state, that profile measurements might be able to be used as prognostic indicators and that these measures were easy for clinicians to relate to. It makes sense for clinicians to discuss patient improvements using the profile dimensions (physical mobility, pain, sleep, energy, social isolation and emotional reactions) rather than in terms of utility measurements. In principle it would be possible to go back to the descriptors that are used to define the utility values concerned.

Although the attributes of profile measures outlined above are important, it appears that they relate more to the clinical interest in the study than to the broader policy or planning implications. It could be argued that if an evaluation seeks to provide information useful for both clinical and planning decisions, it should incorporate clinical quality of life measures and utility assessments.

Is it right to construct "league tables" of health care interventions in terms of cost per quality-adjusted life-year?

Economic evaluation, which relates mainly to planning decisions, strives to obtain comparative assessments of costs and consequences across a

Table 2 *"League Table"* of costs and benefits of selected medical procedures[a]

Procedure	Present value of extra cost per QALY gained (£)
Pacemaker implantation for heart block	700
Hip replacement	750
Valve replacement for aortic stenosis	950
CABG for severe angina with LMD	1,040
CABG for moderate angina with 3 VD	2,400
Kidney transplantation (cadaver)	3,000
Heart transplantation	5,000
Home haemodialysis	11,000
CABG for mild angina 2 VD	12,600
Hospital haemodialysis	14,000

[a]Adapted from Williams, 1985.[28]

wide range of programmes. The logic, outlined earlier, is that because resources are scarce, priorities for health service investments need to be assigned.

Because many evaluations have been performed, it is not surprising that there has been a tendency to construct "league tables" of interventions in terms of their cost per quality-adjusted life-year. One such ordering of programmes by Williams is presented in Table 2.[28] Is this justifiable, and what are the pitfalls? It is important to note that most authors merely present data for debate and do not specify any "cut-off" point beyond which programmes should not be provided. One exception to this rule is the paper by Kaplan and Bush where the authors suggest a kind of policy "triage".[31] Programmes with a cost of less than $20,000 per well year are considered "cost-effective by current standards"; those with a cost per well year in excess of $100,000 are considered "questionable in comparison with other health care expenditures", and those with costs in between are considered "controversial but possibly justifiable." However, most authors merely seek to assess how their study results compare with others. Sinclair used this approach to point out that neonatal intensive care for babies of birth-weight less than 1000 g was *not* expensive in terms of cost per quality-adjusted life-year, when compared to investments being made in other fields.[37] Comparisons between health care, environmental protection, and occupational health and safety are particularly instructive. Judging by the policy decisions that have been contemplated, the community is willing to pay much greater sums to save lives in these other fields.[38]

One of the main messages to be gleaned from such league tables is "never mind the quality (of the evidence), feel the width." That is, choices in the allocation of resources within health care, and between health care and other fields, are being made all the time. But are they being made consistently? Improvement in the quantity and quality of economic evaluations to a stage where this debate can be entered into brings with it increased responsibilities. Therefore, it is important to outline the main issues that those using these data should address.

First, many of the league tables are constructed using studies performed at different times and places. Presumably these use different methodology, too, although it is often hard to tell from published work exactly how costs and consequences were assessed. Apart from differences in the methods of measuring utilities, there are likely to be crucial differences in the formulation of the cost-effectiveness or cost-utility model and the costing methodology employed. Contentious issues are whether one should include production gains and losses, and whether one should include the medical care costs in added years of life. Methodological decisions on some of these issues may have a more profound impact on study results than the choice of utility measurement technique.

Second, it must be remembered that the studies merely give a "snapshot" of the costs and consequences of the intervention at a given stage of its development. Further refinements in the future may substantially improve benefits or reduce costs, thereby improving the cost per QALY figure.

Third, there are many factors to be taken into account when making health care resource allocation decisions. The criterion of equity was mentioned earlier. Investing in health care programmes that have the lowest cost per QALY implies a maximization principle. That is, to produce the largest improvement in health status given the resources at the disposal of the health care system. The implication of considering also the equity criterion would be that one might invest in programmes that had relatively high costs per QALY if they were targeted at disadvantaged groups. The construction of league tables of cost per QALY embodies some degree of equity since a QALY gained is valued the same no matter who receives it. However, it is important to be aware of inadvertently biasing the analysis against groups such as the elderly, chronic sick, unemployed or women by including production gains and losses in the analysis. In Fig. 1, the equity criterion would lead one to prefer $(C_1 - B_1)/U$ as the formulation of the cost-utility model. This was the approach adopted by Williams.[28] As far as he was concerned, the onus would be on those choosing to adopt a different value standpoint to state what this was.

Finally, one of the hesitations many have about league tables is that comparisons are made across such disparate fields. Does it really make sense to compare a long-term care programme for the elderly with heart transplantation? Perhaps an equally promising approach, hinted at by Williams, would be to explore the relative value of investments *within* fields.[28] This approach would focus on the relative efficiency of alternative techniques used by those in the same medical specialism. It would highlight those procedures which are more cost-effective than alternatives and those which appear to be marginally useful, when compared to the potential alternative uses of the same resources. For example, Williams calculated that coronary artery bypass surgery for moderate angina with one vessel disease would cost $12,000 per quality-adjusted life-year gained, whereas percutaneous transluminal coronary angioplasty for the same indication would cost only $3400 per QALY gained.[28]

Ultimately the broader choices will have to be addressed. But given the state of development of economic evaluation in health care and the need to secure active participation of clinical researchers and practitioners, it makes sense to tackle the more limited issues first. However, as the quantity and quality of evidence improves the obligation on decision makers to consider it must surely increase.

CONCLUSIONS

The main objective of this paper has been to discuss the relevance of quality of life measurement in clinical and epidemiological research to resource allocation decisions in health care. The discussion has centred on economic evaluation, the form of health services research which most directly pertains to decisions about the allocation of resources, and the use of the quality-adjusted life-year in economic evaluation.

The main conclusions are as follows. First, it should be acknowledged that there are two co-existing resource allocation processes in health care: planning decisions made on behalf of the community as a whole, and clinical decisions made on behalf of the individual patient. Potentially, clinical and epidemiological research and economic evaluation have a relevance to both resource allocation processes. However, the emphasis in clinical research is on influencing the clinical decision process. In economic evaluation it is on influencing the planning decision process. Nevertheless, the interrelationships between research and decision making can be quite complex.

In clinical and epidemiological research, resource allocation decisions would be improved if more trials included quality of life measures and if more trials incorporated an economic component. This would help policy makers and clinicians make decisions about the rational diffusion and use of health technologies. It might also be worthwhile to consider undertaking utility assessments on patients when economic evaluation is being performed alongside the clinical trial. However, since economic evaluation relates mainly to planning decisions, the relevant utility values will usually be those of the general public or their elected representatives.

Of the various forms of economic evaluation, cost-utility analysis, where the consequences of interventions are expressed in terms of the quality-adjusted life-years gained, is the most promising approach for all but the most limited choices. More empirical work is required in utility measurement, but economic analysts should investigate, through sensitivity analysis, whether it is the utility values which have the most impact on study results. Other factors, such as the range of costs and consequences included in the economic model, or the methods of estimating costs, might have a more profound influence on the study. If this is true, an expensive empirical investiation involving utility measurements may not be justified.

The comparison of health care interventions in terms of their cost per quality-adjusted life-year should be encouraged. However, the fact that such comparisons are being made places greater burdens on analysts to improve methodological standards and to communicate their results to decision makers more intelligently. Attention should be paid to standardization of economic evaluation methodology. Although methodological controversies will always be present and analysts might use different formulations of the cost-utility model, studies should be undertaken in a way that would present results in a standard format for comparative purposes. Those commissioning research have an important role in encouraging such standardization.

In communicating results to decision makers, investigators must highlight the importance of other factors, such as equity, and value judgements about these factors implied by the economic model used. It may be more productive to concentrate on the choices within medical specialisms than between them.

Early economic evaluations in health care, which were predominantly of the cost-benefit type, were likened to "horse and rabbit stew." Because the range of costs and benefits estimated was so limited, it was argued that it was pointless to obtain an accurate estimate of a small proportion of the relevant factors (the rabbit) when there was a much greater proportion (the horse) about which nothing was known. With the rapid growth of cost-utility analysis, economic evaluators are in danger of preparing a more palatable meal without being able to tell the customer (the decision maker) how to eat it.

REFERENCES

1 Banta, H.D., Behney, C.J., Willems, J.S.: *Toward Rational Technology in Medicine*. New York: Springer, 1981

2 Culyer, A.J., Horisberger, B. (Eds): *Economic and Medical Evaluation of Health Care Technologies*. Berlin: Springer-Verlag, 1983
3 Owen, D.: *In Sickness and in Health*. London: Quartet Books, 1976
4 Department of Clinical Epidemiology and Biostatistics: How to read clinical journals. V: To distinguish useful from useless or even harmful therapy. *Can. Med. Assoc. J.* 124: 1156–1162, 1981
5 Mosteller, F.: Innovation and evaluation. *Science* 211: 881–886, 1981
6 Guyatt, G., Drummond, M.G., Feeny, D., Tugwell, P. *et al.*: Guidelines for the clinical and economic evaluation of health care technologies. *Soc. Sci. Med.* 22: 393–408, 1986
7 Acton, J.P.: *Measuring the Social Impact of Heart and Circulatory Disease Programs: Preliminary Framework and Estimates*. Report R-1697-NHLI. Rand Corporation: Santa Monica, 1975
8 Jones-Lee, M.W.: *The Value of Life: An Economic Analysis*. London: Martin Robertson, 1976
9 Weinstein, M.C.: Economic assessment of medical practices and technologies. *Med. Decis. Making* 1: 309–330, 1981
10 Warner, K.E., Luce, B.R.: *Cost-benefit and Cost-effectiveness Analysis in Health Care*. Ann Arbor: Health Administration Press, 1982
11 Drummond, M.F.: *Studies in Economic Appraisal in Health Care*. Oxford: Oxford Medical Publications, 1981
12 Drummond, M.F., Ludbrook, A., Lowson, K.V., Steele, A.: *Studies in Economic Appraisal in Health Care*. Volume two. Oxford: Oxford Medical Publications, 1986
13 Department of Clinical Epidemiology and Biostatistics: How to read clinical journals. VII: To understand economic evaluation (Part B). *Can. Med. Assoc. J.* 130: 1542–1549, 1984
14 Ludbrook, A.: A cost-effectiveness analysis of the treatment of chronic renal failure. *Appl. Econ.* 13: 337–350, 1981
15 Torrance, G.W.: Utility approach to measuring health-related quality of life. *J. Chron. Dis.* 40:593–600, 1987
16 Culyer, A.J., Maynard, A.K.: Cost-effectiveness of duodenal ulcer treatment. *Soc. Sci. Med.* 15C: 3–11, 1981
17 Drummond, M.F., Stoddart, G.L.: Economic analysis and clinical trials. *Controlled Clin. Trials* 5: 115–128, 1984
18 Weinstein, M.C., Stason, W.B.: Foundations of cost-effectiveness analysis for health and medical practices. *N. Engl. J. Med.* 296: 716–721, 1977
19 Drummond, M.F.: *Principles of Economic Appraisal in Health Care*. Oxford: Oxford Medical Publications, 1980
20 Buxton, M.J., Acheson, R., Caine, N., Gibson, S., O'Brien, B.: *Study of the Costs and Benefits of the Heart Transplant Programmes at Harefield and Papworth Hospitals*. London: HMSO, 1985
21 Culyer, A.J.: *Need and the National Health Service*. London: Martin Robertson, 1976. Chapter 4
22 Chapalain, M-T.: Perinatality. French cost-benefit studies and decisions on handicap and prevention. In *Major Mental Handicap: Methods and Costs of Prevention*. London: CIBA Foundation Symposium, 1978

transplant programmes: quality of life data and their relationship to survival analysis. London: Health Economics Research Group, Brunel University, 1986 (mimeo)

24 Stason, W.B., Weinstein, M.C.: Allocation of resources to manage hypertension. *N. Engl. J. Med.* 296: 732–739, 1977

25 Weinstein, M.C.: Estrogen used in postmenopausal women – costs, risks and benefits. *N. Engl. J. Med.* 303: 308–316, 1980

26 Willems, J.S., Sanders, C.R., Riddiough, M.A., Bell, J.C.: Cost-effectiveness of vaccination against pneumococcal pneumonia. *N. Engl. J. Med.* 303(10): 553–559, 1980

27 Churchill, D.N., Lemon, B.C., Torrance, G.W.: A cost-effectiveness analysis of continuous ambulatory peritoneal dialysis and hospital hemodialysis. *Med Decis. Making* 4: 489–500, 1984

28 Williams, A.: Economics of coronary artery bypass grafting. *Br. Med. J.* 291: 326–329, 1985

29 Boyle, M.H., Torrance, G.W., Sinclair, J.C., Horwood, S.P.: Economic evaluation of neonatal intensive care of very-low-birth-weight infants. *N. Engl. J. Med.* 308: 1330–1337, 1983

30 Paterson, M.: Measuring the socio-economic benefits of auranofin. In *Measuring the Social Benefits of Medicine*, Teeling-Smith, G. (Ed.). London: Office of Health Economics, 1983

31 Kaplan, R.M., Bush, J.W.: Health related quality of life measurement for evaluation research and policy analysis. *Health Psychol.* 1: 61–80, 1982

32 Sackett, D.L., Torrance, G.W.: The utility of different health states as perceived by the general public. *J. Chron. Dis.* 31: 697–704, 1978

33 Wolfson, A.D., Sinclair, A.J., Bombardier, C., McGeer, A.: Preference measurement for functional status in stroke patients: inter-rater and inter-technique comparisons. In *Values and Long-term Care*, Kane, R., Kane, R. (Eds). Lexington, Mass.: D.C. Heath Publishers, 1982

34 Kind, P., Rosser, R., Williams, A.: Valuation of quality of life: some psychometric evidence. In *The Value of Life and Safety*, Jones-Lee, M.W. (Ed.). Amsterdam: Elsevier/North-Holland, 1982

35 Thompson, M.S., Cohen, A.B.: Should we measure personal valuations of perinatal outcomes? In *Clinical and Economic Evaluation of Perinatal Programs*. Mead Johnson Symposium on Perinatal and Developmental Medicine No. 20. Symposium held in Vail, Colorado, 6–10 June, 1982

36 Guyatt, G., Bombardier, C., Tugwell, P.X.: Measuring disease-specific quality of life in clinical trials. Hamilton (Ont.): Department of Clinical Epidemiology and Biostatistics, McMaster University, 1986 (mimeo)

37 Sinclair, J.C.: Personal communication, 1984

38 Graham, J.D., Vaupel, J.W.: Value of life: what difference does it make? *Risk Anal.* 1: 89–95, 1981

25

ECONOMIC EVALUATION OF NEONATAL INTENSIVE CARE OF VERY-LOW-BIRTH-WEIGHT INFANTS*

Michael H. Boyle, George W. Torrance, John C. Sinclair, Sargent P. Horwood

Neonatal intensive care results in both increased survival of low-birth-weight infants and increased costs for their care. Despite the high cost, an economic evaluation – in which the increment in health benefits resulting from neonatal intensive care is related to the increment in cost – has not been reported.[1]

We carried out an economic evaluation of neonatal intensive care of very-low-birth-weight (< 1500 g) infants born to residents in a defined region. We restricted the target population to infants whose birth weight was less than 1500 g, because the introduction of intensive care is reported to have had particularly important effects on both mortality and costs in this group.[2-5] We adopted the societal perspective – i.e., we measured all the costs and benefits of providing neonatal intensive care, regardless of who pays or who benefits. Moreover, we projected the long-term consequences (benefits and costs) for the entire life of the infants in the cohorts. We used the techniques of cost-benefit analysis, in which outcomes are converted to dollars; cost-effectiveness analysis, in which outcomes are measured in units of health; and cost–utility analysis, in which the social value of the outcomes is measured. We compared the findings before and after the introduction of neonatal intensive care in our population. The comparisons were made from birth to the time of hospital discharge, to age 15, and to the time of death.

METHODS

Setting and population

All infants weighing 500 to 1499 g at birth who were born live to residents of Hamilton-Wentworth County during the periods July 1964 to December 1969 (373 infants) and January 1973 to December 1977 (265

* First published in *The New England Journal of Medicine*, Vol. 308 (1983), 1330–7.
© The New England Journal of Medicine. Reprinted by permission.

infants) were included in the study. Those years were chosen to separate clearly the periods before and after the introduction of neonatal intensive care in Hamilton-Wentworth County. Infants were stratified into two classes of birth weight – 1000 to 1499 g and 500 to 999 g.

Hamilton-Wentworth is an urban, industrial county in southern Ontario with an estimated population of 410,000 in 1977. Before the introduction of neonatal intensive care, very-low-birth-weight infants born to county residents accounted for 0.95 percent of all live births, and neonatal mortality in this weight group was 58.7 percent.[6] These birth-rate and mortality-rate figures are typical of the experience that was reported for the 1960s from other geographic areas in the United States, Canada, and England.[7-9]

Additional details about the setting of the study and the population studied appear elsewhere.[6]

Program description

The McMaster regional perinatal program, introduced during the period 1970 to 1972, provides consultation and care for high-risk mothers and newborns in south-central Ontario. The objectives of the program conform to current recommendations for the regional development of perinatal health services.[10,11] These recommendations recognize three levels of risk requiring stepwise increments in the complexity and cost of perinatal health services: Level I, normal or low risk; Level II, moderate risk; and Level III, high risk. The regional perinatal center, which includes the regional neonatal-intensive-care unit, opened at the beginning of 1973 at the new McMaster University Medical Center. The unit is staffed and equipped to provide Level III care. Two other hospitals in the county (Henderson and St. Joseph's) are staffed and equipped to provide Level II perinatal care, and they maintain close affiliation with the regional center. An ambulance service is readily available to transport mothers and babies to the regional center.

Neonatal intensive care of very-low-birth-weight infants was implemented by applying a number of specific elements of neonatal care whose efficacy has been established through randomized controlled trials.[1] These practices, involving mainly the respiratory, nutritional, and environmental aspects of management, were implemented to different degrees at the three hospitals participating in the program; specifically, long-term tracheal intubation and assisted ventilation were performed only at the regional center.

All very-low-birth-weight infants delivered in Hamilton-Wentworth before the introduction of neonatal intensive care (during the period 1964 to 1969) were treated in either Henderson or St. Joseph's Hospital. After the introduction of neonatal intensive care (during the period 1973 to 1977), 43 percent of all very-low-birth-weight infants born to county residents were delivered in the regional perinatal center, and an additional 25 percent were transferred to the center after birth for specialized care. Thus, 68 percent of the 1973-to-1977 cohort actually received care in the regional neonatal-intensive-care unit.

Health outcomes

Mortality was determined at final discharge of newborns from the hospital. Among children discharged from the hospital, 121 of 150 survivors from 1964 to 1969 (81 percent) and 134 of 151 survivors from 1973 to 1977 (89 percent) were located and surveyed by mailed question-naire. Ages at follow-up ranged from 9 to 14 years for the 1964-to-1969 cohort and 1½ to 6 years for the 1973-to-1977 cohort. The mortality and morbidity outcomes of the cohorts have been reported.[6]

A classification of health states was developed to measure the health of survivors according to their physical function (six possible levels), role function (five levels), social and emotional function (four levels), and health problems (eight levels). Thus, there were $6 \times 5 \times 4 \times 8 = 960$ distinct possible health states. This classification was used in a home interview to describe the outcomes to date for a random sample of the survivors drawn from each cohort.

The relative value that members of society attach to the various possible health states of survivors was determined through utility measurements. Specifically, the aggregate social preference (utility) for each of the 960 possible health states in the classification system was determined in a random sample of parents of Hamilton, Ontario, schoolchildren;[12] strati-fication was employed for educational placement (regular or special) and the sex of the parent. The respondent was asked to rate the desirability or undesirability of a health state relative to other health states and relative to the reference states "healthy" and "dead." Conventionally, utility values are scaled from 1 (normal health) to 0 (dead); however, parents rated some chronic dysfunctional states in children as worse than death. Therefore, our range of utility values extends from 1 to −0.39. These utilities were used to adjust life-years for quality. For example, a life-year in a state judged to be 0.75 on the utility scale would represent 0.75 quality-adjusted life-years.

Costs

Neonatal-intensive-care costs   All costs were expressed in 1978 Canadian dollars. Costs of neonatal care were measured for each of the three Hamilton hospitals (McMaster University Medical Center, Henderson Hospital, and St. Joseph's Hospital) providing neonatal care. We estimated the cost of an episode of care by identifying at each hospital the relevant service departments (e.g., neonatal, radiology, or operating room), specifying the most appropriate unit for the measurement of service output (e.g., patient days, radiology-department work units, or operations), and using 1978 financial and service data to determine a fully allocated unit price for each service (e.g., dollars per patient day, dollars per work unit, or dollars per operation). The actual cost for each infant was determined by recording the quantity of services used by the infant, multiplying the quantity by the unit price of the service, and summing across all services. Because unit prices were fully allocated, they reflect not only the direct costs of care (e.g., salaries, wages, and supplies) but an appropriate share of the costs of support departments (e.g., administration and housekeeping) and overhead items (e.g., employee benefits and equipment depreciation). The simultaneous-equation method was used to allocate all costs among support departments serving each other.[13] A detailed description of our method of costing neonatal care is available.[14]

Other neonatal-care costs included physician charges, costs of convalescent care in community hospitals outside Hamilton, and costs of ambulance transport. Physician charges were obtained from billings to the Ontario Health Insurance Plan. Hospital-specific per diem rates[15] served to approximate the costs of hospital care outside the neonatal units.

Follow-up and projected costs and earnings Follow-up costs are the costs of resources consumed by children after discharge from the hospital as newborns and include both health-care costs (hospital, medical, dental, and drugs) and other costs (institutional, special services, appliances, the extra cost of special education, and miscellaneous items). Earnings are the anticipated lifetime earnings of survivors.

We interviewed parents to determine the types and quantity of services used by surviving children, studied the sources of these services, and determined a price per unit. Prices were all expressed in 1978 Canadian dollars. So that comparable information might be available in both cohorts, it was necessary to estimate missing cost data for older children and to forecast costs and effects not yet observed for younger children. Our own data served as the basis for these estimates and projections for the period up to and including age 15.

Forecasts of lifetime outcomes and costs were made independently by two developmental pediatricians using the health history that was available for each child. The projections included life expectancy, future functioning in terms of the health-state-classification system, productivity as a percentage of normal productivity, consumption of health services as a percentage of normal consumption, and living arrangements (i.e., independent living, parental or custodial care in a community setting, or institutionalization). So that the projections would reflect their uncertainty about the future, the pediatricians were asked to specify a probability distribution of outcomes in each forecast rather than a point estimate. Normal age-specific and sex-specific earnings were estimated on the basis of 1971 census data on individual income[16] indexed to 1978 according to the change in average weekly earnings.[17] Ontario health-care expenditures for 1978,[18] adjusted to reflect age-specific and sex-specific health-care costs,[19] were used to define normal consumption of health services. Yearly costs for a handicapped child receiving parental care at home were estimated to be $8,462, comprising the cost of food, shelter, and clothing[20] and an opportunity cost for the provision of parental care.[21] Yearly costs for institutional care were estimated to be $22,816 (Source: Ontario Ministry of Community and Social Services).

Analyses

See Appendix for more detailed explanation of analytic models.

We calculated the incremental costs, effects, and earnings associated with the provision of neonatal intensive care in Hamilton-Wentworth County. Analyses were done up to the following points: discharge of the newborn from the hospital, age 15, and death. Costs included neonatal-intensive-care costs and follow-up costs to the health-care sector and other sectors. Effects included numbers of lives saved, life-years gained, and quality-adjusted life-years gained. Earnings were subtracted from costs to yield a net economic cost.

We undertook three types of analysis: cost–effectiveness analysis, which investigates the additional cost and the additional net economic cost per life saved and per life-year gained from the provision of neonatal intensive care; cost–utility analysis, which investigates the additional cost and the additional net economic cost per quality-adjusted life-year gained; and cost–benefit analysis, which investigates the net economic benefit in dollars of intensive neonatal care over nonintensive care.[22–24]

A neonatal-intensive-care program requires the early expenditure of large sums of money to achieve later gains (e.g., in numbers of life-years or productivity). Therefore, a discount rate of 5 percent per annum was applied to costs, earnings, and effects (numbers of life-years and quality-adjusted life-years) occurring in the future in order to convert the future values to their equivalent present value.[25] For example, if C_n is the cost in year n, the equivalent present value is $C_n/(1.05)^{n-1}$.

Sensitivity analyses[26] were performed on all results to determine the robustness of the findings in the presence of major changes in key factors.

Table 1 *Health outcomes for very-low-birth-weight infants born before and after the introduction of neonatal intensive care, according to birth-weight class (undiscounted)*

Period	Birth weight 1000–1499 g		Birth weight 500–999 g	
	Before intensive care (1964–69) n = 213	Intensive care (1973–77) n = 167	Before intensive care (1964–69) n = 160	Intensive care (1973–77) n = 98
To hospital discharge				
Survivors (%)	62.4	77.2	10.6	22.4
To age 15 (projected)				
Life-years/live birth	9.0	11.1	1.46	3.37
QALYs*/live birth	6.4	8.1	1.22	1.80
To death (projected)				
Life-years/live birth	38.8	47.7	6.6	13.0
QALYs*/live birth	27.4	36.0	5.5	9.1

*QALY denotes quality-adjusted life-years.

Specifically, the following four factors were each varied independently over the given range to determine the impact on the findings: the discount rate (from 0 to 10 percent); life expectancy within the extremes of our forecasts; loss to follow-up, assuming that all those lost had major damage or that all were normal; and utility values over their range of uncertainty.[12]

Health outcomes

The rate of survival to hospital discharge increased with neonatal intensive care. Among infants weighing 1000 to 1499 g, 133 of 213 (62.4 percent) survived without intensive care as compared with 129 of 167 infants (77.2 percent) who survived in the intensive care era (Table 1). Among infants weighing 500 to 999 g, the survival rate with intensive care increased from 17 of 160 (10.6 percent) to 22 of 98 (22.4 percent).

Life-years per live birth (projected to age 15 and to death) also increased with neonatal intensive care. This was true for both birth-weight groups and for both crude and quality-adjusted life-years. However, the increase in quality-adjusted life-years was considerably less than that in unadjusted life-years for the group weighing 500 to 999 g.

Table 2 *Economic outcomes according to birth-weight class (undiscounted)* *

Costs/live birth	Birth weight 1000–1499 g		Birth weight 500–999 g	
	Before intensive care (1964–69) n = 213	Intensive care (1973–77) n = 167	Before intensive care (1964–69) n = 160	Intensive care (1973–77) n = 98
To hospital discharge Health care	5,400	14,200	1,500	13,600
To age 15 (projected) Health care	8,100	18,700	1,800	18,000
Other	4,000	2,000	200	1,900
Total cost	12,100	20,700	2,000	19,900
To death (projected) Health care	45,400	61,500	9,500	28,600
Other	47,100	38,600	1,500	15,000
Total cost	92,500	100,100	11,000	43,600
Earnings/live birth To death (projected)	122,200	154,500	19,200	48,100

*Values are expressed in 1978 Canadian dollars. Multiply by 0.877 to calculate equivalent 1978 U.S. dollars.

Costs

Table 2 shows the costs per live birth as measured until the time of discharge from the hospital and as projected to age 15 and to death. Projected lifetime earnings per live birth are also given.

Costs were greatly increased with provision of neonatal intensive care. For example, in the group weighing 1000 to 1499 g the cost of care until the time of hospital discharge before the introduction of neonatal intensive care was $5,400 per live birth, whereas the neonatal-intensive-care program cost $14,200 per live birth. In the group weighing 500 to 999 g, the cost of care until hospital discharge before the introduction of intensive care was $1,500 per live birth, as compared with $13,600 per live birth in the intensive-care program.

Economic evaluation

The data from Tables 1 and 2 have been used in Tables 3 and 4 to calculate the various measures of economic evaluation of neonatal intensive care. Table 3 can be computed directly from the data in Tables 1 and 2. Table 4

Table 3 *Measures of economic evaluation of neonatal intensive care, according to birth-weight class (undiscounted)* *

Period	Birth weight class	
	1000–1499 g	500–999 g
	$	
To hospital discharge		
Cost/additional survivor at hospital discharge	59,500†	102,500
To age 15 (projected)		
Cost/life-year gained	4,100†	9,400
Cost/QALY‡ gained	5,100	30,900
To death (projected)		
Cost/life-year gained	900	5,100
Cost/QALY‡ gained	900	9,100
Net economic benefit (loss)/live birth	24,700	(3,700)
Net economic cost/life-year gained	NA§	600
Net economic cost/QALY‡ gained	NA§	1,000

*Values are expressed in 1978 Canadian dollars. Multiply by 0.877 to calculate equivalent 1978 U.S. dollars.
†Table 3 can be directly reconstructed from Tables 1 and 2, using the formulas in the Appendix. For example, 59,500 = (14,200 − 5,400)/(0.772 − 0.624); 4,100 = (20,700 − 12,100)/(11.1 − 9.0).
‡QALY denotes quality-adjusted life-years.
§NA denotes not applicable.

Table 4 *Measures of economic evaluation of neonatal intensive care, according to birth-weight class (5 percent discount rate)* *

Period	Birth weight class	
	1000–1499 g	500–999 g
	$	
To hospital discharge†		
Cost/additional survivor at hospital discharge	59,500	102,500
To age 15 (projected)		
Cost/life-year gained	6,100	12,200
Cost/QALY‡ gained	7,700	40,100
To death (projected)		
Cost/life-year gained	2,900	9,300
Cost/QALY‡ gained	3,200	22,400
Net economic benefit (loss)/live birth	(2,600)	(16,100)
Net economic cost/life-year gained	900	7,300
Net economic cost/QALY‡ gained	1,000	17,500

*Values are expressed in 1978 Canadian dollars. Multiply by 0.877 to calculate equivalent 1978 U.S. dollars.
†All costs and effects occurred in year one.
‡QALY denotes quality-adjusted life-years.

differs from Table 3 in that future costs (those beyond the first year), earnings, and effects (numbers of life-years and quality-adjusted life-years) are discounted at a rate of 5 percent per annum. Since neonatal intensive care has high initial costs in order to achieve later gains in numbers of life-years, numbers of quality-adjusted life-years, and productivity, discounting affects the later gains more than the initial costs and adversely affects the measures of economic evaluation.

Cost-effectiveness (5 percent discount rate) For the group weighing 1000 to 1499 g at birth, the incremental cost of the neonatal-intensive-care program was $59,000 per additional survivor at hospital discharge, $6,100 per life-year gained until age 15, and $2,900 per life-year gained over the projected lifetime. When the increased future earnings were netted against costs as a "cost recovery," the net economic cost was reduced to $900 per life-year gained. For the group weighing 500 to 999 g at birth the intensive-care program cost $102,500 per additional survivor at hospital discharge, $12,200 per life-year gained until age 15, and $9,300 per life-year gained over the patient's lifetime. The net economic cost of intensive care was $7,300 per life-year gained.

Cost–utility (5 percent discount rate) Among the infants weighing 1000 to 1499 g at birth, the neonatal-intensive-care program cost $7,700 per quality-adjusted life-year gained until age 15 and $3,200 per quality-adjusted life-year gained over the projected lifetime. The net economic cost was $1,000 per quality-adjusted life-year gained. For infants weighing 500 to 999 g at birth, the figures were $40,100 per quality-adjusted life-year gained until age 15 and $22,400 per quality-adjusted life-year gained over the projected lifetime. The net economic cost of intensive care was $17,500 per quality-adjusted life-year gained.

Cost–benefit (5 percent discount rate) For both birth-weight groups, the provision of neonatal intensive care resulted in an increase in cost that was greater than the increase in projected earnings. For the group weighing 1000 to 1499 g, the net economic loss was $2,600 per live birth. For the group weighing 500 to 999 g, the net economic loss was $16,100 per live birth.

Analyses by 250-g subgroups A breakdown of the group weighing 1000 to 1499 g revealed that the subgroup weighing 1000 to 1249 g had the larger gains in survival to hospital discharge, life-years, and quality-adjusted life-years. Although the subgroup weighing 1250 to 1499 g had a smaller gain in survival and other health outcomes, their care also incurred only a modest additional cost. As a result, most measures of economic evaluation were more favorable for the 1250-to-1499-g subgroup; in fact, intensive care of this subgroup resulted in a net economic benefit of $1,150 per live birth, whereas intensive care of the babies weighing 1000 to 1249 g resulted in a net economic loss of $5,500 per live birth (Fig. 1).

A breakdown of the group weighing 500 to 999 g revealed more dramatic differences. Gains in survival to hospital discharge in life-years, and in quality-adjusted life-years were almost totally confined to the subgroup weighing 750 to 999 g. However, the gain in the number of life years was not nearly matched by the gain in the number of quality-adjusted life-years. As a result, the increments in both hospital costs and postdischarge costs were very much higher in the subgroup weighing 750 to 999 g than in the subgroup weighing under 750 g. In fact, cost–benefit analysis showed that intensive care of the 750-to-999-g subgroup resulted in a net economic loss of $25,000 per live birth (Fig. 1), which was by far the largest net economic loss calculated for any subgroup.

Sensitivity analysis   Sensitivity analyses were performed for all measures of economic evaluation. As the discount rate was increased from 0 to 10

Figure 1 Net economic benefit of neonatal intensive care according to 250-g subgroups, at a 5 per cent discount rate.
Values are expressed in 1978 Canadian dollars (per live birth in birth-weight class). Multiply by 0.877 to calculate equivalent 1978 U.S. dollars

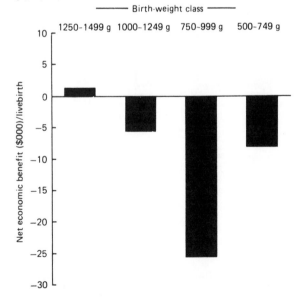

percent all measures of economic evaluation for each weight group became less favorable. In the group weighing 1000 to 1499 g, the net economic benefit per live birth was positive at discount rates lower than approximately 3½ percent and negative at higher discount rates; in the group weighing 500 to 999 g, the net economic benefit per live birth was negative at a discount rate of zero and became even more negative as the discount rate was increased (Fig. 2). All measures of economic evaluation were relatively insensitive to variation in life expectancy. As the assumption regarding the status of those lost to follow-up was changed from "all damaged" to "all normal," the measures of economic evaluation were not much affected except for a substantial improvement in the cost—utility measures for the group weighing 500 to 999 g (Fig. 2, cost/QALY

Figure 2 Sensitivity to four factors for cost/quality-adjusted life-year (QALY) gained and net economic benefit/live birth, both over the lifetime.
The four factors and their range of uncertainty are A, discount rate (0 percent to 10 percent); B, life expectancy (low to high); C, loss to follow-up (all damaged to all normal); and D, utility values (lower bound to upper bound). In the figure, the base-case values (Table 4) are shown as a heavy bar. The columns indicate the magnitudes of factor effects taken one at a time. The direction of each effect is indicated at the top and the bottom of the column. Interpretations of the directions of effects must allow for the incremental nature of the analysis; for example, different losses to follow-up in the two time periods between the two weight groups cause the direction of the effect of factor C to change between the two weight groups.

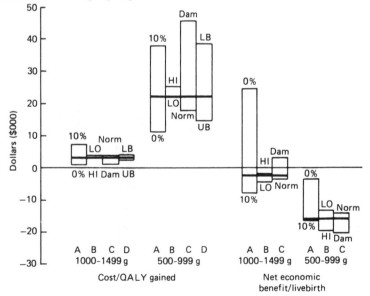

[quality-adjusted life-years] gained). As the utility values were increased through their range of uncertainty, all cost–utility results improved; the change was relatively minor for the 1000-to-1499-g group, but substantial for the 500-to-999-g group (Fig. 2, cost/QALY gained). In each of these cases (discount rate, life expectancy, loss to follow-up, and utility values) the direction of the difference between the two weight groups was unaffected by changes in the factor.

DISCUSSION

Neonatal intensive care of very-low-birth-weight infants born to residents of Hamilton-Wentworth County resulted in both increased survival and increased costs. By every measure of economic evaluation, it was economically more favorable to provide intensive care for the relatively heavier infants (weighing 1000 to 1499 g at birth) than for those weighing 500 to 999 g. This finding is in general agreement with the predictions of Budetti and co-workers.[27] There was a projected net economic loss (when a 5 percent discount rate was used) resulting from the neonatal intensive care of each weight group.

We believe that our findings about health outcomes can be generalized to the neonatal intensive care of very-low-birth-weight infants in similar urban settings during the period studied. We included all very-low-birth-weight infants born to residents of a defined region in order to avoid the referral bias inherent in the inclusion only of mothers and infants admitted to our Level III perinatal center.[6] We carried out birth-weight-specific comparisons to minimize confounding from factors such as maternal age, parity, and socio-economic status, which influence neonatal mortality primarily by affecting the birth-weight distribution of live births.[28] Moreover, we ascertained that factors that could influence birth-weight-specific mortality risk at the time of birth – including gestational age, use of tocolytic drugs or glucocorticoids prenatally, mode of delivery, multiple pregnancy, infant sex, one-minute Apgar score, and presence of respiratory-distress syndrome – did not make an important contribution to the difference in mortality between the 1964-to-1969 and the 1973-to-1977 cohorts.[6]

With regard to the generalizability of our economic outcomes (costs and earnings), several points are relevant. Although our cost data are all expressed in 1978 Canadian dollars, these can be converted to United States dollars by means of the 1978 conversion rate of 0.877 U.S. dollars per Canadian dollar and they can be converted to current dollars by means of an appropriate price index (e.g., the medical-care subsection of the consumer price index for health-care costs, the overall consumer price index for other costs, and the index of average earnings for earnings figures). Moreover, generalizability is enhanced because our cost data are collected without regard to who pays. Thus, our findings are independent of the financing mechanisms in a particular jurisdiction. On the other hand, our costs are a function of the level of intensity of our particular program, and jurisdictions with different levels of intensity should expect different costs (and probably different outcomes). Similarly, sparsely populated regions have programs with features different from ours and may well have different overall costs.

The accuracy of the data is related inversely to the length of follow-up. The data for the period from birth to hospital discharge are based on actual measurements; the data for the period from birth to age 15 are based on a combination of measurements and projections; and the data for the period from birth to death are based on projections from our forecasters. Moreover, the data rely in part on parental recall of costs and events, and the direction of any bias resulting from this is uncertain. On the one hand, parents of the 1964-to-1969 cohort may have been more likely to forget both costs and temporary periods of dysfunction. However, children in the 1973-to-1977 cohort may yet have dysfunction and incur costs not predicted by their present health states.

The economic evaluation measures (Table 4) reflects the major tangible factors. However, there are many intangible factors not included in these measures that affect the value of neonatal-intensive-care programs for very-low-birth-weight infants. These include (for example) the emotional impact on families of infant deaths or dysfunctional children; the outlook for future successful pregnancies; and the gains in knowledge and skills that come from working on the most difficult cases and that can then be applied more generally.

A major finding of this study – that by every economic measure neonatal intensive care for infants weighing 1000 to 1499 g is superior to neonatal intensive care for infants weighing 500 to 999 g – is robust with respect to all sensitivity analyses investigated. The result is unchanged by the selection of any discount rate in the range investigated, by the assumption about life expectancy, by the assumption about the condition of children lost to follow-up, or by the assumption about the utility values.

We emphasize that this evaluation is an economic one, which considers both outcomes and costs. A very different conclusion could result if only clinical outcomes were considered. For example, neonatal intensive care of infants weighing 750 to 999 g at birth resulted in the largest gain in survival rate for any subgroup (from 19 percent to 43 percent). However, neonatal intensive care of this same subgroup also produced a net economic loss that was the largest for any subgroup ($25,500 per live birth). Thus, the introduction of the economic perspective leads to a quite different conclusion about the effects of neonatal intensive care than does consideration from a purely clinical perspective.

What can we conclude about the overall economic viability of neonatal intensive care and about its ranking as compared with other programs? Cost–benefit analysis has the advantage of not requiring external com- parison. If the net economic benefit is positive and the health outcomes are positive, the program both pays for itself economically and improves health and is therefore deserving of support. This is the case for the infants weighing 1000 to 1499 g at discount rates of less than $3\frac{1}{2}$ percent. Thus, if the test discount rate is below $3\frac{1}{2}$ percent, neonatal intensive care for infants weighing 1000 to 1499 g is economically justified. Although test discount rates that low are frequently advocated by economists,[29] most governments recommended a higher rate.[30,31]

A program that does not meet the cost–benefit criterion (neonatal intensive care for infants weighing 1000 to 1499 g at discount rates above $3\frac{1}{2}$ percent and neonatal intensive care for infants weighing 500 to 999 g at any discount rate) represents a net drain on society's resources – that is, the program consumes more resources than it saves or creates. Then the question (from a social perspective) is, "How much is society willing to pay for improved health outcomes?" Many health programs are consciously supported by society if the positive effects (health and otherwise) are judged to be sufficient to justify the resource expenditures. Examples include most geriatric programs, dialysis and kidney- transplantation programs, and many others. Cost–effectiveness and cost– utility analyses can be used to compare such programs if comparable methodology has been used.

A number of studies have been reported that present the same economic-evaluation measures as our study: for example, cost per life- year gained over the lifetime,[32,33] cost per quality-adjusted life-year gained over the lifetime,[34,35] and net economic cost per quality-adjusted life-year gained over the lifetime.[36] Although these studies may be roughly comparable to ours, we prefer not to make direct comparisons because of methodologic differences. A judgment concerning the relative economic value of neonatal intensive care of very-low-birth-weight infants will require the economic evaluation of other health programs by similar methods. Such studies should measure incremental costs and incremental outcomes for actual patients in the program as compared with those not in the program. Costs should be measured comprehensively and from the point of view of society as a whole. Outcomes should be measured according to numbers of lives saved, life-years gained, and also, prefer- ably, quality-adjusted life-years gained. Quality-adjustment factors should be real, not hypothetical. Future costs, earnings, and outcomes should be discounted at an appropriate discount rate; the choice of a 5 percent rate would permit direct comparison with the results of this study. The more such studies are undertaken with a common methodology and reported in the literature, the more we will all be able to make valid comparisons among alternatives competing for our limited health-care resources.

The findings of our study have several potential applications. Countries or regions with insufficient present capacity to provide intensive care for all very-low-birth-weight infants may wish to give priority to infants in the group weighing 1000 to 1499 g at birth. Societies with undeveloped facilities for the intensive care of very-low-birth-weight infants may choose to develop first the capacity to provide neonatal intensive care for infants weighing 1000 to 1499 g. Clearly, the rationing of neonatal intensive care – i.e., its preferential provision to those most likely to benefit or to those from whom society is most likely to benefit – raises important ethical questions that require discussion.

Our findings have application also to the identification of problem areas requiring further research; moreover, the methods of economic evaluation are applicable to the evaluation of preventive or therapeutic innovations. New approaches to the prevention of extreme prematurity and to neonatal intensive care of babies weighing under 1000 g at birth are clearly needed and in fact are being introduced frequently. Future studies that seek to determine the effectiveness of such innovations may also undertake to determine their efficiency, using the techniques of economic evaluation.

APPENDIX

Analytic models (see also references 22 through 24)

Basic outcome data (Tables 1 and 2)

S = Proportion of cohort (live births) surviving to hospital discharge.

Y = Life-years/live birth. The total number of life-years from the cohort projected to age 15 or to death and divided by the number of live births. When discounting is used, future life-years (beyond the first year) are converted to their equivalent present value (see formula in Methods) before being totaled and divided.

Q = QALYs/live birth. Same as Y, except the life-years are quality-adjusted according to the known or projected health states of the patients.

C = Cost/live birth. The total cost for the cohort for health care and for disability-related items, divided by the number of live births. Costs are totaled up to the point of hospital discharge, to age 15, and to death. When discounting is used, future costs (beyond the first year) are converted to their equivalent present value (see formula in Methods) before being totaled and divided.

W = Earnings/live birth. The total earnings (wages) for the cohort projected over the lifetime and divided by the number of live births. When discounting is used, future earnings are converted to their present value (see formula in Methods) before being totaled and divided.

Subscripts 1 and 2 on the above symbols represent the two programs studied; subscript 1 represents the period before intensive care (1964 to 1969), and subscript 2 represents the intensive-care period (1973 to 1977).

Incremental data $\Delta S = S_2 - S_1$, additional survivors per live birth in the group with neonatal intensive care as compared with the group without intensive care. Similarly,

$\Delta Y = Y_2 - y_1$, additional life-years per live birth.

$\Delta Q = Q_2 - Q_1$, additional quality-adjusted life-years (QUALYs) per live birth.

$\Delta C = C_2 - C_1$, additional cost per live birth.

$\Delta W = W_2 - W_1$, additional earnings per live birth.

Economic evaluation models (Tables 3 and 4)

Cost–effectiveness analysis Three cost–effectiveness ratios (C/E) are calculated, the second one for two projected time periods (to age 15 and to death).

C/E = $\Delta C / \Delta S$, additional cost per life saved.

C/E = $\Delta C / \Delta Y$, additional cost per life-year gained.

C/E = $(\Delta C - \Delta W) / \Delta Y$, additional net economic cost per life-year gained.

Cost–Utility Analysis Two cost–utility ratios (C/U) are calculated, the first one for two projected time periods (to age 15 and to death).

C/U = $\Delta C / \Delta Q$, additional cost per QALY gained.

C/U = $(\Delta C - \Delta W) / \Delta Q$, additional net economic cost per QALY gained.

Cost–benefit analysis The net economic benefit (NEB) of neonatal intensive care is calculated.

NED = $\Delta W - \Delta C$

REFERENCES

1 Sinclair, J.C., Torrance, G.W., Boyle, M.H., Horwood, S.P., Saigal, S., Sackett, D.L. Evaluation of neonatal-intensive-care programs. *N. Engl. J. Med.* 1981; 305:489–94.

2 Pomerance, J.J., Ukrainski, C.T., Ukra, T., Henderson, D.H., Nash, A.H., Meredith, J.L. Cost of living for infants weighing 1,000 grams or less at birth. *Pediatrics* 1978; 61:908–10.

3 McCarthy, J.T., Koops, B.L., Honeyfield, P.R., Butterfield, L.J. Who pays the bill for neonatal intensive care? *J. Pediatr.* 1979; 95:755–61.

4 Phibbs, C.S., Williams, R.L., Phibbs, R.H. Newborn risk factors and costs of neonatal intensive care. *Pediatrics* 1981; 68:313–21.

5 Yu, V.Y.H., Bajuk, B. Medical expenses of neonatal intensive care for very low birthweight infants. *Aust. Paediatr. J.* 1981; 17:183–5.

6 Horwood, S.P., Boyle, M.H., Torrance, G.W., Sinclair, J.C. Mortality and morbidity of 500- to 1,499-gram birth weight infants live-born to residents of a defined geographical region before and after neonatal intensive care. *Pediatrics* 1982; 69:613–29.

7 Kleinman, J.C., Kovar, M.G., Feldman, J.J., Young, C.A. A comparison of 1960 and 1973-1974 early neonatal mortality in selected states. *Am. J. Epidemiol.* 1978; 108:454–69.

8 Usher, R. Changing mortality rates with perinatal intensive care and regionalization. *Semin. Perinatol.* 1977; 1:309–19.

9 Steiner, E.S., Sanders, E.M., Phillips, E.C.K., Maddock, C.R. Very low birth weight children at school age: comparison of neonatal management methods. *Br. Med. J.* 1980; 281:1237–40.

10 Swyer, P.R. The regional organisation of special care for the neonate. *Pediatr. Clin. North Am.* 1970; 17:761–76.

11 Committee on Perinatal Health. Toward improving the outcome of pregnancy: recommendations for the regional development of maternal and perinatal health services. White Plains, N.Y.: The National Foundation – March of Dimes, 1976.

12 Torrance, G.W., Boyle, M.H., Horwood, S.P. Application of multi-attribute utility theory to measure social preferences for health states. *Operations Res.* 1982; 30:1043–69.

13 Kaplan, R.S. Variable and self-service costs in reciprocal allocation models. *Accounting Rev.* 1973; 48:738–48.

14 Boyle, M.H., Torrance, G.W., Horwood, S.P., Sinclair, J.C. A cost analysis of providing neonatal intensive care to 500-1,499 gram birth-weight infants. Hamilton, Ont.: Program for Quantitative Studies in Economics and Population, Faculty of Social Sciences, McMaster University, 1982. (Research report no. 51).

15 Hospital Statistics 1977/78. Toronto: Ontario Ministry of Health, 1978.

16 1971 Census of Canada. Income of individuals by sex, age, marital status and period of immigration. (Catalogue 94-760 Volume III (Part 6) (Bulletin 3.6-2).) Ottawa: Statistics Canada, 1975.

17 Employment, Earnings and Hours. (Catalogue 72-002.) Ottawa: Statistics Canada, 1980.

18 Ontario Ministry of Treasury and Economics. Ontario Statistics 1980, Toronto, 1980.

19 Denton, F.T., Spencer, B.G. Health-care costs when the population changes. *Can. J. Economics* 1975; 8:34–48.

20 Culley, J.D., Settles, B.H., Von Name, J.B. Understanding and measuring the cost of foster care. Newark, N.J.: Bureau of Economic and Business Research, University of Delaware, 1975.

21 Kaegi, E.A.R. Prenatal diagnosis and selective therapeutic abortion in the prevention of Down's syndrome – an evaluation emphasizing medical and economic issues. M.Sc. Thesis, McMaster University, Hamilton, Ontario, 1976.

22 Warner, K.E., Luce, B.R. *Cost-benefit and cost effectiveness analysis in health*

care: principle, practice, and potential. Ann Arbor, Mich.: Health Administration Press, 1982.

23 Drummond, M.F. *Principles of economic appraisal in health care.* Oxford: Oxford University Press, 1980.

24 Weinstein, M.C., Stason, W.B. Foundations of cost-effectiveness analysis for health and medical practices. *N. Engl. J. Med.* 1977; 296:716–21,

25 Cost-benefit and cost effectiveness analysis in health care,[22] p. 93.

26 Cost-benefit and cost effectiveness analysis in health care,[22] p. 100.

27 Budetti, P., McManus, P., Barrand, N., Heinen, L.A. The costs and effectiveness of neonatal intensive care. Washington, D.C.: Congressional Office of Technology Assessment, U.S. Government Printing Office, 1981, p. 41.

28 Lee, K-S., Paneth, N., Gartner, L.M., Pearlmann, M.A., Gruss, L. Neonatal mortality: an analysis of the recent improvement in the United States. *Am. J. Public Health* 1980; 70:15–21.

29 Cost-benefit and cost effectiveness analysis in health care,[22] p. 97.

30 Treasury Board. Benefit-cost analysis guide. Ottawa: Ministry of Supply and Services, 1976.

31 Her Majesty's Treasury. Investment appraisal and discounting techniques and the use of the test discount rate in the public sector. Edinburgh: Her Majesty's Stationery Office Press, 1980.

32 Cretin, S. Cost/benefit analysis of treatment and prevention of myocardial infarction. *Health Serv. Res.* 1977; 12:174–89.

33 Torrance, G.W., Zipursky, A. Economic evaluation of treatment with anti-D. McMaster University, Hamilton, Ont.: Department of Pediatrics and Faculty of Business, 1977.

34 Weinstein, M.C. Estrogen use in postmenopausal women – costs, risks, and benefits. *N. Engl. J. Med.* 1980; 303:308–16.

35 Stason, W.B., Weinstein, M.C. Allocation of resources to manage hypertension. *N. Engl. J. Med.* 1977; 296:732–9.

36 Torrance, G.W., Sackett, D.L., Thomas, W.H. Utility maximization model for program evaluation: a demonstration application. In: Berg, R.L. ed. Health status indexes: proceedings of a conference conducted by Health Services Research, Tuscon, Arizona, October 1–4, 1972. Chicago: Hospital Research and Educational Trust, 1973:156–72.

26

———— ~ ————

AN ANALYTIC APPROACH TO RESOLVING PROBLEMS IN MEDICAL ETHICS*

Daniel Candee, Bill Puka

The past decade has seen a substantial increase in recognizing the importance of moral factors in making decisions about patient illness. Along with this recognition has come an increased need for physicians to have a systematic method with which to think about and resolve moral problems in medicine. Several techniques have been developed, reviewed by Callahan.[1] However, nearly all of these techniques use the format of open-ended discussion of cases involving problematic moral issues. As such, they typically serve to expand the participants' thinking about moral issues, but they do not necessarily focus on making an actual decision. In this paper, we suggest a method which aims at providing a systematic series of question an individual must ask in order to arrive at a well-reasoned moral decision. The method, which we will call the analytic approach, borrows certain concepts from traditional theories of ethics, and attempts to apply them systematically to making decisions about current ethical problems.

Traditional moral theories are neither procedures nor decision-making rules. Their chief task has been to explain and justify moral beliefs in order to develop consistency, plausibility, and completeness in our moral views. The needs of explanation and justification which they serve are different from the needs of decision-making. Part of what allows general principles of explanation to be meaningful is a conscious ignoring of the peculiarities of each situation. However, while moral theories are meant to be fundamental and abstract, their principles might, at least, be used as conceptual aids in making moral decisions. This may move us part of the way down the decision-making path in a manner that is more comprehensive and well-reasoned than is opinion or intuition.

Broadly speaking, moral thought traditionally takes two general approaches to answering the basic question in normative ethics, "What is the right thing to do?" The first approach, teleology usually defines

* Reprinted from *Journal of Medical Ethics*, 2 (1984), 61–70. © Journal of Medical Ethics. Reprinted by permission.

"right" in terms of the good produced as the consequences of an action. The most prominent form of teleology, utilitarianism, bids one calculate the probable results of performing various actions relevant to a situation and choose one that will maximize the ratio of benefit over harm produced. The second major approach, deontology, defines "right" by considering intrinsic features of an action, largely independent of its consequences. We will draw on three main concerns of deontological theory here: 1) fulfilling one's duties in a situation, 2) respecting the rights and autonomy of others (regardless of the consequences), and 3) treating others with equal justice. These concerns are organized usefully in the logic of Kant's categorical imperative and principle of respect. Roughly these direct us to act only on rationales that we can generalize to similar situations and which can be consented to rationally by anyone similarly situated (or affected by such actions). Put another way, they advise us to respect everyone's capacity to determine and pursue her or his goals, never treating people as mere means or tools to our ends.

Despite their differences, both orientations are accepted by moral philosophers as worthy of serious consideration. Both strive to be logical, internally consistent, and to yield similar decisions in morally similar situations. Just as theories of natural science strive to explain the natural world by a set of interrelated logical principles, so ethical theories strive to explain the moral world by constructing their own principles.

In order to demonstrate how these two major types of moral theory might be used to resolve a bioethical problem, let us consider a particular situation. (We make no pretence at presenting an orthodox version of either type of theory since neither was designed as a decision mechanism. Further, the extensive variations within each type prevent any one approach from being properly representative of either.) Our goal is to suggest two broad sets of concerns (utility and justice) that must be considered in making moral decisions of any kind. These concerns correspond to those that have distinguished the two major approaches to moral philosophy through the ages.

In 1971 at Johns Hopkins Hospital, a baby was born who, shortly after birth, was clinically diagnosed to have Down's syndrome (mongolism), a condition associated with mental retardation. An additional confirmation of the clinical diagnosis through chromosomal analysis, which takes several weeks to perform, was not carried out. The baby also had duodenal atresia, a constriction of a portion of the intestine that prevents the passage of food. It is fatal if not surgically corrected! Surgery for this condition carries a relatively small risk.

The mother of the baby, a nurse, was so distressed on learning the diagnosis, that she refused to give consent for the operation to remove the intestinal blockage. Her husband accepted the decision, believing that as a nurse, his wife was more knowledgeable about this matter than he. The physician in the case indicated to the parents that children with Down's syndrome often had IQs of between 50 and 80, could perform simple jobs, were usually happy, and could live a long time. This failed to change their minds. The doctors at the hospital did not attempt to thwart the parents' decision through a court order. In the hospital, after about two weeks, the child died of starvation.[2]

Were the doctors at Hopkins right or wrong to have allowed the baby to starve? We begin resolving the dilemma by consulting the process of moral decision-making outlined in Table 1. The first step according to both the utilitarian and the deontological viewpoints is to gather claims, i.e., to determine who wants what. As a practical matter, we will have to limit the scope of persons whose interests can be considered. Among those persons who will be directly affected by the present decision are the parents, who would like to avoid the difficulty of rearing a retarded baby, the doctors, who are willing to accede to the wishes of the parents, and the baby who, we can assume, would like to live as normal a life as possible.

Step two, determining feasible alternatives, is greatly influenced by the presentation of claims. Within limits set by the environment, we can usually act in a way that satisfies the exclusive claims of either party or partially satisfies the claims of both. The purpose of moral decision-making is to determine which of the feasible alternatives is morally best. In the present case, the alternatives would seem to include performing surgery, allowing the baby to die (passive euthanasia), or actually ending the baby's life (active euthanasia).

Utilitarian approach

At step three, utilitarian and deontological approaches diverge. Deontology determines the most moral action by setting forth the rights, duties, and principles involved in a situation and by trying to determine which take precedence. By contrast, utilitarian theory determines which actions will lead to the greatest ratio of benefit to harm for all persons involved in a dilemma. (This can be done for each act or by formulating a rule which, if followed regularly in similar situations, would be likely to maximize good.) In order to calculate the utilitarian ratio it is necessary to predict the possible outcomes (consequences) of each action, the probability of each outcome occurring, and the desirability of those outcomes for the child and for the parents and for society (Table 1, steps 3–6). The presentation of the utilitarian approach will rely heavily on the method outlined in Brody.[3]

Table 1 *Steps in the moral reasoning process*

Teleological (utilitarian) approach	Deontological approach
(1) Gather general claims	(1) Gather general claims
(2) List feasible alternatives	(2) List feasible alternatives
(3) Predict consequences (outcomes) of each action	(3) List relevant rights-claims, duties and principles
(4) Determine probability of each outcome occurring	(4) Establish validity of rights-claims
(5) Assign value to each outcome (determine basis of valuing)	(5) Determine priorities and balance claims
(6) Determine utilities (probability multiplied by the ascribed value of the various outcomes)	

Three possible outcomes are considered for each alternative action. These range from the best to the worst possible results measured in terms of the goal that a particular alternative was designed to achieve. The feasible alternatives, predicted outcomes and associated probabilities are the same from the perspective of both parents and child. They are presented in Table 2, columns 1 and 2, and are repeated in Table 3, columns 1 and 2. The outcomes from the perspective of society differ, as we shall see shortly.

Looking at Table 2, we see that the best outcome if surgery is done is that the child will be intellectually normal. However, the probability of this event occurring has been estimated to be only two chances out of 100. Indeed, the best outcome will occur only if the initial diagnosis, which was not checked by chromosomal analysis, was in error. Probability estimates are made on information derived from either an experienced person, or preferably, the research literature. In this case, studies reviewed by Rynders, Spiker, and Horrobin[4] have established that a randomly chosen baby who has been correctly diagnosed as having Down's syndrome will have an equal chance of developing an IQ in the range of 30 to 50 as it will of developing one in the range of 50 to 80. Since we are allowing for the two per cent chance that the child will be normal, we will consider the likelihood of the less desirable outcomes occurring to be .49 each.

Similarly, the probability that each of the other outcomes listed in Table 2 will occur can also be estimated. Where research literature or an experienced person is not available (as in predicting the probability of a baby dying quickly without food), an educated guess (based, perhaps, on related experiences) must be made. In medicine, as in all fields, actions must sometimes be taken with far less than perfect knowledge of the resulting consequences. However, to make no estimate at all substitutes prejudice and happenstance for rationality.

D. Candee and B. Puka

Table 2 Utility of alternative medical treatments (Child's perspective)

Alternative treatment	Outcome	Probability	Value	Utility	Alt. value	Alt. utility
	Normal IQ	.02	1.00	.02	(1.00)	(.02)
	60 IQ	.49	1.00	.49	(.50)	(.25)
Surgery	40 IQ	.49	1.00	.49	(.20)	(.10)
	Total utility			1.00		(.37)
	Die quickly	.10	.30	.03		
Passive	Die slowly	.80	.10	.08		
euthanasia	Die very slowly and painfully	.10	.00	.00		
	Total utility			.11		
	Die quickly	1.00	.30	.30		
Active	Die slowly	.00	.10	.30		
euthanasia	Die very slowly and painfully	.00	.00	.00		
	Total utility			.30		

Table 3 Utility of alternative medical treatments (Parents' perspective)

Alternative treatment	Outcome	Probability	Value	Utility	Alt. value	Alt. utility
	Normal IQ	.02	1.00	.02	(1.00)	(.02)
	60 IQ	.49	.30	.15	(.00)	(.00)
Surgery	40 IQ	.49	.10	.05	(.00)	(.00)
	Total utility			.22		(.02)
	Die quickly	.10	.50	.05		
Passive	Die slowly	.80	.50	.40		
euthanasia	Die very slowly and painfully	.10	.00	.00		
	Total utility			.45		
	Die quickly	1.00	.50	.50		
Active	Die slowly	.00	.50	.00		
euthanasia	Die very slowly and painfully	.00	.00	.00		
	Total utility			.50		

Up to this point, we have simply analysed the moral problem and assembled relevant data. We have made no value judgements. The fourth step in the utilitarian approach is to assign values to each possible outcome. In the present problem, we must consider the "value" of life for a retarded person. How does living with an IQ of 60, for example, compare to living with a normal IQ, with an IQ of 40, or not living at all?

The answer to these questions depends largely on whose viewpoint is being taken. It might seem natural to start with the child's viewpoint, but can a neonate, much less a retarded one, assess the "value" of life? This situation reveals an issue that must be addressed whenever one is calculating utilities. Should we consider the subjective value of a behaviour to an individual, or make a more objective assessment of what that behaviour is worth?

In the present case, there are three main reasons for considering the full subjective value of behaviour to the child. Perhaps most important is the common observation that retarded persons of any age do not find living painful in itself and give no indication that they would prefer to die. Moreover, just as the positive joys of life are limited for retarded people, so are the sorrows. On balance, a retarded person might find his or her life as pleasurable as a mentally normal person. Lastly, since the other people in the dilemma are adults, they have only a part of their lives ahead of them. In comparison, the neonate has its entire life ahead.

The argument for limiting the value of the child's life rests on a more "objective" or "comparative" approach. Using this approach we leave the particular neonate's perspective and compare the life of a retarded person to that of a normal individual. Since the retarded person cannot experience the full range of human reactions, the quality of his or her life activities seems diminished. Retarded persons themselves often recognize that much is missing in their experiences. Thus, if the goal of utilitarianism is to produce the greatest overall good, then by this reasoning, the life of the retarded neonate should be counted less than the life of a fully functioning adult.

There can be no resolution of this issue within the scope of this paper. Both arguments have merit. Some readers will undoubtedly favour the subjective approach, others will favour the objective one. What we wish to emphasize here is that no matter which solution is ultimately chosen, all persons at this point in the utilitarian calculation must address the question: "value of behaviour to whom?" in assigning value to behaviour.

In order to demonstrate that the steps in the utilitarian process are the same regardless of which values are assigned we will go through the solution twice, first choosing values that stem from the subjective viewpoint, then choosing values stemming from the objective point of view. From the subjective viewpoint the value of life, as seen on behalf of a severely retarded child, will be immense. We may quantify this value judgement by giving the outcomes of living with either a normal, a 60 IQ, or a 40 IQ a weight of 1.0 on a scale of zero to one (Table 2, column 3).

In comparison to the outcomes for surgery, the possible outcomes for euthanasia are much less desirable, when assessed on behalf of the child. Clearly, the worst outcome would be to die slowly and painfully. This outcome can be given a value of zero (Table 2, passive euthanasia, column 4). In comparison, the prospect of dying slowly and with less pain is a slightly more palatable choice. Thus, our "rational infant" may give it a value of .10. However, the prospect of a quick and pain-free death should be the least objectionable euthanasia outcome and may be valued even higher, say .30, by the child.

Based on the probabilities and values assumed in Table 2, we are now able to calculate the total utilities for each feasible alternative. This is done by multiplying the value of each possible outcome by its associated probability and then summing across outcomes within each alternative. The resulting utilities are contained in the fifth column of Table 2. As shown, performing the atresia operation is, from the child's subjective point of view, of much greater utility than either of the other two choices.

Now let us shift ground for a moment and assume that a reasoner takes an "objective" view of the value of life. In that case, the values assigned to the outcomes of living with an IQ of 60 or 40 will be much lower. Such values are listed under the "alternative value" column in Table 2. They reflect the fact that, objectively, the quality of life for a mentally disabled person is considerably less than for a person of normal intelligence. The utility of each outcome given the "alternative value" is that value multiplied by the probability of the outcome occurring. The probabilities remain as they were in column 3. The new "alternative utilities" are given in Table 2, column 6.

The particular values a person chooses depend on his or her philosophical and religious beliefs and on his or her perception of the world. However, what binds together all persons who solve the dilemma in the spirit of consequentialism is that all will follow the same logic and all will have to wrestle with the same philosophical and factual problems.

Regardless of which set of utilities is accepted in Table 2, the child's point of view is only one among several that should be considered. Table 3 presents the utilities of each outcome from the viewpoint of the parents. The first question which arises here is whether the parents' perspective should carry twice as much weight as the child's. A strict utilitarian approach would count each person's utilities equally. Thus, if there are two parents their combined perspective would carry twice as much weight as the child's. However, from a functional point of view the parents act in unison, not in isolation. It is easier for one parent to rear a retarded child if he or she has the help of the other. For this reason, it makes sense to treat the parents' perspective as one.

The situation can be handled statistically by considering the value of each outcome under the parents' perspective as the interaction of the value of that outcome to each parent alone. For example, we might estimate the value of rearing a child with an IQ of 60 would be .55 for each individual parent. The interaction would, therefore, be .55 (value to one parent) × .55 (value to other parent) = .30 (value from parents' perspective). It is this figure (.30) that appears as the value for the second outcome under surgery on Table 3.

In practice, what we are suggesting is that instead of estimating the value to each parent individually the value from the parents' perspective be estimated directly. Where individuals act as a functional group it seems best to assign values in terms of that group. This technique will be especially helpful when we consider the effect of each alternative on society.

Returning to Table 3, surgery, we see that while the prospect of having a child with an IQ of 60 is a lowly valued outcome (.30) the prospect of caring for a youngster with an IQ of 40 is valued even less. As for euthanasia alternatives, the outcome of dying quickly would seem to be valued about the same as that of dying slowly. While the former involves less pain to the child, the latter may be perceived by the parents as removing some of the responsibility for the baby's death from their shoulders. As before, the parents would place no value on the prospect of a painful death for their child. Notice that while the value weightings changed considerably from Table 2 (child's viewpoint) to Table 3 (parents' viewpoint) the probabilities remained the same. Value judgements may be different for each moral reasoner. Probabilities, within limits set by consulting different sources of information, are not.

Again, as we did for the child's perspective, we present alternative utilities based on parents who might posit different values for rearing a mentally defective child. Columns 6 and 7 of Table 3 present alternative values and utilities for parents who give no value to rearing a child whose IQ is significantly less than normal. Again, our point is not to advocate one solution or the other but to demonstrate the process of utilitarian reasoning.

In addition to the parents' and child's perspectives, a third perspective, that of society, may also be considered. While society consists of millions of individuals, it may be better to treat them as a unit. After all, individuals will not be directly involved in paying for or caring for a child who may be institutionalized or may need special services. Those decisions will be made in the name of society by agency officials. It matters little to any single member of society whether a normal child is added to the rolls of a public school or to the rolls of an institution for the mentally disabled. The impact comes only on the level of a national or community budget.

Again, the idea of treating groups as an interaction of individuals seems to make sense. A very slight difference in value to any single individual between adding a normal or disabled child to the world (for example, 1.0 vs 0.99) will become meaningful when each figure is multiplied exponentially by the number of people in society. Rather than trying to perform this elaborate calculation we again recommend estimating the value of each outcome directly from the viewpoint of society. The values for the three surgery outcomes are shown in the first three rows of Table 4. The cumulative effect of the difficulties that would fall upon a society having to provide for a mentally disabled child can be seen in the dramatically lower value given to the 60 and 40 IQ outcomes compared to the normal IQ outcome. The lower values reflect the cost of special services and possible institutionalization for the child.

When we turn to the euthanasia outcomes we notice that the possible outcomes have changed from Tables 2 and 3. What does it mean for society to be concerned with the outcome of this particular child dying? The effect would seem to lie in the consequences that this case would have for other similar cases. Thus, the best we could hope for under the passive euthanasia alternative would be that this case would set a precedent allowing persons who have good reason to die to do so. As previously discussed, the value of setting a precedent which would allow for a quick death (outcome 1 under both the passive and active euthanasia alternatives) and a slow death (outcome 2) is about the same (.5). However, as was true in Tables 2 and 3, the probability of active euthanasia leading to a quick death is much greater than it is for passive euthanasia. The most interesting outcome of the euthanasia alternatives is outcome 3, the possibility that the guidelines established by the present case may prove inadequate to distinguish between euthanasia that is in the patient's best interest from cases where it is not. One of the greatest public fears concerning euthanasia is that persons who may want to be saved will be allowed to die. This is another version of the "slippery slope" argument. The purpose of presenting it here is to recognize the worst danger entailed by euthanasia and to estimate the probability of its occurrence as a consequence of either the passive or active euthanasia approaches. As can be seen in Table 4 (outcome 3), we consider the risk of inappropriate guidelines to be greater in the case of active euthanasia than in the case of passive euthanasia. There is more risk of committing an error that cannot be undone if active euthanasia is used. Thus, despite the relief in suffering that active euthanasia may provide to a given individual it is a riskier and hence less useful alternative from society's point of view. However, compared to surgery and the likelihood that a mentally disabled child will be added to the world both forms of euthanasia are more desirable.

The final step in the utilitarian approach is to combine the total utilities for each alternative as seen by the parents, by the child, and by society. Doing so (Table 5) reveals that, given the probabilities and original set of values, surgery is the most useful option. This is due primarily to the clear advantage that the opportunity to live has for the child, even though it is

Table 4 *Utility of alternative medical treatments (Society's perspective)*

Alternative treatment	Outcome	Probability	Value	Utility
Surgery	Normal IQ	.02	1.00	.02
	60 IQ	.49	.10	.05
	40 IQ	.49	.00	.00
	Total utility			.07
Passive euthanasia	Allow people to die quickly for whom it would be best	.10	.50	.05
	Allow people to die slowly for whom it would be best	.80	.50	.40
	Lead to people being left to die for whom it would not be best	.10	.00	.00
	Total utility			.45
Active euthanasia	Allow people to die quickly for whom it would be best	.80	.50	.40
	Allow people to die slowly for whom it would be best	.00	.50	.00
	Lead to people being killed for whom it would not be best	.20	.00	.00
	Total utility			.40

Table 5 *Utility of alternative medical treatments (Combined perspectives)*

| Alternative treatment | | Utility for | | |
	Child	Parents	Society	Combined
Using original utilities[a]				
Surgery	1.00	.22	.07	1.29
Passive euthanasia	.11	.45	.45	1.01
Active euthanasia	.30	.50	.40	1.20
Using alternative utilities[b]				
Surgery	.37	.02	.07	.46
Passive euthanasia	.11	.45	.45	1.01
Active euthanasia	.30	.50	.40	1.20

[a] See total utilities for each alternative Tables 2–4.
[b] See total utility in parentheses for surgery alternatives, Tables 2 and 3. Other utilities are same as original.

recognized that the child will almost certainly be mentally disabled. In comparison, the disadvantages of surgery to the parents and to the society are not as great.

However, if we accept the alternative utilities shown in Table 5, we arrive at a different conclusion. A comparison of these utilities indicates that euthanasia, particularly active euthanasia, is the preferred choice. The change between the two sets of utilities in Table 5 rests primarily on the value that the child himself would give to living with an IQ significantly below normal. If that value is high, then the surgery alternative has a great utility (see child utility column). If it is not, then the surgery alternative becomes least attractive. A smaller but still significant change between the original and alternative utilities is the contribution made to the surgery alternative by the parents. If the parents find some value in rearing a mentally disabled child (as in the original utilities) then the surgery alternative is more likely to be useful. If they do not (as in the alternative utilities) then the surgery alternative becomes less useful.

Deontological approach

Having considered a teleological approach to solving the dilemma, let us now turn to the perspective of deontology. As stated earlier, deontology denies what teleology asserts. That is to say, in the deontological perspective, the moral rightness of an act is determined not by the consequences it produces, but by qualities intrinsic to the act itself. The particular qualities that we will consider here are the basic human rights and duties that impinge on a situation. We shall organize our thinking about the deontological approach around two questions: "What rights are claimed, and by what principles are they valid?", and "What duties are owed by whom and to whom?" (Table 1, steps 3 and 4).

In answer to the first question, three rights-claims seem relevant to this situation: the child's claim to life, the parents' claim to liberty in their own lives, and the parents' claim to the freedom of being able to make decisions affecting their child.

We will look first at the child's claim of having a right to life. On what basis should we recognize this right? There is, of course, no simple answer. It is often argued that rights are associated with the status of personhood. But how is personhood defined? It seems reasonable to us that, since personhood is being used as a moral category here, to qualify as a person an individual must have the essential characteristics that distinguish us as a species capable of morality. These characteristics include the capacity to prefer one set of goods over another and the capacity to be treated and to treat others with respect or concern. Further, there must be a sense of self or at least a sense of being alive. Together, these characteristics constitute having "a point of view". To speak of a rights-claim presumes that ignoring that claim would cause a significant harm to, or loss or infringement of that individual's point of view.

It is difficult to determine whether a retarded neonate qualifies as a person by these criteria. Some of the difficulty is simply due to the child's status as a neonate. Are its faculties cognitively or subjectively complex enough to represent a "point of view"? The neonate may discriminate pleasant from unpleasant stimuli, but does it really care about the difference? Further complications are caused by the problem of mental retardation. Will the retarded neonate ever develop a sufficient sense of self?

There is no doubt that the retarded neonate can be a recipient of moral concern, that she or he is a moral person in this respect. Yet, can he or she function even as a minimally active moral participant – showing respect, honouring rights, and fulfilling duties? A small animal can be trained to obey rules and we may be duty-bound to care about its welfare, but to have a right to life (a claim against even being painlessly killed) one may have to be able to reciprocate in practices of mutual respect. In this way, arguments can be made both for and against according the child the right to life. While we suspect that most moral reasoners will support the pro-right position in this situation, it also may be argued that the child only has a right not to be harmed. Neither right in itself leads inexorably to only one treatment alternative. The stance taken here may lead to either surgery or euthanasia depending on how one assesses all of the right-claims taken together.

The second rights-claim we should consider concerns the parents' liberty. Clearly, rearing a retarded child places especially serious limits on the activities of its parents. It forces them to re-orientate their lifestyles radically and thus prevents them from exercising their right to liberty fully. In determining the validity of that claim, we must first recognize that the mere curtailment of liberty does not in itself represent a right violation. A right is a claim against others interfering unjustly. If the parents have a *duty* to rear the child, then the interference is justified. Similarly, the mere fact that the parents may *feel* constrained to rear the child, once euthanasia is ruled out, does not constitute a rights violation. So long as they are not coerced into such an action, their rights are not violated.

On the other hand, forcing the parents to keep and rear the baby when they have no special duty to do so would violate their rights. To determine if this is the case let us proceed with the third and fourth steps in the determination of duties.

The relevant duties seem to be from the parents and from society toward the child. (We will ignore the possibility, because it is slim, that the child has duties to commit suicide or seek foster care to avoid burdening its parents. After all, it did not bring itself or its disabilities into existence or into its parents' lives.)

Considering the parents first, there is a generally recognized special duty of parents to sustain the lives of their children. But does this duty extend to sustaining the life of a retarded neonate? The major argument for extending the duty is based on the fact that the parents brought the child into the world as a dependant. There are generally recognized practices in this culture pertinent to the nuclear family which many would argue include rearing retarded children. Assuming that the parents knew what these expectations were before the act of conception, they can now be held responsible for fulfilling them. Given this argument, those who also believe the child has a right to life may look to the parents to honour the right by authorizing surgery.

Let us now consider the opposite argument, a case against extending the parents' special duty to cover this situation. Such an argument might contend that the special obligation of parents to care for their children holds only for such behaviour that can reasonably be expected to accompany parenthood. Since the parents could not reasonably have expected that their child would be born retarded, with accompanying duodenal atresia, they cannot be held fully responsible for sustaining its life. Persons holding this view may concede that the parents have a special obligation to do more for the retarded child than they would be expected to do for a normal child, including purchasing special equipment, providing a special education, and making an extreme effort to find a surrogate home for the child. But, according to this argument, they do not have an ultimate obligation to raise the child personally or to shoulder all the financial burden of having someone else raise the child.

If the parents do not have the ultimate responsibility for rearing the child, who does? If we recognize a general duty to sustain the lives of persons, as do most deontologists, then all members of the community would have an obligation to contribute to raising the child. Often this obligation is discharged by supporting public institutions for the mentally handicapped. However, there may be no efficient mechanism for enforcing this obligation or for maintaining a reasonable quality of life at such institutions. In that case, we may arrive at a situation in which rights and duties are not reciprocal. The child may indeed have a right to life but no one may have a special obligation to make extreme sacrifices in order to sustain that life. In that case, the situation becomes a tragedy for the neonate and he or she may be left to die.

The third rights-claim to consider is the parents' will to determine the fate of their child. The claim takes two forms. One form holds that parents should be allowed to choose any action they consider "reasonable" for their child. Since this claim rests on the parents' special relationship to the child, it should be limited by their special duty. As we have said, if the parents recognize the child as having a right to life, then their special duty extends at least as far as trying to find some means to sustain that life. The parents may be justified in asserting the freedom to select the nature of that sustenance (for example, natural family, institutionalization, adoption) but they cannot claim a right to avoid the search entirely and let the child die. Should the search prove unsuccessful, then the parents may be in a position to let the child die simply by refusing to be the only persons to step in and actually sustain the child's life. Notice, though, that if this possibility exists, it would seem to apply only in cases where the child creates certain difficulties that could not reasonably have been unexpected by the parents before it was born. It is unlikely that an argument could be made for letting a normal child die.

The second form of the parents' claim holds that regardless of the wisdom of their views, no other party has a greater right to determine the fate of their child than they do. Again, the claim rests on the special relationship of parent and child. But, in this case, the doctors also have a special relationship with the child, that of doctor and patient. The doctors, too, hold the child's interests in their trust. Thus, while the parents may be justified in asserting that their view should be equal to any other, a further case must be made to show that it is superior. Where the decisions of two parties, each having a special relationship to the child, differ, a third party who is specially equipped for deciding such issues, might be consulted. That party might consist of the courts or of an ethics committee. Of course, the function of that body should not be to decide the case in *lieu* of persons having special relationships with the child. Rather, it should adjudicate the arguments raised by the specially related persons.

Summary and conclusions   We have now pursued two approaches to moral decision-making and arrived at both decisions to perform and not to perform the atresia operation on the basis of each of them. In the case of the utilitarian approach, the difference in recommended actions hinged on differences in assigning values to the various alternatives. In the case of the deontological approach the difference hinged on the limits one sets on claims both to rights and to duties. Our goal has not been to convince the reader that one or the other action-choice is correct, but rather to suggest a way in which two broad sets of concerns (utility and justice) can be systematically considered in the course of making moral decisions. In doing so, we selected only certain tenets of each approach. We made simplifying assumptions and knowingly omitted certain content complications. However, we have tried to organize an individual's moral decision-making around certain ordered steps and questions that can readily be applied to solving problems in medical ethics.

The value of such an approach to students in general and to health professionals in particular seems to be three-fold. First, no decision reached through the systematic application of a valid ethical approach will be arbitrary. In the process of our reasoning, we have specified those perceptions of facts that must be made if a decision to perform or not to perform the operation is to be made. Thus, given the same value judgements and the same factual perceptions, all persons using a single ethical approach in a consistent manner should arrive at a similar moral decision in the case. Second, it encourages the health professional to adopt a logical, systematic approach to moral or social problems just as he or she would in solving professional (for example, medical or legal) ones. Third, the use of systematic thinking increases the chances that the decision the reasoner finally reaches will be both consistent with the reasoner's own values and in the best interests of the client.

An individual may not actually go through the process of constructing utilitarian tables or listing all claims, rights, and duties in every moral dilemma. A simple list of pros and cons, and a consideration of one or two rights will probably suffice in most cases. But, having seen the process that underlies detailed ethical reasoning, the health professional is in a better position to guide her thought and to know which questions must be answered before she or he can rest comfortably with any moral decision.

REFERENCES

1 Callahan, D., *The teachings of ethics in higher education: a report by the Hastings Center.* Hastings-on Hudson, NY: Institute of Society, Ethics, and Life Sciences, The Hastings Center, 1980.
2 Reiser, S., Dyck, A., Curran, W. *Ethics in medicine.* Cambridge, Mass.: MIT Press, 1977.
3 Brody, H. *Ethical decisions in medicine.* Boston, Mass.: Little, Brown & Company, 1976: Chapter 2.
4 Rynders, J., Spiker, D., Horrobin, M. Underestimating the educability of Downs's syndrome children: examination of methodological problems in recent literature. *American journal of mental deficiencies* 1978; 5: 440–448.

COMMENTARY

Charles Fletcher *Emeritus Professor of Clinical Epidemiology, University of London*

This paper gives detailed consideration to two separate ethical approaches to deciding on the management of a newborn baby with Down's syndrome and duodenal atresia: the options considered are curative operation; allowing the baby to die with or without control of distress and actively dispatching it either by quick, slow or painfully slow methods. Logical thinking about each of the main approaches teleological (or utilitarian) and deontological (or moral-duty based) is urged along the steps outlined in Table 1. In the utilitarian analysis the reasoning is supported by numerical ratings of the values to baby, parents and society of the alternative actions which are then multiplied by their probabilities of occurrence to derive a "utility" score for each of them. These are then added up to give a final set of utility scores (Table 5) first adopting a "subjective" and then an "objective" view of what the baby's wishes might or should be. In the deontological analysis the rights and duties of the same three parties are considered without any numerical trans-formation. The authors give no guidance about which their own choice of action would be, they simply urge that their logical processes should be followed, suggesting that these are analogous to the processes by which decisions are taken in clinical diagnosis or treatment or in legal thinking. The ultimate decision, they admit, will depend upon individual value judgements. They propose no way of combining the two analyses nor do they suggest which should be given the greater weight.

This advocacy of logical analysis of ethical quandaries is one which will commend itself to many practitioners in the caring professions. But the basis of and detailed prosecution of their analyses are open to criticism.

i) They pay no attention to the consequences of alternative decisions on the members of the clinical team. For them active euthanasia is ruled out if for no other reason by the risk of a charge of murder as in the recent Arthur case in Derby and of the endless legal disputes that have followed such decisions in the USA. The authors admit that their consideration of the particular example they give is not complete (they ignore, for instance, the diminished life expectancy of a baby with Down's syndrome which will reduce the "values" of preserving its life). Nor do they consider the alternative of having the baby adopted, after surgery, by foster parents with values quite different from those of the parents in this case.

ii) In the utilitarian analysis the numerical transformations of the three main alternative actions seem both spurious and unnecessary. Even if the crude numbers given to the "values" and the more securely based probabilities are accepted their combination to produce the utilities have little value for comparison with each other without some estimate of their errors, so that significant differences between them could be determined. The bland statement in relation to Table 5 that the utility figure of 1.29 for surgery is "greater" than 1.20 for active euthanasia is absurd. Without knowledge of the potential errors of these figures they have no more meaning that a "simple list of pros and cons' which the authors eventually admit "will suffice in most cases", (but without saying which sort of cases will benefit from a numerical analysis and why). The dramatic change in the eventual utilities brought about by a change from the "subjective" to the "objective" view of the baby's valuation of survival shows how insecure these figures are. They also treat the values of the two parents as one. This is of uncertain validity even if they agree, but what if they disagree?

iii) The authors' claim that their proposed method is akin to that used by doctors and lawyers in reaching their opinions is invalid. I do not think doctors ever give numerical values to the values and probabilities of occurrence of the consequences of alternative diagnostic and therapeutic decisions that they take. If they did they would realize that they should work out some statistical technique to enable them to interpret differences between the numbers.

iv) No explanation is given about how doctors could decide whether passive euthanasia would be rapid or slow. No doctor would permit a slow, painful death for a baby so this alternative is nonsense: it is presumably put in to provide three alternatives for each section of the Table. The objection applies even more strongly to active euthanasia.

v) In their deontological analysis of the problem the authors are concerned with the rights and duties of the child, the parents, and society: given their predilection for numbers it is not clear why they reject numerical ratings here for they are concerned with greater or lesser rights and duties which could be transformed into semi-quantitative scales such as are used by sociologists and psychologists in studies of opinions and moods. Perhaps after all they agree with Wordsworth that "high Heaven rejects the lore of nicely calculated less or more". They advance no firm opinion on the rights of a subnormal neonate which, they say, must depend on whether it can be regarded as a "person". They conclude only that they "suspect that most moral reasoners will support the pro-right position". Nor do they attempt to adjudicate on the conflict of views between those who think that all humans, from the moment of fertilization to the seventh age, "sans teeth, sans eyes, sans taste, sans everything", have a complete right to life which must be preserved at all costs and those who believe that the quality of life must be taken into account together with the cost in deciding whether to prolong it.

vi) They say that "at the time of conception" (i.e. of intercourse?) the parents must have had an expectation of having a retarded child so the parents must now be responsible for rearing it. But at the time of conception they might already have decided that if this happened they would not wish to do so.

vii) The authors present their two ethical approaches to the problem without giving any indication of how they might be combined, nor of how one might be reasoned to be better than the other. Most doctors who do stop to consider the ethics of their decisions before they act, ponder on the moral as well as the practical consequences for harm and benefit of the alternatives which they face. In considering prompt killing of a subnormal neonate (which scores so high in Table 5) they would temper their consideration by wondering if they had any right or duty to do this. For virtually all of them the moral duty not to kill would outweigh any beneficial consequences of killing. The authors state that "given the same value judgements and the same factual perception all persons using a single ethical approach 'will reach a similar moral decision'." This is a tenuous supposition; and if both approaches are used and the conclusions differ – what then?

Some readers would have welcomed a more dialectical discussion of these keenly debated conflicts of opinion than the authors' unresolved though interesting presentation of some, but not all viewpoints.

After a doctor's decision to allow a Down's neonate with a tracheo-oesophageal fistula to die in deference to the parents' wishes in April, 1982 in the USA there was nationwide controversy and the United States Department of Health and Human Services issued a letter to hospitals stating that it was unlawful to withhold nutrition, or medical or surgical treatment required to correct a life-threatening condition if such withholding was "based upon the fact that the infant is handicapped; and the handicap does not render treatment or nutritional sustenance medically contraindicated".[1] These guidelines have been opposed by paediatricians yet several States are considering juvenile protection acts which will limit doctors' choices.[2] If an improved and more effective version of the procedures recommended by the authors were developed perhaps the rights groups might be more willing to accept the decisions of doctors who use them. Certainly if the authors' plea to doctors to think about ethical decisions with the same logical care as they use in reaching their clinical decisions were heeded and if they could persuade members of organizations such as "Life", who have closed minds on ethical matters, to use critical logic in examining the basis for their prejudices a large step forward would have been taken.

REFERENCES

1 Beauchamp, T.L., Childress, J.F. *Principles of biomedical ethics.* Oxford: Oxford University Press, 1983, 2nd edition: 310.
2 Duncan, G. Squeal rules in the nursery. *British medical journal* 1983: 287; 1204.

27

~

ETHICS AND RESOURCE ALLOCATION: AN ECONOMIST'S VIEW*

A. McGuire

INTRODUCTION

This paper, concerned as it is with ethics and resource allocation, has the potential to be "all things to all men". I want to establish very quickly the parameters of the present study. I shall be principally concerned with medical ethics and their role as a mechanism in the allocation processes relating to health care resources. In this sense I wish to address the role of medical ethics in the allocation of health care resources. The paper will attempt to show that medical ethics have been dominated by "individualistic" ethical codes which do not fully consider questions relating to resource allocation at a social level. It will be stated that the structure of the health care sector augments these "individualistic" ethics. Furthermore it will be suggested that different actors in this sector address different questions of resource allocation in particular with respect to different time periods and that this serves to further enhance the influence of "individualistic" ethical codes in the sector.

Central to the paper is the concept of economic efficiency, in that when discussing resource allocation it will be taken as given that resources should be allocated in the most efficient manner. That is allocation is aimed at maximizing the benefits to society from the resources available. I take this objective as given in health care and do not debate its merit. It should also be noted that economic inefficiency can arise in two distinct ways: *technical* inefficiency which is due to excessive input usage in a production process whereas *allocative* inefficiency results from employing inputs in a production process in a way which does not maximize the social value of the output obtained. It is important to distinguish between these forms of economic inefficiency, particularly as it is argued below that the influence of medical ethics upon resource allocation in the health care sector is currently confined to problems of technical inefficiency with potential ill-effects on allocative efficiency.

* First published in *Social Science and Medicine*, 22 (1986), 1167–74. © Pergamon Journals Ltd. Reprinted by permission.

ETHICAL CONSIDERATIONS

Before discussing medical ethics specifically a little should be said about ethics more generally. Jonsen and Hellegers [1, p. 4] define ethics as "an academic discipline, a systematic set of prescriptions that constitute the intellectual instruments for the analysis of morality". They suggest that ethics "provides not only a descriptive discipline of morality but a normative one as well, for its analysis purports to reveal the roots of obligation and value appreciation, thereby exposing not how men do *in fact* behave, but how *in principle* they should behave" [1, p. 4]. In fact a third aspect of ethics, metaethics concerned with the logic of moral reasoning and the definition of ethical terms, could also enter the definition of ethics itself but we shall not be concerned with this aspect. The normative characteristic of ethics is crucially important as it means that ethical standards *per se* are not necessarily functional, in the sense of defining specific actions. They do, I would argue, nevertheless serve to dictate the limits of actions.

Veatch[2] maintains: "The components of a complex theory of ethics will answer such questions as what moral rules apply to specific ethical cases, what ethical principles stand behind the rules, how seriously the rules should be taken, and what constitutes the fundamental meaning and justification of the ethical principles". This present study will focus upon a particular aspect of the theory of ethics, that is the application of moral rules to specific actions. In this case the actions are concerned with resource allocation in health care.

Turning more specifically to medical ethics, Jonsen and Hellegers suggest that "traditionally medical ethics has dwelt mostly within the theories of virtue and of duty" [1, p. 5], essentially individualistic ethics. Of these, duty is arguably the more important, in that it is only after moral duty has been defined, albeit, in a normative sense, that virtue, the distinctive characteristic associated with the practice of duty, may be defined. Jonsen and Hellegers continue by stating that "the nature of contemporary medicine demands that they be complemented by the third essential theory – the common good" [1, p. 5], which clearly relates ethics to a social level. These authors claim [1, p. 12] that the lack of an ethics of the common good means that there is an absence of "the ethical issues arising from the intersection of multiple actions in institutions and society" and that "an adequate definition (of medical ethics) calls for an explicit reflection on the morality of institutions and the relationship, and possible clash, between social values and individual values".

For Jonsen and Hellegers the reason why the doctrine of the common good is important is that it is this aspect of ethics that allows consideration of "how the institutional structure can be designed so as to avoid conflict, how to reconcile discord, and how to compensate unjust harm" [1, p. 13]. Admirable as these causes are, they are to the economist incomplete. Economists would need to add "and aid economic efficiency".

It has to be recognized that economic efficiency can only be defined with respect to some social objective. Furthermore there may be a distinction between the *specified* objective and the *attainable* objective. The former may not equate with the latter as the process of attainment will be effected by the constraints encountered in the allocation process. Thus, although no social outcome should be ruled out as infeasible when the specification of objectives takes place, the constraints met during allocation may well, in the event determine the actual outcome. This is of course merely stating the obvious, however, it is critical to our analysis.[3]

The addition of the goal of economic efficiency does, as was alluded to by Jonsen and Hellegers, raise some potential difficulties in reconciling the ethics of the common good with the individualistic ethics of virtue and duty. In particular, having stated that economic efficiency can only be defined with respect to an objective and may only be measured with regard to outcome, we can see that the ethics of the common good, in as much as it relates to efficiently provided social outcomes, must now be concerned with a choice of actions on the basis of the *consequences* of these actions. Indeed this is fundamental to the approach taken by economists in problems of resource allocation: a utilitarian approach is normally adopted whereby the economist is concerned with the maximization of the social benefits from health care over the social costs associated with the production of these benefits. On the other hand, the more individualistic ethical characteristics (those which, I would argue, are dominant in the health care sector) associated with virtue and duty are less concerned with the recommendation of a choice of action on the basis of consequences, than with the moral processes involved in undertaking that action. Thus the concept of duty is not wholly derivative from the associated consequence and, indeed, need not necessarily be related to the concept of the social or common good.

Indeed in comparing deontological theories, which I would define as those associated with the individualistic ethics of virtue and duty, and utilitarian theories Beauchamp and Childress[4] state that

utilitarianism conceives the moral life in terms of means-to-ends reasoning. It asks: "What is our objective?" and "How can we most effectively and efficiently realize the objective of the production of the greatest possible good?" This conception of the moral life in terms of means to ends relates well to such empirical sciences as economics. Deontologists in contrast, hold not only that there are standards independent of the ends for judging the means, but that it is a fundamental mistake to conceive the moral life in terms of means and ends – a matter of the wrong starting point.

A further aspect of ethical theories is that, again to arrive at a more normative position, they may be formulated in terms of specific rules concerning how duty ought to be undertaken. However, no matter how strict the rules are it is likely that examples of exceptions to the rules can always be found. Thus Ross, a rule-deontologist, attempts to overcome this difficulty, with regard to the individualistic ethical position, by distinguishing between *actual* duty and *prima facie* duty, the former relating to the obligations that ought to be undertaken in a particular situation recognizing however that these obligations may be subjected to conflicting duties or "exceptions to the rule". The latter relates to the obligations that would be undertaken if there were not conflicting or exceptional circumstances. Thus "Ross suggests that one can formulate a number of moral rules that hold without exception as rules of *prima facie*, though not of actual duty".[4]

In defining medical ethics then, in line with Jonsen and Hellegers,[1] we perceive a potential conflict in ethical demands between the individualistic and the utilitarian ethical stipulations. For the moment however it is necessary to reiterate that we are only interested in the normative aspects of medical ethics. This is because I would hold that it is these aspects which define the boundaries of action undertaken by the medical practitioner in the health care sector. These aspects do not dictate the conduct of the clinician but they do serve to define potential conduct. Before turning to consider (medical) ethical conduct explicitly I want first to consider the structure of the health care market as this also plays an important role in determining the importance of (medical) ethical conduct in the resource allocation process in the health care sector.

STRUCTURAL SETTING

We have already noted that specified objectives may not equate with attainable objectives because of the existence of constraints in the resource allocation process which inhibit the achievement of specified objectives. A particularly important set of constraints which affect any allocation process relate to property rights holding. Property rights are held to specify the effective rights of an individual to undertake action, for example decisions concerning the production of goods and services (e.g. health care), and make effective claims upon the rewards (both positive and negative) of the outcomes of these actions.[5] In this sense, as Furubotn and Pejovich [6, p. 1139] remark

property rights do not refer to relations between men and things but, rather, *to the sanctioned behavioral relations among men that arise from the existence of things and pertain to their use.* Property rights assignments specify the norms of behaviour with respect to things that each and every person must observe in his interactions with other persons, or bear the cost for nonobservance. The prevailing system of property rights in the community can be described, then, as the set of economic and social relations defining the position of each individual with respect to the utilisation of scarce resources.

Thus, in accepting the pattern of property rights holdings as a constraint we may state that the economically efficient allocation of resources in any sector cannot be defined in abstraction from the distribution of property rights. In this sense we are defining a particular set of rights – i.e. property rights to resource allocation and utilization – as constraining the attainment of any specified objective function and the efficient allocation of resources associated with that objective function.

To outline the importance of property rights in the health care sector it is necessary to consider the structure of this sector. Although economists have suggested a number of models for analyzing behaviour in the health care sector the vast majority have been deficient in that they have not given adequate attention to structural conditions. Indeed, in my opinion only two economic models have given sufficient attention to such conditions and it is these models that underlie the approach undertaken below – these are the models developed by Evans[7] and Harris.[8]

In the analysis of the vast majority of sectors of any economy, traditional "neo-classical" economics has focused largely upon the exchange mechanisms that allocate resources through the market for any good or service. Thus, as Evans[7] states,

The traditional analysis of market structure in a particular industry presupposes a bilateral relationship between two classes of independent transactors, the producers (or suppliers) of a particular set of commodities, and the buyers (or consumers). The set of exchange relationships between these two *is* the market . . .

As he goes on to emphasize, analysis of exchange is complicated in the health care sector, not only because of the lack of readily identifiable prices which are considered crucial to the analysis of exchange, but also because this particular sector is inadequately characterized by interactions between pairs of transactors and a clearer exposition of exchange would recognize the multilateral agreement that exists between actors in this sector. Consideration must thus be given to the *non-market* relationships that exist between transactors. For example there must be recognition of the agency relationship that exists between patients and doctors which arises from the asymmetry of information by these actors. The clinician, who holds more information, not only on diagnosis but also on outcome, acts as an agent for the patient to aid in the process of demand and, in turn, the act of consumption. A distinct relationship also exists between the health care providers and the government, in that the government, at least in many European countries, provides financial resources whilst also acting as a regulator of the health care market, yet simultaneously delegates a substantial degree of "self-government" to the medical profession. The existence of such non-market transactions means that any analysis of this sector which is based purely upon market exchange is deficient. Production and consumption in the health care market overlap, and, as I shall state below different actors may, simultaneously, be involved in both processes.

The Harris model[8] is important in that, although concentrating on one particular part of the health care market, the hospital, it emphasizes that production in the health care sector is geared towards *short-run* resource allocation. This arises largely from the nature of the good health care – it is difficult to store, in that being a service it is difficult to build up inventories, and it is poorly substitutable across broad categories of patient, in that being an intermediate demand good related to health status, production will vary across diagnostic cases, and possibly even across individuals within the same diagnostic category. Moreover uncertainty plays a crucial role in diagnosis and treatment. As such production is geared to the short-run; fire-fighting as Harris has described it.

None of this implies that all medical decision-making or treatment involves an aspect of fire-fighting. It is merely to emphasize the importance of this aspect in that it is the ever present limit of potential fire-fighting action which would seem to legitimize clinical freedom with respect to resource allocation as it relates to production (supply of treatment).

Thus we have a sectoral structure where multilateral relationships and short-run allocation decisions dominate. Indeed we could identify the major actors as in Fig. 1. However not only are the relationships in this sector multilateral, unlike other goods and services where exchange between producers and consumers is governed by allocation via recourse to market prices, in the health care sector there are a number of important,

Figure 1 Structure of the health care sector (after Evans)[7]

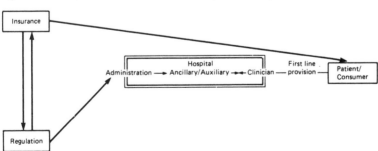

perhaps dominant non-market (i.e. non-price) interactions. Furthermore in analyzing the role of the various actors in the health care sector we find a conflict of interests arising from property rights holdings with respect to resource utilisation which are spread across different characteristics of the health care market, particularly with respect to different time periods.

Thus, referring to Fig. 1, the left hand side of the diagram identifies the insurance and regulating bodies. In fact the latter may also be identified as the legislators if we take the regulators to mean government. These bodies combine to act as budget-holders for the health-care market. These actors, in playing the roles of legislators, budget-holders and regulators, determine the quantities of resources available in the sector, for example through the supply of resources which enable the uptake of specialized labour and capital resources, as well as frequently acting as *de facto* owners of health care resources. Thus the insurance and regulating bodies can influence economic efficiency through their role in providing funds, controlling capacity levels, determining staffing levels, etc. This control has, at least until recently, normally been exercised over the *long-run* period. In other words such bodies are removed from short-run allocation problems and have normally not been concerned with such problems, concentrating instead on resource allocation in the long-run.

The roles performed by these bodies have replaced a number of market relationships with non-market relationships which thus assume greater importance in the health care sector. Managerial and entrepreneurial decisions taken at arm's length from the place of production then, take on added significance and, importantly, these decisions have normally referred to long-run resource allocation problems. In that the regulating bodies are presumably acting for society at large we may assume that they are attempting to maximize the social welfare accruing from the consumption of health care. Indeed in some countries, for example the U.K., this assumption holds for the insurance body as well given that the government has direct control over this function.

The consumer enters the structural picture on an individual level as a patient who, through the existence of an asymmetry of information, forms an agency relationship with the doctor. The doctor's role derives from his specialized knowledge of the relationship between health care and health status. Thus the doctor can identify the necessary level of production of health care (i.e. the supply of treatment) and simultaneously, in his capacity as agent, specify to the patient the amount of consumption of health care (i.e. the demand for treatment) necessary to improve his/her health status. However even the doctor's assessment of the treatment requirements is not perfect and he/she thus becomes a part bearer in the risk of outcome associated with the production process. The existence of the agency relationship and this risk bearing function mean that the doctor becomes a property rights holder in the patient's utility function (allowing him/her to help determine the level of consumption and thus the level of satisfaction/welfare attached to the commodity health care). However these property rights must remain indirect in that only the patient/consumer can properly determine the relationship between utility and health care, and utility and health status.[9]

The perfect agency relationship, i.e. one which allows an optimal outcome for the patient if the doctor were acting perfectly prudently, is clearly difficult to attain. This difficulty would almost certainly manifest itself even if we had no doubts about the *content* of the doctor's utility function (i.e. what gives the doctor satisfaction/increased welfare, e.g. income, status, patient outcome, etc.), or the possibility of conflict between the doctor's utility function and the pursuit of the patient's maximum utility. There is clearly a major problem here which relates to the doctor's ability to judge perfectly the existence and weights to be attached to the various aggregate characteristics of the commodity health care. In essence the doctor is trained to act as the patient's agent with respect to the patient's health; and he/she is not, nor can he/she be, a perfect agent with respect to the patient's time, the patient's family's time or indeed the patient's family's utility associated with the patient's health.

Nevertheless the knowledge of the relationship between health care and health status allows the doctor to make judgements concerning the effectiveness of health production, and therefore the amount of resources required in treatment. (Note that there is not necessarily an interest in the cost of supplying these resources.) As part of this judgement and through the part transfer from consumer (patient) to supplier (doctor) of the holding on the risk of outcome, the doctor gains strong property rights in the determination of the health care production process necessary to satisfy "need" in any particular individual patient. (How this leaves the influences of these same property rights on the determination of the social welfare function in health care is something we will return to. For the moment emphasis is on the needs of the individual patient.)

Thus the doctor is predominantly concerned with *short-run* resource allocation problems related to input usage rather than input cost (i.e. the concern here is with technical efficiency rather than allocative efficiency). In this sense the doctor's behavior is dictated by the *tactical* level at which he/she operates. In contrast the regulators and insurance bodies retain overall control of long-run resource allocation, and can be stated to operate at the *strategic* level. During periods of financial clemency there may well be little apparent conflict between tactical and strategic approaches. However during periods of financial stringency it is likely that conflict will become more visible.

Thus the relationships that exist between doctors, hospital administrators, functional budget holders, ancillary departments and government agencies have a direct bearing on allocative efficiency, that is efficiency with regard to maximizing the value of the output from the available resources, both short-run and long-run, and in turn technical efficiency, that is efficiency relating to minimum resource usage and finally on effectiveness, that is the impact of the inputs on health status. The government and insurance authorities however retain *overall* control of long-run allocative efficiency. Yet when such agencies are tightening resource constraints (e.g. budgets) this will encroach more and more upon short-run allocative efficiency. In turn this may affect technical efficiency and thereby effectiveness. This will occur both directly through the effect that changes in budget allowances have upon the production process (e.g. the purchase of technologically advanced equipment) and through putting strain upon the existing relationships, and consequently the property rights holdings in the hospital. Thus any change in the conditions under which problems of short-run resource allocation are resolved (i.e. the economic conditions, see above), must affect the structure of property rights holdings. Thus actors who are strictly at arm's length from the production of the good health care, as their concern moves from long-run allocative efficiency to short-run allocative efficiency, may affect the distribution of the property rights holdings and thus the composition of output in that sector.

Doctors' property rights in the determination of community needs ought to be much less than for individual patient needs. Indeed I would suggest that it is illegitimate for clinicians to attempt to extend their property rights to the determination of the former. It is just such attempted extension which is a crucial factor in the confusion engendered by debates about need. Indeed doctors' determination to classify needs as "objective" would seem on occasion to be a deliberate attempt at obfuscation regarding the legitimate province for doctors' property rights. Consequently in the debate about need (see, for example, [10] and [11]) I would not want to endorse the view that need be banished nor necessarily accept its return from exile as an unadulterated blessing. Rather what is required is to set property rights and needs together in the one model but this will not be attempted in this particular paper, at least in detail.

The picture is further complicated by the fact that although the regulating and legislative bodies (i.e. the government) do have substantial control over the health care sector, an important delegation of self-government has been awarded to doctors. As Evans [9, p. 335] states

Individual providers are required to belong to professional organisations which regulate their conduct, deploying the full coercive power of the state. Although this delegation is in principle subject to review, traditionally and still in most jurisdictions the professional organisation functions to a significant extent as a private government, enjoying considerable independence in its limited area.

Thus not only do doctors have strong property rights holdings in the consumption process (as the consumer/patient's agent) *and* in the production process (by determining the relationship between health care and health status) these property rights holdings are heavily protected through the delegation of self-government.

We noted that the analysis of exchange in this sector is difficult as value cannot easily be transformed and that the exchange processes are dominated by non-market relationships. This leads to the identification of the doctor as playing a critical role in both the consumption and production processes and thus resource allocation in this sector. This role I have argued is dominated by short-run allocation problems concerned with the amount of inputs utilized in the act of production/consumption (i.e. technical efficiency). Because of the nature of his/her role, that is the short-run (fire-fighting) identification of the applicable relationship between health care and health status (i.e. the treatment) for the individual, the uncertainty (risk of outcome) associated with this choice, and the structural conditions of the health care sector, medical ethics have come to be dominated by the individualistic aspects of virtue and duty to the neglect of ethical considerations associated with the "common good". In order to fully appreciate this it is necessary to analyze (medical) ethical conduct in the health care sector.

ETHICAL CONDUCT

The structural environment of the health care sector has then a dominant influence on conduct. The aim of this section is to analyze how the structural setting affects one aspect of clinical conduct, medical ethics, and to try to reconcile such conduct with economic analysis. As stated above I view medical ethics as a key element in the structure of property rights holdings in the hospital sector with regard to the specification of the production and consumption processes.

The agency relationship is central to the understanding of the health care sector. Arrow [12, p. 37] suggested a number of years ago that "Medicine along with the other professions, is distinctive in that the specialisation is in sheer information". Thus because of his/her lack of information the consumer/patient enters into an agency agreement in an effort to ascertain the required health care to improve health status. However evaluation of performance cannot be conducted *ex ante*. This is because of the complexity of the processes required to ascertain patient need (e.g. because of the uncertainty arising from random factors and/or environmental considerations). In other words performance cannot be estimated at a time when the agency relationship is entered into. The ethical standards of the medical profession are used as a means of specifying that the agency will undertake all that is possible and necessary to fulfil individual patient need. Thus as Arrow [12, p. 37] continues "the usual reasons why the market acts as a check to ensure quality operate here with very weak force. It is for this reason that the ethical indoctrination of physicians is of such crucial importance. The control that is exercised ordinarily by informed buyers is replaced by internalized values".

In this context Harris [8, p. 473], whose model is developed for the U.S.A., states that "one function of the fee-for-service system is to seal the ethical bond between doctor and patient". This may operate in two ways: firstly and most obviously, but nevertheless unconvincing to my mind, as a means of validating an ex post check on performance (i.e. the patients ask whether he/she received value for money); and secondly, as a means of separating doctors from the full consequences of resource allocation implications associated with the specified treatment and in effect helping both to confirm and to clarify the distribution of property rights holding between doctor and patient. It is this latter aspect that Harris emphasizes. Thus in the context of analyzing the economics of the hospital Harris [8, p. 474] argues that there is "a strong ethical presumption that the doctor be left alone to do whatever is necessary for the patient's well-being. Somehow, the doctor must be isolated from the rest of the hospital, even though he is really part of it . . . This problem is solved by setting up a separate contract between the patient and the hospital-supplier".

Although Harris is specifically concerned with the hospital I would argue that, not only does this sector dominate and therefore play an influential role on the rest of the health care sector, but that similar processes are at work across the whole of the health care sector.

In the U.S.A. the increase in clarity of this separation of property rights through the fee-for-service system is enhanced by the fact that the doctor is not a hospital employee, but rather an agent employed directly by the patient. In the U.K., for example, the clinician is an employee of the Regional Health Authority and not the hospital. This particular mechanism is thus relatively weak in the U.K. Of much greater importance is the third party (insured body) payment mechanism which is funded through general taxation which helps to remove the price–exchange–resource implication aspect from the doctor–patient relationship.'

Even so, medical ethics may assume a more important role in this structural setting in acting as a means to reassure the patient that the doctor is working in the patient's "best interest", even although this "best interest" may be misspecified by the doctor as it is narrowly defined to relate only to the relationship between health care and health status. All other arguments in the patient's utility function which help form "best interest" are abstracted away by the doctor. The doctor can indeed determine the technically correct relationship between health status and health care required by the patient. However only the patient can convert this relationship into utility gains.

Harris [8, p. 473] considers a further relevant element, what he describes as the "moral burden of ultimate responsibility for the outcome of the case". This arises from the agency relationship and manifests itself through medical ethics. This special negative aspect of the consumption/production process he suggests inevitably occurs "in an arrangement in which one makes repeated marginal decisions about life and death". It arises because first, the good we are concerned with is a regrettable and second, there is an acceptance of the risk bearing by the doctor. It follows that the ethical code may be interpreted as an attempt to internalize this negative aspect which arises from the agency relationship.

At the same time the medical ethical code allows individual doctors to know that they have acted broadly as their peers would have done. Strictly this does nothing to reduce the risk holding by the doctor; but it does affect his perception of the cost of doing so. In other words the nontransferability of the risk bearing by doctors to other actors in the production process may mean that medical ethics acts as a substitute for risk sharing. There is no opportunity in the health care sector for specialization in risk bearing across different actors with different degrees of risk aversion.

Medical ethics, when viewed from the perspective of the profession as a whole, may therefore be seen as the mechanism for self-regulation. Although the state does have overall regulatory control, there is a very important transfer of regulatory control from the state to the medical profession "in the form of rights to self-government" [7, p. 335]. Thus in this sense also medical ethics regulates medical conduct. Yet again it does nothing to reduce the risk holding by doctors, but it may serve to reduce the variance of outcome and in this way act as an *ex ante* check on performance.

There are therefore a number of dimensions to medical ethics. First and foremost they underpin the non-market relationships (i.e. the agency relationship and the right to self-government), in the health care sector. The doctor, through these non-market relationships, assumes a very strong position in the health care sector in that the determination of the relationship between health care and health status allows him both to hold strong property rights over the production process and entry into the patient/consumer utility function. The decentralized structure of the health care sector serves to augment the role of medical ethics, in that a number of important production/consumption decisions must be made at the individual level.

PERFORMANCE

The distinction between resource allocation decisions taken at the strategic and the tactical levels, we have argued, becomes particularly important at times when resource constraints (e.g. budgets) are being tightened. It is during such periods that a fundamental dichotomy in performance can be best observed. Given his individualistic ethical position the doctor tends to stress performance criteria with regard to the relationship between health care and health status in terms of the effectiveness of treatment at the *individual* level. The health system planner, on the other hand, ought to have a tendency towards defining performance not only in terms of broad effectiveness but also in terms of economic efficiency and distributional equity.

With regard to the last it is important to note that a common criticism of the utilitarian stance is that it ignores distributional issues and thus issues of equity, concern being restricted to maximizing benefits rather than the analysis of their distribution. However as we stated above ethical theories may be formulated with regard to specific rules. With regard to equity (however defined) the utilitarian may argue that his/her primary consideration is to the efficient allocation of resources which maximizes benefits and that the distributional questions relating to the performance of such actions must be addressed at the social level. In other words equity issues must be considered at a governmental level as it is only at this level that aggregate (i.e. society wide) issues can be addressed. Thus once moral rules concerning distributional matters have been set the utilitarian economist can set about maximizing the benefits from health care resources. To some this may seem an easy solution, for example we side-step issues concerning Kantian principles of justice and their relation to health care. However it is not the main focus of our narrower study and must be left for a later debate.

Our concern is rather, to differentiate the issues of performance (i.e. the efficiency of resource allocation) with respect to the different moral aspects contained within the boundaries of medical ethics. Of particular importance is how the earlier distinction made between actual duty and prima facie duty is important to health care resource allocation. If the ethic of the common good could be internalized within prima facie duty for the individual doctor, it would mean that the doctor *ought* to weigh up the social costs and benefits associated with each individual treatment, i.e. there would be a reconciliation of individual and social utilitarian objectives. However the doctor is constantly faced with the short-run allocation problems (i.e. the fire-fighting). The individual ethical aspects of virtue and duty which underpin the non-market relationships centred upon the clinician (i.e. the agency relationship and the self-governing aspect) lead to strong property rights holdings in the production *and* consumption processes in the health care sector. This probably means that there is little hope of such an internalization of the ethic of the common good. This ethic still has a role to play, *but in its own right*, and predominantly as a legitimization of the aspect of self-government for the profession. Therefore, not surprisingly, its role is normally subjugated to the ethics of virtue and duty.

However as resource constraints have become more binding there has been a movement of the actors normally concerned with long-run allocation problems, i.e. the overall regulators, legislators and insurance bodies, into the short-run arena. This has affected the property rights holdings of doctors in the production process through limiting or at least attempting to limit, their claims to resources. Such actions will undoubtedly have a bearing upon the behaviour of the doctor. If the resource constraints relate merely to policies associated with budgetary restraint it is unlikely that medical decisions and hence short-run resource allocation processes will move easily into line. Indeed co-operative bargaining between parties within the health care sector may cease and accompanying inefficiencies rapidly be realized. The major difficulty is that such policies are difficult to reconcile with *all* aspects of medical ethics.

Alternatively if resource constraints are pursued in particular areas (e.g. the hospital sector – remembering its dominant influence in the health care sector) in an attempt to follow an ethic of the common good, it is difficult to suggest how this policy and pursuit can be reconciled with the ethics of virtue and duty. One possible solution could be the introduction of a "health code" ethic based upon cost–benefit analysis aimed at pursuing the "common good".

The introduction of the cost–benefit approach, which is essentially the issue, into the health care sector has been constrained, at least in part, by the methodological difficulties in measuring benefits. More importantly in our view, the current property rights structure has prevented the cost–benefit approach from entering production decisions. This is largely because the position of the doctor in demanding/specifying a particular point on the health care production possibility curve is backed by a strong, but narrowly defined, code of medical ethics.

If our underlying thesis is correct then it ought to be the case that the ethical code and the doctor's property rights holdings will be strongest where the health care good is an intermediate, immediately demanded and poorly substitutable. This description of the health care good would seem most true in the acute sector but less so in, say, geriatrics. The relative strength of the doctor's property rights holdings would seem to follow a similar distribution. Thus the acute sector had dominated the hospital sector, and indeed the health care market.

Generally, it is not surprising that medical and ethical constraints are dominant in this sector nor that (as Harris suggests) some traditional economic indicators may be capable of being misinterpreted in this sector: "Hospitals with apparent capacity excesses or cost overruns may actually be in a deceptively stable equilibrium". Policy needs to be directed at changing, but not overruling, these constraints such that social preferences count more than currently. The difficulty is of course to comprehend what happens to output as the constraints, and thus the equilibrium, changes.

As suggested above there are at least two roads open. One solution would be to shift the basis of the medical ethical code towards greater concern for social, as opposed to individual welfare.

An alternative solution is not to widen the basis of medical ethics, but to restrict its use to the short-run resource allocation questions of the medical arena. To assist this process, and strengthens the property rights holdings by administrators and politicians over long-run resource allocation decisions, I would advocate a "health care ethical code" based, in essence, upon economic appraisal. The implementation of either solution will be difficult as it is not surprising that the medical profession, at a time of increasing financial constraint, will increase their recourse to existing ethical codes and are reluctant to embrace the alien concept of cost–benefit analysis. From the doctor's standpoint the pressures of financial stringency are the worst of all reasons for marrying medical and economic objectives. Indeed as an economist it is not difficult to sympathize with this particular perspective.

REFERENCES

1 Jonsen, A.R. and Hellegers, A.E. Conceptual foundations for an ethics of medical care. In *Ethics of Medical Care* (Edited by Tancredi, L.R.). Institute of Medicine, Washington, 1974).
2 Veatch, R.M. *A Theory of Medical Ethics*. Basic Books, New York, 1980.
3 Hammond, P.J. Utilitarianism, uncertainty and information. In *Utilitarianism and Beyond* (Edited by Sen, A. and Williams, B.). Cambridge University Press, Cambridge, 1982.
4 Beauchamp, T.L. and Childress, J.F. *Principles of Biomedical Ethics*. Oxford University Press, New York, 1979.
5 McKean, R. Property rights within government and devices to increase governmental efficiency. *South. Econ. J.* 39, 175–186, 1976.
6 Furubotn, E. and Pejovich, S. Property rights and economic theory: a survey of recent literature. *J. Econ. Lit.* 10, 1138–1159, 1972.

7 Evans, R.G. Incomplete vertical integration: the distinctive structure of the health care industry. In *Health, Economics and Health Economics* (Edited by van der Gaag, J. and Perlman, M.). North Holland, Amsterdam, 1981.

8 Harris, J. The internal organisation of hospitals: some economic implications. *Bell J. Econ.* **8,** 467–482.

9 Evans, R.G. and Wolfson, A.D. Faith, hope and charity: health care in the utility function. University of British Columbia, Discussion Paper No. 08–46, 1980.

10 Culyer, A.J. *Need and the National Health Service.* Martin Robertson, London, 1976.

11 Williams, A. Need – an economic exegesis. In *Economic Aspects of Health Services* (Edited by Culyer, A.J. and Wright, K.G.). Martin Robertson, London, 1978.

12 Arrow, K.J. Government decision making and the preciousness of life. In *Ethics and Medical Care* (Edited by Tancredi, L.C.). Institute of Medicine, Washington, 1984.

28

————— ∼ —————

INFORMED CONSENT: COURT VIEWPOINTS AND MEDICAL DECISION MAKING*

Dennis J. Mazur

Appellate decisions set precedent for future legal decisions within a particular state and often prove influential in other states. We surveyed the appellate judicial decisions about medical informed consent from 1957 to 1983 in three influential states (California, Massachusetts, and New York) to examine the trends in outcomes. This period of time was selected to get an assessment of court decisions approximately ten years before and after a key Federal Court decision in medical informed consent.

Before 1972, the courts in these three states held to a "medical community" standard for deciding what should be disclosed: seven of the 11 appellate decisions were in favor of the physician. After 1972, these courts adopted a "reasonable person" standard (to be discussed later): eight of 12 of these court decisions were in favor of the patient. An increasing number of courts are following these appellate standards and going from the physician-based standard to that of the "reasonable person." The standards of medical informed consent across states, however, are still in flux. Andrews has noted that the requirements of informed consent have been codified in 23 states, with the remaining states having adopted informed consent laws for special procedures.[1] The changing standards of informed consent suggest that this may be a valuable time to re-examine the concept.

Medical informed consent, whether considered in the physician's office, at the patient's bedside, or in the courts, may be viewed as a problem in medical decision making. For decision analysts, medical informed consent presents a challenging intersection of problems such as employing methodologies for adequately analyzing preferences for outcomes in medical intervention and staying within the situational constraints on communication between patients and physicians. Decision analytic research has already investigated certain topics clearly relevant to informed consent such as patient preferences for certain vs. uncertain

* First published in *Medical Decision Making*, 6 (1986), 224–30. © Society for Medical Decision Making. Reprinted by permission.

outcomes[10] and patient reactions to uncertainty.[6] Prior to examining a decision analytic approach to informed consent, it is helpful to review the standards for (medical) risk disclosure as they have evolved in the medical-legal doctrine of informed consent. It is also informative to examine prior applications of decision analysis in the medical-legal setting.

PREVIOUS DECISION ANALYTIC APPLICATIONS IN THE MEDICAL–LEGAL SETTING: NEGLIGENCE LAW

Decision analysts have previously been interested in the application of decision analytic principles with respect to negligence law as it applies to physicians. The law considers two types of physician negligence: 1) negligence in practicing medicine (malpractice) and 2) negligence in informing patients prior to a medical intervention (informed consent). Over ten years ago, Forst proposed expected utility criteria for establishing the existence of negligence in malpractice and informed consent and for determining the proper amount of compensation.[11]

Forst based his application of medical decision analysis to negligence law on four notions: 1) outcomes (positive and negative) for the procedure, 2) a single index that summarizes the decision maker's relative displeasure (or disutility) for that outcome, 3) the best available judgment regarding the probability of occurrence of that outcome, and finally, 4) computing the expected disutility for each alternative medical intervention in accordance with the standard formula for calculating a mathematical expectation.[11]

Forst was interested in the "extent of disclosure ... appropriate in a particular instance."[11] His proposal "attempts to ease the physician's burden ... in this matter by incorporating the patient's preference *without having to inform* the patient *of the risks* he faces [my italics]."[11]

It is important to understand Forst's application of medical decision analysis within the context of the standards for informed consent during the time in which he was writing. This was an era where the dominant standards were based on "custom and practice of physicians within a community," "what a reasonable doctor discusses under the circumstances," and the disclosure that is determined by "good medical practice".[11] Since then, as discussed more fully later, there have been considerable changes in the legal concepts operative in many stages regarding what is to be revealed explicitly to patients about medical risk.

Others have also examined a decision analytic approach to physician negligence. Recently, Brusztajen et al. considered the "reasonable and prudent" criterion of negligence law.[3] These authors point out that decision analysis can be a useful tool in structuring 1) the choices presented to the patient, and 2) the physician's own ongoing summary and review of the prudence of the clinical decision itself.[3] Before further examining potential applications of decision analysis to informed consent, it is useful to examine in more detail how the type of information required in medical informed consent and the standards by which medical informed consent is judged have both been shifting in the courts.

THE COURTS AND MEDICAL INFORMED CONSENT

OVERVIEW OF FOUR VIEWPOINTS

The origins of informed consent: consent to procedure

Although discussions of what the "reasonable physician" would do in terms of informing patients appeared in 1767,[24] the legal concept of adequate medical informed consent originated in surgical cases in the early 1900s,[19,22] The courts told physicians that they would be judged on 1) whether the patient – prior to assenting – was told what was to be done in the surgical intervention, and 2) whether any changes were made in the originally proposed surgery – in absence of emergency – unless consented to by the patient or someone authorized by the patient. Thus, surgeons were charged with accurately describing what they intended to do during surgery and getting assent. Failure to do this constituted "unauthorized touching" of the patient and was considered "battery" or *intentional harm* to the patient.[22]

Beginning in the late 19th century,[21,30] continuing through the 1900s,[19,22] and up until the early 1950s, the law specified the physician's obligation as primarily to obtain permission prior to performing a medical intervention. This protected the patient's right to be told about the *nature* of the medical *intervention* (what the physician intended to do).

Standards regarding informed consent: from physician-oriented to patient-oriented standards

Physician-oriented criteria. Between 1900 and 1972, what constituted an adequate medical informed consent was determined by the medical community.[7,9] Physicians were responsible for informing patients only to the extent that their peers informed their patients. If physicians failed to adhere to these standards, they were viewed by the courts as negligent in disclosure, rather than as intentionally harming their patients. The "community of peers" standard (medical community standard) is still reflected in recent court decisions in certain states.[31] However, the trend today in many states is away from such a profession-based standard of disclosure toward more patient-oriented criteria.

Patient-oriented jury-defined criteria: "reasonable person" standard. In 1972, the *Canterbury* v. *Spence* decision in the District of Columbia withdrew from the medical profession the right to determine what must be disclosed to patients.[4] In taking this position, the court reaffirmed the patient's right of self-determination: "every human being of adult years and sound mind has a right to determine what shall be done with his own body ..."* The court concluded that the right of self-determination demands that the law, and not physicians, set standards regarding what is to be revealed to patients.[4] The court also recognized that individual patient differences (knowledge, familiarity with medicine and its concepts) generate unique requirements for information.

The court considered the prior standard of mutual physician agreement to be too ill-defined. It also doubted the reality of any discernible custom among physicians.[4] The court decided that what constituted adequate information for informed consent was what a "reasonable person" would want to know. The court said that "[a] risk is thus material [and should be disclosed] when a reasonable person, in what the physician knows or should know to be the patient's position, would be likely to attach significance to the risk or cluster of risks in deciding whether to forego the proposed [procedure]."† The determination of what the "reasonable person" would want to know is to be made by a jury.

Patient-oriented patient-defined criteria: "individual preference" standard. Within the "reasonable person" standard, there is the possibility of further development of informed consent in the courts toward an "individual preference" standard. This would involve a patient's being informed on the basis of his individual attitudes.

Increased specification of types of information

It was not until the late 1950s[23] that patients were given legal rights of access to information beyond that related to the nature of the medical intervention. Courts began to extend to patients rights of access to additional types of information: what would happen 1) without intervention, 2) with alternative interventions, and 3) with the intervention described in terms of a) outcomes (positive and negative), and b) an outcome's probability or chance of occurrence.

---

* The *Canterbury* court cited agreement with *Schloendorff* v. *Society of New York Hospital*, 211 N.Y. 125, 105 N.E. 92, 93 (1914) and other cases.
† The *Canterbury* court cited agreement with Waltz & Scheuneman, Informed consent to therapy, 64 N.W.U.I. Rev. 628, 639–640 (1970).

INTERPRETING THE COURT STANDARDS: THREE INFORMATIVE
CASES

Three California cases from the past 25 years were selected to illustrate
the concepts relevant to consideration of medical risk important in
clarifying the "reasonable man" standard. One decision was made before
Canterbury, one in the same time period as *Canterbury*, and one after
Canterbury.

Case 1. Tangora *v.* Matanky *(1964): Inherent risk and rare events.*

In *Tangora* v. *Matanky*, the appellate court used physician-oriented
criteria to decide whether adequate information had been given prior to
obtaining consent. In *Tangora*, the patient died of anaphylaxis after an
intramuscular injection of penicillin.[26] The physcian was alleged to have
been negligent because he failed to tell the patient that this rare event
could occur. This issue was settled by physcian experts who testified that
the physcian's peers did not consider it important to explain this danger to
their patients.

The community of physicians considered it unimportant to explain the
danger of anaphylactic shock from penicillin, and the court agreed on the
basis of the judicial concept of "inherent risk." Although the courts in
1964 did not have an operational definition of risk, the courts did isolate
the specific category of "inherent risks," which they gave a special status.

The courts have defined inherent risk by example. The *Tangora v.
Matanky* court stated:

... To prove that the result rarely occurs ... is not enough. It must also be shown
that the result is not an inherent risk of the operation or treatment ... medical
experts ... testified that in a small percentage of cases an injection of penicillin
results in an anaphylactic shock ... and that occurs in the absence of any
negligence of the doctor. Substantial evidence in this case establishes that an
anaphylactic shock, while rare, is an inherent risk in the use of penicillin.*

The *Tangora* court ruled that such a rare inherent risk did not have to be
explained to patients.

The *Tangora* court's interpretation of "inherent risk" did not clarify
whether its concept was to include mishaps due to technical error so long
as they do not occur more often than expected by the standard of
community practice. Conversely, the court did not clarify whether inherent risks are to be defined solely as accidents of Nature that are unrelated
to the technical performance of the procedure in the best of hands.

---

* The appellate opinion cited in reference both: *Siverson* v. *Weber*, 57 Cal. 2d.834, the
Supreme court at page 839 (22 Cal. Rptr. 337, 372 P. 2d 97); and *Surabian* v. *Lorenz*, 229
Cal. App. 2d 462 at 466 (40 Cal. Rptr. 410).

Case 2. Cobbs *v.* Grant *(1972): community Standards of disclosure.*

The California counterpart of the *Canterbury* decision is *Cobbs* v. *Grant,* 1972.[5] The patient, after surgery for duodenal ulcer disease, required three additional emergency operations: for splenic injury during the first operation, for a newly developed ulcer, and for internal bleeding. The physician was alleged to be negligent because he did not explain any of the inherent risks of the surgery.

The appellate court, influenced by *Canterbury,* decided that standards of disclosure should be determined by the "community at large," rather than be set by the medical community [quoting the trial court's instruction to the jury]:

... A physician's duty to disclose is not governed by the standard practice in the [physician] community; rather it is a duty imposed by law.[5]

It is also clear from *Cobbs* that although to the physician the need for a particular treatment may seem evident, it is still "the prerogative of the patient ... to determine for himself the direction in which he believes his interests lie."[5]

The *Cobbs* v. *Grant* court describes two roles for the physician in informed consent. First, the physician is asked to recommend a particular set of actions for the patient based on the clinician's *medical experience* and a thorough understanding of established medical knowledge. Second, the physician is seen as a *decision analyst,* giving the patient a structured summary of "the therapeutic alternatives and their hazards"[5]:

A medical doctor, being the expert, appreciates the risk inherent in the procedure he is prescribing, the risks of a decision not to undergo the treatment, and the probability of successful outcome of the treatment. But once this information has been disclosed, that aspect of the doctor's expert function has been performed. The weighing of these risks against the individual subjective fears and hopes of the patient is not an expert skill. Such evaluation and decision is a nonmedical judgment reserved to the patient alone.[5]

Cobbs v. *Grant* asserts that 1) the patient has a central role in the decision making process, and 2) the patient should understand the possible outcomes and know the chance that each will occur.

Case 3. McKinney *v.* Nash *(1981): Statistical definitions of materiality*

In the post-*Canterbury* case of *McKinney* v. *Nash* (1981),[16] the patient suffered bilateral testicular atrophy and impotence following hernia surgery. The patient had been told only that it would be a simple operation and that there would be "no problem."

The appellate court addressed the question of how frequent and serious a complication must be to become material to the patient. Expert witnesses testified that the incidence of postoperative bilateral testicular atrophy was approximately 0.1%. The court held that this incidence constituted a "minimal" level of risk and that it was therefore potentially acceptable to "reasonable men."

McKinney v. *Nash* said the following:

The low incidence of testicular atrophy (bilateral testicular atrophy can be expected in one-tenth of 1 percent of patients) weights against materiality.[16]

Thus, the court seemed to suggest that *materiality* can be defined in terms of a defined range of probability of a complication. The court also rendered a judgment about the seriousness of the complication. The court stated that "the seriousness of testicular atrophy is debatable as well."[16]

In defining risk, the original *Canterbury* decision held that "the factors contributing significance to the dangerousness of a medical technique are, of course, the incidence of injury and the degree of harm threatened."[*] *McKinney* v. *Nash* went beyond the concepts of chance of outcome and extent of harm. The court recognized that the individual patient may reasonably regard even low-probability events as important. The attitudes of individuals must be considered in determining materiality:

... Yet we cannot say, as a matter of law, that a jury reasonably could find that knowledge of this risk was not material to plaintiff's decision . . .[16]

Thus, the court appeared to define the significance of risk of a procedure in terms of the probability that an outcome will occur and an *individual's* preference for that outcome.

Thus, in the law there are increasing commitments toward more knowledgeable participation of patients in the decision-making process related to their own medical care. There are, however, attendant problems with the move toward more knowledgeable participation by patients. For example, how much information does the patient want? Over what time interval does he want to be informed? Does he want all types of information available given to him? Can both the patient and the physician adequately comprehend the implications of the available information (especially probabilistic information) and its quality? These three appellate cases were selected to illustrate important issues related to 1) public policy and ethical implications related to further clarifying the concept of informed consent, and 2) decision analytic implications related to further clarification of patient–physician consideration of *medical risk* in informed consent.

---

[*] *Canterbury* cited Comment, Informed consent in medical malpractice, 55 Calif. L. Rev. 1396, 1407 n.68 (1967).

PUBLIC POLICY AND ETHICAL IMPLICATIONS OF THE CASES

Katz has discussed how the different standards of medical informed consent conflict in terms of their public policy and ethical implications.[13] He sees a tension between physician-based and patient-based standards in terms of the former's assuring patients' custody and care from physicians, and the latter's protecting patients' rights of self-determination in medicine.[13] Who should make the decisions in medical care – expert or recipient? Is there a need for physicians – as experts in medicine – to control the situation in terms of medical recommendations, and a need for patients – as experts in their own preferences – to control the situation in terms of willingness to accept medical risk? Katz feels that there is a problem with physicians' inattention to their patients' right and need to make their own decisions in medicine.[13] Part of the issue is the need for specification of the domain where patients should be given options by physicians. It is important to remember that physicians themselves have specific problems with both understanding and communicating issues related to medical risk.

DECISION ANALYTIC IMPLICATIONS OF THE CASES

Courts, such as *Canterbury* and *Tangora*, have focused on the issue of "inherent risks" of a medical procedure. The courts have not given a strict definition of "inherent risk," but they have defined the concept by example. In *Tangora* v. *Matanky*, from a decision analytic view, the physician – when creating a decision tree – does not distinguish between inherent risks and the risk of a technical mishap. The patient should be told of inherent risks and be allowed to decide whether a risk is acceptable, even if it is "inherent" in the procedure. Common risks of commonly performed procedures are in fact germane to patient decision making even if they are "inherent" in the procedure.

In *Cobbs* v. *Grant*, the physician was seen as providing the patient a structured analysis which was a synthesis of medical knowledge and his own experience. Such an analysis contained at least reference to alternative outcomes and their chance of occurrence. The patient was then seen as the final determiner of his own interests in the medical intervention.

The *McKinney* v. *Nash* court shares two perspectives with decision analysis. First, risk must be separated into three components: a) the nature of the outcome, b) the chance that the outcome will occur, and c) the individual patient's attitude toward the nature of the outcome and the chance that it will occur. Second, the competent patient may reasonably regard low-probability outcomes as significant. Thus, *McKinney* v. *Nash* interprets "reasonableness" not in terms of what a mythical "average" reasonable person would want, but in terms of the *individual's* attitudes. The *McKinney* v. *Nash* court's concern for the uniqueness of the individual is good decision analysis. This, however, raises the issue of whether individual decision making can ever become a legal principle in a system of law that is based on precedent.

THE DECISION PROBLEM IN "CURRENT" INFORMED CONSENT

THREE MAJOR COMPONENTS

The decision problem in informed consent has three major aspects: description of the intervention (its alternatives, outcomes, and complications), definition of risk, and translation of concepts and values. First, there is the "descriptive problem": Does the patient understand the physician's description of the proposed diagnostic procedure or therapy? Second, there is the problem of the basis for defining the risks that are pertinent to the decision to give consent: How to decide which individual patient preferences to take into account to determine what risks are presented? Finally, there is the problem of "translation"; Can the physician accurately translate his or her understanding of the probabilities of morbidity/mortality to the patient and can the patient convey his or her preferences to the physician?

DECISION ANALYSIS: POTENTIAL CONTRIBUTIONS

Decision analysis does offer – in certain of its forms – an *explicit* formulation of outcomes and probabilities. By *explicit* here we mean explicit to the patient as well as to the decision analyst. Yet, different decision analysts can apply the decision analytic process to medical informed consent in different ways, some ways more explicit than others in terms of their abilities to be understood by both patients and physicians, as well as the decision analyst.

"INFORMAL" VS. "FORMAL" USES OF DECISION ANALYSIS

With the legal move toward more knowledgeable patient participation in informed consent and more concern with individual patient preference regarding what risk is to be borne in medical intervention, decision analysis can benefit this process both informally and formally. Informally the decision analytic branched tree structure allows the orientation of the patient to the notion of alternative outcomes with their probabilities of occurrence. Informal uses of decision analysis include the explicit revelation of outcomes and probabilities without necessarily calculating expected utilities (or disutilities). Also, the continued development of decision analysis methodologies for elicitation of patient preference with regard to quality of life (category scaling,[29] time trade-off,[27] and direct questioning of objectives[8]) may reveal these as important techniques in aiding patients' assessments of their own preferences. Formally, decision analysis' calculation of expected utilities with the standard formulas for mathematical expectation and sensitivity analysis provide a framework for evaluating adequacy of the medical decision, i.e., in terms of what is to be done in the individual patient's case regarding medical intervention. Bursztajn et al. found a tension between the more and less formal uses of decision analysis in this context.[2] Decision analysis has important potential uses in both informal and formal areas of medical risk revelation and in judging the quality of the medical decision making.

SPECIFIC ISSUES FOR DECISION ANALYSTS

The constraints on communication between patient and physician in informed consent generate specific research questions for decision analysts. These research questions are aimed at further developing an understanding of the *basic components* of medical informed consent. The two pragmatic issues which face decision analysts regarding informed consent are: 1) what can be done at the present time *with the research available* to improve medical informed consent, and 2) what areas involving *explicit* communication about medical risk demand further clarification.

Time and place for informed consent

Lidz *et al.* have suggested that the goal of involving patients in decisions about their own care is most difficult to obtain in acutely ill hospitalized patients, after diagnosis and prior to therapy.[15] One positive suggestion is to begin to discuss issues of patient preferences in the physician's office when the need for a diagnostic procedure is first suspected.

Time and patient preferences

Time relates to patient preferences and informed consent in two additional ways. One is the recognition that patient preferences may change over time and that allowing the patient a longer time interval of deliberation may be in order. The second issue is one that is also addressed by the courts: the emergent circumstance is an invalid setting for achieving an adequate informed consent in the law.[4]

Minimal sets of concepts

Key requirements of a decision analytic approach to medical informed consent involve ensuring individual physicians' and patients' adequate *conceptual understanding* of outcomes and *probabilities*, and, in addition, *assessing patients* regarding what they have understood after such revelations. Patients may be unwilling to ask questions related to medicial risk, but physicians should prompt patients with questions to assess their understanding. This is, of course, more feasible in non-urgent and non-emergent circumstances.

Description of outcomes

With regard to outcomes, physicians should assure themselves that each patient understands what it is like to have the particular outcome in question, e.g., a stroke, severe nausea, etc. In addition, patients should be given reasonable estimates of the outcome's likelihood of occurrence. To be adequately presented, outcomes should be described in terms of their 1) nature, 2) anticipated severity, 3) anticipated duration, and 4) anticipated effects on the natural course of the existing medical condition. This should be done in the specific context of the outcome's reasonable likelihood of occurrence in the patient's own case. Thus, an outcome cannot be adequately described without immediate reference to its likelihood of occurrence.

Language of probability

Issues related to probability include: 1) clear communication with the patient regarding *what is chance or probability*; that many issues in medical decision making are very much like taking a chance in non-medical risk-taking ventures; 2) establishing the patient's understanding and facility with *numerical equivalences* (percentages vs. fractions vs. number of patients out of 100 vs. number of patients out of 1000); and 3) becoming clearer on possible errors of interpretation using *qualitative vs. quantitative* expressions of chance or probability. Nakao and Axelrod have illustrated the disparate views physicians hold with regard to their own use of common qualitative expressions of probability (verbal modifiers expressing frequency), e.g., an event's frequency of occurrence described qualitatively as "rare," "common," or "frequent."[20] Fryback[12] emphasizes the need for improvement in standards of *quantitative* communication about likelihoods in terms of probabilities. He also emphasizes the positive view – shared by Lichtenstein, Fischhoff, and Phillips[14] – that probability estimates on the part of both physicians and patients can be improved by training with feedback. Only after understanding is achieved in terms of our expressions of chance, likelihood, etc., can we hope to further develop patient and physician understanding and successful use of uncertainty bands and ranges of variation of statistical interpretations of data sets.

Framing

Decision analytic research into framing of outcomes strongly suggests that specific care must be taken in describing events to patients, in terms of both the patient's chances of surviving and his or her chances of suffering a specific morbidity,[17] and the chances of surviving or sustaining a complication in the short term vs. the long term.[18] Without presenting both versions to the patient, a physician or decision analyst may not be certain that the most has been done in attempting to clarify the numbers to the patient and combatting the "framing" bias as just one of the commonly held biases inherent in the heuristics of everyday decision making.

Language of preference

Physicians also need to consider how best to elicit and understand a patient's attitudes toward outcomes. There should be a specific *language* of preference in order to better communicate attitudes about outcomes in medicine. The first component of this language of preference is a language of *comparisons* where patients can be assisted in comparing outcomes. For patients to compare risks of procedure, they must be presented with 1) adequate descriptions of those outcomes, and 2) understandable notions regarding the chances that the outcomes will occur in their particular case. The second part of such a language of preference consists of understanding the *relations* that can hold between outcomes. Important research in this area should be conducted to better understand to what extent *consistency* is an important aspect of patient decision making. Are patient preferences consistent with the axioms of decision analysis (e.g., Forst's statement of the axioms[11])? As well, are patient preferences consistent over time, in both the short term and the long term?

A third direction in the development of a language of preference involves the notion of *relative risk* and its place, if any, within a decision analytic framework. Although certain investigators have postulated the importance of using relative risk in terms of individuals' better understanding risk in their own lives,[28] other investigators do not consider relative risk to be expressible within the decision problem.[25]

Potential conflicts of interest

As suggested earlier, the dependency of the courts on precedent-based decision making may force the major task of change onto decision analysts working with physicians and their patients. In addition, decision analysts must bear in mind that potential charges of conflict of interest may be raised: physicians who are at the same time caring for their patients, recommending medical intervention, both diagnostic and therapeutic, and who are also eliciting patient preferences regarding outcomes. This can be seen most clearly in terms of the context of the surgeon/decision analyst who recommends the surgery, elicits the patient's preferences regarding surgery, and performs the surgery. The role of the physician as both the care provider and the preference elicitor of the same patient may be very difficult to coordinate, not only in terms of time, but in terms of impartiality of viewpoints in decision making.

CONCLUSION

For both physicians and the courts, the concepts of decision analysis may play a crucial role in the evolution of medical informed consent. Decision analytic research could help to create a more precise legal framework for guiding physicians in their relationship with the society they have sworn to serve.

REFERENCES

1 Andrews, L.B.: Informed consent statutes and the decision-making process. *J. Legal Med.* 5:163–217, 1984
2 Bursztajn, H., Feinbloom, R.I., Hamm, R.M. *et al.*: *Medical Choices, Medical Chances. How Patients, Families, and Physicians Can Cope with Uncertainty.* New York, Delacorte, 1981
3 Bursztajn, H., Hamm, R.M., Gutheil, T.G. *et al.*: The decision analytic approach to medical malpractice law: formal proposals and informal syntheses. *Med. Decis. Making* 4:401–414, 1984
4 *Canterbury* v. *Spence*, 464 F.2d 772–789 (D.C. Cir. 1972)
5 *Cobbs* v. *Grant*, 8 Cal. 3d 229–243, 503 P.2d 1, 104 Cal. Rptr. 505 (1972)
6 Curley, S.P., Eraker, S.A., Yates, J.F.: An investigation of patient's reactions to therapeutic uncertainty. *Med. Decis. Making* 4:501–511, 1984
7 *Danielson* v. *Roche*, 109 Cal. App. 2d 832, 835, 241 P.2d 1028, 1030 (1952)
8 Detsky, A.S., McLaughlin, J.R., Abrams, H.B. *et al.*: Quality of life of patients on long-term total parenteral nutrition at home. *J. Gen. Intern. Med.* 1:26–33, 1986
9 *Engelking* v. *Carlson*, 13 Cal. 2d 216, 88 P.2d 695 (1939)
10 Eraker, S.A., Soc, H.C.: Assessment of patients' preferences for therapeutic outcomes. *Med. Decis. Making* 1:29–39, 1981

11 Forst, B.E.: Decision analysis and medical malpractice. *Operations Res.* Jan–Feb 1974, pp. 1–12

12 Fryback, D.G.: Decision maker, quantify thyself! *Med. Decis. Making* 5:51–60, 1985

13 Katz, J.: *The Silent World of Doctor and Patient.* New York, Free Press, 1984

14 Lichtenstein, S., Fischhoff, B., Phillips, L.D.: Calibration of probabilities: the state of the art to 1980. *In:* Kahneman, D., Slovic, P., Tversky, A. (eds): *Judgment under Uncertainty: Heuristics and Biases.* New York, Cambridge University Press, 1982, pp. 331–333

15 Lidz, C.W., Meisel, A., Osterweis, M. *et al.:* Barriers to informed consent. *Ann. Intern. Med.* 99:539–543, 1983

16 *McKinney v. Nash,* 120 Cal. App. 3d 428–441, 174 Cal. Rptr. 642 (1981)

17 McNeil, B.J., Pauker, S.G., Sox, H.C. *et al.:* On the elicitation of preferences for alternative therapies. *N. Engl. J. Med.* 306:1259–1262, 1982

18 McNeil, B.J., Weichselbaum, R., Pauker, S.G.: Fallacy of the five-year survival in lung cancer. *N. Engl. J. Med.* 299:1397–1401, 1978

19 *Mohr v. Williams,* 95 Minn. 261, 104 N.W. 12 (1905)

20 Nakao, M.A., Axelrod, S.: Numbers are better than words: verbal specifications of frequency have no place in medicine. *Am. J. Med.* 74: 1061–1065, 1983

21 *Pettigrew v. Lewis,* 46 Kan. 78, 26 Pac. 458 (1891)

22 *Pratt v. Davis,* 244, Ill. 300, 79 N.E. 562 (1906)

23 *Salgo v. Leland Stanford Jr. University Board of Trustees,* 154 Cal. App. 2d 560, 578, 317, P.2d 170, 181 (Cal. Dis. Ct. App. 1957)

24 *Slater v. Baker & Stapleton,* 2 Wils. K.B. 359, 95 Eng. Rep. 860 (1767)

25 Slovic, P., Fischhoff, B., Lichtenstein, S.: Facts versus fears: understanding perceived risk. *In:* Kahneman, D., Slovic, P., Tversky, A. (eds): *Judgment under Uncertainty: Heuristics and Biases.* New York, Cambridge University Press, 1982, p. 484

26 *Tangora v. Matanky,* 231 Cal. App. 2d 468–474, 42 Cal. Rptr. 348 (1964)

27 Torrance, G.W., Thomas, W.K., Sackett, D.L.: A utility maximization model for evaluation of health care programs. *Health Serv. Res.* 7:118–133, 1972

28 Wilson, R.: Analyzing the daily risks of life. *Technol. Rev.* 81:40–46, 1979

29 Wolfson, A.D., Sinclair, A.J., Bombardier, C. *et al.:* Preference measurements for functional status in stroke patients: inter-rater and inter-technique comparisons. *In:* Kane, R.L., Kane, R.A. (eds): *Values and Long Term Care.* Lexington, Massachusetts, Lexington Books, 1982

30 *Wurdemann v. Barnes.* 92 Wis. 206, 66 N.W. 111 (1896)

31 *Young v. Yarn,* 136 Ga. App. 737, 222 S.E.2d 113 (1975)

29

———— ~ ————

FORGIVE AND REMEMBER:
MANAGING MEDICAL FAILURE*

Charles L. Bosk

Failure to perform competently as a professional means two different things. First, there is failure to apply correctly the body of theoretic knowledge on which professional action rests. Failures of this sort are errors in techniques. For surgeons, we have identified two varieties of this type of error – technical and judgmental. Second, there is failure to follow the code of conduct on which professional action rests. Failures of this sort are moral in nature. Again for surgeons we have identified two varieties of moral failure – normative and quasi-normative. Moral failure is more often the subject of serious social control efforts than errors in techniques. This is to say, social control of the profession subordinates technical performance to moral performance. In conclusion, we shall examine this finding.

After giving brief definitions of each type of error I shall examine the technical-moral distinction itself to see why moral breaches are considered more serious than technical ones. Then I shall relate type of error to its conspicuousness and to the response it evokes. I shall demonstrate that moral errors are more conspicuous than technical ones and that they arouse a stronger response. A discussion of these relationships informs us how professionals interpret their charter, tells us what license and mandate mean to the professional, and informs us what professionals mean when they claim to exercise professional self-control.

TECHNICAL ERRORS

When a surgeon makes a technical error, he is performing his role conscientiously but his skills fall short of what the task requires. Technical errors are expected to happen to everyone, but rarely. They are expected to happen to everyone because surgeons understand that theirs is at best an imperfectly applied science. At times, interventions fail because tech-

---

* First published as Chap. 6, with brief extracts from Chap. 2 in *Forgive and remember: Managing medical failure* (1979). © The University of Chicago Press. Reprinted by permission.

niques have been less than perfectly performed. Certain failures of technique are expected as a routine and calculable part of the work environment: they are built into training.

For an error to be defined as technical, two conditions must be met. First the error has to be speedily noticed, reported, and treated. Such a chain of events serves as a signal of the subordinate's good intentions at the same time that it allows treatment of the problem before it becomes unmanageable. The same objective condition reported immediately on one occasion and later on another will meet with a different response from attendings.

A second condition must be met for failure to be defined as technical; mistakes must not be frequently made by the same person. When an individual makes mistakes frequently, he cannot legitimately claim that a momentary lapse occurred.

JUDGMENTAL ERRORS

A judgmental error occurs when an incorrect strategy of treatment is chosen. In these cases judgment is not always incorrect in any absolute sense; the surgeon, given the clinical evidence available at the time, may have chosen an eminently reasonable course of action, but the result – a death or complication – forces the surgeon to consider whether some alternative might have been more profitably employed. Clinical results, not scientific reasoning, determine how correct judgment is. Surgeons have an aphorism that expresses this: "Excellent surgery makes dead patients." By this they state most flat-footedly their understanding that textbook principles of care have to be compromised to meet the immediate situation, that results and not the elegance of a clinical blueprint separate acceptable from unacceptable practice.

The two most common judgmental errors that attendings make are (1) overly heroic surgery, and (2) the failure to operate when the situation demands. Overly heroic surgery involves the decision to operate when the patient cannot tolerate the procedure. This decision to operate is a surgeon's commitment to his skills; it is also a moral–ethical decision about what "tolerable" risk is and a decision about what the proper role of the physician is – whether he is charged with merely sustaining life or whether he may subject his patients to great risk in order to upgrade the quality of life. Needless to say, these are not easy or pleasant decisions.

NORMATIVE ERRORS

A normative error occurs when a surgeon has, in the eyes of others, failed to discharge his role obligations conscientiously. Technical and judgmental errors are errors in a role; normative errors signal error in assuming a role. These errors are not distributed throughout the division of labor but are almost exclusively subordinate errors. Normative error occurs when, in the attending's judgment, a houseofficer's conduct violates the working understandings on which action rests. When a normative error occurs, the mistake renders it impossible to consider the person making it – in legal terms – a just and reasonably prudent individual. Viewed sociologically, normative errors challenge tacit background assumptions about how reality in a scene is constructed.

Normative errors are taken seriously by housestaff and attendings. Housestaff fear normative error much more than they do technical and judgmental errors. They fear that normative errors destroy their credibility as responsible workers; they fear bad recommendations and other negative sanctions.

A technical or judgmental error then says something to an attending about a recruit's level of training; a normative error says something about the recruit himself.

QUASI-NORMATIVE ERRORS

Normative errors are breaches of standards of performance that all attendings share: quasi-normative errors are eccentric and attending-specific. Each attending has certain protocols that he and he alone follows. A subordinate who does not follow these rules mocks his superordinate's authority; his behavior is a claim that his judgment is as adequate as his superior's; and even though in no absolute sense can one claim that a mistake has been made, a subordinate who makes a quasi-normative error risks his reputation as a trustworthy recruit.

There are many decisions which surgeons are forced to make in the absence of scientifically established criteria. Great uncertainty surrounds much medical behavior. From their own clinical experience and from medical journals, attendings marshal evidence to support one approach to a particular problem as opposed to another. However, the evidence is far from conclusive, debate continues, and a consensus fails to emerge. Some attendings approach a problem in one fashion with very good results; others have equally good results with a competing approach. Despite the open-ended nature of the question "Which approach is better?", attendings in their everyday behavior can be quite dogmatic. Attendings believe that housestaff are on *their* services to learn *their* approach to the surgical management of disease. On other services, they can learn *other* approaches.

TECHNICAL VS. MORAL ERRORS

Embedded in this ethnographic account is the contrast between technical errors, on the one hand, and moral errors, on the other. Throughout we have seen that moral errors are more harshly treated. At the recurrent everyday level, technical errors are the occasion for restitutive sanctions while moral errors are an occasion for repressive ones. Superiors "support" those that make technical errors and "degrade" those who make moral ones. At the career level those who make technical errors are allowed to remain in the medical elite although they may not become surgeons, while those who make moral errors are banished from elite ranks although they are allowed to become surgeons elsewhere. Why is it that techniques are subordinated to morals? This is not a finding that the literature on professions with its emphasis on increasing specialization and cognitive rationality prepares us for. If anything, as the profession of medicine becomes more scientific, specialized, and bureaucratized, we would expect the opposite. As far as control of performance is concerned, we would expect impersonal evaluations of techniques to have priority over personal judgments of an individual's moral performance. How are we to account for the fact that the opposite is the case?

The explanation lies in the nature of the professional–client relationship. The professional agrees to apply his expertise to the client's problem in a manner that takes care not to abuse and/or exploit the client's helplessness. The professional agrees to protect the client's best interests. The physician does not promise to cure. The lawyer does not promise to win the case. The most that either can promise is to help as best he can and in a fashion consistent with the highest standards of the community. Now, in most professional–client relationships, the client has a great deal at stake. In fact, so much hangs in the balance that suspicion of the professional's motives and the appropriateness of his conduct is always a possibility. To defend against this, the professional proves how secondary his personal considerations are by placing himself in his client's service. He is available when the occasion demands. Moreover, professionals work to cultivate the impression that the only case they have of interest is the one before them now – the client being served at the moment.[1] A professional's claim that he will not benefit from the client's compromised position is backed by the sacrifices of time and energy that he makes for his client. In making these sacrifices, he matches what his client has at stake by a considerable investment of his own.

When things go awry, when the professional's efforts to aid his client fail whatever the reason, the professional's last line of defense – should he doubt himself, should his colleagues question him, should his clients or their representatives accuse him – is that he did everything possible. "Doing everything possible" is a moral defense and not a technical one. The individual claims his conduct is beyond question – that he did everything any other member of his profession might have done in similar circumstances – and that failure is accidental, incidental, and random. He claims that the case deviates so far from the average that it should be discarded from any sample of his normal performance. He argues that its inclusion so skews the sample of his normal work that one might be led to make unwarrantable inferences about his professional worth. The claim that he "did everything possible" is basically a claim to ethical conduct. When he claims that he did everything possible, the professional claims that he acted in good faith. Although results are open to debate, his conduct is not.

The challenges of "good faith behavior" come from three different sources, each at a different level of social organization. First, an individual can doubt himself. Here the claim of "good faith behavior" acts as an individual defense. The individual who convinces himself that he met all the obligations of his office assuages a guilty conscience. Second, a group of colleagues may question an individual's results. This is the professional group exercising its license and mandate. The group standard for what comprises "everything possible" may be stricter or harsher than an individual's. At Pacific the group standard demands sacrifices and imposes on the individual the obligation to recognize problems beyond his level of skill and to route these problems to the proper expert. These last two obligations are meant to assure the widest dispersal of high-quality care. Personal pride or self-interest then does not interfere with the ability to act in a client's interest. The ideal network of professionals is one in which each member in turn is expected to defer to his more knowledgeable colleague in order that skills and problems are properly and speedily aligned. Therefore, the moral behavior of doing everything possible is a guarantee of high-quality technical care. The third challenge of "good faith behavior" comes from outside the profession. Its formal expression is in the legal system. The rules of evidence for what constitutes good faith behavior are established by law rather than being part of an unwritten code. Here we confine ourselves to the professional code in general and to challenges of professionals in the organization specifically. We are concerned with the relation of the group to those members whose action is questioned.

The professional's last line of defense is a moral one because it is proper moral performance alone that substantiates a claim to proper technical performance when events mock such a claim. It is not the patient dying but the patient dying when the doctor on call fails to answer his pages that makes it impossible to sustain a case of acting in the patient's interest. It is not losing the suit but losing the suit when representing a defendant while having substantial holdings in the plaintiff's company that mocks a claim of impartial justice. Moral error breaches a professional's contract with his client. He has not acted in good faith. He has done less than he should have. Such conduct is not honest and defensible but undercuts all the presumptions on which the professional-client relationship is based. For this reason moral errors are treated more seriously than technical ones. They undercut the very fabric of client-professional and professional-professional relationships. Hence the control of technical performance is subordinated to the control of moral performance; without the over-arching moral system, the technical system is not amenable to control.

Two observations suffice to show the precedence of morals over techniques. First, the claims to excellence made by superordinates at Pacific are based not only on a technical superiority but also a moral superiority. They speak of "sweating blood" for patients or "really busting their butts on this one." The hours they work are a source of complaint but also a source of pride. Attendings feel it is their willingness to do more than their less luminous colleagues which distinguishes them more than anything else. It is this pride in working harder and doing more than others rather than a pride in the advanced medical technology available to them which informs their characterization of Pacific being a better hospital than others. Second, there is the following curious fact. The statistical limit which separates acceptable from unacceptable techni-cal performance has never been firmly established. We do not know how many wound infections make a surgeon incompetent, nor do we know how much undiseased tissue he must remove before his honesty is thrown into question. Here professional standards are not established. Yet the minimum number of moral breaches needed to dismiss a professional from practice is clear-cut: one will do. One breach of professional ethics is all that is necessary to expel a physician from a hospital's staff or disbar a lawyer. In practice, of course, it is rare that a single infraction is so severe as to warrant this response.

The argument should not be pushed too far. We are not claiming that technical performance is unimportant. We are saying that normative, that is, moral, standards are the organizing principle of a professional com-munity. It is worth noting that technical and moral performances are poles of a continuum. In some professions the continuum is quite truncated and any technical error is also a moral one: air-traffic controll-ers are a good example. In other professions, the continuum is quite long, so long that "not busting your butt" and not doing everything possible – restraining rescuer impulses – can be interpreted as part of proper therapy: psychiatry is a good example. The fact that this is the case allows professionals to accept the occasional technical error even when its consequences for the patient may be grave; defends them psychologically, socially, and legally against charges of exploiting a client's helplessness; and assures the client that his best interests are cared for.

CONSPICUOUS PERFORMANCES

The above proof is a rather slender peg on which to hang an argument. We need to demonstrate that the technical control of performance is subordinated to moral controls with stronger data than any we have put forth. In the introduction I claimed that one good reason for studying surgeons in order to investigate social control processes was that their performances were inherently more conspicuous than those of physicians in other specialties. Simply stated, what a surgeon does is more obvious than what a psychiatrist does. We accept as a commensense assumption that for performance to be labeled "deviant," it has to be somehow observable. Of all medical performances, surgical ones are most observable. After all, it is only these performances that are said to take place in a theater. If our contention is correct that in the concern for social control there is subordination of technical performances to moral ones, we would expect the control of techniques to be a less conspicuous part of the environment than control of morals.

This is, in fact, what we found. Surgeons are loath to judge the technical performance of others. Surgeons routinely condemn results without condemning the performance. They claim that "unless they were there they do not know what kind of situation the surgeon faced, what kinds of factors may have compromised his ability to perform the optimal procedure." They add that "they cannot say for certain what they would have done in the same situation." Because of the multitude of factors that influence judgment and confound results, the social control of techniques remains inconspicuous. When and where it occurs, such control is built into the fabric of everyday life as minidiscussions of surgical problems, as anecdotes or horror stories, as hypothetical questions for future considerations, or as mild rebukes. Individuals are not separated from the work group nor is action seen as in any way "nonnormal" by members of the surgical service.

The fact that controls of techniques are not a conspicuous feature of group life underscores the problematic and probabilistic nature of medical practice, what Fox (1957a) identifies as the theme of uncertainty in medicine. There are three sources of uncertainty. There are inherent limits to medical knowledge itself; there is the inability of any one physician to master the entire corpus of available knowledge; and there is the difficulty in deciding in any particular case between the limits of the science and the limits of the person. When failure is technical, its source lies in one or some combination of these three sources of uncertainty. To cope with his own uncertainty and to suspend judgment about the failure of others is something practitioners learn early in a medical career. In an unpublished paper on the autopsy as a rite of passage, Fox (1957b) points out that prosecutors are careful to specify, in cases where premortem diagnoses do not accord with postmortem findings, the good clinical evidence which informs incorrect diagnosis and treatment. Pathologists are careful not to impugn the motives, skills, or intelligence of the clinician involved.

The point here is that one learns that such a thing as honest errors exist and that all physicians make them. These things happen. There are generally good reasons that one can suggest post hoc for them. It is therefore not proper to damn such results with hindsight. When physicians act in "good faith," the reasons for failure are routinely recoverable and excusable. Moreover, it is assumed that the physician acting in good faith will learn from his failures. There is a general reluctance to let a technical failure be a conspicuous occasion for social control since its sources are so variegated, since the decisions demanded are so subtle and complex, since it happens to everyone, and since it is believed that the responsible physician will draw the proper lessons from the evidence.

While the social control of technical performance is inconspicuous, the control of moral performance is a very conspicuous feature of the environment. With errors of technique, it is never completely clear whether the fault lies in the individual or in the field. However, when the error is a moral one – a case of being improperly oriented to tasks at hand – an individual's liability is quite clear. The social control of moral performance is quite conspicuous. Dedication, hard work, and a proper reverence for role obligations are all readily apparent. A want of interest or enthusiasm in a subordinate is quickly noticed by a superior. From this evidence, superordinates are quick to infer that an underling has serious problems that will interfere with his becoming a high-quality physician. The subordinate's good faith is put into question by his behavior. The judgments that are suspended for errors in technique are not suspended here.

There are three senses in which moral performance and its control are more conspicuous than technical performance and its control. First, subordinates are constantly revealing their moral worth to superiors in a variety of manners: by their degree of attentiveness as they hold retractors,[2] by their affect as they discuss clinical problems, by their rapport with patients, and by their resourcefulness in getting things done. Superiors take all these as indicators of a person's moral performance. Differences in moral performance among subordinates are often greater than differences in technical performance, especially given the restrictions of a strictly regulated division of labor. Moral performance is more conspicuous than technical performance to begin with because superiors find it easier to read a subordinate's moral performance than this technical performance. Deficiencies in moral performance say more about an individual's capacity to improve and become a reliable colleague than do deficiencies in technical performance, which may speak to momentary and easily correctable shortcomings.

The heightened meaningfulness of moral performance over technical performance leads to a second way in which moral performance is highly conspicuous as a basis of social control: namely, moral performance seems more consequential in career-tracking decisions than technical skill. Letters of recommendation or condemnation cite moral character more commonly than mastery of the body of knowledge on which the profession rests.

Despite being talked to several times by Dr. Grant and myself, this man has a tendency to regard the patient as just so much operative experience, and if he is not doing the "cutting and sewing," he is just not interested. He avoids the operating room when he is not going to be the operating surgeon, and takes little interest in cases that he does not find appealing or challenging. In short, he has not performed with the maturity and dependability that one expects of a resident of his maturity in years and apparently this is merely a continuation of past problems . . . At this juncture, I just cannot visualize him as a chief resident in surgery as I would be afraid of his slipshod methods and his cavalier attitudes toward responsibility and toward his patients

(Department of Surgery).

Letters of praise routinely cite an individual's flexibility, dependability, and sensibility. When asked what they look for in housestaff, attendings cite what they call the three A's: "availability, affability, and ability – in that order." At the promotion meeting, the cutting edge in problematic cases was a person's moral performance. Moral performance governs the sorting of trainees into professional networks. There is a double irony in the fact that technical performance is less conspicuous than moral performance as a basis of social control. One would, of course, assume that moral worth is more difficult to infer from behavior than technical worth rather than vice versa. Is it not believed that, after all, character resides in a more hidden recess of the self than technical skills? Furthermore, the outsider would hardly expect the attention paid to moral performance given the prevailing definitions of the professional as a technical expert who applies a body of theoretic knowledge to perform certain functions valued by the society in general (Parsons 1949, p. 372).

There is a third way in which controls of moral performance are more conspicuous than controls of technical performance. Controls of technical performance are "built into" the everyday performance of tasks. Controls of moral performance are not. They are quite extraordinary disturbances in group life at the recurrent everyday level. They are characterized by the superordinate's assault on guilty parties. Public humiliations and dressing-downs, sarcastic and mock-ironic remarks, or a pointed ignoring of the guilty party are all tactics superiors use to treat moral breaches. This all contrasts sharply with the handling of technical failure, for handling this failure blends into ongoing activity and seems a routine part of it. The manner in which a superordinate handles a moral lapse – his bracketing of the event as something memorable and distasteful – makes these breaches a more conspicuous feature of the environment than technical failures.

Perhaps the greater conspicuousness of moral error relative to technical error is merely an artifact of my research site, which is, after all, a training institution charged with the socialization of recruits. In the world of independent practice, this relationship would not hold up. This objection is an empirical one but empirically I do not have nor did I set out to gather the data to silence the objection. However, I do know that the number of technical errors is much greater than the number of disciplinary actions taken by hospital boards or state medical societies. I suspect that one reason for this is that for error to be considered culpable, technical failure must be wedded to a moral breach. Professionals restrict colleagues – and the extent of this restriction is for our particular purposes beside the point – for abusing the "good faith" requirement of professional action. The restriction of colleagues in other settings – its patterns and extent – is certainly a question for future research. Study of other medical settings and of other professions is of course needed. It would be foolhardy and wrong to argue that my site selection did not limit the generalizability of my data in any way. However, it also provided several advantages, the most important of which was to show professional controls in their most basic forms.

FORGIVENESS AND PUNISHMENT

There is a second feature of group life that supports our contention that the control of techniques is subordinated to the control of morals: namely, there is a differential response to these breaches. Superordinates tend to be tolerant and forgiving of technical error and intolerant and unforgiving of moral error. This pattern of response shows us how moral competence acts as the organizing principle of a professional community.

Forgiveness and punishment of breaches are two mechanisms for establishing group membership or the boundaries of the professional group. This first is an inclusion mechanism; the second, one of exclusion. Distinct identity as a group depends on the operation of both mechanisms. If we are to understand the nature of a professional community, we need to look at both mechanisms.

Technical offenses are forgiven by superordinates. This leniency promotes cohesion among members of the work force. Forgiveness itself operates as a deterrence to further technical error. First, it obligates the subordinate who is forgiven to the superordinate who shows him mercy. To repay this obligation, the subordinate becomes more vigilant in the immediate future. Following a technical error, it is quite common for a subordinate to spend extra time with each patient on work rounds double-checking to make sure results are satisfactory. Second, when a subordinate sees his technical errors are forgiven, he recognizes that he has no incentive to hide them. He is less likely, therefore, to compound his problems by attempting to treat problems that are over his head for fear of superordinate reprisal. Forgiveness encourages "help-seeking" behavior and removes the stigma from uncertainty.

Forgiveness also serves to reintegrate offenders into the group. We see this most directly in the "hair-shirt" ritual that is part of the Mortality and Morbidity Conference. The self-criticism, confession, and forgiveness that are all part of this ceremony allow the offender to reenter the group. The "hair-shirt" ritual promotes group solidarity. In tightly knit communal groups such ceremonies are a regular part of group life. For example, forms of this practice are found in monasteries or the rural communes of China. "Hair-shirt" rituals are a form of public exorcism. Through them, whatever demons that led to incorrect practice are driven from the group.

There are parallels in the treatment of errors in technique by superordinates and subordinates. The houseofficer confesses to his attending. The attending confesses to the entire collegium, which is his superordinate. Both humble themselves and in turn both are forgiven and embraced. Forgiveness binds the confessor to the group and exacts a pledge from him to live up to standards in the future. Since in time all make errors in techniques, all are obliged in time to go before the group and humble themselves. Through this process of confession and forgiveness the group exacts the allegiance of all its members to its standards.

By the same token, the group can afford to be merciful in the face of technical error since its members openly confess them. First, such confession is ipso facto proof that an individual adheres to group standards and knows what the expectations for his behavior are. Second, such confessions serve as proof that an individual is punishing himself for his faults. Therefore, forgiveness serves to limit self-criticism and prevent an individual from being immobilized by guilt. Forgiveness helps individuals mobilize for action after failure has stripped them of a sense of mastery. Forgiveness helps individuals cope with the problematic features of medical practice. It is a necessary part of group life which sustains commitments and mobilizes actors in the face of inevitable failure.

Superordinate reaction to moral errors is severe and intolerant. Superordinates punish those who make moral errors. In the short run, they shame these individuals. The degradation of the subordinate who makes a moral error places him outside the group. The onus then falls on the subordinate to show that his lapse was only temporary and not representative of his work. He must show that he "has learned his lesson and been properly put in his place." Those who cannot demonstrate this in the long run are excommunicated from the group of surgeons at Pacific. Demonstrations that one has learned his place are signaled by increased deference to superordinate authority, greater attention to detail, and closer ties with nurses and patients. One makes a highly visible show to the superordinate that one is genuinely repentant.

Superordinate intervention and sanction are necessary for moral lapses but not for technical ones for a simple reason. When technical errors are made, the individual acknowledges his subordination to the group by the gesture of confession and self-criticism. He voluntarily humbles himself. He bows, lowers himself, in the face of group standards. This is not the case for moral errors. As we have seen, the cutting edge that defines moral errors is an individual's failure to acknowledge the underling status which the requirement of "good faith" behavior imposes. The failure to route problems properly because of professional pride or the failure to confess error and admit shortcomings – these are features of moral error but not of technical error. When he makes a moral error, the subordinate shows by his conduct that he does not acknowledge his subordination to the group and its standards. Under such conditions, the superordinate forcefully reminds him of this subordination. The anger that superordinates show on such occasions derives from the manner in which the subordinate has mocked the community and its values.

Just as the group can afford to be merciful in the face of technical error since an individual is contrite, submits himself to group authority, and pledges to do better, the group must be merciless in the face of moral error since an individual is prideful, contemptuous of the group's authority, and offers no assurance of future improvement. The authorities of the group must punish the offender in the second case since there is nothing that suggests the desire or resources for self-improvement. Moral errors disqualify one from civil treatment by the group. Such errors exclude one from the group. One is expected to learn quickly what is forbidden from the fierce response it evokes. Superordinates expect such behavior to be quickly extinguished. When the behavior is not extinguished in the individual, the individual is extinguished in the group.

Forgiveness and punishment are the poles of a continuum on which responses to deviant acts can be arrayed. Discussions of the function of deviance for group formation often emphasize one pole of the continuum to the exclusion of the other. For example, Bensman and Gerver (1963) discuss the importance that forgiving deviance in a factory has for creating group solidarity, while Erikson (1966) discusses the importance of punishment in Puritan New England for maintaining group identity. However, what both studies fail to appreciate fully is that both forgiveness and punishment are different sides of the same coin and that both are necessary if a group is to sustain a distinct identity and boundaries. The proper task of analysis is not to celebrate one process at the expense of the other, but rather to see which violations mobilize one mechanism and which mobilize the other. Forgiveness and punishment always coexist in different proportions in different communities at different times. The task of analysis is to explain these variations.

CORPORATE VS. INDIVIDUAL SELF-CONTROL

We are now in a position to state how professional self-control operates. Professionals forgive errors that are defined as involving techniques. The operations of control for these errors is inconspicuous; it is built into the everyday activities of the work group. Professionals punish errors that are defined as moral. The operation of controls is here quite conspicuous; it is set apart from everyday activities. This is to say that professionals interpret their mandate to control performance as an injunction to maintain a community of high moral standards. Those who show that they are unreliable, incapable of sacrifice, and unable to act in "good faith" in the patient's interest are excluded from the network of elite surgeons and granted only a limited mandate. Those who prove themselves reliable, capable of sacrifice, and able to act in "good faith" are invited into the elite professional network and granted an extensive mandate. In the control of work, technical performance is subordinated to moral performance. Simply stated, physicians do not expect the application of medical knowledge to be perfect. There will always be honest errors. However, physicians do expect perfect compliance as their best defense and remedy for the honest and inevitable errors they will all occasionally make. Negligence is defined in terms of clinical norms – moral values – and not technical standards.

Unfortunately, we cannot allow matters to rest here. In the term *professional self control*, there is linguistic ambiguity. Read as *professional-self control*, it connotes the individual professional's ability to handle responsibility. It underscores the fact that the client can trust that the professional will restrain his own desire for gain and act in the client's interest. When the emphasis is on the professional-self, the term celebrates the moral stature to which the individual has grown. Read as *professional self-control*, the term underscores the corporate responsibility of the profession to regulate its own internal affairs. This reading emphasizes the contract between the profession and lay society. The ambiguity of the term reflects an underlying ambiguity over the interpretation of license and mandate. We cannot make clear with a hyphen what is an inherently problematic feature of social life.

However, we can point out problems raised by this ambiguity by juxtaposing these two different readings of *professional self control*. From the emphasis in the education of surgeons on character building and the moral development of surgeons, it is clear that the profession places much weight on professional-self control, or the individual's control of his professional self. As superordinates see it, the goal of training is to turn out, after five years, individuals with the capacity to display this professional-self control. We know that education is an imperfect mechanism of social control and that not everyone develops this control. We have seen that those who do not develop these controls are downwardly mobile in professional networks. The question becomes: Who or what controls these individuals as they pursue their careers? What does the corporate control of individual professionals look like when viewed in a setting less exclusive than Pacific Hospital and across settings for the profession as a whole? We do know of the hesitancy of the profession to establish standards which discriminate unacceptable from acceptable performance and of the well-documented tendency (Friedson and Rhea 1972; cf. also chapter 5 above) of the profession to punish by exclusion, thus protecting a few professionals but hardly lay society from less than adequate performance. This suggests to us that there is a hypertrophy of professional-self control and an atrophy of professional self-control.

The hypertrophy of individual self-control and the atrophy of corporate self-control becomes all the more apparent when we focus on the surgery department rather than on the individual service as the unit of analysis, when we look more closely at quasi-normative errors, and when we examine the reactions of the surgeons at Pacific to the "dumps" of their colleagues at other institutions. Analyzing controls on a service, we find a system in which attendings exercise authority without hesitation. Subordinates' errors are discovered and corrected by superordinates. If the error is technical or judgmental, sanctions are restitutive; actions are taken to restore the situation to normal. If the error is normative or quasi-normative, sanctions are repressive; actions are taken which punish the guilty party. In this ritual drama of social control, housestaff and attendings never exchange roles. Superordinates discover breaches and they discover them of subordinates and never of each other. These interactive patterns do not mean that attending surgeons are such moral and technical virtuosos that they never commit breaches which offend the sensibilities of colleagues or even of subordinates. Rather, these patterns speak to the symbolic importance of the completion of training and to the attainment of staff position as a form of moral licensing. Further, such patterns indicate how firmly the norm of autonomy is embedded in medical culture. On a surgical service, professional controls exist in a hierarchical relationship composed of one set of subordinates and two superordinates who are somewhat independent of each other. The domain of social control is limited; each service is a self-consciously isolated unit. The boundaries of the authority system are the scope of each attending's authority. For all intents and purposes these boundaries are never breached. Attending surgeons do not meddle in each other's affairs, unless explicitly asked for advice on a case, or unless making a dramatic gesture of deference to another attending such as first-assisting in a procedure to learn a new technique. At all other times, the respect and freedom which attendings accord each other in organizing their services gives controls their self-consciously isolated quality. Services, then, are the locus of control and not the department. What from one perspective is a detailed and harsh system of controls is, from another, a system in which corporate responsibility is virtually absent and in which individuals are given great license. Within the surgery department at Pacific, quality of care is almost totally dependent on the skills and conscience of individual practitioners and almost independent of any structural constraints save that of hierarchy. Here it is important to remember that a formal hierarchy does not observably govern interaction among attendings on different services the way that it constrains the behavior of individuals on specific services. Individuals on services act within a well-defined hierarchy, while individuals at a department level do not. However well behavior is controlled at the service level, at the department level there are no formal devices, save the Mortality and Morbidity Conference, to ensure a uniform quality of care. The Mortality and Morbidity Conference is, of course, a retrospective review of behavior. The surgery department at Pacific, with its highly elaborated conception of autonomy, individual self-control, and its relative absence of corporate controls, is an exquisite miniature of the way medical controls work in general (Friedson 1975).

Rather than merely decry this state of affairs, we are in a position to explain why individual conscience is so well articulated as a control and why corporate devices are so underdeveloped. An understanding of two key mechanisms is crucial here: (1) the attending's authority and (2) quasi-normative error. We have described each service as an independent authority system with the boundaries consisting of the attending's authority. The attending's authority rests on his legal responsibility to the patient. The physician's fiduciary trust is not just a feature of sociological description, it is also embedded within our legal system. So, despite the face that he makes many of the everyday treatment decisions and that he is responsible for much of the service's operation, the subordinate in a legal sense has no autonomy. He is merely an extension of the attending. When an attending punishes a houseofficer, he is punishing his subordinate as an appendage of himself, as his representative to the patient. In disciplining a houseofficer, the attending is displaying the invisible standards he applies to himself. The superordinate-subordinate relationship permits the dramaturgical depiction of conscience at very little cost to the superordinate. The authority of the attending rests here on his right to care for patients in the manner that he deems proper. This is a power that the houseofficer cannot yet claim because he has not yet earned it. He does not have a full professional self. License, the granting of the great personal autonomy, the giving of the right of individuality to the professional himself, is awarded only after training is completed. An attending feels free to reprimand houseofficers as if they were children and often for no better reason than "I'm the boss and that's the way I want things done," for the houseofficer has not passed fully through the sets of rites, rituals, and ordeals that transform outsiders into insiders and make colleagues out of subordinates. But the crucial point is: once such a transformation occurs, a professional self is seen as something inviolable. Corporate responsibility is discharged through the socialization and education of recruits. Just as it is inappropriate for parents to meddle in the lives of their grown children, surgeons view meddling as inappropriate surveillance of the performance of those released from training. In a way, the attending position on social control may be characterized as follows: For the five years they are home – while they are housestaff – you work hard with them, you try to provide a good environment, you send them out and you hope for the best. The corporate responsibility of the profession is not seen to extend beyond raising one generation of surgeons after another from professional infancy to professional adulthood.

However, as in any socialization period that takes a substantial portion of time, the relations among the generations is marked by conflict. Quasi-normative errors as a symbolization of this inequality among the generations allow us to understand this conflict more fully. A complete professional self is one that has earned the right to organize its work in a manner that it sees fit. This right belongs to attendings; it does not yet belong to houseofficers, although they often claim it. Quasi-normative errors act on two distinct levels as boundary-maintaining devices that uphold the privileges of rank for attendings. First, such idiosyncratic standards of proper practice establish the right of the attendings on each service to employ their own best judgment in carrying out their work. What it is "wrong" for housestaff to do on one service, an attending on another service may do as a matter of standard procedure. The judgment, maturity, honesty, and suitability for a surgical career of a houseofficer who makes repeated quasi-normative errors would be open to question. Yet attending A and attending B view the differences between themselves as nothing more than an artifact of training, clinical experience, individual philosophy, personality – in a word, as a difference in style. In this setting, differences of style among colleagues are recognized as legitimate. To reduce many matters of disagreement about proper practice to questions of style removes them as a serious topic for discussion, or possibly control. For while one may like or dislike a style, one very rarely finds in a style cause for moral outrage and social control. That large area surgeons relegate to style when evaluating one another (and error when judging subordinates) serves to underscore their autonomy as professionals while diminishing the range of practices seen as open to public debate and control. Quasi-normative errors – that is, the stylistic idiosyncracies of attendings – serve to isolate the surgical services from one another.

Second, and perhaps in the long run more significant, is the way quasi-normative error serves as a device to maintain the boundary between attending and housestaff. The attending has the power to impose his will on a situation whatever the merits of the arguments a houseofficer may muster to defend his course of action. At an everyday level, events treated as matters of style among colleagues are treated as matters of morals between ranks. The fact that attendings react in a similar fashion to normative errors, where there is consensus within the collegium, and also react similarly to quasi-normative errors where there is no consensus, may have several regrettable consequences. It may mean, in the first place, that the moral lessons of normative error have not been properly internalized. Housestaff mistakenly link similarities of response to similarities of stimulus and confuse genuine norms with quasi-norms. They treat all repressive sanction as flowing from the arbitrary, capricious, dogmatic, and unreasonably autocratic personalities of attendings rather than from deeply held common sentiments shared by a community of fellow surgeons. In this case, they would be unable to develop strong commitment to the community norms since they would be unable to perceive that such norms exist. All shortcomings become attributable to personality and style. In the second place, the treatment of quasi-normative error cultivates in housestaff an appreciation for the pains of subordination. The completion of training signifies being out from under. The houseofficer, in talking about the future of a prospective surgeon, emphasizes his freedom to make his own decisions, his freedom from others' eccentricities, and his freedom from the opinions of others. Here, quasi-normative error weakens a future surgeon's ties to a colleague community and at the same time fails to instill a finely etched sense of what constitutes good and bad practice. Independence, freedom, and professional autonomy become completely egoistic; the ritual passage of residency can fail to transmit the culture to the recruit. Furthermore, quasi-normative error serves as a gloss for attendings to lean on the authority of their office rather than their expertise. Labeling a behavior a quasi-normative error closes off discussion of its appropriateness without an assessment of its merits. Such labeling prevents the give-and-take necessary to keep attendings sharp. Finally, quasi-normative error can depress housestaff initiative and zeal and thereby encourage the mindless following of routines.

The behavior of the surgeons at Pacific to the "dumps" of colleagues elsewhere is yet another indicator of how undeveloped corporate responsibility is within the profession. "Dumps" are mismanaged patients sent to Pacific from other hospitals. Basically, surgeons do not publicly condemn or reprimand the most outrageous performances. Their rationale is twofold: (1) if the surgeon is a responsible, ethical colleague, he knows he has made a hash out of the case, so there is, as the surgeons say, "no reason to rub his nose in it"; or, alternatively, if he is not responsible and ethically competent, then the dumping surgeon is a "bandit" and nothing anyone says will change him; and (2) either way one has it, if one complains and makes "dumping" unpleasant and difficult for the surgeon in trouble, he would rather bury his problems before suffering the "bad manners" of Pacific staff and seeking help for them. Silence, then, is seen as the response that best protects patients. At Pacific, the response of superordinates to "dumps" is to crack the whip harder over the heads of their subordinates in the hope that negligence is a generational problem and that their redoubled efforts to establish professional-self controls, a well-articulated sense of individual responsibility, will eradicate such lackadaisical behaviors. All the while, the attendings at Pacific fail to instill such controls in some subordinates and release them from training – and from their watchful eyes – to send dumps to Pacific in the future. The problem is not, as some have claimed (Barber *et al.* 1973; Gray 1975; Crane 1975) an absence of any socialization, controls, or ethical sense in the profession; the problem is rather a system which celebrates individual conscience as a control while ignoring corporate responsibility. The profession of medicine needs to develop structural remedies – or structure socialization – in a way that brings into balance both the corporate and the individual dimensions of control. Adequate controls in the profession exist only to the degree that a corporate moral sense is cultivated equal to the individual moral sense.

SUMMING UP

In this report we have described the system of controls that regulates behavior among surgeons. We have discovered what these controls are, how they are enforced, how they have far-reaching consequences for channeling fledgling surgeons into different career paths, and how these standards are learned by subordinates. We have seen why the controls which do obtain in the professional are so uneven. Being matters of conscience, they may be very strongly internalized by individuals or they may be only weakly present.

The findings of this report differ from those of others in ways that should be made clear. First, Freidson (1970) and others who follow him emphasize the hesitation with which controls operate and the mildness of most punishments. The position of those who emphasize "professional dominance" give sociological credence to Shaw's famous dictum that "all professions are conspiracies against the laity." We have found, however, that these patterns cannot be explained adequately as maneuvers by the profession to retain a stranglehold on the market. What we have found is that the hesitation and mildness which surrounds controls are best understood in light of the way a surgeon's knowledge about the world is structured. The uncertainty which the surgeon routinely faces in making a diagnosis and pinpointing a precise causative agent for therapeutic misadventure accounts for a great deal when explaining why surgeons discipline errant colleagues as they do and when explaining why normative rather than technical breaches are the more serious errors. In short, in understanding social control in a profession I feel it is best not to stray too far from the cognitive frameworks the profession itself employs to make sense of the world. To take the role of the other impels us to look at how the other constructs his world. We need to know which objects in this world are taken for granted, which are problematic, and which are considered irrelevant for the purposes at hand. If, in the study of lower-class deviance, it is unwarrantable to bootleg everyday definitions of right and wrong into our work, it is just as inadmissable to do so in the case of high-status professionals. One of the strengths of this report, not common in other works, is that it attempts to take the sociology of knowledge of modern medicine seriously, the better to see how the nature of a particular cognitive realm structures values, attitudes, and practice with regard to error. A sophisticated sociology of medicine must have some familiarity with, at the very least, the nature of medical reasoning in order to appreciate the coded language in which colleagues raise questions, communicate approval, shoulder blame, and hurl accusations at each other. I am not saying that all studies in the sociology of medicine should necessarily display this understanding of the physician's phenomenal world; I am saying that only we need to place a greater emphasis on such understanding in the future than we have in the past. As sociologists, it is peculiar that we have such appreciation for the "symbolic" interaction and linguistic codes of corner boys, prostitutes, drug users, fences, members of communes, and so on, and so little appreciation of and tolerance for the same dimensions of action among physicians.

The recent work of Barber, Crane, and Gray claims that physicians receive almost no ethical training through their socialization. My claim is that postgraduate training of surgeons is above all things an ethical training. Subordinates are harshly disciplined when they violate the ethical standards of the discipline. They are promoted and accepted into the ranks as colleagues on the basis of their ethical fitness. It is true that the moral standards demanded and the superordinate's self-interest converge here to a great degree. Nevertheless, the point remains that normative standards of dedication, interest, and thoroughness are applied in evaluating subordinates rather than narrowly technical standards. Moreover, ethical dilemmas such as how to most appropriately manage the terminal patient are discussed during rounds. The moral and ethical dimensions of training are not bracketed from all other concerns but are instead built into everyday clinical life. It is unwarrantable to infer from absence of formal courses, seminars, and so on that ethical "training" is relegated merely to the informal structure of role learning. Perhaps one of the reasons that Barber, Crane, and Gray missed the ethical dimension of training is that their survey research methodology is too distant from the rhythms of everyday life to capture this dimension of action. Time and again surgeons express their feelings by indirection – the horror story is a good example. To understand how surgeons debate ethical concerns requires knowledge of that same coded language surgeons use to discuss error. I am not suggesting that sociological analysis is a subtle, new form of mysticism which requires a divining of the real meaning lurking beneath the surface of interaction. On the contrary, I suggest that sociological analysis begins with an understanding of what actors mean when they talk to each other. Such knowledge requires a respect for the word and gesture as units of social meaning, a respect that rests on our understanding of the *gestalt* which structures any word's meaning. Since we expect each occupation to have a unique *gestalt* based on its typical work problems, we expect members of occupational groups to speak to each other in their own coded ways. To learn the language of an occupational group, to learn its ways, we need to spend time observing how they meet the routine contingencies of the workplace.

Once we learn the ways workers speak to each other in the workplace, we see things that were previously obscure. A third difference in this report from others concerns the nature of in-group solidarity among professionals. We commonly believe that physicians maintain a conspiracy of silence, protecting incompetent colleagues by shielding their mistakes from the lay public. This account makes clear that this silence is not merely a feature of professional-client relations, but that is is also a feature of the public confessional, the Mortality and Morbidity Conference. When an attending "puts on the hair shirt," he takes blanket responsibility for a case. He maintains a conspiracy of silence. He does not publicly announce which subordinates made which errors. The in-group solidarity of the service as a working group would be crushed by such an open betrayal of its confidences. In a sense, Mortality and Morbidity conferences such as Pacific's serve as a model of the lesson "we don't tell tales" as well as "we openly admit our mistakes and strive to correct them." Conspiracies of silence are not in and of themselves evil things. They are, however, harmful when they allow a group to practice without any incentives to curb their excesses. A problem exists for the profession of medicine when the lessons of silence are learned without the concomitant lesson that the professional himself has the responsibility to correct his errors. Professional responsibility is itself thought of as individual and not corporate responsibility.

This last point leads me to make a concluding recommendation. I feel that improved performance is desirable, necessary and possible in the social control of medicine. Such performance rests on the profession's developing a corporate sense equal to its individual sense. While it is impossible to specify, in a step-by-step fashion, a program for accomplishing this, my account makes clear what elements contribute to an effective control system. First, there must be some hierarchy, or a functional equivalent, that permits question-answer sequences, what we call the competence quizzes of rounds, about the appropriateness of different treatment modalities. Second, some face-to-face interaction is necessary. Physicians need to feel part of the same community and answerable to one another. Third, there must be public forums for discussing problems and allocating blame. Such forums create as well as sustain a community by giving members a sense of their shared identity. Fourth, the community needs some control of sanctions so that it is able to control malefactors within its own ranks. The dilemmas involved in handling "dumps," or in dismissing subordinates from Pacific only to lose the capacity to restrain them, need resolution. At present, a physician's conscience is not only his guide but the patient's only protection. The patient deserves the protection of not only the individual's but also the collectivity's conscience. Beyond that, the profession as a whole needs to raise its conscience about its public responsibilities. The collectivity needs to promote the structural changes that will build stronger accounting mechanisms into everyday practice.

NOTES

1 Young physicians are taught techniques that encourage the patient to think he is "special" to the physician – always sit when visiting patients in their rooms,

escort them from your clinic personally, develop a theme from their lives and structure discussion around it.

2 Retractors are known in the argot of surgery as "idiotstick." The phrase conveys the degree of skill necessary to hold them properly. The maintenance of interest while standing at attention and keeping the patient's flesh clear of the operative field for hours on end is no easy task. However, superordinates take an inability to do this as an indication that an individual does not care about becoming a surgeon. Further, flagging interest insults the attending who is operating: he expects that his art will be appreciated for art's sake, if not merely for the utilitarian lessons a subordinate may learn.

REFERENCES

Barber, Bernard; Lally, John J.; Makarushka, Julia Loughlin; and Sullivan, Daniel. *Research on Human Subjects: Problems of Social Control in Medical Experimentation.* New York: Russel Sage, 1973.

Bensman, Joseph, and Gerver, Israel. "Crime and Punishment in the Factory: The Function of Deviancy in Maintaining a Social System." *American Sociological Review* 28(1963):588–99.

Crane, Diana. *The Sanctity of Social Life.* New York: Russel Sage, 1975.

Erikson, K.T. *Wayward Puritans.* New York: John Wiley: 1966.

Fox, Renée C. "Training for Uncertainty." In *The Student-Physician,* edited by Robert K. Merton, George Reader, and Patricia Kendall. Cambridge: Harvard University Press, 1957a, pp. 207–41.

"The Autopsy: Its Place in the Attitude-Learning of Second-Year Medical Students." Department of Sociology, University of Pennsylvania, 1957b, unpublished.

Friedson, Eliot. *Professional Dominance: The Social Structure of Medical Care.* New York: Atherton, 1970.

Doctoring Together. New York: Elsevier, 1975.

Friedson, Eliot, and Rhea, Buford. "Processes of Control in a Company Equals." In *Medical Men and Their Work,* edited by Eliot Freidson and Judith Lorber. Chicago: Aldine-Atherton, 1972, pp. 185–89.

Gray, Bradford H. *Human Subjects in Medical Experimentation.* New York: John Wiley, 1975.

Parsons, Talcott. *Essays in Sociological Theory.* New York: Free Press, 1949.

30

~

WHY DOCTORS DON'T DISCLOSE
UNCERTAINTY*

Jay Katz

Since the 1760's, whenever judges and counsel have dined at Sargeants' Inn Hall, the traditional toast to "the glorious memory of King William" has been followed by one to "the glorious uncertainty of the law."[1] The toast was first proposed in honor of Chief Justice Lord Mansfield, who had unsettled the legal community by overruling several long established legal precedents and by introducing a number of innovations in the practices of his court. The simultaneous celebration of authority and uncertainty was no accident. Nor was it a coincidence that uncertainty was celebrated when it would only engender momentary laughter before being drowned in ale and wine. This story from legal history serves as a reminder that the disquiet over uncertainty is not restricted to the medical profession.

With the exception of Renèe Fox's pioneering studies,[2] the impact of uncertainty on professional practices has received little systematic attention from either lawyers or physicians. On reflection, this is not surprising. It is a fact of life that human beings find it difficult to maintain a consistent, self-conscious appreciation of the extent to which uncertainty accompanies them on their daily rounds and to integrate that uncertainty with whatever certainties inform their conduct. Physicians are not exempt from this human proclivity. They will acknowledge medicine's uncertainty once its presence is forced into conscious awareness, yet at the same time will continue to conduct their practices as if uncertainty did not exist.

THE GAP BETWEEN THEORY AND PRACTICE

Medical knowledge is engulfed and infiltrated by uncertainty. In *Clinical Judgment* Alvan Feinstein has argued persuasively that:

[al]though anticoagulants, antibiotics, hypotensive agents, insulin, and steroids have been available for 15 to 40 years, many of their true effects on patients and

* First published *Hastings Centre Report*, 14 (1984), 35–44. © 1984 Jay Katz. Reprinted with permission of The Free Press, a division of Macmillan, Inc. from *The Silent World of Doctor and Patient* by Jay Katz.

diseases are unknown or equivocal. Clinicians are still uncertain about the best means of treatment for even such routine problems as a common cold, a sprained back, a fractured hip, a peptic ulcer, a stroke, a myocardial infarction, an obstetrical delivery, or an acute psychiatric depression . . . At a time of potent drugs and formidable surgery, the exact effects of many therapeutic procedures are dubious and shrouded in dissension – often documented either by the unquantified data of "experience" or by grandiose statistics whose mathematical formulations are so clinically naive that any significance is purely numerical rather than biologic.[3]

Yet the reality of medical uncertainty is generally brushed aside as doctors move from its theoretical contemplation to its clinical application in therapy and, even more so, in talking with their patients.

A conversation with a surgeon-friend illustrates this point. We first discussed at some length all the uncertainties that plague the treatment of breast cancer. We readily agreed on what was known, unknown, or conjectural about the varieties of therapeutic modalities offered to patients, such as surgery, radiation, and chemotherapy. I then asked how he would speak with a patient about the treatment of breast cancer. Since he had faced this difficult assignment only a few days earlier, he related to me this recent experience.

At the beginning of their encounter, he had briefly mentioned a number of available treatment alternatives. He added that he had done so without indicating that any of the alternatives to radical surgery deserved serious consideration. Instead, he had quickly impressed on his patient the need for submitting to this operation. I commented that he had given short shrift to other treatment approaches even though a few minutes earlier he had agreed with me that we still are so ignorant about which treatment is best. He seemed startled by my comment but responded with little hesitation that ours had been a theoretical discussion, of little relevance to practice. Moreover, he added emphatically that, in the light of present knowledge, radical surgery was the best treatment.

He then asked me what I might have done instead. I told him that I would have first clearly acknowledged our ignorance about which treatment is best. I would then have laid out all treatment modalities in considerable detail and discussed them with the patient. Eventually I would have made a recommendation but only after I had first elicited her preference *and* the reasons for her choice. Holding back for a while on giving her my recommendation would have served two purposes: one, to prevent her being pressured by my professional authority to accept my recommendation; and, two, to provide an additional opportunity to explore – if she had come to a decision unsupported either by the facts I had presented or her stated needs – why she had chosen that particular treatment. We would then have been better situated to clarify whether her decision was affected by a lack of understanding of what I had said or whether I had insufficiently appreciated her wishes, needs, and expectations. He responded that the patient we had been discussing – indeed, most of his patients – would not tolerate such explorations. Patients, he went on to say, do not have the capacity to understand such complex matters and, moreover, such conversations would cause them anxiety and intolerable pain. He also pointed to the specific danger of his patient choosing an inappropriate treatment because it seemed more pleasing in the short run, even if it were not in her best interest in the long run. I was particularly struck by his real concern about not causing his patient any pain. Yet, I also silently wondered whether he would have been equally, if not more, pained by having to converse with her about his certainties and uncertainties as to the choice of treatment.

In scrutinizing these two conversations, the surgeon's with his patient and mine with him, I was struck by a number of puzzling facts: First, he and I had been able to talk about the uncertainties surrounding the treatment of breast cancer without undue difficulty. We had agreed that nobody knew what is *the* one best treatment and we had also been able to discuss the specific indications and contraindications of various treatment modalities, their risks and benefits. While we could not do so with complete certainty, we conversed quite intelligibly, and without using many technical terms, about what was known and unknown about the likelihood of recurrence, advantages and disadvantages of deferring adjuvant therapies, like chemotherapy, to a later time, and about the impact of various treatments on longevity. In short, he and I could identify reasonably well the certainties and uncertainties inherent in the various approaches to the treatment of breast cancer. Yet, as he moved from theory to practice, my surgeon-friend – both in his conversation with me and with his patient – suddenly seemed to forget all that he had said about uncertainty. He spoke instead with considerable certainty, but no explanation, about the indication for only one form of treatment: radical mastectomy.

Second, when I challenged him about the discrepancy between his theoretical awareness of uncertainty and his certainty about what was best for his patient, he momentarily seemed surprised that I ever would raise that issue. In response to my challenge, he did not address the tensions between theory and practice, but remarked without elaboration that they are separate domains which do not need to be bridged. It seemed to me, as he turned his attention to the clinical problem, that he had suddenly become aware of the existence of uncertainty, that uncertainty had become split off and removed from consciousness.

Third, once challenged, my surgeon-friend spoke with conviction about how his patient could neither comprehend nor tolerate an exploration of the certainties and uncertainties inherent in the treatment of breast cancer. At the same time he admitted that he hardly knew his patient. He hastened to add, however, that his lack of familiarity with this particular patient was of little moment, because on the basis of considerable "clinical experience," he had learned that patients neither wish to nor can engage in such conversations. When I asked him to give me some examples of when he had tried to converse with patients about such matters, he paused for a while and then said that these incidents had happened so long ago that he could not clearly remember them. The certainty he had expressed about the choice of treatment seemed to be powerfully reinforced by convictions that related not to matters of medical knowledge but to his views about patients and the proper management of the physician-patient relationship.

In trying to make sense out of these observations, three problems that uncertainty of medical knowledge poses for physician-patient decision making deserve separate attention. One is engendered by the interrelationship between certainty and uncertainty inherent in medical knowledge itself. Uncertainty here raises the question: is medicine sufficiently advanced so that doctors can be aware of, and distinguish between, opinions and recommendations based on certainty, uncertainty, or a mixture of both? The second problem is created by disclosures of uncertainties to patients. Disclosure of uncertainty here raises two questions: Can patients comprehend medicine's "esoteric" knowledge, in general, and its accompanying certainties and uncertainties, in particular? And is the impact on patients of such disclosures ultimately beneficial or detrimental? The third problem is created by the impact on physicians of a greater awareness of uncertainty. Awareness of uncertainty here raises the question: would contemplation of medical uncertainties diminish physicians' effectiveness as healers? The fear is that doctors might become so obsessed by questions and doubts that they could no longer act with the necessary dispatch and conviction.

THE DISREGARD OF UNCERTAINTY

Beyond these three specific problems, a more general problem requires attention. Recall that my surgeon-friend initially was not only quite conscious of the uncertainties inherent in the treatment of breast cancer but also could separate uncertainty from certainty reasonably well. Moreover, whenever he disregarded the problem of uncertainty of knowledge and was challenged, he became aware of it once again. Thus a closer scrutiny of our conversation suggests the influence of two modes of thought on what he said to me: he could be fully conscious of, or oblivious to, the uncertainties of medical knowledge. He was more conscious of uncertainty when he addressed theoretical issues and oblivious of uncertainty when he was preoccupied with practical concerns.

The mode of thought that ignores uncertainty found expression in his recounting of how much he had impressed on his patient the need for radical surgery. It is hard to tell, without inquiry, whether he had momentarily, and without awareness, repressed all his knowledge about uncertainty – that is, denied uncertainty – or whether he was aware of uncertainty and for other reasons decided not to consider it. For now I only wish to point to the fact that it is possible not only to deny uncertainty but also quickly and effectively to suppress the emergence of any thoughts about uncertainty out of a conviction that it is to be eschewed in the practice of medicine. The distinguishing characteristic of this mode of thought is that the physician will tell a false or incomplete story not only to his patient but to himself as well.

The mode of thought that consciously considers uncertainty found expression when my surgeon-friend, once challenged by me, became immediately aware of medicine's uncertainties but proceeded to offer a number of justifications for his personal and professional beliefs. At these times, he did not tell a false story to himself, but felt, based on his "clinical experience" acquired during training and practice, that patients needed to be told a false or incomplete story. It is important to distinguish between these two modes of thought, because denial and habitual suppression of uncertainty make significant information unavailable to physicians themselves; even if they want to, they cannot impart such information to patients. Keeping uncertainty to oneself for other reasons, on the other hand, does not create this problem. Moreover, the reasons for withholding information about uncertainty may point to complex problems about the practice of medicine that deserve examination in their own right.

Our conversation also illustrates that uncertainty of medical knowledge itself is not at issue. To be sure, our conversation would have proceeded along different lines if medicine were not beset by pervasive uncertainties. One may wish it to be otherwise but this does not change the fact that uncertainty of knowledge will for a long time remain an essential characteristic of the practice of medicine. In fact, my surgeon-friend and I were able to talk comfortably and intelligibly about certainty and uncertainty. He only disregarded uncertainty when he was speaking about or to the patient. The actual or intrapsychic presence of the patient might have made him shift from one mode of thought to the other. In the presence of his patient his awareness of uncertainty became compromised, which precluded contemplation of the idea of acknowledging uncertainty to her. Thus the problem posed by uncertainty of knowledge for mutual decision making is how to keep the existence of uncertainty clearly in mind and not replace it by certainty whenever one moves from theoretical to practical considerations. Put another way, the problem is not uncertainty of medical knowledge but the capacity to remain aware of, and the willingness to acknowledge, uncertainty.

The defenses that physicians employ against an awareness of uncertainty have been well described by Renée Fox, who has made important contributions to the study of medical uncertainty. She identified "three basic types of uncertainty" that isolate particular stresses that affect physicians:

The first results from incomplete or imperfect mastery of available knowledge. No one can have at his command all skills and all knowledge of the lore of medicine. The second depends upon limitations in current medical knowledge. There are innumerable questions to which no physician, however well trained, can as yet provide answers. A third source of uncertainty derives from the first two. This consists of difficulty in distinguishing between personal ignorance or ineptitude and the limitations of present medical knowledge.[4]

Fox emphasized the stresses caused by deficiencies in individual and collective professional knowledge, as well as by the difficulty of making clear distinctions between these two sets of deficiencies.

In her detailed study of doctors and patients on "Ward-F Second," a metabolic research unit, Fox documented the pervasive presence of uncertainty as a third party.[5] The doctors who worked on this ward were deeply committed to getting the better of uncertainty and they persevered despite many failures and the considerable stress that their dual obligations as investigators and clinicians imposed on them. Since the stresses were quite noticeable, Fox became intrigued to learn more about how the doctors coped with the stresses of uncertainty. She identified some of the defenses physicians employed against uncertainty – the "counterphobic impious grim joking . . . to come to terms with the most stressful aspects of their situation" and "the game of chance . . . the wagering behavior in which they engage" when predictions were hazardous. She emphasized that they devised "nonempirical or magical techniques to 'enable them to carry out their . . . tasks with confidence and poise.'"

The failure to acknowledge uncertainty could have resulted from a denial of uncertainty, from traditional ideas about the ethical conduct of physicians toward patients which can exist side by side with an awareness of uncertainty, or from habitual thoughts about the proper exercise of one's professional responsibilities which quickly suppress any budding awareness of uncertainty. The difficulty of making such distinctions has led me to encompass all three under the term *disregard of uncertainty*. The important lesson to be learned from Fox's study, as is equally true for the conversation with my surgeon-friend, is how pervasive the disregard of uncertainty becomes whenever uncertainty ceases to be merely theoretical and impinges on "the stressful aspects of [the doctor's] situation" in actual clinical encounters. Fox's observations compellingly illustrate the difficulties of coping with uncertainty, if by coping is meant "struggling with, contending with," and not trying to put it out of mind. Thus, while the very existence of uncertainty imposes burdens on physicians, the greater burden is the obligation to keep these uncertainties in mind and to acknowledge them to patients.

Another example, provided by George Crile, Jr., illustrates a more total denial of uncertainty, caused by psychological forces that are deeply embedded in the unconscious and difficult to overcome. The existence of such defensive operations defines some of the limits of human capacities to become aware of uncertainty. These limits must be accepted, although the restrictions they impose on awareness can be moderated. Crile wrote that his father, George Crile, Sr., a renowned surgeon of the early twentieth century under whom he trained, "*never* did a radical mastectomy."[6] Instead, his father always employed a less mutilating surgical procedure. George Crile, Jr., continued, "[d]uring my residency at the Cleveland Clinic, I was also exposed to the influence of Dr. Tom Jones, who *always* did a radical mastectomy. Being a rebellious child, I discounted my father's ideas, adopted the Jones technique, and for seventeen years I performed only radical mastectomies." Now, however, Crile concluded, "[c]onventional radical mastectomies are not done" at the Cleveland Clinic.

Having been trained by his father and Jones, Crile was aware of the uncertainties that surrounded the proper treatment of breast cancer, but he was compelled to deny uncertainty and substitute an uncompromising certainty in its place for powerful personal reasons. His conversion raises many questions. In now following his father, has he merely become a compliant child? How can he know? Or, put differently, to what extent can he demand that patients trust him implicitly since he was so readily affected by oedipal conflicts, which he fought out over the bodies of countless Jocastas? Indeed, to what extent do many surgeons, trained by other illustrious "fathers," replicate this struggle by performing only procedures prescribed by their elders' paternal authority, to which they submit passively because they have not sufficiently resolved their conflicts with their biological fathers? I enlist these psychological considerations both to emphasize how these and other powerful forces can defeat an awareness of uncertainty and to encourage a more self-conscious and reflective recognition of the constant presence of uncertainty in medical practice. Such heightened awareness may alert physicians to the fact that something may be amiss whenever single-mindedness dominates their therapeutic interventions.

The denial of uncertainty, the proclivity to substitute certainty for uncertainty, is one of the most remarkable human psychological traits. It is both adaptive and maladaptive, and therefore both guides and misguides. In one of his earlier works, *The Interpretation of Dreams*, Freud observed how, immediately upon awakening, the dreamer distorts the senselessness of his dream as dreamt by giving it a coherence that it did not possess. He wrote:

[I]t is our normal thinking that . . . approaches the content of dreams with a demand that it must be intelligible . . .

* * *

It is the nature of our waking thought to establish order in material of that kind, to set up relations in it and to make it conform to our expectations of an intelligible whole . . . An adept in sleight of hand can trick us by relying upon this intellectual habit of ours. In our efforts at making an intelligible pattern of the sense-impressions that are offered to us, we often fall into the strangest errors or even falsify the truth about the material before us.[7]

Similarly, other studies have demonstrated how witnesses at scenes of accidents unwittingly fill in their incomplete perceptions and recollections with "data" that will give coherence to both their certainties and uncertainties about what has transpired.

Human beings' defensive and adaptive needs to make both their internal and external worlds intelligible, to shun incomprehensibility, doubt, and uncertainty, are formidable. In dreams, it is the simultaneous presence of contradictory, "absurd" and irrational unconscious thoughts and of more accustomed rational thoughts – all of which make up the content of dreams – that is largely denied. Witnesses to accidents defend against the faulty nature of their external sense perceptions. Both examples illustrate the pervasive and fateful human need to remain in control over one's internal and external worlds by seemingly understanding them, even at the expense of falsifying the data.

Physicians' denial of awareness of uncertainty serves similar purposes: it makes matters seem clearer, more understandable, and more certain than they are; it makes action possible. There are limits to living with uncertainty. It can paralyze action. This is particularly true, as John Dewey noted, in practical affairs, as in the practice of medicine, where decisions must be made. He chided his fellow-philosophers on their futile quest for certainty to obtain relief from the tremendous insecurities of human existence. He argued that "the idea of any complete synthesis of knowledge upon an intellectual basis" is an impossible quest. "Man has never had such a varied body of knowledge in his possession before, and probably never before has been so uncertain and so perplexed as to what his knowledge means, what it points to in action and in consequences."[8] This insight did not suggest to Dewey an abandonment of the quest for greater certainty. He concluded instead that it is "the vital office of present philosophy . . . to search out and disclose the obstructions; to criticize the habits of mind which stand in the way [of] the development of an [integrated] system of thought." This objective, too, has its limits because of the constant admixture of certainty and uncertainty. Nevertheless, it should be the "vital office" of scientific medicine to develop systems of thought and action that will permit physicians to account more fully for both the certainties and uncertainties that shape their practices. To achieve such an objective will not prove easy, for formidable obstacles, to which I now turn, impede the awareness and acknowledgement of uncertainty in the practice of medicine . . .

CONFORMITY AND ORTHODOXY

Conformity and orthodoxy, playing the game according to the tenets of the group to which students wish to belong, are encouraged in medical, as in all professional, education; they further compromise awareness of uncertainty. I recall that during my first year at medical school we were one day instructed by the faculty of one distinguished university hospital that anticoagulant therapy was the treatment of choice for threatening pulmonary embolization and that any other therapy constituted unprofessional conduct, while at another equally distinguished hospital, we were informed that the only correct treatment was the surgical ligation of the inflamed veins. One could view such an exposure to controversy as training for uncertainty. I believe it is not. In neither hospital were we exposed to the complexities of decision making in the light of each hospital's successes and failures with this treatment as contrasted with alternative treatments; nor were we encouraged to keep an open mind. In both we were educated for dogmatic certainty, for adopting one school of thought or the other, and for playing the game according to the venerable, though contradictory, rules that each institution sought to impose on its staff, students, and patients.

Kathleen Knafl and Gary Burkett described similar events in the training of orthopedic residents.[9] For example, a not unusual controversy over the indications for subjecting a 13-month-old girl to a leg-lengthening procedure led to the following stand-off. A fourth year resident, quoting from the scientific literature that favored one particular approach, was interrupted by the attending surgeon: "I know that's what he says, but that's *not the way we do it here.*" Then another attending surgeon interjected, "[t]hat's *the way some of us do it!*" Again, this is not an example of teaching uncertainty: rather, it is an illustration of the rejection of scientific controversy in favor of personal preferences, of teaching conformity to one point of view or another. It was done by an appeal to clinical judgment and clinical experience. However important they are in their own right, clinical judgment and the adoption of one school of thought harbor their own built-in dangers. They constitute effective defenses against uncertainty. As Donald Light, Jr., observed:

Clinical judgment and emphasizing technique redefine competence and mistakes in terms of technique ... But good technique in turn rests with the clinical judgment of the professional, which is essentially individual judgment. Thus in gaining control over their work by acquiring a treatment philosophy and exercising individual judgment without question, professionals run the danger of gaining too much control over the uncertainties of their work by becoming insensitive to complexities in diagnosis, treatment, and ¢lients relations.[10]

The assertion of clinical wisdom, based on personal experience, is difficult to refuse; it can only be arbitrarily accepted or arbitrarily rejected.

Little seems to have changed with regard to "training for uncertainty" since Fox's studies and my experiences as a medical student. A few years ago in a seminar at the Yale Law School a young surgeon who had recently completed his training with a renowned surgeon, one of the most uncompromising advocates of radical breast surgery, joined my class of law students. During our discussion of a great many medical articles on the controversy over the treatment of breast cancer, he was unusually quiet. I finally turned to him and invited his comments. In an uncharacteristic outburst of temper, he pounded the table and practically shouted, "Anything but radical mastectomy is criminal conduct!" Subsequently, though still firmly committed to his views, he apologized for his "unpardonable" behavior. I thanked him because he had provided me and my students with a rare opportunity to experience the relentless power of deeply held personal and professional beliefs. Such orthodoxy will always remain a foe of an awareness and acknowledgment of uncertainty. As Thomas Kuhn has documented in his book, *The Structure of Scientific Revolutions*, shifts in paradigms may overturn orthodoxy, but only to clear the way for the establishment of a new orthodoxy.[11] One can only acknowledge this dynamic phenomenon and resist its excesses as best one can.

SPECIALIZATION

In addition to the pressures of socialization and conformity, specialization, so prevalent in contemporary medical practice, contributes in its own way to the flight from uncertainty. Although specialization is to begin with an adaptive response to the vastness of medical knowledge, which no practitioner can master in its entirety, and, thus, ostensibly is an attempt to cope better with some forms of uncertainty, it paradoxically makes a significant contribution of its own to a spurious sense of certainty. Specialization tends to narrow diagnostic vision and to foster beliefs in the superior effectiveness of treatments prescribed by one's own specialty. This effect of specialization is reflected in the contemporary treatment of most diseases. Again, breast cancer provides a good illustration. Surgeons, radiation therapists and chemotherapists are in vehement disagreement over the respective merits of their treatments, usually without sufficiently doubting the effectiveness of their own treatment or respecting their competitors' treatment. As a consequence, a chance first encounter by a patient with one or another therapist may influence the treatment ultimately "chosen," regardless of what the patient might have chosen if provided with other options that are equally approved medically.

The public, and professionals as well, need to become more aware of the fact that many disparate groups now live under medicine's tent. Contemporary medicine is not a unitary profession but a federation of professions with differing ideologies and senses of mission. The diversification has changed medical practices. At the turn of the century, when allopathic physicians were first given an exclusive legislative mandate to superintend the health care of the nation, allopathic medical practices were more uniform. A clearer appreciation by patients that, in today's world, uncertainty over the treatment of breast cancer can lead one specialist to recommend surgery and others to recommend radiation treatment or chemotherapy – all of which may be viable alternatives – could in itself moderate the evils of specialization.

Great tensions are created by the conflict between the quest for certainty and the reality of uncertainty. The resolution of these tensions in favor of certainty have been abetted by a number of assumptions of what constitutes good patient care. I now want to explore some of the assumptions that emphasize the importance of faith, hope, and reassurance, rather than of ambiguity and doubts, in the treatment of disease.

THE PLACEBO EFFECT OF THE PHYSICIAN

The importance that physicians have attributed throughout medical history to faith, hope and reassurance seems to demand that doctors be bearers of certainty and good news. Therefore, the idea of acknowledging to patients the limitations of medical knowledge and of doctors' capacities to relieve suffering is opposed by an ancient tradition. The controversy over the employment of placebos, whose effectiveness supposedly depends so much on the certainty with which they are prescribed by doctors and accepted by patients, provides a specific example of the tensions between faith and certainty, on the one hand, and acknowledgment of uncertainty, on the other. Therefore, an examination of the function of placebos in the contemporary practice of medicine – since their employment can be viewed as an attempt to hide lack of knowledge and uncertainty – may contribute to setting limits on the need for certainty in physician-patient interactions.

Traditionally placebos have been defined as any pills, potions or procedures whose effectiveness is not attributable to their pharmacologic or specific properties.[12] This definition only scratches the surface. Let me postpone looking more deeply into the definition and ask a question first: Why has the use of placebos been defended so apologetically and embarrassedly by their advocates and been attacked so vehemently by their opponents? That their use constitutes deceptive practice cannot be the whole answer, for the need for deception in the practice of medicine has had many defenders. For example, the lack of full disclosure of postoperative risks is justified on the ground of speeding recovery. Nor can the answer be found in the nonscientific basis of placebo treatments, for doctors continue to employ therapeutic agents such as steroids, chemotherapy and antibiotics for many diseases, even though the scientific rationale for their use remains obscure. Recently, one of my students made the astute observation that the controversy over placebos brings to the surface more acutely and undeniably the discomfort physicians have generally experienced over the fact that the effectiveness of so many of their practices is strongly influenced by symbolic powers that reside in the silent laying on of hands and is not merely a result of their scientific treatments.[13] The demonstrable effectiveness of placebos affirms this reality and contradicts the prevailing idea that only biological agents and specific physical interventions are curative. Moreover, placebos point to the need to assign psychological influences emanating from doctors, and not only from patients, a respectful place in the cure of disease. Thus, the discomfort that placebos engender in the hearts and minds of physicians may have to do less with an uneasiness over dishonesty, full disclosure, or a lack of knowledge of their scientific rationale, and more with a disquiet over the implications of placebo treatments for the overall practice of medicine.

For example, if placebos were to be acknowledged as effective in their own right, it would expose large gaps in medicine's and doctors' knowledge about underlying mechanisms of cure and relief from suffering. Whatever embarrassment such admissions would create, acknowledgment of placebos' effectiveness would also demand their incorporation into the practice of medicine as significant adjuvants to good medical care. To keep such disturbing problems out of mind, physicians either have interdicted the employment of placebos altogether or have used them furtively or secretly. Placebos deserve a different fate. Physicians must ask: What is the inherent strength in placebos that makes them such a powerful ally to treatment? It cannot reside in the pill itself, for by definition it is an inert substance . . .

If physicians themselves are the placebos, then they are powerful therapeutic agents in their own right. Their effectiveness is probably augmented by the positive transferences patients bring to their interactions with physicians. It is also likely that the placebo effect is unconsciously mediated. Deep in patients' unconscious, physicians are veiwed as miracle workers, patterned after the fantasied all-caring parents of infancy. Medicine, after all, was born in magic and religion, and the doctor-priest-magician-parent unity that persists in patients' unconscious cannot be broken. The placebo effect therefore attests to the power of the unconscious. Yet, patients are defined by their consciousness as well. On a conscious level, patients are aware of the limitations of medicine and physicians. They have learned of these limitations from personal suffering, from illnesses and deaths of loved ones. Patients know that miracles are only occasionally the lot of mankind. They may hope for miracles, but they are also resigned to the reality of their rarity.

Two interrelated questions can now be asked: Will acknowledgment of the limitations of medicine and of physicians undermine the placebo effect? And will not expressions of hope and reassurance cement faith and augment the placebo effect? Let me first comment on the second question. It can only be answered affirmatively. The evidence of the positive impact of a doctor's reassuring pronouncements on patients is overwhelming. Thus when the placebo effect and the patients' self-healing capacities work together and patients get well, one can only ask: Why not accept this remarkable gift that human nature has bestowed on us? But often patients do not improve. Then they can only feel deeply disappointed and deceived. Are hope and reassurance worth this price?

A new question arises: Can hope and reassurance be offered to patients without resorting to deception and without inviting disappointment? Or put in terms of my initial question: must acknowledgment of the limitations of medicine and of physicians undermine the placebo effect? Here the answer is not as clear. Such acknowledgments may indeed reduce that initial sense of well-being that magnificent promises engender. Yet, acknowledgment of limitations leaves plenty of room for hope and faith. Patients do get well. The unconscious and transference here come to the aid of physicians and patients. Both factors will exert their influence if physicians can be trusted. Moreover, uncertainty itself comes to the aid of their interactions because it too leaves room for hope and faith. Therefore it may turn out that an acknowledgment of uncertainty will enhance physicians' therapeutic effectiveness, because it demonstrates honesty in the face of uncertainty and a willingness to be more engaged with their patients than is possible when communications are beset by evasions, half-truths, and even lies. Patients hear these things, even if they dismiss them at first and bask in the heady transference feelings that . . . are prominent early in treatment. It must also be recognized that the failure to acknowledge uncertainty can create a sense of psychological abandonment in patients that is as real as physical abandonment, for the withholding of crucial information compromises intimacy, and physicians and patients can only engage in arm's-length transactions. If that happens, the placebo effect is undermined rather than strengthened.

If one surveys these unresolved questions, another one arises that may point us in the right direction: What kinds of faith, hope, and reassurance do patients wish to place in and obtain from a doctor? The answer may very well turn out to be that patients hope that physicians can be trusted to observe carefully, to treat them with care, to alleviate unnecessary suffering, to discuss with them the implications of uncertainty's inevitable presence, to give the unpredictable forces of nature a helping hand, and, above all, to remain honestly present and not abandon patients when they need them most . . .

INTERVENTION OR DELAY

. . . Physicians have also justified their tendency to intervene on the ground that patients demand that something be done for them. Doctors have overlooked, however, the contributions of their own long-standing preference for resolving any ambiguity about treatment in favor of intervention to the creation of such "demands." Fostering such expectations in patients makes acknowledgment of uncertainty about action or delay unnecessary, since both parties seemingly share the same preference. Yet, the preference for treatment over watchful waiting has many consequences. It can make patients out of persons who do not need to be so confirmed and who should be educated to rely more on their own self-healing capacities. It exposes such patients unnecessarily to the iatrogenic complications of the powerful treatments of modern medical technology, when either no treatment or a less drastic therapy is a viable alternative.

In a posthumously published paper, Franz J. Ingelfinger, the editor of *The New England Journal of Medicine*, noted the high incidence of patients' visits to doctors for illnesses that are either self-limited or beyond the curative capabilities of medicine.[14] He quoted the frequently given high figure of 90 percent, but since "substantiating data [were] fragmentary," he did not state whether he believed the figure to be actually that high. His observations attest to the importance of an unexplored phenomenon. They also attest to the need for physicians not only to become more aware of their ignorance about when to delay and when to intervene, but also to acknowledge these uncertainties to patients. The high rate of "unnecessary" surgery, of resort to antibiotics and to tranquilizers, bears testimony to physicians' propensity to resolve uncertainty and ambiguity by action rather than inaction. To turn the tide requires a massive reeducation of physicians and patients. Both must learn that there is considerable value in living with uncertainty and not resolving it peremptorily in favor of action. The latter course imposes its own risks to life and health and its own considerable economic costs to individuals and society. Lest I am misunderstood, let me note that I favor neither action nor delay, but only the proposition that both are meaningful alternatives and that ultimately a patient must decide which route to follow. The traditional certainty with which intervention has been defended has obscured the uncertainties which beset such recommendations.

THE CONFLICT BETWEEN ART AND SCIENCE

A related problem resides in the uncertainty of whether to base the practice of medicine on its modern science, its ancient art, or both. Even though the age of science has been with us for over one hundred years, the commitment to its scientific principles, appearances notwithstanding, is not solidly established within the medical profession. A telling example is the recent rush to coronary bypass surgery, a costly and hazardous procedure, based largely on clinical judgments rather than carefully controlled and reasonably conclusive experimental studies.[15] Nor have many older procedures, like tonsillectomies and hysterectomies, been subjected to rigorous verification despite considerable doubts about whether such interventions are indicated as frequently as they are being performed.[16] The uncertainties tend to be resolved by appeals to clinical judgment – the practice of the art of medicine – even though medicine's science, which is a better judge of the merits of the procedure than is clinical experience, cannot confirm such judgments. At a minimum, the conflicts between medicine's art and science should be brought to patients' awareness.

PROFESSIONAL AUTHORITARIANISM AND THE MASK OF INFALLIBILITY

The lack of acknowledgment of uncertainty to patients is also reinforced by the traditional authoritarian relationship that governs interactions between physicians and patients and that doctors seek to foster. Professing certainty serves purposes of maintaining professional power and control over the medical decision-making process as well as of maintaining an aura of infallibility. Physicians' power and control are maintained not only by projecting a greater sense of certainty than is warranted but also by leaving patients in a state of uncertainty, not in the sense of shared uncertainties but in the sense of keeping patients in the dark. In a review article that is critical of such practices, H. Waitzkin and J.D. Stoeckle have persuasively argued that

a physician's ability to preserve his own power over the patient in the doctor-patient relationship depends largely on his ability to control the patient's uncertainty. The physician enhances his power to the extent that he can maintain the patient's uncertainty about the course of illness, efficacy of therapy or specific future actions of the physician himself.

* * *

. . . The less uncertain the patient becomes about the nature of his illness and the effects of treatment, the less willing he may be to relinquish decision-making power to the physician . . .[17]

Doctors' acknowledgment of their uncertainties would significantly lessen this source of patient manipulation.

Donning a "mask of infallibility" is another way of maintaining professional control. Samuel Gorovitz and Alasdair MacIntyre observed that "[a]t present the typical patient is systematically encouraged that *his* physician will not make a mistake, even though what the physician does may not achieve the desired medical objectives and even though it cannot be denied that some physicians do make mistakes."[18] They went on to point out that

[t]he first reaction of physicians to the invitation to dispense with the mask of infallibility is likely to be a humane alarm at the insecurity that a frank acceptance of medical fallibility might engender in the patient. But we wonder whether the present situation, in which the expectations of patients are so very often disappointed during medical treatment, is not a greater source of insecurity.

Physicians would admit to each other in private that infallibility eludes them, but they would at the same time also assert that they often have to conduct themselves *vis-à-vis* patients as if they possessed it. Masks can deceive not only the audience but the actor as well. The mask of infallibility makes it more difficult than it otherwise would be for physicians to explore their own doubts and uncertainties, and precludes acknowledging them to patients. Moreover, since infallibility is cousin to omnipotence, patients often are unwittingly led to expect too much from doctors' interventions and later will bitterly complain about the result obtained. Physicians then generally overlook the fact that such "ungrateful patients" are their own creation.

Acknowledgments of fallibility could bring uncertainties into the open and reduce the possibility of a misunderstanding based on mixed messages in doctors' orders, which occur whenever doubts remain unexpressed.

More generally, it could reduce the existing gulf of inequality between physicians and patients and make its own contribution to a better appreciation that both are voyagers on the high sea of uncertainty. The extent to which patients can and wish to interact with doctors on such an unaccustomed basis ... is unclear. At a minimum, however, some patients do wish to be treated in this manner. It will only become apparent how many patients feel this way once the curtain of silence, of mistrust in patients' capacities to engage in such conversations, is lifted.

THE FEAR OF QUACKS AND CONCERN OVER COSTS

Two additional arguments that physicians have advanced against the acknowledgment of uncertainty deserve consideration. One speaks to fears that such revelations will drive patients into the arms of quacks who promise so much more, and the other speaks to concerns about the economic costs of more thorough-going conversations between physicians and patients. With respect to the first argument, I do not wish to suggest that a shift in professional practices toward greater acknowledgment of uncertainty will satisfy all patients or indeed, that it will not penalize some patients for whom blind faith in physicians is therapeutic
...

Perhaps those patients who need miracles do not belong in doctors' offices. Yet physicians have all too unquestioningly accepted the burden of being healers to all the ills of mankind. This self-imposed duty, based in part on the highest motives of not turning suffering persons away, is also in need of reexamination. The commonly advanced justifications that patients have nowhere else to turn or that they must be kept away from nonphysician healers who will only endanger their health by administering quack remedies are unsatisfactory.

If, after doctors have acknowledged their limitations and promised only that they will try to do their best, patients decide to turn to faith healers, so be it. Physicians should not foreclose such moves by patients, if only to reassure the vast majority of patients who remain in their care that physicians will exercise only those skills they truly possess. Acting out of fear that any acknowledgement of medicine's limitations will drive patients into the arms of quacks has its own dangers. In promising more than medicine can deliver, physicians adopt the practices of quacks and are themselves transformed into quacks.

With respect to the economic argument, let me first observe that, particularly in recent years, physicians have been accused along with quacks of being guided more by economic than therapeutic considerations in the conduct of their practices. It has been asserted, for example, that the performance of radical surgery for breast cancer over less extensive procedures is influenced too much by the higher fees that the former operation commands, that appropriate referrals to other medical specialists are impeded by prospects of losing a fee, and that organized medicine's fight against nonmedical practitioners, including quacks, is dictated largely by economic considerations. While there is truth in these contentions, too much has been made of them; other less obvious but equally important issues that affect therapeutic practices adversely have been overlooked. I have been chided, and correctly so, that in my prior writings I have made too little of these economic pressures. At the same time, I still hold to the view that doctors' unwillingness to come to terms with their uncertainties about what properly falls within the domain of scientific medicine – whether to base their evaluation of a patient's condition on scientific or intuitive grounds, whether to delay or to intervene, and whether or not to share with patients their bafflements and even ignorance – influence their propensity to err on the side of intervention as much as do economic considerations. In not facing up to all these issues, doctors and patients have become victims of too many unnecessary interventions. That there is money to be made out of all this is true, but it is not the whole story.

Physicians themselves have employed economic arguments by contending that greater fidelity to disclosure and consent will be costly both in physicians' time and patients' fees. While the concern over cost must be taken seriously, it is not at all clear how much time conversation will take once doctors know what needs to be talked about, and how and why they should talk.

Moreover, physicians have always maintained that cost should not be an impediment to good patient care. If conversation with patients constitutes good patient care, then the expense can be justified on this ground. Physicians have not been averse to justifying the high costs of renal dialysis and coronary bypass surgery on the grounds that they are essential to good patient care. Furthermore, conversations about medical uncertainty may in fact reduce costs, for patients may decline interventions once they learn that they are optional rather than medically necessary. Once these and other issues have been scrutinized it may turn out that physicians' concerns over the economic costs of conversation may also mask an underlying concern: avoidance of the uncomfortable role of being the bearer of uncertainty . . .

COPING WITH UNCERTAINTY

The question of how to moderate the defensive disregard of uncertainty must now be addressed. Not surprisingly, the poet, John Keats, points the way. As Freud frequently observed, writers and poets are possessed of remarkable psychological insights from which we can profit. Shortly before Christmas of 1817, Keats wrote to his brothers about a "disquisition" he had had with his friend Charles Wentworth Dilke, a very intelligent but highly doctrinaire young man:

I had not a dispute but a disquisition with Dilke on various subjects; several things dove-tailed in my mind, and at once it struck me what quality went to form a Man of Achievement, especially in Literature, and which Shakespeare possessed so enormously – I mean *Negative Capability*, that is, when a man is capable of being in uncertainties, mysteries, doubts, without any irritable reaching after fact and reason . . .[19]

He went on to say that "if pursued through volumes, [it] would perhaps take us no further than this, that with a great poet the sense of Beauty overcomes every other consideration, or rather obliterates all consideration."

In an essay on Keats's letters, Lionel Trilling observed that Keats tried to convey that in obliterating "all considerations of what is disagreeable or painful," one betrays the sense of Beauty, resulting in "a statement that really has no meaning."[20] Trilling juxtaposed Keats's letter to his brothers with his famous poem "Ode on a Grecian Urn" and its closing lines

'Beauty is truth, truth beauty,' – that is all Ye Know on earth, and all ye need to know.[21]

Trilling went on to observe that, like Shakespeare and other great poets, Keats looked at human life not only in terms of beauty but also in terms of its "ugly or painful truth."[22] Thus, unlike Dilke, whom Keats described as "a man who cannot feel that he has a personal identity unless he has made up his mind about everything," Keats emphasized the capacity for negative capability, "the faculty of not having to make up one's mind about everything." Trilling commented that this capacity depends "upon the sense of one's personal identity and is the sign of personal identity. Only the self that is certain of its existence, of its identity, can do without the armor of systematic certainties. To remain content with half-knowledge is to remain with contradictory knowledges; it is to believe that 'sorrow is wisdom' and also that 'wisdom is folly.'"

Keats knew illness; he had not walked the hospital wards for nothing. He was concerned with the "truth which is to be discovered between the contradiction of love and death, between the sense of personal identity and the certainty of pain and extinction." Physicians need to be like poets and in two senses. They are practitioners of the art of medicine, an art akin to that of the poets, who seek to discover beauty in its life-affirming and life-destroying dimensions. Yet, they are also practitioners of the science of medicine who seek to discover truth in the beauty of discovery and in the ugliness of ignorance.

Thus, physicians need to be educated not only to "a more reasonable awareness of uncertainty, a less dogmatic clinging to presumed certainties, a greater ability to face uncertainty with equanimity,"[23] as John C. Whitehorn has put it, but also to learning how to remain "in uncertainties, mysteries, doubts, without any irritable reaching after fact and reason."[24] What has been neglected in professional training is learning how truly to cope with uncertainties, how to avoid paying mere lip service to them and becoming paralyzed by them . . .

It is possible to escape the tyranny of first impressions and naive preconceptions. Consider once again Halsted's radical mastectomy or coronary bypass surgery or the implantation of pacemakers. A greater appreciation of inevitable medical uncertainty could have led to more modest initial claims of the effectiveness of these procedures and to their less aggressive employment until effectiveness had been more clearly established. The example of penicillin, so frequently cited as a warning against delay, is not apposite. Its effectiveness was quickly established for a great many conditions that had been beyond medical control before its discovery. That its administration also had other consequences, discovered only later, like allergic sensitivity reactions or resistance to effectiveness, only speaks to what is true for all medical interventions: they must be administered judiciously.

If greater awareness and acknowledgment of uncertainty are too much to ask, at least it must be recognized that, in physician-patient interactions, professionals' defenses against ignorance and uncertainty are a greater problem than patients' ignorance. Such recognition will shift the burden of improving their conversations from patients to doctors. Moreover, shifting the focus from the uncertainty of medical knowledge to the ways in which professionals have coped with these uncertainties again places the burden on medicine's practitioners.

Patients' supposed intolerance of medical uncertainties may thus turn out to be a reflection less of an inherent incapacity to live with this tragic fact and more of an identification with the perceived incapacity of physicians to live with it. Patients' supposed intolerance may turn out to be significantly affected by a projection of physicians' intolerance onto patients. If so, then new paths can open up for trust. It could now travel along a two way street, from patient to doctor and from doctor to patient. Trust could be grounded in a mutual recognition of the capacities and incapacities of both parties for coping with human (professional and patient) vulnerabilities engendered by uncertainty . . .

REFERENCES

1   100 *Gentleman's Magazine* 98 (August, 1930).
2   See, generally, Fox, R., *Experiment Perilous: Physicians and Patients Facing the Unknown* (Glencoe, Ill.: Free Press, 1959); Fox, R. and Swazey, J., *The*

Courage to Fail: A Social View of Organ Transplants and Dialysis (Chicago: University of Chicago Press, 1974 and 1978 [2nd ed.]); Fox, R., "Training for Uncertainty," In: *The Student-Physician*, eds. R. Merton, G. Reader, and P. Kendall (Cambridge: Harvard University Press, 1957), p. 207.

3 Feinstein, A., *Clinical Judgment* (Baltimore: Williams & Wilkins Co. 1967), pp. 23–24.

4 Fox, R., "Training for Uncertainty," *supra* note 2, pp. 208–209.

5 Fox, R., *Experiment Perilous, supra* note 2.

6 Crile, G., Jr., "How Much Surgery for Breast Cancer?", *Modern Medicine* (June 11, 1973), p. 32.

7 Freud, S., "The Interpretation of Dreams," 5 *The Standard Edition of the Complete Psychological Works of Sigmund Freud* (London: Hogarth Press, 1953), p. 499.

8 Dewey, J., *The Quest for Certainty: A Study of the Relation of Knowledge and Ation* (New York: Minton, Balch and Company, 1928), pp. 312–313.

9 Knafl, K. and Burkett, G., "Professional Socialization in a Surgical Specialty: Acquiring Medical Judgment," 9 *Social Science and Medicine* 397 (1975).

10 Light, D. Jr., "Uncertainty and Control in Professional Training," 20 *Journal of Health and Social Behavior* 310 (1979), p. 320.

11 Kuhn, T., *The Structure of Scientific Revolutions*. (Chicago: University of Chicago Press, 1970) (2nd ed.).

12 Wolf, S., "The Pharmacology of Placebos," 11 *Pharmacological Reviews* 689 (1959). Also see generally, Bok, S., "The Ethics of Giving Placebos," 231 *Scientific American* 17 (1974); Bok, S., *Lying: Moral Choice in Public and Private Life* (New York: Random House, 1978).

13 Remarks of Dr. Dean Hashimoto, then a second year student at Yale Law School.

14 Ingelfinger, F., "Arrogance," 303 *New England Journal of Medicine* 1507 (1980), p. 1509.

15 See, for example, Braunwald, E., "Coronary-Artery Surgery at the Cross-roads," 297 *New England Journal of Medicine* 661 (1977); McIntosh, H. and Garcia, J., "The First Decade of Aortocoronary Bypass Grafting, 1967–1977: A Review," 57 *Circulation* 405 (1978): "Effects of Coronary-Artery Bypass Grafting on Survival: Implications of the Randomized Coronary Artery Surgery Study," 309 *New England Journal of Medicine*, 1181, 1983.

16 See, for example, Bakwin, "Pseudodoxia Pediatrica," 232 *New England Journal of Medicine* 691 (1945).

17 Waitzkin, H. and Stoeckle, J., "The Communication of Information about Illness: Clinical, Sociological, and Methodological Considerations," 8 *Advances in Psychosomatic Medicine* 180 (1972), p. 187–188.

18 Gorovitz, S. and MacIntyre, A., "Toward a Theory of Medical Fallibility," 1 *Journal of Medicine and Philosophy* 51 (1976).

19 Forman, M., *The Letters of John Keats*. (London: Oxford University Press, 1931), p. 72.

20 Trilling, L., *The Opposing Self* (New York: Viking Press, 1955), p. 35.

21 Keats, J., "Ode on a Grecian Urn." In: *The Major Poets: English and American*, C. Coffin ed. (New York: Harcourt, Brace & World, 1954).

22 Trilling, *supra* note 20, p. 37.
23 Whitehorn, J.C., "Educating for Uncertainty," 7 *Perspectives in Biology and Medicine* 118 (1963), p. 122.
24 Forman, *supra* note 19, p. 72.